ST PAUL'S
EPISTLES TO THE THESSALONIANS

ST PAUL'S
EPISTLES TO THE THESSALONIANS

THE GREEK TEXT
WITH
INTRODUCTION AND NOTES

BY

GEORGE MILLIGAN, D.D.

MINISTER OF CAPUTH, PERTHSHIRE

Eugene, Oregon

Wipf and Stock Publishers
199 W 8th Ave, Suite 3
Eugene, OR 97401

St. Paul's Epistles to the Thessalonians
The Greek Text with Introduction and Notes
By Milligan, George
Copyright©1908 by Milligan, George
ISBN: 1-59752-241-4
Publication date 6/8/2005
Previously published by Macmillan and Co., 1908

αὐτὸс δὲ ὁ θεὸс τῆс εἰρήνηс ἁγιάсαι ὑμᾶс ὁλοτελεῖс, καὶ ὁλόκληρον ὑμῶν τὸ πνεῦμα καὶ ἡ ψυχὴ καὶ τὸ сῶμα ἀμέμπτωс ἐν τῇ παρουсίᾳ τοῦ κυρίου ἡμῶν Ἰηсοῦ Χριстοῦ τηρηθείη. πιсτὸс ὁ καλῶν ὑμᾶс, ὃс καὶ ποιήсει.

TO

MY MOTHER

ὡς ἐὰν τροφὸς θάλπῃ τὰ ἑαυτῆς τέκνα.

πάντα Δοκιμάζετε.

προσεύχεσθε... ἵνα ὁ λόγος τοῦ κυρίου τρέχῃ καὶ δοξάζηται.

PREFACE.

THE Epistles to the Thessalonians can hardly be said to have received at the hands of English scholars the attention they deserve, in view not only of their own intrinsic interest, but of the place which they occupy in the Sacred Canon. They are generally believed to be the earliest of St Paul's extant Epistles, and, if so, are, in all probability, the oldest Christian documents of importance that have come down to us. Certainly no other of the Pauline writings give us a clearer idea of the character of the Apostle's missionary preaching, or present a more living picture of the surroundings of the primitive Christian Church. A detailed study of their contents is essential, therefore, to a proper understanding of the Apostolic Age, and forms the best introduction to the more developed interpretation of Christian thought, which we are accustomed to describe as Paulinism.

This must be made the excuse for the length at which certain subjects bearing on St Paul's language and teaching as a whole are dealt with in the Introduction, and also for the numerous references to recent literature dealing with these points, which will be found especially in the foot-notes. Writing as I have had to do far from a Library, the difficulty I have experienced in keeping abreast of the advances of modern scholarship has led me to believe that those similarly situated may be glad to be directed to the sources where they are most likely to find help.

The Text adopted for the Commentary is the Greek Text of Westcott and Hort which, through the kind permission of

Messrs Macmillan and Co., has been reproduced here exactly as it stands in the latest authoritative revision. Full note has, however, been taken of all variants of importance, and for the convenience of students a brief summary has been given of the Authorities for the Text in Introduction VII.

In Introduction VIII. there will be found a selected list of the more important Commentaries on the Epistles, and of various Monographs dealing with special points raised by them. My obligations to these are undoubtedly greater than I have been able to acknowledge; but I have not thought it advisable to overload my Notes by discussing or quoting the views of others, except where this seemed to be really demanded. An exception has been made in the case of the rich and terse comments of the patristic writers, and such later expositors as Calvin and Bengel: and the Latin translations of Beza, Estius, and others have been freely cited, wherever they threw light on the exact meaning of the original.

In addition, moreover, to the ordinary sources of help, there are two which have been so largely used in the following work that they may be specially mentioned.

The publication within recent years of large collections of Inscriptions and Papyri has now made possible a thorough re-study of the Pauline language in the light of contemporary documents. Upon the general questions that are thereby raised, such as the disappearance of much that used to be known as 'Biblical Greek,' and the existence or non-existence of 'Semitisms' in the Greek New Testament, this is not the place to enter: they will be found fully stated in the writings of such experts as Professors Deissmann and Thumb, and Dr J. H. Moulton, and, from a more conservative point of view, of the lamented Dr Friedrich Blass. All that we are meanwhile concerned with is the light thrown upon St Paul's letters by the constant occurrence in them of words and phrases, which are now proved to have formed part of the common stock of the Apostle's own time, even when it is equally clear that their meaning has been deepened and enriched in his hands, partly through the influence of the Greek Old Testament, and partly through the power of his own Christian consciousness.

Much work has still to be done before the full extent of the new lexical discoveries can be properly estimated; but the citations in the following pages may at least serve to draw increased attention to the richness of the field that is being gradually opened up before the New Testament student. A full list of the collections made use of with the names of their distinguished editors will be found in Index III. 1 (*a*) and (*b*).

In the second place, as regards St Paul's thought, or, more exactly, the form in which his thought often clothes itself, we are again enabled to judge how largely he was a man of his own time, through the convenient editions of later Jewish literature, which we owe to the labours of the contributors to Kautzsch's *Apokryphen* and *Pseudepigraphen* of the Old Testament in Germany, and of Dr R. H. Charles in England. There may be a tendency perhaps in certain quarters to over-estimate this dependence, and to lose sight of the far more significant extent to which the Apostle was influenced by the canonical books of the Greek Old Testament. At the same time, more particularly in writings so largely eschatological in their character as our two Epistles, it is a constant source of interest to trace the parallels that exist between them and contemporary apocalyptic literature. A list of citations, with the titles of the editions that have been used, is given in Index III. 2.

In a work which has ventured to intrude upon so much new and debateable ground, I can hardly hope not to have fallen into many errors both of judgment and of fact, and that these are not more numerous is due only to the generous help of many well-known scholars. I desire to thank in particular my friends Dr J. H. Moulton of Didsbury College, Manchester, and Mr J. H. A. Hart of St John's College, Cambridge, who, amidst their own engrossing duties, have found time to read the proofs, and have favoured me with many valuable criticisms and suggestions, and Dr A. Souter of Mansfield College, Oxford, who has ungrudgingly placed at my disposal his knowledge and experience, more particularly in connexion with the textual and critical portions of the work. Nor can I forget the unfailing courtesy and attention of the officials of the Cambridge University Press, and the skill of their compositors and readers.

It is not easy to part with the work, which has been an almost constant companion for a number of years: and I never was more conscious of its shortcomings than now, on the eve of publication. I can only hope that, in spite of these, it may awaken in others a little of the interest it has been to myself, and may prove a small contribution to the better understanding of Epistles which let us so fully into the heart of the great Apostle, and whose message, notwithstanding the strange forms in which it is sometimes cast, is still fraught with such deep significance for the Church of to-day.

G. M.

CAPUTH MANSE,
   PERTHSHIRE.
      January, 1908.

CONTENTS.

INTRODUCTION.

		PAGE
I.	The City of Thessalonica	xxi
II.	St Paul and the Thessalonian Church	xxvi
III.	General Character and Contents of the Epistles	xli
IV.	Language, Style, and Literary Affinities	lii
V.	Doctrine	lxiii
VI.	Authenticity and Integrity	lxxii
VII.	Authorities for the Text	xciii
VIII.	Commentaries	cii

TEXT AND NOTES.

Analysis of 1 Thessalonians 2
Text and Notes of 1 Thessalonians 3
Analysis of 2 Thessalonians 84
Text and Notes of 2 Thessalonians 85

ADDITIONAL NOTES.

A.	St Paul as a Letter-Writer	121
B.	Did St Paul use the Epistolary Plural?	131
C.	The Thessalonian Friends of St Paul	133
D.	The Divine Names in the Epistles	135
E.	On the history of εὐαγγέλιον, εὐαγγελίζομαι	141
F.	Παρουσία. Ἐπιφάνεια. Ἀποκάλυψις	145
G.	On ἀτακτέω and its cognates	152
H.	On the meanings of κατέχω	155
I.	The Biblical Doctrine of Antichrist	158
J.	The history of the interpretation of 2 Thess. ii. 1—12	166

INDEXES.

- I. Subjects 177
- II. Authors 179
- III. References 183
    - 1. Inscriptions and Papyri 183
        - (a) Inscriptions 183
        - (b) Papyri 184
    - 2. Judaistic Writings 188
- IV. Greek Words 191

ABBREVIATIONS.

THE following list of abbreviations applies for the most part to lexical and grammatical works, and to periodical publications; but the full titles of a few other books have been added for convenience of reference, especially where it seemed of importance to specify the exact editions made use of.

For abbreviations in connexion with Authorities for the Text and Commentators, see Introduction VII. and VIII. The abbreviations for the Inscriptions and the Papyri are explained in Index III. 1 (a) and (b), and for Judaistic writings in Index III. 2.

A sufficiently full title to identify other books quoted is given as a rule on the occasion of their first mention: see the references under Index II. Authors.

It may be added that the quotations from the LXX. follow throughout the text of the smaller Cambridge Septuagint *The Old Testament in Greek* edited by H. B. Swete, 3 vols., Cambridge, 1887—1894, and the quotations from the N.T. *The New Testament in the original Greek* revised by B. F. Westcott and F. J. A. Hort, vol. i. Text, London, 1898.

The Concordance of Hatch and Redpath has been used for the Greek O.T., and that of Moulton and Geden for the N.T.

By I. i. 1 is to be understood 1 Thess. i. 1, and by II. i. 1, 2 Thess. i. 1.

Abbott *Joh. Gr.* = *Johannine Grammar*, by Edwin A. Abbott. London, 1906.

Am. J. of Th. = *The American Journal of Theology*. Chicago, 1897—.

Anz *Subsidia* = *Subsidia ad cognoscendum Graecorum sermonem vulgarem e Pentateuchi versione Alexandrina repetita*, by H. Anz. Halle, 1894.

ABBREVIATIONS

Archiv = *Archiv für Papyrusforschung*, ed. U. Wilcken. Leipzig, 1901—.

Aristeas = *Aristeae ad Philocratem Epistula*, ed. P. Wendland. Leipzig, 1900.

B.C.H. = *Bulletin de correspondance hellénique*. Paris and Athens, 1877—.

B.D.B. = *A Hebrew and English Lexicon of the Old Testament*, by Drs Brown, Driver, and Briggs. Oxford, 1906.

Blass = *Grammar of New Testament Greek*, by F. Blass. Eng. Tr. by H. St John Thackeray. 2nd Edit. London, 1905.

Bousset, W. = *Die Religion des Judentums im neutestamentlichen Zeitalter*. 2nd Edit. enlarged and re-arranged. Berlin, 1906.

Burton = *Syntax of the Moods and Tenses of New Testament Greek*, by E. D. Burton. 2nd Edit. Edinburgh, 1894.

Buttmann = *A Grammar of the New Testament Greek*, by A. Buttmann. Eng. Tr. by J. H. Thayer. Andover, 1873.

C.G.T. = *Cambridge Greek Testament for Schools and Colleges*.

Conybeare *Selections* = *Selections from the Septuagint* (with a Grammar of Septuagint Greek) by F. C. Conybeare and St George Stock. Boston, 1906.

C.R. = *The Classical Review*. London, 1887—.

Cremer = *Biblico-Theological Lexicon of New Testament Greek*, by H. Cremer. Eng. Tr. by W. Urwick. 4th Edit. Edinburgh, 1895.

Crönert = *Memoria Graeca Herculanensis*, by G. Crönert. Leipzig, 1903.

Dalman *Worte* = *Die Worte Jesu*, by G. Dalman. Leipzig, 1898. Eng. Tr. by D. M. Kay. Edinburgh, 1902.

Deissmann *BS.* = *Bible Studies* by G. A. Deissmann. Eng. edit. by A. Grieve. Edinburgh, 1901.

Deissmann *Hellenisierung* = *Die Hellenisierung des Semitischen Monotheismus*, by G. A. Deissmann. Leipzig, 1903.

Deissmann *in Christo* = *Die neutestamentliche formel "in Christo Jesu,"* by G. A. Deissmann. Marburg, 1892.

Deissmann *New Light on the N.T.* = *New Light on the New Testament from Records of the Graeco-Roman Period*, by G. A. Deissmann, tr. by L. R. M. Strachan. Edinburgh, 1907.

ABBREVIATIONS

Dieterich *Untersuchungen* = *Untersuchungen zur Geschichte der griechischen Sprache, von der hellenistischen Zeit bis zum 10. Jahrh. n. Chr.*, by K. Dieterich. Leipzig, 1898 (*Byzantinisches Archiv*, Heft i.).

Encyc. Bibl. = *Encyclopaedia Biblica*, edited by T. K. Cheyne and J. S. Black. 4 vols. London, 1899—1903.

E.G.T. = *The Expositor's Greek Testament*, edited by W. Robertson Nicoll. Vols. i.—iii. London, 1897—1903.

Exp. = *The Expositor.* London, 1875—. Cited by series, volume, and page.

Exp. T. = *The Expository Times.* Edinburgh, 1889—.

Field *Notes* = *Notes on the Translation of the New Testament* (being *Otium Norvicense* iii.), by F. Field. Cambridge, 1899.

Gildersleeve *Syntax* = *Syntax of Classical Greek*, by B. L. Gildersleeve and C. W. E. Miller. Pt. i. New York, 1900.

Gradenwitz *Einführung* = *Einführung in die Papyruskunde*, by O. Gradenwitz. Heft i. Leipzig, 1900.

Grimm-Thayer = *A Greek-English Lexicon of the New Testament*, being Grimm's Wilke's *Clavis Novi Testamenti*, tr. and enlarged by J. H. Thayer. 2nd Edit. Edinburgh, 1890.

Hastings' *D.B.* = *Dictionary of the Bible*, edited by James Hastings. 5 vols. Edinburgh, 1898—1904.

Hatch *Essays* = *Essays in Biblical Greek*, by Edwin Hatch. Oxford, 1889.

Hatzidakis = *Einleitung in die Neugriechische Grammatik*, by G. N. Hatzidakis. Leipzig, 1892.

Hauck *RE.*[3] = Herzog's *Realencyclopädie*, 3rd Edit. by A. Hauck. Leipzig, 1896—.

Hermann *Vig.* = Vigerus *de Idiotismis*, ed. G. Hermannus. Leipzig, 1802.

Herwerden = *Lexicon Graecum suppletorium et dialecticum*, by H. van Herwerden. Lugd. Batav., 1902. *Appendix*, 1904. *Nova addenda* in *Mélanges Nicole* (Geneva, 1905) pp. 241—260.

Hesychius = *Hesychii Alexandrini Lexicon*, ed. M. Schmidt. Jena, 1867.

Jannaris = *An Historical Greek Grammar*, by A. N. Jannaris. London, 1897.

Jelf = *A Grammar of the Greek Language*, by W. E. Jelf. 3rd Edit. London, 1861.

J.H.S. = *The Journal of Hellenic Studies*. London, 1880—.

J.Q.R. = *The Jewish Quarterly Review*. London, 1889—.

J.T.S. = *The Journal of Theological Studies*. London, 1900—.

Kennedy *Sources* = *Sources of New Testament Greek*, by H. A. A. Kennedy. Edinburgh, 1895.

Kennedy *Last Things* = *St Paul's Conceptions of the Last Things*, by H. A. A. Kennedy. London, 1904.

Kühner[3] = *Ausführliche Grammatik der griechischen Sprache*, by R. Kühner. *Elementar- und Formenlehre*, ed. F. Blass. 2 vols. Hanover, 1890, 1892. *Satzlehre*, ed. B. Gerth. 2 vols. 1898, 1904.

Kuhring = *De Praepositionum Graecarum in Chartis Aegyptiis Usu*, by G. Kuhring. Bonn, 1906.

Lob. *Phryn.* = *Phrynichi Ecloga*, ed. C. A. Lobeck. Leipzig, 1820.

LS. = *A Greek-English Lexicon*, by H. G. Liddell and R. Scott. 6th Edit. Oxford, 1869.

Mayser = *Grammatik der Griechischen Papyri aus der Ptolemäerzeit*, by E. Mayser. Leipzig, 1906.

Meisterhans = *Grammatik der attischen Inschriften*, by K. Meisterhans. 3rd Edit. by E. Schwyzer. Berlin, 1900.

Mél. Nic. = *Mélanges Nicole*. (A collection of studies in classical philology and in archaeology dedicated to Prof. J. Nicole). Geneva, 1905.

Moeris = *Moeridis Lexicon Atticum*, ed. J. Pierson. Lugd. Batav. 1759.

Moulton *Prolegg.* = *A Grammar of New Testament Greek*, by J. H. Moulton. Vol. i. *Prolegomena*. 2nd Edit. Edinburgh, 1906.

Nägeli = *Der Wortschatz des Apostels Paulus*, by Th. Nägeli. Göttingen, 1905. See p. lv n.[2].

Norden *Kunstprosa* = *Die antike Kunstprosa vom vi. Jahrhundert v. Chr. bis in die Zeit der Renaissance*, by E. Norden. 2 vols. Leipzig, 1898. See p. lvii n.[5].

Ramsay *C. and B.* = *The Cities and Bishoprics of Phrygia*, by W. M. Ramsay. Vol. i. in two parts. Oxford, 1895—97.

Reitzenstein *Poimandres = Poimandres: Studien zur Griechisch-Ägyptischen und Frühchristlichen Literatur*, by R. Reitzenstein. Leipzig, 1904.

Roberts-Gardner = *An Introduction to Greek Epigraphy*. Part II. *The Inscriptions of Attica*. Edited by E. S. Roberts and E. A. Gardner. Cambridge, 1905.

Rutherford *N.P. = The New Phrynichus*, by W. G. Rutherford. London, 1881.

Schmid *Attic. = Der Atticismus in seinen Hauptvertretern von Dionysius von Halikarnass bis auf den zweiten Philostratus*, by W. Schmid. 4 vols and Register. Stuttgart, 1887—97.

Schürer[3] = *Geschichte des Jüdischen Volkes im Zeitalter Jesu Christi*, by E. Schürer. 3rd and 4th Edit. Leipzig, 1901—02. Eng. Tr. of the 2nd Edit. Edinburgh, 1890—91.

SH. = *A Critical and Exegetical Commentary on the Epistle to the Romans*, by W. Sanday and A. C. Headlam. 5th Edit. Edinburgh, 1902.

SK. = *Studien und Kritiken*. Gotha, 1828—.

Soph. Lex. = *Greek Lexicon of the Roman and Byzantine Periods*, by E. A. Sophocles. Memorial edition. New York, 1887.

Stephanus *Thesaurus = Thesaurus Graecae Linguae*, by H. Stephanus. 8 vols. and Glossary and Index. London, 1816—26.

Suicer *Thesaurus = Thesaurus Ecclesiasticus e Patribus Graecis*, by J. C. Suicer. Amsterdam, 1682.

Suidas = *Suidae Lexicon*, ed. I. Bekker. Berlin, 1854.

Thieme = *Die Inschriften von Magnesia am Mäander und das Neue Testament*, by G. Thieme. Göttingen, 1906.

Thumb *Hellen. = Die Griechische Sprache im Zeitalter des Hellenismus*, by A. Thumb. Strassburg, 1901.

Trench *Syn. = Synonyms of the New Testament*, by R. C. Trench. New Edition. London, 1901.

Viteau = *Étude sur le grec du Nouveau Testament*, by J. Viteau. Vol. i. *Le Verbe: Syntaxe des Prépositions*; Vol. ii. *Sujet, Complément et Attribut*. Paris, 1893—96.

Volz *Jüd. Eschat. = Jüdische Eschatologie von Daniel bis Akiba*, by P. Volz. Tübingen, 1903.

Votaw = *The Use of the Infinitive in Biblical Greek*, by C. W. Votaw. Chicago, 1896.

Weber *Jüd. Theologie* = *Jüdische Theologie auf Grund des Talmud und verwandter Schriften*, being the 2nd Edition by F. Delitzsch and G. Schnedermann of F. Weber's *System der altsynagogalen palästinischen Theologie* or *Die Lehren des Talmud*. Leipzig, 1897.

WH. or WH.² = *The New Testament in the original Greek*, by B. F. Westcott and F. J. A. Hort. Vol. i. *Text*; vol. ii. *Introduction and Appendix* containing *Notes on Select Readings* &c. Revised Editions. London, 1898 and 1896.

Wilcken *Ostr.* = *Griechische Ostraka* by U. Wilcken. 2 vols. Leipzig, 1899.

Witk. *Epp.* = *Epistulae Privatae Graecae*, ed. S. Witkowski. Leipzig, 1906. See p. 129.

WM. = *A Treatise on the Grammar of New Testament Greek*, by G. B. Winer, tr. and enlarged by W. F. Moulton. 8th Eng. Edit. Edinburgh, 1877.

WSchm. = *Grammatik des neutestamentlichen Sprachidioms*, by G. B. Winer. 8th Edit. newly revised by P. W. Schmiedel (in progress). Göttingen, 1894—.

Zahn *Einl.* = *Einleitung in das Neue Testament*. Vol. i. 2nd Edit. Leipzig, 1900; vol. ii. 1st Edit. 1899.

Z.N.T.W. = *Zeitschrift für die neutestamentliche Wissenschaft.* Giessen, 1900—.

INTRODUCTION

INTRODUCTION

I.

THE CITY OF THESSALONICA[1].

Σοί με, Θρηϊκίης σκυληφόρε, Θεσσαλονίκη,
μήτηρ ἡ πάσης πέμψε Μακηδονίης.
                Antipater of Thessalonica
                (time of Augustus).

Thessalonica was built close to the site of the ancient town of Therma or Therme, so named from the hot mineral springs which still exist in the vicinity, and at the head of the Gulf called after it the Thermaic Gulf[2]. Accounts differ as to the origin of the new city, but, according to the most probable story, it was founded by Cassander, the son-in-law of Philip of Macedon, about the year 315 B.C. and was called by him Thessalonica in honour of his wife, the step-sister of Alexander the Great[3]. Its earliest inhabitants were drawn not

The Foundation of Thessalonica.

---

[1] The principal authority for the history of Thessalonica is Tafel's *Historia Thessalonicae* (Tübing., 1835), afterwards prefixed as *Prolegomena* to his elaborate monograph *De Thessalonica ejusque agro. Dissertatio geographica* (Berol., 1839). Accounts of the geography and antiquities of the region are to be found in Cousinéry *Voyage dans la Macédoine* i. p. 23 ff. (Paris, 1831), Leake *Travels in Northern Greece* iii. p. 235 ff. (1835), Heuzey et Daumet *Mission Archéologique de Macédoine* (Paris, 1876), and Duchesne et Bayet *Mémoire sur une Mission au Mont Athos* (Paris, 1876). See also Lightfoot *Biblical Essays* p. 253 ff., and the artt. 'Thessalonica' in the *Encycl. Bibl.* and in Hastings' *D.B.* The present appearance and condition of the town are graphically described by G. F. Abbott in *The Tale of a Tour in Macedonia* (1903).

[2] Herod. vii. 121 Θέρμη δὲ τῇ ἐν τῷ Θερμαίῳ κόλπῳ οἰκημένῃ, ἀπ' ἧς καὶ ὁ κόλπος οὗτος τὴν ἐπωνυμίην ἔχει.

[3] Strabo 330 ἣ πρότερον Θέρμη ἐκαλεῖτο. κτίσμα δ' ἐστὶν Κασσάνδρου,

only from Therme, but from several of the neighbouring cities on the shores of the Gulf[1], and there is ample evidence that it soon rose to be a place of very considerable importance. It owed this in large measure to the natural advantages of its situation, commanding, as it did, on the landward side the rich plain of the Strymon, on which there also converged the three plains, watered respectively by the Axias, the Lydias, and the Haliacmon, and being furnished towards the sea with a good natural harbour.

When, accordingly, in 168 B.C. Macedonia was conquered by the Romans, and divided into four districts, Thessalonica, 'celeberrima urbs,' was made the capital of *Macedonia Secunda*[2]. And when, a few years later, 146 B.C., the different districts were united into a single province, it became virtually the capital of the whole.

Thessalonica under Roman rule,

Under Roman rule the prosperity of the city continued to advance rapidly. Its situation on the great *Via Egnatia*[3], about midway between Dyrrachium on the Adriatic and the river Hebrus in Thrace, brought it into such direct contact with the stream of traffic that was continually passing along that busy highway between Rome and her Eastern dependencies, that Cicero can speak of its inhabitants as 'placed in the lap of the Empire[4]'; and it was here that he himself sought refuge in the quaestor's house during his exile[5].

On the outbreak of the First Civil War (49 B.C.), Thessalonica was the head-quarters of the Pompeian party[6], but during the Second was found on the side of Octavius and Antonius[7], and, when their cause triumphed, was declared by way of reward a free city[8]. The consequence was that, unlike

ὃς ἐπὶ τῷ ὀνόματι τῆς ἑαυτοῦ γυναικός, παιδὸς δὲ Φιλίππου τοῦ 'Αμυντίου, ὠνόμασεν. The new title (under the form Θετταλονίκη) is first found in Polyb. xxiii. 4. 4, 11. 2 &c. Other accounts of the foundation of the city will be found in Tafel p. v.

[1] Strabo *l.c.*, Plin. *N.H.* iv. 17.
[2] Liv. xlv. 29, 30.
[3] See Tafel *Via militaris Romanorum Egnatia* (Tübing. 1842).
[4] 'Thessalonicenses positi in gremio imperii nostri' (*de prov. Consul.* 2).
[5] *Pro Planc.* 41.
[6] Dion Cass. xli. 18.
[7] Plut. *Brut.* 46, Appian *Bell. Civ.* iv. 118.
[8] 'Thessalonica liberae condicionis' (Plin. *N.H.* iv. 17). Coins have been discovered with the inscription Θεσσαλονικεων ελευθεριας (-ρια), which probably refers to this fact (Tafel p. xxviii f.).

THE CITY OF THESSALONICA

its neighbour Philippi, which was a Roman colony, Thessalonica remained an essentially Greek city, having the right to summon its own assembly[1], and being ruled by its own magistrates, who, according to the account in Acts, were known by the somewhat unusual title of politarchs[2]. This fact, formerly urged against St Luke's accuracy, has in recent years been triumphantly vindicated by the discovery of various inscriptions in which it reappears[3].

Other proofs of the flourishing state of Thessalonica are afforded by Strabo who, writing about a quarter of a century before St Paul's visit, describes it as the most populous of the Macedonian cities of his time, a description that is confirmed a century later by Lucian[4]. *at the beginning of the Christian era,*

Of St Paul's connexion with Thessalonica, and the circumstances attending the introduction of Christianity into it, we shall have occasion to speak later. Meanwhile it may be well to summarize briefly the story of the city's fortunes down to the present time.

About the middle of the third century it was erected into a colony, and, according to Duchesne, it probably received about the same time the title of metropolis of Macedonia[5]. Before *in the third and fourth centuries,*

---

[1] Ac. xvii. 5 τὸν δῆμον (cf. xix. 30, 33, of Ephesus). As throwing further light on the political constitution of Thessalonica, an interesting inscription, belonging to 143 A.D., may be recalled, where mention is made not only of its politarchs (see below), but of the decrees passed ὑπὸ τῆς κρατίσ[της βουλ]ῆς καὶ τοῦ δήμου (Duchesne p. 10).

[2] Ac. xvii. 6.

[3] The most important of these, which was found on a Roman Arch (since demolished), is now preserved in the British Museum. It is reproduced, with a history of the various transcriptions that have from time to time appeared, by Prof. E. DeWitt Burton in an important art. on 'The Politarchs' in the *Amer. Journ. of Theol.* ii. (1898), p. 598 ff. (summarized in Hastings' *D.B.* under 'Rulers of the City'). From this art. it would appear that the number of politarchs in Thessalonica in N.T. times was either five or six, and further that the office was by no means confined to Thessalonica, as is sometimes erroneously assumed. To Burton's evidence we can now add the occurrence of the title on an Egyptian papyrus-letter from Oxyrhynchus, belonging to the beginning of the first century, where the writer claims that his correspondent had made some promise through the 'politarch' Theophilus (P.Oxy. 745, 4 ὡς καὶ ὑπέσχου διὰ τοῦ πολειτάρχου Θεοφίλου).

[4] Strabo 323 Θεσσαλονίκειας, Μακεδονικῆς πόλεως, ἣ νῦν μάλιστα τῶν ἄλλων εὐανδρεῖ, Luc. *Asin. aur.* 46 πόλεως τῶν ἐν Μακεδονίᾳ τῆς μεγίστης Θεσσαλονίκης.

[5] The title occurs as early as Strabo 330 ἣ δὲ μητρόπολις τῆς νῦν Μακεδονίας ἐστί, but, in view of the fact that both

xxiv   THE EPISTLES TO THE THESSALONIANS

the foundation of Constantinople, it seems even to have been thought of as the possible capital of the world[1].

Its patron-saint Demetrius was martyred about 304 A.D.[2], and towards the close of the same century (389 A.D.) Thessalonica again received unhappy prominence through the ruthless massacre of at least seven thousand of its inhabitants by the order of the Emperor Theodosius, an act for which he was refused absolution by Ambrose, Bishop of Milan, until, after the lapse of eight months, he performed the most abject penance.

in the Middle Ages,   In the following century Theodoret describes Thessalonica as 'the greatest and most populous' city of the district[3], and the place which it gradually acquired in the history of the Church is shown by the fact that Cameniata in the tenth century bestows upon it, as its special right, the proud title of 'the orthodox city[4],' a designation it continued to deserve throughout the Middle Ages, when, according to its historian Tafel, it proved itself 'fax quaedam humanitatis ... fideique Christianae promotrix[5].'

Amongst its great names during this period none was more illustrious than that of Eustathius, who was not only the foremost scholar of his age, but, as archbishop of Thessalonica from 1175 to c. 1192, proved himself 'a man of political insight, and a bold and far-seeing reformer[6].'

Meanwhile the outward fortunes of the city were very varied,

---

contemporary and later inscriptions speak of Thessalonica simply as πόλις, Duchesne (p. 14 f.) thinks that Strabo's words, if not the gloss of a copyist, are best understood figuratively: cf. Jacobs *Anth. Gr.* ii. p. 152, no. 428 (time of Augustus) Θεσσαλονίκη, μήτηρ ἡ πάσης...Μακηδονίης.

[1] 'Before the foundation of Constantinople, Thessalonica is mentioned by Cedrenus (p. 283), and Sardica by Zonaras, as the intended capital' (Gibbon *Decline and Fall* c. xvii.).

[2] The splendid church erected in his honour is now a Turkish mosque.

[3] Theodoret *H.E.* v. 17 Θεσσαλονίκη πόλις ἐστὶ μεγίστη καὶ πολυάνθρωπος.

[4] Cameniata *De excidio Thessaloni-*

censi § 3 ἐν δὲ τοῦτο πρῶτον καὶ ἰδιαίτατον διεδείκνυτο, τὸ ὀρθόδοξον αὐτὴν καὶ εἶναι καὶ ὀνομάζεσθαι καὶ τούτῳ μᾶλλον ἤπερ τοῖς ἄλλοις σεμνύνεσθαι. According to Tafel (p. xlvi), the name is due to the city's obstinate defence of image-worship against the iconoclastic Emperors in the eighth and ninth centuries. Lightfoot (*Bibl. Essays* p. 268 f.) prefers to connect it with the stalwart resistance which Thessalonica offered to successive Gothic and Slavonic invasions, and to its active efforts for the conversion of the invaders.

[5] *Praef.* p. 3.

[6] J. E. Sandys *Hist. of Class. Scholarship*[2] p. 421.

but finally, after being plundered by the Saracens in 904, falling into the hands of the Normans and Tancred in 1185, and being placed under the protection of the Venetian Republic in 1422, it was taken by the Turks under Amurath II. in 1430, and has remained ever since in their possession.

At the present time under the popular name of Saloniki or (Turkish) Selanik[1], it is the second city in European Turkey, and carries on a large and flourishing trade. A recent traveller, after a careful examination of the statistics on the spot, estimated the number of its inhabitants a few years ago at 150,000, of whom he considered that no fewer than 90,000 were Jews[2]. These Jews are not, however, to be thought of as the direct descendants of the Jews of St Paul's day, but are Spanish Jews whose ancestors found refuge here when the Jews were expelled from Spain under Ferdinand and Isabella. They still speak a kind of Spanish 'much damaged by wear and tear, and picturesquely patched up with Turkish and other foreign elements[3],' and occupy a distinct *mahallah* or quarter of the city. Their importance is shown by the fact that they possess about thirty synagogues, as compared with about an equal number of Turkish mosques and twelve Christian churches, while a large part of the trade of the city is in their hands.

The Greek influence on the town, however, notwithstanding the comparatively small number of Greek inhabitants, is still predominant, so that 'on the whole, Salonica may be said still to be what it has been for more than twenty centuries— a centre of Hellenic influence and civilisation[4].'

---

[1] The old name of Θεσσαλονίκη is still used by all Greeks of any education. In the heading of letters this is often abbreviated into Θ/νίκη.

[2] Abbott p. 19 f. These figures are very considerably higher than the usual official returns, but, in a communication to the present writer, Mr Abbott states that in dealing with Turkish statistics two things must be kept in mind: first, that the Jews, who have no political ambitions, endeavour to minimize their numbers in order to avoid taxation; secondly, that the Christians often exaggerate theirs for political reasons.

[3] Abbott p. 20.

[4] *Ibid.* p. 21.

II.

ST PAUL AND THE THESSALONIAN CHURCH.

Αὐτὸν γὰρ αὐχεῖ Θεσσαλονίκη τὸν Παῦλον ἔχειν τῆς εὐσεβείας διδάσκαλον, τὸ σκεῦος τῆς ἐκλογῆς...ἐν αὐτῇ μᾶλλον τὸν τῆς θεογνωσίας σπόρον κατέβαλε, καὶ πολύχουν ἀποδίδοσθαι τὸν τῆς πίστεως καρπὸν διεσπούδασε.

Cameniata *De excidio Thessalonicensi* § 3.

'It is this close combination of cosmopolitan Judaism with cosmopolitan Hellenism which afforded the new religion its non-local, non-parochial hot-beds, and fitted it (humanly speaking) for the acceptance of the world.'

J. P. Mahaffy *The Silver Age of the Greek World* (1906) p. 317.

1. The Foundation of the Thessalonian Church.

1. It was during what is generally known as his Second Missionary Journey that St Paul first visited Thessalonica, and founded the Christian Church there. Obliged to leave Philippi, the Apostle along with Silas and, in all probability, Timothy, turned his face towards the South, and, following the line of the Great Egnatian Road which here runs through scenery of great natural beauty[1], pushed on steadily over the hundred miles that separated Philippi from Thessalonica[2]. In the latter busy seaport with its varied population and strenuous life St Paul would find just such a scene of work as he most desired. At once along with his companions he entered on an active mission amongst the Jews of the place, frequenting the Synagogue on three successive Sabbath days (ἐπὶ σάββατα τρία, Ac. xvii. 2) and reasoning in friendly intercourse (διελέξατο) with the assembled worshippers[3].

---

[1] Renan *St Paul* (1869) p. 154 f.

[2] According to the *Antonine Itinerary*, the actual distances were from Philippi to Amphipolis thirty-three miles, from Amphipolis to Apollonia thirty miles, and from Apollonia to Thessalonica thirty-seven miles, and in consequence it has been conjectured that Amphipolis and Apollonia (Ac. xvii. 1) formed the Apostle's successive resting-places for the night. But, as the ordinary rate for travellers on foot did not exceed sixteen to twenty Roman miles a day (Ramsay in Hastings' *D.B.* v. p. 386), the whole journey probably occupied from five to six days.

[3] Amongst the inscriptions found at Thessalonica is a fragment of uncertain

In doing so, as was natural with such an audience, the Apostle found a common starting-point in the Jewish Scriptures, expounding and quoting them to prove (διανοίγων καὶ παρατιθέμενος) that the Christ, for whom the Jews had been taught to look, ought to suffer and to rise again from the dead, and then passing on to show that these things were indeed fulfilled in the historical Jesus whom he had now come to proclaim (v. 3). Nor was this all, but, to judge from the nature of the charge afterwards brought against the missionaries ('saying that there is another King, Jesus' v. 7), special stress would seem to have been laid on the doctrine of the Kingdom which had played so large a part in the teaching of Jesus Himself, and above all, as we see clearly from the two Epistles afterwards addressed to the Thessalonian Church, upon its speedy and final establishment by the glorious return of its now exalted and heavenly King.

So far as the Jews were concerned, the immediate effect of this preaching was small, but, in addition to the 'some' of them who were persuaded, the historian of the Acts mentions other two classes who 'consorted' with the Apostles, or more exactly 'were allotted' to them by Divine favour (προσεκληρώθησαν), namely, 'of the devout Greeks a great multitude, and of the chief women not a few' (v. 4). Both these classes were of Gentile birth[1]. And this in itself prepares us for the further fact, not referred to in Acts, but amply attested by the contents of St Paul's own Epistles, that, on the comparative failure of this Jewish mission, the Apostles turned directly to the Gentile inhabitants of the town, and prosecuted their teaching amongst them with a far larger degree of success (cf. I. i. 9, ii. 14.)[2].

date, but as late as imperial times, which reads 'ΓΩΓΗΕΒΡ συν]αγωγὴ 'Εβρ[αίων], see J.H.S. xviii. (1898), p. 333.

[1] Dr Hort indeed thinks that the 'chief women' were probably the Jewish wives of heathen men of distinction as in Ac. xiii. 50 (Jud. Christianity p. 89), but on that occasion the women were found ranked against the Apostles, and in the present instance it is more natural to think of them as of Macedonian extraction (cf. Knowling E.G.T. ad loc.). For the important part played by women in Macedonia see Lightfoot Philippians[2] p. 55 f., Ramsay St Paul the Traveller and the Roman Citizen p. 227.

[2] The Lukan and Pauline accounts would be brought into closer harmony if in Ac. xvii. 4 we could adopt Ram-

How long St Paul continued his work amongst the Gentiles in Thessalonica we can only conjecture, but there are various particulars that indicate that it may well have extended over several months. Thus, apart from the two separate occasions on which he received help from Philippi (Phil. iv. 15 f.), a fact in itself pointing to a considerable lapse of time, the Apostle evidently found it worth his while to settle down for a time to his ordinary trade, and thereby secure the opportunity not only of instructing his converts as a whole in the main Christian truths (I. i. 9 f.), but of dealing directly and personally with them (I. ii. 7, 11; see further p. xlv). There is also evidence of a certain amount of organization in the newly-formed community either immediately previous to or after the missionaries' departure (I. v. 12 ff.). Nor is it without significance as showing how widely St Paul had succeeded in making his presence and influence felt outside the circle of his own immediate followers that 'the city,' evidently 'all the city' (A.V.), though there is no warrant for 'all' in the original, was set in an uproar by the attack made against him (*v.* 5).

Attack upon St Paul.
The primary instigators of this attack were the Jews who, moved by jealousy of the success attending St Paul's preaching, but unable of themselves to thwart it, enlisted on their side 'certain vile fellows of the rabble,' the *lazzaroni* of the market-place, who must have been very numerous in such a city as Thessalonica, and with their aid assaulted the house of Jason, in which apparently the Apostles were lodging. It had been their intention to bring them before that assembly of the people which, in virtue of their *libera condicio* (see p. xxii n.[8]), the Thessalonians were privileged to hold. But means had been found for the Apostles' escape, and the mob had to content themselves with wreaking their vengeance on Jason and certain others of the brethren by bringing them before the politarchs, or city-magistrates, on the charge of being revolutionaries—'these that have turned the world upside down' (*v.* 6)—and more particularly of acting 'contrary to the decrees of Caesar, saying that there is another King, Jesus' (*v.* 7).

say's emendation of the text, resulting from a comparison of A with D, πολλοί τῶν σεβομένων καὶ Ἑλλήνων πλῆθος

πολύ (*St Paul* p. 235); but the reading is wanting in MS. authority, nor is it required on internal grounds.

ST PAUL AND THE THESSALONIAN CHURCH xxix

The charge was cleverly planned, and in itself clearly betrays the Jewish prompting which, as we have just seen, underlay the whole riot, for only Jews thought of the Messiah as King, and could thus have accused the Apostles of proclaiming Jesus as 'another' King. At the same time no charge was more likely to arouse the hostility of the Greek magistrates[1]. As in the case of Pilate, when a similar accusation was laid before him against the Lord Himself (Lk. xxiii. 2, Jo. xix. 12, 15), the politarchs would be very sensitive to any appearance of tolerating treason against the honour of the Emperor, and it says much for their desire to administer justice impartially that they contented themselves with requiring that 'security,' probably in the form of a pecuniary surety or bond, should be taken from Jason and the others that the peace of the city should not be further disturbed[2]. Moderate, however, though this decision was[3], it made it impossible for St Paul to remain in Thessalonica without the risk of involving his friends in serious troubles, and possibly of arousing active official opposition to his whole work, and accordingly along with Silas he departed by night for the important city of Beroea[4], whither he was followed soon after by Timothy.

2. The missionaries' reception there was even more encouraging than at Thessalonica. No longer 'some' but 'many' of the Jews believed, and along with them 'of the Greek women of honourable estate, and of men, not a few' (v. 12). But the work was not long allowed to go on in peace. The bitter malice of the Thessalonian Jews followed St Paul here, and so successful were they in again 'stirring up and troubling the multitudes' that the brethren sent for the Apostle to go

2. Departure from Thessalonica. Beroea.

---

[1] 'Nec Caesaribus honor' is one of the complaints of Tacitus against the Jews (*Hist.* v. 5). And Just. M. *Apol.* I. 11 (Otto) proves how necessary the first Christians found it to show that by 'kingdom' they understood nothing 'human' (οὐκ εἰς τὸ νῦν τὰς ἐλπίδας ἔχομεν).

[2] Ac. xvii. 9. The phrase λαμβάνειν τὸ ἱκανόν, which Blass (*Acta Apostolorum* p. 187) traces to Latin influence *satisdare, satis accipere*, can now be illustrated from the inscriptions, e.g. *O.G.I.S.* 484, 50 (ii./A.D.) τὸ ἱκαν[ὸν πρὸ κρίσ]εως λ[α]μβάνεσθαι, 629, 101 (ii./A.D.) οὗ[τος τ]ὸ ἱκανὸν λαμβανέτω.

[3] Ramsay describes it as 'the mildest that was prudent in the circumstances' (*St Paul* p. 230).

[4] In an inscription discovered at Beroea belonging to ii./A.D., the city is described as ἡ σεμνοτάτη μητρόπολις τῆς Μακεδονίας καὶ δὶς νεωκόρος Βέροια (*Rev. d. Études grecques* xv. p. 142).

Athens.	'as far as to the sea,' where, probably at Dium, some of them embarked along with him for Athens (*v.* 14 f.).
3. Movements of Silas and Timothy.	3. Meanwhile Silas and Timothy remained behind at Beroea, perhaps to prosecute the newly started work, possibly also to know when it would be safe for St Paul to return to Thessalonica, but in any case with instructions to rejoin him as quickly as possible. If we had only the account in Acts to guide us, we might imagine that they were not able to accomplish this until St Paul reached Corinth (cf. Ac. xviii. 5). But again the historical narrative requires to be supplemented by the Apostle's own Epistle. For the mention of the despatch of Timothy on a special mission to Thessalonica while St Paul was still at Athens shows us that he at least had previously rejoined the Apostle there (I. iii. 1 f.); and if so, it is probable that Silas had also done the same in accordance with the urgent message already sent to both (Ac. xvii. 15). And if we can think of the despatch of Silas himself shortly afterwards on a similar errand, perhaps to Philippi, with which at the time St Paul was in communication (Phil. iv. 15), we can understand, in accordance with the definite statements of Ac. xviii. 5, how on the conclusion of their respective missions the two messengers 'came down from Macedonia' to St Paul at Corinth, to which city he had gone on alone from Athens[1].
Timothy's report from Thessalonica.	The report which Timothy brought back from Thessalonica, supplemented possibly by a letter from the Thessalonians themselves addressed to St Paul[2], was evidently in the main highly satisfactory. The Thessalonians, to judge from the Epistle afterwards addressed to them, which is our only definite source of information, had proved themselves worthy of their 'election' not only in the manner in which they themselves had received the Gospel, but in the 'ensample' they

---

[1] Cf. Paley *Hor. Paul.* c. ix. 4. It is of course possible that St Paul only sent instructions from Athens to Timothy and Silas while still at Beroea to proceed thence on their respective missions, and consequently that it was actually *first* at Corinth that they rejoined him. But the explanation given above seems more natural, especially in view of the emphatic καταλειφθῆναι 'left behind' of I. iii. 1, suggesting the immediately previous presence of his companions with the writer (see note *ad loc.*).

[2] For an interesting attempt to reconstruct this letter see Rendel Harris 'A Study in Letter-writing,' *Exp.* v. viii. p. 161 ff., and cf. Add. Note A, 'St Paul as a Letter-Writer, p. 126.'

had subsequently set to believers throughout Macedonia and Achaia (I. i. 4 ff.). At the same time they were exposed to certain dangers requiring immediate attention if they were indeed to prove a 'crown of glorying' at the Parousia of the Lord Jesus (I. ii. 19).

4. Thus it would appear that no sooner had St Paul and his companions left Thessalonica than suspicions had begun to be cast upon the whole course of their Apostolic ministry, with the obvious intention of diverting the Thessalonian believers from their allegiance. Nowhere are we expressly told who were the authors of these insinuations. And in consequence many have referred them to the *heathen* population of Thessalonica[1] who would naturally resent bitterly the defection of their fellow-countrymen from the old standards of faith and morals. But if so, it hardly seems likely that their opposition would have taken this particular form, or, even supposing it had, that it would have had much effect upon the Christian converts. These last could not but know that their fellow-countrymen's zeal against the Apostles was dictated not only by prejudice, but by ignorance of the facts of the case, and they would hardly allow themselves to be led astray by those who had never put themselves in the way of discovering what was the real character and teaching of the men they were so eager to traduce.

If, however, the attacks came from a *Jewish* source, the case would be very different. The Thessalonian Jews would be able to claim that in virtue of their own past history, and the 'oracles' that had been committed to their fathers, they were in a better position to decide than any newly admitted Gentile converts could possibly be, what was the true relation of the Apostles' teaching to the whole course of that Divine revelation, of which it claimed to be the natural and necessary fulfilment. We must not indeed suppose that their attacks assumed the definite form which St Paul had afterwards to face in connexion with his Judaistic opponents in Galatia and elsewhere. Of this there is as yet no trace in the Epistles before us[2]. On the other hand we can easily understand how

4. Circumstances leading to the writing of 1 Thessalonians. Insinuations directed against St Paul

by the Jewish inhabitants of Thessalonica.

---

[1] So e.g. Clemen, *Paulus* (1904) ii. p. 181 f.

[2] Jülicher *Introd. to the N.T.* Eng. Tr. p. 58 'The new converts were threatened, not by a false Gospel, but by rabid hatred of any Gospel.'

ready the Jewish inhabitants of Thessalonica would be by open assertion and covert hint to throw discredit on the Apostle's character and credentials with the object of undermining as far as possible the effect of his work[3].

It is this latter consideration indeed, which alone enables us to understand the large place which St Paul devotes to this subject in his Epistle. It may seem strange at first sight that he should have thought it worth while to defend himself and his companions from attacks coming from a source so manifestly inspired by unworthy motives. But the Apostle could not but recognize that much more than his own personal honour was at stake. The whole future of the Gospel at Thessalonica would be endangered, if these 'perverse and wicked men' (II. iii. 2) were allowed to get their way. And therefore it was that he found it necessary for the Word's sake, if not for his own, that they should not only be answered, but repudiated and condemned in the most emphatic manner (I. ii. 15 f.).

Persecution of the Thessalonian Christians.

Nor was this the only point on which Timothy's report caused St Paul grave concern. The persecution, which the Apostle had foretold as the lot of Christ's people everywhere, had evidently fallen in full measure on the young Thessalonian community (I. iii. 3 ff.). And though as yet there were no signs of active backsliding, but rather the contrary, St Paul dreaded that such a state of things might not continue, and that his converts might suffer themselves to be 'lured away' (v. 3) from that standing fast in the Lord (v. 8), through which alone they could hope to obtain full and complete salvation at the Lord's appearing (v. 13, cf. v. 9). The exhortation of a father therefore (ii. 11) was required, as well as the tender dealing of a mother (ii. 7), and this all the more in view of certain other matters of a more directly practical kind, on which Timothy had evidently represented the Thessalonians as requiring further guidance.

---

[1] Cf. B. Weiss 'The Present Status of the Inquiry concerning the Genuineness of the Pauline Epistles' in *Amer. Journ. of Theol.* i. (1897) p. 332 f.— a paper in which there are many suggestive remarks regarding the Epistles before us.

ST PAUL AND THE THESSALONIAN CHURCH xxxiii

These concerned in the first place their moral conduct. Christian believers though they were, the Thessalonians had not yet learned the completeness of the severance which their new faith demanded from various habits and practices they had hitherto been accustomed to regard as 'indifferent,' nor the necessity of a quiet, orderly continuance in the work and relationships of their daily life, notwithstanding the speedy coming of their Lord for which they had been taught to look (iv. 1—12). *Their moral*

And then as regards that coming itself, there were at least two points on which the Apostle's previous instruction required to be supplemented. *and doctrinal difficulties,*

In the first place the Thessalonians had to be reassured on a question which was giving them grave concern, and on which apparently they had definitely asked St Paul's opinion. What of those of their number who were falling asleep while as yet Christ had not come? Would they in consequence be shut out from the glory by which His coming would be attended[1]? By no means, so the Apostle hastened to comfort them, in one of the few pictorial representations of the Last Things that occur in his writings; they would rather be the first to share in that glory. For not till the 'dead in Christ' had risen, would the living be caught up along with them to meet the descending Lord in the air (iv. 13—18).

In the second place, as regarded the time of that coming, which to the Thessalonians in their eager love for Christ might seem to be unaccountably delayed, St Paul recalled what they ought never to have forgotten, that the Day of the Lord would come as a surprise, and that in consequence their present duty was not to be over-anxious on a point regarding which no certain knowledge was possible, but rather to watch and be sober, putting on the triple armour of faith and love and hope—a hope grounded on God's gracious purposes towards them, and on the redemptive work of Christ through which

---

[1] The same problem meets us in 4 Ezra v. 41 f. (ed. Bensly): 'Et dixi: sed ecce, domine, tu praees his qui in fine sunt, et quid facient qui ante nos sunt aut nos aut hi qui post nos? Et dixit ad me: coronae adsimilabo iudicium meum; sicut non nouissimorum tarditas, sic nec priorum uelocitas.' See further note *ad* I. iv. 15.

xxxiv   THE EPISTLES TO THE THESSALONIANS

and failure in internal discipline.
alone the fulfilment of these purposes had been rendered possible (v. 1—11).

Nor was this all, but as appears from the closing section of the Epistle, St Paul had evidently also been informed of certain difficulties that had arisen in the internal discipline of the young community, and in consequence seized the opportunity of reinforcing the authority of those who had been placed in positions of trust, and of laying down certain general rules of holy living, by means of which the well-being of the whole community might be secured, and its members be 'preserved entire, without blame' at the coming of the Lord Jesus Christ (v. 12—23).

The Epistle a substitute for a personal visit.
Such then would seem to have been the circumstances which led up to the writing of this Epistle, and the manner in which St Paul met them. Nothing indeed can be clearer from the Epistle itself than how much the Apostle regretted having to fall back upon this method of communicating with his beloved converts. Gladly would he rather have revisited them in person, and indeed, as he expressly tells them, on two occasions he had actually made the attempt, but in vain— 'Satan hindered us' (ii. 18). No other course then remained open for him but to have resort to a letter, a means of conveying religious truth which he had made peculiarly his own[1], and of which he had doubtless frequently availed himself before in communicating with the Churches he had founded[2].

Written in the name of all the missionaries.
It is noteworthy too, how closely on the present occasion St Paul associated Silas and Timothy with himself in the writing of the Epistle. For not only do their names occur along with his own in the Address in accordance with a favourite and characteristic practice[3], but the first person plural

---

[1] See further Add. Note A, 'St Paul as a Letter-Writer.'

[2] Note the emphatic ἐν πάσῃ ἐπιστολῇ in II. iii. 17, which naturally implies more than a single precursor (Sanday *Inspiration* p. 336), and 'On the Probability that many of St Paul's Epistles have been lost' see Jowett *The Epistles of St Paul to the Thessalonians*[2] &c. (1859) i. p. 195 ff. On the other hand I. v. 27, II. ii. 15, iii. 17 f. have been taken as implying that the habit of sending important Epistles was new (Weiss *Introd. to the N.T.*, Eng. Tr. i. p. 204; cf. von Soden *Hist. of Early Christian Literature* Eng. Tr. p. 27 f.).

[3] Cf. Cic. *ad Att.* ix. 7 A. Farrar (*St Paul* i. p. 579) recalls the saying of Origen that the concurrence of Paul

is maintained throughout both this Epistle and its successor with a regularity to which we have no subsequent parallel[1]. It will be well therefore to recognize this fact in our subsequent exposition of the Epistle's teaching, and to refer the views there expressed to all three Apostles, even though St Paul must be regarded as their primary and principal author.

5. This same consideration helps also to establish what our previous account of St Paul's movements has made sufficiently clear, that it was at Corinth that the First Epistle to the Thessalonians was written, for it was there, as we have seen, that Silas and Timothy rejoined him on the conclusion of their respective missions, nor, so far at least as we can gather from the Lukan account, was there any subsequent period in their history when the three missionaries were together in one place, and consequently in a position to act as joint-sponsors of the letter.

5. Place of writing of 1 Thessalonians.

With this view the internal evidence of the Epistle itself is in complete harmony. To place it earlier, as for example at Athens, in accordance with the 'subscription' in certain MSS. and followed by the A.V., would hardly leave time for all that had taken place in the Church at Thessalonica after the Apostles' departure (ii. 14, iii. 1—6), and, above all, for the influence the Thessalonian believers had been able to exert on the surrounding district (i. 7 f., iv. 10). On the other hand, to place it subsequent to St Paul's departure from Corinth where he remained a year and a half (Ac. xviii. 11), is obviously inconsistent with the freshness that marks his references to his Thessalonian friends (i. 5, ii. 1 ff.), and with his express statement that as yet he had been separated from them only 'for a short season' (ii. 17).

6. If then we are correct in regarding Corinth as the place of writing of the Epistle, and are prepared further to think of a comparatively early period in the Apostle's sojourn there, the exact date will be determined by the view taken of the chronology of St Paul's life. It is a subject on which authorities

6. Date.

---

and Silas flashed out the lightning of these Epistles (*Hom. V. in Jerem.* 588 b).

[1] See further Add. Note B, 'Did St Paul use the Epistolary Plural?'

widely differ, but the general tendency is to throw the dates backward rather than forward, and we shall probably not be far wrong if we place the writing of our Epistle somewhere about 50—51 A.D.

>Harnack (*Chronol. d. altchr. Litt.* (1897) i. p. 239 n.¹) dates the two Epistles as early as 48—49, and in this he is followed by McGiffert (art. 'Thessalonians (Epistles to)' in *Encyc. Bibl.* col. 5037). The 'Chronology of the N.T.' advocated by Turner in Hastings' *D.B.*, which has met with wide acceptance, would throw them forward a year (50), while Ramsay (*St Paul* p. 254) prefers 51—52, the earlier of these dates being also supported by St Paul's latest biographer Clemen (see his *Paulus* i. p. 398). W. Brückner (*Chronol.* p. 193 ff.), while dating the four chief Epistles as late as 61—62, agrees that, if 1 Thessalonians is really the work of St Paul, it must be carried back to a much earlier period in the Apostle's life, when his theological system was not yet fully developed; cf. Menegoz *Le Péché et la Rédemption d'après Saint Paul* (Paris, 1882) p. 4.

1 Thessalonians probably the earliest extant Pauline Epistle.

On this view too of the date, we are probably justified in regarding 1 Thessalonians as the earliest of St Paul's extant Epistles. It is impossible indeed to ignore the fact that in recent years this honour has been claimed with increasing persistency for the Epistle to the Galatians by a very influential band of scholars. And, if we are prepared to admit the South Galatian address of that Epistle, there is no doubt that a place can be found for it previous to the above-mentioned date, and, further, that this position is favoured by the often striking coincidences between its language and the incidents of the First Missionary Journey, and more specially the speech delivered by the Apostle at Pisidian Antioch in the course of it[1].

On the other hand, if such resemblances in language and thought are to be reckoned with, how are we to explain the fact that in the Thessalonian Epistle, written, according to most of the supporters of this view, very shortly after Galatians (see small print below), there is an almost complete absence of any trace of the distinctive doctrinal positions of that Epistle? No doubt the differences in the circumstances under which the

---

[1] The various arguments that bear upon the exact date of Galatians will be found carefully stated by Knowling *The Testimony of St Paul to Christ* (1905) p. 28 ff.; see also Moffatt *Hist. N.T.* p. 125 f.

two Epistles were written, and the particular ends they had in view, may account for much of this dissimilarity. At the same time, while not psychologically impossible, it is surely most unlikely that the same writer—and he too a writer of St Paul's keen emotional nature—should show no signs in this (according to this view) later Epistle of the conflict through which he had just been passing, and on which he had been led to take up so strong and decided a position.

If, however, in accordance with the older view, 1 Thessalonians along with its successor to the same Church can still be placed first, all is clear. As an example of St Paul's missionary teaching, written before the acuter controversies of his later years had forced themselves upon him, and made inevitable the presentment of the old truths in a new way, it stands in its natural relation to the earlier missionary discourses of Acts, which in so many respects it resembles, while the Epistle to the Galatians ranks itself along with the other great doctrinal Epistles to the Corinthians and the Romans, whether, with the majority of modern critics, we place it first amongst these, or, with Bishop Lightfoot, in an intermediate position between 2 Corinthians and Romans.

> Considerable variety of opinion exists among the supporters of the priority of Galatians as to the exact date to be assigned to it. Dr Vernon Bartlet (*Exp.* v. x. p. 263 ff., *Apost. Age* p. 84 ff.), reviving a view suggested by Calvin, thinks that it was written at Antioch on St Paul's way to the Council of Jerusalem. The same conclusion was arrived at, much about the same time, on independent grounds by the Romanist Dr Weber (see his *Die Abfassung des Galaterbriefes vor dem Apostel-Konzil*, Ravensburg, 1900, summarized in *J.T.S.* iii. (1902) p. 630 ff.), and recently has formed the main thesis of Mr Douglas Round's Essay *The Date of St Paul's Epistle to the Galatians* (Cambridge, 1906). As a rule, however, a period *subsequent* to the Council of Jerusalem is preferred—McGiffert (*Hist. of Christianity in the Apost. Age* p. 226 ff.) dating the Epistle from Antioch before St Paul departed on his Second Missionary Journey, Clemen (as against his own earlier view, *Chronol.* p. 199 ff.) assigning it rather to the Apostle's stay in Athens (*Paulus* i. p. 396 ff., ii. p. 164 ff.), and Zahn (*Einl. in d. N.T.* i. p. 139 ff.) and Rendall (*Exp.* IV. ix. p. 254) carrying it forward to the beginning of the visit to Corinth in the course of the same journey. On this last view it can only have preceded the Thessalonian Epistles by a few weeks, or at most

xxxviii THE EPISTLES TO THE THESSALONIANS

months (cf. Bacon *Introd. to the N.T.* p. 57 f.). The later, and more widely accepted, dates assigned to Galatians have no direct bearing upon the point before us, except in so far as they emphasize that we are there dealing with a wholly different 'type' of teaching from that which meets us in the Thessalonian Epistles.

7. Despatch of 1 Thessalonians.

7. St Paul makes no mention of how his Epistle was sent to Thessalonica, but at a time when there was no regular system of posts except for imperial purposes, it can only have been by the hand of a personal courier or friend[1]. And it was perhaps through him on his return that the Apostle received the news which led to the writing of his second Epistle.

8. Circumstances leading to the writing of 2 Thessalonians.

8. That news was evidently of a somewhat mingled character. On the one hand, there were not wanting traces of an exceedingly growing faith and of an abounding love on the Thessalonians' part (II. i. 3) together with an endurance under continued persecution which called forth the Apostle's warmest praise, and seemed in his eyes a happy augury of his converts' future bliss at the revelation of the Lord Jesus from heaven (i. 4—12). But as against this, there were only too evident signs that the thought of the imminence of that revelation was still exercising a disturbing influence over the Thessalonians' daily conduct. So far from their excitement having been allayed by St Paul's first letter, as he hoped it would have been, the reverse would seem rather to have been the case, and not only so, but their restlessness had been still further fomented by certain pneumatic utterances, and even by carefully reasoned words and a letter, one or all of them shielding themselves under the Apostle's name and authority, to the effect that the Day of the Lord was not only imminent, but was actually come (ii. 2).

In these circumstances then, what more natural than that St Paul should seize the opportunity of once more recalling to his converts another aspect of his eschatological teaching, of which he had been in the habit of speaking (ἔλεγον, ii. 5) while with them, but of which apparently they had lost sight? Sudden and unexpected though the coming of the Day of the Lord would be, it would nevertheless be preceded by certain

---

[1] See further Add. Note A, 'St Paul as a Letter-Writer,' p. 130.

clearly-defined signs, foremost amongst which was the appearance of the Man of lawlessness, who for the time being was held in check, but whose revelation was to be looked for as the final precursor of the end. With the details of this crowning revelation of evil, we are not at present concerned. It is enough that in the very thought of it St Paul found an additional argument alike for a continued steadfastness on the part of his converts (ii. 13—16), and for a quiet and orderly walk, as contrasted with the disorderliness which certain idlers and busybodies in their midst were displaying (iii. 1—15).

9. More need hardly be said as to the circumstances in which this Second Epistle was written, for the general similarity between it and its predecessor, to which fuller reference will have to be made afterwards (see p. lxxx ff.), shows that in the main the historical conditions of the Thessalonian Church were very little altered[1], and that consequently the Second Epistle must have been written not many months after the First. We therefore date it also from Corinth within the period already specified 50—51 A.D.

9. Place of writing and Date of 2 Thessalonians.

The idea first advocated by Grotius (*Annot. in N.T.* ii. p. 715 ff.), and adopted by Ewald (*Sendschreiben des Paulus* p. 17 f.), Laurent (*NTliche Stud.* p. 49 ff.), and (from his own standpoint) Baur (*Paul,* Eng. Tr. ii. p. 336 ff.), that 2 Thessalonians was written *before* 1 Thessalonians can no longer be said to have any serious supporters. Thus, without attaching too great weight to such passages as II. ii. 2, 15 which, if not directly referring to 1 Thessalonians, are best explained by its existence, it is excluded by I. ii. 17—iii. 6 which could hardly have been written by St Paul, if he had previously addressed a letter to Thessalonica. The whole relationship indeed of 2 to 1 Thessalonians is of a secondary character alike on its literary side, and in the picture presented of the 'developed' circumstances of the Church, as shown by the heightened praise (II. i. 4: I. ii. 14) and blame (II. iii. 6 f.: I. iv. 11), which these circumstances now called forth.

2 Thessalonians not prior to 1 Thessalonians.

---

[1] 'Wir treffen...Stimmungen, Erwartungen, Bestrebungen, Lebensformen nach der lobens- wie tadelnswerthen Seite hin an, in denen wir alten Bekannten wiederbegegnen. Nur Alles, Gutes wie Verkehrtes,...in einer über das bisher bekannte Mass hinaus gehobenen Steigerung.' Klöpper *Der zweite Brief an die Thessalonicher* (reprinted from *Theologische Studien und Skizzen aus Ostpreussen* ii. p. 73 ff.) p. 17.

10. St Paul's subsequent connexion with Thessalonica.

10. Regarding St Paul's subsequent connexion with the Thessalonian Church we have no definite information, but it is hardly possible to doubt that on more than one occasion he was able to carry out his ardently cherished desire of revisiting in person his friends there. Thus he would naturally pass through the city both coming and going on his Third Missionary Journey (Ac. xx. 1 ff.), and if we accept the belief in a renewed period of active work on the part of the Apostle between a first and second Roman imprisonment, he would be almost certain to stop at Thessalonica on the occasion of that journey to Philippi which he had previously carefully planned in the event of his again finding himself a free man (Phil. i. 26, ii. 24). Nor, once more, could Thessalonica fail to be included in his programme if he ever paid that last visit to Macedonia, to which he alludes in his First Epistle to Timothy (i. 3)[1].

---

[1] See further Add. Note C, 'The Thessalonian Friends of St Paul.'

III.

GENERAL CHARACTER AND CONTENTS OF THE EPISTLES.

'Jeder einzelne paulinische Brief ist eine christliche That und will als solche verstanden sein.'
W. BORNEMANN *Die Thessalonicherbriefe* p. 256.

1. From what has already been said of the circumstances under which the Epistles to the Thessalonians were written, it must be clear that they are in no sense literary documents, still less theological treatises, but genuine letters intended to meet passing needs, and with no thought of any wider audience than those to whom they were originally addressed[1]. Of all the N.T. Epistles which have come down to us, they are amongst the most 'personal,' and illustrate to perfection the 'stenographed conversation' which Renan claims as a distinctive feature of the Pauline style[2].

1. The Epistles are true letters,

Greatly however as this adds to the living interest of the Epistles, it is one main source of their difficulties. For, whether or not they form only part of a correspondence that was passing between St Paul and the Thessalonian Church (cf. p. xxx), they so abound in allusions to what the Thessa-

---

[1] On the whole question of Letter *versus* Epistle in the case of the Pauline literature see especially Deissmann *BS.* p. 3 ff., and on the danger of carrying the distinction too far cf. Lock *The Bible and Christian Life* p. 114 ff., and Ramsay *The Letters to the Seven Churches* (1904) p. 22 ff.

The fact is that the Pauline Epistles require a new category: while letters, they are distinctively *religious* letters, approaching more nearly to the Pas-

toral Letter addressed by a Church to its members, or a minister to his congregation, than to what we understand by the 'letter' of ordinary correspondence.

[2] *Saint Paul* (ed. 1869) p. 231 f., 'Le style épistolaire de Paul est le plus personnel qu'il y ait jamais eu.... On dirait une rapide conversation sténographiée et reproduite sans corrections.'

lonians already know, or have been asking, that it is hardly too much to say, that the more familiar the subjects with which they deal were to their first readers, the more veiled they are from us[1].

'occasional' in their origin,

It is a complete mistake, however, to suppose that because our Epistles are thus 'occasional' writings in the strict sense of the word, they are therefore marked by that poverty of subject-matter which has sometimes been urged against them. On the contrary, if, as we shall have occasion to see more fully again, what we have come to regard as the distinctive doctrines of Paulinism are awanting, and awanting because the special circumstances demanding them had not yet arisen, the Epistles are nevertheless filled with definite religious teaching. Combined with the speeches in Acts, which in so many respects they recall[2], they contain the best evidence we possess as to the general character of St Paul's missionary preaching to Gentiles[3].

but filled with definite religious teaching.

It is not possible to illustrate this at length here, but I. i. 9 f. may be referred to as a convenient summary of the earliest Pauline teaching with its two *foci* of Monotheism, the belief in the one living and true God, as distinguished from

---

[1] The student will not regret being reminded of John Locke's famous 'Essay for the understanding of St Paul's Epistles, by consulting St Paul himself,' prefixed to his *Paraphrase and Notes* on certain of the Epistles (London, 1823): cf. especially p. 4, 'The nature of epistolary writings in general disposes the writer to pass by the mentioning of many things, as well known to him to whom his letter is addressed, which are necessary to be laid open to a stranger, to make him comprehend what is said: and it not seldom falls out that a well-penned letter, which is very easy and intelligible to the receiver, is very obscure to a stranger, who hardly knows what to make of it....Add to this, that in many places it is manifest he answers letters sent, and questions proposed to him, which, if we had, would much better clear those passages that relate to them than all the learned notes of critics and commentators, who in after-times fill us with their conjectures; for very often, as to the matter in hand, they are nothing else.'

[2] Cf. e.g. for linguistic parallels 1 Thess. i. 9 with Ac. xiv. 15; 1 Thess. i. 10 with Ac. xvii. 31; 1 Thess. iii. 4 with Ac. xiv. 22; 1 Thess. v. 9 with Ac. xx. 28: and for the general similarity of teaching see Sabatier *L'Apôtre Paul* (Strassburg, 1870) pp. 85—97, Eng. Tr. pp. 95—111.

[3] Prof. B. W. Bacon, while agreeing as to the generally 'missionary' character of the Epistles, points out that 'Paul's attitude in them is that of confirmer rather than proclaimer of the Gospel' (*The Story of St Paul*, London, 1905, p. 230).

III.

GENERAL CHARACTER AND CONTENTS OF THE EPISTLES.

'Jeder einzelne paulinische Brief ist eine christliche That und will als solche verstanden sein.'
W. BORNEMANN *Die Thessalonicherbriefe* p. 256.

1. From what has already been said of the circumstances under which the Epistles to the Thessalonians were written, it must be clear that they are in no sense literary documents, still less theological treatises, but genuine letters intended to meet passing needs, and with no thought of any wider audience than those to whom they were originally addressed[1]. Of all the N.T. Epistles which have come down to us, they are amongst the most 'personal,' and illustrate to perfection the 'stenographed conversation' which Renan claims as a distinctive feature of the Pauline style[2].

1. The Epistles are true letters,

Greatly however as this adds to the living interest of the Epistles, it is one main source of their difficulties. For, whether or not they form only part of a correspondence that was passing between St Paul and the Thessalonian Church (cf. p. xxx), they so abound in allusions to what the Thessa-

---

[1] On the whole question of Letter *versus* Epistle in the case of the Pauline literature see especially Deissmann *BS.* p. 3 ff., and on the danger of carrying the distinction too far cf. Lock *The Bible and Christian Life* p. 114 ff., and Ramsay *The Letters to the Seven Churches* (1904) p. 22 ff.

The fact is that the Pauline Epistles require a new category: while letters, they are distinctively *religious* letters, approaching more nearly to the Pastoral Letter addressed by a Church to its members, or a minister to his congregation, than to what we understand by the 'letter' of ordinary correspondence.

[2] *Saint Paul* (ed. 1869) p. 231 f., 'Le style épistolaire de Paul est le plus personnel qu'il y ait jamais eu.... On dirait une rapide conversation sténographiée et reproduite sans corrections.'

lonians already know, or have been asking, that it is hardly too much to say, that the more familiar the subjects with which they deal were to their first readers, the more veiled they are from us[1].

'occasional' in their origin,

It is a complete mistake, however, to suppose that because our Epistles are thus 'occasional' writings in the strict sense of the word, they are therefore marked by that poverty of subject-matter which has sometimes been urged against them. On the contrary, if, as we shall have occasion to see more fully again, what we have come to regard as the distinctive doctrines of Paulinism are awanting, and awanting because the special

but filled with definite religious teaching.

circumstances demanding them had not yet arisen, the Epistles are nevertheless filled with definite religious teaching. Combined with the speeches in Acts, which in so many respects they recall[2], they contain the best evidence we possess as to the general character of St Paul's missionary preaching to Gentiles[3].

It is not possible to illustrate this at length here, but I. i. 9 f. may be referred to as a convenient summary of the earliest Pauline teaching with its two *foci* of Monotheism, the belief in the one living and true God, as distinguished from

---

[1] The student will not regret being reminded of John Locke's famous 'Essay for the understanding of St Paul's Epistles, by consulting St Paul himself,' prefixed to his *Paraphrase and Notes* on certain of the Epistles (London, 1823): cf. especially p. 4, 'The nature of epistolary writings in general disposes the writer to pass by the mentioning of many things, as well known to him to whom his letter is addressed, which are necessary to be laid open to a stranger, to make him comprehend what is said: and it not seldom falls out that a well-penned letter, which is very easy and intelligible to the receiver, is very obscure to a stranger, who hardly knows what to make of it....Add to this, that in many places it is manifest he answers letters sent, and questions proposed to him, which, if we had, would much better clear those passages that relate to them than all the learned notes of critics and commentators, who in after-times fill us with their conjectures; for very often, as to the matter in hand, they are nothing else.'

[2] Cf. e.g. for linguistic parallels 1 Thess. i. 9 with Ac. xiv. 15; 1 Thess. i. 10 with Ac. xvii. 31; 1 Thess. iii. 4 with Ac. xiv. 22; 1 Thess. v. 9 with Ac. xx. 28: and for the general similarity of teaching see Sabatier *L'Apôtre Paul* (Strassburg, 1870) pp. 85—97, Eng. Tr. pp. 95—111.

[3] Prof. B. W. Bacon, while agreeing as to the generally 'missionary' character of the Epistles, points out that 'Paul's attitude in them is that of confirmer rather than proclaimer of the Gospel' (*The Story of St Paul*, London, 1905, p. 230).

CHARACTER AND CONTENTS OF THE EPISTLES xliii

the vain idols of heathenism, and the Judgment, as heralded by the Parousia of God's Son from heaven, who had already proved Himself the only complete Rescuer from the coming Wrath. In these great truths, proclaimed not argumentatively, but 'in power and in the Holy Spirit and in much assurance' (I. i. 5), the missionaries found the most effective means of reaching the consciences, and satisfying the religious instincts of their heathen auditors, and so of preparing the way for other and fuller aspects of Christian doctrine.

The consequence is that while our Epistles do not exhibit the constructive or dialectic skill of the Epistle to the Romans, or approach the mystical heights of the Epistle to the Ephesians, they reveal with marvellous clearness what has well been called the 'pastoral' instinct of the great Apostle[1], and present an unrivalled picture alike of his own missionary character and aims, and of the nature of the community he is addressing.

2. In none other indeed of his Epistles, unless it be in the companion Epistle to a Macedonian Church, the Epistle to the Philippians, or in the *apologia* of the Second Epistle to the Corinthians, does the real Paul stand out more clearly before us in all the charm of his rich and varied personality. We see his intense affection for his young converts (I. ii. 7 f., 17 ff., iii. 5—10, II. i. 4), and his desire for their sympathy and prayers (I. v. 25, II. iii. 1 f.); his keen sensitiveness as to what others are saying of him, and the confident assertion of the purity of his motives (I. ii. 1—12); his proud claim of what is due to him as an Apostle of Christ (I. ii. 6), and his willingness to forego this right in view of the higher interests of his work (I. ii. 9, II. iii. 8 f.); his longing desire for the Thessalonians' progress in spiritual things (I. iii. 11 ff., II. i. 11 f.), and the fierceness of his indignation against those who were hindering the cause of Christ (I. ii. 15 f., iv. 6, II. iii. 2): and we notice how through all St Paul is constrained and ruled by his own

2. The picture they present of St Paul in his personal character,

---

[1] Dr Vernon Bartlet (Hastings' *D.B.* i. p. 730) finds that 'the true cause' of all the Pauline Epistles 'lay deep in the same spirit as breathes in 1 Th., the essentially "pastoral" instinct.... Of a temper too ardent for the more studied forms of writing, St Paul could yet by letter, and so on the spur of occasion, concentrate all his wealth of thought, feeling, and maturing experience upon some particular religious situation, and sweep away the difficulty or danger.'

sense of union with his Risen Lord, and dependence on His authority (I. iv. 1 f., II. iii. 6, 12).

and in the spirit,   Very noteworthy too are the tact and the courtesy which the Apostle everywhere displays. So far from being the 'very disagreeable personage both to himself and others,' whom Nietzsche so perversely discovers[1], he shows the most painstaking desire to do full justice not only to his fellow-workers (cf. p. xxxiv f.), but also to his readers. With an intensity of feeling, that finds difficulty in expressing itself (I. iii. 9), he gives thanks for *all* (I. i. 2 f., cf. II. i. 3): *all*, notwithstanding the presence of weak and faulty believers amongst them, are treated as sons of light, and of the day (I. v. 5): and it is to *all*, with evident emphasis (cf. I. v. 28), that the closing greeting of his second and severer Epistle is sent (II. iii. 18)—even the man who is showing signs of setting aside his authority is still a 'brother' (II. iii. 14 f.).

This last form of address, indeed, forms one of the Epistles' most noticeable features. It is throughout as 'brothers' that St Paul regards his readers, and he never starts a new line of thought without reminding them of the fact, as if to bring home to them in the clearest manner, that all these questions concerned both them and him alike[2].

Hence too, in the appeals which he addresses to them, St Paul never loses an opportunity of going back upon his readers' previous knowledge (I. i. 5, ii. 1 f., 5, 9, 11, iii. 3 f., iv. 2, v. 2, II. ii. 5 f., iii. 7). And when he finds it necessary to exhort, he almost goes out of his way to show his appreciation of the zeal the young community has already displayed (I. iv. 1, 10, v. 11, II. iii. 4).

and methods of his missionary work.   And if such is the spirit of St Paul's missionary work, an equally clear light is thrown upon its methods. Driven from Philippi, the Apostle might naturally, for a time at any rate, have turned to some quieter and more obscure spot; but instead, in characteristic fashion, he boldly carried forward his

---

[1] *Morgenröte* i. § 68.

[2] Ἀδελφοί, as an address, occurs 21 times in our Epistles. Notice too the subtle change from the 2nd to the 1st pers. plur. in I. iii. 2 f., iv. 6 f., 13 f., v. 5, II. i. 11 f., by which the missionaries, almost unconsciously, identify themselves with their converts.

message to what was, in many ways, the most important city of the district, in order that from it as a centre the influence of his message might penetrate into the whole of the surrounding country[1].

This is not, however, to say that St Paul at once entered on an open and active *propaganda* amongst the varied population of Thessalonica. To have done so would only have been to court defeat; and even the preaching in the Synagogue, to which in the first instance he trusted for arresting attention, formed only a part, and perhaps the less important part of his work. That consisted rather in quiet and friendly converse with all whom his message had reached. And our Epistles enable us to picture him during those long hours of toil for his daily support[2], to which the fear of proving burdensome to others had driven him, gathering round him little companies of anxious inquirers, and with the authority of a father, and the tenderness of a mother, dealing with their individual needs (I. ii. 11)[3].

Hence the closeness of the bonds between St Paul and his Thessalonian converts: in no forced sense of the phrase they were literally his 'greater self.' To be parted from them was to

[1] The Apostle's preference for 'towns' is in entire accord with the statesman-like ideal, which from the first he had set before himself, of gradually Christianizing the Roman Empire: cf. Ramsay *Pauline and other Studies* (London, 1906) p. 49 ff., Lock *St Paul the Master-Builder* (London, 1899) Lect. i. and ii., and for a full account of 'missionary methods in the time of the Apostles' with special reference to St Paul see Zahn *Skizzen aus dem Leben der Alten Kirche*[2] (Erlangen, 1898) p. 76 ff. (translated in *Exp.* VI. vii., viii., and VII. iv.), and Harnack *Die Mission und Ausbreitung des Christentums* (Leipzig, 1902), Eng. Tr. by Moffatt under title *The Expansion of Christianity* (London, 1904).

By 'the whole of Macedonia' (I. iv. 10) we naturally understand the whole of the Roman province of that name, in accordance with St Paul's regular usage of similar terms elsewhere, e.g. Asia (Rom. xvi. 5), Achaia (Rom. xv. 26), Illyricum (Rom. xv. 19).

[2] On the exact nature of this work the Epistles throw no light, but it was probably tent-making (cf. Ac. xviii. 3), though it would appear that the material used was not, as is generally imagined, cloth or felt but leather: cf. the old designation of Paul as σκυτότομος (reff. in Suicer *Thesaurus* s.v.), and see further Zahn art. 'Paulus' in Hauck *RE.*[3] xv. p. 70 f.

[3] Cf. P. Wernle *Paulus als Heidenmissionär* (Freiburg i. B., 1899) p. 22 f., E. von Dobschütz *Probleme des Apostolischen Zeitalters* (Leipzig, 1904) p. 60. The whole of the section on 'The Organization of the Mission' with its graphic description of the Apostolic 'cure of souls' in Weinel's *St Paul* Eng. Tr. p. 200 ff. is full of interest.

suffer 'bereavement' of the acutest kind (I. ii. 17): to hear of their continued well-doing was to 'live' (I. iii. 8): to see them again was his 'constant' and 'very exceeding' prayer (I. iii. 10).

Surely there can be no difficulty in recognizing here the portrait of one who 'though he was Paul, was also a man[1],' and who, in the fine phrase of another early writer, carried 'music' with him wherever his influence penetrated[2].

3. The Thessalonian community— in the freshness of its first faith,

3. Hardly less striking than the picture of their writer is the picture of their first readers which our Epistles present—a picture all the more interesting because here alone in the Pauline writings we are brought face to face with a young Christian community in all the freshness and bloom of its first faith. The Thessalonians, who were by nature of a simple and sturdy type of character[3], had evidently accepted with peculiar eagerness the Apostolic message, and even amidst surrounding persecution had continued to display a characteristic fidelity[4], which was found deserving of all praise (I. i. 6 f., II. i. 4 ff.).

in its 'shortcomings' in moral conduct and order,

There were however various 'shortcomings' (ὑστερήματα I. iii. 10) in their faith which required attention: while it is characteristic of them in common with all the early Pauline communities, that not at once had they succeeded in freeing themselves from some even of the grosser sins of their old pagan surroundings (I. iv. 3—8)[5]. Nor was this all, but in their very enthusiasm for their new faith with its bright assurance of

---

[1] Chrys. εἰ καὶ Παῦλος ἦν ἀλλ' ἄνθρωπος ἦν.

[2] Isidore *Epp.* ii. 124 ὁ γῆν καὶ θάλασσαν ῥυθμίσας.

[3] Cf. Renan *Saint Paul* p. 136 ff.

[4] Mommsen *Hist. of Rome* Bk. III. ch. 8, Eng. Tr. ii. p. 229: 'In steadfast resistance to the public enemy under whatever name, in unshaken fidelity towards their native country and their hereditary government, and in persevering courage amidst the severest trials, no nation in ancient history bears so close a resemblance to the Roman people as the Macedonians' (cited by Lightfoot *Bibl. Essays* p. 248 n.[5]).

[5] In addition to possessing all the temptations of a great seaport, Thessalonica was notoriously in antiquity as one of the seats of the Cabiri, or Cabeiri, mysterious deities, whose worship was attended with grossly immoral rites: cf. Firmicus *de Err. Prof. Relig.* c. 11, 'Hunc eundem (Corybantem) Macedonum colit stulta persuasio. Hic est Cabirus, cui Thessalonicenses quondam cruento ore cruentis manibus supplicabant' (cited by Tafel p. xxxiii). Full particulars regarding the Cabiri will be found in Lobeck *Aglaopham.* iii. ch. 5, p. 1202 ff.: see also Lightfoot *ut s.* p. 257 f.

CHARACTER AND CONTENTS OF THE EPISTLES xlvii

(as they believed) an immediate Parousia of the Lord, the Thessalonian believers were showing a spirit of restlessness and excitement, which was leading to the neglect of their daily work and duty, and at the same time making them impatient of the restraints their leaders were seeking to lay upon them[1].

On both points, therefore, we find St Paul addressing to them words of prudence and moderation, enforcing, on the one hand, the dignity and consecration of labour (I. iv. 11 f., II. iii. 6 ff.)[2], and, on the other, checking the self-assertive spirit, which threatened to disturb the peace of the whole community (I. v. 12 f., II. iii. 6).

For it is very noticeable that it is the community *as a whole* which principally bulks in the Apostle's thoughts. Even though there are already clear traces of a certain class who were 'to all appearance office-bearers of the Ecclesia,' the services which they rendered 'were not essentially different from services which members of the Ecclesia, simply as brethren, were to render each other. *They* too were to admonish the disorderly, as also to do the converse work of encouraging the feeble-minded. *They* too were to make the cause of the weak their own, to sustain them, which is at least

in its responsible membership,

---

[1] As showing how these faults, with the still more marked virtues of hospitality and brotherly-love, continued to prevail in the Macedonian Church long after the Apostle's time, Archbishop Alexander (Speaker's *Comm. on the N.T.* iii. p. 701) refers to Hieron. *Comm. in Ep. ad Gal.* Lib. ii. cap. ii. opp. tom. vii. 356, ed. Migne: 'Haec ex parte *usque hodiè* permanere, non potest dubitari, qui Achaiam viderit. Macedones in charitate laudantur, et hospitalitate ac susceptione fratrum. Unde ad eos scribitur 1 Thess. iv. 9. Sed reprehenduntur... (Ibid. 10, 11). Quod ne quis putet officio magis docentis, quam *vitio gentis* admonitum, in secundâ ad eosdem inculcat ac replicat (2 Thess. iii. 10—12).'

[2] This is the more noteworthy when we remember that in old Greek thought labour was never regarded otherwise than as a necessity: cf. e.g. Aristotle's contemptuous allusion to 'those who live, as their name denotes, ἀπὸ τῶν χειρῶν' (*Pol.* III. iv. 2). According to Bigg (*The Church's Task in the Roman Empire* p. 72) Dion Chrysostom 'is the only classical author who speaks with understanding sympathy of the labouring poor.' For the very different Jewish attitude towards all forms of honest work see F. Delitzsch *Jüdisches Handwerkerleben zur Zeit Jesu* (translated into English as *Jewish Artisan Life in the Time of Christ* in the Unit Library, 1902), Edersheim *Sketches of Jewish Social Life* c. xi., and cf. Taylor *Sayings of the Jewish Fathers*[2] (Cambridge, 1897) pp. 18 f., 141.

one side, if not more, of the "helpful leadership" of the Elders; as well as to show long-suffering towards all[1].'

in the simplicity of its worship, And if thus we have here only the first beginnings of later Church-organization, so Christian worship comes before us in its simplest and most comprehensive form. The principal stress is laid upon such primary religious duties as praise, prayer, and instruction in which all are invited to take part (I. v. 11). And as the kiss of peace is to be extended to all the brethren (I. v. 26), it is again upon all that the closing benediction rests (II. iii. 18).

and in the extent of its Christian liberality. The very fact too that the Thessalonian believers require to be warned against the danger of indiscriminate bounty (II. iii. 10 f.) shows that, though themselves drawn principally from the poorer and working classes, they had from the first risen to a full sense of their obligation in the matter of Christian giving. And that the same trait continued to distinguish their later history is proved by the warmth of St Paul's commendation of the Macedonian Churches who, 'according to their power,...yea and beyond their power,' had responded to his appeal on behalf of the poor brethren in Judaea (2 Cor. viii. 1 ff.).

4. Absence of plan in the Epistles. 4. It is obvious from what has been said regarding the general character of our Epistles that it is vain to look in them for any definite plan. Their contents are too personal, too varied, to submit themselves to any such restraint. At the same time a distinct method and progress of thought is clearly traceable in them, so far at least as their leading topics are concerned. And though reference has already been made to most of these, it may be convenient for the student to have them briefly presented again in the order in which they occur[2].

5. General structure of 1 Thessalonians. 5. Beginning with a greeting which happily combines the new watchword of 'Grace' with the old Hebraic salutation of 'Peace,' St Paul and his fellow-writers give thanks with striking

---

[1] Hort *The Christian Ecclesia* p. 126 ff.; cf. Weinel *St Paul*, Eng. Tr. p. 213, 'In the Pauline communities the "oversight" and the "admonishing" were still conceived of as services of love which one man rendered to his neighbour—notice the first *and* in the quotation from 1 Thessalonians v. [12 ff.].'

[2] See also the Analyses prefixed to the two Epistles, pp. 2, 84.

CHARACTER AND CONTENTS OF THE EPISTLES

warmth for the spiritual state of their Thessalonian brethren. i. 1.
And then, as if conscious that it is useless to say anything i. 2—10.
further until they have set themselves right with their converts, they proceed to refute certain calumnies, which, so they have been informed, are being circulated against themselves.

Their *apologia* takes, as is natural, the form of an ii. 1—12.
historical narrative of their ministry at Thessalonica, and is marked by frequent appeals to their converts' own knowledge of what its character had been. This has the further advantage ii. 13—16.
of giving the Apostles the opportunity of again gratefully recognizing how readily the Thessalonians on their part have accepted the Word of God, and with what brave endurance they have faced the consequent persecution.

Returning to more personal matters, St Paul affirms his ii. 17—20.
own and his companions' great desire to see again those who have proved such a 'glory' to them. Only when this was iii. 1—10.
clearly proved to be impossible had he consented to allow Timothy to act as his ambassador. And now that he has returned with the 'good news' of the Thessalonians' faith and love, words fail the missionaries to express their deep sense of thanksgiving and joy. So far moreover from Timothy's report leading them to acquiesce in their own enforced absence, it has rather increased their desire to see their young converts face to face, and to complete the good work begun in them. God alone can secure this. And accordingly it is their constant prayer that He will open up their way of return, and that iii. 11—13.
meanwhile the hearts of the tried and afflicted Church may be stablished in holiness, in view of the approaching Parousia of the Lord.

A second, and more didactic, portion of the Epistle follows, iv. 1.
in which the writers proceed to furnish fresh guidance for their readers in all that pertains to their Christian calling. In particular they warn them against the immorality, which was iv. 2—8.
then so marked a feature in Greek city-life, and, while gladly recognizing their spirit of charity and brotherly-love, they iv. 9—12.
summon all to diligence in their own work, that thereby they may preserve an honourable independence, and gain the respect of their heathen neighbours.

THE EPISTLES TO THE THESSALONIANS

iv. 13—18. Their fears regarding those of their number who meanwhile are falling on sleep are met with the assurance that, so far from these being shut out from Christ's glory on His Return, they
v. 1—11. will rather be the first to share in it. And then the suddenness of that Return, of which the Thessalonians have already been so fully warned, is made the basis of a practical appeal to watchfulness and sobriety.
v. 12—22. Various exhortations, still addressed to the community as a whole, with reference to their attitude to their leaders, and to their more feeble brethren, follow, along with some general
v. 23, 24. rules of Christian living. And the whole is sealed once more with a characteristic prayer to the God of peace.
v. 25—28. Finally, the Epistle is brought to a close with a salutation and benediction.

6. General structure of 2 Thessalonians.
i. 1, 2.
i. 3—5.
6. The Second Epistle follows on very similar lines. After the opening address and greeting, the writers again give thanks for the Thessalonians' state, dwelling with pride on their progress, as proved especially by their patient endurance under persecution. They bid them remember that that persecution, so far from leading them to think that God had forgotten them, should rather encourage them to look forward with confidence to the final reward by which their present sufferings
i. 6—10. will be crowned. And this, in its turn, leads to a graphic picture of what will result alike to believers and unbelievers
i. 11, 12. when the Lord appears. A prayer, to which the Apostles are giving constant expression, that it may be well with the Thessalonian Church in that Day, is interjected.

ii. 1, 2. The writers then proceed to what is the most distinctive feature of their second letter. They have learned that their former teaching regarding the Parousia, supplemented from other sources for which they disown all responsibility, has been the unwitting cause of an undue restlessness and excitement on the Thessalonians' part. Accordingly, while saying nothing to shake the belief in the suddenness of the Parousia, they remind their readers of what they had clearly taught them before, that it will be preceded by certain well-defined signs. Amongst
ii. 3—12. these the principal place is given to the appearance of the Man of lawlessness, as the full and crowning manifestation of the evil already working in their midst. For the present that

manifestation is held in check by a restraining power, but how long this power will last no one can tell.

In any case, they urge, the Thessalonians must stand firm ii. 13—15. and hold fast the traditions they have already been taught, in humble dependence upon the God, Who alone can give them unfailing consolation, and strengthen them to do and to say all that is right.

To the same God let them also pray on the Apostles' iii. 1—5. behalf. And meanwhile, in conformity with the example the Apostles themselves have set them, let them apply themselves iii. 6—15. with diligence to their daily work, shunning every disorderly brother, and at all times and in all ways seeking the 'peace' iii. 16. which is the peculiar property of 'the Lord of peace,' and which it is again the writers' prayer that He may bestow upon them all.

The whole is then confirmed by an autographic salutation iii. 17, 18. and benediction in St Paul's own handwriting.

IV.

LANGUAGE, STYLE, AND LITERARY AFFINITIES.

Οἶδε γὰρ ἡ σοφία τοῦ μεγάλου Παύλου πρὸς τὸ δοκοῦν κεχρῆσθαι κατ' ἐξουσίαν τοῖς ῥήμασι καὶ τῷ ἰδίῳ τῆς διανοίας εἱρμῷ προσαρμόζειν τὰς τῶν ῥημάτων ἐμφάσεις, κἂν πρὸς ἄλλας τινὰς ἐννοίας ἡ συνήθεια τὴν κατάχρησιν τῶν λέξεων φέρῃ.

Gregory of Nyssa *Opp.* Migne II. 1303.

i. *Language.*

i. Language.

General character of vocabulary.

The two Epistles to the Thessalonians contain in all about 460 different words. Of these 27 are ἅπαξ λεγόμενα in the N.T., and 27 are used by St Paul alone amongst the N.T. writers. A still larger number (37) are peculiar to the Pauline writings along with the Gospel and Acts of St Luke, and the Epistle to the Hebrews.

Passing to the question of meaning, the influence of the Greek O. T. is unmistakable in the case of a very considerable number of words. With regard to others, we are led to look rather to the ordinary colloquial usage of the Apostle's time for the exact sense he is desirous to convey.

N.T. ἅπαξ λεγόμενα in the Epistles. 1 Thessalonians.

The following is a list of the ἅπαξ λεγόμενα referred to. In this case it will be convenient to take each Epistle separately, and to arrange the words in the order in which they occur.

1 Thessalonians: ἐξηχέω* (i. 8), ἀναμένειν* (i. 10), προπάσχω (ii. 2), κολακία (ii. 5), τροφός* (ii. 7), ὁμείρομαι* (ii. 8), συμφυλέτης (ii. 14), ἀπορφανίζομαι (ii. 17), σαίνομαι (iii. 3), ὑπερβαίνω* (iv. 6), θεοδίδακτος (iv. 9), περιλείπομαι* (iv. 15), κέλευσμα* (iv. 16), ἄτακτος* (v. 14), ὀλιγόψυχος* (v. 14), ὁλοτελής (v. 23), ἐνορκίζω (v. 27).

Of these 17 words, nine, which are distinguished by an asterisk, are found in the LXX.; four (κολακία, προπάσχω, σαίνομαι, ἀπορφανίζομαι) are found in good Gk. writers, and a fifth (ὁλοτελής) in Plutarch; while ἐνορκίζω is found in the A text of 2 Esdr. xxiii. (xiii.) 25 (cf. ἔνορκος, 2 Esdr. xvi. (vi.) 18). There thus remain

LANGUAGE, STYLE, AND LITERARY AFFINITIES liii

only two words which can be regarded as free formations of the Apostle's own—θεοδίδακτος and συμφυλέτης. The former, framed on the analogy of θεόκτιστος (2 Macc. vi. 23), probably contains a reminiscence of Isa. liv. 13 διδακτὸς θεοῦ. The latter (for class. φυλέτης) may be compared with συνμαθήτης (Jo. xi. 16), συνπολίτης (Eph. ii. 19), and with σύμφυλος in **Aq.** Zech. xiii. 7 : see further Lob. *Phryn.* p. 471, Rutherford *N.P.* p. 255 f. for the prevalence of similar compounds in late Gk.

2 Thessalonians: ὑπεραυξάνω (i. 3), ἐνκαυχάομαι* (i. 4), ἔνδειγμα (i. 5), τίνω* (i. 9), ἐνδοξάζομαι* (i. 10, 12), ἀτάκτως (iii. 6, 11), ἀτακτέω (iii. 7), περιεργάζομαι* (iii. 11), καλοποιέω (iii. 13), σημειόομαι* (iii. 14). 2 Thessalonians.

Of these 10 words, five are again found in the LXX., three (ἀτακτέω, ἀτάκτως, ἔνδειγμα) are found in the ordinary Gk. of the Apostle's time, καλοποιέω is found as a variant in Lev. v. 4, while ὑπεραυξάνω is found several times in late Gk., and is in thorough harmony with the Pauline love for compounds in ὑπερ-.

The total number of words, which have not yet been quoted from any other source than the two Epistles, is thus reduced to the two words already discussed in connexion with 1 Thess.[1], while the Epistles' 27 ἅπαξ λεγόμενα in the N.T. compare very favourably with the 41 (4?), which, according to the calculation in Grimm-Thayer, are to be found in St Paul's other Epistle to a Macedonian Church, the Epistle to the Philippians[2].

To the foregoing lists there may be added a number of words or phrases, occurring in the Epistles, which are used elsewhere in the N.T. only by St Paul. Words or phrases confined to St Paul in the N.T.

ἀγαθωσύνη, ἁγιωσύνη, ἀδιαλείπτως, ἄρα οὖν, εἴπερ, ἔκδικος, ἐνέργεια, ἐξαπατάω, ἐπιβαρέω, ἐπιφάνεια (Pastorals), εὐσχημόνως, θάλπω, μή πως, μνεία, μόχθος, ὄλεθρος, πάθος, περικεφαλαία, πλεονεκτέω, προΐστημι, προλέγω, στέγω, στέλλομαι, συναναμίγνυμαι, ὑπεραίρομαι, ὑπερεκπερισσοῦ, φιλοτιμέομαι.

Along with these, the following may be noted as occurring only in St Paul and the Lukan writings, or in St Paul and the Ep. to the Hebrews, or in all three combined. or to St Paul along with St Luke and the Ep. to the Hebrews.

ἄγων, αἱρέομαι, αἰφνίδιος, ἄμεμπτος, ἀναιρέω, ἀνταποδίδωμι, ἀξιόω, ἀποδείκνυμι, ἀποστασία, ἀσφάλεια, ἄτοπος, διαμαρτύρομαι, ἐκδιώκω,

---

[1] It should be hardly necessary to point out that ἅπαξ εὑρημένα is a fitter designation of such words than ἅπαξ εἰρημένα, in view of the constant reduction in the words hitherto believed to be peculiar to the Gk. Bible: see Deissmann 'Hellenistisches Griechisch' in Hauck *R.E.*³ vii. p. 636.

[2] Schmidt (*Der erste Thessalonicherbrief* p. 82) has drawn attention to the interesting fact that there are several words and phrases in 1 Thess. which are used elsewhere by St Paul in the same sense only in the Ep. to the Philippians: e.g. πρόφασις (ii. 5; Phil. i. 18), ἐπιθυμία (in good sense ii. 17; Phil. i. 23), καὶ ἅπαξ καὶ δίς (ii. 18; Phil. iv. 16), στέφανος (metaph. ii. 19; Phil. iv. 1), κεῖσθαι εἰς (metaph. iii. 3; Phil. i. 16), ἐρωτᾶν (ask, iv. 1, v. 12; Phil. iv. 3).

liv   THE EPISTLES TO THE THESSALONIANS

ἐκφεύγω, ἐνίστημι, ἐνκακέω, ἐπισυναγωγή, ἐφίστημι, ἡσυχάζω, ἡσυχία, καθάπερ, καταξιόομαι, καταργέω, κατευθύνω, μαρτύρομαι, μεθύσκομαι, μεταδίδωμι, μιμητής, νουθετέω, παραγγελία, παρρησιάζομαι, περισσοτέρως, πληροφορία, προεῖπον, σέβασμα, τοιγαροῦν, ὑστέρημα.

Words found with a special meaning   From this brief notice of the peculiarities of the Pauline diction as illustrated by our Epistles, we may turn to one or two lists of words which are used in them for the first time in the N.T. in a special sense. Their history, which is traced more fully in the Textual or Additional Notes, is of importance as throwing light upon the main sources of the Apostle's vocabulary.

owing to the influence of the LXX.,   Amongst these a first place must be given to the words, whose meaning here is due apparently in the first instance to the sense in which they were used in the Greek O.T. (including the Apocrypha), though in the case of many of them full allowance must also be made for the fact that they formed part of the 'common' dialect of the Apostle's time.

The following are typical examples: ἀγαθωσύνη, ἀγάπη, ἄγγελος, ἁγιάζω, ἁγιασμός, ἅγιος, ἀθετέω, ἀνάγκη, ἀνομία, ἄνομος, ἀποκαλύπτω, ἀποκάλυψις, ἀποστασία, ἀπώλεια, διάβολος, δόξα, δοξάζω, δουλεύω, δωρεάν ('gratis'), ἔθνη, εἴδωλον, εἰρήνη, ἔκδικος, ἐκκλησία, ἐνδοξάζομαι, ἐνκαυχάομαι, ἐντρέπω (metaph.), ἐξουθενέω, εὐαγγελίζομαι, εὐδοκέω, εὐδοκία, ζάω ('bene vivo' I. iii. 8), θέλημα, θλῖψις, θροέομαι, καρδία, καταξιόω, κατευθύνω (metaph.), καύχησις, κοιμάομαι (metaph.), ὀλιγόψυχος, ὁλόκληρος, ὄνομα, πειράζω, περικεφαλαία, περιπατέω (metaph.), περιποίησις, πίστις, πονηρός, προσευχή, σαλεύω (metaph.), σέβασμα, στέλλομαι, στέφανος (metaph.), στηρίζω, ὑπομονή, ψυχή, χάρις.

or technical usage in other connexions.   Other expressions which, starting from a technical or quasi-technical sense in classical or late Gk., have come to be adopted as technical terms of the Christian religion are ἀδελφός, ἀπόστολος, διάκονος, ἐνέργεια, ἐπιφάνεια, μνείαν ποιεῖσθαι, μυστήριον, παρουσία.

Words illustrated by the non-literary records of the Apostle's time.   Finally regard must be had to the large number of words and phrases upon which much additional light has been thrown by the discovery of such non-literary records as the Greek inscriptions of the Eastern Provinces of the Roman Empire, and the papyrus-letters of Egypt.

Evidence of this will be found on practically every page of the following Commentary. Here it must suffice to draw attention to such interesting examples as are afforded by—

ἀγαπητός, αἰώνιος, ἄμεμπτος, ἀμέμπτως, ἀπάντησις, ἀποδείκνυμι, ἀρέσκειν (τινι), ἀσπάζομαι, ἀσπασμός, ἀτακτέω (and its cognates), ἄτοπος, δίκη, εἶδος, ἐν (instrumental), ἐνίστημι, ἐνορκίζω, ἐξουσία, ἐπιβαρέω, ἐρωτάω ('rogo'), εὐσχημόνως, εὐχαριστέω, κατέχω, κύριος, παράδοσις, παρακαλέω, προΐσταμαι, σημειόομαι, τύπος, υἱὸς θεοῦ, φιλοτιμέομαι.

General conclusion.   Deductions from mere lists of words are always dangerous, and in any case it is obviously impossible to form any definite conclusions as to the nature and the sources of the Pauline vocabulary on the evidence of two short Epistles. This much however is clear that the Apostle had an ample Greek vocabulary at his command, and, notwithstanding his Jewish origin and upbringing, had learned to use Greek as virtually a second mother-tongue. Not only did he speak freely in Greek, but apparently he thought in Greek, and was able to adapt to his own special purposes the words he found in current use[1].

On the other hand, our Epistles do nothing to confirm (though they may not disprove) the idea that St Paul had received a thorough Greek education. There are no quotations in them from ancient Greek authors, and at most two or three words (such as ἀπορφανίζομαι) for which only classical, as distinguished from late Greek, authority has been produced. And the general impression which they convey is that for his 'Wortschatz,' or stock of words, St Paul, when not directly indebted to the Greek O.T., was mainly dependent upon the living, spoken tongue of his own day, borrowing from time to time more or less consciously from ethical writers, but otherwise showing little or no dependence upon the literature of classical or later times[2].

---

[1] On St Paul's indebtedness to Hellenism see especially Canon Hicks's classical essay 'St Paul and Hellenism' in *Studia Biblica et Ecclesiastica* iv. (Oxford, 1896), and E. Curtius's paper on 'Paulus in Athen' in his *Gesammelte Abhandlungen* ii. p. 527 ff. (Berlin, 1894), translated in *Exp.* vii. iv. p. 436 ff. Cf. also Sir W. M. Ramsay's articles on 'Tarsus' in *Exp.* vii. i. and ii., and the same writer's articles on 'St Paul's Philosophy of History,' and 'Paulinism in the Graeco-Roman world' in the *Contemporary Review*, Sept. and Oct. 1907.

[2] Cf. especially Nägeli *Der Wortschatz des Apostels Paulus* (Göttingen, 1905) where, after a careful examination of Pauline words, falling under the first five letters of the alphabet, the writer comes to the conclusion that for his vocabulary the Apostle was mainly indebted not to 'literary theory,' but to 'life' (p. 28). In the same way von Dobschütz (*Die urchristlichen Gemeinden* p. 279) draws attention to the striking manner ('in frappanter Weise') in which the special ethical terms of Greek philosophy are wanting in the Pauline writings: cf. A. Carr 'The use of pagan ethical terms in the N.T.,' *Exp.* v. ix. p. 443 ff. It must be kept in view, however, that, if more of the Stoic literature of the period had survived, this conclusion might require to be considerably modified.

lvi   THE EPISTLES TO THE THESSALONIANS

ii. *Style*.   ii. *Style*.

The general style of the Epistles confirms what has just been said regarding their vocabulary. There is certainly in them none of the studied rhetorical art or skilfully framed dialect, with which the Apostle is sometimes credited elsewhere[1]. St Paul was too much concerned with what he had to say to be able to think of mere literary devices[2]. And the drawn-out sentences (I. i. 2 ff., ii. 14 ff., II. i. 6 ff., ii. 8 ff.), the constant ellipses (I. i. 8, ii. 11, iv. 4 ff., 14, II. i. 3, 9, ii. 7, iii. 6), the manner in which he 'goes off' at a word (I. ii. 14 f., v. 8 f., II. i. 10), the inversion of metaphors (I. ii. 7ᵇ, v. 2, 4), not only bear evidence to the intensity of the writer's feelings at the time, but are in themselves valuable proofs of 'unstudied epistolary genuineness[3].'

The general style of the Epistles is direct

and regular.

This is very far, however, from saying that either Epistle shows signs of carelessness, or is wanting in well-ordered passages which, if not comparable to, at least prepare the way for the splendid outbursts of some of the later Epistles (cf. e.g. I. ii. 3 ff., II. iii. 1 ff.). St Paul had evidently that highest gift of a great writer, the instinctive feeling for the right word, and

---

[1] See, e.g., J. Weiss *Beiträge zur Paulinischen Rhetorik* (Göttingen, 1897), where certain sections more particularly of the Epp. to the Corinthians and Romans are analyzed with the view of showing their artistic and even rhythmical arrangement, and cf. Blass's attempt (*Die Rhythmen der asianischen und römischen Kunstprosa*, Leipzig, 1905) to find 'Asianic rhythm' in Romans and other Pauline writings, including 1 Thessalonians.

[2] 'Kunstliteratur' and 'Paulusbriefe' are, as Deissmann puts it, 'inkommensurable Grössen' (*Hellenisierung*, p. 168 n.⁴).

[3] The very closeness indeed of the literary dependence of 2 Thess. upon the earlier Epistle, and the consequent stiltedness of style to which this sometimes leads (notably in II. i. 3—10), so far from disproving that Epistle's authenticity, may be turned into an argument in favour of it. St Paul had evidently not the pen of a ready writer, and when he had once found an expression suited to his purpose found it very difficult to vary it. What more natural than that the words and phrases which, during that anxious time of waiting for the return of Timothy, he had been turning over in his mind as the most suitable to address to his beloved Thessalonians, should have remained in his memory, and have risen almost unconsciously to his lips, as he dictated his second letter to the same Church so shortly afterwards? For a somewhat similar argument applied to the relation of Colossians and Ephesians see Dr Sanday's art. on 'Colossians' in Smith's *D.B.*² i. pt. 1, p. 630.

even when writing, as he does here, in his most 'normal' style[1], and with an almost complete absence of the rhetorical figures, so largely practised in his day[2], he does not hesitate to avail himself of the more popular methods of adding point or emphasis to what he wants to say[3], by the skilful arrangement of his words (e.g. I. v. 3, II. ii. 6), by compressed word-pictures (I. i. 8 ἐξήχηται, ii. 2 ἀγῶνι, ii. 17 ἀπορφανισθέντες, II. iii. 1 τρέχῃ), by interpolated questions (I. ii. 19, iii. 6 (?), 9 f.), and even by plays on words (I. ii. 4, II. iii. 2 f., 11).

No effort indeed is wanting on the writer's part to bring home to his readers the extent of his heart-felt gratitude on their behalf, and his concern for their highest welfare. And here, as in all the other Pauline writings, we readily recognize that the arresting charm of the Apostle's style is principally due to 'the man behind[4],' and that the highest form of all eloquence, 'the rhetoric of the heart,' is speaking to us[5].

iii. *Literary Affinities.*

iii. *Literary Affinities*

What has just been said will prepare us not to expect in our Epistles any direct affinities with the more distinctly literary works of St Paul's or of previous times. There are, however, two sources which have left such an unmistakable

---

[1] See Lightfoot *Journ. of Class. and Sacr. Philol.* iii. (1857) p. 302.

[2] Cf., however, the *meiosis* in I. ii. 15, II. iii. 2, 7, the *chiasmus* in I. v. 6, and the intentional *anakolouthon* in II. ii. 7.

[3] In Dr A. J. Wilson's paper on 'Emphasis in the N.T.' in the *J.T.S.* viii. p. 75 ff., some of the finer methods of expression, beloved by Paul, are well brought out.

[4] Even Heinrici in his well-known discussion 'Zum Hellenismus des Paulus' (in his commentary on 2 Corinthians in Meyer vi.[8], Göttingen, 1900), while emphasizing the Apostle's points of contact with the rhetorical methods of his contemporaries, quotes with approval the words of Gregory of Nyssa prefixed as a heading to this section, and adds pointedly, 'Des Paulus Stil ist individuell und packend...Kein Klassiker, kein Hellenist hat so geschrieben, auch nicht ein Kirchenvater. Der von seinem Herrn überwältigte hellenistische Jude steht für sich da.' Cf. also the words of U. von Wilamowitz-Moellendorff as cited on p. 121 of this work.

[5] There are some good remarks on this point in Norden's great work on *Die antike Kunstprosa* ii. p. 509 f., though in pronouncing the Pauline Epistles 'unhellenisch,' he falls into the fundamental error of treating them as 'Kunstprosa' instead of in direct connexion with the non-literary texts of the time: cf. Deissmann in the *Theologische Rundschau* v. (1902) p. 66 ff.

impress upon the Apostle's language, as well as thought, that they cannot be passed over here. They are (1) the Greek O.T., (2) certain Sayings of Jesus.

(1) with the Greek O.T.

(1) We have seen already how dependent St Paul was on the LXX. for many of his most characteristic words. But his indebtedness does not stop there. So minute was his acquaintance with its phraseology, so completely had it passed *in sucum et sanguinem*, that, though in these alone of all his Epistles there is no direct quotation from the O.T., there are whole passages which are little more than a mosaic of O.T. words and expressions. Two short passages may serve to illustrate this.

as illustrated by 1 Thess. i. 8—10

The first is St Paul's description of the result of his ministry in Thessalonica in 1 Thess. i. 8—10.

i. 8 ἀφ' ὑμῶν γὰρ ἐξήχηται ὁ λόγος τοῦ κυρίου.

Joel iii. (iv.) 14 ἤχοι ἐξήχησαν ἐν τῇ κοιλάδι τῆς δίκης. 3 Macc. iii. 2 V φήμη δυσμενὴς ἐξηχεῖτο.

ib. ἐν παντὶ τόπῳ ἡ πίστις ὑμῶν ἡ πρὸς τὸν θεὸν ἐξελήλυθεν.

Ps. xviii. (xix.) 5 εἰς πᾶσαν τὴν γῆν ἐξῆλθεν ὁ φθόγγος αὐτῶν.

i. 9 ὁποίαν εἴσοδον ἔσχομεν πρὸς ὑμᾶς.

4 Regn. xix. 27 τὴν εἴσοδόν σου ἔγνων.

ib. καὶ πῶς ἐπεστρέψατε πρὸς τὸν θεὸν ἀπὸ τῶν εἰδώλων.

Isa. xliv. 22 ἐπιστράφητι πρὸς μέ, καὶ λυτρώσομαί σε. Jer. iii. 22 ἐπιστράφητε...δοῦλοι ἡμεῖς ἐσόμεθά σοι, ὅτι σὺ Κύριος ὁ θεὸς ἡμῶν εἶ.

ib. δουλεύειν θεῷ ζῶντι καὶ ἀληθινῷ.

Jos. iii. 10 ἐν τούτῳ γνώσεσθε ὅτι θεὸς ζῶν ἐν ὑμῖν. Dan. vi. 26 λατρεύοντες τῷ θεῷ...αὐτὸς γάρ ἐστι θεὸς...ζῶν εἰς γενεὰς γενεῶν. Isa. lxv. 16 εὐλογήσουσιν γὰρ τὸν θεὸν τὸν ἀληθινόν.

i. 10 ἀναμένειν τὸν υἱὸν αὐτοῦ ἐκ τῶν οὐρανῶν.

Isa. lix. 11 ἀνεμείναμεν κρίσιν.

ib. Ἰησοῦν τὸν ῥυόμενον ἡμᾶς.

Sap. xvi. 8 σὺ εἶ ὁ ῥυόμενος ἐκ παντὸς κακοῦ. Ps. cxxxix. (cxl.) 1 ἀπὸ ἀνδρὸς ἀδίκου ῥῦσαί με.

ib. ἐκ τῆς ὀργῆς τῆς ἐρχομένης.

Isa. xiii. 9 ἰδοὺ γὰρ ἡμέρα Κυρίου ἔρχεται ἀνίατος θυμοῦ καὶ ὀργῆς.

and 2 Thess. i. 6—10

Our second passage is the great picture of approaching Judgment in 2 Thess. i. 6—10. Here, as generally in the eschatological passages of the Epistles, the O.T. basis of the whole conception is even more marked.

LANGUAGE, STYLE, AND LITERARY AFFINITIES

i. 6 εἴπερ δίκαιον παρὰ θεῷ ἀνταποδοῦναι τοῖς θλίβουσιν ὑμᾶς θλῖψιν.

Isa. lxvi. 4 τὰς ἁμαρτίας ἀνταποδώσω αὐτοῖς. *ib.* 6 φωνὴ Κυρίου ἀνταποδιδόντος ἀνταπόδοσιν τοῖς ἀντικειμένοις. Lam. iii. 64 ἀποδώσεις αὐτοῖς ἀνταπόδομα, Κύριε, κατὰ τὰ ἔργα τῶν χειρῶν αὐτῶν. Cf. Obad. 15.

i. 7 καὶ ὑμῖν τοῖς θλιβομένοις ἄνεσιν μεθ' ἡμῶν ἐν τῇ ἀποκαλύψει τοῦ κυρίου Ἰησοῦ ἀπ' οὐρανοῦ.

Isa. xix. 20 κεκράξονται πρὸς Κύριον διὰ τοὺς θλίβοντας αὐτούς, καὶ ἀποστελεῖ αὐτοῖς ἄνθρωπον ὃς σώσει αὐτούς, κρίνων σώσει αὐτούς.

i. 7, 8 μετ' ἀγγέλων δυνάμεως αὐτοῦ ἐν πυρὶ φλογός.

Ex. iii. 2 ὤφθη δὲ αὐτῷ ἄγγελος Κυρίου ἐν πυρὶ φλογός. Sir. viii. 10 (13) μὴ ἐμπυρισθῇς ἐν πυρὶ φλογὸς αὐτοῦ.

i. 8 διδόντος ἐκδίκησιν τοῖς μὴ εἰδόσι θεὸν καὶ τοῖς μὴ ὑπακούουσιν τῷ εὐαγγελίῳ τοῦ κυρίου ἡμῶν Ἰησοῦ.

Isa. lxvi. 15 ἰδοὺ γὰρ Κύριος ὡς πῦρ ἥξει,...ἀποδοῦναι ἐν θυμῷ ἐκδίκησιν αὐτοῦ...ἐν φλογὶ πυρός. Jer. xxv. 12 ἐκδικήσω τὸ ἔθνος ἐκεῖνο. Jer. x. 25 ἔκχεον τὸν θυμόν σου ἐπὶ ἔθνη τὰ μὴ εἰδότα σε καὶ ἐπὶ γενεὰς αἳ τὸ ὄνομά σου οὐκ ἐπεκαλέσαντο.

i. 9 οἵτινες δίκην τίσουσιν.

Prov. xxvii. 12 ἄφρονες δὲ ἐπελθόντες ζημίαν τίσουσιν.

ib. ὄλεθρον αἰώνιον.

4 Macc. x. 15 τὸν αἰώνιον τοῦ τυράννου ὄλεθρον.

ib. ἀπὸ προσώπου τοῦ κυρίου καὶ ἀπὸ τῆς δόξης τῆς ἰσχύος αὐτοῦ.

Isa. ii. 10 ἀπὸ προσώπου τοῦ φόβου Κυρίου καὶ ἀπὸ τῆς δόξης τῆς ἰσχύος αὐτοῦ (cf. *vv.* 19, 21).

i. 10 ὅταν ἔλθῃ ἐνδοξασθῆναι ἐν τοῖς ἁγίοις αὐτοῦ καὶ θαυμασθῆναι ἐν πᾶσιν τοῖς πιστεύσασιν.

Ps. lxxxviii. (lxxxix.) 8 ὁ θεὸς ἐνδοξαζόμενος ἐν βουλῇ ἁγίων. Ps. lxvii. (lxviii.) 36 θαυμαστὸς ὁ θεὸς ἐν τοῖς ὁσίοις αὐτοῦ. Ezek. xxviii. 22 Τάδε λέγει Κύριος...ἐνδοξασθήσομαι ἐν σοί,...ἐν τῷ ποιῆσαί με ἐν σοὶ κρίματα, καὶ ἁγιασθήσομαι ἐν σοί.

ib. ἐν τῇ ἡμέρᾳ ἐκείνῃ.

Zeph. i. 7 εὐλαβεῖσθε ἀπὸ προσώπου Κυρίου τοῦ θεοῦ, διότι ἐγγὺς ἡμέρα τοῦ κυρίου. Isa. ii. 19 f. ἀπὸ τῆς δόξης τῆς ἰσχύος αὐτοῦ, ὅταν ἀναστῇ θραῦσαι τὴν γῆν. τῇ γὰρ ἡμέρᾳ ἐκείνῃ κτλ.

(2) More important still is the relation of the Apostle's language in our Epistles to certain Words of the Lord that have come down to us in the Gospels. For without taking any

(2) with the Words of Jesus.

note of some of the subtler resemblances that have been detected here, there still remain sufficient to show that St Paul must have been well acquainted with the actual words of Jesus, and in all probability had actually some written collection of them in his possession[1].

The following are some of the most obvious examples:

I. ii. 7 ἐγενήθημεν νήπιοι ἐν μέσῳ ὑμῶν.

ii. 12 τοῦ θεοῦ τοῦ καλοῦντος ὑμᾶς εἰς τὴν ἑαυτοῦ βασιλείαν καὶ δόξαν.

ii. 14 ff. τῶν Ἰουδαίων, τῶν καὶ τὸν κύριον ἀποκτεινάντων Ἰησοῦν καὶ τοὺς προφήτας...εἰς τὸ ἀναπληρῶσαι αὐτῶν τὰς ἁμαρτίας πάντοτε.

iii. 13 ἐν τῇ παρουσίᾳ τοῦ κυρίου ἡμῶν Ἰησοῦ μετὰ πάντων τῶν ἁγίων αὐτοῦ.

iv. 8 ὁ ἀθετῶν οὐκ ἄνθρωπον ἀθετεῖ ἀλλὰ τὸν θεόν.

iv. 9 περὶ δὲ τῆς φιλαδελφίας...ὑμεῖς θεοδίδακτοί ἐστε εἰς τὸ ἀγαπᾶν ἀλλήλους.

iv. 16 f. αὐτὸς ὁ κύριος...ἐν σάλπιγγι θεοῦ καταβήσεται ἀπ' οὐρανοῦ ...ἔπειτα ἡμεῖς οἱ ζῶντες...ἁρπαγησόμεθα ἐν νεφέλαις εἰς ἀπάντησιν τοῦ κυρίου εἰς ἀέρα.

v. 1 περὶ δὲ τῶν χρόνων καὶ τῶν καιρῶν.

Lk. xxii. 27 Ἐγὼ δὲ ἐν μέσῳ ὑμῶν εἰμὶ ὡς ὁ διακονῶν.

Mt. xxii. 3 (the Parable of the Marriage Feast) καὶ ἀπέστειλεν τοὺς δούλους αὐτοῦ καλέσαι τοὺς κεκλημένους εἰς τοὺς γάμους.

Mt. xxiii. 31 f. υἱοί ἐστε τῶν φονευσάντων τοὺς προφήτας. καὶ ὑμεῖς πληρώσατε τὸ μέτρον τῶν πατέρων ὑμῶν. Cf. the Parable of the Vineyard Mt. xxi. 33 ff. and parallels.

Mt. xvi. 27 μέλλει γὰρ ὁ υἱὸς τοῦ ἀνθρώπου ἔρχεσθαι ἐν τῇ δόξῃ τοῦ πατρὸς αὐτοῦ μετὰ τῶν ἀγγέλων αὐτοῦ (Mk. viii. 38 μετὰ τῶν ἀγγέλων τῶν ἁγίων, Lk. ix. 26 τοῦ πατρὸς καὶ τῶν ἁγίων ἀγγέλων).

Lk. x. 16 ὁ ἀθετῶν ὑμᾶς ἐμὲ ἀθετεῖ· ὁ δὲ ἐμὲ ἀθετῶν ἀθετεῖ τὸν ἀποστείλαντά με.

Mt. xxiii. 8 πάντες δὲ ὑμεῖς ἀδελφοί ἐστε. Cf. Jo. xv. 12 αὕτη ἐστὶν ἡ ἐντολὴ ἡ ἐμὴ ἵνα ἀγαπᾶτε ἀλλήλους.

Mt. xxiv. 30 f. (Mk. xiii. 26 f., Lk. xxi. 27) ὄψονται τὸν υἱὸν τοῦ ἀνθρώπου ἐρχόμενον ἐπὶ τῶν νεφελῶν τοῦ οὐρανοῦ...καὶ ἀποστελεῖ τοὺς ἀγγέλους αὐτοῦ μετὰ σάλπιγγος μεγάλης, καὶ ἐπισυνάξουσιν τοὺς ἐκλεκτοὺς αὐτοῦ κτλ. Mt. xxv. 6 ἰδοὺ ὁ νυμφίος, ἐξέρχεσθε εἰς ἀπάντησιν.

Mt xxiv. 36 περὶ δὲ τῆς ἡμέρας ἐκείνης καὶ ὥρας.

which, however, many of the coincidences suggested seem to be very precarious.

[1] See especially A. Resch *Der Paulinismus und die Logia Jesu* (*Text. u. Unters.* N.F. xii.) Leipzig, 1904— a valuable collection of materials, in

v. 2 ἡμέρα Κυρίου ὡς κλέπτης ἐν νυκτὶ οὕτως ἔρχεται.	Mt. xxiv. 43 (Lk. xii. 39) εἰ ᾔδει ὁ οἰκοδεσπότης ποίᾳ φυλακῇ ὁ κλέπτης ἔρχεται.
v. 3 τότε αἰφνίδιος αὐτοῖς ἐπίσταται ὄλεθρος.	Lk. xxi. 34 μή ποτε…ἐπιστῇ ἐφ' ὑμᾶς ἐφνίδιος ἡ ἡμέρα ἐκείνη ὡς παγίς.
v. 5 πάντες γὰρ ὑμεῖς υἱοὶ φωτός ἐστε.	Lk. xvi. 8 τοὺς υἱοὺς τοῦ φωτός. Cf. Jo. xii. 36 πιστεύετε εἰς τὸ φῶς, ἵνα υἱοὶ φωτὸς γένησθε.
v. 6 γρηγορῶμεν.	Mt. xxiv. 42 γρηγορεῖτε οὖν.
v. 7 οἱ μεθυσκόμενοι νυκτὸς μεθύουσιν.	Mt. xxiv. 48 f. (Lk. xii. 45) ὁ κακὸς δοῦλος…πίνῃ μετὰ τῶν μεθυόντων.
v. 11 οἰκοδομεῖτε εἷς τὸν ἕνα.	Mt. xvi. 18 ἐπὶ ταύτῃ τῇ πέτρᾳ οἰκοδομήσω μου τὴν ἐκκλησίαν.
v. 13 εἰρηνεύετε ἐν ἑαυτοῖς.	Mk. ix. 50 εἰρηνεύετε ἐν ἀλλήλοις.
v. 18 τοῦτο γὰρ θέλημα θεοῦ.	Mt. vii. 21 ὁ ποιῶν τὸ θέλημα τοῦ πατρός μου (cf. xii. 50).
II. i. 5 εἰς τὸ καταξιωθῆναι ὑμᾶς τῆς βασιλείας τοῦ θεοῦ.	Lk. xx. 35 οἱ δὲ καταξιωθέντες τοῦ αἰῶνος ἐκείνου τυχεῖν.
i. 7 ἐν τῇ ἀποκαλύψει τοῦ κυρίου Ἰησοῦ ἀπ' οὐρανοῦ.	Lk. xvii. 30 ᾗ ἡμέρᾳ ὁ υἱὸς τοῦ ἀνθρώπου ἀποκαλύπτεται.
i. 12 ὅπως ἐνδοξασθῇ τὸ ὄνομα τοῦ κυρίου ἡμῶν Ἰησοῦ ἐν ὑμῖν, καὶ ὑμεῖς ἐν αὐτῷ.	Primarily dependent on the LXX. (cf. Isai. lxvi. 5), but see John xvii. 1, 10, 21 ff.
ii. 1 ἡμῶν ἐπισυναγωγῆς ἐπ' αὐτόν.	Mt. xxiv. 31 ἐπισυνάξουσιν τοὺς ἐκλεκτοὺς αὐτοῦ[1].
ii. 2 μηδὲ θροεῖσθαι.	Mt. xxiv. 6 μὴ θροεῖσθε.
ii. 3 μή τις ὑμᾶς ἐξαπατήσῃ.	Mt. xxiv. 4 βλέπετε μή τις ὑμᾶς πλανήσῃ.
ib. ἀποκαλυφθῇ ὁ ἄνθρωπος τῆς ἀνομίας.	Mt. xxiv. 12 διὰ τὸ πληθυνθῆναι τὴν ἀνομίαν.
ii. 4 ὁ ἀντικείμενος…ὥστε αὐτὸν εἰς τὸν ναὸν τοῦ θεοῦ καθίσαι.	Mt. xxiv. 15 τὸ βδέλυγμα τῆς ἐρημώσεως…ἑστὸς ἐν τόπῳ ἁγίῳ.
ii. 9 f. οὗ ἐστιν ἡ παρουσία κατ' ἐνέργειαν τοῦ Σατανᾶ ἐν πάσῃ δυνάμει καὶ σημείοις καὶ τέρασιν ψεύδους καὶ ἐν πάσῃ ἀπάτῃ ἀδικίας τοῖς ἀπολλυμένοις.	Mt. xxiv. 24 ἐγερθήσονται γὰρ ψευδόχριστοι καὶ ψευδοπροφῆται, καὶ δώσουσιν σημεῖα μεγάλα καὶ τέρατα ὥστε πλανᾶσθαι εἰ δυνατὸν καὶ τοὺς ἐκλεκτούς.
ii. 11 ἐνέργειαν πλάνης εἰς τὸ πιστεῦσαι αὐτοὺς τῷ ψεύδει.	Mt. xxiv. 4 βλέπετε μή τις ὑμᾶς πλανήσῃ.
iii. 3 ὁ κύριος, ὅς…φυλάξει ἀπὸ τοῦ πονηροῦ[2].	Mt. vi. 13 ῥῦσαι ἡμᾶς ἀπὸ τοῦ πονηροῦ.

[1] 'It is no exaggeration to say that Matt. xxiv. is the most instructive commentary on the chapter before us [2 Thess. ii.].' Kennedy *St Paul's Conceptions of the Last Things* (London, 1904) p. 56.

[2] For possible references to *Agrapha* of Jesus see 1 Thess. iii. 5, v. 4, 21 f., 2 Thess. iii. 10 with the notes *ad loca*.

Jesus and Paul.

Upon the larger question, the relation in which so-called 'Paulinism' stands to the original teaching of Jesus, it is impossible to enter here[1]. But no one can take account of the foregoing parallels, and of much that will come before us in the course of this Commentary, without realizing how conscious the disciple was throughout of his complete dependence upon his Master. His whole 'gospel,' when not directly inspired by the living Lord Himself (cf. I. iv. 15 ἐν λόγῳ Κυρίου with note *ad loc.*), was firmly rooted in his knowledge of the life and words of the historic Jesus, or, perhaps we should rather say, upon that knowledge as conditioned by his own sense of union with the Risen Christ, and interpreted in the light of his own growing Christian experience.

---

[1] Those who desire to pursue the subject may be referred to three important monographs which have appeared lately—P. Feine *Jesus Christ und Paulus* (Leipzig, 1902), M. Goguel *L'Apôtre Paul et Jésus-Christ* (Paris, 1904), and R. J. Knowling *The Testimony of St Paul to Christ* (London, 1905). See also Dr R. J. Drummond's Kerr Lectures on *The Relation of the Apostolic Teaching to the Teaching of Christ* (Edinburgh, 1900). In his pamphlet *Jesus und Paulus* (Tübingen, 1906) Kaftan has replied to the 'Jesus or Paul' attitude of Bousset's *Jesus* and Wrede's *Paulus* in the recent German series of *Religionsgeschichtliche Volksbücher*. See also A. Jülicher's *Paulus und Jesus* (1907) in the same series, where the writer states his conclusion in the words, 'Paulus hat also seine Theologie nicht an die Stelle der Religion Jesu gesetzt, sondern rings um sie her' (p. 72).

V.

DOCTRINE.

'Doctrinae divinae vis confluit in amorem.'
Bengel *ad* 1 Thess. iv. 9.

1. The Epistles to the Thessalonians are generally regarded as the least dogmatic of all the Pauline Epistles, and it is true that there is no mention in them of such distinctive aspects of 'Paulinism' as the contrasts between law and gospel, faith-righteousness and work-righteousness, and flesh and spirit—that the term 'justification' is wholly wanting—and that even the Apostle's favourite watchword of 'grace,' which is found twice as often in his writings as in all the rest of the New Testament, occurs only in two passages (II. i. 12, ii. 16), apart from the more formal salutations and benedictions.   1. The simple theology of the Epistles.

This is very far, however, from saying that St Paul had not by this time reached the definite system of Christian truth which, even when not expressed, lies at the base of all his writings. He had now been engaged for a period of nearly fifteen years in active missionary work, and if he does not find it necessary to lay special stress here on certain doctrines which later emerged into prominence owing to the controversies in which he found himself engaged, this is mainly due to the circumstances under which the Epistles were written[1].

Addressing as he was a small working-class community, composed principally of Gentile Christians, and surrounded   Reasons for this.

---

[1] In his recent *Essai sur la Christologie de Saint Paul* i. (Paris, 1906) Monteil utters a much-needed warning on the danger of drawing out a chronological chart of the Apostle's growth in Christian truth from his writings, which were conditioned throughout by the special needs to which they were addressed. 'Paul was above all not a doctor and a theologian, but an apostle; far less occupied with framing a system of dogma and theology, than with announcing the gospel of salvation' (p. 12).

by all the temptations of a great commercial seaport, St Paul recognized that what his converts stood most in need of was encouragement, combined with certain very definite warnings against the undue excitement they were displaying owing to a mistaken application of his former teaching. And consequently he fell back upon the main elements of that teaching, with the view not only of showing in what it really consisted, but of leading his readers on to the higher truths for which he had been preparing them. So far, therefore, from the simple theology which the Epistles contain, as compared, for example, with the more argumentative methods of the Epistles to the Galatians or Romans, throwing any doubt on their authenticity, as Menegoz seems tempted to think[1], it is precisely what we should expect in the circumstances[2], while the many points of contact which the Epistles exhibit with the language and teaching of the missionary discourses of Acts afford striking confirmation of the credibility of both (cf. p. xlii).

2. Doctrine of God.

2. In view then of the surroundings of his Thessalonian converts, we are not surprised to find the Apostle laying very special stress on the doctrine of God or rather of 'the God,' as contrasted with the many and vain gods whom formerly they worshipped[3].

It is from this God, as St Paul and his companions are

---

[1] *Le Péché et la Rédemption d'après Saint Paul*, p. 4.

[2] It is only from this point of view that we can accept such statements as that the Epistles contain 'a first sketch of Paul's doctrine' (Sabatier *L'Apôtre Paul* p. 95, E. Tr. p. 109), or that they form 'a kind of Christian primer' (Bruce *St Paul's Conception of Christianity* p. 15). Schmidt's statement is more exact: 'To sum up: the dogmatic system of the Apostle is for obvious reasons not fully unfolded in this Epistle but merely touched on incidentally, but this is done in thoroughly Pauline fashion' (*Der erste Thessalonicherbrief*, p. 78).

[3] It should be noted, however, that the old view (Letronne *Œuvres* i. p. 8) that ὁ θεός, taken absolutely and without any further designation, is confined to Christian documents is now disproved on the evidence of the papyri: cf. Wilcken *Archiv* i. p. 436, where such passages are cited as B. G. U. 27, 10 ff. ('certainly heathen' —ii./A.D.) καὶ παρεδέξατο ἡμᾶς ὁ τόπος ὡς ὁ θεὸς ἤθελεν, and B. G. U. 246, 12 f. ('very probably heathen'—ii./iii. A.D.) ἐντυγχάνω τῷ θεῷ ὑπὲρ ὑμῶν.

For similar evidence from the inscriptions see Ramsay *C. and B.* i. p. 498 f., where expressions like 'thou shalt not wrong the God' (σὺ μὴ ἀδικήσεις τὸν θεόν), and 'may he not escape the notice of the God' (μὴ λάθοιτο τὸν θεόν), used to prevent the violation of Christian tombs, are shown to be based on pagan models: see further pp. 147, 150 ff.

DOCTRINE

never tired of asserting, that they themselves have derived 'the gospel' which they declare (I. ii. 2 ff.)[1], and, as they have been 'approved' by God Himself for this purpose (v. 4), so it is to His verdict that in the last instance they submit themselves (vv. 4, 10). How complete indeed their sense of dependence is appears in the emphatic manner in which on four distinct occasions the missionaries turn from the thought of their own efforts to the true Author of all grace and peace (I. iii. 11, v. 23, II. ii. 16, iii. 16)[2]. And it is to Him similarly that throughout the Epistles they refer the Thessalonians for all that concerns their own Christian life. They, who formerly were amongst those 'who knew not the God' (I. iv. 5; cf. II. i. 8), have now turned to 'a God living and true' (I. i. 9), and as their 'faith to Godward' (I. i. 8) is entirely due to the 'call' which 'the God' Himself has addressed to them (I. i. 4, II. ii. 13), so it is of Him that they must continue to walk worthily, if finally they are to reach the kingdom and glory to which His 'call' is summoning them (I. ii. 12, II. i. 5). Any failure in this can only be due to themselves, and not to God, for He is 'faithful' to accomplish the work which He Himself has begun (I. v. 24; cf. II. iii. 3), and it is 'in the very presence of God'—before His all-seeing and all-searching eye—an emphatic phrase used nowhere else in the Pauline Epistles (cf. 2 Cor. v. 10),—that the highest human hopes are consummated (I. i. 3, iii. 9, 13; cf. ii. 19).

It is very noticeable too as showing the nature of the conception which St Paul had already formed of the Deity, that frequently in these his oldest extant epistles he describes God as 'Father,' and that too in a way to suggest that the term was already in general use, and in need of no explanation (I. i. 1, iii. 11, 13, II. i. 1 f., ii. 16). Not only does he thereby forge a fresh link between his own teaching and the teaching of Jesus (cf. p. lix ff.), but, by the manner in which he associates

---

[1] The actual phrase (τὸ) εὐαγγέλιον (τοῦ) θεοῦ occurs elsewhere in the Pauline Epistles only in Rom. i. 1, xv. 16, 2 Cor. xi. 7; cf. 1 Tim. i. 11.

[2] Cf. also II. iii. 5 where, before uttering the παραγγελία of v. 6 which would naturally follow on v. 4, the Apostles interject a prayer.

Bengel (ad I. iii. 11) remarks very beautifully: 'Utraque epistola ad Thessalonicenses fere singula capita singulis suspiriis obsignata habet.'

the Father with the glorified Lord, he takes what has been called 'the first decisive step' towards the later Christian doctrine of the Trinity[1].

3. Doctrine of Christ.

3. Nothing indeed can exceed the exalted place assigned to the Person of Christ even in these markedly monotheistic writings. For though, in accordance with general Pauline practice, He is only once directly spoken of as the 'Son' of God[2], He is united with the Father in a manner which leaves no doubt as to the essential equality which the writer regards as subsisting between them. It is 'in the Lord Jesus Christ' as well as 'in God the Father' that the Church's life consists (I. i. 1, II. i. 1; cf. I. ii. 14): to both Father and Son (I. iii. 11) and even to Son and Father (II. ii. 16 f.), followed by a verb in the singular, that the missionaries address their prayers: and from Both that the highest blessing proceeds (I. i. 1, v. 28, II. i. 2, iii. 18)[3].

The fact too that Christ, even when standing alone, should be regarded as the immediate Author of His people's spiritual growth and establishment in holiness in view of His Second Coming is most significant[4], especially when taken along with

---

[1] Sanday, art. 'Jesus Christ' in Hastings' *D. B.* ii. p. 648; cf. the same writer's *The Life of Christ in Recent Research* (1907), p. 131 f.

[2] As a matter of fact, the full term (ὁ) υἱὸς (τοῦ) θεοῦ occurs elsewhere in the Pauline Epistles only in Rom. i. 4, 2 Cor. i. 19, Gal. ii. 20, Eph. iv. 13, though Christ is referred to as 'Son' on various other occasions (cf. 1 Cor. i. 9, xv. 28, Gal. i. 16, iv. 4, 6, Rom. i. 3, 9, v. 10, viii. 3, 29, 32, Col. i. 13). The comparative rarity of the title may perhaps be due to the fact that it had already been assumed by the Roman Emperors, as when a papyrus-fragment (*B. G. U.* 174) of the year 7 A.D. begins ἔτους ἕ[κ]του καὶ τριακοστοῦ [τῆς] Καίσαρος κρατήσεως θεοῦ υἱ[ό]ν (for υἱοῦ) with evident reference to the Emperor Augustus (Deissmann *BS.* p. 166 f.): cf. Magn. 157ᵇ, 3 f. τὸν υἱὸν τοῦ μεγίστου θεῶν, where the μεγ. θεῶν is Claudius, and his 'son' Nero! On the other hand the 'heathen' usage of the term may have stamped itself on the Apostle's mind, and determined him to recover it to its proper use.

[3] In view of the constant tendency to underrate the Christology of St Paul's earlier writings, it may be well to quote the weighty testimony of Bishop Lightfoot: 'The Christology of the Colossian Epistle is in no way different from that of the Apostle's earlier letters....The doctrine is practically involved in the opening and closing words of his earliest extant epistle (1 Thess. i. 1, v. 28)' (*Colossians*[2] p. 122).

[4] On prayer addressed to Christ in the Early Church see Zahn *Skizzen*[2] p. 271 ff., A. Seeberg *Die Anbetung des 'Herrn' bei Paulus* (1891), and the short tract in *Biblischen Zeit- und Streitfragen* by A. Juncker *Das Gebet bei Paulus* (1905) p. 10 ff.

the part assigned to Him at that Coming. For though Christ is never directly spoken of as Judge in our Epistles, and the final issues are ascribed to God (II. ii. 11 f.) in accordance with the general Jewish belief of the time [1], it is clearly implied that in the work of Judgment the Son also will have a part (I. iii. 13, iv. 6, 17, v. 2 f., II. i. 7 f., ii. 8)[2]. In this connexion, as constantly elsewhere throughout the Epistles, He is described as ὁ κύριος, a title which was the common term for God amongst the Jews of the time, but which is here apparently confined to the Person of the glorified Lord[3], while the identical expressions, which the Hebrew prophets were in the habit of using of God, are directly transferred to Him (e.g. I. v. 2, II. i. 7).

Other evidence, pointing in the same direction, is to be found in the facts that it is from Christ, no less than from God, that the Apostles claim to have derived their commission (I. ii. 7; cf. iii. 2, v. 12), and 'through the Lord Jesus' that they enforce their charges (I. iv. 1 f.[4]; cf. v. 27, II. iii. 6, 12),

---

[1] Cf. e.g. 4 Ezra vi. 6 'facta sunt haec per me et non per alium, ut et finis per me et non per alium'; *Orac. Sib.* iv. 40 ff. ἀλλ' ὁπότ' ἂν δὴ κόσμου καὶ θνητῶν ἔλθῃ κρίσις, ἣν θεὸς αὐτὸς ποιήσει.

Elsewhere, however, more particularly in Enoch, judgment is represented as entrusted to the Messiah, cf. xlv. 3, lxii. 2, lxix. 27 'And he sat on the throne of his glory, and the sum of judgment was committed unto him, the Son of Man': see also *Apoc. Bar.* lxxii. 2, *Orac. Sib.* iii. 286 f., and, on the whole subject, Volz *Jüd. Eschat.* p. 259 f., Holtzmann *Neutest. Theol.* i. p. 262.

[2] For the later teaching of the Apostle to the same effect cf. Rom. ii. 16, 1 Cor. i. 8, iv. 5, 2 Cor. i. 14, v. 10, x. 18; and for its significance on the lips of one who had been brought up a strict Jewish monotheist see Colani *Jésus-Christ et les Croyances Messianiques de son temps* (1864) p. 155, 'Pour un juif, dire que Jésus présidera au jugement, c'était à peu près dire qu'il est le créateur. Aussi je ne sais pas de preuve plus éclatante de l'immense impression produite par le Galiléen que ce simple fait...un pharisien, comme l'avait été Paul, a pu voir en lui le juge des vivants et des morts.'

[3] Briggs *The Messiah of the Apostles* p. 86 n.[6], 'The change of usage by Paul in applying Lord so exclusively to Christ and in carefully abstaining from using it for God the Father was a radical change of an importance which it is hard for any one to exaggerate. It involved the practical substitution of the sovereignty of the Messiah for the sovereignty of God during the Messianic age.' It would perhaps be more exact to say that St Paul regarded the κυριότης of the world as exercised 'through' the Messiah during the period specified. See further Addit. Note D, p. 136 ff.

[4] On the *causal* force of διά in this passage cf. WM. p. 474, n.[3], 'the Apostle was not acting in his own person, but as moved through Christ,' and see

THE EPISTLES TO THE THESSALONIANS

while the Thessalonians' prayers are specially asked that 'the word of the Lord' Jesus may 'spread rapidly, and be received everywhere with honour' (II. iii. 1).

4. Doctrine of the Holy Spirit.
4. This living activity which the power of God (I. ii. 13), or of Christ (I. i. 8, II. iii. 1), can alone impart to the Word is no less clearly marked in connexion with the part assigned to the Third Person of the Holy Trinity, as when the Spirit is made the ground of the 'much assurance' in which the Thessalonians had received the Apostolic Gospel (I. i. 5), of the 'joy' which, notwithstanding much affliction, they had been enabled to display (I. i. 6), and of those charismatic gifts and utterances which, in view of recent abuses, they were at the moment in danger of despising (I. v. 19 f.).

On the other hand, to fall into sins of uncleanness was to reject 'the God,' Whose gift the indwelling Spirit was (I. iv. 7 f.), and to come short of that complete sanctification which was the Spirit's peculiar work (II. ii. 13).

5. Soteriology.
5. When we pass to the region of Soteriology, it is certainly somewhat surprising at first sight to discover that the great doctrine of redemption through the Death of Christ is only once mentioned, and then in the most general way (I. v. 10). At the same time, if only from what St Paul himself tells us regarding his contemporary preaching at Corinth (1 Cor. i. 17 ff., ii. 1 f.), it is clear that this truth was already fully present to the Apostle's own mind, and had been previously proclaimed and accepted at Thessalonica. Else what meaning could his readers have attached to the indirect but significant allusion to Jesus as 'the Rescuer' out of the coming Wrath (I. i. 10), or to the definition of the Christian Faith as rooted in the historic facts of the Death and Resurrection of Jesus (I. iv. 14)?

If too the other great Pauline soteriological doctrine of the union of believers with Christ is not stated here with the same precision that we find in some of the later Epistles, it is certainly implied, as, for example, in the description of the 'Church of the Thessalonians (which is)...in the Lord Jesus

---

A. Schettler *Die paulinische Formel 'durch Christus'* (Tübingen, 1907) p. 53, 'Hinter seinem schwachen Wort steht die Autorität Jesu.'

Christ' (I. i. 1, II. i. 1), or in the emphatic manner in which 'life with Christ' is shown to be the result of the believer's redemption (I. v. 10, ἵνα...ἅμα σὺν αὐτῷ ζήσωμεν)[1], and the final goal of all his hopes (I. iv. 17 καὶ οὕτως πάντοτε σὺν κυρίῳ ἐσόμεθα).

6. It is from this latter point of view indeed, as a prize awaiting the believer in the future, that the 'obtaining of salvation' is principally viewed in our Epistles (I. v. 9, II. ii. 14). The whole outlook is eschatological[2]: and the definite announcement of the Parousia of the Lord rounds off each step in the Apostolic argument (I. ii. 19, iii. 13, iv. 15, v. 23, II. ii. 1 ff.).

<small>6. Eschatology.</small>

Nor can there be any doubt that, in common with all the other Apostolic writers, St Paul regards this Parousia as close at hand (I. iv. 15)[3], though at the same time he is careful to emphasize that the main fact regarding it is that it will be unexpected (I. v. 1), and even in his second letter, in entire keeping with the want of system which distinguishes so much of his eschatology both here and elsewhere[4], the Apostle finds

---

[1] On this important passage see further E. Schäder *Die Bedeutung des lebendigen Christus für die Rechtfertigung nach Paulus* (Gütersloh, 1893) p. 33 f.

[2] Upon 'the vital bearing of St Paul's eschatological outlook upon his theology as a whole' see especially Dr H. A. A. Kennedy's valuable monograph *St Paul's Conceptions of the Last Things* (London, 1904). There are some significant remarks in Prof. Shailer Mathews' *The Messianic Hope in the New Testament* (Chicago, 1905), Part III. c. ii., 'The Eschatological Messianism of Paul.'

[3] Cf. Jas. v. 8, 1 Pet. iv. 7, Heb. x. 25, Rev. i. 1, and for the teaching of our Lord Himself, on which doubtless in the last instance this belief rested, cf. Mt. xvi. 28, Mk. xiv. 62, Lk. xxi. 28. Wellhausen in his *Einleitung in die drei ersten Evangelien* (1905) seeks to minimize this dependence, e.g. 'The eschatological hope acquired its intensity first through the oldest Christians, who attached ('hefteten') it to the Person of Jesus' (p. 107); but see Sanday *Recent Research* p. 157 ff.

In any case it should be noted that a belief in the near approach of the End is naturally characteristic of apocalyptic writing, cf. e.g. 4 Ezra viii. 61 'Quapropter iudicium meum modo appropinquat,' *Apoc. Bar.* xx. 6 'For they [the times] will come and will not tarry': see further Volz *Jüd. Eschat.* p. 163 f., Holtzmann *Neutest. Theol.* ii. p. 188.

[4] Cf. Deissmann (*Theol. Lit. Zeitung*, 1898, Sp. 14): 'What is called the "Eschatology" of Paul has little that is "Eschatological" about it.... Paul did not write *de novissimis*....One must be prepared for a surging hither and thither of great thoughts, feelings, expectations' (cited by Kennedy *op. cit.* p. 21 n.[2]).

room for a parousia of Anti-Christ—a supreme manifestation of the power of evil then at work in the world—by which the Parousia of the Christ will be preceded (II. ii. 3 ff.).

Upon the significance of this picture of 'wickedness incarnate' it will be necessary to dwell at length later[1]. In the meantime it is sufficient to notice that final and complete victory rests with the returning Lord. As He descends from heaven accompanied by His ministering angels (II. i. 7, cf. I. iii. 13)[2], He is met by His risen and living saints (I. iv. 16f.): they enter into 'rest' (II. i. 7), and 'eternal destruction' falls upon the ungodly (II. i. 9).

It is only natural that in depicting the events of that Great Day St Paul should avail himself freely of the figurative language borrowed from the Old Testament, and the later apocalyptic writings of the Jews[3]. But this only serves to set in bolder relief the generally spiritual character of his conception, and the 'fine tact' which enabled him to adapt all that was best in the thought of his time for Christian service[4]. His whole interest in the Parousia proceeds along 'redemptive' lines[5], and his main concern for his converts is that, having found complete deliverance in Jesus *now*, they will be lifted out of the reach of *future* judgment (I. i. 10), and so enjoy that uninterrupted 'life' which, as we have already

---

[1] See Addit. Notes I and J, and to the literature cited there add Ramsay *Exp.* VII. iv. p. 417 ff., where the interesting suggestion is thrown out that the true key to the cryptic utterance of II. ii. 3 ff. is to be found in the twofold light in which St Paul had already begun to regard the Roman Emperor, as the present servant of the Church, in restraining the existing powers of disorder, but as no less its future and irreconcilable foe, when the idolatry of the Imperial cult—an Emperor sitting 'in the sanctuary of God, setting himself forth as God'—had reached its height.

[2] On the Pauline angelology see especially O. Everling *Die paulinische Angelologie und Dämonologie* (Göttingen, 1888).

[3] A useful collection of Jewish parallels will be found in E. Teichmann's *Die Paulinischen Vorstellungen von Auferstehung und Gericht und ihre Beziehung zur Jüdischen Apokalyptik* (Freiburg i. B. 1896).

[4] See A. Titius *Die Neutestamentliche Lehre von der Seligkeit*, ii. *Der Paulinismus* (Tübingen, 1900) p. 47 ff.

The above limitation must be kept in view in estimating such dicta as— 'On no subject, perhaps, was St Paul, in his way of thinking, more a man of his time than on that of eschatology' (Bruce *op. cit.* p. 379); 'Everywhere we recognize the Jewish expectation of the future' (Weinel *St Paul* p. 44).

[5] Kennedy *op. cit.* p. 160 n.[1].

seen, he regards as the peculiar possession of Christ's people (I. v. 10, iv. 17)[1].

7. Hence, to pass to a last point, the emphasis laid throughout on the moral conditions through which alone this 'life' can be reached or enjoyed. St Paul knows nothing of the crude divorce between religion and morality, which is sometimes so strangely attributed to him: his whole attitude is rather 'a shout of triumph' as to the reality of the alliance existing between them[2]. It is not the mere 'word of hearing' that constitutes 'the believer,' but the word 'doing its work' within the heart (I. ii. 13). And, as it is from the personal relation of the soul to God, that the necessary pleasing of God can alone spring (I. iv. 1, cf. ii. 14 f.), so, on the other hand, where God teaches, practice must inevitably follow (I. iv. 9 f., note the emphatic καὶ γάρ). So far indeed from 'faith'·being separated from 'works,' it is in its results that it is principally viewed here (I. i. 3, II. i. 11), and in immediate conjunction with the great Christian duty of 'love' (I. iii. 6, v. 8). And as 'sanctification' is God's 'will' for His people (I. iv. 3), this 'sanctification' must extend alike to the entire 'spirit and soul and body' if the Thessalonians hope to be preserved 'without blame' at the Parousia of their Lord (I. v. 23).

7. Ethical teaching.

---

[1] For the manner in which the thought of 'life' dominates the higher teaching of Jewish Apocalyptic, see W. Bousset *Die Religion des Judentums im neutestamentlichen Zeitalter* (Berlin, 1906) p. 316, and cf. Volz *op. cit.* p. 306.

The same thought is very prominent in the wonderfully pure faith of Zoroaster: cf. Söderblom *La Vie Future d'après le Mazdéisme* (Paris, 1901) p. 269, 'Le rêve le plus cher de la piété mazdéenne était celui de la vie éternelle dans un corps purifié, incorruptible, sur une terre nouvelle, délivrée de tout ce que la souille encore.'

The whole relation of Persian to Jewish and Christian eschatology is full of interest, but cannot be followed out here. In addition to Söderblom's book, the student will find much illustrative material in E. Böklen *Die Verwandtschaft der Jüdisch-Christlichen mit der Parsischen Eschatologie* (Göttingen, 1902): see also Dr J. H. Moulton's art. 'Zoroastrianism' in Hastings' *D.B.* iv. p. 988 f. Several of the more striking parallels, such as the foregoing, are noted by Kennedy *op. cit.*, especially pp. 321 n.[1], 330 n.[2], 336 n.[2]. On the influence of Mazdeism upon pagan thought see especially F. Cumont *Les Religions Orientales dans le Paganisme Romain* (Paris, 1907) c. vi. with the valuable bibliographical notes.

[2] A. Jülicher *Die Religion Jesu und die Anfänge des Christentums* p. 86 (in *Die Kultur der Gegenwart*, I. 4, Berlin, 1906).

VI.

THE AUTHENTICITY AND INTEGRITY OF THE EPISTLES.

Hitherto we have been assuming the authenticity of the Epistles to the Thessalonians in accordance with tradition and the general verdict of the whole Christian Church up to a comparatively recent period. Nor, so far as we have come, have we discovered anything in the Epistles themselves to throw serious doubt on this conclusion. At the same time it is impossible any longer to ignore that it is now frequently challenged, more particularly with regard to the Second Epistle. And though many of the points raised are dependent on the exact interpretation of various words and phrases to which we have still to turn, it may be well in the meantime to set forth the external evidence on which the claims of both Epistles to genuineness rest, and to examine as far as possible the principal objections that have been brought against them. For this purpose it will be necessary to treat them separately.

I. THE AUTHENTICITY AND INTEGRITY OF 1 THESSALONIANS.

Authenticity of 1 Thessalonians.
1. External evidence.

1. The external evidence in favour of 1 Thessalonians is not so strong as we might have expected, nor can it be carried back to such an early date as in the case of many of the other N.T. writings. Thus, though there is a certain resemblance between its eschatological teaching and the Didache, it is by no means clear that the writer of the latter actually used it. Nor do the frequently-cited passages from the Apostolic Fathers amount to much, though two passages in Ignatius, and one in the *Shepherd of Hermas* may perhaps be taken as showing acquaintance with its contents. Much more important testi-

mony in its favour is the fact that it is contained in the Canon of Marcion (c. 140 A.D.), and in the Syriac Vulgate and Old Latin Versions. In the Muratorian Fragment on the Canon (c. 170 A.D.) it is placed sixth in the list of St Paul's Epistles. Irenaeus (c. 180 A.D.) is, so far as we know, the first writer to quote it by name.

> For a possible reminiscence of iv. 15—17 in Didache xvi. 6 f. see the note on iv. 16. The passages from Ignatius are *Rom.* ii. 1 οὐ γὰρ θέλω ὑμᾶς ἀνθρωπαρεσκῆσαι ἀλλὰ Θεῷ ἀρέσαι, cf. ii. 4 οὐχ ὡς ἀνθρώποις ἀρέσκοντες, ἀλλὰ θεῷ, and *Eph.* x. 1 ἀδιαλείπτως προσεύχεσθε (where however the reading is doubtful), cf. v. 17 ἀδιαλείπτως προσεύχεσθε[1]: and the passage from Hermas is *Vis.* III. ix. 10 παιδεύετε οὖν ἀλλήλους καὶ εἰρηνεύετε ἐν αὐτοῖς, cf. v. 13 f. εἰρηνεύετε ἐν ἑαυτοῖς· παρακαλοῦμεν δὲ ὑμᾶς, ἀδελφοί, νουθετεῖτε.... For the evidence of Marcion see Tert. *adv. Marc.* v. 15, Epiphan. *Haer.* xlii. 9. Can. Murat. 'ad tensaolenecinsis sexta.' In *adv. Haer.* v. vi. 1 Irenaeus quotes v. 23 as the words of the 'Apostle' 'in prima epistola ad Thessalonicenses'; cf. also v. xxx. 2, Clem. Al. *Paed.* i. p. 88 D (ed. Sylburg), Tert. *de Res. Carn.* c. 24.

It is not necessary to carry the evidence further down, for, apart from the frequent references to the Epistles which are to be found in the writings of the Fathers from Irenaeus onwards (see small print above), the very existence of 2 Thessalonians, whatever its exact date, implies the recognition of the Pauline authorship of the First Epistle at a very early period in the history of the Church—a recognition moreover which it continued uninterruptedly to enjoy until the middle of last century.

2. The first to raise doubts regarding it was Schrader (*Der Apostel Paulus*, Leipzig 1836), who proceeded on purely subjective grounds. And in this he was followed by F. C. Baur, who developed the attack against both Epistles with great vigour in his *Paulus, der Apostel Jesu Christi* (Stuttgart 1845, Eng. Tr. 2 vols., London, 1873—75). Baur indeed afterwards saw reason to modify his views regarding the relation of the two Epistles (in the *Theol. Jahrbücher*, xiv. 1855, p. 141 ff., see his *Paul*, Eng. Tr. ii. p. 314 ff.), but the objections which

2. Objections to the Epistle's authenticity.

---

[1] 'The evidence that Ignatius knew 1 Thessalonians is almost *nil*.' The *N.T. in the Apost. Fathers* (Oxford, 1905) p. 74.

he originally raised may still be said to form the principal storehouse from which arguments against the authenticity of the First Epistle are drawn, and on that account deserve mention.

In themselves they are of a somewhat varied character, and embrace such points as the meagreness of the Epistle's contents, and their close dependence on the narrative in Acts, the striking similarity to the Corinthian Epistles in thought and language, the un-Pauline character of such passages as ii. 14 ff., iv. 14 ff., and the traces of a later date implied in the description of the Thessalonian Church.

If, however, the view that has already been taken of the circumstances attending the writing of the Epistle is correct (p. xxxi ff.), none of these objections should cause much difficulty. What more natural, for example, than that, writing as he did to vindicate his own and his companions' character, St Paul should dwell at considerable length on the nature of their ministry at Thessalonica? And if general agreement in historical details with St Luke's account is only what we would then look for, the no less striking apparent divergences (cf. pp. xxvii, xxx) are in themselves strong proof that we have the work not of a mere imitator, but rather of an independent and more fully informed narrator. Nor are the frequent resemblances to the Corinthian Epistles to be wondered at, when we remember the short interval of time that elapsed between their composition, and the closely similar situations that they were designed to meet. The violent polemic against the Jews (ii. 14 ff.) is no doubt startling in view of the Apostle's general attitude towards his fellow-countrymen, but it may be sufficiently accounted for by the strenuous opposition which at the time they were offering to him in his work (note the pres. participles ἀρεσκόντων, κωλυόντων, and cf. p. xxxi f.)[1]. Nor is there any need to refer *v.* 16ᶜ to the destruction of Jerusalem. The language is too vague to be understood of any such literal and outward event, and, as we shall see again, clearly refers to the 'judgment' passed upon the Jewish people in the rejection of their Messiah. Similarly the 'concrete representation' of the Last Things in iv. 14 ff. is not enough, as indeed Baur himself admits, to brand the Epistle as un-apostolic, and may easily be due to an early and apparently transitory stage in St Paul's eschatological thought. And

---

[1] According to B. Weiss (*Apokalyptische Studien* in *SK.*, 1869, p. 24) 'Es war die Periode der schärfsten Spannung zwischen ihm und seinem Volke, das den abtrünnigen Vorkämpfer des Christentums mit dem wildesten Fanaticismus verfolgte.'

finally, the statements regarding the rapid growth and widely-extended influence of the Thessalonian Church (i. 7 f., iv. 10), even if no account be taken of the Apostle's constant tendency to exhibit his converts in the most favourable possible light (iii. 6, 12, iv. 1), are in entire accord with what we know of the Macedonian character (see p. xlvi), and the natural advantages Thessalonica enjoyed for an active missionary propaganda (see p. xxii).

There seems to be nothing therefore in these objections to cause any serious difficulty[1]. And even if they were much stronger than they are, they would be more than counter-balanced by the tone and character of the Epistle as a whole[2]. There is an unmistakable ring of reality about its more personal passages, a revelation alike of writer and readers, to which no imitator could ever have attained. Nor again is it possible to conceive how any one writing *after* what had come to be regarded as the distinctive truths of Paulinism were widely known could so skilfully have avoided their introduction into a letter purporting to be written by the Apostle[3]. Only in such an actual historical situation as we have tried to depict is an adequate explanation of the Epistle's *raison d'être* forthcoming. And only in St Paul himself can we find a writer who could have succeeded in so impressing his personality upon what he wrote, combined with the freedom in thought and expression which in themselves are so distinctive of an original author. Is it likely too that any one writing long after the expectation had been falsified would have endangered his credibility by ascribing to St Paul language, which certainly on the face of it implies that the writer looked for the Parousia during his own lifetime (iv. 15)?

---

[1] Steck's supposed discovery (*Jahrbücher f. protest. Theologie* 1883, p. 509 ff.) of the λόγος κυρίου of iv. 15 in 4 Ezra v. 41 f. (cited on p. xxxiii, n.¹), and the consequent carrying forward of the writing of 1 Thess. to at least 100 A.D., is of no greater weight, as the relation between the passages is of the most general kind, and by no means demands any theory of literary dependence: see further Bornemann p. 310 ff.

[2] See especially von Soden's careful study 'Der erste Thessalonicherbrief' in *SK.*, 1885, p. 263 ff. Cf. Jülicher *Einl. in d. N.T.* p. 37, Eng. Tr. p. 58, 'In opposition to the school of Baur the genuineness of the Epistle should be upheld as unquestionable. In style, vocabulary and attitude it approaches as nearly as possible to the four Principal Epistles.'

[3] Cf. Knowling *The Testimony of St Paul to Christ* (1905) p. 21 f.

lxxvi THE EPISTLES TO THE THESSALONIANS

3. Present agreement as to its authenticity.

3. It is only therefore what we should expect, when we find that the claims of 1 Thessalonians to be regarded as an authentic work of the Apostle Paul are now freely admitted by practically all N.T. scholars of importance, its opponents being limited to those who deny the genuineness of all the Pauline Epistles[1].

and integrity.

Nor, apart from the wider question of its authenticity, does there seem any good ground for doubting the general integrity of the Epistle in the form in which it has come down to us. Schmiedel indeed suggests that ii. 15 f. is an interpolation, and others, who accept the passage as a whole, are inclined to throw doubt on the last clause of v. 16 as possibly an 'editorial comment,' added after the destruction of Jerusalem had taken place[2]. But for neither position is there any real warrant (see notes *ad loca*); while v. 27, which has also been suspected, is, whatever the exact interpretation given to it, in thorough accord with the strained and anxious mood, through which at the time the Apostle was passing (p. xxxi ff.)[3].

II. THE AUTHENTICITY AND INTEGRITY OF 2 THESSALONIANS.

Authenticity of 2 Thessalonians.

On the other hand the authenticity and integrity of 2 Thessalonians stand on a different footing, and raise questions of a more difficult character. And, that being so, it is satisfactory to find that the external evidence on its behalf is both earlier and fuller than in the case of the First Epistle.

1. External evidence.

1. Thus, leaving aside possible references in the Didache and Ignatius, there are two passages in Polycarp both of which appear to have this Epistle directly in view. It is true that in the first the writer supposes himself to be quoting words originally addressed to the Philippians, but the words (see below) are only found in 2 Thessalonians, and Polycarp may easily have confused between the two Macedonian Churches,

---

[1] E.g. van Manen art. 'Paul' in *Encyc. Bibl.* See the thorough-going refutation of such extreme positions by Knowling *op. cit.* p. 7 ff., as well as in his earlier work *The Witness of the Epistles* (1892) p. 133 ff.

[2] Moffatt *Hist. N.T.* p. 626.

[3] See further C. Clemen *Die Einheitlichkeit der paulinischen Briefe* (Göttingen, 1894) p. 13 ff.

or possibly in view of their vicinity have looked upon Philippi and Thessalonica as forming in reality one community[1]. In the second, it is hardly possible to doubt that he is consciously adapting a passage of 2 Thessalonians for his purpose, though unfortunately here, as in the foregoing passage, the Greek original is lost. Coming further down we find the Epistle again vouched for in the Canon of Marcion, in the Syriac Vulgate and Old Latin Versions, and in the Muratorian Fragment, while the references to it in early Christian literature are both numerous and clear. Thus there seems an obvious reference to its principal eschatological passage in Justin Martyr's *Dialogue with Trypho*, and an interesting passage in the *Epistle Vienne and Lyons* points even more strongly in the same direction. Irenaeus is again the first to mention it directly by name.

> With iii. 8 ff. cf. Didache xii. 3, and with ii. 3 ff. cf. Didache xvi. 6 ff. The passage from Ignatius is *Rom.* x. 3 ἔρρωσθε εἰς τέλος ἐν ὑπομονῇ Ἰησοῦ Χριστοῦ, cf. iii. 5 εἰς τὴν ὑπομονὴν τοῦ χριστοῦ. It is doubtful, however, whether ὑπομονή is to be understood in the same sense in both passages (see note *ad loc.*). With i. 4 ὥστε αὐτοὺς ἡμᾶς ἐν ὑμῖν ἐγκαυχᾶσθαι ἐν τ. ἐκκλησίαις τ. θεοῦ cf. Polyc. *Ep.* xi. 3 'ego autem nihil tale sensi in vobis vel audivi, in quibus laboravit beatus Paulus, qui estis in principio epistulae ejus: de vobis etenim gloriatur in omnibus ecclesiis[2]'; and with iii. 15 καὶ μὴ ὡς ἐχθρὸν ἡγεῖσθε ἀλλὰ νουθετεῖτε ὡς ἀδελφόν, cf. *Ep.* xi. 4 'et non sicut inimicos tales existimetis.' The passage from Justin is *Dial.* 110 (ed. Otto) ὅταν καὶ ὁ τῆς ἀποστασίας ἄνθρωπος, ὁ καὶ εἰς τὸν ὕψιστον ἔξαλλα λαλῶν, ἐπὶ τῆς γῆς ἄνομα τολμήσῃ εἰς ἡμᾶς τοὺς Χριστιανούς, and the passage from the *Ep. Vienne and Lyons* (ap. Eus. *H. E.* v. 1) ἐνέσκηψεν ὁ ἀντικείμενος, προοιμιαζόμενος ἤδη τὴν μέλλουσαν ἔσεσθαι παρουσίαν αὐτοῦ...Χριστὸς... καταργῶν τὸν ἀντικείμενον...οἱ υἱοὶ τῆς ἀπωλείας: cf. ii. 3 ff. In *adv. Haer.* III. vii. 2 Irenaeus introduces a quotation from ii. 8 with the words 'et iterum in secunda ad Thessalonicenses, de Antichristo dicens, [Apostolus] ait': cf. also Clem. Al. *Strom.* v. p. 554 (ed. Sylburg), Tert. *de Res. Carn.* c. 24.

2. On external grounds then the Epistle is amply vouched for, but the internal difficulties are here of a much more serious

2. Internal evidence.

---

[1] Cf. Zahn *Geschichte des Neutest. Kanons* i. p. 815.

[2] 'The present tense of *gloriatur* also suggests that he is quoting' (*The N.T. in the Ap. Fathers* p. 95).

character than in the case of 1 Thessalonians, and have in recent years been presented with a skill and force that make the question of the Epistle's authenticity one of the most interesting and keenly debated points in modern N.T. criticism.

The attack was started by J. E. Ch. Schmidt (in his *Bibliothek f. Kritik und Exegese des N.T.* Hadamar 1801, and then in his *Einleit. in das N.T.* Giessen 1804), and his objections were revived by de Wette in the earlier editions of his *Lehrbuch der histor.-krit. Einleit. in die kanonischen Bücher des N.T*s., but afterwards abandoned in the fourth edition (1842), and in his *Exegetisches Handbuch* (1841) where the Epistle's authenticity is fully recognized. Meanwhile, however, doubts had again been raised by Kern (*Tübing. Zeitschr. f. Theol.* ii. 1839) who was closely followed by Baur (*Paulus*, 1845), both writers seeing in the Epistle a fictitious writing, dependent on the Apocalypse, and containing features borrowed from the person and history of Nero: while Hilgenfeld (*Einl. in d. N.T.* 1875, p. 642 ff.) went further, carrying its composition as far down as Trajan's time, a position with which in the main Bahnsen (*Jahrb. f. protest. Theol.* 1880, p. 681 ff.) agreed.

Others in more recent times who have denied the Epistle's authenticity are Weizsäcker, Pfleiderer, Schmiedel, Holtzmann, and Wrede, and, in part, P. W. Schmidt and Dr Samuel Davidson. On the other hand it has gained the support of Harnack, Jülicher, and Clemen, has been vigorously defended by Zahn, and is now treated as genuine by the great majority of commentators in Germany, including its latest expositors Bornemann and Wohlenberg, as well as by the general consensus of N.T. scholarship both in this country and America[1].

It cannot be denied however that many who support this conclusion do so with a certain amount of hesitation, and only because of the still greater difficulties attending any rival theory. And it may be well therefore to subject the more important arguments that have been urged against the Epistle to a fresh examination with the view of seeing how far they are really well-grounded. In the main they are derived from (1) its language and style, (2) its literary relationship to 1 Thessalonians, and (3) the character of its doctrinal contents.

The Epistle objected to on the ground of

---

[1] Dr Charles, who refers to the Epistle 'with some hesitation' in his Jowett Lectures on *Eschatology* (1899) p. 380, is now satisfied as to its genuineness: see e.g. his *Ascension of Isaiah* (1900) p. lxii. On the other hand Dr McGiffert (*Encyc. Bibl.* art. 'Thessalonians' col. 5045) speaks of its genuineness as 'beset with serious difficulties' and 'at best very doubtful.'

AUTHENTICITY AND INTEGRITY OF THE EPISTLES lxxix

(1) In itself the vocabulary of the Epistle is by no means remarkable. The words peculiar to it among N.T. writings number only 10, as compared with 17 in 1 Thessalonians, nor do any of them cause any real difficulty (cf. p. liii). And this is the more noteworthy when we remember the unique character of some of its apocalyptic passages, and the marked tendency observable in other of the N.T. writings towards diversity of language and style in dealing with similar topics[1].

<small>(1) Language and style.</small>

But while the vocabulary is thus in the main genuinely Pauline, various words and phrases are often pointed to as used in an un-Pauline manner.

Thus it is said that in i. 11 (ἵνα ὑμᾶς ἀξιώσῃ τῆς κλήσεως ὁ θεὸς ἡμῶν) κλῆσις refers to the final call to participation in future blessedness instead of, as is usual in St Paul, to the initial act of the Christian's life. But even if this future reference be admitted, which is by no means certain, we have at least a partial parallel in Phil. iii. 14 διώκω εἰς τὸ βραβεῖον τῆς ἄνω κλήσεως τοῦ θεοῦ ἐν Χριστῷ Ἰησοῦ, and in any case we can hardly refuse to the word a latitude of application which St Paul might so naturally have extended to it. Nor again surely can any one seriously urge that, because on two occasions the Apostle used the verb ἐξελέξατο with reference to the Divine election (1 Cor. i. 27 f., Eph. i. 4), he could not therefore have used εἵλατο in ii. 13 (ὅτι εἵλατο ὑμᾶς ὁ θεὸς ἀπ' ἀρχῆς εἰς σωτηρίαν), a verb which, as we know from other evidence (Phil. i. 22), he was in the habit of employing, and which from its special reference to the destiny or vocation of the chosen was peculiarly appropriate in the present passage. Still more idle is the objection to ἰσχύς in i. 9 (ἀπὸ τῆς δόξης τῆς ἰσχύος αὐτοῦ) for the more usual δύναμις, for not only is ἰσχύς vouched for by Eph. i. 19, vi. 10, but in the Thessalonian passage it is actually a quotation from Isa. ii. 10. And if any importance is to be attached to the solitary appearance of ἐνκαυχᾶσθαι (i. 4) instead of καυχᾶσθαι, which is found more than thirty times in the Pauline Epistles, or to the combination ὄλεθρος αἰώνιος (i. 9), which St Paul does not again use, but which is in perfect keeping with the language of the Old Testament, and more particularly with that of Jesus, on which in the whole passage the writer shows himself so dependent, or to the admittedly difficult construction ὅτι ἐπιστεύθη τὸ μαρτύριον ἡμῶν ἐφ' ὑμᾶς (i. 10: see note *ad loc.*)—do not these and similar anomalies tell at least as much for as against Pauline authorship, for is it likely that any imitator would have endangered the credibility of his work by making use of them?

---

[1] Cf. Lightfoot *Notes on Epistles of St Paul* p. 72 f.

The same might be said of the variation that appears in certain familiar formulas or phrases between our Epistle and 1 Thessalonians, even if other explanations of the changes were not forthcoming. Thus in the opening thanksgiving, when instead of the simple εὐχαριστοῦμεν of I. i. 2 we find εὐχαριστεῖν ὀφείλομεν in i. 3 and again in ii. 13, this, apart from the added emphasis, is in entire accord with the more formal style of the whole Second Epistle, to which reference will have to be made again. And in the closing invocation the substitution of ὁ κύριος τῆς εἰρήνης (iii. 16) for ὁ θεὸς τῆς εἰρήνης (I. v. 23), taken along with the similar interchange of Persons in ii. 13 and I. i. 4, may well be due to the prominent place which the exalted Lord was occupying at the moment in St Paul's thoughts in view of His glorious Return. In any case it seems evident that throughout this Epistle ὁ κύριος is to be referred to Christ and not to God, so that there is at least no exception here to the general Pauline practice (see Add. Note D).

Other examples of so-called inconsistencies with the language of the first Epistle hardly need to be mentioned. When hostile criticism has to fall back on *minutiae* such as these, unless they are supported by other and stronger evidence than any we have yet discovered, that is in itself a confession of the insufficiency of its case. And it will be generally conceded that this Epistle, taken as a whole, so far as its language and style are concerned, leaves upon the mind of any unbiassed reader the impression of a genuinely Pauline work[1]. For not only are there abundant traces of the Apostle's characteristic phraseology and manner, as has been clearly shown by Dr Jowett and others[2], but the whole Epistle reflects that indefinable original atmosphere which a great writer imparts to his work, and which, in this instance, we are accustomed to associate with the name of St Paul.

(2) Literary dependence

(2) On the other hand, the very closeness of our Epistle's resemblance to 1 Thessalonians has been made the ground of

---

[1] Cf. Jülicher *Einl. in d. N.T.* p. 40, Eng. Tr. p. 62, 'The least important of these arguments [against the genuineness of the Epistle] are those referring to the phraseology, for on the whole the style is so thoroughly Pauline that one might indeed admire the forger who could imitate it so ingeniously.'

[2] Jowett *The Epistles of St Paul to the Thessalonians*, &c., 2nd Ed. i. p. 148 f. According to Reuss *Hist. of the N.T.*, ed. Houghton, p. 75 'For every "unpauline" expression the concordance shows ten Pauline.'

AUTHENTICITY AND INTEGRITY OF THE EPISTLES lxxxi

a second objection to its authenticity. For the literary dependence between the two Epistles has been declared to be of such a character that the question comes to be not, 'Could one man have written both Epistles?' but, 'Is it likely that one man writing to the same people at what must have been a very short interval of time would repeat himself to so large an extent? Or, even if this is conceivable under certain circumstances, is it likely in the case of a writer so richly endowed and so fertile in thought as the Apostle Paul?'

on 1 Thessalonians,

The first to raise this difficulty pointedly was Weizsäcker[1], and his arguments have recently been strongly emphasized by H. Holtzmann[2] and W. Wrede[3]. And the objection is at least an interesting one, for, when taken in conjunction with other peculiarities of the Epistle, it lends itself very easily to the idea of an imitator or forger, who, in order to gain credence for certain views he wished to express, encased them, so to speak, in the framework of a generally accepted Pauline Epistle. To this supposition we shall have to return later, but in the meantime before expressing any opinion upon it, we must notice clearly how far the resemblances between the two Epistles really extend.

Both Epistles begin with a salutation in almost identical terms, and marked by a form of address which the Apostle does not employ again (I. i. 1; II. i. 1, 2).

This is followed by the customary thanksgiving, expressed again in a way found nowhere else in St Paul, and based on practically the same grounds as regards the Thessalonians' state (I. i. 2 ff.; II. i. 3 f.).

A section follows in the main peculiar in thought to the Second Epistle (i. 5—12), but exhibiting many parallels of language with the First, while the transition to the great revelation of chap. ii. is marked by a form of appeal (ἐρωτῶμεν δὲ ὑμᾶς, ἀδελφοί, ii. 1) which is found in the Pauline Epistles outside these two Epistles only in Phil. iv. 3.

The revelation referred to—the section regarding the Man of lawlessness, ii. 1—12—stands so entirely by itself as regards

[1] *Das Apostolische Zeitalter*[2] p. 249 f., Eng. Tr. i. p. 295 f. ('The fact that the genuineness of the epistle has been strenuously assailed is not surprising, but inevitable. The reason for this is found, above all, in its striking relation to the first letter' p. 295).
[2] *Z.N.T.W.* ii. (1901), p. 97 ff.
[3] *Die Echtheit des zweiten Thessalonicherbriefs* (*Texte und Untersuchungen*, N.F. ix. 2), Leipzig, 1903.

f 2

contents, that it is frequently spoken of as constituting the *raison d'être* of the whole Epistle. But, apart from other Pauline peculiarities of language which it exhibits, it is interesting to notice in connexion with the point before us, that we find here the same reminiscences by the writer of a visit to his readers, and of what he had said when with them, that we have already met in 1 Thessalonians (ii. 5 οὐ μνημονεύετε ὅτι ἔτι ὢν πρὸς ὑμᾶς ταῦτα ἔλεγον ὑμῖν; cf. I. iii. 4 καὶ γὰρ ὅτε πρὸς ὑμᾶς ἦμεν, προελέγομεν ὑμῖν): this does not occur again in the Pauline Epistles.

No sooner, moreover, has the writer of the Second Epistle finished this, his main theme, than he utters a fervid thanksgiving and prayer for his readers (ii. 13 f.), after the manner of I. ii. 13, in which several of the characteristic words and phrases scattered through the First Epistle are re-echoed.

Similar resemblances may also be traced in the exhortation that follows to stand firm and to hold fast the traditions they have been taught (ii. 15; I. iv. 1), and more especially in the remarkable invocation of ii. 16, which corresponds both in form and place with I. iii. 11, though there, in accordance with the usual practice, ὁ θεὸς καὶ πατὴρ ἡμῶν comes before ὁ κύριος ἡμῶν Ἰησοῦς: while the prayer in iii. 5 ὁ δὲ κύριος κατευθύναι ὑμῶν τὰς καρδίας may be compared with I. iii. 11 αὐτὸς δὲ ὁ θεὸς ... κατευθύναι τὴν ὁδὸν ἡμῶν, the only other passage in the Pauline writings where the verb κατευθύνειν is found, though it is to be noted that it is used in different connexions in the two passages.

The closing section iii. 6—15, like the closing section I. v. 1 ff., is occupied with a practical exhortation, which in the main follows independent lines, though we are again struck with the recurrence here of various turns of expression and thought with which the First Epistle has already made us familiar—such as the warning against *disorderly walking* (iii. 6, 7, 11; I. v. 14); the call to *imitate* the writer's mode of life (iii. 7, 9; I. i. 6 f.); and the reference to the Apostle's *labouring night and day* that they might not prove themselves *burdensome* to their converts (iii. 8; I. ii. 9), to which the Second Epistle adds the further thought of providing an example to the restless and idle (iii. 9).

Both Epistles end with an invocation to 'the Lord (God, 1 Thess.) of peace,' and with the customary Pauline benediction (II. iii. 16, 18; I. v. 23, 28).

The resemblances between the two writings are thus very striking, and justice can hardly be said to have been done to them as a rule by the upholders of the Pauline authorship of the Second Epistle. At the same time, care must be taken that they are not pressed too far. Even our brief review has indicated what an examination of Wrede's carefully prepared Tables makes still more evident, that at most the parallelism between the two Epistles cannot be said to extend to more than one-third of their whole contents. And from this, again, there fall to be deducted such points of contact as are afforded by the salutation at the beginning, the benediction at the close, the phrases of transition from one subject to another, and similar formal expressions, where a close resemblance of language is not only natural but probable[1].

Nor must it be forgotten that even where certain sections of the Second Epistle correspond in their general contents to certain sections of the First, the actual parallelisms in language are by no means always found within these corresponding sections, but have frequently to be drawn from the two Epistles as wholes. And not only so, but they often occur in such different connexions as to suggest not so much the slavish copying by one man of another, as rather the free handling by the same writer of certain familiar words and phrases[2].

The same may be said of the differences of *tone*, combined with the similarities of expression, between the two Epistles of which certain critics have made so much. It is quite true that in certain particulars the general tone of Second Thessalonians is more official and severe than the tone of First Thessalonians, though warm and personal passages are not wanting (e.g., i. 11, ii. 16 f., iii. 3—5), and that at places the writer seems in difficulties as regards both his language and his grammar[3].

But while these facts, taken by themselves, might be evidence of a later writer clumsily imitating another man's work[4],

[1] According to Schmiedel (*Hand-Commentar zum N.T.* II. i. p. 8), out of not quite 825 words in Second Thessalonians over 150 correspond literally, and over 30, with slight variations, with the vocabulary of First Thessalonians: not surely a very large number when the circumstances of the Epistle's composition are kept in view.

[2] See further a review by Wernle of Wrede's pamphlet in the *Göttingische gelehrte Anzeigen*, 1905, p. 347 ff. (summarized in *Exp.* VII. ii. p. 91 f.).

[3] Commenting on i. 3—10, Bornemann remarks: 'Man hat das Gefühl, als sei er nicht sofort mit seinen Worten ins rechte Gleis gekommen und müsse, zum Teil mit den Worten seines früheren Briefes, zum Teil mit alttestamentlichen und liturgischen Wendungen erst den Zug seiner Gedanken rangieren und sammeln' (*Die Thessalonicherbriefe* p. 328).

[4] 'Künstliche oder vielmehr verkünstelte Nacharbeit.' Holtzmann *l.c.* p. 100.

they may be equally well accounted for by a change in the mood of the same writer, and in the circumstances of those to whom he writes.

St Paul was, we know, subject to great alternations of feeling, and when he wrote 2 Thessalonians, not only was he no longer under the influence of the same glad rebound from anxiety regarding the Thessalonians' state that he experienced when he wrote his First Epistle, but there is also evidence that at the time he was personally much harassed by 'unreasonable and evil men' at Corinth (iii. 2; Acts xviii. 12 ff.). Moreover, as regards the recipients of the letter, there are undoubted traces in the Second Epistle that, between the time of its writing and the writing of the First, St Paul had heard of an increasing restlessness among his converts—a business which was no business (μηδὲν ἐργαζομένους ἀλλὰ περιεργαζομένους, iii. 11)—which might well justify more authoritative and severe warnings on his part, without however implying the later Church-discipline ('Kirchenzucht') which Schmiedel tries to discover in them.

Nor is it quite fair, as is generally done by those who lay stress on the closeness of the literary dependence between the two Thessalonian Epistles, to speak of it as without a parallel in early Christian literature. For, to those who admit their authenticity, we have within the circle of the Pauline Epistles themselves the kindred Epistles to the Ephesians and Colossians, exhibiting an identity of thought and language, such as to make them, notwithstanding their admitted differences in aim, almost duplicates of each other. And if St Paul could thus repeat himself in two contemporary Epistles, addressed if not to the same Church at least to the same district, why should not a like similarity run through two other Epistles, written at an interval according to the traditional view of at most a few months, and dealing with a situation which, if differing in certain particulars, was in the main unchanged (cf. p. lvi n.[3])?

A further effort to explain the extent of the resemblances between the two Epistles has also been made by the suggestion that St Paul had re-read the First immediately before writing the Second Epistle, or more precisely that he had in his hands the rough draft which his amanuensis had prepared of his first letter—a clean copy having been despatched to Thessalonica—and that he drew freely from it in dictating the terms of the second letter[1].

One cannot say that this is impossible, and there would certainly be nothing according to the literary canons of the time to prevent a writer thus freely borrowing from his own previous work. But the very ingenuity of the suggestion is against it, and presupposes that the Apostle attached a greater importance to his own writings than their strictly occasional character warrants.

It is safer therefore to be content with such general explanations as have already been offered, or frankly to admit that the resemblances between the two Epistles constitute an interesting but, in our present state of ignorance regarding the exact circumstances of their writing, an insoluble literary problem. This however in no way militates against the Pauline authorship of the Second, unless other and more definite grounds for disputing it can be produced.

(3) Such grounds, it is said, are to be found in the Epistle's doctrinal contents, as being, in the first place, inconsistent with the clear teaching of 1 Thessalonians, and, in the second, in themselves of such a character, that it is not possible to think of St Paul's having written them.

(3) Doctrinal contents. These are said to be

(a) As regards the charge of inconsistency with 1 Thessalonians, that rests in the main on an alleged change of attitude with reference to the nearness of the Parousia. In 1 Thessalonians the Parousia is represented as close at hand, and there is no mention of any sign by which it is to be preceded; but in 2 Thessalonians we are distinctly told that it will not take place until the Man of lawlessness has been revealed[2].

(a) inconsistent with 1 Thessalonians,

To this it is generally replied that the two pictures are not really inconsistent, and that while there is nothing in the

---

[1] 'Für den vielbeschäftigten und seines erregbaren Temperaments bewussten Pl lag gerade in diesem Fall nichts näher, als das Concept des 1 Th, wenn ein solches vorhanden war, noch einmal durchzulesen, ehe er den 2 Th diktirte' (Zahn *Einl. in das N.T.* i. p. 179).

[2] Cf. G. Hollmann *Die Unechtheit des zweiten Thessalonicherbriefs* in *Z. N. T. W.* v. (1904), p. 29 ff.

lxxxvi THE EPISTLES TO THE THESSALONIANS

teaching regarding the Parousia in 1 Thessalonians to exclude the prior coming of the Man of lawlessness, there is equally nothing in his coming as depicted in the Second Epistle to delay unduly the expected Parousia of the First: all that is said is that Christ will not come just yet[1].

But while there is undoubted force in this—and parallels for the conjunction of the two views, or rather for the two aspects of the same truth may be cited from our Lord's eschatological discourse (Mt. xxiv. 29 ff.), and from the Apocalypse of St John (Rev. iii. 1 ff., vi. 1 ff.)—it is better not to attempt to reconcile the two positions too literally. There are many indications that St Paul's eschatological views were at this time in a state of flux, and that his teaching concerning the Last Things was determined by practical and not theological motives, without much regard as to how far that teaching presented a consistent whole[2]. And it may well have been that in the short time that had elapsed between the writing of 1 and 2 Thessalonians he had heard of circumstances in his converts' state, which led him to emphasize afresh an aspect of the Parousia, on which he had dwelt when in Thessalonica (ii. 5), but of which they had apparently lost sight, and which may also have gained a new significance in his own mind.

(b) un-Pauline.

(b) Even, however, if the point be thus turned against the charge of inconsistency, the question still remains whether it is at all likely that St Paul, supposing him to have been the writer, would have so far departed from his general mode of thought in this particular passage, ii. 1—12. In none of his other New Testament writings do we find him laying stress on the 'signs' preceding the end; nor does the person of

---

[1] Baur admitted this in his earlier and, it seems to us, correcter view of the relation of the two Epistles on this point. 'It is perfectly conceivable,' he says, 'that one and the same writer, if he lived so much in the thought of the *parousia* as the two Epistles testify, should have looked at this mysterious subject in different circumstances and from different points of view, and so expressed himself regarding it in different ways' (*Paulus* p. 488, Eng. Tr. ii. p. 93). On 'how confused a maze of eschatological conceptions could co-exist often in one and the same person,' see Wernle *Beginnings of Christianity* Eng. Tr. i. p. 25.

[2] Cf. Vischer *Die Paulusbriefe* (1904) p. 71 'Wo eine überschwängliche Hoffnung spricht, darf man nicht juristische Präzision erwarten.'

Antichrist, with whom in general his conception corresponds, though the actual name is not used, again appear in his Epistles except in the incidental notice of 2 Cor. vi. 15 (τίς δὲ συμφώνησις Χριστοῦ πρὸς Βελίαρ;). But this in itself is not sufficient ground for maintaining that St Paul can never have shared what we know to have been a widely spread belief of his time (comp. 1 Jo. ii. 18, 22, iv. 3, 2 Jo. 7, Rev. xii. 13; Gfrörer *Jahr. des Heils* ii. p. 257). And if he did not again lay the same stress on it, that may have been either because he had outgrown the belief in this particular form, or because he did not again find himself confronted with circumstances which made such teaching either necessary or desirable.

Of course if the historical situation lying at the background of this teaching is to be sought in the antinomian Gnostic heresies of the second century, as Hilgenfeld, Bahnsen and Pfleiderer have from various points of view maintained, or even in the popular legend of *Nero redivivus*, which has been widely believed from Kern and Baur down to P. Schmidt and Schmiedel, the Pauline authorship of the Epistle at once falls to the ground.

But, as has already been indicated, the doctrine of Antichrist did not come into existence with Montanism, but was firmly rooted in Jewish soil even before the Christian era; while, as regards the Nero-hypothesis, the recent researches of Gunkel[1], Bousset[2], and Charles[3] have made clear that it was at a much later date than the interests of this theory require, that those traits belonging to Antichrist were transferred to Nero, which alone could make him a fitting basis for the Pauline conception.

Nor can this conception be derived from the Johannine Apocalypse, as was at one time freely held[4]. It is now very generally admitted by critics of all schools that the 'hindrance' to the Man of lawlessness, of which the writer speaks, is to be

---

[1] *Schöpfung und Chaos* p. 221 ff.

[2] *Der Antichrist* p. 13 f., Eng. Tr. p. 21 f. See also art. 'Antichrist' in *Encyc. Bibl.*

[3] *The Ascension of Isaiah* p. lxi ff. 'Schmiedel's view which regards 2 Thess. ii. 1—12...as a Beliar-Neronic myth (68—70 A.D.) is at conflict with the law of development as well as with all the evidence accessible on the subject' (p. lxii. n.¹).

[4] E.g. Hilgenfeld *Einl. in d. N.T.* p. 647 ff. Later critics, while regarding the close affinity of the Thessalonian picture with Rev. xiii. &c. as unmistakable, are careful not to assert actual literary dependence; cf. Holtzmann *Neutest. Theologie* ii. p. 191, Pfleiderer *Urchristentum*² i. p. 97 f. (Eng. Tr. i. p. 138).

found in the influence of the Roman Government, in perfect keeping with such later Pauline passages as Rom. xiii. 1—7. But if so, it will be at once recognized how wholly different this is from the description of Rome given in the Apocalypse, drunk with 'the blood of prophets and of saints, and of all that have been slain upon the earth' (Rev. xviii. 24; cf. vi. 9 ff., vii. 14, xiv. 8, xvi. 19)[1].

The whole conception indeed, as it meets us here, is purely religious, not political, and it is in the Old Testament, in the teaching of Jesus, and, more particularly as regards form, in certain Jewish apocalyptic beliefs, that its roots are to be found (see further Add. Note I, p. 158 ff.).

Further than this it is impossible to go at present without entering on many of the vexed questions of interpretation which the passage raises. But if what has just been said is correct, it will be seen that, obscure though the passage undoubtedly is, there is still nothing in it to make its Pauline authorship impossible, or even improbable; while its genuine Pauline style, and its natural place in the argument of the Epistle, are strong evidence in favour of the traditional view.

3. Rival Theories regarding the origin and intention of 2 Thessalonians. The Epistle is said (1) to bear traces of interpolation,

3. In this general conclusion we are confirmed by the unsatisfactory and conflicting nature of the rival theories which are offered of the origin and intention of 2 Thessalonians by those who deny its authenticity—theories which land us in greater difficulties than any they serve to remove. Incidental notice has been taken of some of these theories already, but there are three in particular which call for further remark[2].

(1) There is, in the first place, the theory of Interpolation, which has been so frequently resorted to lately to explain, or explain away, difficulties in New Testament interpretation, and which in the present instance has at least this in its favour,

---

[1] 'A representation of Rome as a *protecting* power, "restraining" Belial, even temporarily, is inconceivable after July, 64 A.D.' (Bacon *Introd. to the N.T.* p. 78).

[2] On the necessity of the impugners' of the Epistle's authenticity supplying us with an intelligible account of its origin, see Bornemann *Komm.* p. 478, and cf. Wrede's frank admission, 'Vor allem darf es nicht bei der blossen Negation bleiben: es muss gefragt werden, wie der Brief positiv als pseudonymes Schriftstück zu begreifen ist' (p. 3).

that we have abundant signs of its presence in the apocalyptic literature of the period. May it not then have been at work here?

May not, as P. Schmidt suggests, i. 1—14, ii. 1, 2ᵃ, ii. 13—18 have formed a true Pauline Epistle, into which a later writer interpolated the two passages which have caused most difficulty, i. 5—12 and ii. 1—12[1]?

But apart altogether from the arbitrariness of any such theory, and the total absence of MS. evidence in support of it, the result is to leave a letter so shorn of all its distinctive features that it is difficult to see how St Paul could ever have thought of writing it[2]. And further, a careful study of the Epistle as a whole shows that these two sections are so closely related both to what immediately precedes, and to what follows, that they cannot be separated from them without violence.

(2) Of greater interest is the view which Spitta develops in a striking study on the Epistle contained in his *Zur Geschichte und Litteratur des Urchristentums* i. p. 111 ff. Starting from the 'inferiority' of the Second Epistle to the First, he holds that, with the exception of the authenticating paragraph at the end (iii. 17, 18), it is the work not of St Paul, but of Timothy. And in this way he thinks that he finds an adequate explanation both of its generally Pauline character and of its peculiarities—of the former, because it was written by Timothy in close correspondence with St Paul and by his commission: of the latter, because the Jewish cast of its apocalyptic passages is in thorough harmony with what we learn elsewhere regarding Timothy's Jewish upbringing (Ac. xvi. 1, 2 Tim. i. 5, iii. 14 f.).

(2) to be the work of Timothy.

But, to take the last point first, was Timothy after all more of a Jew than St Paul? And difficult though it may be to reconcile on paper the attitude towards the Jews which underlies ii. 1—2 with that afterwards elaborated in Rom. xi.,

---

[1] *Der erste Thessalonicherbrief* p. 111 ff. (Berlin, 1885).
[2] So strongly does Hausrath feel this, that apparently he regards ii. 1—12 as the genuine Pauline fragment ('Grundlage'), which was afterwards worked up into an Epistle (*Neutest. Zeitgesch.*[2] iii. p. 198, Eng. Tr. iii. p. 215).

Dr Moffatt properly insists that 'it would be psychologically false to deny the compatibility of both positions at different periods within a single personality[1].' By the time Romans xi. came to be written, the Apostle was 'more dispassionate and patriotic,' or rather had attained to wider views of the possibilities God had in store for the chosen people.

It is in the want, however, of any satisfactory direct evidence in support of it that the real weakness of Spitta's theory may be seen. For the verse on which he relies so much will certainly not bear the strain put upon it—'Remember ye not, that when I was yet (ἔτι) with you, I told you these things?' (ii. 5). The ἔτι, so Spitta argues, points to a time very shortly before that at which the writer is writing[2]. And as Timothy had been at Thessalonica more recently than St Paul, the reference is thought to be naturally to his visit. But is there any need so to restrict ἔτι? All that it implies is the desire on the writer's part to carry his readers back with him to the time when he was with them, whenever that time may have been. And further, is it conceivable that ἔλεγον can be understood of any other than the leading writer St Paul, more particularly in view of the admitted reference of the first person singular to him in II. iii. 17 and I. iii. 5, v. 27, the only other passages in the two Epistles where it is used? Had Timothy wished to distinguish himself here from his two companions, Paul and Silvanus, would he not certainly have added his name ἐγὼ ὁ Τιμόθεος, or some such expression, and not have trusted to the Thessalonians' recognizing his handwriting as different from that of St Paul in the closing paragraph (iii. 17, 18), as Spitta is driven to suggest[3].

That Timothy may on this occasion have acted as St Paul's amanuensis is of course possible; and it is perhaps in the

[1] *Hist. N.T.* p. 626.
[2] 'Auf eine Anwesenheit in Thessalonich, welche bereits längere Zeit vergangen ist, passt der Ausdruck nicht' (p. 124).
[3] 'Ein Missverständniss war ja für die Briefempfänger nicht wohl möglich, davon zu geschweigen, dass sie des Timotheus Handschrift werden gekannt haben im Unterschied von der des Paulus in der Schlussbemerkung, 3, 18. Somit ergiebt es sich mit ziemlicher Sicherheit, dass der im Namen von Paulus, Silvanus und Timotheus ausgegangene 2. Thess.-Brief von den letzter dieser drei abgefasst und von den ersten nur mit einen eigenhändigen Schlusswort versehen ist' (p. 125).

AUTHENTICITY AND INTEGRITY OF THE EPISTLES xci

thought of a change of amanuensis from (say) Silvanus in the First Epistle that some of our Epistle's linguistic peculiarities may find an explanation (cf. Add. Note A, p. 125 f.). But this is very different from supposing that Timothy was actually its author, or that the Apostle set his own seal to views with which he was not wholly in agreement, as Spitta's theory requires.

(3) If then the writer was not St Paul, there is nothing left for us but to fall back upon the suggestion which has been urged from time to time in various forms, that the Epistle is the work of an unknown writer, who, anxious to gain currency for his own views regarding the Last Things, imbedded them in a framework skilfully drawn from St Paul's genuine Epistle. *(3) to be forgery.*

We have seen already the objections attending any such theory, in so far as it is connected with a definite historical situation such as the expected return of Nero. But apart altogether from such considerations, is it likely that a fictitious Epistle addressed on this showing to a Church which had already an authentic Epistle of St Paul's, and in which many of the original recipients may well have been alive, would ever have gained currency as the Apostle's?

So strongly does Wrede, the latest exponent of the theory, feel this that he suggests that the Epistle was never intended for Thessalonica at all, but that the unknown writer simply made a general use of 1 Thessalonians, as, owing to its apocalyptic character, best serving the purpose he had in view (pp. 38 ff., 68). So that it comes to this: That this Epistle, so amply vouched for in antiquity, is nothing but a barefaced forgery[1]—written in the name of St Paul by one who was not St Paul—invested with the authority of the Apostle, though designed to correct views currently attributed to the Apostle— and addressed to the Church of Thessalonica, though having another and a very different circle of readers in view. Surely there are more 'misses' here than any 'hits,' with which,

---

[1] It is unfortunate to have to use the word 'forgery'—round which such definite associations have now gathered —in connexion with our problem; but no other word brings out so well the deliberate attempt of one man to use the name and authority of another in his writing. In view of iii. 17, 18, there can be no talk here of a harmless pseudonymous writing. Cf. Wrede p. 86: 'Stammt der zweite Thessalonicherbrief nicht von Paulus, so ist er eine Fälschung.'

according to the most charitable interpretation of it, the theory can be credited!

Nor does the view of forgery, so improbable in itself, derive any real help from two passages which are often cited in support of it, and as in themselves conclusive against the Epistle's genuineness.

The first of these is ii. 2: 'To the end that ye be not readily shaken from your reason, nor yet be disturbed either by spirit, or by word, or by epistle as from us, as if the day of the Lord is now present.' But even if the difficult clause, μήτε δι' ἐπιστολῆς ὡς δι' ἡμῶν, be taken as referring to the possible existence of a pretended or forged epistle, and is not merely the exhausting by the writer of the different ways by which the Thessalonians might have been disturbed—spirit, word, letter, it represents at most just such a vague suspicion as might have crossed St Paul's mind (cf. I. v. 27), but which would have been exceedingly unnatural in one who was himself engaged in passing off a spurious letter.

The same may be said of iii. 17: 'The salutation of me Paul with mine own hand, which is the token in every epistle: so I write.' The particular form of authentication used here is unique among the Pauline Epistles; and if it had been the work of a forger, would he not have been more careful to follow St Paul's general usage, as it meets us in 1 Cor. xvi. 21, or Col. iv. 18? 'But if Paul wrote the words, they express his intention; and this intention was satisfactorily fulfilled if he always added the benediction in his own handwriting[1].'

4. General conclusion.

4. On the whole then, without any desire to minimize the difficulties surrounding the literary character and much of the contents of this remarkable Epistle, there seems to be nothing in them to throw undue suspicion on its genuineness; while the failure of those who reject it to present any adequate explanation of how it arose, or of the authority it undoubtedly possessed in the Early Church, is in itself strong presumptive evidence that the traditional view is correct, and that we have here an authentic work of the Apostle Paul.

---

[1] Drummond *The Epistles of Paul the Apostle to the Thessalonians* &c. (in *International Handbooks to the N.T.*) p. 13.

VII.

AUTHORITIES FOR THE TEXT.

The text adopted for the following commentary is the Greek text of Westcott and Hort: it approximates therefore closely to the type of text represented by אB. In these circumstances it has not been thought necessary to provide a complete *apparatus criticus*; but wherever the Editors have shown any doubt as to the true reading by the use of brackets or the insertion of marginal readings, the leading authorities on both sides have been cited. These authorities have as a rule been taken from the great collection of Tischendorf (*Nov. Test. Graec.*[8] ii. Leipzig, 1872), or from Friedrich Zimmer's useful monograph *Der Text der Thessalonicherbriefe* (Quedlinburg, 1893), and the citations, more particularly in the case of the versions, have, as far as possible, been verified, and sometimes corrected, by a comparison with the best available texts of the originals[1].

It will be kept in view that the accompanying lists aim only at enumerating the authorities actually cited in the *apparatus* or textual commentary.

I. GREEK MSS.

The text is contained in whole, or in part, in the following MSS.

i. *Primary Uncials.*

    א. Codex Sinaiticus, saec. iv. Discovered by Tischendorf in the Convent of St Catherine on Mt Sinai, and

---

[1] In this connexion I desire to express my indebtedness to Mr Norman McLean, Christ's College, Cambridge, and the Rev. A. E. Brooke, B.D., King's College, Cambridge, who have kindly verified the citations from the Syriac, Armenian, and Aethiopic, and from the Egyptian versions respectively.

now at St Petersburg. The MS. has been corrected by various hands, of which ℵ^a is nearly contemporary, ℵ^b belongs probably to the sixth century, and ℵ^c to the beginning of the seventh. Ed. Tischendorf, Leipzig, 1864.

A. Codex Alexandrinus, saec. v. Originally at Alexandria. Presented by Cyril Lucar, Patriarch of Constantinople, to Charles I. in 1628, and deposited in the British Museum in 1753. Issued in autotype facsimile by E. M. Thompson, London, 1879.

B. Codex Vaticanus, saec. iv. Generally believed to be the oldest extant MS. of the Greek Bible. O. von Gebhardt dates it c. 331, A. Rahlfs (*Theol. Literaturzeitung*, 1899, p. 556) soon after 367. Probably of Egyptian origin, though there are also strong grounds for inclining to a connexion with the Eusebian library at Caesarea (Kenyon, *Text. Criticism of the N.T.*, p. 66 ff.; cf. SH. p. lxvii f.). The MS. has been one of the great treasures of the Vatican Library since shortly after its foundation, and was issued in phototype by J. Cozza-Luzi and others (Rome, 1889), and better in photographed facsimile by Hoepli (Milan, 1904).

C. Codex Ephraemi rescriptus, saec. v. A Palimpsest, much mutilated. The remains of the Greek Text, underlying the works of Ephraim the Syrian († 373), were deciphered and published by Tischendorf, Leipzig, 1843. Of our Epistles the fragment 1 Thess. i. 1— ii. 9 is all that survives. The original MS. is now in Paris.

D (D$_2$). Codex Claromontanus, saec. vi. A Graeco-Latin MS. from the monastery of Clermont, near Beauvais, and now at Paris. Its type of text is closely akin to EFG, and 'all probably go back to one common archetype, the origin of which is attributed to Italy' (Kenyon, p. 81)[1]. Of its correctors D^b dates from about the seventh, and D^c from the ninth or tenth century. Ed. Tischendorf, Leipzig, 1852.

G (G$_3$). Codex Boernerianus, saec. ix. A Graeco-Latin MS., so named from Prof. C. F. Boerner, who bought it in 1705; now at Dresden. For the conjectural history of the MS. see SH. p. lxiv, and for its relation to D and the Gothic version, *ibid*. p. lxix f. Ed. Matthaei, Meissen, 1791.

---

[1] A. Souter (*J. T. S.* vi. p. 240 ff.) argues that D belongs to Sardinia.

AUTHORITIES FOR THE TEXT

H(H₃). Codex Coislinianus, saec. vi. Originally in the library of the Laura on Mt Athos. Forty-one leaves still exist, scattered through various libraries, and in addition the text of twenty-two pages has been recovered from the 'offsets' left by them on the pages opposite. The fragment at Kieff contains 1 Thess. ii. 9—13, iv. 5—11. The subscription connects the MS. with Euthalius, on whom see especially Dean Armitage Robinson, *Euthaliana* (*Texts and Studies*, iii. 3), Cambridge, 1895; cf. SH. p. lxviii f., von Dobschütz in *Zeitschrift für Kirchengeschichte*, xix. 2, von Soden, *Die Schriften des Neuen Testaments* (1902), i. p. 637 ff., Turner in Hastings' *D.B.* v. p. 524 ff., Conybeare in *Z.N.T.W.* v. (1904) p. 39˙ff., Robinson in *J.T.S.* vi. p. 87 ff. The text was edited by Omont, *Notices et Extraits*, xxxiii. pt. i. p. 141 ff., with the St Petersburg offsets, the Paris and Turin offsets by Robinson (*Euthaliana*, p. 48 ff.), and the recently recovered Athos offsets by Prof. Kirsopp Lake, *Facsimiles of the Athos Fragments of Codex H of the Pauline Epistles* (Oxford, 1905).

No account has been taken of E(E₃) and F(F₂) in accordance with Hort's judgment that the former in its Greek text is simply a transcript of D(D₂), and the latter, as certainly, a transcript of G(G₃), or 'an inferior copy of the same immediate exemplar' (*Intr.*² § 203).

ii. *Secondary Uncials.*

K(K₂). Codex Mosquensis, saec. ix. Moscow.

L(L₂). Codex Angelicus, saec. ix. Rome.

P(P₂). Codex Porphyrianus, saec. ix. St Petersburg. Wants 1 Thess. iii. 5 μηκετι...ημεις οι iv. 17. Ed. Tischendorf in *Mon. Sacr. Ined.*, Nov. Coll., v., Leipzig, 1865, pp. 58—364.

iii. *Minuscules.*

According to von Soden (*Die Schriften des N.T.* i. p. 44) there are now about 630 cursive MSS. available for the Pauline Epistles. The following are a few of the most important.

4** (= Acts 4): saec. xv, now in Basle, Univ. A.N. iv. 5.

6 (= Gosp. 6, Acts 6): saec. xi, in Paris, Bibl. Nat. Gr. 112.

17 (= Gosp. 33, Acts 13): saec. xi, in Paris, Bibl. Nat. Gr. 14. Deserves special notice (Hort, *Intr.*² § 212).

23: A.D. 1056, in Paris, Bibl. Nat. Coisl. Gr. 28.

31 (= Acts 25, Apoc. 7): A.D. 1087, in London, Brit. Mus. Harl. 5537.

37 (= Gosp. 69, Acts 31, Apoc. 14): saec. xv, in Leicester, Library of the Town Council. 'Has many Non-Alexandrian, Pre-Syrian readings of both kinds' (Hort, *Intr.*² § 212). For the history of this interesting MS. see Scrivener, *Codex Augiensis* (Cambridge, 1859), Introd. p. xl ff. and Appendix, J. Rendel Harris, *Origin of the Leicester Codex* (Cambridge, 1887).

47: saec. xi, in Oxford, Bodl. Roe 16.

67 (= Acts 66, Apoc. 34): saec. xi, in Vienna, Imp. Gr. th. 302.

67**: very ancient readings in the margins of 67, which have no other cursive attestation. Hort (*Intr.*² § 212) regards them as akin to M^{paul}, though they cannot have been derived from the text of M^{paul} itself.

71: saec. xii, in Vienna, Imp. Gr. th. 61.

73 (= Acts 68): saec. xiii, in Upsala, Univ. MS. Gr. 1.

116 (= Acts 101): saec. xiii, in Moscow, Syn. 333.

137 (= Gosp. 263, Acts 117): saec. xiii, in Paris, Nat. Gr. 61*.

154 (= Acts 126): saec. xi, in Paris, Nat. Gr. 217.

For Athos, Laura 184 B. 64 (saec. x) = *a* 78 of von Soden's list, see Sect. III under Origen.

II. VERSIONS.

The ancient Versions are as follows.

i. *Latin.*

(1) Old Latin (Lat Vet Vg or O.L.). The history of the Old Latin version (or versions) is still involved in many perplexities: it must be sufficient to refer here to the exhaustive art. by Dr H. A. A. Kennedy in Hastings' *D.B.* iii. p. 47 ff., where Antioch is suggested as its original home. Mr C. H. Turner and Prof. Souter, on the other hand, are emphatic for Rome, while the majority of modern critics may be said to favour the theory of an African origin. The extant fragments of the version have been collected by the Benedictine, P. Sabatier, in his monumental work *Bibliorum sacrorum latinae versiones seu vetus Italica* (Rheims, 1739—49). See also L. Ziegler, *Die lateinischen Bibelübersetzungen vor Hieronymus*, Munich, 1879.

The following authorities for the Pauline Epistles have been cited.

d: Latin version of D (Cod. Claromontanus). 'The genuine Old Latin character of the text is indicated by its frequent agreement with the quotations of Lucifer of Cagliari († 370)' (F. C. Burkitt, *Encyc. Bibl.* col. 4995).

f: Latin version of F (Cod. Augiensis).

g: Latin version of G (Cod. Boernerianus).

m: the so-called *Speculum*, a treatise falsely assigned to St Augustine, which contains extracts from a Spanish text, akin to the Bible used by Priscillian (see Hort as quoted in Gregory, *Textkritik des Neuen Testamentes* (1902), ii. p. 606). Ed. by Weihrich in Vienna *Corpus script. eccles. Lat.* xii. 1887.

r^2: A fragment, belonging to the seventh century, preserved at Munich. Contains 1 Thess. i. 1—10.

(2) Vulgate (Vg). A revision by Jerome of the Old Latin to bring it closer to the Greek text he possessed ('Graecae fidei auctoritati reddidi Novum Testamentum'). The authoritative edition of the Roman Church, issued by Clement VIII. in 1592, has been reprinted by Nestle (Stuttgart, 1906) in a very convenient form with a carefully selected *apparatus*. The great critical edition of the N.T., which is being prepared by Bishop J. Wordsworth and the Rev. H. J. White has not yet advanced beyond the Acts (Oxford, 1889—).

(2) Vulgate.

The readings of the Vulgate MSS. (Vg^{codd}) will be found (partly) in Nestle, and more fully detailed in Tischendorf.

ii. *Syriac.* ii. *Syriac.*

There is naturally no translation of the Bible which has more interest for us than the Syriac, though we must be careful not to identify this dialect of the Euphrates valley with the Aramaic spoken by our Lord: see especially Burkitt, *Evangelion da Mepharreshe*, vol. ii. (Cambridge, 1904). The history of its various versions, and of the vexed questions raised by them, is fully discussed in the same writer's art. 'Text and Versions' in the *Encyc. Bibl.* col. 4998—5006.

We are here concerned only with two of these versions.

(1) Syr (Pesh) = the Syriac Vulgate or *Peshitta*, i.e. 'the simple,' so named apparently to distinguish it from subsequent editions 'which were furnished with marginal variants and other critical apparatus.' Burkitt regards it as the work of Rabbūla bishop of Edessa (or some one deputed by him) between 411 and 435 A.D. Edd. Leusden and Schaaf (1709); S. Lee (1816). The new critical edition of Mr G. H. Gwilliam

(1) The *Peshitta*.

xcviii THE EPISTLES TO THE THESSALONIANS

has not yet advanced beyond the Gospels (Oxford, 1901). For the 'Place of the Peshitto Version in the Apparatus Criticus of the N.T.' see the same writer's art. in *Studia Biblica et Ecclesiastica*, v. iii. Oxford, 1903.

(2) The Harclean.
(2) Syr (Harcl). A recension made by Thomas of Harkel in 616 of the older Philoxenian version of 508. The text is 'remarkable for its excessive literalness,' and follows 'almost invariably that of the later Greek MSS.' (Burkitt). It is cited by Tischendorf as syr$^{p(osterior)}$, and is edited by J. White as *Versio Syriaca Philoxeniana*, Oxford, 1778—1803.

Of great importance are certain readings in the margin of the foregoing version.

(Syr (Harcl mg.)) derived from 'three (v.l. two) approved and accurate Greek copies' in the monastery of the Enatonians near Alexandria (Hort, *Intr.*² § 215).

iii. *Armenian.*
iii. *Armenian.*

The existing Armenian Vulgate (Arm) is a revision about the middle of the fifth century of certain original translations based upon the Old Syriac (Robinson, *Euthaliana*, p. 72 ff.). The Greek text used for this revision was apparently closely akin to ℵB. Ed. Zohrab, Venice, 1805.

iv. *Egyptian.*
(1) Bohairic.
iv. *Egyptian.*
(1) Bohairic (Boh = me (Memphitic) WH., = cop (Coptic) Tisch.). A very early date has sometimes been assigned to this version, but recent research points rather to the sixth or seventh century (Burkitt, *Encyc. Bibl.* col. 5008). The Pauline Epistles have been edited by G. Horner in vol. iii. of his Bohairic N.T., Oxford, 1905.

(2) Sahidic.
(2) Sahidic (Sah = the (Thebaic) WH.). Now believed to be older than the Bohairic version, going back at least to the early part of the fourth century. The N.T. exists only in fragments, which have not yet been collected into a formal edition. [It is understood that G. Horner is preparing one for the Clarendon Press.] Ciasca's collections have been used in the verification of the citations in the present volume.

v. *Aethiopic.*
v. *Aethiopic.*

The date of the Aethiopic version (Aeth) is again uncertain. It may be as early as the fourth century, but is more generally assigned to the end of the fifth (Scrivener, *Introd. to the Crit. of the N.T.*⁴ ii. p. 154). The text from an edition printed at Rome in 1548—9 is to be found in Walton's *Polyglott*, also in an edition prepared by T. Pell Platt (for the Bible Society) in 1830.

AUTHORITIES FOR THE TEXT

vi. *Gothic.*

The Gothic version (Go) was made for the Goths by Ulfilas, who succeeded Theophilus as their Bishop in 348. The translation follows with great fidelity a Greek text, evidently closely akin to the secondary uncials (KLP). It may however have been modified by the influence of the Latin versions, and 'for textual purposes, therefore, its evidence must be used with care' (Kenyon, *Text. Crit.* p. 204). Edd. Gabelentz and Loebe, Leipzig, 1836—43.

III. FATHERS.

The following particulars regarding the patristic authorities cited have been drawn, with additions, from Gregory's *Textkritik*, ii. p. 770 ff.[1] Migne, *P. L.*, has been used to denote Migne, *Patrologiae Cursus Completus*, Latin series, Paris, 1844—64, and Migne, *P.G.*, the corresponding Greek series, Paris, 1857—66.

Amb = Ambrose, Bishop of Milan, 374—397. Ed. Migne, *P. L.* xiv.—xvii. (1845). A considerable portion of what will henceforward be the authoritative edition of his works has already appeared in the Vienna *Corpus*, under the care of K. Schenkl, and latterly of H. Schenkl, Vienna, 1896—.

Ambst (or Ambrstr) = Ambrosiaster (see under List of Commentaries). The text used, pending the issue of the critical edition by H. Brewer S. J. in the Vienna *Corpus*, has been that of Migne, *P.L.* xvii., but the text has been critically revised for this edition with MSS. Bodl. 756 (of the eleventh century) and 689 (of the twelfth century) by A. Souter. The Commentary from which this complete text of St Paul's Epistles is extracted was issued in Rome between 366 and 384 A.D., and contains the (Old-Latin) text commonly used in Rome at that date, and revised by Jerome to make the Vulgate. A study of this text has been published in A. Souter's *Study of Ambrosiaster* (in *Texts and Studies*, vii.), Cambridge, 1905, and the author's conclusions have been accepted by Prof. Kirsopp Lake of Leiden (*Review of Theology and Philosophy* ii. [1906—1907] p. 620 f.).

Ath = Athanasius, Bishop of Alexandria († 373). Ed. Migne, *P. G.* xxv.—xxviii.

---

[1] Reference may also now be made to the same writer's graphic *Canon and Text of the New Testament* (Edinburgh, 1907).

Bas = Basil the Great, Bishop of Caesarea in Cappadocia, †379. The Benedictine edition of his works under the care of J. Garnier appeared at Paris, 1721—30.

Chr = John Chrysostom, Bishop of Constantinople, †407. For the various readings contained in MSS. of Chrysostom (Chr^{codd}) see Tischendorf. Collations of these were published by Matthaei in his critical edition of the N.T. (1803—07). See further under List of Commentaries.

Clem = Homilies of the Pseudo-Clement. Ed. P. de Lagarde, Leipzig, 1865. For the general history of 'The Clementine Literature' see A. C. Headlam in *J.T.S.* iii. p. 41 ff.

Const = Apostolic Constitutions. Edd. P. de Lagarde, Leipzig, 1862; F. X. Funk, *Didascalia et Constitutiones Apostolorum*, Paderborn, 1906.

Cypr = Cyprian, Bishop of Carthage, †258. Ed. W. Hartel in the Vienna *Corpus*, 1868—71.

Cyr-Alex = Cyril, Bishop of Alexandria, 412—444. Ed. Migne, *P.G.* lxviii.—lxxvii.

Cyr-Hier = Cyril, Bishop of Jerusalem, 350—386. Edd. Migne, *P.L.* xxxiii.; W. C. Reischl and J. Rupp, Munich, 1848—60; Photius Alexandrides, Jerusalem, 1867—8.

Did = Didymus of Alexandria, †394 or 399. Ed. Migne, *P.G.* xxxix.

Ephr = Ephraim the Syrian, †373. A Latin translation of the Armenian version of his Commentaries on the Pauline Epistles was edited by the Mechitarist Fathers, Venice, 1893. See also F. H. Woods 'An Examination of the N.T. Quotations of Ephrem Syrus' in *Stud. Bibl. et Eccles.* iii. p. 105 ff.; Oxford, 1891.

Eus = Eusebius of Caesarea, †340. Ed. Migne, *P.G.* xix.—xxiv. A new edition of his works has begun to appear in the Berlin series of Ante-Nicene Greek Fathers.

Hier = Sophronius Eusebius Hieronymus, best known as Jerome, †420. Edd. Migne, *P.L.* xxii.—xxx.; Vallarsi, Verona, 1734—42.

Hipp = Hippolytus of Rome, †235. Edd. Migne, *P.G.* x.; Bonwetsch and Achelis (in the Berlin series), Leipzig, 1897—.

Iren^{lat} = Latin version, not later than the fourth century, of Irenaeus' work *Adversus omnes haereses*, written c. 180. Edd. Stieren, Leipzig, 1853; W. W. Harvey, Cambridge, 1857.

Macar = Macarius, an Egyptian ascetic, †389. His homilies are published in Migne, *P.G.* xxxiv.: cf. *J.T.S.* viii. p. 85 ff. This Macarius must be carefully distinguished from Macarius Magnes, whose date is probably a quarter of a century later: see *J.T.S.* ii. p. 610 f., viii. pp. 401 ff., 546 ff., Schalkhausser, *Makarios von Magnesia* (Leipzig, 1907).

Orig = Origen, head of the catechetical school in Alexandria, †254. Edd. Lommatzsch, Berlin, 1831—48; P. Koetschau, E. Klostermann, and E. Preuschen (in the Berlin series). Leipzig, 1899—. See also von der Goltz, *Eine textkritische Arbeit des 10. bez. 6. Jahrhunderts* (*Texte und Unters.*, N.F. II. 4, 1899), which describes MS. Athos, Laura 184. B. 64 (saec. X), a manuscript of the Acts, Catholic, and Pauline Epistles, which has preserved for us many interesting readings of Origen.

Orig[lat] = The free Latin version of Origen's works by Jerome and others.

Ps-Ath = Writings wrongly ascribed to Athanasius, and contained in the Benedictine edition of Athanasius' works vol. ii.

Tert = Tertullian, †*c*. 240. Edd. Migne, *P.L.* i.—iii.; Oehler, Leipzig, 1853—4; A. Reifferscheid, G. Wissowa and E. Kroymann (in the Vienna *Corpus*), Vienna, 1890—.

Thdt = Theodoret, a Syrian monk, Bishop of Cyrus, †*c*. 457. See List of Commentaries.

Theod-Mops[lat] = Latin version of Theodore, Bishop of Mopsuestia in Cilicia, †*c*. 429. See List of Commentaries.

Vig = Vigilius, an African bishop, flourished *c*. 484. Ed. Migne, *P.L.* lxii. The authorship of works under this name is disputed.

VIII.

SELECTED LIST OF COMMENTARIES.

Literature on the Epistles. The literature relating to our Epistles is dealt with very fully by Bornemann in his *Die Thessalonicherbriefe*, which replaces the work of Lünemann in the new edition of Meyer's *Kritisch-exegetischer Kommentar*: see pp. 1—7 and 538 ff. The following list consists for the most part of those Commentaries which have been used in the preparation of this volume, the editions specified being those to which the present writer has had access, though occasionally for the sake of completeness other works have been included. For fuller information regarding the Greek Patristic Commentaries it is sufficient to refer to Mr C. H. Turner's exhaustive article in the supplementary volume of Hastings' *D.B.* The new and valuable facts regarding the Latin writers have been supplied through the kindness of Prof. A. Souter.

i. *Greek Writers.*

I. GREEK WRITERS.

(1) Earlier Period.

(1) Earlier Period.

ORIGEN († 253). From the list of Origen's works given by Jerome (*Ep.* xxxiii.) it appears that Origen wrote a Commentary on 1 Thess. in 3 books, and on 2 Thess. in 1 book. Of these unfortunately only fragments now survive. Jerome himself (*Ep.* cxix.) has preserved one relating to 1 Thess. iv. 15—17: and from the same source we learn that Theodore of Heraclea, Apollinaris, and Diodore of Tarsus also commented on 1 Thess.

CHRYSOSTOM, JOHN (Chrys.). Chrysostom († 407) is generally ranked as the greatest of the early Pauline interpreters, more particularly on the homiletic side. 'He is at once a true exegete and a true orator, a combination found in such perfection perhaps nowhere else' (Swete, *Patristic Study*, p. 104). His *Homilies* on the Thessalonian Epistles appear to have been preached as episcopal utterances at Constanti-

SELECTED LIST OF COMMENTARIES ciii

nople. They are printed in Migne, *P. G.* lxii., and in a critical edition by F. Field, Oxford, 1855. An English translation under the editorship of C. M. (Charles Marriott) was published at Oxford in 1843 in the *Library of the Fathers*.

THEODORE OF MOPSUESTIA (Th. Mops.). Theodore, Bishop of Mopsuestia (†*c*. 429), was after the death of Chrysostom the most influential teacher in the Eastern Church. By his Nestorian followers he was known as *par excellence* 'the Interpreter,' a title which he deserved from his rigid avoidance of the allegorical method, and constant endeavour to discover the literal and historical meaning of the Sacred Writings. The Greek version of his Commentary on the Pauline Epistles exists only in fragments, preserved in the Catenae, but a Latin version (sixth century?) embracing ten of the Epistles, including 1, 2 Thess., is extant. It has been edited with a valuable Introduction and Notes by Prof. H. B. Swete (Cambridge, 1880—82).

THEODORET OF CYRRHUS (Thdt.), a third great writer of the Antiochene school (†*c*. 457). According to his own statement Theodoret intended his Commentary on the Pauline Epistles to be little more than an abridgement of the works of Chrysostom and Theodore, whom he describes as τοὺς τῆς οἰκουμένης φωστῆρας. But he has done his work with such 'appreciation, terseness of expression, and good sense' that, according to Bishop Lightfoot (*Gal.*¹⁰ p. 230), 'if the absence of faults were a just standard of merit' his Commentaries 'would deserve the first place.' The Commentary on 1, 2 Thess. will be found in vol. v. of the complete edition of Theodoret's works by J. L. Schulze, Halle, 1769—74. It was also edited by C. Marriott, Oxford, 1870.

(2) Later Period.

OECUMENIUS (Oecum.), Bishop of Tricca in Thessaly. His date is uncertain, but Turner (*l.c.* p. 523) places the Catena on St Paul as in all probability within the limits 560—640. The original Catena draws largely from Chrysostom, while later recensions embody copious extracts from Photius, Patriarch of Constantinople (*c*. 820—*c*. 891). Printed in Migne, *P. G.* cxviii.—cxix.

THEOPHYLACT (Thphl.), Archbishop of Achridia (*Ochrida*) in Bulgaria, *c*. 1075. His Commentary on the Pauline Epistles follows Chrysostom in the main, but with 'a certain independence': ed. A. Lindsell, London, 1636.

EUTHYMIUS ZIGABENUS (Euth. Zig.), a younger contemporary of Theophylact, *c*. 1115. Ed. Nicolas Kalogeras, late Archbishop of Patras, Athens, 1887.

ii. Latin Writers.

II. LATIN WRITERS[1].

AMBROSIASTER (Ambrstr. or Ambst.). Regarding the identity of the so-called 'Ambrosiaster' there has been much difference of opinion, but the view most widely held in the present day is one suggested by the French scholar Dom Morin of Maredsous, Belgium, in the *Revue d'Histoire et de Littérature religieuses* for 1899, pp. 97—121, that he was Isaac, a converted Jew, who lived in Rome during the pontificate of Damasus (366—384)[2]. His Commentary on the Pauline Epistles, from which a complete Old Latin text can be derived, has been pronounced by Jülicher (article '*Ambrosiaster*' in Pauly-Wissowa's *Real-Encyclopädie*) to be the best on St Paul's Epistles prior to the Reformation, and Harnack (*Sitzungsberichte der Kgl. Preuss. Akad. der Wissenschaften*, 1903, p. 212) regards it and the *Quaestiones Veteris et Novi Testamenti*, now assigned to 'Ambrosiaster,' though printed amongst the works of St Augustine (*e.g.* Migne, *P.L.* xxxv.), as the greatest literary product of the Latin Church between Cyprian and Jerome. For editions see the note on p. xcix.

PELAGIUS (Pelag.). Amongst the works of Jerome (Migne, *P.L.* xxx. p. 670 ff.) there is a series of commentaries on the Pauline Epistles, which contain some of the quotations which Augustine and Marius Mercator, his contemporaries, make from a commentary of Pelagius (†*c.* 440). The older scholars were divided in opinion on the subject of the Pseudo-Jerome commentary. Some regarded it as the work of Pelagius; others as the commentary of Pelagius after it had been expurgated by Cassiodorus and his pupils[3]. A few years ago Prof. Zimmer of Berlin discovered at St Gall what is a nearer approach to the original commentary than Pseudo-Jerome, but even this form is interpolated. According to Souter (*The Commentary of Pelagius on the Epistles of Paul* [London, 1907] p. 15 ff.) the anonymous MS. cxix. of the Grand Ducal Library at Karlsruhe (saec. ix) is the only pure copy of Pelagius extant, the Pseudo-Jerome commentary being an expansion of the original Pelagius on the longer epistles. Pending the appearance of his edition,

---

[1] The most valuable guide to Latin commentators on the Pauline Epistles down to the time of Luther is Denifle's *Luther und Luthertum*, Erster Band (II Abt.), *Quellenbelege* (Mainz, 1905).

[2] The later view of Morin (*Revue Bénédictine*, 1903, pp. 113—131) that he was Decimius Hilarianus Hilarius, a layman and proconsul, supported, with caution, by Souter, *Study of Ambrosiaster*, p. 183 ff., has been rejected by later critics.

[3] This latter view must be given up, as Pseudo-Jerome contains many Pelagian traces: further, Turner has suggested (*J.H.S.* iv. (1902—3) p. 141), and Souter has proved (*The Commentary of Pelagius* (Proceedings of British Academy, vol. ii. p. 20) that we possess Cassiodorus' revision under the name of Primasius (Migne, *P.L.* lxviii.).

SELECTED LIST OF COMMENTARIES

the student is recommended to correct the corrupt text of Migne by the help of the collation of the St Gall MS. in Zimmer's *Pelagius in Irland* (Berlin, 1901).

III. REFORMATION PERIOD.

(1) Protestant Writers.

ERASMUS, DESIDERIUS († 1536) issued his first edition of the Greek N.T. (*ap. Io. Frobenium*) at Basle in 1516. It was accompanied by a new Latin translation and annotations. The more popular *Paraphrasis in Epp. Pauli omnes* appeared a few years later.

CALVIN, JOHN († 1564), 'the greatest of the commentators of the Reformation' (SH. p. ciii.). His *Commentarii in omnes epistolas Pauli Apostoli* was first published at Strassburg in 1539. The numerous citations in the present work are taken from vol. vi. of Tholuck's complete edition of the N.T. Commentaries (Berlin, no date).

BEZA, THEODORE († 1605). Beza's first edition of the Greek N.T. with translation and annotations was published by H. Stephanus in 1565 (*sine loco*), and in 1642 a new edition 'ad quartam (1598) conformata' was issued from Daniel's Press at Cambridge. The Bible Society's convenient reprint (Berlin, 1905) of this Cambridge edition has been followed here.

(2) Roman Catholic Writers.

ESTIUS, W. (Est.), Provost and Chancellor of Douay († 1613). His *In omnes beati Pauli...Epistolas commentaria* were published after his death (Douay, 1614—16, new ed. Paris, 1672—76). They form 'a valuable exposition of the Epistles in the Augustinian spirit' (Reuss).

CORNELIUS A LAPIDE († 1637). *Commentaria in...omnes d. Pauli epistolas.* Antwerp, 1635.

GROTIUS, H. (De Groot, † 1645), Dutch statesman and theologian. His *Annotationes* on the whole Bible were first published in his *Opp. theol.* (Basle, 1732). The *Ann. in N.T.* appeared separately, Paris, 1641. See also the *Critici Sacri*.

IV. POST-REFORMATION PERIOD.

BENGEL, J. A. (Beng.) † 1752. *Gnomon Novi Testamenti*, Ed. 3 adjuv. J. Steudel, London, 1855.

WETSTEIN, J. J. († 1754). His edition of the *Novum Testamentum Graecum* (Amsterdam, 1751—52) is still invaluable for its large collection of illustrations drawn from Jewish, Greek, and Latin sources. A new and revised edition is among the great *desiderata* for N.T. *apparatus*.

V. MODERN PERIOD.

It will be convenient to classify the writers of this Period as (1) German and (2) English, and to arrange the names in each section in alphabetical, rather than in chronological, order.

(1) German Writers.

BORNEMANN, W.: *Die Thessalonicherbriefe* in the new edition of Meyer's *Kommentar* (Göttingen, 1894)—the fullest modern Commentary on the Epistles, and a great storehouse of materials for all subsequent editors. It has not been translated into English.

DE WETTE, W. M. L.: *Briefe an die Thessalonicher*, 3te Aufl. von W. Moeller in *Exeg. Handb. zum N.T.* II. iii. Leipzig, 1864.

GOEBEL, SIEGFRIED: *Die Briefe P. an d. Thess.* in *Neutest. Schriften*, i. pp. 1—37. 2te Aufl. Gotha, 1897. Brief Notes.

HOFMANN, J. C. K. von: *Thessalonicherbriefe* in *Die heilige Schrift Neuen Testaments*, i. Nördlingen, 1869.

KOCH, A.: *Commentar über d. ersten Brief d. Apostels Paulus an d. Thessalonicher.* Berlin, 1849.

LÜNEMANN, G.: *Die Briefe an d. Thessalonicher* in Meyer's *Kommentar.* Engl. Tr. by Dr P. J. Gloag from the 3rd German edition. Edinburgh, 1880.

PELT, L.: *Epistolae Pauli Apostoli ad Thessalonicenses.* Griefswald, 1830. Rich in patristic references.

SCHMIDT, P.: *Der erste Thessalonicherbrief.* Berlin, 1885. A small book of 128 pages, but containing, in addition to a textual commentary, helpful discussions on the language and historical situation of the Epistle, and an excursus on 2 Thess., intended to show that it had been subject to interpolation.

SCHMIEDEL, P. W.: *Die Briefe an die Thessalonicher* in the *Hand-Commentar zum N.T.* II. i. Freiburg im B., 1891. A marvel of condensation, especially in the very useful Introductions. The authenticity of 2 Thess. is denied.

SCHOTT, H. A.: *Epistolae Pauli ad Thessalonicenses et Galatas.* Leipzig, 1834.

WEISS, BERNARD: *Die Paulinische Briefe*, 2te Aufl. Leipzig, 1902. A revised Text with brief but suggestive Notes.

WOHLENBERG, G.: *Der erste und zweite Thessalonicherbrief* in Zahn's *Kommentar zum N.T.* Leipzig, 1903. The most recent German commentary of importance on the Epistles. The general line of thought is brought out clearly, and there

SELECTED LIST OF COMMENTARIES cvii

is much valuable lexical material contained in the footnotes, but the Introduction is very brief, and the question of authenticity is practically ignored altogether.

The German translations of Luther (from Theile and Stier's *N. T. Tetraglotton*) and Weizsäcker (*Das neue Testament übersetzt*, 9te Aufl. Tübingen, 1900) have also been frequently cited.

It is understood that Prof. von Dobschütz of Strassburg is preparing still another edition of the Epistles for Meyer's *Kommentar*.

(2) English Writers.

ALFORD, H. (Alf.): *The Greek Testament*, iii. 2nd ed. London, 1857.

DRUMMOND, JAMES: *The Epistles of Paul the Apostle to the Thessalonians* in *International Handbooks to the N.T.* ii. New York, 1899.

EADIE, JOHN: *A Commentary on the Greek Text of the Epistles of Paul to the Thessalonians*. London, 1877.

ELLICOTT, C. J.: *St Paul's Epistles to the Thessalonians*, 4th ed. London, 1880. Rich in lexical and grammatical material, with a revised translation and many interesting citations from the old English Versions. There is practically no Introduction.

FINDLAY, G. G.: *The Epistles to the Thessalonians* in the *Cambridge Bible for Schools and Colleges*, 1891, and more recently (1904) in the *Cambridge Greek Testament*. It is only the latter book, which is substantially a new work, that has been cited in the present volume. The Commentary is marked by the writer's well-known qualities as an expositor—careful attention to the text combined with great theological suggestiveness—and, within the limits imposed by the Series to which it belongs, this is probably the most convenient edition of the Epistles for students.

JOWETT, B.: *The Epistles of St Paul to the Thessalonians, Galatians, Romans*. 2nd ed. London, 1859. Contains various striking Essays on such subjects as 'Evils in the Church of the Apostolical Age,' 'On the Belief in the Coming of Christ in the Apostolical Age,' and 'On the Man of Sin.'

LIGHTFOOT, J. B. (Lft.): The Notes on 1, 2 Thess. occupy pp. 1—136 of Bishop Lightfoot's posthumously published *Notes on Epistles of St Paul* (London, 1895), and combined with the same writer's art. 'Thessalonians, Epistles to the' in Smith's *D. B.* and his Essays on 'The Churches of Macedonia' and 'The Church of Thessalonica' in *Biblical Essays* (London, 1893) p. 235 ff. make up a mass of invaluable material relating to the Epistles, to which subsequent workers find it difficult sufficiently to express their indebtedness.

VAUGHAN, C. J.: *The First Epistle to the Thessalonians.* Cambridge, 1865. The first part of an Edition (apparently never carried further) of the Pauline Epistles for English readers, containing a literal new translation and short notes.

WORDSWORTH, C.: *The New Testament in the original Greek,* Part iii. London, 1859.

In addition to the foregoing, Commentaries on the Epistles have been contributed by Archbishop Alexander to *The Speaker's Commentary* (London, 1881), by Canon A. J. Mason to Bishop Ellicott's *New Testament Commentary for English Readers* (London, no date), by Principal Marcus Dods to Schaff's *Popular Commentary on the New Testament* (Edinburgh, 1882), by Dr P. J. Gloag to *The Pulpit Commentary* (London, 1887), and by Dr W. F. Adeney to *The Century Bible* (Edinburgh, no date).

In his *First* and *Second Epistle to the Thessalonians* (London, 1899 and 1900) the Rev. G. W. Garrod has provided careful Analyses of the Epistles with brief Notes for the special use of students in the Church Training Colleges.

Amongst more recent homiletical literature dealing with the Epistles, mention may be made of Dr John Lillie's *Lectures on the Epistles of Paul to the Thessalonians* (Edinburgh, 1863), of Dr John Hutchison's *Lectures on the Epistles to the Thessalonians* (Edinburgh, 1884), an interesting series of discourses founded on a careful exegesis of the text, and of Prof. Denney's volume in *The Expositor's Bible* (London, 1892), where the theological side of the Epistles is brought out with great clearness and suggestiveness.

A volume on the Epistles by Professor Frame, of Union Theological Seminary, New York, is announced by Messrs T. and T. Clark in connexion with the *International Critical Commentary.*

vi. *Special Studies.*

VI. SPECIAL STUDIES.

Studies or Monographs dealing with particular points in the Epistles are referred to under the relative sections, but the titles and aims of a few of the more important may be collected here.

ASKWITH, E. H.: *An Introduction to the Thessalonian Epistles.* London, 1892. A defence of their genuineness with a new view of the eschatology of 2 Thess.

BRÜNIG, W.: *Die Sprachform des zweiten Thessalonicherbriefes.* Naumburg a. S., 1903. Aims at showing its truly Pauline character.

KLÖPPER, A.: *Der zweite Brief an die Thessalonicher* (from *Theol. Studien und Skizzen aus Ostpreussen*). Königsberg, 1889. A somewhat discursive plea for the Pauline authorship.

SELECTED LIST OF COMMENTARIES   cix

SODEN, H. VON : *Der erste Thessalonicherbrief* in *SK.*, 1885, p. 263 ff. Contains a full defence of the authenticity of the Epistle.

SPITTA, F. : *Der zweite Brief an die Thessalonicher* in *Zur Geschichte und Litteratur des Urchristentums,* i. p. 109 ff. (Göttingen, 1893). Suggests that Paul left the actual composition of the Epistle to Timothy, who made use in his work of a Jewish apocalypse of the time of Caligula.

VIES, A. B. VAN DER : *De beiden brieven aan de Thessalonicensen, historisch-kritisch onderzoek naar hunnen oorsprung.* Leiden, 1865.

WESTRIK, T. F. : *De echtheid van den tweeden brief aan de Thessalonicensen.* Utrecht, 1879. 'Especially useful on the question of style' (Moffatt). The present writer has been unable to make any use of either of the foregoing.

WREDE, W.: *Die Echtheit des zweiten Thessalonicherbriefs* (in *Texte und Untersuchungen,* N.F. ix. 2), Leipzig, 1903. A strong attack on the Epistle's authenticity, principally on the ground of its literary dependence on 1 Thess.

ZIMMER, F.: *Der Text der Thessalonicherbriefe.* Quedlinburg, 1893. A revised Text with Critical Apparatus, and discussion of the characteristics of the various authorities.

ZIMMER, F.: 1 *Thess.* ii. 3—8 *erklärt* in *Theologische Studien* B. Weiss *dargebracht,* p. 248 ff. Göttingen, 1897. Designed to show the rich results of a thoroughgoing exegesis applied to the Epistles.

οὕτως ἔςται ἡ παρογςία τοῦ γἱοῦ τοῦ ἀνθρώπογ.

Ἀδιαλείπτως οὖν προσκαρτερῶμεν τῇ ἐλπίδι ἡμῶν καὶ τῷ ἀρραβῶνι τῆς δικαιοσύνης ἡμῶν, ὅς ἐστι Χριστὸς Ἰησοῦς.
POLYCARP.

ὅτι οὐκ ἔθετο ἡμᾶς ὁ θεὸς εἰς ὀργὴν ἀλλὰ εἰς περιποίηςιν ςωτηρίας διὰ τοῦ κγρίογ ἡμῶν Ἰηςοῦ Χριςτοῦ.

ΠΡΟΣ ΘΕΣΣΑΛΟΝΙΚΕΙΣ Α

ANALYSIS.

I. ADDRESS AND GREETING. i. 1.

II. HISTORICAL AND PERSONAL. i. 2—iii. 13.

1. THANKSGIVING FOR THE GOOD ESTATE OF THE THESSALONIAN CHURCH. i. 2—10.
2. GENERAL CHARACTER OF THE APOSTOLIC MINISTRY AT THESSALONICA. ii. 1—12.
3. RENEWED THANKSGIVING FOR THE SUCCESS ATTENDING THE APOSTOLIC MINISTRY AT THESSALONICA. ii. 13—16.
4. SUBSEQUENT RELATION OF THE APOSTLES TO THE THESSALONIAN CHURCH. ii. 17—iii. 10.
    (1) Their Desire to revisit Thessalonica and its Cause. ii. 17—20.
    (2) The Mission and Return of Timothy. iii. 1—10.
5. PRAYER. iii. 11—13.

III. HORTATORY AND DOCTRINAL. iv. 1—v. 24.

1. LESSONS IN CHRISTIAN MORALS. iv. 1—12.
    (1) General Exhortation. iv. 1, 2.
    (2) Warning against Impurity. iv. 3—8.
    (3) Encouragement in Brotherly Love. iv. 9, 10^a.
    (4) Call to Quiet Work. iv. 10^b—12.
2. TEACHING CONCERNING THEM THAT ARE ASLEEP AND THE ADVENT OF CHRIST. iv. 13—18.
3. TEACHING CONCERNING THE SUDDENNESS OF THE ADVENT AND THE NEED OF WATCHFULNESS. v. 1—11.
4. VARIOUS PRECEPTS WITH REGARD TO CHURCH LIFE AND HOLY LIVING. v. 12—22.
5. PRAYER. v. 23, 24.

IV. CONCLUDING INJUNCTIONS AND BENEDICTION. v. 25—28.

ΠΡΟΣ ΘΕΣΣΑΛΟΝΙΚΕΙΣ Α

ΠΑΥΛΟΣ καὶ Cιλουανὸς καὶ Τιμόθεος τῇ ἐκκλησίᾳ Θεσσαλονικέων ἐν θεῷ πατρὶ καὶ κυρίῳ Ἰησοῦ Χριστῷ· χάρις ὑμῖν καὶ εἰρήνη.

TITLE. The heading ΠΡΟΣ ΘΕΣΣΑΛΟΝΙΚΕΙΣ (B* -ΝΕΙΚ-) A′ is found in ℵABK 17 Go Boh. D prefixes ΑΡΧΕΤΑΙ, while in G this is amplified to ΑΡΧΕΤΑΙ ΠΡΟΣ ΘΕΣΣΑΛΟΝΙΚΑΙΟΥΣ Α′ ΠΡΩΤΗ ΕΠΙΣΤΟΛΗ. In the *Can. Murat.* the Epistle is referred to as 'ad tensaolenecinsis.' Beza, to whom, along with the Elzevir editions, the received forms of the titles of the Pauline Epistles are due, has 'Pauli Apostoli Epistola Prima ad THESSALONICENSES.'

I. 1. ADDRESS AND GREETING.

1. 'Paul and Silvanus and Timothy to the assembly of the Thessalonians who acknowledge God as Father and Jesus Christ as Lord, and are gathered together in this twofold Name, we send you the new greeting with the old. Grace, the source of all good, be unto you, and with grace Peace, the crown of all blessings.'

1. Παῦλος κ. Σιλουανὸς κ. Τιμόθεος] For the combination of names see Intr. p. xxxiv f. In neither of the Thessalonian Epp. nor in the Ep. to the Philippians does St Paul add, as elsewhere, his official title ἀπόστολος, doubtless owing to the special footing of friendship on which he stood to the Macedonian Churches, and to the fact that his authority had never been seriously questioned among them.

Σιλουανός (Σιλβανός DG, as regularly in the papyri), the Gentile by-name of the Σιλᾶς (for accent, WSchm. p. 74) of Ac. xv. 22—xviii. 5 (see Deissmann *BS.* p. 315 n.²), and the form always used by St Paul, is here mentioned before Timothy, both because he was already known as 'a chief man among the brethren' (Ac. xv. 22, cf. *v.* 32), and because he had taken a more prominent part in the founding of the Thessalonian Church (Ac. xvii. 4, 10). After St Paul's departure from Corinth (Ac. xviii. 18) Silvanus does not again appear in connexion with him. He is generally identified with the Silvanus of 1 Pet. v. 12. For an attempt to distinguish the Pauline Silvanus from the Jerusalem Silas, see Weizsäcker *Ap. Zeitalter*² p. 256 (Engl. Tr. i. p. 292 f.), and as against this Zahn *Einl. in d. N.T.* i. p. 148 ff. In the traditional lists of the 'Seventy,' compiled by Ps.-Dorotheus, Silas and Silvanus appear as distinct individuals, the former as Bishop of Corinth, the latter as Bishop of Thessalonica (Fabric. *Lux Evang.* p. 117).

Timothy joined St Paul on his second missionary journey at Lystra (Ac. xvi. 1 ff.), and though he is not specially mentioned either at Philippi (Ac. xvi. 19), or at Thessalonica (Ac. xvii. 4, 10), this was probably due to his subordinate position at the time. We read of him as left behind at Beroea (Ac. xvii. 14). Apparently he rejoined St Paul at Athens (1 Thess. iii. 1), and after a special mission to Thessalonica followed him to Corinth (Ac. xviii. 5): see further Intr. p. xxx. With occasional short interruptions he was the Apostle's constant companion to the end of his life, and is associated with him in the opening of six of his Epp. (1, 2 Thess., 2 Cor., Phil., Col., Philemon), and mentioned in the concluding chapters of other two (Rom., 1 Cor.): cf. also Heb. xiii. 23. Two Epp. were addressed specially to him. For the light in which he was regarded by St Paul see the note on iii. 2.

τῇ ἐκκλησίᾳ Θεσσαλονικέων] a form of address peculiar to these Epp. (cf. II. i. 1), and in which the thought of the *local* gathering of believers is still prominent. In the Corinthian Epp. St Paul prefers to connect the Ecclesia with the name of the place where it is situated τ. ἐκκλησίᾳ τ. θεοῦ τ. οὔσῃ ἐν Κορίνθῳ (1 Cor. i. 2, 2 Cor. i. 1, cf. Gal. i. 2 τ. ἐκκλησίαις τ. Γαλατίας), as if he were thinking rather of the one Church of Christ as it was represented there in a particular spot. In the addresses of the Epp. of the Captivity all mention of the Ecclesia is dropped, and some such general designations as πᾶσι τ. ἁγίοις (Phil.) or τ. ἁγίοις κ. πιστοῖς (Eph., Col.) are substituted: cf. however Philem. 2. For the Biblical history of the word ἐκκλησία, which meant originally any public assembly of citizens summoned by a herald, see especially Hort *The Christian Ecclesia* (1898) p. 1 ff.

ἐν θεῷ πατρί κτλ.] a defining clause connected with ἐκκλησίᾳ, the absence of any uniting art. (τῇ) helping to give more unity to the conception (WM. p. 169 f.). In themselves the words bring out the truly *Christian* origin and character of the Ecclesia spoken of as compared with the many ἐκκλησίαι, religious and civil, which existed at the time at Thessalonica. Grot.:

'quae exstitit, id agente Deo Patre et Christo'; Calv.: 'non alibi quaerendam esse Ecclesiam, nisi ubi praeest Deus, ubi Christus regnat.'

On the formula θεὸς πατήρ in the salutations of the N.T. Epp. see Hort's note on 1 Pet. i. 2, and on the union here of θεῷ πατρί and Κυρ. Ἰησ. Χρ. under a common vinculum (ἐν) see Intr. p. lxvi.

The whole phrase is an expanded form of the characteristic Pauline formula ἐν Χριστῷ Ἰησοῦ by which, as Deissmann has shown (*Die neutestamentliche Formel* '*in Christo Jesu*,' Marburg 1892), the Apostle emphasizes that all Christians are locally united 'within the pneumatic body of Christ,' in so far as they together build up His body.

The different titles applied to the Lord throughout the Epp. are discussed in Add. Note D.

χάρις ὑμῖν κ. εἰρήνη] a greeting doubtless suggested by the union of the ordinary Gk. and Heb. forms of salutation (cf. 2 Macc. i. 1), though both are deepened and spiritualized. Thus χαίρειν (cf. Ac. xv. 23, xxiii. 26, Jas. i. 1) now gives place to χάρις, a word which, without losing sight of the Hellenic charm and joy associated with the older formula, is the regular Pauline expression for the Divine favour as shown in all its freeness and universality; while εἰρήνη, so far from being a mere phrase of social intercourse (cf. Judg. xix. 20, 2 Esdr. iv. 17), is not even confined to its general O.T. sense of harmony restored between God and man (e.g. Num. vi. 26), but has definitely in view that harmony as secured through the person and the work of Christ (cf. Jo. xiv. 27). On the varied meanings of χάρις in the Biblical writings see especially Robinson *Eph.* p. 221 ff., and for the corresponding growth in the sense of εἰρήνη see SH. p. 15 f.

This same form of greeting is found in all the Pauline Epp. except 1, 2 Tim. where ἔλεος is added (cf. 2 Jo. 3).

THE FIRST EPISTLE TO THE THESSALONIANS

² Εὐχαριστοῦμεν τῷ θεῷ πάντοτε περὶ πάντων ὑμῶν
μνείαν ποιούμενοι ἐπὶ τῶν προσευχῶν ἡμῶν, ἀδιαλείπτως

It occurs also in 1, 2 Pet. In Jas. we have the simple χαίρειν, and in Jude ἔλεος κ. εἰρήνη κ. ἀγάπη. On St Paul's use of current epistolary phrases see Add. Note A, and for an elaborate discussion on the Apostolic Greeting see F. Zimmer in Luthardt's *Zeitschrift* 1886 p. 443 ff.
It will be noticed that the T.R. clause ἀπὸ θεοῦ πατρός κτλ. is omitted by WH. in accordance with BG 47 73. Its insertion (אAC(?)DKLP) is clearly due to the desire to assimilate the shorter reading to the later Pauline practice: cf. II. i. 2.

I. 2—III. 13. HISTORICAL AND PERSONAL.

I. 2—10. THANKSGIVING FOR THE GOOD ESTATE OF THE THESSALONIAN CHURCH.

The Address is followed by the customary Thanksgiving, which is found in all the Pauline Epp. except Gal. and the Pastorals (cf. however 2 Tim. i. 3). At the same time it is again clear that we have here no mere conventional formula, nor even a *captatio benevolentiae* as in the ancient speeches intended to win over the readers, but rather an earnest effort on the part of the writers to raise the thoughts of their converts to the God on whom they are wholly dependent, and in consequence to rouse them to fresh efforts. The warmth of the thanksgiving on the present occasion, which is most nearly paralleled by Phil. i. 3 ff., is proved by its being a 'constant' attitude (πάντοτε), and by its including 'all,' irrespective of position or spiritual progress (περὶ πάντων ὑμῶν).

2—5. 'We thank the one God at all times for you all, making mention of you unceasingly when we are engaged in prayer. And indeed we have good cause to do so, for the thought of your Christian life is for us a constant fragrant memory as we recall how your faith proves itself in active work, and your love spends itself in toilsome service for others, and your hope is directed in all patience and perseverance to the time when Christ shall be revealed. Nor is this all, but, Brothers beloved by God, who know better than we the true character of your election to Christian privileges? Its reality was proved by the power beyond mere words with which our preaching came home to you—preaching, moreover, which we felt to be inspired by the Divine ardour of the Holy Spirit, and by a perfect conviction on our part of the truth of our message, as indeed you yourselves know from the manner of men we proved ourselves to be for your sakes.'

2. Εὐχαριστοῦμεν κτλ.] Εὐχαριστεῖν, originally 'do a good turn to,' in the sense of expressing gratitude is confined to late writers ('pro *gratias agere* ante Polybium usurpavit nemo' Lob. *Phryn.* p. 18). It is very common in the papyri, e.g. P.Amh. 133, 2 ff. (ii./A.D.) πρὸ τῶν ὅλων ἀσπάζομαί σε καὶ εὐχαριστῶ σοι ὅτι ἐδήλωσάς μοι τὴν ὑγείαν σου. In mod. Gk. it appears in the form ὐκαριστῶ.

For εὐχ. πάντοτε cf. II. i. 3, ii. 13, 1 Cor. i. 4, Eph. v. 20, Phil. i. 3 f., and for the force of the art. before θεῷ see Intr. p. lxiv.

μνείαν ποιούμενοι κτλ.] the first of three conditional or modal clauses describing the nature of the perpetual thanksgiving. For μνείαν ποιεῖσθαι in the sense of 'make mention of' cf. Rom. i. 9, Eph. i. 16, Philem. 4, and for an interesting instance of its use in the papyri in connexion with prayer, see *B.G.U.* 632, 5 ff. (ii./A.D.) μνίαν σου ποιούμενος παρὰ τοῖς [ἐν]θάδε θεοῖς ἐκομισάμην [ἐ]ν ἐπι[σ]τόλιον.... The

³μνημονεύοντες ὑμῶν τοῦ ἔργου τῆς πίστεως καὶ τοῦ κόπου τῆς ἀγάπης καὶ τῆς ὑπομονῆς τῆς ἐλπίδος τοῦ

phrase occurs frequently in the inscriptions, e.g. Magn. 90, 16 f. (ii./B.C.) [ὁ δ]ῆμος φαίνηται μνείαν ποιούμενος τῶν...κρινάντων τὰς κρίσε[ι]ς. In the passage before us the customary gen. (ὑμῶν) is not inserted after μνείαν, probably on account of the immediately preceding περὶ πάντων ὑμῶν: cf. Eph. i. 16.

In the N.T. προσευχή, when referring to the act of prayer, is used only of prayer to God, and is a more general term than δέησις. The prep. ἐπί retains here a slightly local sense 'at,' 'when engaged in,' cf. Rom. i. 10. For a somewhat similar use of εἰς see the ancient Christian letter reprinted in P.Heid. 6, 11 f. (iv./A.D.) ἵνα μνημον[ε]ύης μοι εἰς τὰς ἁγίας σου εὐχάς.

ἀδιαλείπτως] The exact connexion of ἀδιαλείπτως is disputed. WH. and many modern editors (Tisch., Weiss, Nestle) follow Chrys. and the Gk. commentators in referring it to the following μνημονεύοντες, but on the analogy of Rom. i. 9 (cf. 2 Tim. i. 3) it is perhaps better taken as qualifying μν. ποιούμ. (Syr., Vg.), a connexion that is further supported by the position of corresponding phrases in the papyri, e.g. P.Lond. I. 42, 5 f. (ii./B.C.) οἱ ἐν οἴκῳ πάντες σου διαπαντὸς μνείαν ποιούμενοι. The word itself which is confined to late Gk. (e.g. Polyb. ix. 3. 8) is used in the N.T. only by St Paul, and always in connexion with prayer or thanksgiving (ii. 13, v. 17, Rom. i. 9; cf. Ign. *Eph.* x. ὑπὲρ τῶν ἄλλων δὲ ἀνθρώπων ἀδιαλείπτως προσεύχεσθε).

3. μνημονεύοντες] 'remembering' (Vg.*memores*, Est.*memoria recolentes*) in accordance with the general N.T. usage of the verb when construed with the gen., cf. Lk. xvii. 32, Ac. xx. 35, Gal. ii. 10. When construed with the acc. as in ii. 9, Mt. xvi. 9, 2 Tim. ii. 8, Rev. xviii. 5, it is rather 'hold in remembrance.' In Heb. xi. 22 with περί it is = 'make mention of,' perhaps also in the same sense with the simple gen. in v. 15 (see Westcott *ad l.*).

This second participial clause introduces us to the first mention of the famous Pauline triad of graces, viewed however not in themselves but in their results, the gen. in each case being subjective, so that the meaning is practically, 'remembering how your faith works, and your love toils, and your hope endures' (cf. Blass, p. 96). The whole is thus a 'brevis Christianismi veri definitio' (Calv.), while the order in which the graces are here mentioned is not only in itself the natural order (cf. v. 8 and Col. i. 4, 5 with Lft.'s note, 'Faith rests on the past; love works in the present; hope looks to the future'), but assigns to hope the prominence we would expect in an Ep. devoted so largely to eschatological teaching: cf. for the same order of results Rev. ii. 2 οἶδα τὰ ἔργα σου, καὶ τὸν κόπον καὶ τὴν ὑπομονήν σου.

ὑμῶν] placed first for emphasis and to be repeated with each of the three clauses.

τ. ἔργου τ. πίστεως] not to be limited to any particular act of faith, but comprehending the whole Christian lifework, as it is ruled and energized by faith, cf. II. i. 11, Gal. v. 6 (πίστις δι' ἀγάπης ἐνεργουμένη), Jas. ii. 18 ff.

The meaning of πίστις in the N.T. and in some Jewish writings is discussed by SH. p. 31 ff.: see also the careful note in Lietzmann *Römerbrief* p. 24 f. (in *Handbuch zum N.T.* III. 1, 1906).

καὶ τ. κόπου τ. ἀγάπης] As distinguished from ἔργον, κόπος brings out not only the issue of work, but the cost associated with it: cf. its use in the vernacular for πόνος, e.g. B.G.U. 844, 10 f. (i./A.D.) κόπους γάρ μο[ι] παρέχει

κυρίου ἡμῶν Ἰησοῦ Χριστοῦ ἔμπροσθεν τοῦ θεοῦ καὶ
πατρὸς ἡμῶν, ⁴εἰδότες, ἀδελφοὶ ἠγαπημένοι ὑπὸ [τοῦ]

I 4 τοῦ om BDGL al

ἀσθενοῦντες. It is thus here the laborious toil (Grot. *molesti labores*) from which love in its zeal for others does not shrink; cf. Rev. ii. 2 f. For the use made of the word by St Paul to describe the character of his own life cf. ii. 9, iii. 5, II. iii. 8, 2 Cor. vi. 5, xi. 23, 27, and for the corresponding verb κοπιάω see the note on v. 12.

Ἀγάπη, not found in class. writers, is one of the great words of the N.T., where it is taken over from the LXX. to describe the new religious-ethical principle of love that Christianity has created (cf. SH. p. 374 ff.). The contention however, that it is a word actually 'born within the bosom of revealed religion' can no longer be rigidly maintained: cf. Deissmann *BS.* p. 198 ff., and see further Ramsay *Cities and Bishoprics of Phrygia* i. p. 492, also *Exp. T.* ix. p. 567 f.

καὶ τ. ὑπομονῆς τ. ἐλπίδος] Ὑπομονή, though not unknown to profane literature, has also come like ἀγάπη to be closely associated with a distinctively Christian virtue. It is more than passive 'patience' (O.L. *patientia*) under trial, and is rather a 'verbum bellicum' pointing to the heroic 'endurance,' the manly 'constancy' (Vg. *sustinentia*), with which the Christian believer faces the difficulties that beset him in the world: cf. II. i. 4, iii. 5, Rom. v. 3 f., 2 Cor. vi. 4, Heb. xii. 1, Rev. i. 9; and for a full discussion of ὑπομονή and its synonyms see Trench *Syn.* § liii.

τ. κυρίου ἡμῶν κτλ.] The sentence would naturally have finished with ἐλπίδος, but in characteristic fashion St Paul lengthens it out by the addition of two clauses, both of which are best taken as dependent on ἐλπίδος alone, rather than on all three substantives. The first clause sets before us the true object of hope—τ. κυρίου ἡμ. Ἰησ. Χρ. (gen. obj.), in accordance with the teaching of the whole Ep. which centres Christian hope in the thought of the speedy Parousia of Christ: cf. Col. i. 27 Χριστὸς ἐν ὑμῖν, ἡ ἐλπὶς τῆς δόξης, and see Intr. p. lxix f. The second clause emphasizes the Divine presence in which this hope is manifested—ἔμπροσθεν τ. θεοῦ κ. πατρὸς ἡμῶν, words which may be rendered either 'before God and our Father,' or 'before our God and Father.' The latter rendering is preferable, as the art., in itself unnecessary, is apparently introduced to bind the two clauses together, and to connect both with ἡμῶν: cf. Gal. i. 4 (with Lft.'s note), Phil. iv. 20, the only other places where the exact phrase occurs.

The strongly affirmatory ἔμπροσθεν τ. θεοῦ κτλ. is characteristic of this Ep., cf. ii. 19 (τ. κυρίου), iii. 9, 13. For the more usual ἐνώπιον τ. θεοῦ see Rom. xiv. 22, 1 Cor. i. 29 *al*.

4. εἰδότες...] 'having come to know...,' a third participial clause, conveying the writers' *assured* knowledge (contrast γνῶναι, iii. 5) of the Thessalonians' election, and introducing a description of the signs by which that knowledge has been reached, and is still enjoyed.

ἀδελφοὶ ἠγαπημένοι κτλ.] The ordinary address of ἀδελφοί, which is very common in these Epp., and seems always to be used with a certain emphasis attaching to it (Intr. p. xliv), is here enriched by the addition of ἠγαπ. ὑπὸ [τοῦ] θεοῦ (cf. II. ii. 13 ἠγαπ. ὑπὸ Κυρίου), a phrase which in this exact form is not found elsewhere in the N.T. (cf. Jude 1 τοῖς ἐν θεῷ πατρὶ ἠγαπημένοις), but occurs in the LXX. Sir. xlv. 1 ἠγαπημένον ὑπὸ (ἀπὸ ℵ)

θεοῦ, τὴν ἐκλογὴν ὑμῶν, ⁵ὅτι τὸ εὐαγγέλιον ἡμῶν οὐκ
ἐγενήθη εἰς ὑμᾶς ἐν λόγῳ μόνον ἀλλὰ καὶ ἐν δυνάμει καὶ
ἐν πνεύματι ἁγίῳ καὶ πληροφορίᾳ πολλῇ, καθὼς οἴδατε

θεοῦ κ. ἀνθρώπων: cf. also its use of Ptolemy in *O.G.I.S.* 90, 4 al. (ii./B.C. —the Rosetta stone) ἠγαπημένου ὑπὸ τοῦ Φθᾶ. To connect ὑπὸ [τοῦ] θεοῦ with τ. ἐκλογὴν ὑμ. as in the A.V. is inadmissible both on account of the order of the words, and because in St Paul's sense any other ἐκλογή than by God is inconceivable.

The use of ἀδελφοί in the N.T. to denote members of the same religious community, fellow-Christians, was probably taken over from Judaism (Ac. ii. 29, 37, iii. 17 &c.), and from the practice of the Lord Himself (cf. Mt. xii. 48, xxiii. 8); but it can also be illustrated from the ordinary language of the Apostles' time. Thus in P.Tor. I. 1, 20 (ii./B.C.) the members of a society which had to perform a part of the ceremony in embalming bodies are described as ἀδελφοὶ οἱ τὰς λειτουργίας ἐν ταῖς νεκρίαις παρεχόμενοι, and in P.Par. 42, 1 &c. (ii./B.C.) the same designation is applied to the 'fellows' of a religious corporation established in the Serapeum of Memphis. See further Kenyon *British Museum Papyri* I. p. 31, Ramsay *C. and B.* i. pp. 96 ff., 630, and for the evidence of the inscriptions cf. *I.G.S.I.* 956 B.

According to Harnack, the term, as a mutual designation by Christians of one another, fell into general disuse in the course of the 3rd cent., while, as applied by ecclesiastics to the laity, it came to be confined (much as it now is) to sermons (*Mission und Ausbreitung des Christentums* (1902), pp. 291, 303 (Engl. Tr. ii. pp. 9 f., 31 f.)).

τ. ἐκλογὴν ὑμῶν] There is nothing in the passage to enable us to decide whether this ἐκλογή is to be carried back to God's eternal decree (cf. Eph. i. 4), or whether it refers only to the actual admission of the Thessalonians into the Church. As however it is clearly stated to be a matter of the writers' own knowledge (εἰδότες), the thought of the historical call must certainly be included. Th. Mops.: 'electi estis (hoc est, quemadmodum ad fidem accessistis).'

'Εκλογή itself, which is not found in the LXX. (cf. however **Aq.** Isa. xxii. 7; **Sm.**, **Th.** Isa. xxxvii. 24, and for the verb Isa. xlix. 7), occurs elsewhere in the N.T. six times, and always with reference to the Divine choice (Ac. ix. 15, Rom. ix. 11, xi. 5, 7, 28, 2 Pet. i. 10). For an apparent instance of its use with reference to man's choosing see Pss. Sol. ix. 7 τὰ ἔργα ἡμῶν ἐν ἐκλογῇ καὶ ἐξουσίᾳ τῆς ψυχῆς ἡμῶν (with Ryle and James' note). The corresponding verb ἐκλέγεσθαι is found in the Pauline Epp. only 1 Cor. i. 27 f., Eph. i. 4.

5. ὅτι] 'how that,' the demonstrative ὅτι introducing a description not of the ground of the Thessalonians' election, but of the signs by which it was known to the Apostles—these being found (1) in the power and assurance with which they themselves had been enabled to preach at Thessalonica (*v.* 5), and (2) in the eagerness and joyfulness with which the Thessalonians had believed (*v.* 6). For this use of ὅτι with εἰδέναι cf. ii. 1, Rom. xiii. 11, 1 Cor. xvi. 15, 2 Cor. xii. 3 f.

τὸ εὐαγγέλιον ἡμῶν] i.e. 'the gospel which we preach,' with reference to the contents of the Apostles' message rather than to the act of declaring it, for though the Apostles might be the bearers of the message (ii. 4, 9, II. ii. 14), in its origin it was God's (ii. 2, 8, 9), and in its substance Christ's (iii. 2, II. i. 8). In this connexion the use of

I 6] THE FIRST EPISTLE TO THE THESSALONIANS 9

οἶοι ἐγενήθημεν ᵀ ὑμῖν δι' ὑμᾶς· ⁶καὶ ὑμεῖς μιμηταὶ ἡμῶν

5 ὑμῖν ℵACP 17 31 67** al Boh: ἐν ὑμῖν BDGKL al pler d r² g Vg Ephr Chr Thdt Ambst Theod-Mops^lat al

ἐγενήθη (for form, WM. p. 102), one of the characteristic words of the Epp. (8 times against 13 in the remaining Pauline Epp. of which two are quotations from the LXX.), is significant as pointing to a result reached through the working of an outside force, though no stress can be laid in this connexion on the pass. form which in the N.T., as in late Gk. generally, is used interchangeably with the midd.: cf. e.g. Eph. iii. 7 with Col. i. 23, 25, and for the evidence of the inscriptions see Magn. 105 (ii./B.C.) where γενηθῆναι appears seven times for γενέσθαι (Thieme, p. 13). Similarly, in accordance with the tendency in late Gk. to substitute prepositional phrases for the simple cases, εἰς ὑμᾶς can hardly be taken as equivalent to more than ὑμῖν: cf. ii. 9, 1 Pet. i. 25.

For the history of the word εὐαγγέλιον see Add. Note E.

οὐκ...ἐν λόγῳ μόνον κτλ.] The influence in which the Gospel came to the Thessalonians, is now stated first negatively (οὐκ ἐν λόγ. μόν.) and then positively in a series of closely related substantival clauses, the first (ἐν δυνάμει) laying stress on the effective power with which the Gospel was brought home to the Thessalonians, the second and third (ἐν πνεύμ. ἁγ. κ. πληροφ. πολλῇ: note the common preposition) on the Divine fervour which the Spirit had been the means of enkindling (cf. Eph. v. 18), and of which 'much assurance' was the characteristic mark.

For the contrast between λόγος and δύναμις cf. 1 Cor. ii. 4, iv. 20, and for the phrase πνεῦμα ἅγιον where ἅγιον retains its full force as marking the essential characteristic of the Spirit spoken of cf. 2 Cor. vi. 6, 1 Pet.

i. 12 (with Hort's note), and see also Weber *Jüdische Theologie* (1897) p. 190 ff.

πληροφορίᾳ] Πληροφορία (not found in class. writers or LXX.) is here used in its characteristic N.T. sense of 'full assurance' or 'confidence' ('in muche certaintie of persuasion' Genevan N.T. 1557), cf. Col. ii. 2, Heb. vi. 11, x. 22; Clem. R. *Cor.* xlii. 3 μετὰ πληροφορίας πνεύματος ἁγίου ἐξῆλθον, εὐαγγελιζόμενοι.

The corresponding verb is found five times in the Pauline Epp., and elsewhere in the N.T. only in Lk. i. 1. An interesting ex. of its use is afforded by P.Amh. 66, 42 f. (ii./A.D.) in an account of certain judicial proceedings where the complainer, having failed to make good his accusation, is invited by the strategus to bring forward his witnesses to support it—ἵνα δὲ καὶ νῦν πληροφορήσω ἐλθέτωσαν οὓς ἄγεις, 'but now also to give you full satisfaction, let the persons whom you bring come.' In mod. Gk. πληροφορία denotes simply 'information': cf. for an approximating use of the verb in this sense Rom. iv. 21.

καθὼς οἴδατε] καθώς (a late form for Attic καθά, Lob. *Phryn.* p. 426, Rutherford *N. P.* p. 495) introducing an epexegesis of what has preceded, cf. 1 Cor. i. 6. For the appeal to the Thessalonians' own knowledge see Intr. p. xliv.

οἶοι ἐγενήθημεν κτλ.] 'what manner of men we proved ourselves to you for your sakes'—οἶοι pointing to the spiritual power of the preachers, and δι' ὑμᾶς (Vg. *propter vos*, Beza *vestri causâ*) bringing out the interest and advantage of those for whom, according to God's purpose, that power was exercised (cf. P.Grenf. I. 15, 9 f. (ii./B.C.)).

ἐγενήθητε καὶ τοῦ κυρίου, δεξάμενοι τὸν λόγον ἐν θλίψει πολλῇ μετὰ χαρᾶς πνεύματος ἁγίου, ⁷ὥστε γενέσθαι

ἐσόμεθα διὰ σὲ [βεβοηθημέ]ναι). For ἐγενήθημεν see above, and for the general thought cf. 2 Cor. iv. 7—15. The omission of ἐν before ὑμῖν (see crit. note) may have been due to the influence of -θημεν, while its retention (WH. mg.) is further favoured by the antithetical δι' ὑμᾶς: see Findlay's crit. note where iii. 7, iv. 14, 2 Cor. i. 11, 20, iii. 18, Rom. i. 17 are cited for the like Pauline *play* upon prepositions.

6, 7. 'As regards yourselves further, you on your own part also gave proof of your election by showing yourselves imitators of us—yes, and not of us only, but of the Lord. We refer more particularly to your attitude towards the Word, which was marked by a deep inward joy notwithstanding much outward affliction. So unmistakably indeed did you exhibit this spirit that you became an ensample to all Christian believers both in Macedonia and in Achaia.'

6. καὶ ὑμεῖς μιμηταί κτλ.] A second proof of the Thessalonians' ἐκλογή, which, instead of being thrown into a second subordinate clause dependent on εἰδότες, is stated in a separate sentence. Ὑμεῖς is emphatic, 'You on your part,' while the periphrasis with ἐγενήθητε again lays stress on the moral responsibility of those spoken of (cf. Gildersleeve *Syntax* §§ 61, 141). Μιμηταί 'imitators' (R.V.) rather than 'followers' (A.V. and all previous Engl. versions): cf. ii. 14; 1 Cor. iv. 16, xi. 1, Eph. v. 1, Heb. vi. 12, the only other places where the word is found in the N.T., and see also Xen. *Mem.* i. 6. 3 οἱ διδάσκαλοι τοὺς μαθητὰς μιμητὰς ἑαυτῶν ἀποδεικνύουσιν (cited by Koch). For the corresponding verb see II. iii. 7, 9. The compound συνμιμητής is found in Phil. iii. 17.

κ. τοῦ κυρίου] Ambrstr. '*ipsius Domini*,' Beng.: 'Christi, qui Patris apostolum egit, et verbum de coelo attulit, et sub adversis docuit'—a clause added to prevent any possible misunderstanding by showing the real source of what the Thessalonians were called upon to imitate: cf. 1 Cor. xi. 1, Eph. v. 1, and for the title τοῦ κυρίου see Add. Note D.

δεξάμενοι τὸν λόγον] The special ground of imitation is now stated, consisting not only in the 'ready reception' (Vg. *excipientes*, Calv. *amplexi estis*) of 'the word' but in the interwoven affliction and joy with which that reception was accompanied. For δέχομαι see ii. 13 note.

θλίψει] Θλῖψις (or θλῖψις, WSchm. p. 68) like the Lat. *tribulatio*, is a good ex. of a word transformed to meet a special want in the religious vocabulary. Occurring very rarely in profane Gk. writers even of a late period, and then only in the literal sense of 'pressure,' it is found frequently both in the LXX. and N.T. to denote the 'affliction,' 'trial,' which is the true believer's lot in the world; cf. Rom. v. 3, viii. 35, xii. 12, 2 Cor. i. 4. For the existence of these afflictions at Thessalonica cf. iii. 3, 7, II. i. 4 ff.; and see Intr. p. xxxii.

μετὰ χαρᾶς πνεύματος ἁγίου] Πνεύματος gen. of originating cause, 'joy inspired by, proceeding from the Holy Spirit': cf. Rom. xiv. 17 χαρὰ ἐν πνεύματι ἁγίῳ, xv. 13, Gal. v. 22. Thdt.: πάντων μέγιστον τὸ...πνευματικῆς ἡδονῆς ἐμφορεῖσθαι.

For this union of suffering and joy as marking 'a new aeon' in the world's history, see for St Paul's own case 2 Cor. vi. 10, Col. i. 24, and for the Macedonian Churches generally 2 Cor. viii. 1, 2; cf. also 1 Pet. iv. 13.

Μετά with gen. to denote *manner* is very frequent in the Κοινή, e.g. P. Oxy. 292, 5f. (i./A.D.) δι' παρακαλῶ σε μετὰ πάσης δυνάμεως (other exx. in Kuhring, p. 34).

ὑμᾶς ⌜τύπον⌝ πᾶσιν τοῖς πιστεύουσιν ἐν τῇ Μακεδονίᾳ

7 τύπον BD* 6 17 67** al d r² g Vg Syr (Pesh) Sah (?) Boh (?) Arm Aeth Ephr Ambst Theod-Mops^lat al: τύπους ℵACGKLP 37 al pler g Syr (Harcl) Chr Thdt al

7. ὥστε γενέσθαι] The inf. introduced by ὥστε is here consecutive, and points to a result actually reached and not merely contemplated (Votaw, p. 13)—this result being further viewed in its direct dependence upon the previously-mentioned cause. Ὥστε is found with the ind. with a somewhat similar force in Jo. iii. 16, Gal. ii. 13, but as a rule when so construed the conjunction (as in class. Gk., Jelf § 863) does little more than draw attention to the result as a new *fact* without emphasizing its *connexion* with what went before: see Moulton *Prolegg.* p. 209 f.

. ύπον] 'an ensample,' the use of the sing. showing that it is the community as a whole that is thought of: cf. II. iii. 9, Didache iv. 11 ὑμεῖς δὲ [οἱ] δοῦλοι ὑποταγήσεσθε τοῖς κυρίοις ὑμῶν ὡς τύπῳ θεοῦ.... The v.l. τύπους (WH. mg.) probably arose from assimilation to ὑμᾶς.

In itself τύπος (τύπτω) meant originally the 'mark' of a blow (cf. Jo. xx. 25 τ. τύπον τ. ἥλων), and from being frequently used to denote the 'stamp' struck by a die came to be applied to the 'figure' which a stamp bears, or more generally to any 'copy' or 'image.' Hence by a natural transition from effect to cause, it got the meaning of 'pattern,' 'model,' and finally of 'type' in the more special Bibl. sense of a person or event prefiguring someone or something in the future. For the history of the word and its synonyms see Radford *Exp.* v. vi. p. 377 ff., and add the interesting use of the word in the inscriptions to denote the 'models' in silver of different parts of the body, presented as votive offerings to the god through whose agency those parts had been healed; see Roberts-Gardner p. 161 with reference to *C.I.A.* II. 403 (iii./B.C.).

πᾶσιν τ. πιστεύουσιν] 'to all believers,' the part. with the art. being practically equivalent to a substantive; cf. ii. 10, II. i. 10 (τ. πιστεύσασι), and for the similar technical use of οἱ πιστοί (1 Tim. iv. 12) see Harnack *Miss. u. Ausbr.* p. 289 (Engl. Tr. ii. p. 6 f.).

ἐν τῇ Μακεδονίᾳ κτλ.] The repetition of the art. shows that the writers are here thinking of Macedonia and Achaia as the two distinct though neighbouring provinces into which after 142 B.C. Greece was divided, whereas in the next verse they are classed together as embracing European Greece as a whole (cf. Ac. xix. 21, Rom. xv. 26).

For the extension of the Gospel throughout Macedonia cf. iv. 10, and for the existence of believers in Achaia see such passages as Ac. xvii. 34, xviii. 8, 2 Cor. i. 1. It heightened the praise of the Thessalonians that it was to 'nations so great and so famed for wisdom' (Thdt.) that they served as an ensample.

8—10. Further confirmation of what has just been stated in *v.* 7.

'We say this of your ensample, for indeed our experience has been that from you as a centre the word of the Lord has sounded out like a clear and ringing trumpet-blast in the districts just mentioned, and not only so, but your faith in the one true God has gone forth everywhere. Common report indeed speaks so fully of this that it is unnecessary that we ourselves should add anything. All are prepared to testify that as the result of our mission amongst you, you have turned from many false idols to the service of one God who is both living and true, and are confidently waiting for the return of His Son out of the heavens. We mean of course Jesus, whom God raised from the dead, and

καὶ ἐν τῇ Ἀχαΐᾳ. ⁸ἀφ' ὑμῶν γὰρ ἐξήχηται ὁ λόγος τοῦ κυρίου οὐ μόνον ἐν τῇ Μακεδονίᾳ καὶ Ἀχαΐᾳ, ἀλλ'

to whom we all have learned to look as our Rescuer from the Wrath that is even now coming.'

8. ἀφ' ὑμῶν] 'from you as a centre' (cf. 1 Cor. xiv. 36), rather than 'by your instrumentality' as missionaries, which would naturally, though not necessarily (Blass p. 125), have been ὑφ' ὑμῶν.

ἐξήχηται] Ἐξηχέω. ἅπ. λεγ. N.T., is found in the LXX. Joel iii. (iv.) 14, 3 Macc. iii. 2 V, Sir. xl. 13 ὡς βροντὴ μεγάλη ἐν ὑετῷ ἐξηχήσει, cf. Philo *in Flacc.* § 6 (ii. p. 522 M.) ἐκ περιεστῶτος ἐν κύκλῳ πλήθους ἐξήχει βοή τις ἄτοπος. The Engl. verss. from Tindale (with the exception of Rheims 'was bruited') agree in the rendering 'sounded out' (Beza *personuit*, Erasm. *exsonuit*, sive *eburcinatus est*), pointing to the clear, ringing nature of the report as of a trumpet (Chrys. ὥσπερ σάλπιγγος λαμπρὸν ἠχούσης). Lft. finds the underlying metaphor rather in the sound of thunder (cf. Sir. xl. 13 quoted above and Pollux i. 118 ἐξήχησεν βροντή), and recalls Jerome's description of St Paul's own words, 'non verba sed tonitrua' (*Ep.* 48).

ὁ λόγος τοῦ κυρίου] a familiar O.T. phrase for a prophetic utterance, used here with direct reference to the Gospel-message ('a word having the Lord for its origin, its centre, and its end' Eadie) which had been received by the Thessalonians, and which they had been the means of diffusing to others. The exact phrase, though frequent in Ac., is used elsewhere by St Paul only II. iii. 1. Afterwards he prefers ὁ λόγος τ. θεοῦ, and once, in Col. iii. 16, ὁ. λόγος τ. χριστοῦ (mg. κυρίου).

οὐ μόνον ἐν τῇ Μακεδονίᾳ κτλ.] If we follow the usual punctuation, the construction of the rest of the sentence is irregular, as instead of ἐν π. τόπῳ standing in opposition to ἐν τ. Μακ. κ.

Ἀχ. we find a new subject introduced. It has accordingly been proposed to place a colon after τ. κυρίου, dividing v. 8 into two parts. The first part ἀφ' ὑμῶν...κυρίου then gives the reason of v. 7, and the second part takes up the preceding ἐξήχηται, and works it out according to locality. This yields good sense, but it is simpler to find here another ex. of St Paul's impetuous style. He had meant to stop at τόπῳ, but in his desire to make a forcible climax he lengthens out the sentence.

As regards the fact, the situation of Thessalonica made it an excellent centre for missionary enterprise (Intr. p. xxii), while it is possible as further explaining the hyperbole ἐν παντὶ τόπῳ (cf. Rom. i. 8, xvi. 19, 2 Cor. ii. 14, Col. i. 6, 23) that St Paul had just heard from Aquila and Priscilla, who had recently arrived in Corinth from Rome, that the faith of the Thessalonians was already known there (so Wieseler *Chronol.* p. 42).

The preposition ἐν following a verb of motion may have a certain significance as indicating the *permanence* of the report in the regions indicated (WM. p. 514), a fact that is also implied in the use of the perf. ἐξελήλυθεν, but the point cannot be pressed in view of the frequent occurrence of ἐν for εἰς in late Gk.: see the exx. in Hatzidakis p. 210, e.g. Acta Joh. (Zahn) 36 ἤλθομεν ἐν τῷ τόπῳ, to which Moulton (*Prolegg.* p. 234) adds the early P.Par. 10, 2 f. (ii./B.C.) παῖς ἀνακεχώρηκεν ἐν Ἀλεξανδρείᾳ. For the corresponding εἰς for ἐν cf. *B.G.U.* 385, 5 f. (ii.—iii./A.D.) ἡ θυγά[τ]ηρ μου ἰς Ἀλεξανδρείαν ἔσσι.

Ἐξέρχομαι is used in a similar connexion in Rom. x. 18 (LXX.), 1 Cor. xiv. 36, and, like the preceding ἐξηχέω, conveys the idea of rapid, striking progress. Chrys.: ὥσπερ γὰρ περὶ

19] THE FIRST EPISTLE TO THE THESSALONIANS 13

ἐν παντὶ τόπῳ ἡ πίστις ὑμῶν ἡ πρὸς τὸν θεὸν ἐξελήλυθεν, ὥστε μὴ χρείαν ἔχειν ἡμᾶς λαλεῖν τι· ⁹αὐτοὶ γὰρ
περὶ ⌐ἡμῶν¬ ἀπαγγέλλουσιν ὁποίαν εἴσοδον ἔσχομεν πρὸς
ὑμᾶς, καὶ πῶς ἐπεστρέψατε πρὸς τὸν θεὸν ἀπὸ τῶν

9 ἡμῶν] ὑμῶν B al d Sah Thdt al

ἐμψύχου τινὸς διαλεγόμενος, οὕτως εἶπεν, 'ἐξελήλυθεν'· οὕτως ἦν σφοδρὰ καὶ ἐνεργής.

ἡ πίστις ὑμ. ἡ πρὸς τ. θεόν] The connecting art. ἡ is here inserted before the defining clause to prevent ambiguity (Blass p. 160), while the definite τὸν θεόν emphasizes 'the God' towards whom the Thessalonians' faith is directed in contrast with their previous attitude towards τὰ εἴδωλα (v. 9).

ὥστε μὴ χρείαν κτλ.] On ὥστε with inf. see v. 7 note, and for χρείαν ἔχειν followed by the simple inf. cf. iv. 9, v. 1, Mt. iii. 14, xiv. 16, also Heb. v. 12. λαλεῖν can hardly be distinguished here from λέγειν, but in accordance with its original reference to personal, friendly intercourse, it perhaps draws attention to the free and open nature of the communication thought of. The verb is especially characteristic of the Fourth Gospel, where it is assigned to Christ thirty-three times in the sense of Jo. xviii. 20 ἐγὼ παρρησίᾳ λελάληκα τῷ κόσμῳ...καὶ ἐν κρυπτῷ ἐλάλησα οὐδέν, and see Abbott *Joh. Grammar* p. 203.

9. αὐτοὶ γάρ] i.e. the men of Macedonia and elsewhere. For an ingenious conjecture that the reading of the verse ought to be αὐτοὶ γὰρ ἀπαγγέλλετε... with reference to a letter sent by the Thessalonians to St Paul see Rendel Harris, *Exp.* v. viii. p. 170 f., and cf. Intr. p. xxx.

ὁποίαν εἴσοδον] 'what sort of entrance'—εἴσοδον being used of the 'act of entering' (ii. 1, Ac. xiii. 24) rather than of the 'means of entering' (Heb. x. 19, 2 Pet. i. 11), while the indirect interrogative ὁποίαν (WM. p. 209 n.³) points to the nature of that entrance, how happy and successful it was (*v.* 5).

For the disappearance of ὁποῖος from common Gk. (elsewhere in N.T. only Ac. xxvi. 29, Gal. ii. 6, 1 Cor. iii. 13, Jas. i. 24) see WSchm. p. 191, Meisterhans p. 237. It is found in the curious combination ὅτι ὁποίαν in P.Gen. 54, 1 ff. (iii./A.D.) οἶδας...ὅτι ὁποίαν προέρεσιν ἔχω καὶ οἶδας...ὅτι γν[ώ]μη ὁποία ἐστίν.

καὶ πῶς ἐπεστρέψατε κτλ.] 'and how you turned...' not 'returned' (as in A.V. 1611), ἐπι- having here apparently simply a *directive* force, cf. Rev. i. 12. For the bearing of the whole clause on the generally *Gentile* character of the Thessalonian Church see Intr. p. xlii f. The thought of *manner* (Chrys.: εὐκόλως, μετὰ πολλῆς τῆς σφοδρότητος) if not wholly wanting in πῶς is certainly not prominent, as in late Gk. the word is practically = ὅτι (Blass p. 230, Hatzidakis p. 19).

Ἐπιστρέφειν, while frequent in Acts of Gentiles turning to God, is not again used by St Paul in this sense; contrast Gal. iv. 9, 2 Cor. iii. 16, the only other places in his Epp. where it occurs. To indicate the fact of conversion the Apostle preferred as a rule such general terms as πιστεύειν, ὑπακούειν, perhaps as emphasizing not the mere turning away from error, but the positive laying hold of truth. That however this latter condition was fulfilled in the Thessalonians' case is proved by the description that follows of their Christian life under the twofold aspect of doing and of waiting, of active service and of confident hope.

εἰδώλων δουλεύειν θεῷ ζῶντι καὶ ἀληθινῷ, ¹⁰καὶ ἀναμένειν
τὸν υἱὸν αὐτοῦ ἐκ τῶν οὐρανῶν, ὃν ἤγειρεν ἐκ [τῶν]

10 τῶν om AC al Eus

δουλεύειν θεῷ ζῶντι κτλ.] 'to serve God living and true,' the absence of the art. drawing attention to God in His character rather than in His person, and δουλεύειν (inf. of purpose) pointing to complete, whole-hearted service: cf. Rom. xii. 11, xiv. 18, xvi. 18, Eph. vi. 7, Col. iii. 24, and for the thought Jer. iii. 22 ἐπιστράφητε...ἰδοὺ δοῦλοι ἡμεῖς ἐσόμεθά σοι, ὅτι σὺ Κύριος ὁ θεὸς ἡμῶν εἶ. [Eng. Ch. Cat.: 'My duty towards God is... to serve Him truly all the days of my life.']

Δουλεύειν is apparently never used in a religious sense in pagan literature: cf. however ἱερόδουλοι as a designation of the votaries of Aphrodite at Corinth.

Under ζῶντι in accordance with the regular O.T. conception (Deut. v. 26, Jos. iii. 10, Dan. vi. 20, 26; cf. Sanday *Exp. T.* xvi. p. 153 ff.) must be included not merely the being, but the activity or power of God (Ac. xiv. 15, 2 Cor. iii. 3, Heb. ix. 14; cf. Grill *Untersuchungen über die Entstehung des vierten Evangeliums* (1902) i. p. 237); while ἀληθινῷ (here only in St Paul) is 'true' in the sense of 'real' (Jo. xvii. 3, 1 Jo. v. 20; cf. Trench *Syn.* § viii.), the 'very' God of the creeds as distinguished from false gods who are mere empty shams and shows (εἴδωλα, in LXX. for אֱלִילִים *nothings* Lev. xix. 4 &c., and הֲבָלִים *breaths* Deut. xxxii. 21, Jer. xvi. 19 &c.). Thdt.: ζῶντα μὲν αὐτὸν ὠνόμασεν, ὡς ἐκείνων [τῶν εἰδώλων] οὐ ζώντων· ἀληθινὸν δέ, ὡς ἐκείνων ψευδῶς θεῶν καλουμένων.

10. καὶ ἀναμένειν τὸν υἱὸν αὐτοῦ] 'Ἀναμένειν, ἅπ. λεγ. N.T., but fairly frequent in the LXX., e.g. Job vii. 2, Isa. lix. 11 ἀνεμείναμεν κρίσιν, and see also the instructive parallel from Aesch. *Eum.* 243 ἀναμένω τέλος δίκης (cited by Chase *The Lord's Prayer* p. 72 n.²). The leading thought here seems to be to wait for one whose coming is expected (Beng.: 'de eo dicitur, qui abiit ita, ut venturus sit'), perhaps with the added idea of patience and confidence (ἀνα-, Winer *de verb. comp.* pt. iii. p. 15). In Ac. i. 4 περιμένειν is found in the same sense. The more general word is ἀπεκδέχεσθαι, 1 Cor. i. 7, Phil. iii. 20. Calv.: 'Ergo quisque in vitae sanctae cursu perseverare volet, totam mentem applicet ad spem adventus Christi.'

For τὸν υἱὸν αὐτοῦ—the only place in these Epp. where Christ is so described—see Intr. p. lxvi.

ἐκ τῶν οὐρανῶν] 'out of the heavens' (Wycl. *fro heuenes*: Tind. and the other Engl. verss. preserve the sing.). The plur. may be a mere Hebraism, the corresponding Heb. word שָׁמַיִם being plur. in form, but it is possible that St Paul's language here, as elsewhere, is influenced by the Rabbinic theory of a plurality of heavens, generally regarded as seven in number, through which 'the Beloved' ascends and descends: cf. especially *The Ascension of Isaiah* vi.—xi., and on the whole subject see Morfill and Charles *Book of the Secrets of Enoch* p. xxxff., Cumont *Religions orient.* (1907) p. 152. This reference must not however be pressed in view of the fact that the sing. actually occurs oftener than the plur. (11: 10) in the Pauline writings: note particularly the use of the sing. in practically the same context as here in iv. 16, II. i. 7.

It may be added as showing the difference in usage among the N.T. writers that in St Matthew's Gospel the plur. is used more than twice as

νεκρῶν, Ἰησοῦν τὸν ῥυόμενον ἡμᾶς ἐκ τῆς ὀργῆς τῆς ἐρχομένης.

often as the sing. (55:27), while in the Apocalypse out of 52 occurrences of the word only one is in the plur. (xii. 12), and that in a passage under the direct influence of the LXX. (Isa. xliv. 23, xlix. 13, cf. also Dan. iii. 59), where the plur. οὐρανοί (like our colloquial *heavens*) is frequently used of the visible sky, especially in the Pss. (e.g. viii. 4, xviii. (xix.) 2; cf. F. W. Mozley *The Psalter of the Church* (1905) p. 4).

For the use of the art. before οὐρανῶν in the present passage cf. Mt. iii. 17, Mk. i. 11 (WSchm. p. 162).

ὃν ἤγειρεν ἐκ [τῶν] νεκρῶν] 'whom He (sc. God) raised out of the dead'—the resurrection of Jesus being traced as always in the Pauline teaching to the direct act of God, cf. 1 Cor. vi. 14, xv. 15, Gal. i. 1 &c. It is to be noted that in the present passage the thought of the resurrection is introduced not as the *argumentum palmarium* for the Divine Sonship (as in Rom. i. 4), but, in accordance with the context, as the necessary prelude to Christ's Return, and the general resurrection by which it will be accompanied: cf. Rom. viii. 11, 1 Cor. xv. 20 ff., 2 Cor. iv. 14, Col. i. 18, and especially the words spoken at Athens so shortly before Ac. xvii. 31. Calv.: 'in hunc finem resurrexit Christus, ut eiusdem gloriae nos omnes tandem consortes faciat, qui sumus eius membra.'

For ἐγείρειν cf. iv. 14 note, and for the phrase ἐκ [τῶν] νεκρῶν (elsewhere with art. only Eph. v. 14, Col. i. 18) see WSchm. p. 163.

Ἰησοῦν τὸν ῥυόμενον ἡμᾶς] It is the historical Jesus (Add. Note D) Who acts as 'our Rescuer' (cf. Rom. xi. 26 from LXX. Isa. lix. 20), the thought of deliverance by *power* being apparently always associated with ῥύεσθαι in the Bibl. writings (cf. Gen. xlviii. 16, Rom. vii. 24, xv. 31, 2 Cor. i. 10,

2 Tim. iv. 17 f.), while the following ἐκ (contrast ἀπό II. iii. 2) emphasizes its *completeness* in the present instance—'He brings us altogether out of the reach of future judgment'; cf. Sap. xvi. 8 and see Ps.-Clem. vi. 7 ποιοῦντες γὰρ τὸ θέλημα τοῦ Χριστοῦ εὑρήσομεν ἀνάπαυσιν· εἰ δὲ μήγε οὐδὲν ἡμᾶς ῥύσεται ἐκ τῆς αἰωνίου κολάσεως (cited by Chase *The Lord's Prayer* p. 79, where the constructions of ῥύεσθαι are fully discussed).

ἐκ τ. ὀργῆς τ. ἐρχομένης] 'out of the wrath that is coming'—τῆς ὀργῆς, as in ii. 16, Rom. iii. 5, v. 9, ix. 22, xiii. 5, being used absolutely of the Divine wrath, and in accordance with the context (ἀναμέν. τ. υἱόν κτλ.) and the general N.T. usage, having here the definite eschatological reference for which the language of the prophetic writings has prepared us, cf. e.g. Isa. ii. 10—22, Zeph. iii. 8 ff., and see further Ritschl *Rechtfertigung u. Versöhnung*[3] ii. p. 142 ff. A similar application of the term is found in Judaistic literature, e.g. *Book of Jubilees* xxiv. 30 ('nor one that will be saved on the day of the wrath of judgment'), *Secrets of Enoch* xliv. 2 ('the great wrath of the Lord shall consume him'), and for classical usage cf. Eur. *Hipp.* 438 ὀργαὶ δ' εἰς σ' ἐπέσκηψαν θεᾶς.

This wrath is further described as τῆς ἐρχομένης (cf. Eph. v. 6, Col. iii. 6), the repeated art. drawing attention to 'coming' as its essential feature, while both verb and tense bring out the certainty and perhaps the nearness of its approach (cf. v. 2 note).

Needless to say it is no angry resentment that is thought of, but the hostility to sin which is as necessary a part of God's nature as His love; cf. Isa. lxi. 8, Zech. viii. 17, and see Lact. *de irâ Dei* 5: 'nam si deus non irascitur impiis et iniustis, nec pios

II. ¹Αὐτοὶ γὰρ οἴδατε, ἀδελφοί, τὴν εἴσοδον ἡμῶν τὴν πρὸς ὑμᾶς ὅτι οὐ κενὴ γέγονεν, ²ἀλλὰ προπαθόντες καὶ ὑβρισθέντες καθὼς οἴδατε ἐν Φιλίπποις ἐπαρρησιασάμεθα ἐν τῷ θεῷ ἡμῶν λαλῆσαι πρὸς ὑμᾶς τὸ εὐαγγέ-

utique iustosque diligit.... In rebus enim diversis, aut in utramque partem moveri necesse est, aut in neutram.'

On the bearing of *vv.* 9, 10 on the missionary teaching of St Paul see Intr. p. xlii f.

II. 1—12. GENERAL CHARACTER OF THE APOSTOLIC MINISTRY AT THESSALONICA.

Having borne witness to the reality of the 'election' of their Thessalonian converts, the Apostles now turn to deal more particularly with certain charges that had been brought against themselves after their departure from Thessalonica, and of which they had heard probably through Timothy (Intr. p. xxx). This section of the Epistle accordingly takes the form of an 'apologia,' or a vindication on the part of St Paul and his companions of their Apostolic claims, in so far as these were evidenced by their entrance into Thessalonica (*vv.* 1, 2), the general character of their preaching (*vv.* 3, 4), and its particular methods (*vv.* 5—12). Compare with the whole section, both for language and tone, 2 Cor. iv. 1—6.

1, 2. 'Why speak however of the report of others, seeing that we can confidently appeal to your own experience as to the effective character of our ministry. For even though we were subjected to shameful contumely, as you well know, at Philippi, nevertheless we boldly declared to you the Gospel of God. Not that this boldness was our own. It came to us from God, and so upheld us in the midst of the opposition we encountered.'

1. Αὐτοὶ γὰρ οἴδατε κτλ.] An appeal again to the Thessalonians' own ex-perience (cf. i. 5), as distinguished from the report of others (αὐτοί emph.), and strengthened in the present instance by the repetition of the significant ἀδελφοί (cf. i. 4); while the resumptive γάρ refers back to i. 9ª, and in meaning is almost = 'however.'

οὐ κενὴ γέγονεν] 'hath not been found vain'—the reference being to the essential content of the Apostles' preaching rather than to its results. (Chrys.: οὐκ ἀνθρωπίνη, οὐδὲ ἡ τυχοῦσα; Beng.: '*non inanis*, sed plena virtutis.') That however an enduring result was secured is proved by the perf. γέγονεν. For κενός in this sense cf. 1 Cor. xv. 10 and see Trench *Syn.* § xlix., and for the form of the sentence by which οἴδατε claims in anticipation the subj. of γέγονεν for its object see WM. p. 781.

2. ἀλλὰ προπαθόντες κτλ.] See Ac. xvi. 19 ff., Phil. i. 30. Προπαθόντες (class., ἅπ. λεγ. N.T.) finds its full explanation in the second participle which is almost = ὥστε καὶ ὑβρισθῆναι: cf. Dem. *c. Conon. ad init.* ὑβρισθείς, ὦ ἄνδρες δικασταί, καὶ παθὼν ὑπὸ Κόνωνος (cited by Wetstein). More than the bodily suffering it was the personal indignity that had been offered to him as a Roman citizen (cf. Cic. *in Verr.* v. 66 'scelus verberare [civem Romanum]') that had awakened a sense of *contumely* in St Paul's mind. For a similar use of ὑβρίζειν cf. Mt. xxii. 6, Lk. xviii. 32, Ac. xiv. 5, 2 Macc. xiv. 42, 3 Macc. vi. 9. The somewhat awkward repetition of καθὼς οἴδατε after οἴδατε (*v.* 1) brings out strongly the writers' desire to carry their readers along with them (Intr. p. xliv).

ἐπαρρησιασάμεθα ἐν τῷ θεῷ κτλ.] In itself ἐπαρρησιασάμεθα may refer gene-

λιον τοῦ θεοῦ ἐν πολλῷ ἀγῶνι. ³ἡ γὰρ παράκλησις ἡμῶν οὐκ ἐκ πλάνης οὐδὲ ἐξ ἀκαθαρσίας οὐδὲ ἐν δόλῳ, ⁴ἀλλὰ

rally to the Apostles' whole attitude, but as the verb is always used elsewhere in the N.T. (Ac.⁷, Eph.¹) of the bold proclamation of the Gospel it is better to give it the full meaning 'became bold of speech' (aor. of inception, Kühner³ § 386. 5), the nature of this boldness being further brought out by the explanatory inf. λαλῆσαι (i. 8 note), while the added clause ἐν τ. θεῷ ἡμ. points to its true source. Oecum.: διὰ τὸν ἐνδυναμοῦντα θεὸν τοῦτο ποιῆσαι τεθαρρήκαμεν.

The expression 'our God' is rare in the Pauline Epp., occurring elsewhere only in iii. 9, II. i. 11, 12, 1 Cor. vi. 11: it is common in the Apocalypse.

ἐν πολλῷ ἀγῶνι] 'in much conflict'—the reference, as the context shows, being to the *external* dangers to which the Apostles had been subjected (O.L. *in multo certamine*) rather than to any *internal* fears on their part (Vg. *in multa sollicitudine*, cf. Col. ii. 1): cf. Phil. i. 30 τὸν αὐτὸν ἀγῶνα ἔχοντες οἷον εἴδετε ἐν ἐμοί, 1 Tim. vi. 12 ἀγωνίζου τὸν καλὸν ἀγῶνα τῆς πίστεως. The metaphor, as in the case of the allied ἀθλεῖν, ἄθλησις (2 Tim. ii. 5, Heb. x. 32), is derived from the athletic ground: cf. Epict. *Diss.* iv. 4. 30 where life is compared to an Olympic festival in which God has given us the opportunity of showing of what stuff we are made—ἐλθὲ ἤδη ἐπὶ τὸν ἀγῶνα, δεῖξον ἡμῖν τί ἔμαθες, πῶς ἤθλησας.

3—7ᵃ. 'We said that we were bold in God, and that it was the Gospel of God we preached, and we said rightly, for our whole appeal to you is not rooted in error, neither has it any connexion with licentious and delusive practices (as was the case with some of your old religious teachers). On the contrary, as those who have been approved by the all-seeing God Himself we were entrusted with His Gospel. It is this indeed which makes us independent of all merely human considerations. And consequently we did not at any time play the part of flatterers, as you well know, nor, and here we call God Himself to witness, did we under any fair outward pretext conceal an inward spirit of covetousness. On the contrary worldly glory either at your hands or at the hands of others was so little in our thoughts, that we did not even demand the support and honour to which as Apostles of Christ we were entitled.'

3. παράκλησις] Vg. Ambrstr. *exhortatio*, Tert. *aduocatio*. Though closely allied with διδαχή (Chrys.) or διδασκαλία (Thdt.), παράκλησις is not to be identified with either, but implies something more in the nature of an appeal (Euth. Zig.: ἡ διδασκαλία, ἡ πρὸς τὸ πιστεῦσαι προτροπή), having for its object the direct benefit of those addressed, and which may be either hortatory or consolatory according to circumstances: cf. the almost technical use of λόγος παρακλήσεως in Ac. xiii. 15. In the present instance παράκλησις is what Bengel finely calls 'totum praeconium evangelicum, passionum dulcedine tinctum.'

A characteristic use of the word in ordinary life is cited by Wohlenberg from Polyb. iii. 109. 6 f., where with reference to the address of Aemilius Paulus to the soldiers before the battle of Cannae it is said that for the hired soldier ὁ τῆς παρακλήσεως τρόπος is necessary, but that for those who fight for life and country no such exhortation is required—ὑπομνήσεως μόνον, παρακλήσεως δ' οὔ, προσδεῖ. For the corresponding verb παρακαλεῖν see the note on *v.* 11.

οὐκ ἐκ πλάνης] 'does not arise out of error,' πλάνης, as ἐκ (not ἐν) proves, being used, as apparently always in

καθὼς δεδοκιμάσμεθα ὑπὸ τοῦ θεοῦ πιστευθῆναι τὸ εὐαγγέλιον οὕτως λαλοῦμεν, οὐχ ὡς ἀνθρώποις ἀρέσκοντες

the N.T., in the pass. sense of 'error' rather than in the act. sense of 'deceit.' In contrast with false teachers who are not only 'deceivers' but 'deceived' (πλανῶντες κ. πλανώμενοι 2 Tim. iii. 13) the Apostles know whom they have believed (2 Tim. i. 12), and are confident in 'the word of the truth of the gospel' (Col. i. 5) which they have been called upon to declare (cf. Eph. iv. 14 f., and see also 1 Jo. iv. 6).

οὐδὲ ἐξ ἀκαθαρσίας] 'nor out of uncleanness'—the reference being not to 'covetousness,' a meaning of ἀκαθαρσία for which no sufficient warrant can be produced, nor even to 'impure motives,' but to actual 'impurity,' 'sensuality' (cf. iv. 7, Rom. vi. 19), the 'disclaimer, startling as it may seem,' being not 'unneeded amidst the impurities consecrated by the religions of the day' (Lft.): see further Intr. p. xlvi.

οὐδὲ ἐν δόλῳ] a new and distinct negative clause (οὐδέ, Buttmann p. 366), the ἐν, as distinguished from the preceding ἐκ (bis) of the originating cause, drawing attention rather to the general habit or method of the Apostles' working. Unlike the ἐργάται δόλιοι with whom at the time they were confronted (2 Cor. xi. 13, cf. ii. 17, iv. 2), and with whose 'guile' they were sometimes charged (2 Cor. xii. 16), they had never used unworthy means for ensnaring (δόλος from same root as δέλεαρ *a bait*, Curtius *Gr. Etym.* § 271) their converts. Thdt.: οὔτε μὴν δόλῳ χρώμενοι συνεργῷ εἰς ὄλεθρον ὑμᾶς θηρεύομεν. For the absence of δόλος as a mark of Christ Himself see 1 Pet. ii. 22 (Isa. liii. 9): cf. also Jo. i. 47.

4. ἀλλὰ καθὼς δεδοκιμάσμεθα κτλ.] 'but according as we have been approved by God.' Δοκιμάζω means originally 'put to the test' (cf. *v.* 4[b], 1 Cor. iii. 13), but in the N.T. generally conveys the added thought that the test has been successfully surmounted (Rom. i. 28, ii. 18, xiv. 22), in accordance with the technical use of the word to describe the passing as fit for election to a public office, e.g. Plato *Legg.* vi. 765 c, D οὓς ἂν καὶ ψῆφος ἡ τῶν δοκιμαζόντων δοκιμάσῃ· ἐὰν δέ τις ἀποδοκιμασθῇ κτλ., and from the inscriptions such a passage as *C.I.A.* III. 23, 30 ff. νόμος ἐραν[ισ]τῶν· [μη]δενὶ ἐ[ξ]έστω (ε)ἰσι[έν]αι [εἰς] τὴν σεμνοτά[τ]ην σύνοδον τῶν ἐρανιστῶν π[ρὶ]ν ἂν δοκιμασθῇ: cf. Magn. 113, 9 ff. ἀνὴρ δεδοκιμασμένος τοῖς θείοις κριτηρίοις τῶν Σεβαστῶν ἐπί τε τῇ τέχνῃ κτλ. In the LXX. the idea of *approval* is as a rule wanting, but cf. 2 Macc. iv. 3 διά τινος τῶν ὑπὸ τοῦ Σίμωνος δεδοκιμασμένων, 'through one of Simon's *tried* (or trusted) followers.'

In the present passage the verb is almost = ἀξιοῦν (II. i. 11), though we must beware of finding here any suggestion of *innate* fitness on the Apostles' part (Chrys.: εἰ μὴ εἶδε παντὸς ἀπηλλαγμένους βιωτικοῦ, οὐκ ἂν ἡμᾶς εἵλετο). The whole point is that their preaching is to be referred entirely to God as its source, in contrast with the sources previously disowned: they had been, and still were, 'entrusted' with it ('nicht befunden... sondern genommen' Hofmann).

πιστευθῆναι τὸ εὐαγγέλιον] For this use of πιστεύομαι cf. Rom. iii. 2, Gal. ii. 7, 1 Tim. i. 11, Tit. i. 3, and for the construction see WM. p. 287. Πιστεύομαι c. gen. as sometimes in late Gk. (e.g. Polyb. vi. 56. 13 πιστευθεὶς ταλάντου) does not occur in the N.T.

οὕτως] not the antecedent to the following ὡς, but = 'in the same manner,' 'in accordance therewith' with reference to the Divine commission just spoken of; cf. Mt. v. 16, Eph. v. 28.

οὐχ ὡς ἀνθρώποις ἀρέσκοντες] not a mere restatement of the preceding

ἀλλὰ θεῷ τῷ ΔΟΚΙΜΑΖΟΝΤΙ ΤΑΣ ΚΑΡΔΙΑΣ ἡμῶν. ⁵οὔτε γάρ ποτε ἐν λόγῳ κολακίας ἐγενήθημεν, καθὼς οἴδατε, οὔτε

clause in another light according to a favourite Pauline practice (cf. Col. i. 5ᵇ, 6), but an independent clause describing the manner of the Apostles' preaching in contrast with the charge of ἐν δόλῳ, and rendered more emphatic by the substitution of οὐ for the more regular μή with the participle. On this construction for the statement of a definite fact see Moulton *Prolegg.* p. 231 f., where it is fully illustrated from the papyri, e.g. P.Oxy. 726, 10 f. (ii./A.D.) οὐ δυνάμενος δι' ἀ[σ]θένειαν πλεῦσαι, 'since he is unable through sickness to make the voyage.' For the general thought cf. Ps. lii.(liii.) 6, Pss. Sol. iv. 8 ἀνακαλύψαι ὁ θεὸς τὰ ἔργα ἀνθρώπων ἀνθρωπαρέσκων. In no case must ἀρέσκοντες be weakened into 'seeking to please.' The statement is absolute, and the verb here betrays something of the idea of actual *service* in the interests of others (cf. Rom. xv. 1, 3, 1 Cor. x. 33), which we find associated with it in late Gk. Thus in monumental inscriptions the words ἀρέσαντες τῇ πόλει, τῇ πατρίδι &c., are used to describe those who have proved themselves of use to the commonwealth as in *O.G.I.S.* 646, 12 (Palmyra, iii./A.D.) ἀρέσαντα τῇ τε αὐτῇ βουλῇ καὶ τῷ δήμῳ.

ἀλλὰ θεῷ τῷ δοκιμάζοντι κτλ.] Δοκιμάζοντι chosen here with reference to the preceding δεδοκιμάσμεθα (for a similar word-play cf. Jer. vi. 30) shows a tendency to relapse into its original meaning of 'prove,' 'try' (Beza *Deo exploranti*, Est. 'vtpote cordium nostrorum inspectoris et exploratorem'): cf. Jer. xi. 20 Κύριε κρίνων δίκαια, δοκιμάζων νεφροὺς καὶ καρδίας.

Καρδία, according to Bibl. usage, is the focus of the personal life, the centre of all, intellectual as well as emotional, that goes to make up the moral character, and is thus equivalent to the inner, hidden man known to God alone, cf. 1 Regn. xvi. 7, Ac. i. 24, Rom. viii. 27, Rev. ii. 23, and see art. 'Heart' in Hastings' *D.B.* The use of the plur. here and of ψυχάς (v. 8) cannot be explained by the attraction of the plur. verb, but shows that throughout St Paul is thinking of his fellow-preachers at Thessalonica as well as of himself (Intr. p. xxxiv f.).

5. οὔτε...ἐν λόγῳ κολακίας ἐγενήθημεν] 'For neither at any time did we fall into the use of speech of flattery'—λόγῳ being clearly the preachers' own 'discourse' or 'teaching' at Thessalonica, and not the 'report' of others regarding it.

Κολακία (for form, WH.² *Notes* p. 160) ἅπ. λεγ. N.T., though common in class. writers, carries with it the idea of the tortuous methods by which one man seeks to gain influence over another, generally for selfish ends. Thus Aristotle defines the κόλαξ: ὁ δ' ὅπως ὠφέλειά τις αὐτῷ γίγνηται εἰς χρήματα καὶ ὅσα διὰ χρημάτων, κόλαξ (*Eth. Nic.* iv. 12. 9): cf. Theophr. *Charact.* 2 τὴν δὲ κολακείαν ὑπολάβοι ἄν τις ὁμιλίαν αἰσχρὰν εἶναι, συμφέρουσαν δὲ τῷ κολακεύοντι. How easily such a charge might be brought against the Apostles is evident from what we know of the conduct of the heathen rhetoricians of the day, cf. Dion Cass. *Hist. Rom.* lxxi. 35, Dion Chrys. *Orat.* xxxii. p. 403.

For a new work περὶ κολακείας by Philodemus the Epicurean (50 B.C.) see *Rhein. Museum* lvi. p. 623.

For γίνεσθαι ἐν (*versari in*) meaning entrance into and continuance in a given state or condition cf. Rom. xvi. 7, 1 Cor. ii. 3, 2 Cor. iii. 7, Phil. ii. 7, 1 Tim. ii. 14, Sus. 8 ἐγένοντο ἐν ἐπιθυμίᾳ αὐτῆς.

προφάσει πλεονεξίας, θεὸς μάρτυς, ⁶οὔτε ζητοῦντες ἐξ ἀνθρώπων δόξαν, οὔτε ἀφ' ὑμῶν οὔτε ἀπ' ἄλλων, ⁷δυνάμενοι
ἐν βάρει εἶναι ὡς Χριστοῦ ἀπόστολοι· ἀλλὰ ἐγενήθημεν

προφάσει πλεονεξίας] i.e. 'the cloak of which covetousness avails itself.' Had covetousness been the preachers' motive it would have hidden itself under some outward pretext (cf. Hor. *Epist.* I. xvi. 45 'introrsum turpem, speciosum pelle decora'). Beng.: '*praetextu* specioso, quo tegeremus *avaritiam*.'

Πρόφασις (wrongly rendered *occasio* Vg., Clarom., Calv., Est.) is the ostensible reason for which a thing is done, and generally points to a false reason as opposed to the true, cf. εἴτε προφάσει εἴτε ἀληθείᾳ Phil. i. 18, and the class. parallels there adduced by Wetstein, and see also P.Oxy. 237. vi. 31, vii. 11, 13, 16 (ii./A.D.); while πλεονεξία, though often associated by St Paul with sins of the flesh (Eph. iv. 19, v. 3, cf. 1 Cor. v. 9 ff., vi. 9 f., and see also Musonius p. 90 (ed. Hense) ὁ θεός...ἀήττητος μὲν ἡδονῆς, ἀήττητος δὲ πλεονεξίας), is in itself simply 'covetousness,' being distinguished from φιλαργυρία 'avarice' as the wider and more active sin: see Lft.'s note on Col. iii. 5 where it is explained as 'entire disregard for the rights of others.'

θεὸς μάρτυς] Cf. *v.* 10, also Rom. i. 9, 2 Cor. i. 23, Phil. i. 8. Chrys.: ὅπερ ἦν δῆλον, αὐτοὺς καλεῖ μάρτυρας...ὅπερ δὲ ἄδηλον ἦν...θεὸν καλεῖ μάρτυρα. Dr Dods aptly compares Cromwell's declaration to his first Parliament: 'That I lie not in matter of fact, is known to very many; but whether I tell a lie in my heart, as labouring to represent to you what was not upon my heart, I say, the Lord be judge.'

6. οὔτε ζητοῦντες κτλ.] Upon the repudiation of covetousness follows naturally the repudiation of worldly ambition (cf. Ac. xx. 19, 2 Cor. iv. 5, Eph. iv. 2). Calv.: 'duo enim sunt isti fontes, ex quibus manat totius ministerii corruptio.' For ζητεῖν in the sense of selfish seeking cf. Rom. x. 3, 1 Cor. x. 24, 33, xiii. 5, 2 Cor. xii. 14, Phil. ii. 21, and for δόξα in its original sense of 'good opinion' see note on *v.* 12. In Hellenistic Gk. ἐξ and ἀπό are frequently used interchangeably (WM. p. 512, Moulton *Prolegg.* p. 237, Meisterhans p. 212): in accordance however with the earlier distinction between them ἐξ may here point to the ultimate source, and ἀπό rather to the more immediate agents (Ambrstr. *ex hominibus...a uobis*).

It should be noted that what the Apostles disclaim is the *desire* of popularity. Th. Mops.: 'cautissime enim posuit *non quaerentes*; hoc est, "non auspicantes hoc," nec hanc habentes actus nostri intentionem.'

7ᵃ. δυνάμενοι ἐν βάρει εἶναι] 'when we might have been burdensome' (Wycl. *whanne we...my3ten haue be in charge*)—a concessive part. clause subordinate to the preceding ζητοῦντες. Most modern editors follow the A.V. in regarding this clause as part of *v.* 6.

Βάρος is here understood (1) in its simple meaning of 'weight,' 'burden' (Vg. *oneri esse*), with reference to the Apostles' right of maintenance, cf. *v.* 9, and see further II. iii. 8, 1 Cor. ix. 11, 2 Cor. xi. 7 ff., Gal. vi. 6, also Jos. *Antt.* I. 250 (xvi. 2) οὐδὲ γὰρ ἔσεσθαι βαρὺς ...δαπάναις ἰδίαις χρησάμενος; or (2) in its derived sense of 'authority,' 'dignity' (Clarom. *in gravitate* [honore] *esse*), pointing to the honour they might have expected to receive at the Thessalonians' hands, cf. 2 Cor. iv. 17 βάρος δόξης, Polyb. iv. 32. 7 πρὸς τὸ βάρος τὸ Λακεδαιμονίων, Diod. Sic. iv. 61 διὰ τὸ βάρος τῆς πόλεως. The two meanings are however compatible,

νήπιοι ἐν μέσῳ ὑμῶν, ὡς ἐὰν τροφὸς θάλπῃ τὰ ἑαυτῆς

and it is probable that St Paul plays here on the double sense of the phrase: cf. the Latin proverb 'Honos propter onus.'

ὡς Χριστοῦ ἀπόστολοι] Χριστοῦ poss. gen., placed emphatically first to show whose Apostles they were, and why therefore they were entitled to claim honour (cf. Add. Note D). For the title ἀπόστολοι here including Silvanus and Timothy almost in the sense of our *missionaries* cf. Ac. xiv. 4, 14, Rom. xvi. 7, 2 Cor. viii. 23, xi. 13, Phil. ii. 25, Rev. ii. 2, Didache xi. 3 f.; and for the wider use of the word generally see Lft. *Gal.*¹⁰ p. 92 ff., Harnack *Die Lehre der zwölf Apostel* p. 93 ff., Hort *Ecclesia* p. 22 ff.

In class. Gk. ἀπόστολος generally denotes 'a fleet,' 'an expedition' (cf. Dittenberger *Sylloge*² 153, an Attic inscription iv./B.C., and see *Archiv* iii. p. 221), but it occurs in Herodotus in the sense of 'messenger,' 'envoy' (i. 21, cf. v. 38), and is found with the same meaning in 3 Regn. xiv. 6A ἐγώ εἰμι ἀπόστολος πρός σε σκληρός (cf. **Sm.** Isa. xviii. 2). See also the interesting fragment in P.Par. p. 411 f. (ii./B.C.), where, if we can accept the editor's restoration of the missing letters, we read of a public official who had sent to a delinquent a messenger (ἀπόστολον) bearing the orders he had disregarded—[ἐπεσ]ταλκότων ἡμῶν πρός σε τὸν ἀπ[όστολον]. Upon the existence of 'apostles' among the Jews see Harnack *Miss. u. Ausbr.* p. 237 ff. (Engl. Tr. i. p. 409 ff.), and cf. Krauss *Die jüdischen Apostel* in *J.Q.R.* 1905, p. 370 ff.

7ᵇ—12. A positive counterpart to the previously-mentioned hostile charges.

7ᵇ, 8. 'Nay, we went further, for to establish a sure bond of sympathy with you we showed ourselves ready to act the part of children in your midst. Or we may put it in this way—we yearned over you with the same tender affection that a nursing-mother displays towards her children. With such deep affection indeed did we long after you that we shared with you not only the Gospel of God, but also our very lives—so dear had you proved yourselves to us.'

7ᵇ. ἀλλὰ ἐγενήθημεν νήπιοι κτλ.] The reading here is doubtful. If νήπιοι (א*BC*D*G *minusc. aliq.*) be adopted, the whole clause is the avowal on the writers' part of their becoming as children to children, speaking what St Augustine describes as 'decurtata et mutilata verba' (*de catech. rud.* 15), baby-language to those who were still babes in the faith: cf. Origen on Mt. xv. 17 ὁ ἀπόστολος ἐγένετο νήπιος καὶ παραπλήσιος τροφῷ θαλπούσῃ τὸ ἑαυτῆς παιδίον καὶ λαλούσῃ λόγους ὡς παιδίον διὰ τὸ παιδίον. On the other hand, if the well-attested ἤπιοι (אᶜAC^bD^cKLP 17 &c.) be preferred, the Apostolic 'gentleness' is placed in striking contrast with the slanders that had been insinuated against them (*vv.* 5, 6): cf. 2 Tim. ii. 24 where ἤπιος εἶναι is mentioned as a mark of the true pastor. This agreement with the context leads most modern editors and commentators to favour ἤπιοι, especially as the reading νήπιοι can be easily explained as due to *dittography* of the final ν of ἐγενήθημεν. WH.² (*Notes* p. 128), on the other hand, point out that 'the second ν might be inserted or omitted with equal facility,' and that 'the change from the bold image to the tame and facile adjective is characteristic of the difference between St Paul and the Syrian revisers.'

ἐν μέσῳ ὑμῶν] i.e. 'as one of yourselves,' 'without any undue assumption of authority.' Beng.: 'non agebant, quasi ex cathedra.' Cf. our Lord's own words: Ἐγὼ δὲ ἐν μέσῳ ὑμῶν εἰμι ὡς ὁ διακονῶν (Lk. xxii. 27).

τέκνα· ⁸οὕτως ὁμειρόμενοι ὑμῶν ηὐδοκοῦμεν μεταδοῦναι

ὡς ἐὰν τροφὸς θάλπῃ κτλ.] 'as if a nurse were cherishing her own children': cf. Gal. iv. 19. By a sudden change of metaphor by no means uncommon in the Pauline writings (cf. v. 2, 4, 2 Cor. iii. 13 ff.) the attitude of the Apostles is now described as that of a 'nurse,' or rather a 'nursing-mother' towards her children. Th. Mops.: '"nutricem" uero hoc in loco matrem dixit quae filios suos nutrit': cf. Aug. *Serm.* xxiii. 3. Too much stress however in this connexion must not be laid on ἑαυτῆς which in late Gk. has lost much of its emphatic force: cf. the common legal formula in the papyri by which a woman appears μετὰ κυρίου τοῦ ἑαυτῆς ἀνδρός, e.g. P.Grenf. I. 18, 4 f. (ii./B.C.).

Τροφός, ἅπ. λεγ. N.T., occurs in the LXX., Gen. xxxv. 8, 4 Regn. xi. 2, 2 Chron. xxii. 11, Isa. xlix. 23 as the translation of מֵינֶקֶת; cf. also *B.G.U.* 297, 12 ff. (i./A.D.) where a nurse acknowledges that she had received τὰ τροφεῖα καὶ τὰ ἔλαια καὶ τὸν ἱματισμὸν καὶ τἆλλα ὅσα καθήκει δίδοσθαι τροφῷ τοῦ τῆς γαλακτοτροφίας διετοῦς χρόνου καὶ τιθηνήσεως μηνῶν ἓξ κτλ. For τροφός = μήτηρ see Kaibel *Epigrammata Graeca* (1878) 247, 7 (i./ii. A.D.). The poetic θάλπω, elsewhere in N.T. only Eph. v. 29 (ἐκτρέφει κ. θάλπει), means properly 'to warm,' and thence, like the Lat. *fovere*, comes to signify 'cherish,' 'foster': cf. Deut. xxii. 6 καὶ ἡ μήτηρ θάλπῃ ἐπὶ τῶν νοσσῶν, and for its metaphorical use see *O.G.I.S.* 194, 6 (i./B.C.) τὴν πόλιν ἔθαλψε. It may be added that, while the sense seems to favour the use of ἐάν as the ordinary conditional particle, it is possible that we have here an instance of the late use of ἐάν for ἄν (WM. p. 390), ὡς ἐάν then implying '*a standing contingency*,—"as it may be (may be seen) at any time"' (Findlay). For early instances of this use

of ἐάν from the Κοινή cf. P.Petr. III. 43 (2), iii. 4 (iii./B.C.) ὅσωι ἐὰν πλεῖον εὕρῃι, P.Grenf. I. 18, 27 (ii./B.C.) ἐξ οὗ ἐὰν αἱρῆται, and see further Moulton *Prolegg.* pp. 43, 234, Mayser p. 152 f.

8. οὕτως ὁμειρόμενοι ὑμῶν] 'even so being eagerly desirous of you' (Vg. *ita desiderantes vos*, Beza *ita cupidi vestri*). Ὁμείρομαι (for breathing, WH.² *Notes* p. 151) is not found elsewhere in the Bibl. writings except in Job iii. 21 (cf. **Sm.** Ps. lxii. (lxiii.) 2). The common derivation from ὁμοῦ and εἴρειν (hence Thpht. = προσδεδεμένοι, Oecum. = ἀντεχόμενοι ὑμῶν) is philologically impossible, and Dr J. H. Moulton suggests rather the √ smer 'to remember' (Skt. *smirti* 'memory,' *smarâmi* 'I remember,' Lat. *memor*) with a prepositional element, and compares as parallel formations δύρομαι and ὀδύρομαι, κέλλω and ὀκέλλω, ὀ-μόργνυμι, ὠ-κεανός (ptc. of ὠ-κεῖμαι 'to lie around'). Wohlenberg conjectures that it may here be used 'as a term of endearment' ('edles Kosewort') derived from the language of the nursery: cf. note on νήπιοι (*v.* 7). For the construction with the gen. in the case of verbs of 'longing' see Kühner³ § 416, 4 b.

ηὐδοκοῦμεν] The absence of ἄν with ηὐδοκοῦμεν (for augment, WH.² *Notes* p. 169, WSchm. p. 101) points to a result actually reached, while the verb itself which is only found in late Gk. (in LXX. frequently for רָצָה) draws attention to the hearty goodwill attending the writer's attitude 'were well-pleased' (Vg. *cupide volebamus*). Cf. the use of εὐδοκεῖν in 1 Cor. i. 21, x. 5, Gal. i. 15, with reference to God, and in Rom. xv. 26 f., 2 Cor. v. 8, xii. 10 with reference to man; see also the note on εὐδοκία II. i. 11, and for a full discussion of both words Fritzsche *Röm.* ii. p. 369 ff. An interesting ex. of εὐδοκεῖν is afforded by P.Lond. I. 3, 6 ff. (ii./B.C.) ηὐδόκησάς με τῆς τιμ[ῆς

ὑμῖν οὐ μόνον τὸ εὐαγγέλιον τοῦ θεοῦ ἀλλὰ καὶ τὰς ἑαυτῶν ψυχάς, διότι ἀγαπητοὶ ἡμῖν ἐγενήθητε· 9 μνημονεύετε γάρ, ἀδελφοί, τὸν κόπον ἡμῶν καὶ τὸν μόχθον·

τ]οῦ ἡμίσους τοῦ [τρί]τοῦ λογείας τῶν κειμένων νεκρῶν, apparently = 'thou hast granted me the honour of the half of the offerings collected for the dead (mummies).' In legal documents the verb is frequent in the sense of 'give consent,' e.g. in the marriage-contract P.Oxy. 496, 8 (ii./A.D.) where the husband is not allowed to dispose of certain property χωρὶς εὐδοκούσης τῆς γαμουμένης, 'without the consent of the bride': see further Gradenwitz *Einführung* i. p. 160 ff.

τὰς ἑαυτῶν ψυχάς] 'our very lives,' 'our very selves'—ψυχάς (for plur. cf. *v.* 4 note) according to its ordinary Bibl. usage laying stress on what belonged essentially to the writers' personality (Beng.: 'anima nostra cupiebat quasi immeare in animam vestram'): cf. Mk. viii. 35, 2 Cor. xii. 15, Sir. xxxv. 23 (xxxii. 27) ἐν παντὶ ἔργῳ πίστευε τῇ ψυχῇ σου, and for a full discussion of ψυχή in the LXX. see Hatch *Essays* p. 101 ff.

For the reflexive ἑαυτῶν referring to the 1st pers. plur. cf. II. iii. 9 (note), Rom. viii. 23, 2 Cor. i. 9, iii. 5 &c. (WM. p. 187, WSchm. p. 204); and see P.Par. 47, 26 (ii./B.C.) αὐτοὺς δεδώκαμεν, P.Tebt. 47, 30 f. (ii./B.C.) ἵν' ἡμεῖς μὲν κομισώμεθα τὰ ἑαυτῶν (Mayser, p. 303).

διότι ἀγαπητοί κτλ.] Out of the Apostles' intercourse with the Thessalonians a relationship of love (ἀγαπ. used by St Paul of his converts in all groups of his Epp.) had been developed once for all (aor. ἐγενήθητε) which had led to the consequent ηὐδοκοῦμεν κτλ.

Διότι (*propterea quod*) has apparently always a *causal* force in the N.T. (Wilke *ntl. Rhet.* p. 251), though in the LXX. and late Gk. generally it is also frequently found in a sense differing little from ὅτι 'that': cf. 2 Macc. vii. 37 ἐξομολογήσασθαι διότι μόνος αὐτὸς θεός ἐστιν, B.G.U. 1011. ii. 15 ff. (ii./B.C.) διότι γὰρ πολ[λὰ] ληρώι[δη] καὶ ψευδῆ προσαγ[γ]έλ[λε]ται κατανοεῖς καὶ αὐτός, and for similar evidence from the Attic inscriptions, where διότι never = 'because,' see Meisterhans, p. 252 f. On the other hand in P.Tebt. 24, 34 (ii./B.C.) καὶ διότι must have its full causal force. In mod. Gk. the word is used instead of γάρ, a meaning which Fritzsche (*Röm.* i. p. 57) finds even in such passages as Ac. xviii. 10, Rom. i. 19 (cf. Blass p. 274); see also 1 Pet. iii. 10 where γάρ is used to introduce a quotation from the O.T. instead of διότι which is preferred in i. 16, 24, ii. 6. Jebb (in Vincent and Dickson *Mod. Gk.*² App. p. 338) cites the passage before us along with Gal. ii. 16 to illustrate the ease of the colloquial transition.

9. 'That this is no idle vaunt you yourselves very well know, for you cannot have forgotten our self-sacrificing labours amongst you, how, even while working night and day for our own maintenance so as not unduly to burden you, we preached to you the Gospel of God.'

9. μνημονεύετε γάρ κτλ.] For μνημονεύω c. acc. see i. 3 note, and for ἀδελφοί see i. 4 note.

κόπος (i. 3 note) and μόχθος are found together again in II. iii. 8, 2 Cor. xi. 27, the former pointing to the 'weariness' or 'fatigue' resulting from continual labour, the latter rather to the 'hardship' or 'struggle' involved in it. The similarity in sound between the words is well brought out in the rendering 'toil and moil' (Lft.).

νυκτὸς καὶ ἡμέρας ἐργαζόμενοι πρὸς τὸ μὴ ἐπιβαρῆσαί
τινα ὑμῶν ἐκηρύξαμεν εἰς ὑμᾶς τὸ εὐαγγέλιον τοῦ θεοῦ.
[10] ὑμεῖς μάρτυρες καὶ ὁ θεός, ὡς ὁσίως καὶ δικαίως καὶ

νυκτ. κ. ἡμ. ἐργαζόμενοι] An explanatory clause which gains in force through the absence of any connecting particle. For the fact cf. Ac. xviii. 3, and for the picture here presented of St Paul's missionary activity see Intr. p. xlv.
It may be noted that νυκτὸς κ. ἡμέρας (gen. of *time*) is the regular order of the words in St Paul (iii. 10, II. iii. 8, 1 Tim. v. 5, 2 Tim. i. 3). In the Apocalypse on the other hand we find always ἡμέρας κ. νυκτός (iv. 8, vii. 15 &c.), and so in St Luke (xviii. 7, Ac. ix. 24). When however St Luke adopts the acc., the order is changed νύκτα κ. ἡμέραν (ii. 37, Ac. xx. 31, xxvi. 7).

πρὸς τὸ μὴ ἐπιβαρῆσαι κτλ.] 'in order that we might not burden any of you': cf. II. iii. 7 ff. for an additional reason for these self-denying labours.

The late Gk. ἐπιβαρεῖν is used only figuratively in the N.T. (II. iii. 8, 2 Cor. ii. 5) and is nearly = καταβαρεῖν (2 Cor. xii. 16, cf. 2 Regn. xiii. 25), though the preposition in ἐπιβαρεῖν is mainly directive (*onus imponere*), in καταβαρεῖν rather perfective 'to weigh a man to the ground.' For its use in the inscriptions cf. Magn. 113, 15 f. where a certain physician Tyrannus is said to have behaved ὡς μηδένα ὑφ' αὑτοῦ παρὰ τὴν ἀξίαν τοῦ καθ' ἑαυτὸν μεγέθους ἐπιβεβαρῆσθαι, and for the simple verb βαρεῖν (2 Esdr. xv. (v.) 15, 1 Tim. v. 16) in the same sense, cf. *I.G.S.I.* 830, 15 (Puteoli ii./A.D.) ἵνα μὴ τὴν πόλιν βαρῶμεν. In the late P.Oxy. 126, 8 (vi./A.D.) one Stephanous undertakes to 'burden herself' (βαρέσαι τὸ ἐμὸν ὄνομα) with certain imposts hitherto paid by her father.

On πρὸς τό with inf. signifying not mere result but subjective purpose see WM. p. 414, Moulton *Prolegg.* p. 218 ff.

10—12. 'We are not afraid indeed to appeal alike in your sight and in the sight of God to the whole character of our relations with you. All believers will be ready to testify how these were marked throughout by holiness and righteousness, and how careful we were to give no offence in anything. Indeed, as you very well know, we acted the part of a father to each one of you, as we exhorted, and encouraged, and solemnly charged, according to your several requirements, in order that you might respond to your privileges, and your whole lives be worthy of the God who is calling you to share in His kingdom and glory.'

10. ὑμεῖς μάρτυρες κτλ.] The two former appeals to the witness of men (*v.* 1) and of God (*v.* 5) are now united in confirmation of the whole character of the Apostolic ministry.

ὡς ὁσίως κτλ.] In accordance with the distinction found in Plato (*Gorg.* 507 B) and other Gk. writers, it has been common to describe ὁσίως as indicating duty towards God, and δικαίως duty towards men. But the distinction, which even in class. Gk. is sometimes lost sight of, must not be pressed in the N.T., where all righteousness is recognized as one, 'growing out of a single root, and obedient to a single law' (Trench *Syn.* p. 307). Accordingly ὁσίως and δικαίως are best regarded as descriptive of the Apostles' attitude towards both God and man from its *positive* side, that attitude being viewed first from a religious (ὁσίως) and then from a moral (δικαίως) standpoint, while the following ἀμέμπτως from the *negative* side emphasizes their general blamelessness in these same two respects.

As regards the individual expres-

ἀμέμπτως ὑμῖν τοῖς πιστεύουσιν ἐγενήθημεν, ¹¹καθάπερ οἴδατε ὡς ἕνα ἕκαστον ὑμῶν ὡς πατὴρ τέκνα ἑαυτοῦ ¹²παρακαλοῦντες ὑμᾶς καὶ παραμυθούμενοι καὶ μαρτυρό-

sions, ὁσίως is found only here in the N.T., while ἀμέμπτως occurs again in v. 23 (cf. iii. 13 WH. marg.). Both ἄμεμπτος and -ως are common in the inscriptions and papyri, e.g. *O.G.I.S.* 485, 14 ἁγνῶς καὶ ἀμέμπτως. For the combination ὁσίως κ. δικαίως see further *A pol. Arist.* xv. *sub fine*, also P.Par. 63. viii. 13 f. (ii./B.C.) where a letter-writer makes a claim for himself as having ὁσίως καὶ...δικαίως [πολι]τευσά-μενος before the gods, and for ἀμέμπτως κ. ὁσίως cf. Clem. R. *Cor.* xliv. 4.

On ὡς see Blass p. 230, and for the use of the adverbs instead of the corresponding adjectives, as bringing out more fully the mode and manner of ἐγενήθημεν (Ambrstr. *facti sumus*), cf. 1 Cor. xvi. 10 ἵνα ἀφόβως γένηται πρὸς ὑμᾶς.

ὑμῖν τ. πιστεύουσιν] Cf. i. 7. The clause is not 'pointless' (Jowett), but is to be closely connected with ἐγενή-θημεν (cf. Rom. vii. 3), as marking the impression the missionaries made upon their Thessalonian converts, whatever might be the judgment of others. Thdt.: οὐ γὰρ εἶπεν, ἄμεμπτοι πᾶσιν ὤφθημεν, ἀλλ' Ὑμῖν τοῖς πιστεύ-ουσι.

11. καθάπερ οἴδατε] The expressive καθάπερ ('die schärfste aller Gleichheitspartikeln' Meisterhans p. 257) is found in the N.T. only in the first two groups of the Pauline Epp. (16 times) and in Heb. iv. 2: cf. P.Hib. 49, 6 f. (iii./B.C.) καθάπερ ἔγραψα and the common legal formula καθάπερ ἐγ δίκης 'as if in accordance with a legal decision' (e.g. P.Amh. 46, 13 (ii./B.C.)). In the Decrees τὰ μὲν ἄλλα καθάπερ ὁ δεῖνα 'was the usual introduction to an amendment proposed in the Ecclesia to a probouleuma' (Roberts-Gardner p. 18): e.g. *C.I.G.* 84, 6 f. Κέφαλος εἶπε· τὰ μὲν ἄλλα καθά-περ τῇ βουλεῖ· ἀναγράψαι δὲ....

ὡς ἕνα κτλ.] The construction is irregular but, if this is not to be taken as an instance of the Hellenistic use of the part. for the ind. (cf. Moulton *Prolegg.* p. 222 f.), we may either resume ἐγενήθημεν (*v.* 10) after ὡς, leaving both ἕνα ἕκ. and ὑμᾶς to be governed by the following participles, or still better supply such a finite verb as ἐνουθετοῦμεν which the writer lost sight of owing to the extended participial clause.

Ἕνα ἕκαστον (Vg. *unumquemque*), an intensified form of ἕκαστον, marks the individual character of the Apostles' ministry. Chrys.: βαβαί, ἐν τοσούτῳ πλήθει μηδένα παραλιπεῖν, μὴ μικρόν, μὴ μέγαν, μὴ πλούσιον, μὴ πένητα.

ὡς πατὴρ κτλ.] an appropriate change from the figure of the nursing-mother (*v.* 7) in view of the thought of instruction which is now prominent. Pelag.: 'parvulos nutrix fovet : proficientes vero jam pater instituit.'

12. παρακαλοῦντες ὑμᾶς κτλ.] 'exhorting you and encouraging and testifying'—a clause which, contrary to the usual verse-division, is included by WH. in *v.* 12. Παρακαλεῖν, like παράκλησις (*v.* 3 note), is a favourite word with St Paul, occurring no less than ten times in these Epp. with the double meaning of 'exhort' and 'comfort.' The former idea is prominent here, while the succeeding παραμυθού-μενοι (elsewhere in N.T. only in v. 14, Jo. xi. 19, 31, cf. 2 Macc. xv. 9) is addressed to the feelings rather than to the will. For a similar combination of the corresponding nouns see 1 Cor. xiv. 3, Phil. ii. 1.

Μαρτύρεσθαι, properly 'summon to witness,' and then absolutely 'asseve-

μενοι, εἰς τὸ περιπατεῖν ὑμᾶς ἀξίως τοῦ θεοῦ τοῦ ⌜καλοῦντος⌝ ὑμᾶς εἰς τὴν ἑαυτοῦ βασιλείαν καὶ δόξαν.

II 12 καλοῦντος BDGHKLP 17 al pler d g Syr (Harcl mg) Chr ⅔ Ambst Ephr al: καλέσαντος ℵA 23 31 al pauc Vg Go Syr (Pesh Harcl) Sah Boh Arm Theod-Mops^lat

rate,' 'protest,' from which it is an easy transition to the meaning 'conjure,' 'solemnly charge' which suits best the present passage and Eph. iv. 17: see Hort on 1 Pet. i. 11 who cites in support of this rendering Plut. ii. 19 B (of Homer) ἐν δὲ τῷ προδιαβάλλειν μόνον οὐ μαρτύρεται καὶ διαγορεύει μήτε χρῆσθαι κτλ. 'solemnly warns not to use'—a charge as in the presence of God. An interesting parallel is also afforded by P.Oxy. 471, 64 f. (ii./A.D.) μαρτύρονται κύριε τὴν σὴν τύχην, where however the editors translate 'they bear evidence,' as if it were the commoner μαρτυροῦσι. According to Lft. (ad loc., cf. note on Gal. v. 3) μαρτύρομαι has never this latter sense in the N.T. any more than in class. Gk., but that the two words were sometimes confused in late Gk. is proved by such a passage as P.Amh. 141, 17 f. (iv./A.D.) τοσοῦτο μαρτυραμένη [κ]αὶ ἀξιοῦσα τῆς παρὰ σοῦ ἐκδικείας τυχεῖν, where we can only translate 'bearing witness to the facts and praying to obtain satisfaction by you.'

εἰς τὸ περιπατεῖν κτλ.] On εἰς τό with the inf. expressing here not so much the *purpose* as the *content* of the foregoing charge see Moulton *Prolegg.* p. 218 ff., where the varying shades of meaning attached to this phrase in the Pauline writings are fully discussed.

Περιπατεῖν with reference to general moral conduct occurs thirty-two times in the Pauline Epp., and twelve times in the writings of St John (Gosp.², Epp.¹⁰). St Luke prefers πορεύεσθαι (Gosp.² Ac.²) for this purpose, as do St Peter and St Jude. The metaphor though not unknown in class. Gk. (cf. Xen. *Cyr.* ii. 2. 24 ἡ πονηρία διὰ τῶν παραυτίκα ἡδονῶν πορευομένη, and the essentially similar metaph. use of

ἀναστρέφεσθαι, ἀναστροφή) is Hebraistic in origin: cf. the early designation of Christianity as ἡ ὁδός (Ac. ix. 2 &c.) in keeping with the common metaphorical use of the word in the LXX.

For the use of the pres. inf. περιπατεῖν (v.l. -τῆσαι D^cKL) see Blass p. 195 n¹. For περιπατεῖν ἀξίως cf. Eph. iv. 1, and for ἀξίως with gen. of a person cf. Rom. xvi. 2, Col. i. 10, 3 Jo. 6. The exact phrase ἀξίως τοῦ θεοῦ is found in the Pergamene inscription 248, 7 ff. (ii./B.C.) where Athenaios, a priest of Dionysios and Sabazius, is extolled as συ[ν]τετελεκότος τὰ ἱερὰ...εὐσεβῶς [μ]έγ καὶ ἀξίως τοῦ θεοῦ (see Deissmann *BS.* p. 248).

Thieme (p. 21) cites similar exx. from the Magnesian inscriptions, e.g. 33, 30 ἀξίως [τ]ῆ[ς] θ[ε]ᾶς (Gonnos in Thessaly iii./B.C.), 85, 10 f. ἀξίως τῆς τε Ἀρτέμιδος...καὶ [τοῦ] δήμου (Tralles); but rightly draws attention to the difference of spirit underlying the appeal of the Christian Apostle to his converts to walk worthily of the Gospel, and the praise which a Greek commune bestows on the ambassadors of another state for acting ἀξίως τῆς θεᾶς καὶ τοῦ δήμου.

τοῦ καλοῦντος] 'who is calling,' the verb being used in its technical sense of 'call to the kingdom' with the further idea, as throughout the Pauline Epp., that the calling as God's act has been effectual (Rom. viii. 30, 1 Cor. i. 9). The use of the pres. part. instead of the more common aor. (καλέσαντος, WH. mg.) in this connexion (cf. iv. 7, Gal. i. 6, 15, v. 13, but not v. 8) may be due to the fact that the whole phrase is practically='our caller' (cf. i. 10, and see Rom. ix. 11 where ἐκ τοῦ καλοῦντος is contrasted with ἐξ ἔργων), but is perhaps sufficiently ex-

plained by the eschatological reference of the present passage. Believers are continually being called to an inheritance on which they have not yet fully entered, but of which they are assured (cf. v. 24).

On the different uses of καλέω see SH. p. 241 f.

εἰς τ. ἑαυτοῦ βασιλείαν κτλ.] Though there are undoubted instances in the Pauline Epp. of βασιλεία as the *present* kingdom of God's grace (Rom. xiv. 17, 1 Cor. iv. 20, Col. i. 13), its reference in the main is to the *future* (II. i. 5, 1 Cor. vi. 9, xv. 50, Gal. v. 21, 2 Tim. iv. 1, 18), and that this is the case here is shown by its inclusion with the eschatological δόξα under one art. The two expressions must not however be united as if = 'His own kingdom of glory,' or even 'His own kingdom culminating in His glory,' but point rather to two manifestations of God's power, the first of His *rule*, the second of His *glory*. On ἑαυτοῦ which seems here to retain its full emphasis see note on *v.* 7, and on St Paul's teaching regarding the 'kingdom' at Thessalonica see Intr. p. xxvii.

Δόξα, in class. Gk. = 'opinion,' 'good opinion' (cf. *v.* 6), through the influence of the LXX. where it is commonly used to translate Heb. כָּבוֹד 'honour,' 'glory,' came to be applied in the N.T. to the full manifestation of God's glory ('*Gloria*, divinitas conspicua'—Beng. on Ac. vii. 2), or more specially to that glory as revealed to men in the Divine majesty and goodness (e.g. Eph. i. 6, 12, 17, iii. 16, Col. i. 11 with Lft.'s note). From this it was a natural transition to the future bliss or glory that awaits God's people, the ethical conception being still always predominant: cf. Rom. v. 2 ἐπ' ἐλπίδι τ. δόξης τ. θεοῦ, viii. 18 πρὸς τ. μέλλουσαν δόξαν ἀποκαλυφθῆναι εἰς ἡμᾶς. This sense of the word can also be illustrated from post-canonical literature by such passages as *Apoc. Bar.* xv. 8 'For this world is to them a trouble and a weariness with much labour; and that accordingly which is to come, a crown with great glory'; xlviii. 49 'And I will recount their blessedness and not be silent in celebrating their glory, which is reserved for them'; and especially 4 Ezra vii. 42 where the state of the blessed is described as 'neque nitorem neque claritatem neque lucem' but only 'splendorem claritatis altissimi' [perhaps = ἀπαύγασμα δόξης Ὑψίστου, SH. p. 85].

For the Bibl. history of the word δόξα see further Kennedy *Last Things* p. 299 ff., and for the possibility that δόξα may originally have had a 'realistic' meaning in the ordinary Gk. of the day though no actual instance of this use has yet been found, see Deissmann *Hellenisierung* p. 165 f., where its use as a name for women and ships (F. Bechtel, *Die attischen Frauennamen* (1902) p. 132) is cited as a partial parallel.

In the passage before us the whole phrase τ. καλοῦντος κτλ. shows affinity with the 'invitation' in the Parable of the Supper, Mt. xxii. 1 ff., Lk. xiv. 16 ff.: cf. Dalman *Worte* p. 97 (Engl. Tr. p. 118 f.) where similar exx. are adduced from Jewish literature.

II. 13—16. RENEWED THANKSGIVING FOR THE SUCCESS ATTENDING THE APOSTOLIC MINISTRY AT THESSALONICA.

Because their ministry had been attended with so much toil and zeal (*vv.* 1—12), the Apostles are now all the more ready to renew their thanksgiving to God that the Thessalonians had not come short either in their ready acceptance of the Gospel-message (*v.* 13), or in their endurance under persecution (*v.* 14)—the latter thought leading to a vehement condemnation of the persecuting Jews (*vv.* 15, 16).

13, 14. 'Seeing then that we on our part have bestowed so much labour and affection upon you, we are

¹³ Καὶ διὰ τοῦτο καὶ ἡμεῖς εὐχαριστοῦμεν τῷ θεῷ ἀδιαλείπτως, ὅτι παραλαβόντες λόγον ἀκοῆς παρ' ἡμῶν τοῦ θεοῦ ἐδέξασθε οὐ λόγον ἀνθρώπων ἀλλὰ καθὼς ἀληθῶς ἐστὶν λόγον θεοῦ, ὃς καὶ ἐνεργεῖται ἐν ὑμῖν τοῖς

the more unceasingly thankful that you yourselves have not come short in the act of receiving. Nay rather when the "word of hearing" was delivered to you, it became something more than the "word of hearing." We might be its bearers, but God was its author. And in welcoming it as you did, it proved itself no mere human message, but a Divine power in all believing hearts. How true this is your own lives testified in that, after the example of the Christian Churches of Judæa, you underwent the same sufferings at the hands of your fellow-countrymen that they did at the hands of the unbelieving Jews.'

13. καὶ ἡμεῖς] 'we on our part'—καί denoting the *response* of the Apostles to the favourable character of the news they had received: cf. iii. 5, Col. i. 9 (with Lft.'s note). For a different view according to which καί really belongs to the verb see Lietzmann on *Rom*. iii. 7 (in *Handb. z. N.T.* iii. 1 (1906)).

ὅτι παραλαβόντες κτλ.] ὅτι not so much causal (II. i. 10, ii. 13), as introducing the subject-matter of the εὐχαριστία, namely that the Thessalonians had not only outwardly *received* (παραλαβόντες) the Apostolic message, but had inwardly *welcomed* (ἐδέξασθε) it, and that too not as the word of men, but as the word of God. For a similar use of παραλαμβάνω in the Pauline Epp. cf. iv. 1, II. iii. 6, Gal. i. 9, 12, 1 Cor. xv. 1, 3, Phil. iv. 9, Col. ii. 6, and for δέχομαι of willing, hearty reception cf. i. 6, II. ii. 10, 1 Cor. ii. 14, 2 Cor. viii. 17, Gal. iv. 14. In the present passage the Vg. makes no attempt to mark the difference of the verbs (*accepissetis...accepistis*),

but Clarom. has *percepissetis...excepistis*, and Ambrstr. *accepissetis... suscepistis*.

λόγον ἀκοῆς] 'Ακοῆς may be understood in the active sense of 'a hearing' (cf. Gal. iii. 2, where it is contrasted with ἔργων) in keeping with the part here assigned to the Thessalonians themselves, but it is better taken in its (ordinary) passive sense of 'a message' spoken and heard (Vg. *verbum auditûs*): cf. Rom. x. 16 (LXX. Isa. liii. 1), Heb. iv. 2.

παρ' ἡμῶν] to be connected with παραλαβόντες, notwithstanding the interjected λόγ. ἀκοῆς, as indicating the *immediate* source of the message delivered and received, while the emphatic τοῦ θεοῦ is added to point to its *real* source lest the Apostles should seem to be making undue claims (cf. 1 Cor. ii. 13).

οὐ λόγον ἀνθρώπων κτλ.] To understand ὡς before λόγ. ἀνθρ. (as A.V., R.V.) is unnecessary, and fails to bring out as clearly as the absolute rendering the real character of the message here referred to. For (ὁ) λόγος (τοῦ) θεοῦ with reference to the preaching of the Gospel cf. 2 Tim. ii. 9, Apoc. i. 9, and for the whole clause cf. *Apol. Arist*. xvi. οὐ γὰρ ἀνθρώπων ῥήματα λαλοῦσιν [οἱ χριστιανοί], ἀλλὰ τὰ τοῦ θεοῦ.

ὃς καὶ ἐνεργεῖται] 'which also is set in operation' (Clarom., Ambrstr. *quod operatur*)—ἐνεργεῖται being best understood in the pass. sense in which it is frequently found in late Gk. (e.g. Polyb. i. 13. 5, ix. 12. 3), and which brings out more clearly than the midd., which is generally found here, the Divine agency that is at work. For this energizing power of God's

πιστεύουσιν. ¹⁴ὑμεῖς γὰρ μιμηταὶ ἐγενήθητε, ἀδελφοί, τῶν ἐκκλησιῶν τοῦ θεοῦ τῶν οὐσῶν ἐν τῇ Ἰουδαίᾳ ἐν Χριστῷ Ἰησοῦ, ὅτι τὰ αὐτὰ ἐπάθετε καὶ ὑμεῖς ὑπὸ τῶν ἰδίων συμφυλετῶν καθὼς καὶ αὐτοὶ ὑπὸ τῶν Ἰουδαίων,

word cf. Heb. iv. 12, Jas. i. 21, 1 Pet. i. 23, Isa. lv. 11; and for a valuable note on the use of ἐνεργεῖν and its cognates in the N.T. see Robinson *Eph.* p. 241 ff.

ἐν ὑμῖν τ. πιστεύουσιν] a clause added to emphasize that, powerful though the word of God is, it can only operate where a believing attitude exists and continues: cf. *v.* 10, and for the thought see Mt. xiii. 23, 58, Heb. iv. 2.

14. ὑμεῖς γάρ κτλ.] A practical confirmation of the ἐνέργεια just spoken of. The Thessalonians in their turn (ὑμεῖς emph.) had shown themselves not idle hearers, but active 'imitators' of the Churches of God in Judaea, which are apparently specially mentioned here simply because they were the earliest Christian communities, and had throughout their history been exposed to severe hostility.

For the added clause ἐν Χρ. Ἰησ. cf. i. 1 note, and for similar appeals to the lessons of past sufferings cf. 1 Cor. xv. 32, Gal. iii. 4, Heb. x. 32 ff.

ὑπὸ τ. ἰδίων συμφυλετῶν] According to derivation συμφυλέτης (ἅπ. λεγ. N.T.) means literally 'one belonging to the same tribe' (Vg. *contribulibus*), but is evidently used here in a local rather than a racial sense (Ambrstr. *conciuibus*), and need not therefore exclude all reference to those Jews by whom, as we know from Ac. xvii. 5, 13, the persecutions at Thessalonica were first instigated. If so, this would seem to be one of the instances where a certain weakened force must be allowed to ἰδίων (cf. ἑαυτῆς, *v.* 7) in accordance with a not infrequent tendency in Hellenistic Gk., e.g. Job vii. 10 οὐδ᾽ οὐ μὴ ἐπι-στρέψῃ εἰς τὸν ἴδιον οἶκον: cf. Mt. xxii. 5, 1 Cor. vii. 2, and the memorial inscription found at Thessalonica Ἀπολλωνία Νεικῶνι τῷ ἰδίῳ ἀνδρὶ μνήμης χάριν (Heuzey p. 282). See further Deissmann *BS.* p. 123 f., Mayser p. 308, and on the danger of pushing this 'exhausted' ἴδιος too far Moulton *Prolegg.* p. 87 ff.

For the thoroughly class. use of ὑπό with an intrans. verb to point to the author cf. such a passage from the Κοινή as P.Amh. 78, 4 f. (ii./A.D.) βίαν πάσχων ἑκάστοτε ὑπὸ Ἐκύσεως.

καθὼς καὶ αὐτοί κτλ.] Αὐτοί, i.e. the persons included in the collective ἐκκλησιῶν. For the imperfect antecedent cf. WM. p. 181, and for the repetition of καί in order to strengthen the comparison with the immediately preceding καὶ ὑμεῖς cf. Rom. i. 13, Col. iii. 13. Ἰουδαία is here used in its larger sense of all Palestine including Galilee, cf. Lk. iv. 44, Ac. x. 37, Jos. *Antt.* I. 160 (vii. 2) εἰς τὴν τότε μὲν Χαναναίαν λεγομένην νῦν δὲ Ἰουδαίαν, μετῴκησε. Of the precise nature of the sufferings of the Judæan churches after St Paul began his missionary labours we have no record in Acts, but they would doubtless consist in excommunication and social outlawry, as well as in actual legal persecution (cf. Ramsay *C.R.E.* p. 349). In any case the mere mention of 'the Jews' is sufficient to recall to the Apostle what he himself had suffered at the hands of his fellow-countrymen, and accordingly he 'goes off' at the word into a fierce attack upon them.

15, 16. This attack is so different from St Paul's general attitude to his fellow-countrymen (e.g. Rom. x. 1 ff.) that the whole passage has been pronounced an interpolation but without

¹⁵τῶν καὶ τὸν κύριον ἀποκτεινάντων Ἰησοῦν καὶ τοὺς προφήτας καὶ ἡμᾶς ἐκδιωξάντων, καὶ θεῷ μὴ ἀρεσκόντων, καὶ πᾶσιν ἀνθρώποις ἐναντίων, ¹⁶κωλυόντων ἡμᾶς τοῖς

any sufficient warrant (Intr. p. lxxvi). The sharp judgment expressed is due rather to the Apostle's keen sense of the manner in which the Jews had opposed God's will, both in thwarting his own missionary work, and afterwards in seeking to shake the faith of his Thessalonian converts. It is however deserving of notice that this is the only passage in the Pauline writings in which the designation 'the Jews' is used in direct contrast to Christian believers in the sense which St John afterwards made so familiar in his Gospel (i. 19, ii. 18 &c.). For a somewhat similar digression cf. Phil. iii. 2 ff., and for the light in which the Jews are here regarded see Stephen's charge Ac. vii. 51 ff.

15, 16. 'Did we speak of the *Jews* as persecutors? Why, are they not the men at whose door lies the guilt of the death of Jesus, and who in the past drove out the prophets, even as they are now driving out us? The least that can be said of them is that they do not please God, while their well-known hostility to all mankind is shown in the present instance by their deliberately standing in the way of the Gentiles' salvation. But in so doing they are only "filling up the measure of their iniquity" with the result that "the Wrath of God" which they have so fully deserved has reached its final stage.'

15. τῶν καὶ τὸν κύριον κτλ.] The words are skilfully arranged so as to lay emphasis on both κύριον and Ἰησοῦν: it was 'the Lord' whom the Jews slew, 'even Jesus': cf. Ac. ii. 36 and see Add. Note D. For the guilt of the crucifixion as lying at the door of the Jewish people cf. such passages as Lk. xxiv. 20, Jo. xix. 11, Ac. ii. 23, and Gosp. Pet. 7, and for the general thought see our Lord's own parable Mk. xii. 1 ff., which may have suggested his language here to the Apostle. If this latter connexion can be established, it is natural to follow the usual order and place τ. προφήτας also under the government of ἀποκτεινάντων. On the other hand, to avoid the slight anticlimax that is thereby occasioned by the prophets following the Lord Jesus, various modern editors prefer to connect τ. προφήτας with ἡμᾶς under the direct government of ἐκδιωξάντων, an arrangement which has the further advantage of combining closely the prophets and the Apostles as the Divine messengers in the past and the present: cf. Mt. v. 12 οὕτως γὰρ ἐδίωξαν τ. προφήτας τ. πρὸ ὑμῶν, and see also Mt. xxiii. 31, Lk. xi. 47.

The reading ἰδίους, which is found in certain MSS. (D^{bc}KL) before προφήτας, is due not to any doctrinal bias (Tert. *adv. Marc.* v. 15 'licet suos adjectio sit haeretici'), but to a desire for precision of statement: cf. iv. 11, Eph. iv. 28.

καὶ ἡμᾶς ἐκδιωξάντων] 'and drove us out' (Beng.: 'qui persequendo ejecerunt'). For the fact cf. Ac. xvii. 5 ff., 13 ff., and for the force of ἐκδιώκειν (ἅπ. λεγ. N.T.: v.l. Lk. xi. 49) cf. such passages in the LXX. as Deut. vi. 19 ἐκδιώξαι πάντας τοὺς ἐχθρούς σου πρὸ προσώπου σου, Joel ii. 20 καὶ τὸν ἀπὸ βορρᾶ ἐκδιώξω ἀφ' ὑμῶν: see also Thuc. i. 24 ὁ δῆμος αὐτῶν ἐξεδίωξε τοὺς δυνατούς, οἱ δὲ ἀπελθόντες κτλ., Dem. *Or.* xxxii. p. 883 ἐκδιωκόμενος [*scil.* e navi] ῥίπτει ἑαυτὸν εἰς τὴν θάλασσαν.

καὶ θεῷ μὴ ἀρεσκόντων] a notable instance of *meiosis*, cf. II. iii. 2, 7. For the expression which is a favourite one in the Pauline writings cf. *v.* 4, iv. 1, Rom. viii. 8, 2 Cor. v. 9, Col. i. 10.

καὶ πᾶσιν ἀνθρώποις ἐναντίων] the

ἔθνεσιν λαλῆσαι ἵνα σωθῶσιν, εἰς τὸ ἀναπληρῶσαι αὐτῶν

only passage in the N.T. where ἐναντίος is used of persons. The words naturally recall the 'hostile odium' (Tac. *Hist*. v. 5) towards all men with which the Jews have often been charged: cf. Diod. Sic. xxxiv. 1 τοὺς Ἰουδαίους μόνους ἁπάντων ἐθνῶν ἀκοινωνήτους εἶναι, Philostr. *Apoll*. v. 33, Jos. c. *Apion*. II. 121 (10), and the collection of passages in T. Reinach's *Textes...relatifs au Judaïsme* (1895) under the heading 'Misoxénie' in the Index. The reference here however, as the following clause shows, is more limited.

16. κωλυόντων ἡμᾶς κτλ.] 'in that they forbid us to speak to the Gentiles in order that they may be saved.' The emphasis lies on τ. ἔθνεσιν: it was to *the Gentiles* (Wycl. *hethen men*) that the Jews did not wish anything said that had for its object their salvation. Chrys.: εἰ γὰρ τῇ οἰκουμένῃ δεῖ λαλῆσαι, οὗτοι δὲ κωλύουσι, κοινοὶ τῆς οἰκουμένης εἰσὶν ἐχθροί. For the fact cf. Ac. xiii. 45, 50, xvii. 5, 13, xxi. 27 ff. &c., and for a similar instance of ἵνα with its full telic force cf. 1 Cor. x. 33.

On the history of the word ἔθνος, which is here used in its strict LXX. sense of all outside the covenant-people (הַגּוֹיִם), see Kennedy *Sources* p. 98, Nägeli p. 46, and cf. Hicks in *C.R.* i. p. 42 f. where it is shown that ἔθνος first gained significance as a political term after Alexander and his successors began to found cities as outposts of trade and civilization. Then 'Hellenic life found its normal type in the πόλις, and barbarians who lived κατὰ κώμας or in some less organized form were ἔθνη.'

The attitude of the stricter Pharisaism towards other nations is well brought out in such a passage as 4 Ezra vi. 55 f.: 'Haec autem omnia dixi coram te, domine, quoniam dixisti quia propter nos creasti primogenitum saeculum. Residuas autem gentes ab Adam natas dixisti eas nihil esse et quoniam saliuae adsimilatae sunt et sicut stillicidium de uaso similasti habundantiam eorum.'

There are however occasional traces of a more liberal view, e.g. Pss. Sol. xvii. 38, 'He [the Messiah] shall have mercy upon all the nations *that come* before him in fear'; *Apoc. Bar*. i. 4 'I will scatter this people among the Gentiles that they may do good to the Gentiles' (i.e. apparently by making proselytes of them, Charles *ad loc.*).

εἰς τὸ ἀναπληρῶσαι κτλ.] 'in order to fill up the measure of their sins at all times' (Vg. *ut impleant peccata sua semper*). There is no need to depart here from the ordinary sense of εἰς τό with the inf. to denote purpose (cf. v. 12 note), the reference being 'grammatically' to the Jews, but 'theologically' to the eternal purpose of God 'which unfolded itself in this wilful and at last judicial blindness on the part of His chosen people' (Ellic.): cf. Rom. i. 24, and for other exx. of εἰς τό introducing a purpose contemplated not by the doer but by God cf. Rom. i. 20, iv. 11. In acting as they were doing the present Jews were but carrying forward to its completion the work which their fathers had begun (Beng.: 'ut *semper*, ita nunc quoque'), and which had now brought down upon them God's judicial wrath: cf. Gen. xv. 16 οὔπω γὰρ ἀναπεπλήρωνται αἱ ἁμαρτίαι τῶν Ἀμορραίων ἕως τοῦ νῦν, and especially our Lord's own words recorded in Mt. xxiii. 31 f. ὅτι υἱοί ἐστε τῶν φονευσάντων τοὺς προφήτας. καὶ ὑμεῖς πληρώσατε τὸ μέτρον τῶν πατέρων ὑμῶν. The plur. αἱ ἁμαρτίαι laying stress not on specific acts of sin, but on sin in the aggregate, is found in all groups of St Paul's Epp.; cf. Westcott *Eph*. p. 165 f. where the

τὰς ἁμαρτίας πάντοτε. ⌜ἔφθασεν⌝ δὲ ἐπ' αὐτοὺς ἡ ὀργὴ εἰς τέλος.

16 ἔφθασεν ℵAD^bc GKLP cet Orig Eus Chr Thdt al: ἔφθακεν BD* 31 137 154

different Pauline words for 'sin' are classified, and for a non-Christian use of the word see P.Leip. 119, 3 (iii./A.D.) τῶν ἁμαρτιῶ[ν] τὰς πονηρίας συνεχῶ[ς ἀ]νορθουμένων. For the unemphatic αὐτῶν cf. WM. p. 193.

ἔφθασεν δέ κτλ.] 'Tristis exitus' (Beng.). The wrath which in i. 10 was represented as 'coming' is now thought of as actually 'arrived,' thereby marking an 'end' in the history of God's dealings with the Jewish people. For this meaning of φθάνειν, which in late Gk. (perhaps in accordance with its original meaning, cf. Thuc. iii. 49 and see Geldart *Mod. Gk.* p. 206) has entirely lost the sense of anticipation, cf. Rom. ix. 31, 2 Cor. x. 14, Phil. iii. 16, and such passages from the papyri as P.Oxy. 237. vi. 30 f. (ii./A.D.) καὶ ὅτι φθάνει τὸ πρᾶγμα ἀκριβῶς [ἐξ]ητασμένον 'and the fact that a searching enquiry into the affair had already been held,' P.Fior. 9, 9 f. (iii./A.D.) φθάσαντός μου πρὸς τοῖς μναιμίοις (μνημείοις) 'when I had arrived near the tombs.' There is no need to treat the aor. as prophetic, resembling the Heb. perf. of prediction (Findlay): in accordance rather with one of its earliest usages it denotes what has *just happened*, and is thus best rendered in English by the perf. 'is (or has) come,' cf. Moulton *Prolegg.* p. 135, and for the survival of this ancient aor. in mod. Gk. (ἔφθασα = 'here I am') see p. 247. WH. read ἔφθακεν in the margin.

On ἡ ὀργή see the note on i. 10, and for the wrath coming upon (ἐπί) the Jews from above cf. Rom. i. 18 ἀποκαλύπτεται γὰρ ὀργὴ θεοῦ ἀπ' οὐρανοῦ ἐπὶ πᾶσαν ἀσέβειαν. The phrase φθάνειν ἐπί is found elsewhere in the N.T. only Mt. xii. 28, Lk. xi. 20: it occurs six times in the LXX. (Hawkins *Hor. Syn.* p. 51).

εἰς τέλος] an adv. phrase = 'finally,' 'to an end' (Vg. *in finem*, Weizsäcker *zum Ende*), in accordance with the regular N.T. usage (e.g. Mt. x. 22, Lk. xviii. 5, Jo. xiii. 1) supported by many passages in the LXX., e.g. Job xiv. 20, xx. 7, Pss. ix. 7, xlviii. (xlix.) 10 where it represents the Heb. לָנֶצַח. Some translators however prefer the intensive meaning 'to the uttermost,' 'completely' (Hofm. *ganz und gar*, Weiss *im höchsten Grade*), relying on such passages as 2 Chron. xii. 12 (for לְכַלֵּה), xxxi. 1 (for עַד־לְכַלֵּה); cf. also Pss. Sol. i. 1 with Ryle and James's note. In either case the sense remains much the same, namely, that in the case of the Jews the Divine ὀργή (πάλαι ὀφειλομένη κ. προωρισμένη κ. προφητευομένη, Chrys.) had now reached a final and complete end in contrast with the partial judgments which had hitherto been threatened (cf. Jer. iv. 27 συντέλειαν δὲ οὐ μὴ ποιήσω).

In what exactly this 'end' consisted is not so easy to determine, but in no case have we here any *direct* reference to the Fall of Jerusalem as Baur and other impugners of the Epistle's authenticity have tried to show (Intr. p. lxxiv). The whole conception is ethical, the Apostles finding in the determined blindness of the Jewish people with its attendant moral evils an infallible proof that the nation's day of grace was now over, cf. Rom. xi. 7 ff.

For an almost literal verbal parallel to the whole clause cf. *Test. xii patr.* Levi vi. 11 ἔφθασε δὲ αὐτοὺς ἡ ὀργὴ τοῦ θεοῦ εἰς τέλος, whence St Paul may have derived it, if it is not to be regarded as 'a half-stereotyped Rabbinical formula' (Lock, Hastings' *D.B.* iv. p. 746).

¹⁷ Ἡμεῖς δέ, ἀδελφοί, ἀπορφανισθέντες ἀφ' ὑμῶν πρὸς καιρὸν ὥρας, προσώπῳ οὐ καρδίᾳ, περισσοτέρως ἐσπου-

II. 17—III. 10. SUBSEQUENT RELATION OF THE APOSTLES TO THE THESSALONIAN CHURCH.

II. 17—20. Their Desire to revisit Thessalonica and its Cause.

From their outburst against their Jewish opponents the writers return to their relation to their Thessalonian converts, and in a paragraph full of deep feeling give expression to their anxiously-cherished desire to see them again. The paragraph is only loosely connected with the foregoing section, though the emphatic ἡμεῖς δέ (v. 17) may well stand in contrast with the Jews just spoken of. While these had done their utmost to prevent the preaching of the gospel in Thessalonica, the Apostles on their part had been only the more eager to resume their interrupted work. The main stress however is no longer, as in vv. 1—12, on the delivery of the message, but rather on the faith by which it had been received, and which was now in need of encouragement and comfort in view of the sufferings to which the Thessalonians were exposed. In no case does the passage contain an apology for the Apostles' absence, as if on their own account they had deserted the Thessalonian Church. On the contrary the vehemence of the language employed shows how keenly they felt the enforced absence.

17, 18. 'But as for ourselves, Brothers, when we had been bereaved of you for a short season, albeit the separation was in bodily presence, not in heart, we were exceedingly desirous to see you again face to face, and all the more so because of the hindrances we encountered. For when we had resolved to revisit you—so far indeed as I Paul was concerned this resolution was actually

come to on two separate occasions—it was only to find that Satan had effectually blocked our path.'

17. ἀπορφανισθέντες] The metaphor underlying ἀπορφανισθέντες (ἄπ. λεγ. N.T., elsewhere Aesch. *Choeph.* 241, Philo) can hardly be pressed in view of the latitude with which ὀρφανός is often used (e.g. Pind. *Isthm.* 7. 15 ὁ. ἑταίρων), though the closeness of the ties between the Apostles and their converts (cf. ii. 7, 11) makes the special meaning very appropriate here. Th. Mops.: 'desolati a uobis ad instar orphanorum'; Oecum.: ἄνω μὲν εἶπεν, ὅτι, ὡς πατὴρ τέκνα, καὶ ὡς τροφός· ἐνταῦθα δέ, ἀπορφανισθέντες ὅπερ ἐστὶ παίδων, πατέρας ἐπιζητούντων.

πρὸς καιρὸν ὥρας] 'for a space of an hour' (Vg. *ad tempus horae*, Beza *ad temporis momentum*), the combination laying stress on the shortness of the period referred to (cf. 'horae momento' Hor. *Sat.* I. i. 7 f., Plin. *N. H.* vii. 52). For the simple πρὸς καιρόν cf. Luke viii. 13, 1 Cor. vii. 5, and for πρὸς ὥραν cf. 2 Cor. vii. 8, Gal. ii. 5, and for πρός c. acc. to denote the time during which anything lasts cf. πρὸς ὀλίγον (1 Tim. iv. 8), πρὸς τὸ παρόν (Heb. xii. 11), and such a passage from the papyri as *C.P.R.* 32, 9 f. (iii./A.D.) πρὸς μόνον τὸ ἐνεστὸς β' ἔτος μισθώσασθαι.

προσώπῳ οὐ καρδίᾳ] 'a *local* dative ethically used' (Ellic. on Gal. i. 22): cf. WM. p. 270. The same contrast is found in 2 Cor. v. 12: for the thought cf. 1 Cor. v. 3, Col. ii. 5. Grotius cites by way of illustration the line descriptive of lovers, 'Illum absens absentem audituque videtque.'

περισσοτέρως ἐσπουδάσαμεν] 'were more exceedingly anxious'—a sense of *eagerness* being present in the verb ἐσπουδάσαμεν, which we do not usually associate with our Engl. 'endeavoured' (A.V., R.V.). Tindale,

δάσαμεν τὸ πρόσωπον ὑμῶν ἰδεῖν ἐν πολλῇ ἐπιθυμίᾳ. ¹⁸διότι ἠθελήσαμεν ἐλθεῖν πρὸς ὑμᾶς, ἐγὼ μὲν Παῦλος καὶ ἅπαξ καὶ δίς, καὶ ἐνέκοψεν ἡμᾶς ὁ Caτανᾶς. ¹⁹τίς

followed by Cranmer and the Genevan versions, has 'enforsed.' For σπουδάζειν, which in the N.T. is regularly constructed with inf. (in 2 Pet. i. 15 acc. and inf.), cf. Gal. ii. 10, Eph. iv. 3, 2 Tim. ii. 15, Heb. iv. 11, 2 Pet. i. 10, iii. 14.

The comparative περισσοτέρως (for form, WSchm. p. 98) is apparently never used in the Pauline writings without a comparison, either stated or implied, being present to the writer's mind (cf. WM. p. 304 f.). In the present instance this is best found not in the preceding ἀπορφ. ('separation, so far from weakening our desire to see you, has only increased it' Lft.), nor in what the Apostles had learned regarding the persecutions to which the Thessalonians had been exposed (P. Schmidt, Schmiedel), but in the hindrances which, according to the next verse, had been thrown in the way of their return, and which, instead of chilling their ardour, had rather increased it (Bornemann, Wohlenberg).

ἐν πολλῇ ἐπιθυμίᾳ] 'with great desire'—one of the few instances in the N.T. in which ἐπιθυμία is used in a good sense, cf. Lk. xxii. 15, Phil. i. 23, Rev. xviii. 14.

18. διότι ἠθελήσαμεν] 'because we had resolved'—with the idea of active decision or purpose which as a rule distinguishes θέλω in the N.T. from the more passive βούλομαι 'desire,' 'wish.' It is right however to add that by many scholars this distinction is reversed (see the elaborate note in Grimm-Thayer s.v. θέλω), while Blass (p. 54) regards the two words as practically synonymous in the N.T., though his contention that βούλομαι is 'literary' as compared with the more 'popular' (so mod. Greek)

θέλω cannot be maintained in view of the frequent occurrences of the former in the non-literary papyri. For the form θέλω which always stands in the N.T. for the Attic ἐθέλω, and which is always augmented in ἠ-, see WSchm. p. 54. Διότι (v. 8 note) is better separated only by a colon from the preceding clause.

ἐγὼ μὲν Παῦλος] For a similar emphatic introduction of the personal name cf. 2 Cor. x. 1, Gal. v. 2, Eph. iii. 1, Col. i. 23, Philem. 19. For μέν solitarium see Blass p. 267.

κ. ἅπαξ κ. δίς] 'both once and twice' i.e. 'twice' as in Phil. iv. 16; cf. Plato Phaedo 63 D καὶ δὶς καὶ τρίς. Where the first καί is wanting as in Deut. ix. 13, 2 Esdr. xxiii. (xiii.) 20, 1 Macc. iii. 30, the meaning may be more general 'once and again,' 'repeatedly.'

καὶ ἐνέκοψεν κτλ.] On καί here as not adversative (Hermann Vig. p. 521) but 'copulative and contrasting' see Ellic. on Phil. iv. 12 (cf. WM. p. 544 n.¹).

Ἐνκόπτω 'cut into' used originally of breaking up a road to render it impassable, came to mean 'hinder' generally (Hesych.: ἐμποδίζω, διακωλύω); cf. Ac. xxiv. 4, Rom. xv. 22, Gal. v. 7, 1 Pet. iii. 7, and see P.Alex. 4, 1 f. (iii./B.C.) ἡμῖν ἐνκόπτεις καλά. The exact nature of the hindrance is here left undefined, but in accordance with the profound Bibl. view it is referred in the last instance to Satan, as the personal force in whom all evil centres; cf. II. ii. 9, 2 Cor. xii. 7. In the LXX. σατάν is found in the general sense of 'adversary' in 3 Regn. xi. 14 without the art., and in Sir. xxi. 27 (30) with the art.: in the N.T. the name whether with or without the art., always denotes the Adversary κατ' ἐξοχήν. Elsewhere in this Ep. Satan

γὰρ ἡμῶν ἐλπὶς ἢ χαρὰ ἢ στέφανος καυχήσεως—ἢ οὐχὶ καὶ ὑμεῖς—ἔμπροσθεν τοῦ κυρίου ἡμῶν Ἰησοῦ ἐν τῇ αὐτοῦ παρουσίᾳ; ²⁰ ὑμεῖς γάρ ἐστε ἡ δόξα ἡμῶν καὶ ἡ χαρά.

is described as ὁ πειράζων (iii. 5). For the development of the Jewish belief in 'Satan' see *Enc. Bibl.* s.v., and cf. Bousset *Die Religion des Judentums*² (1906) p. 382 ff.

19. 'Nor is this longing on our part to be wondered at. If any deserve to be called our hope or joy or crown of holy boasting at the time when our Lord Himself appears, it is surely you. Yes indeed! you are our glory and our joy.'

19. τίς γὰρ ἡμῶν ἐλπὶς κτλ.] The warmth of the Apostles' feelings towards their converts now finds expression in one of the few rhetorical passages in the Ep. (Intr. p. lvii): cf. Phil. iv. 1. With ἡμῶν ἐλπίς cf. Liv. xxviii. 39 'Scipionem...spem omnem salutemque nostram' (cited by Wetstein).

The phrase στέφ. καυχήσεως (ἀγαλλιάσεως A, Tert. *exultationis*) is borrowed from the LXX. (cf. Prov. xvi. 31, Ezek. xvi. 12, xxiii. 42, where it translates the Heb. עֲטֶרֶת תִּפְאָרֶת), and in accordance with the general Bibl. use of στέφανος is to be understood of the 'wreath' or 'garland of victory' which their converts would prove to the Apostles at the Lord's appearing: cf. for the thought 2 Cor. i. 14, Phil. ii. 16. The distinction between στέφανος 'crown of victory' ('Kranz') and διάδημα 'crown of royalty' ('Krone') must not however be pressed too far (as Trench *Syn.* § xxiii.), for στέφανος is not infrequently used in the latter sense, see Mayor's note on Jas. i. 12, and add the use of στέφανος to denote the 'crown-tax' for the present made to the king on his accession or some other important occasion (cf. 1 Macc. x. 29, and see Wilcken *Ostraka* i. p. 295 ff.). In this latter connexion an

instructive parallel to the passage before us is afforded by P.Petr. II. 39 (*e*), 18 (iii./B.C.) where if we adopt Wilcken's emendation (*ut s.* p. 275) and read ἄλλου (*scil.* στεφάνου) παρουσίας, the reference is to an additional 'crown' given at the king's παρουσία or visit (cf. Add. Note F). For παράληψις τοῦ στεφάνου to denote entering on the priestly office see *B.C.H.* xi. p. 375, and for the general use of the term to denote a 'reward' for services performed see P.Cairo 5, 5 (ii./B.C.) where a certain Peteuris offers a στέφανον χαλκοῦ (τάλαντα) πέντε to the man who secures his freedom; cf. P.Grenf. I. 41, 3 (ii./B.C.), P.Par. 42, 12 (ii./B.C.), and see *Archiv* ii. p. 579.

The figure may also be illustrated from Jewish sources by *Pirqe Aboth* iv. 9, 'R. Çadoq said, Make them [thy disciples] not a crown, to glory in them' (Taylor, *Sayings of the Jewish Fathers*², p. 68).

ἢ οὐχὶ καὶ ὑμεῖς] a rhetorical parenthesis interjected into the main sentence to draw special attention to the position of the Thessalonians. Chrys.: οὐ γὰρ εἶπεν, ὑμεῖς, ἀλλά, " καὶ ὑμεῖς," μετὰ τῶν ἄλλων.

For the unusual use of the disjunctive particle ἤ (wanting in ℵ*) see Blass p. 266.

ἔμπροσθεν τοῦ κυρίου κτλ.] The first definite reference to the Parousia of the Lord Jesus which plays so large a part in these Epp., cf. iii. 13, iv. 15, v. 23, II. ii. 1, 8; Intr. p. lxix.

For the meaning of παρουσία see Add. Note F, and for ἐν not merely 'at the time of,' but 'involved in,' 'as the result of,' cf. 1 Cor. xv. 23 (with Alford's note).

20. ὑμεῖς γάρ ἐστε κτλ.] Γάρ here introduces a confirmatory reply 'Truly,' 'Yes indeed' (cf. 1 Cor. ix.

3—2

III. ¹Διὸ μηκέτι στέγοντες ηὐδοκήσαμεν καταλει-

10; Blass p. 274 f.), while the art. before δόξα marks out the Thessalonians in the language of fond exaggeration as 'the' glory of the Apostles (WSchm. p. 161). In accordance with its general meaning (v. 12 note) and the context (v. 19), the main reference in δόξα must be eschatological, so that the pres. ἐστέ is to be taken as practically = 'you are now and therefore will be.' On the depth of affection displayed in the whole passage Theodoret remarks: ἐπειδὴ μητρὶ ἑαυτὸν ἀπείκασε τιθηνουμένη τὰ βρέφη, τὰ αὐτῆς φθέγγεται ῥήματα. αὐταὶ γὰρ τὰ κομιδῇ νέα παιδία καὶ ἐλπίδα, καὶ χαράν, καὶ τὰ τοιαῦτα προσαγορεύειν εἰώθασι.

III. 1—10. *The Mission and Return of Timothy.*

Hindered in his own desire to revisit Thessalonica, St Paul now recalls how he had done the next best thing in his power by sending Timothy who had already proved himself so faithful a 'minister in the gospel of Christ' to establish his beloved Thessalonians amidst the 'afflictions' which were proving the inevitable accompaniment of their Christian calling (vv. 1—5): while at the same time he can find no adequate words to express his thankfulness at the 'good news' of which Timothy had been the bearer on his return (vv. 6—10).

1—5. 'Unable to bear the thought of this continued separation any longer, we made up our minds—I speak of Silas and myself—to be left behind alone, even though it was in Athens, a city "wholly given to idolatry," while we dispatched Timothy, our true brother in Christ, and called by God Himself to the ministry of the Gospel, in order that he might be the means not only of establishing you more firmly in your present conduct, but also of encouraging you in the heart-possession of the Faith. And there is the more need of this in view of the troubles which (so we hear) are now falling upon you, and by which if you are not on your guard you may be led astray. You cannot surely have forgotten that these are the inevitable lot of Christ's disciples. For even while we were still with you, we warned you clearly that we are bound to encounter trouble. And so it has now proved in your own experience. So anxious however are we still regarding you that—let me say it once more for myself—unable to bear the thought of this continued separation any longer, I sent Timothy to bring back a full report of your faith, lest, as we feared might have been the case, Satan had succeeded in tempting you, and our toil on your account had come to naught.'

1. Διὸ μηκέτι στέγοντες] 'Wherefore no longer bearing' (Vg. *non sustinentes amplius*) viz. the separation referred to in ii. 17 f. Στέγειν originally = 'cover,' and thence either 'keep in' in the sense of 'conceal,' 'hide,' or 'keep off' in the sense of 'bear up under,' 'endure' (Hesych.: στέγει· κρύπτει, συνέχει, βαστάζει, ὑπομένει). Either meaning yields good sense here and in v. 5, but the latter, as Lft. has shown, is to be preferred in view of 1 Cor. ix. 12, xiii. 7, the only other passages in the N.T. where the verb occurs, and its general use in later Gk. e.g. Philo *in Flacc.* § 9 (ii. p. 526 M.) μηκέτι στέγειν δυνάμενοι τὰς ἐνδείας. For the more literal sense of 'ward off' cf. Polyb. iii. 53. 2, Dittenberger *Sylloge*² 318, 24 (ii./B.C.) ἔστεξεν τὴν ἐπιφερομένην τῶν βαρβάρων ὁρμήν.

ηὐδοκήσαμεν καταλειφθῆναι κτλ.] Grot.: '*Triste* hoc, sed tamen hoc *libenter*, feceramus...vestri causa.' For ηὐδοκήσαμεν (Vg. *placuit nobis*) see ii. 8 note, and for καταλειφθῆναι in the sense of being left *behind* owing to the

III 2] THE FIRST EPISTLE TO THE THESSALONIANS 37

φθῆναι ἐν Ἀθήναις μόνοι, ²καὶ ἐπέμψαμεν Τιμόθεον, τὸν ἀδελφὸν ἡμῶν καὶ ⌜διάκονον τοῦ θεοῦ⌝ ἐν τῷ εὐαγγελίῳ τοῦ χριστοῦ, εἰς τὸ στηρίξαι ὑμᾶς καὶ παρακαλέσαι

III 2 διάκονον τοῦ θεοῦ ΝΑΡ 6 67** al Vg Go Boh Syr (Pesh Harcl) Aeth Bas Theod-Mops[lat]: συνεργὸν τοῦ θεοῦ D* 17 d Ephr (?) Ambst: συνεργὸν B Ephr (?)

departure of others cf. [Jo.] viii. 9, Ac. xxv. 14. Hence the verb is frequently used in connexion with dying (Deut. xxviii. 54, Prov. xx. 7, Mk. xii. 19, Lk. xx. 31), and is also the technical term in wills of the Ptolemaic period for 'bequeath,' e.g. P.Petr. I. 11, 9 f. (the will of a cavalry officer) ἐὰν δέ τι ἀνθρώπινον πάθω καταλείπω...τὸν ἵππον καὶ τὰ ὅπλα πτολεμαίῳ[ι]. In the same will, according to Mahaffy's restoration, the testator appoints a certain Demostratus his executor with the formula καταλείπω ἐπίτροπον. In the passage before us the 1st pers. plur. ηὐδοκήσαμεν may be understood of St Paul alone (Add. Note B), but in view of v. 5 (see note) is best referred to St Paul and Silas (cf. Intr. p. xxx). How keenly the two older Apostles felt the departure of their younger companion is proved by the emphatic μόνοι—the sense of loneliness being further deepened by their position in Athens 'urbe videlicet a Deo alienissimâ' (Beng.). [Cf. the now almost proverbial 'Alone in London.'] Calv.: 'signum ergo rari amoris est et anxii desiderii, quod se omni solatio privare non recusat, ut subveniat Thessalonicensibus.'

2. κ. ἐπέμψαμεν Τιμόθεον κτλ.] Timothy is described as ἀδελφός by St Paul in the salutations of 2 Cor., Col., and Philem. (cf. Heb. xiii. 23), but the title διάκονος is not elsewhere bestowed on him exc. in 1 Tim. iv. 6 (καλὸς ἔσῃ διάκονος Χρ. Ἰησοῦ). Here the lofty διάκ. τ. θεοῦ is further defined by ἐν τ. εὐαγγ. τ. χριστοῦ to mark the sphere in which the service or ministry is rendered, viz. 'the Gospel' which has for its object 'the Christ'

as the fulfiller of the one God's gracious purposes on His people's behalf (Add. Note D)—the whole description being intended not so much to emphasize the greatness of the Apostles' sacrifice in parting with Timothy, as to lay stress on the dignity of his mission and prevent the Thessalonians from undervaluing it (cf. 2 Cor. viii. 18 ff., Phil. ii. 20 ff.).

In contrast with δοῦλος or θεράπων, the servant in his relation to a *person*, διάκονος represents rather the servant in relation to his *work* (Trench *Syn.* § ix), and like ἐπίσκοπος (Deissmann, *BS.* p. 230 f.) is already found as a term. techn. in pre-Christian times. Thus in *C.I.G.* II. 3037 along with a ἱερεύς and a ἱέρεια of the δώδεκα θεῶν we hear of two διάκονοι and of a female διάκονος (cf. Rom. xvi. 1), and in Magn. 109 (c. i./B.C.) in a list of sacred functionaries there appear μάγειρος...διάκονος (cf. Thieme p. 17 f.).

The reading διάκ. τ. θεοῦ is however by no means certain in the passage before us, and if the marginal συνεργὸν [τοῦ θεοῦ] is adopted, the thought then finds a striking parallel in 1 Cor. iii. 9 θεοῦ γάρ ἐσμεν συνεργοί, cf. 2 Cor. vi. 1, viii. 23. Weiss (*Textkritik der paulinischen Briefe* (in *Text. u. Unter.* xiv. 3) p. 13) regards the reading of B συνεργόν without τοῦ θεοῦ as the original, on the ground that the genesis of the other variants is thus most easily explained.

εἰς τὸ στηρίξαι κτλ.] Στηρίζειν in its metaph. sense is found only in late Gk., cf. e.g. Epict. *Gnomologium Stobaei* 39 (ed. Schenkl) τοὺς ἐνοικοῦντας εὐνοίᾳ κ. πίστει κ. φιλίᾳ στήριξε. By St Paul, who uses it only in these Epp. and in Rom. (i. 11, xvi. 25), it is

38 THE FIRST EPISTLE TO THE THESSALONIANS [III 3, 4

ὑπὲρ τῆς πίστεως ὑμῶν ³τὸ μηδένα σαίνεσθαι ἐν ταῖς
θλίψεσιν ταύταις. αὐτοὶ γὰρ οἴδατε ὅτι εἰς τοῦτο
κείμεθα· ⁴καὶ γὰρ ὅτε πρὸς ὑμᾶς ἦμεν, προελέγομεν ὑμῖν
ὅτι μέλλομεν θλίβεσθαι, καθὼς καὶ ἐγένετο καὶ οἴδατε.

again combined with παρακαλέσαι (ii. 11 note) in II. ii. 17: for ἐπιστηρίζειν in the same combination cf. Ac. xiv. 22, xv. 32. Swete (*ad* Apoc. iii. 2) classes στηρίζειν with βεβαιοῦν and θεμελιοῦν as technical words in primitive *pastoralia*. For εἰς τό with inf. see the note on ii. 12.

ὑπὲρ τῆς πίστεως ὑμῶν] not 'concerning' (A.V., R.V.) but 'for the furtherance of your faith'—ὑπέρ here retaining something of its original force 'for the advantage or benefit of': contrast II. ii. 1.

3. τὸ μηδένα σαίνεσθαι κτλ.] 'to wit, that no one be led astray in the midst of these afflictions.' Ms. evidence is decisive in favour of τό (not τῷ) which introduces a statement in apposition to the whole foregoing clause, cf. iv. 6. Blass (p. 234) regards the art. as quite superfluous in both passages, but it may be taken as lending more weight to the inf. by making it substantival (cf. iv. 1 and see WM. p. 402 f.).

Σαίνεσθαι (ἄπ. λεγ. N.T.) is generally understood in the sense of 'be moved,' 'be shaken' (Hesych.: κινεῖσθαι, σαλεύεσθαι, ταράττεσθαι), but this is to lose sight unnecessarily of the original meaning of the word. Properly it is used of dogs in the sense of 'wag the tail,' 'fawn' (e.g. *Od.* x. 217 ὅτ' ἂν ἀμφὶ ἄνακτα κύνες ... σαίνωσιν), and hence came to be applied metaphorically to persons, 'fawn upon,' 'beguile' (e.g. Aesch. *Choeph.* 186 σαίνομαι δ' ὑπ' ἐλπίδος). What the Apostles evidently dreaded regarding the Thessalonians was that they would allow themselves to be 'drawn aside,' 'allured' from the right path in the midst of (ἐν) the afflictions (θλίψεσιν, i. 6 note) which were then (ταύταις)

falling upon them (cf. Zahn *Einl.* i. p. 159 f.).

For an entirely different rendering see Severianus (*apud* Cramer *Cat.* vi., p. 353) 'σαίνεσθαι' εἰπὼν τὸ μηδένα ξενίζεσθαι. Lachmann reads μηδὲν ἀσαίνεσθαι. For the reading of FG σιένεσθαι i.e. σιαίνεσθαι 'to be disturbed, troubled,' which has much to recommend it, see Soph. *Lex.* (*s.v.*), and cf. Nestle Z.N.T.W. vii. p. 361 f., and *Exp. T.* xviii. p. 479.

κείμεθα] 'we are appointed.' For κεῖμαι (practically perf. pass. of τίθημι for the rarely used τέθειμαι) in this sense cf. Lk. ii. 34, Phil. i. 16, Josh. iv. 6, and for the general thought see Mk. viii. 34, of which we may here have a reminiscence. The plur., while referring in the first instance to St Paul and his companions along with their Thessalonian converts, embodies a perfectly general statement. Calv.: '*in hoc sumus constituti*, tantundem valet ac si dixisset hac lege nos esse Christianos.'

4. καὶ γὰρ ὅτε πρὸς ὑμᾶς κτλ.] 'For in addition to other considerations when we were with you'—'γὰρ introducing the reason, καί throwing stress upon it' (Ellic.). Πρός is here construed with the acc. even after a verb of rest in accordance with its prevailing use in the N.T. (c. gen. 1, dat. 6, acc. 679, Moulton *Prolegg.* p. 106). Προλέγειν is sometimes understood in the sense of 'tell openly or plainly,' but the ordinary *predictive* force of προ- (Vg. *praedicebamus*) is more in harmony with the following clause: cf. 2 Cor. xiii. 2, Gal. v. 21.

ὅτι μέλλομεν θλίβεσθαι] 'that we are to suffer persecution'—ὅτι introducing the substance of what the

⁵διὰ τοῦτο κἀγὼ μηκέτι στέγων ἔπεμψα εἰς τὸ γνῶναι τὴν ⌜πίστιν ὑμῶν⌝, μή πως ἐπείρασεν ὑμᾶς ὁ πειράζων καὶ εἰς κενὸν γένηται ὁ κόπος ἡμῶν. ⁶″Αρτι δὲ ἐλθόντος

5 πίστιν ὑμῶν ℵADGKLP al pler : ὑμῶν πίστιν B 37 73 116

Apostles foretold, and μέλλομεν (c. pres. inf. as almost always in N.T.) bringing out its Divinely-appointed character : cf. Rom. viii. 13, 18, Gal. iii. 23. A striking parallel both in thought and expression to the whole passage is afforded by Ac. xiv. 22 where Paul and Barnabas are described as ἐπιστηρίζοντες τὰς ψυχὰς τῶν μαθητῶν, παρακαλοῦντες ἐμμένειν τῇ πίστει καὶ ὅτι διὰ πολλῶν θλίψεων δεῖ ἡμᾶς εἰσελθεῖν εἰς τὴν βασιλείαν τοῦ θεοῦ.'

5. διὰ τοῦτο κἀγώ κτλ.] So keenly alive was St Paul to the dangers threatening his beloved Thessalonians that he reiterates his eagerness with regard to the despatch of Timothy, employing now the emphatic 1st pers. sing. 'I also,' 'I on my part,' to bring out still more forcibly his own share in the joint-action already referred to (v. 1). A wholly different turn is given to the verse by Hofmann's suggestion (favoured by Spitta Urchristentum i. p. 121 ff.) that after the despatch of Timothy, and the subsequent departure of Silas, St Paul had still no rest, and in his anxiety despatched *another* messenger or letter on his own account. But if this were so, the fact and nature of this second sending would surely have been more clearly defined, whereas the actual words of vv. 1, 2 seem rather to be expressly repeated, in order to show that the same sending is still in view.

μή πως ἐπείρασεν κτλ.] Μή πως 'lest haply,' a combination found in the N.T. only in the Pauline Epp., and construed here with both ind. and subj.—the former (ἐπείρασεν) describing an action that the writers feared had already taken place, the latter (γένηται) a possible future consequence of that action: see WM. p. 633 f. and for a similar transition only this time from the subj. to the ind. cf. Gal. ii. 2. Findlay prefers to take the clause interrogatively to which there can be no grammatical objection, and which has the advantage of vividness : 'Had the Tempter anyhow tempted you, and would our toil prove in vain ?' For the thought cf. Jas. i. 13 and the agraphon ascribed to Christ in *Hom. Clem.* III. 55, p. 51, 20 τοῖς δὲ οἰομένοις ὅτι ὁ θεὸς πειράζει, ὡς αἱ γραφαὶ λέγουσιν, ἔφη· ὁ πονηρός ἐστιν ὁ πειράζων (Resch *Agrapha* (1889) pp. 115, 233).

ὁ πειράζων] subst. part. applied to Satan as in the history of the Lord's Temptation (Mt. iv. 3) to bring out his characteristic office ('seine nie ruhende Anstrengung' Everling *Angelologie*, p. 78): cf. 1 Cor. vii. 5 ἵνα μὴ πειράζῃ ὑμᾶς ὁ Σατανᾶς. For the distinction between πειράζω (Att. πειράω) and δοκιμάζω (ii. 4 note) see Trench *Syn.* § lxxiv.

εἰς κενόν] 'in vain,' 'to no purpose,' cf. 2 Cor. vi. 1, Gal. ii. 2, Phil. ii. 16.

6—10. 'In view then of the fears just spoken of, imagine our relief when Timothy brought back to us— as he has at this moment done—the tidings of your faith and love and of the kindly remembrance which you are always continuing to cherish of us, reciprocating our longing desire to meet again. To us such a report was a veritable gospel, and through your faith we ourselves were comforted amidst the crushing trials and cares we are encountering in our present work. No news could have

Τιμοθέου πρὸς ἡμᾶς ἀφ' ὑμῶν καὶ εὐαγγελισαμένου ἡμῖν τὴν πίστιν καὶ τὴν ἀγάπην ὑμῶν, καὶ ὅτι ἔχετε μνείαν ἡμῶν ἀγαθὴν πάντοτε ἐπιποθοῦντες ἡμᾶς ἰδεῖν καθάπερ

helped us more, and we seem to be entering on a new lease of life, so long as we hear that you are standing fast in the Lord. Words fail us indeed to express our thanksgiving to God for the joy with which you are filling our hearts in His sight—a joy that is finding unceasing expression in our ardent prayers that we may not only hear of you, but once more see you face to face, and make good any shortcomings in your faith.'

6. Ἄρτι] may be connected grammatically either with ἐλθόντος or with the principal verb παρεκλήθημεν, but the former arrangement is decidedly preferable. Timothy's return had been anxiously waited for, and no sooner had he returned than St Paul proceeded to give vent to the feelings of thankfulness and joy that filled his heart. Beng.: 'statim sub Timothei adventum, recenti gaudio, tenerrimo amore, haec scribit.'

For ἄρτι denoting strictly *present* time ('just now,' 'at this moment') as contrasted with time past or future cf. Jo. ix. 19, 25, Gal. i. 9 f., 1 Cor. xiii. 12, 1 Pet. i. 6, 8, also Epict. *Diss.* ii. 17. 15 ἀφῶμεν ἄρτι τὸν δεύτερον τόπον, *B.G.U.* 594, 5 f. (i./A.D.) μετὰ τὸν θερισμὸ[ν ἐργολ]αβήσομα[ι], ἄρτι γὰρ ἀσθενῶι. See further Lob. *Phryn.* p. 18 ff., Rutherford *N.P.* p. 70 ff.

εὐαγγελισαμένου] 'Participium insigne' (Beng.). So good was Timothy's news that to the Apostles it was a veritable 'gospel.' The point is lost in the Latin verss. which give *adnuntiante* or *cum adnuntiasset*: in the Latin of Th. Mops. however we find *euangelizante*. Chrys.: ὁρᾷς τὴν περιχάρειαν Παύλου; οὐκ εἶπεν, ἀπαγγείλαντος, ἀλλ' 'εὐαγγελισαμένου'· τοσοῦτον ἀγαθὸν ἡγεῖτο τὴν ἐκείνων βεβαίωσιν καὶ τὴν ἀγάπην.

For the history of εὐαγγελίζομαι, which is only found here in the Pauline Epp. in its wider sense, see Add. Note E.

τ. πίστιν κ. τ. ἀγάπην ὑμ.] Calv.: 'totam enim pietatis summam breviter indicat his duobus verbis.' The same combination is found again in v. 8 and several times in the Pastoral Epp. (I Tim. i. 14, ii. 15 &c.), and always in this order (cf. however Philem. 5): on the other hand in Rev. ii. 19 St John characteristically places τ. ἀγάπην first.

καὶ ὅτι ἔχετε κτλ.] Yet a third point in Timothy's good news. Notwithstanding the efforts of the hostile Jews, the Thessalonians had always (πάντοτε) cherished, and were still cherishing (ἔχετε) a 'kindly remembrance' towards their former teachers. For μνείαν ἔχειν 'hold, maintain a recollection' cf. 2 Tim. i. 3, and for ἀγαθός in the sense of 'friendly,' 'well-disposed,' cf. Rom. v. 7 (with Gifford's note), Tit. ii. 5, 1 Pet. ii. 18, and see further on v. 15.

ἐπιποθοῦντες ἡμᾶς ἰδεῖν κτλ.] 'longing to see us...': cf. Rom. i. 11, 2 Tim. i. 4. Ἐπιποθεῖν, a favourite word with St Paul who uses it seven out of the nine times in which it occurs in the N.T. (elsewhere Jas. iv. 5, 1 Pet. ii. 2). It seems to be somewhat stronger than the simple ποθεῖν (not found in N.T.), ἐπι- by marking direction ('idem declarat, quod πόθον ἔχειν ἐπί τινα' Fritzsche *Rom.* i. 11) lending a certain intensity to the idea, though this must not be pressed in view of the fondness of late Gk. for compounds which have lost their strong sense: cf. especially for its use here Diod. Sic. xvii. 101 καὶ παρόντι μὲν οὐ χρησάμενος, ἀπόντα δὲ ἐπιποθήσας.

For καθάπερ see ii. 11 note, and for

καὶ ἡμεῖς ὑμᾶς, ⁷διὰ τοῦτο παρεκλήθημεν, ἀδελφοί, ἐφ' ὑμῖν ἐπὶ πάσῃ τῇ ἀνάγκῃ καὶ θλίψει ἡμῶν διὰ τῆς ὑμῶν πίστεως, ⁸ὅτι νῦν ζῶμεν ἐὰν ὑμεῖς στήκετε ἐν κυρίῳ. ⁹τίνα γὰρ εὐχαριστίαν δυνάμεθα τῷ θεῷ ἀνταποδοῦναι

καί in sentences of comparison cf. WM. p. 548 f.

7. διὰ τοῦτο παρεκλήθημεν κτλ.] 'On this account'—the sing. τοῦτο gathering up as a unity the faith and the love and the kindly remembrance just spoken of—' we were comforted over you,' as the basis on which our παράκλησις rested (cf. 2 Cor. vii. 7). Nor was this all, but the comfort which the Apostles experienced on the Thessalonians' account bore also ἐπὶ πάσῃ τ. ἀνάγκῃ κτλ., from which at the time they themselves were suffering (2 Cor. vi. 4, xii. 10)—ἐπί having again a slightly *local* force, which can, however, hardly be brought out in English.

For ἀνάγκη in its derived sense in Hellenistic Gk. of outward calamity or distress cf. Lk. xxi. 23, 1 Cor. vii. 26, Pss. Sol. v. 8, Dittenberger *Sylloge²* 255, 23 f. ἐν ἀνάγκαις καὶ κακοπαθίαις γένηται, and for the combination with θλίψις (i. 6 note) cf. Job xv. 24, Pss. cvi. (cvii.) 6, cxviii. (cxix.) 143, Zeph. i. 15. How little the Apostles were disturbed by this 'distress and affliction' is proved by the emphatic διὰ τ. ὑμ. πίστεως with which they return to the ground of comfort they have just received, and in so doing prepare the way for the striking declaration of the next verse.

8. ὅτι νῦν ζῶμεν] In view of the preceding ἄρτι (*v.* 6), νῦν is best taken in its full temporal force, and if so ζῶμεν can only refer to the present life lived in the fulness of power and satisfaction (Calv.: 'vivimus, inquit, hoc est recte valemus'): cf. 2 Cor. vi. 9 and for the thought see 2 Cor. iv. 7—15. For a similar use of ζῆν corresponding to the Heb. חָיָה in the pregnant sense of fulness of life in the Divine favour

cf. Deut. viii. 3, Pss. cxviii. (cxix.) 40, 93, cxxxvii. (cxxxviii.) 7, Isa. xxxviii. 16.

ἐὰν ὑμεῖς στήκετε κτλ.] 'if ye stand fast in the Lord' (Beza *si vos perstatis in Domino*; Est. 'si vos in fide Christi Domini constantes permanetis')—the condition on which the Apostles' 'life' depended, and which is expressed by ἐάν with the ind., perhaps to bring out more strongly the writers' confidence that it would certainly be fulfilled.

For other exx. of ἐάν with ind. in the N.T. cf. Lk. xix. 40, Ac. viii. 31, 1 Jo. v. 15, and such passages from the LXX. as Gen. xliv. 30 ἐὰν εἰσπορεύομαι, Job xxii. 3 ἐὰν σὺ ἦσθα. The same irregularity is frequent in the papyri, e.g. P.Tebt. 58, 55 f. (ii./B.C.) ἐὰν δεῖ, P.Amh. 93, 24 (ii./A.D.) ἐὰν φαίνεται (Moulton *Prolegg.* p. 168).

For the late form στήκω (mod. Gk. στέκω) formed from the perf. ἕστηκα cf. II. ii. 15, 1 Cor. xvi. 13, Phil. i. 27, and see WH.² *Notes* p. 176, Dieterich *Untersuchungen* p. 219. Bornemann suggests that in ζῶμεν, ἐὰν ὑμεῖς | στήκετε ἐν κυρίῳ we may have a citation, somewhat altered, from a Jewish or a Christian hymn.

9. τίνα γὰρ εὐχαριστίαν κτλ.] Thdt.: νικᾷ τῆς εὐφροσύνης τὸ μέγεθος τῆς γλώττης τὴν ὑμνῳδίαν. Εὐχαριστία, which in the LXX. is confined to the apocr. books, is used by St Paul twelve times in a theological sense: cf. Rev. iv. 9, vii. 12, where it is found in doxologies, and see Ac. xxiv. 3 for its only other occurrence in the N.T. The word, of which I have as yet found only one ex. in the papyri P.Lond. III. 1178, 25 (ii./A.D.), is frequent in the inscriptions, e.g. *O.G.I.S.* 227, 6 (iii./B.C.) διὰ τὴν τοῦ δήμου εὐχα-

42 THE FIRST EPISTLE TO THE THESSALONIANS [III 10, 11

περὶ ὑμῶν ἐπὶ πάσῃ τῇ χαρᾷ ᾗ χαίρομεν δι' ὑμᾶς ἔμπροσθεν τοῦ θεοῦ ἡμῶν, ¹⁰νυκτὸς καὶ ἡμέρας ὑπερεκπερισσοῦ δεόμενοι εἰς τὸ ἰδεῖν ὑμῶν τὸ πρόσωπον καὶ
καταρτίσαι τὰ ὑστερήματα τῆς πίστεως ὑμῶν;   ¹¹Αὐτὸς

ριστίαν. For its later Christian usage see a note by Dr Hort published in *J.T.S.* iii. p. 594 ff. The ἀντι- in ἀνταποδοῦναι expresses the idea of full, complete return, cf. II. i. 6. The verb is used in a good sense as here in Lk. xiv. 14, Rom. xi. 35 (cf. 2 Cor. vi. 13 ἀντιμισθία), and in a bad sense in Rom. xii. 19, Heb. x. 30 (both from LXX.).

ἐπὶ πάσῃ τ. χαρᾷ κτλ.] For ἐπί pointing to the *basis* of the thanksgiving (O.L. *super omne gaudium* rather than Vg. *in omni gaudio*) see note on *v.* 7. ᾗ χαίρομεν is usually understood as a case of attraction for ἣν χαίρ.: cf. however the cognate dat. in Jo. iii. 29 χαρᾷ χαίρει. Δι' ὑμᾶς 'because of you,' emphasizing more pointedly the περὶ ὑμῶν of the previous clause. '*Ten times*, with an emphasis of affection, is the pronoun ὑμεῖς repeated in *vv.* 6—10' (Findlay).

ἔμπροσθεν τ. θεοῦ ἡμ.] to be connected with χαίρομεν, and deepening the thought of the joy by referring it to its true author. It was because their success in the work entrusted to them was due to 'our God' (ii. 2 note) that the Apostles could thus rejoice 'before' Him.

10. νυκτ. κ. ἡμ....δεόμενοι] a partic. adjunct developing the main thought of the preceding verse. For the phrase νυκτ. κ. ἡμ. see ii. 9 note, and for an interesting parallel, apparently from a heathen source (Intr. p. lxiv), to its use in the present passage cf. *B.G.U.* 246, 11 ff. (ii.—iii./A.D.) οὐκ ἰδότες, ὅτι νυκτὸς καὶ ἡμέρας ἐντυνχάνω τῷ θεῷ ὑπὲρ ὑμῶν.

Ὑπερεκπερισσοῦ (O.L. *superabundantius*, Ambrstr. *abundantissime*) is found elsewhere only in *v.* 13 and Eph. iii. 20. For the form see Buttmann p. 321, and for St Paul's fondness for compounds in ὑπερ- see Ellic. on Eph. iii. 20 and cf. the note on II. i. 3.

Δεόμενοι 'beseeching' stronger than προσευχόμενοι, and embodying a sense of personal need. Except for Mt. ix. 38 the verb is confined in the N.T. to Luke[15] and Paul[6]. It is very common in petitions addressed to ruling sovereigns as distinguished from those addressed to magistrates where ἀξιῶ is preferred, e.g. P.Amh. 33, 21 (ii./B.C.) where certain petitioners appeal to Ptolemy Philometor and Cleopatra II. to rectify a legal irregularity—δεόμεθ' ὑμῶν τῶν μεγίστων θεῶν κτλ.: see further R. Laqueur *Quaestiones Epigraphicae et Papyrologicae Selectae* (1904) p. 3 ff.

εἰς τὸ ἰδεῖν κτλ.] 'to see your face' —the εἰς phrase doing little more here than take the place of a simple inf. as obj. of the foregoing verb (Votaw p. 21).

καταρτίσαι] Καταρτίζειν originally to 'fit' or 'join together' (cf. Mk. i. 19 καταρτίζοντας τὰ δίκτυα) is used in the N.T. especially by St Paul and in the Ep. to the Hebrews in the general sense of 'prepare' or 'perfect' anything for its full destination or use (Rom. ix. 22, 1 Cor. i. 10, Gal. vi. 1, Heb. x. 5 (LXX.), xi. 3), the further thought in the present passage of supplying *what is lacking* being suggested by the accompanying τ. ὑστερήματα τ. πίστ. ὑμ. 'the shortcomings (Wycl. *the thingis that failen*) of your faith.' For ὑστέρημα cf. 1 Cor. xvi. 17, 2 Cor. viii. 13 f., ix. 12, xi. 9, Phil. ii. 30, Col. i. 24, and for πίστις see *v.* 2 note. Calv.:

III 12] THE FIRST EPISTLE TO THE THESSALONIANS 43

δὲ ὁ θεὸς καὶ πατὴρ ἡμῶν καὶ ὁ κύριος ἡμῶν Ἰησοῦς κατευθύναι τὴν ὁδὸν ἡμῶν πρὸς ὑμᾶς· [12]ὑμᾶς δὲ ὁ κύριος

'Hinc etiam patet quam necessaria sit nobis doctrinae assiduitas: neque enim in hoc tantum ordinati sunt doctores, ut uno die vel mense homines adducant ad fidem Christi, sed ut fidem inchoatam perficiant.'

III. 11—13. PRAYER.
This section of the Ep. is now closed with a Prayer which in its two petitions re-echoes the longings of the constant prayer of v. 10.

11—13. 'But after all is said and done, it is to God that we must look for the success of our efforts. May He open up our way to return to you. And in any case, whatever may be the Divine pleasure with regard to us, may the Lord Jesus grant you an increasing and overflowing love not only towards one another but towards all men, after the measure of the love which we on our part are displaying towards you. It is our earnest prayer indeed that this love may be the means of so inwardly strengthening your hearts that your lives may show themselves free from reproach and holy in the sight of the all-seeing God, when the Lord Jesus comes with all His holy ones.'

Αὐτὸς δέ] There is no need to seek any definite contrast for the emphatically placed αὐτός either in δεόμενοι (v. 10) or in Satan who had hitherto been blocking their path (ii. 18). It arises simply from the writers' constant habit of referring everything in the last instance to the direct agency of God, 'Now may God Himself...': see Intr. p. lxv, and for the apparent weakening of αὐτὸς ὁ in Hellen. Gk. see Moulton *Prolegg.* p. 91.

καὶ ὁ κύριος ἡμῶν κτλ.] For the close union of ὁ κύρ. Ἰησ. (Add. Note D) with ὁ θεός κτλ. followed by a verb in the sing. see Intr. p. lxvi.

κατευθύναι 'make straight' rather than 'direct' (Vg. *dirigat*), in accordance with the original meaning of the word, and the removal of the obstacles (ἐνέκοψεν, ii. 18 note) here prayed for. The verb occurs elsewhere in the N.T. only in a metaphorical sense (II. iii. 5, Lk. i. 79), and for a similar use in the LXX. see 1 Chron. xxix. 18, 2 Chron. xix. 3, Ps. xxxvi. (xxxvii.) 23 παρὰ Κυρίου τὰ διαβήματα ἀνθρώπου κατευθύνεται. The opt. κατευθύναι (WSchm. p. 114) is here used without ἄν to express a wish as frequently in these Epp., iii. 12, v. 23, II. ii. 17, iii. 5, 16 (Burton §§ 175, 176).

12. ὑμᾶς δὲ ὁ κύριος...] Ὑμᾶς emphatic, marking the Apostles' desire that whatever the Lord may be proposing as regards themselves ('sive nos veniemus, sive minus' Beng.), the Thessalonians at least will not come short in any good gift. Ὁ κύριος may apply to God, but in view of the general Pauline usage, and the application of the title to Jesus in the preceding clause, it is best understood of Him again: cf. Add. Note D, and for prayer addressed to the Lord Jesus see Intr. p. lxvi.

It is not easy to distinguish between πλεονάσαι and περισσεύσαι (for forms, WSchm. p. 114), but the latter verb is the stronger of the two, implying an *overplus* of love, and hence is often used by St Paul in referring to the Divine grace: cf. Rom. v. 15, 20 (ὑπερπερισσεύειν), 2 Cor. ix. 8, Eph. i. 8, and see Fritzsche *Röm.* i. p. 351. For its use here in connexion with ἀγάπῃ (for dat. cf. Ac. xvi. 5, 2 Cor. iii. 9) cf. Phil. i. 9 ἵνα ἡ ἀγάπη ὑμῶν ἔτι μᾶλλον καὶ μᾶλλον περισσεύῃ ἐν ἐπιγνώσει κτλ., and Bacon's fine saying 'Sola charitas non admittit excessum' (*de augm. Scient.* vii. 3) cited by Gwynn *ad loc.* Chrys.: ὁρᾷς τὴν μανίαν τῆς ἀγάπης

πλεονάσαι καὶ περισσεύσαι τῇ ἀγάπῃ εἰς ἀλλήλους καὶ εἰς πάντας, καθάπερ καὶ ἡμεῖς εἰς ὑμᾶς, ¹³ εἰς τὸ στηρίξαι ὑμῶν τὰς καρδίας ⌈ἀμέμπτους⌉ ἐν ἁγιωσύνῃ ἔμπροσθεν τοῦ θεοῦ καὶ πατρὸς ἡμῶν ἐν τῇ παρουσίᾳ τοῦ κυρίου ἡμῶν Ἰησοῦ μετὰ πάντων τῶν ἁγίων αὐτοῦ.ᵀ

13 ἀμέμπτους] ἀμέμπτως BL 17 31 47 137 Boh (?) Ps-Ath αὐτοῦ solum ℵᶜBDᶜGKL al pler g Vgᶜᵒᵈᵈ ᵃˡⁱᑫ Go Syr (Pesh Harcl) Arm Ephr Chr Thdt Ambst Theod-Mopsˡᵃᵗ: αὐτοῦ ἀμήν ℵ*AD* 37 al pauc d Vg Boh Aeth

τὴν ἀκάθεκτον, τὴν διὰ τῶν ῥημάτων δεικνυμένην; 'Πλεονάσαι, φησί, καὶ περισσεύσαι,' ἀντὶ τοῦ, αὐξῆσαι. This is one of the few passages in the N.T. where περισσεύειν is used *transitively* (Lk. xv. 17, 2 Cor. iv. 15(?), ix. 8, Eph. i. 8): the *transitive* use of πλεονάζειν (contrast II. i. 3) can be paralleled only from the LXX. (Numb. xxvi. 54, Ps. lxx. (lxxi.) 21). As regards the objects of this abounding love on the Thessalonians' part, they are in the first instance their fellow-believers at Thessalonica (εἰς ἀλλήλους), and then all men without distinction (εἰς πάντας), and not merely those of the same faith elsewhere (τ. ὁμοπίστους, Thdt.): cf. v. 15, and for the thought see Rom. xii. 16 f., Gal. vi. 10, 1 Pet. ii. 17.

καθάπερ κ. ἡμεῖς κτλ.] a clause added to strengthen the Apostles' prayer by an appeal to their own example. Thpht.: ἔχετε γὰρ μέτρον καὶ παράδειγμα τῆς ἀγάπης ἡμᾶς. For καθάπερ see ii. 11 note.

13. εἰς τὸ στηρίξαι κτλ.] For εἰς τό with inf. to denote end or purpose see note on ii. 12, and for στηρίξαι see note on iii. 2. The combination στηρίξαι καρδίας is found again in Jas. v. 8, where however there is an appeal to human effort, and not, as generally elsewhere, to the strengthening influence of the Divine working (II. ii. 17, 1 Pet. v. 10, Ps. l. (li.) 14, Sir. vi. 37, Pss. Sol. xvi. 12): cf. also Sir. xxii. 16 (19 f.) καρδία ἐστηριγμένη ἐπὶ διανοήματος βουλῆς ἐν καιρῷ οὐ δειλιάσει.

ἀμέμπτους ἐν ἁγιωσύνῃ] '(so as to be) unblameable in holiness': cf. WM. p. 779. For the force of ἄμεμπτος (ἀμέμπτως, WH. mg.) cf. *C.P.R.* 27 (a marriage-contract—ii./A.D.) αὐτῆς δὲ τῆς Θ. ἄμεμπτον καὶ ἀκατηγόρητον παρεχομένης.

Ἁγιωσύνη (for form, WH.² *Notes* p. 159) is used in the LXX. only of the Divine attributes, e.g. Pss. xxix. (xxx.) 5, xcv. (xcvi.) 6 &c.: cf. 2 Macc. iii. 12 (with reference to the temple) τοὺς πεπιστευκότας τῇ τοῦ τόπου ἁγιωσύνῃ. As distinguished from *ἁγιασμός* the *process* of sanctification (iv. 3 f., 7, II. ii. 13, Heb. xii. 14, 1 Pet. i. 2) ἁγιωσύνη points rather to the resulting *state* (Rom. i. 4, 2 Cor. vii. 1), and is thus closely akin to ἁγιότης (Heb. xii. 20) in which, however, the thought of the abstract quality predominates. An interesting parallel to its use in the passage before us is afforded by *Test. xii. patr.* Levi xviii. 11, where it is said of the saints in Paradise, καὶ πνεῦμα ἁγιωσύνης ἔσται ἐπ' αὐτοῖς. Th. Mops. rightly draws attention to the connexion with the following ἁγίων: 'per quam (sc. sanctitatem) poteritis etiam in futuro die fiduciam ad Deum adsequi, cum ceteris omnibus qui placite conuersantur in uirtute.'

ἔμπροσθεν τ. θεοῦ κτλ.] Two conditions of this 'blamelessness in holiness' on the Thessalonians' part are now stated (1) that it will be realized ἔμπροσθεν τ. θεοῦ κτλ. to whom it is due, and by whom it will be tested (cf. ii. 4), and (2) that this will take place at the Parousia of the Lord Jesus, to which throughout these Epp. the writers point as the goal of all Christian hope (Intr. p. lxix).

μετὰ πάντων τ. ἁγίων αὐτοῦ] There is considerable difference of opinion as to whether we are to understand by οἱ ἅγιοι (1) 'saints' in the sense of just men made perfect, or (2) 'angels,' or (3) a general term including both. The first reference is rendered almost necessary by the regular Pauline use of the term (II. i. 10, 1 Cor. i. 2 &c.), and is supported by the place assigned to holy 'men' in such passages as iv. 14, 1 Cor. vi. 2 (cf. Mt. xix. 28, xx. 21, Rev. ii. 26 f., xx. 4, and Sap. iii. 8 κρινοῦσιν [δικαίων ψυχαὶ] ἔθνη καὶ κρατήσουσιν λαῶν). On the other hand, though οἱ ἅγιοι is nowhere else expressly applied to 'angels' in the N.T., they are so frequently described in this way both in the O.T. and later Jewish literature (see especially Zech. xiv. 5 on which this passage is evidently founded καὶ ἥξει Κύριος ὁ θεός μου, καὶ πάντες οἱ ἅγιοι μετ᾽ αὐτοῦ, and cf. Dan. iv. 10 (13), viii. 13, Pss. Sol. xvii. 49, Enoch i. 9 with Charles's note), and are so expressly associated with the returning Christ elsewhere (cf. II. i. 7, Mt. xiii. 41, Mk. viii. 38 μετὰ τῶν ἀγγέλων τῶν ἁγίων), that it seems impossible to exclude the thought of them altogether here. On the whole therefore the term is best taken in its widest sense as including all (note πάντων), whether glorified men or angels, who will swell the triumph of Christ's Parousia. As further illustrating the vague use of the term, it is of interest to notice that in Didache xvi. 7 its original reference to 'angels' in Zech. xiv. 5 (cited above) is lost sight of, and the passage is applied to risen Christian believers.

For the general thought cf. such passages from Jewish apoc. literature as 4 Ezra vii. 28 : 'reuelabitur enim filius meus Iesus [Syr Ar[1] Messias] cum his qui cum eo, et iocundabit qui relicti sunt annis quadringentis' : xiii. 52 'sic non poterit quisque super terram uidere filium meum uel eos qui cum eo sunt nisi in tempore diei' : *Asc. Isai.* iv. 16, 'But the saints will come with the Lord with their garments which are (now) stored up on high in the seventh heaven : with the Lord they will come, whose spirits are clothed, they will descend and be present in the world, and He will strengthen those, who have been found in the body, together with the saints, in the garments of the saints, and the Lord will minister to those who have kept watch in this world.'

The ἀμήν at the end of the verse (WH. mg.) is well-attested, and its disappearance in certain MSS. may perhaps be traced to the apparent improbability of its occurrence in the middle of an Epistle. 'Videtur αμην hoc loco interiectum offendisse' (Tisch.). On the other hand its addition can be equally readily explained through the influence of liturgical usage.

IV. 1—V. 24. HORTATORY AND DOCTRINAL.

IV. 1—12. LESSONS IN CHRISTIAN MORALS.

With c. iv. we enter on the more directly practical side of the Ep., exhortation and doctrine being closely intermingled (Intr. p. lxxi) with the view of conveying certain great lessons in Christian morals of which the Apostles knew their converts to stand in need.

The section opens with an exhortation of a general character.

IV. 1, 2. General Exhortation.

1, 2. 'And now, Brothers, to apply more directly what we have been saying, we entreat you as friends, nay we exhort you with authority in the Lord, to carry out ever more fully the mode of life which is pleasing to God, as you have already learned it from

46 THE FIRST EPISTLE TO THE THESSALONIANS [IV 1

IV. ¹⌜λοιπόν⌝, ἀδελφοί, ἐρωτῶμεν ὑμᾶς καὶ παρακαλοῦμεν ἐν κυρίῳ 'Ιησοῦ, [ἵνα] καθὼς παρελάβετε παρ'

IV 1 λοιπόν solum B* 17 31 al pauc Vg^codd aliq Syr (Pesh) Boh Arm Orig Chr Theod-Mops^lat: λοιπὸν οὖν ℵADG al pler ἵνα BD*G 17 37 al pauc Lat (Vet Vg) Syr (Pesh) Boh Arm Go Chr ½ Ambst : om ℵAD^cKL al pler Syr (Harcl) Aeth Chr ½ Thdt Theod-Mops^lat al

us. We know indeed that you are doing this, but there is still room for progress, as you cannot but be aware in view of our previous instructions.'

1. Λοιπόν] a colloquial expression frequently used to point forward to a coming conclusion (cf. 2 Cor. xiii. 11, 2 Tim. iv. 8 ; τὸ λοιπ. II. iii. 1, Phil. iv. 8), but in itself doing little more than mark the transition to a new subject as in late Gk. where it is practically equivalent to an emphatic οὖν: cf. Polyb. i. 15. 11 λοιπὸν ἀνάγκη συγχωρεῖν, τὰς ἀρχὰς καὶ τὰς ὑποθέσεις εἶναι ψευδεῖς, Epict. Diss. i. 22. 15 ἄρχομαι λοιπὸν μισεῖν αὐτόν, and the other passages cited by Jannaris Exp. v. viii. p. 429 f. : see also Schmid Attic. iii. p. 135. As showing its frequency as a connecting particle in the Κοινή (cf. B.G.U. 1039, 8 (Byz.))¸ Wilcken remarks that it has passed over into Coptic in this sense (Archiv iii. p. 507). In mod. Gk. λοιπόν has displaced οὖν altogether.

In the present passage οὖν is retained in the text by WH. mg., Tischdf., Zimmer, Nestle. It might easily have dropped out after the -ον of λοιπόν: on the other hand the combination λοιπὸν οὖν is found nowhere else in the N.T., cf. however B.G.U. 1079, 6 ff. (a private letter— i./A.D.) λοιπὸν οὖν ἔλαβον παρὰ το(ῦ) Ἄραβος τὴν ἐπιστολὴν καὶ ἀνέγνων καὶ ἐλυπήθην.

ἐρωτῶμεν ὑμᾶς κτλ.] 'Ερωτᾶν in class. Gk. always = 'interrogare' is frequently used in the N.T. = 'rogare,' cf. v. 12, II. ii. 1, Phil. iv. 3, the only other occurrences of the word in the Pauline writings. This usage is amply vouched for in the Κοινή (e.g. P.Oxy.

292, 7 f. (i./A.D.) ἠρώτησα δὲ καὶ Ἐρμί[α]ν τὸν ἀδελφὸν διὰ γραπτοῦ ἀνηγεί[σθαί] σοι περὶ τούτου, and the other exx. below), and need therefore no longer be traced to the influence of the Heb. שׁאל (cf. Deissmann BS. pp. 195 f., 290 f.). In this, its later sense, ἐρωτᾶν can hardly be distinguished from αἰτεῖν, though by laying greater stress on the person asked than on the thing asked for, it is more appropriate in exhortation (Grimm-Thayer s.v. αἰτέω). The note of urgency underlying its use is heightened here by its conjunction with παρακαλοῦμεν (ii. 11 note), and still more by the addition of ἐν κυρίῳ Ἰησοῦ, pointing to the real source of the writers' authority (cf. Eph. iv. 17).

For the conjunction of the two words in epistolary phrases cf. P.Oxy. 294, 28 f. (i./A.D.) ἐρωτῶ δέ σε καὶ παρακαλ[ῶ γρά]ψει μοι ἀντιφώνησιν περὶ τῶν γενομέν[ων], 744, 6 f. (i./B.C.) ἐρωτῶ σε καὶ παρακαλῶ σε ἐπιμελήθ<ητ>ι τῷ παιδίῳ. The latter papyrus also supplies an instance of ἐρωτάω construed with ἵνα, 13 f. ἐρωτῶ σε οὖν ἵνα μὴ ἀγωνιάσῃς 'I urge you therefore not to worry.'

[ἵνα] καθὼς παρελάβετε] '[that] even as ye received.' If ἵνα is read it should have a comma placed after it to show that it really belongs to the last clause of the verse, where, on account of the long parenthesis, it is repeated. For this semi-final ἵνα when the subject of the prayer is blended with its purpose cf. v. 4, II. i. 11, iii. 1, 2, 2 Cor. i. 17, and for the development of this usage in the later language see Hatzidakis p. 214 ff., Moulton Prolegg. p. 206 ff. A good

IV 2] THE FIRST EPISTLE TO THE THESSALONIANS 47

ἡμῶν τὸ πῶς δεῖ ὑμᾶς περιπατεῖν καὶ ἀρέσκειν θεῷ, καθὼς καὶ περιπατεῖτε,—ἵνα περισσεύητε μᾶλλον. ²οἴδατε γὰρ τίνας παραγγελίας ἐδώκαμεν ὑμῖν διὰ τοῦ κυρίου

ex. from the Κοινή occurs in the Christian papyrus-letter already cited P.Heid. 6, 14 ff. (iv./A.D.) παρακαλῶ [ὁ]ῦν, δέσποτα, ἵνα μνημον[ε]ύης μοι εἰς τὰς ἁγίας σου εὐχάς, ἵνα δυνηθῶμεν μέρος τὸν (ἁμ)αρτιῶν καθαρίσεως.

Παραλαμβάνω as usual lays stress not so much on the manner of the Thessalonians' receiving, as on the contents of what they received : cf. note on ii. 13, and for περιπατεῖν as the result of this teaching see II. iii. 6, Col. ii. 6.

τὸ πῶς δεῖ ὑμᾶς περιπατεῖν κτλ.] In accordance with a usage peculiar to St Luke and St Paul in the N.T. τό (ὅπως without τό FG) is here used to introduce an indirect interrogative sentence (cf. Lk. i. 62, Rom. viii. 26; Blass p. 158), while at the same time in quite class. fashion it binds together all that follows into a kind of substantival object to παρελάβετε (cf. iii. 3, and see further Viteau Étude i. p. 67 f.). The two infinitives are consequently best taken as closely connected, the second stating the necessary result of the first, 'how to walk and (so) please God' (cf. WM. p. 544 n.¹). For περιπατεῖν cf. ii. 12 note, and for ἀρέσκειν θεῷ cf. ii. 4 note. In Ps. xxv. (xxvi.) 3 the LXX. rendering for הִתְהַלָּכְתִּי is εὐηρέστησα.

καθὼς κ. περιπατεῖτε] a clause amply vouched for on ms. authority (אABD* G 17...), and in entire accord with the writers' practice to praise whenever praise is due (Intr. p. xliv), but which, by destroying the regularity of the sentence, leads them to substitute ἵνα περισσεύητε μᾶλλον for the οὕτως καὶ περιπατῆτε which we would otherwise have expected. For a similar irregularity of construction due to the same cause cf. Col. i. 6 (with Lft.'s note), and for the intensive μᾶλλον cf. v. 10, 2 Cor. vii. 13, Phil. i. 23, Mk. vii. 36.

2. παραγγελίας] Παραγγελία (for verb cf. v. 11 note) is found elsewhere in the Pauline Epp. only in 1 Tim. i. 5, 18, where it refers to the whole practical teaching of Christianity. Here the plur. points rather to special precepts (Vg. *praecepta*) or rules of living, which the writers had laid down when in Thessalonica, and which they had referred to the Lord Jesus (διὰ τ. κυρ. Ἰησ.) as the medium through whom alone they could be carried into effect: cf. Rom. xv. 30, 1 Cor. i. 10. Thpht.: οὐκ ἐμὰ γάρ, φησίν, ἃ παρήγγειλα, ἀλλ' ἐκείνου ταῦτα.

For παραγγελία as denoting a 'word of command' received as from a superior officer that it may be passed on to others cf. Xen. *Hell.* ii. 1—4, and for its use more particularly in connexion with instruction cf. Arist. *Eth. Nic.* ii. 2. 4.

IV. 3—8. Warning against Impurity.

From this general exhortation the Apostles proceed to recall more definitely the nature of their former precepts, laying special stress on the Christian duty of sanctification in view of the dangers to which their Thessalonian converts were exposed (Intr. p. xlvi). The will of God regarding this is stated (1) generally (v. 3), and (2) particularly as it affected (a) themselves (vv. 4, 5), and (b) their relation to others (v. 6ᵃ). And the whole warning is enforced by recalling the punishment that will follow its neglect (v. 6ᵇ), and the opposition which the offender is in reality offering alike to his Divine call (v. 7), and the Divine spirit working within him (v. 8).

3—8. 'In particular we call upon

48 THE FIRST EPISTLE TO THE THESSALONIANS [IV 3, 4

Ἰησοῦ. ³Τοῦτο γάρ ἐστιν θέλημα τοῦ θεοῦ, ὁ ἁγιασμὸς ὑμῶν, ἀπέχεσθαι ὑμᾶς ἀπὸ τῆς πορνείας, ⁴εἰδέναι ἕκαστον ὑμῶν τὸ ἑαυτοῦ σκεῦος κτᾶσθαι ἐν ἁγιασμῷ

you to avoid all taint of impurity. For God's purpose regarding you is nothing less than this—that you lead a holy life, abstaining from fornication and learning to gain the mastery over your bodily passions. Lust with its dishonour is the mark of Gentile godlessness. It is a sin which, while it degrades the man himself, brings wrong and injury upon others. And hence, as we have already warned you in the most solemn manner, it incurs the just vengeance of the Lord. Therefore he who deliberately sets aside this warning is setting aside not man but God, Who is the bestower of the Spirit whose distinguishing characteristic is holiness, and of whose presence in your hearts you are already conscious.'

3. Τοῦτο γάρ ἐστιν κτλ.] As regards construction, the emphatic τοῦτο is clearly the subject pointing forward not only to ὁ ἁγιασμός which is in apposition with it, but also to the succeeding inf. clauses by which the nature of the ἁγιασμός is defined, while the predicate is formed by θέλημα τ. θεοῦ, the absence of the art. before θέλημα pointing to the general nature of the conception as compared with the specific παραγγελίαι already spoken of.

Θέλημα (almost entirely confined to Bibl. and late writers), while denoting properly the *result* as distinguished from the *act* of willing (θέλησις), is here used rather in the sense of the Divine purpose (cf. Ac. xxii. 14, Eph. i. 9, v. 17, Col. i. 9, iv. 12) and embraces the thought not only of God's 'commanding' but of His 'enabling' will. 'God works in us and with us, because our sanctification is His will' (Denney). In the same way ἁγιασμός retains here the *active* force which it

always has in the Pauline writings (cf. iii. 13 note), and is = 'that you lead a holy life,' a positive injunction restated from the negative side in the clause that follows.

ἀπέχεσθαι ὑμᾶς κτλ.] a warning rendered necessary by the fact that in the heathen world πορνεία (for form, WH.² *Notes*, p. 160) was so little thought of (Hor. *Sat.* I. 2. 33 ff., Cic. *pro Cael.* 20) that abstinence from it, so far from being regarded as inevitable by the first Christian converts, was rather a thing to be learned : cf. Ac. xv. 20 (with Knowling's note) and see Jowett's Essay 'On the Connexion of Immorality and Idolatry' (*Epp. of St Paul* ii. p. 70 ff.).

Ἀπέχεσθαι (appos. inf., Burton § 386) is here construed with ἀπό, perhaps to emphasize the idea of separation, cf. v. 22, Job i. 1, 8, ii. 3 &c. It is found with the simple gen., as generally in class. Gk., in Ac. xv. 20, 29, 1 Tim. iv. 3, 1 Pet. ii. 11.

For the act. ἀπέχω = 'have wholly,' 'possess,' cf. Phil. iv. 18, Philem. 15, and for its technical use in the papyri and ostraca to denote the receipt of what was due (e.g. *B.G.U.* 612, 2 f. (i./A.D.) ἀπέχω παρ' ὑμῶν τὸν φόρον τοῦ ἐλα[ι]ουργίου, ὧν ἔχετέ [μο]υ ἐν μισθώσει) cf. Deissmann *BS.* p. 229, Wilcken *Ostraka* i. pp. 86, 106 ff., *Archiv* i. p. 77 ff.

4. εἰδέναι ἕκαστον κτλ.] a second inf. clause parallel to the preceding, and emphasizing the truth there stated in greater detail.

The principal difficulty is the meaning to be attached to τὸ ἑαυτ. σκεῦος. Does it refer to (1) 'his own body,' or (2) 'his own wife'? The latter view, advocated by Theodore of Mopsuestia (σκεῦος τὴν ἰδίαν ἑκάστου γαμετὴν ὀνομάζει) and St Augustine ('suum vas

καὶ τιμῇ, ⁵μὴ ἐν πάθει ἐπιθυμίας καθάπερ καὶ τὰ ἔθνη τὰ

possidere, hoc est, uxorem suam' c. *Jul. Pelag.* iv. 10), has been adopted by the great majority of modern commentators, principally it would appear on account of the objections that can be urged against the former. But though supported by certain Rabbinic parallels (e.g. *Megill. Est.* i. 11 'vas meum quo ego utor') and by the occurrence of the phrase κτᾶσθαι γυναῖκα='ducere uxorem' (e.g. Sir. xxxvi. 29 (26), Xen. *Conv.* ii. 10), it is not, it will be admitted, at first sight the natural view, and is suggestive of a lower view of the marriage-state than one would expect in a passage specially directed to enforcing its sanctity (cf. Titius *Neut. Lehre von der Seligkeit* (1900) ii. p. 113). On the whole therefore it seems better to revert to the meaning 'his own body' which was favoured by the Gk. commentators generally (e.g. Thdt. ἐγὼ δὲ νομίζω τὸ ἑκάστου σῶμα οὕτως αὐτὸν κεκληκέναι) as well as by Ambrstr., Pelagius, Calvin, Beza, Grotius; for though no other instance of σκεῦος by itself in this sense can be produced from the N.T., it is sufficiently vouched for by such approximate parallels as 2 Cor. iv. 7 ἔχομεν δὲ τὸν θησαυρὸν τοῦτον ἐν ὀστρακίνοις σκεύεσιν, and by the use of the word in Gk. writers to denote the vessel or instrument of the soul, e.g. Plato *Soph.* 219 A; cf. Philo *quod det. pot. ins.* § 46 (i. p. 186 M.) τὸ τῆς ψυχῆς ἀγγεῖον, τὸ σῶμα.

The most serious objection to this rendering is that it requires us to take κτᾶσθαι in what has hitherto been regarded as the unwarranted meaning of 'possess.' But to judge from the papyri it would seem as if at least in the popular language this meaning was no longer confined to the perf. (κέκτησθαι). Thus in P.Tebt. 5, 241 ff. (ii./B.C.) we find it decreed μηδ' ἄλλους κτᾶσθαι μηδὲ χρᾶσθαι τοῖς...ἐργαλείοις 'nor shall any other persons take possession of or use the tools,' and in

P.Oxy. 259, 6 (i./A.D.) a certain Theon declares on oath that he 'has' thirty days (κτήσεσθαι ἡμ[έ]ρας τριάκοντα) in which to produce a prisoner for whom he has become surety. There seems no reason therefore why κτᾶσθαι should not be used in the passage before us of a man's so 'possessing' or 'taking possession of' his body, as to use it in the fittest way for God's service in thorough keeping with the general Pauline teaching (1 Cor. vi. 15 ff., ix. 17, Rom. xii. 1).

Nor further can it be urged as a 'decisive' objection against this view that it fails to bring out the pointed contrast in which κτᾶσθαι τὸ ἑαυτ. σκεῦος is placed to πορνεία, if only we give its proper weight to the preceding εἰδέναι, for by means of it the condition of purity spoken of is emphasized as a matter of acquired knowledge. (Thpht. : σημείωσαι δὲ καὶ τὸ εἰδέναι· δείκνυσι γὰρ ὅτι ἀσκήσεως καὶ μαθήσεώς ἐστι τὸ σωφρονεῖν.)

For εἰδέναι followed by an inf.= 'know how' cf. Lk. xii. 56, Phil. iv. 12, 1 Pet. v. 9 ; also Soph. *Ajax* 666 f. τοιγὰρ τὸ λοιπὸν εἰσόμεσθα μὲν θεοῖς εἴκειν.

5. μὴ ἐν πάθει ἐπιθυμίας] 'not in lustfulness of desire' (Vg. *non in passione desiderii*, Beza *non in morbo cupiditatis*)—πάθος, according to the usual distinction, denoting the passive state or condition in which the active ἐπιθυμία rules: cf. Col. iii. 5, and see Trench *Syn.* § lxxxvii.

καθάπερ καὶ τὰ ἔθνη κτλ.] Cf. II. i. 8, Gal. iv. 8. This description of τὰ ἔθνη (ii. 16 note) is evidently founded on the LXX. (cf. Ps. lxxviii. (lxxix.) 6, Jer. x. 25), the use of the art. before μὴ εἰδ. pointing to the Gentiles' ignorance of the one true God (τὸν θεόν) as their peculiar property (cf. WSchm. pp. 178, 184), and the cause of their sinfulness. 'Ignorantia, impudicitiae origo.' Rom. i. 24' says Bengel. That, however, St Paul did not regard this ignorance

50   THE FIRST EPISTLE TO THE THESSALONIANS   [IV 6

μὴ εἰδότα τὸν θεόν, ⁶τὸ μὴ ὑπερβαίνειν καὶ πλεονεκτεῖν ἐν τῷ πράγματι τὸν ἀδελφὸν αὐτοῦ, διότι ἔκδικος Κύριος περὶ

as absolute is proved by Rom. i. 19 ff., 28: hence Bengel again, 'Coeli serenitatem adspice : impuritatis taedium te capiet.' For καθάπερ see ii. 11 note, and for the use of καί in comparison see WM. p. 549.

6. τὸ μὴ ὑπερβαίνειν κτλ.] a third inf. clause in apposition with ὁ ἁγιασμός, and parallel therefore to the two preceding clauses, the prefixed τό (see iii. 3 note) leading us to look for a further explanatory statement of the truths already laid down. Ὑπερβαίνειν (ἅπ. λεγ. N.T., cf. II. i. 3 note) may govern ἀδελφόν in the sense of 'get the better of,' but is better taken absolutely = 'transgress,' cf. Plato *Rep.* ii. 366 A ὑπερβαίνοντες καὶ ἁμαρτάνοντες, Eur. *Alc.* 1077 μὴ νῦν ὑπέρβαιν', ἀλλ' ἐναισίμως φέρε. In the present passage the nature of the transgression is defined by the following πλεονεκτεῖν 'take advantage of,' 'overreach,' any reference to unchastity lying not in the word itself, but in the context (cf. πλεονεξία, ii. 5 note). The verb occurs elsewhere in the N.T. only in 2 Cor. ii. 11 (pass.) and in vii. 2, xii. 17 f., where, though intrans. in class. Gk., it is followed as here by a direct obj. in the acc.: cf. for the sense P.Amh. 78, 12 ff. (ii./A.D.) παντοδαπῶς μ[ου] πλεονεκτεῖ ἄνθρωπος ἀ[σ]θενής (α[ὐ]θάδης, Radermacher). The gravity of the charge in the present instance is increased by the fact that it is a (Christian) 'brother' who is wronged : cf. ii. 10.

The expression ἐν τῷ πράγματι has caused difficulty. In the Vg. it is rendered *in negotio* (Wycl. *in chaffaringe,* Luth. *im Handel,* Weizs. *in Geschäften*), and in accordance with this the whole clause has been taken as a warning against defrauding one's brother in matters of business or trade. But no other adequate ex. of πρᾶγμα in this sense in the sing. has been produced, and the words are too closely connected with what precedes and what follows (v. 7 ἀκαθαρσία) to admit of any such transition to a wholly new subject. In ἐν τ. πράγματι therefore we can only find a veiled reference (Corn. a Lap. 'honesta aposiopesis') to 'the matter' on hand, viz. sins of the flesh ; cf. 2 Cor. vii. 11, and see LS. *s.v.* πρᾶξις II. 3. In no case can it be rendered 'in *any* matter' (A.V.). Of this enclitic τῳ (for τινί) there is no clear instance either in the LXX. or N.T. (WSchm. p. 71).

διότι ἔκδικος Κύριος κτλ.] The foregoing warning is now enforced by recalling the punishment which will follow upon its neglect in terms clearly suggested by Deut. xxxii. 35 (Heb.): cf. Rom. xii. 19, Heb. x. 30, and for a class. parallel see Hom. *Batrach.* 97 ἔχει θεὸς ἔκδικον ὄμμα. There is no reason however why, as ordinarily in these Epp., κύριος should not be referred directly to the Lord Jesus through whom God will judge the world: cf. II. i. 7 ff. and see Intr. p. lxvii.

Ἔκδικος, elsewhere in N.T. only Rom. xiii. 4, denoted primarily 'lawless,' 'unjust,' but later passed over into the meaning of 'avenging,' 'an avenger,' in which sense it is found in the apocr. books of the O.T. (Sap. xii. 12, Sir. xxx. 6, cf. 4 Macc. xv. 29). In the papyri it is the regular term for a legal representative, e.g. P.Oxy. 261, 14 f. (i./A.D.) where a certain Demetria appoints her grandson Chaeremon ἔγδικον ἐπί τε πάσης ἐξουσίας 'to appear for her before every authority': see further Gradenwitz *Einführung* i. p. 160, and for a similar use in the inscriptions='advocatus' (cf. Cic. *ad Fam.* xiii. 56) see Michel *Recueil* 459, 19 f. (ii./B.C.) ὑπέμεινεν ἑκουσίως [ἔκ]δικος.

πάντων τούτων, καθὼς καὶ προείπαμεν ὑμῖν καὶ διεμαρτυράμεθα. ⁷οὐ γὰρ ἐκάλεσεν ἡμᾶς ὁ θεὸς ἐπὶ ἀκαθαρσίᾳ ἀλλ' ἐν ἁγιασμῷ. ⁸τοιγαροῦν ὁ ἀθετῶν οὐκ ἄνθρωπον ἀθετεῖ ἀλλὰ τὸν θεὸν τὸν Διδόντα τὸ πνεῦμα αὐτοῦ τὸ ἅΓιον

Seeberg (*Der Katechismus der Urchristenheit* (1903) p. 10 f.) points to this verse as a proof of a traditional catalogue of sins lying at the basis of the Pauline lists, for though only two sins are directly mentioned here, judgment takes place περὶ πάντων τούτων.
προείπαμεν] Cf. iii. 4 note, and for the aor. in -α see WH.² *Notes* p. 171 f., WSchm. p. 111 f.
διεμαρτυράμεθα] Διαμαρτύρομαι, a word of Ionic origin (Nägeli p. 24) and stronger than the simple μαρτύρομαι (ii. 11), is used of solemnly testifying in the sight of God (ἐνώπιον τ. θεοῦ) in 1 Tim. v. 21, 2 Tim. ii. 14, iv. 1, the only other passages in the Pauline writings where it occurs. It is found frequently in the LXX. in this sense (e.g. Deut. iv. 26, viii. 19, 1 Regn. viii. 9), and is used absolutely by St Luke as here in Lk. xvi. 28, Ac. ii. 40; cf. also Heb. ii. 6. Calv.: '*Obtestati sumus:* tanta enim est hominum tarditas, ut nisi acriter perculsi nullo divini iudicii sensu tangantur.'
7. οὐ γὰρ ἐκάλεσεν κτλ.] The emphasis lies on ἐκάλεσεν (cf. ii. 12 note), the thought of the definite Divine call being introduced as an additional reason for the foregoing warning, or, perhaps, in more immediate connexion with the preceding clause, as a justification of the vengeance there threatened.
The interchange of the prepositions ἐπί and ἐν is significant, the former pointing to the object or purpose of the call (cf. Gal. v. 13, Eph. ii. 10, Sap. ii. 23 ὁ θεὸς ἔκτισεν τὸν ἄνθρωπον ἐπ' ἀφθαρσίᾳ), the latter to its essential basis or condition (cf. Eph. iv. 4 with Abbott's note), ἁγιασμός being used in the same active sense as in *vv.* 3, 4.

8. τοιγαροῦν ὁ ἀθετῶν κτλ.] 'Wherefore then the rejecter rejects not man but (the) God'—the compound τοιγαροῦν (class., elsewhere in N.T. only Heb. xii. 1) introducing the conclusion 'with some special emphasis or formality' (Grimm-Thayer *s.v.*).
'Αθετεῖν literally = 'make ἄθετον,' or 'do away with what has been laid down,' refers here to the action of the man who of his own will 'rejects' or 'sets aside' the calling just mentioned (*v.* 7): cf. especially Lk. x. 16 of which we may here have a reminiscence. The verb, which is not approved by the Atticists (frequent in Polyb. e.g. viii. 2. 5 ἀθ. τ. πίστιν, xv. 1. 9 ἀθ. τ. ὅρκους καὶ τ. συνθήκας), occurs other four times in the Pauline writings, always however with reference to things, not persons—τ. σύνεσιν (1 Cor. i. 19), τ. χάριν (Gal. ii. 21), διαθήκην (Gal. iii. 15), τ. πίστιν (1 Tim. v. 12). In the LXX. it represents no fewer than seventeen Heb. originals. For its use in the papyri see P.Tebt. 74, 59 f. (ii./B.C.) ἐμβρόχου τῆς ἐν τῆι ἠθετημένηι ἱερᾷ (cf. 61 (b), 207 note), and in the inscriptions see *O.G.I.S.* 444, 18 ἐὰν δέ τινες τῶν πόλεων ἀθετ[ῶσι] τὸ σύμφωνον.
The absence of the art. before ἄνθρωπον followed as it is by τὸν θεόν deserves notice (cf. Gal. i. 10), while the contrast is further heightened by the use of the absolute negative in the first conception, not to annul it, but rhetorically to direct undivided attention to the second (cf. Mk. ix. 37, Ac. v. 4, 1 Cor. i. 17; WM. p. 622 f.).
τὸν διδόντα κτλ.] The reading here is somewhat uncertain, but the weight of the MS. evidence is in favour of the pres. part. (א*BDG as against AKL for δόντα), the aor. having probably

52 THE FIRST EPISTLE TO THE THESSALONIANS [IV 9

εἰς ἡμᾶς. ⁹ Περὶ δὲ τῆς φιλαδελφίας οὐ χρείαν ἔχετε
γράφειν ὑμῖν, αὐτοὶ γὰρ ὑμεῖς θεοδίδακτοί ἐστε εἰς τὸ

arisen from its occurrence elsewhere in the same connexion (e.g. 2 Cor. i. 22, v. 5). As regards the meaning, the pres. may be taken as pointing to the ever 'fresh accessions of the Holy Spirit' (Lft.) which God imparts, or perhaps better as along with the art. constituting another subst. part. 'the giver of His Holy Spirit.'
For the emphatic τὸ πν. τὸ ἅγ. where the repeated art. lays stress on the ἅγ. in keeping with the main thought of the whole passage cf. Mk. iii. 29, xiii. 11, Eph. iv. 30; while if any weight can be attached to εἰς ὑμᾶς instead of ὑμῖν (cf. i. 5 note) it brings out more pointedly the entrance of the Spirit into the heart and life: cf. Gal. iv. 6, Eph. iii. 16, Ezek. xxxvii. 14 δώσω τὸ πνεῦμά μου εἰς ὑμᾶς καὶ ζήσεσθε, also the interesting reading of D in Mk. i. 10 and parallels, where it is stated that at the Baptism the dove entered *into* Jesus (εἰς αὐτόν), and did not merely rest upon Him (ἐπ' αὐτόν), (Nestle *Exp. T.* xvii. p. 522 n.¹).

IV. 9, 10ª. Encouragement in Brotherly Love.

From impurity, which is at root so cruel and selfish, the Apostles pass by a subtle link of connexion to the practice of brotherly or Christian love, admitting frankly at the same time the Thessalonians' zeal in this respect.

9, 10ª. 'And so again with regard to love of the brethren, that is a subject on which it is not necessary to say much, seeing that as those who are filled with God's Spirit you have already been taught to love: and not only so, but you are actively practising what you have been taught towards all Christian brethren throughout Macedonia.'

9. Περὶ δὲ τῆς φιλαδελφίας] For

περὶ δέ introducing a new subject cf. v. 1. In profane Gk. and the LXX. φιλαδελφία is confined to the mutual love of those who are brothers by common descent (e.g. Luc. *dial. deor.* xxvi. 2, 4 Macc. xiii. 23, 26, xiv. 1) but in the N.T. the word is used in the definite Christian sense of 'love of the brethren,' of all, that is, who are brethren in virtue of the new birth: cf. Rom. xii. 10, Heb. xiii. 1, 1 Pet. i. 22, 2 Pet. i. 7 ἐν δὲ τῇ φιλαδελφίᾳ τὴν ἀγάπην. The last passage is interesting as showing how readily this mutual love amongst believers passed over into the wider ἀγάπη, love for all mankind (cf. iii. 12 note).

οὐ χρείαν κτλ.] not an instance of *paraleipsis*, or a pretending to pass over what in reality is mentioned for the sake of effect (Chrys.: τῷ εἰπεῖν, οὐ χρεία ἐστί, μεῖζον ἐποίησεν ἢ εἰ εἶπεν), but a simple statement of fact. The use of the act. inf. (γράφειν) for the pass. (γράφεσθαι, cf. v. 1) is too amply vouched for in similar combinations to cause any difficulty: see WM. p. 426, Buttmann p. 259 n.¹.

θεοδίδακτοι] The word is ἅπ. λεγ. in the N.T. (cf. Barn. *Ep.* xxi. 6, Tat. *Orat.* c. 29 p. 165 B θεοδιδάκτου δέ μου γενομένης τῆς ψυχῆς, Theoph. *ad Autol.* ii. 9 οἱ δὲ τοῦ θεοῦ ἄνθρωποι... ὑπ' αὐτοῦ τοῦ θεοῦ ἐμπνευσθέντες καὶ σοφισθέντες ἐγένοντο θεοδίδακτοι), and like the corresponding phrase διδακτοὶ τοῦ θεοῦ points not so much to 'one divine communication' as to 'a divine relationship' established between believers and God (see Westcott on Jo. vi. 45): hence it is as those who have been born of God, and whose hearts are in consequence filled by God's spirit that the Thessalonians on their part (αὐτοί.. ὑμεῖς) can no longer help loving; cf. Isa. liv. 13, Jer. xxxviii. (xxxi.) 33 f., Pss. Sol. xvii. 35. Calv.: '*quia divinitus edocti sint*: quo sig-

IV 10, 11] THE FIRST EPISTLE TO THE THESSALONIANS 53

ἀγαπᾶν ἀλλήλους· ¹⁰καὶ γὰρ ποιεῖτε αὐτὸ εἰς πάντας
τοὺς ἀδελφοὺς [τοὺς] ἐν ὅλῃ τῇ Μακεδονίᾳ. Παρακαλοῦμεν δὲ ὑμᾶς, ἀδελφοί, περισσεύειν μᾶλλον, ¹¹καὶ
φιλοτιμεῖσθαι ἡσυχάζειν καὶ πράσσειν τὰ ἴδια καὶ ἐρ-

10 τοὺς ℵᶜBDᵇᶜHKL cet Chr al: om ℵ*AD*G Chrᶜᵒᵈ

nificat insculptam esse eorum cordibus caritatem, ut supervacuae sint literae in charta scriptae.' Beng.: 'doctrinae divinae vis confluit in amorem.'
On εἰς τό as here acting for the epexegetic inf. see Moulton *Prolegg.* p. 219.

10. καὶ γὰρ ποιεῖτε αὐτό κτλ.] 'for indeed ye do it...' καί not losing its force as in the classical καὶ γάρ = 'etenim,' but marking an advance on the preceding statement (Blass p. 275): the Thessalonians have not only been taught, but, looking to the fact that God has been their teacher, they practise (ποιεῖτε) what they have been taught, cf. 1 Jo. iii. 16 ff.

If τούς is omitted before the defining clause ἐν ὅλῃ τ. Μακ., these words are best connected directly with ποιεῖτε, as denoting the region 'in' which the love of the brethren was displayed. For the extent of the region thus referred to ('all Macedonia') see Intr. p. xlv.

10ᵇ—12. *Call to Quiet Work.*

A continued exhortation to the Thessalonians to advance in increasing measure in the practice of the φιλαδελφία whose presence in their midst has just been so fully recognized (v. 10ᵇ), and at the same time to avoid that spirit of restlessness and of inattention to their daily work, of which apparently they had already begun to show traces, and which, if not checked, could not fail to create an unfavourable impression on the minds of unbelievers (vv. 11, 12).

10ᵇ—12. 'This however is not to say that we do not urge you to still further efforts in the practice of this love, while there is one point to which you will do well to pay heed. Instead of giving way further to that restless spirit of which you are already showing signs, make it your earnest aim to preserve a quiet and orderly attitude—attending to your own business, and working with your hands for your own livelihood, even as we directed while still present with you. By so doing you will not only convey a good impression to your unbelieving neighbours, but you will yourselves maintain an honourable independence.'

10ᵇ. Παρακαλοῦμεν δέ κτλ.] For a similar appeal see v. 1, though here the more regular inf. is used after παρακαλ. instead of the ἵνα-construction: cf. P.Oxy. 292, 5 ff. διὸ παρακαλῶ σε μετὰ πάσης δυνάμεως ἔχειν αὐτὸν συνεσταμένον. For περισσεύειν see note on iii. 12, and for μᾶλλον see note on v. 1.

11. καὶ φιλοτιμεῖσθαι ἡσυχάζειν] For a certain amount of restlessness amongst the Thessalonians, apparently owing to their eschatological expectations, see Intr. p. xlvi f.

The verb φιλοτιμεῖσθαι is found again in Rom. xv. 20, 2 Cor. v. 9, and in all three passages seems to have lost its original idea of emulation ('be ambitious'), and to mean little more than 'be zealous,' 'strive eagerly,' in accordance with its usage in late Gk.: cf. Aristeas 79 ἅπαντα φιλοτιμηθέντες εἰς ὑπεροχὴν δόξης τοῦ βασιλέως ποιῆσαι, and see P.Petr. III. 42 H (8) f., 3 f. (iii./B.C.) ἐφιλοτιμοῦ με παραγε[νέσθαι πρὸς σὲ καὶ] ἦλθον, P.Tebt. 410, 10 (i./A.D.) ἐφιλοτ[ι]μοῦ σὺν ἐμοὶ μεῖναι, and for the corresponding adj. P.Petr. I. 29,

γάζεσθαι ταῖς χερσὶν ὑμῶν, καθὼς ὑμῖν παρηγγείλαμεν, [12]ἵνα περιπατῆτε εὐσχημόνως πρὸς τοὺς ἔξω καὶ μηδενὸς χρείαν ἔχητε.

12 (Ptol.) where a steward writes to his employer that he had borrowed four artabae of wheat which a certain Dynis had offered and 'was pressing' (φιλοτίμου ὄντος) to lend. Along with φιλοτιμία, φιλοτιμεῖσθαι is very common in Gk. honorary decrees where its general meaning is 'to act with public spirit,' e.g. *C.I.A.* II. 444, 23 ff. (ii./B.C.) ὅπως οὖν καὶ ἡ βουλὴ καὶ ὁ δῆμος μνημονεύοντες φαίνωνται τῶν εἰς ἑαυτοὺς φιλοτιμουμένων. See also Field *Notes* p. 165, Hicks *C. R.* i. p. 46. With ἡσυχάζειν (a favourite Lukan word, e.g. Lk. xiv. 3, Ac. xi. 18) contrast περιεργάζεσθαι II. iii. 11, and with the striking oxymoron (Beza *et contendatis quieti esse*) cf. Rom. xii. 11 τῇ σπουδῇ μὴ ὀκνηροί, Phil. iv. 7 ἡ εἰρήνη...φρουρήσει, Heb. x. 24 εἰς παροξυσμὸν ἀγάπης.

καὶ πράσσειν τὰ ἴδια] The commentators draw attention to the similar juxtaposition found in Plato *Rep.* vi. 496 D where the philosopher who has escaped from the dangers of political life is described as ἡσυχίαν ἔχων καὶ τὰ αὑτοῦ πράττων, while the general thought is illustrated by another passage from the same book iv. 433 A, τὸ τὰ αὑτοῦ πράττειν καὶ μὴ πολυπραγμονεῖν δικαιοσύνη ἐστί: cf. also Dion Cass. LX. 27 τὴν δὲ δὴ ἡσυχίαν ἄγων, καὶ τὰ ἑαυτοῦ πράττων, ἐσώζετο. In all three passages the more correct τὰ ἑαυτοῦ for τὰ ἴδια (cf. Lk. xviii. 28) may also be noted (cf. Lob. *Phryn.* p. 441).

καὶ ἐργάζεσθαι κτλ.] For the bearing of these words on the general standing of the Thessalonian converts cf. II. iii. 10 f., and for the new dignity imparted by the Gospel to manual labour see Intr. p. xlvii.

In accordance with a tendency of transcribers towards greater precision of statement certain MSS. (ℵ*AD^cKL)

insert ἰδίαις here before χερσίν: cf. note on c. ii. 15.

καθὼς ὑμῖν παρηγγείλαμεν] 'even as we charged you'—the use of the emphatic παραγγέλλειν, which is specially used in class. writers of the orders of military commanders (cf. note on παραγγελία *v.* 2), bringing out the authority with which the Apostles spoke, cf. II. iii. 10 ff. The verb is a favourite with Luke (Gosp.[4] Ac.[11]), and outside these Epp. and 1 Tim. is found elsewhere in the Pauline writings 1 Cor. vii. 10, xi. 17.

12. ἵνα περιπατῆτε κτλ.] The purpose of the foregoing παράκλησις. By avoiding undue interference with the affairs of others, and paying diligent attention to their own work, the Thessalonians would not only present a decorous appearance to their unbelieving neighbours, but themselves enjoy an honourable independence.

Εὐσχημόνως, 'decorously,' 'becomingly,' corresponding to the old Eng. 'honestly' (Vg. *honeste*) of the A.V. here and in Rom. xiii. 13, is found combined with κατὰ τάξιν in 1 Cor. xiv. 40 to express the beauty and harmony that result in the Church from every member's keeping his own place: cf. Aristeas 284 τὰ τοῦ βίου μετ᾽ εὐσχημοσύνης καὶ καταστολῆς γινόμενα, and especially the use of the adj. to denote the Egyptian magistrates who had charge of public morals, e.g. *B.G.U.* 147, 1 (ii.—iii./A.D.) ἀρχεφόδοις καὶ εὐσχήμοσι κώμης, and Wilcken *Ostraka* no. 1153 (Rom.) πέμψατε τοὺς εὐσχήμονας τοὺς ἐπὶ τῶν παροληκμάτων (where see note).

Πρὸς τοὺς ἔξω a phrase derived from the Rabbinical הַחִיצוֹנִים (cf. Schöttgen on 1 Cor. v. 12), and embracing all outside the Christian community whether Gentiles or unbeliev-

IV 13] THE FIRST EPISTLE TO THE THESSALONIANS 55

¹³ Οὐ θέλομεν δὲ ὑμᾶς ἀγνοεῖν, ἀδελφοί, περὶ τῶν

ing Jews, cf. Mk. iv. 11, 1 Cor. v. 12 f., Col. iv. 5, 1 Tim. iii. 7 (ἀπὸ τῶν ἔξωθεν). 'It is characteristic of St Paul to ask, "What will the Gentiles say of us?" a part of the Christian prudence, which was one of the great features of his life' (Jowett). For a similar exhortation with the same end in view cf. 1 Pet. ii. 11 ff. Chrys. thus applies the reproof to his own age: εἰ γὰρ οἱ παρ' ἡμῖν σκανδαλίζονται τούτοις, πολλῷ μᾶλλον οἱ ἔξωθεν...διὸ καὶ χριστεμπόρους καλοῦσιν ἡμᾶς.

καὶ μηδενός κτλ.] Μηδενός may be either masc. or neut. The former in view of the context yields good sense (Wycl. *of no mannes ʒe desire ony thing*): cf. Hieron. *in Gal.* II. c. iii. 'They are sharply censured because they go round idly from house to house, expecting food from others, while they try to make themselves agreeable to this person and that (*singulis*).' On the other hand the use of χρείαν ἔχειν elsewhere with the gen. of the thing (e.g. Mt. vi. 8, Lk. x. 42, Heb. v. 12; cf. Rev. iii. 17 οὐδὲν χρείαν ἔχω) points rather to the rendering 'have need of nothing' (Beza *et nullius indigeatis*): by their own work they would be placed in a position of αὐτάρκεια, cf. II. iii. 8, 12.

IV. 13—V. 11. From the foregoing practical exhortations St Paul turns to two difficulties of a more *doctrinal* character, which, from the manner in which they are introduced, would seem to have been referred directly to him by the Thessalonians, or more probably were brought under his notice by Timothy in view of what he had heard at Thessalonica (Intr. p. xxxiii f.). The first relates to the lot of those dying before the Lord's Return, the second to the time when that Return might be expected. The two sections are closely parallel, each consisting of a question (iv. 13, v. 1): an answer (iv. 14—17, v. 2—10): and a practical exhortation (iv. 18, v. 11).

IV. 13—18. TEACHING CONCERNING THEM THAT ARE ASLEEP AND THE ADVENT OF CHRIST.

13, 14. 'With regard moreover to that other matter which we understand is causing you anxiety, the fate namely of those of your number who are falling on sleep before the coming of the Lord, we are anxious, Brothers, that you should be fully informed. There is no reason why you should sorrow, as those who do not share in your Christian hope cannot fail to do. For as surely as our belief is rooted in the death and resurrection of Jesus, even so we are confident that God will bring along with the returning Jesus those who have fallen on sleep through Him.'

13. Οὐ θέλομεν δέ κτλ.] a phrase used by St Paul to introduce a new and important topic, and always with the impressive addition of ἀδελφοί; cf. Rom. i. 13, xi. 25, 1 Cor. x. 1, xii. 1, 2 Cor. i. 8, and for a near parallel see P.Tebt. 314, 3 (ii./A.D.) πιστεύω σε μὴ ἀγνοεῖν. The corresponding formula γινώσκειν σε θέλω is very common in the papyri, especially in opening a letter after the introductory greeting, e.g. B.G.U. 27, 3 ff. (ii.—iii./A.D.) καὶ διὰ π[α]ντὸς εὔχομαί σε ὑγιένεν καὶ [ἐγὼ?] αὐτὸς ὑγιένω. Γινώσκειν σε θέλω κτλ.

περὶ τῶν κοιμωμένων] 'concerning them that are falling asleep' (Vg. *de dormientibus*)—the pres. part. not only indicating a state of things that was going on, but also lending itself more readily to the thought of a future awakening than the perf. would have done (cf. Lft. *ad loc.*). It was doubtless indeed the extreme appropriateness of the word κοιμᾶσθαι in the latter direction (Thdt.: τῷ γὰρ ὕπνῳ ἐγρήγορσις ἔπεται, Aug. *Serm.* xciii. 6, 'Quare enim dormientes vocantur, nisi quia suo die resuscitantur?') that led St Paul to prefer it to ἀποθνήσκειν in speaking of the

κοιμωμένων, ἵνα μὴ λυπῆσθε καθὼς καὶ οἱ λοιποὶ οἱ μὴ

death of believers who alone are thought of here, though in no case must the underlying figure be pressed as if descriptive of his idea of their intermediate state.

The same metaphor frequently occurs in the earlier O.T. and apocalyptic literature without any reference to the resurrection-hope, e.g. Gen. xlvii. 30, 2 Regn. vii. 12, Jer. xxviii. (li.) 39 (ὕπνον αἰώνιον), *Jubilees* xxiii. 1, xxxvi. 18, *Ass. Mos.* i. 15, x. 14, *Apoc. Bar.* xi. 4, *Test. xii. patr.* Jos. xx. 4 (ἐκοιμήθη ὕπνον αἰώνιον); on the other hand as preparing us for the later Christian use of the term cf. Dan. xii. 2, 2 Macc. xii. 44 f., 4 Ezra vii. 32 'et terra reddet qui in ea dormiunt, et puluis qui in eo silentio habitant.'

On the varied connotation of the term in Jewish eschatology see Volz *Jüd. Eschat.* p. 134, and for the occurrence of the figure in pagan literature, cf. Callim. *Epigr.* x. 1, Hom. *Il.* xi. 241, Soph. *Electr.* 509, Verg. *Aen.* vi. 278 ('consanguineus leti sopor'). See also the striking saying of Gorgias (v./B.C.) in his extreme old age ἤδη με ὁ ὕπνος ἄρχεται παρακατατίθεσθαι τἀδελφῷ (Aelian *V.H.* ii. 35).

The verb (especially ἐκοιμήθην) is very common in Christian inscriptions, e.g. *I.G.S.I.* 549, 1 σὺν θεῷ...ἐκοιμ[ήθη] ἡ δουλὴ τοῦ [θεοῦ] Σαβεῖνα, 68, 1 ἐκοιμήθη ἡ θεοκοίμητος Αἰγεία. The allied subst. κοιμητήριον appears by the middle of the 3rd cent. if not earlier. Thus the formula of dedicating τὸ κοιμ[η]τ[ή]ριον ἕως ἀναστάσεως is found in an inscription at Thessalonica (*C.I.G.* 9439) which Kirchhoff thinks may belong to the 2nd cent., though Ramsay carries it forward to the middle of the 4th (*C. and B.* i. p. 495). The word is often thought to be exclusively Christian, but Roberts-Gardner (p. 513) quote two inscriptions which by the figures of a seven-branched candelabrum are shown to be of Jewish origin. The first of these (*C.I.G.* 9313) runs—Κοιμητήριον Εὐτυχ[ί]ας τῆς μητρὸς Ἀθηνέου κὲ Θεοκτίστου. For the existence of a Jewish colony in Athens cf. Ac. xvii. 17, and see art. 'Athens' in Hastings' *D.B.* by F. C. Conybeare.

καθὼς καὶ οἱ λοιποί] 'even as also the rest,' i.e. 'all who are not believers,' synonymous with οἱ ἔξω (v. 12): cf. Rom. xi. 7, Eph. ii. 3. The clause is often interpreted as='to the same extent as the rest' (Thdt. : τὴν ἀμετρίαν [λύπην] ἐκβάλλει), but this is to strain the Gk. unduly, and we have rather one of the constantly recurring instances in which St Paul 'states his precept broadly, without caring to enter into the qualifications which will suggest themselves at once to thinking men' (Lft.). On the force of καί see ii. 14 note.

οἱ μὴ ἔχοντες κτλ.] The general hopelessness of the pagan world in the presence of death is almost too well-known to require illustration, but see e.g. Aesch. *Eum.* 618 ἅπαξ θανόντος, οὔτις ἔστ' ἀνάστασις, Theocr. *Id.* iv. 42 ἐλπίδες ἐν ζωοῖσιν, ἀνέλπιστοι δὲ θανόντες, Catull. v. 5 f. 'nobis cum semel occidit breuis lux, nox est perpetua una dormienda,' and the touching letter of Cicero *ad Fam.* xiv. 2, which was dated—*Thessalonicae*. The inscriptions tell the same tale, e.g. *I.G.S.I.* 929, 13 κοιμᾶται τὸν αἰώνιον ὕπν(ον), 1879, 11 εὐψυχῶ...ὅστις οὐκ ἤμην καὶ ἐγενόμην, οὐκ εἰμὶ καὶ οὐ λυποῦμαι.

14. No mention has been made of the reason of Gentile hopelessness, but it is clearly traceable to ignorance of the revelation of the one God (cf. Eph. ii. 12 ἐλπίδα μὴ ἔχοντες κ. ἄθεοι ἐν τ. κόσμῳ), and accordingly the Apostles proceed to lay down the real ground of Christian hope. That ground is the death and resurrection of the historic Jesus (cf. Add. Note D),

IV 14, 15] THE FIRST EPISTLE TO THE THESSALONIANS 57

ἔχοντες ἐλπίδα. ¹⁴εἰ γὰρ πιστεύομεν ὅτι Ἰησοῦς ἀπέθανεν καὶ ἀνέστη, οὕτως καὶ ὁ θεὸς τοὺς κοιμηθέντας διὰ τοῦ Ἰησοῦ ἄξει σὺν αὐτῷ.   ¹⁵Τοῦτο γὰρ ὑμῖν λέγομεν

which, by an impressive irregularity of grammatical structure, are here brought into direct relation not with the resurrection of believers, but, in keeping with the general drift of the Ep., with their return with Christ in glory.

εἰ γὰρ πιστεύομεν κτλ.] The use of εἰ in the opening clause of the syllogism instead of throwing any doubt on the belief spoken of, rather makes it more definite, cf. Rom. v. 15, Col. iii. 1, and for the conjunction ἀπέθ. κ. ἀνέστη see Rom. xiv. 9, where it is said in the same sense as here εἰς τοῦτο γὰρ Χριστὸς ἀπέθανεν καὶ ἔζησεν ἵνα καὶ νεκρῶν καὶ ζώντων κυριεύσῃ. The use of ἀπέθανεν in the present passage is specially noticeable in contrast with κοιμᾶσθαι applied to believers (v. 13): it is as if the writers wished to emphasize that because Christ's death was a real death, 'a death of death,' His people's death has been turned into 'sleep.' Chrys.: ἐπειδὴ δὲ ἦλθεν ὁ Χριστός, καὶ ὑπὲρ ζωῆς τοῦ κόσμου ἀπέθανε, οὐκέτι θάνατος καλεῖται λοιπὸν ὁ θάνατος, ἀλλὰ ὕπνος καὶ κοίμησις (de Coemit. et Cruce, Op. ii. 470 ed. Gaume).

It may be noted that only here and in v. 16 does St Paul employ ἀνίστασθαι with reference to resurrection from the dead; cf. also the metaph. use in Eph. v. 14. As a rule he prefers ἐγείρειν, cf. i. 10 and other forty occurrences in his Epp. The subst. ἀνάστασις is found eight times. It is frequent in the inscriptions for the 'erection' of a statue or monument, e.g. Magn. 179, 28 f. ἐπὶ τῇ ἀναστάσει τοῦ ἀνδριάντος.

οὕτως καὶ ὁ θεός] 'so also (we believe that) God,' οὕτως virtually resuming the protasis and καί, which belongs not to the single word 'God' but to the whole clause, serving to strengthen still further the comparison stated in the apodosis (cf. ii. 14 note). Ὁ θεός is emphatic: it is the one true God who, as the raiser-up of Jesus, will raise up His people along with Him, cf. 1 Cor. vi. 14, 2 Cor. iv. 14. In order, however, that He may do so there must be a certain oneness between the Head and His members, and it is to the existence of this connecting link in the case of the Thessalonian believers that the next words point.

τοὺς κοιμηθέντας διὰ τοῦ Ἰησοῦ] 'those that are fallen asleep through Jesus,' κοιμηθέντας being used with a purely midd. sense, and the instrumental διά pointing to Jesus as the mediating link between His people's sleep and their resurrection at the hands of God (cf. διὰ τ. ἐνοικοῦντος αὐτοῦ πνεύματος in a similar connexion in Rom. viii. 11). Stated in full the argument would run: 'so also we believe that those who fell asleep through Jesus, and in consequence were raised by God through Him, will God bring with Him.' This is better than to connect διὰ τ. Ἰησοῦ directly with ἄξει. Such an arrangement, while grammatically possible, is not only contrary to the parallelism of the sentence ('Ιησ. ἀπέθ....τ. κοιμηθ. διὰ τ. Ἰησ.) and to the analogy of the closely following οἱ νεκροὶ ἐν Χρ. (v. 16), but gives a halting and redundant conclusion to the whole sentence: 'God will bring through Jesus along with Him.'

For κοιμηθῆναι see the note on v. 13, and as further illustrating its midd. sense cf. P.Cairo 3, 9 ff. (iii./B.C.) ἡνίκα ἤμελλον κοιμηθῆναι, ἔγραψα ἐπιστόλια β. Dr W. F. Moulton has proposed that in the verse before us the verb may be a true

ἐν λόγῳ κυρίου, ὅτι ἡμεῖς οἱ ζῶντες οἱ περιλειπόμενοι εἰς τὴν παρουσίαν τοῦ κυρίου οὐ μὴ φθάσωμεν τοὺς

passive 'were put to sleep' (see Moulton *Prolegg*. p. 162). But however beautiful the sense that is thus obtained, it is not the one that naturally suggests itself.

ἄξει] '*ducet*, suave verbum : dicitur de viventibus' (Beng.). With the thought cf. *Asc. Isai.* iv. 16 quoted above on iii. 13.

15—18. 'Regarding this, we say, we are confident, for we have it on the direct authority of the Lord Himself that we who are surviving when the Lord comes will not in any way anticipate those who have fallen asleep. What will happen will rather be this. The Lord Himself will descend from heaven with a shout of command, with the voice of an archangel, and with the trumpet-call of God. Then those who died in Christ, and in consequence are still living in Him, shall rise first. And only after that shall we who are surviving be suddenly caught up in the clouds with them to meet the Lord in the air. Thus shall we ever be with the Lord. Wherefore comfort one another with these words.'

15. ἐν λόγῳ κυρίου] The 'word' is often found in some actual saying of the Lord while He was upon the earth, such as Mt. xxiv. 30f. (=Mk. xiii. 26 f., Lk. xxi. 27), xvi. 27, Jo. vi. 39 f., but none of these cover the statement of the present verse, which must certainly be included in the teaching referred to (as against von Soden who finds it only in *v.* 16); while again this very want of similarity with any 'recorded' saying should make us the more chary of postulating an 'unrecorded' one (cf. Ac. xx. 35, and see Ropes *Sprüche Jesu* p. 152 ff.). On the whole, therefore, it is better to fall back upon the thought of a direct revelation granted to the Apostles to meet the special circumstances that had arisen (cf. 1 Cor. ii. 10, 2 Cor. xii. 1 ff., Gal. i. 12, 16, Eph. iii. 3), or more generally to find in this and the following *vv.* the interpretation which, acting under the immediate guidance of the Lord's own spirit ('quasi Eo ipso loquente,' Beza), St Paul and his companions were able to put upon certain current Jewish apocalyptic ideas. On a subject of such importance they naturally felt constrained to appeal to the ultimate source of their authority: cf. 1 Cor. vii. 10 οὐκ ἐγὼ ἀλλὰ ὁ κύριος. Thdt.: οὐ γὰρ οἰκείοις χρώμεθα λογισμοῖς, ἀλλ' ἐκ θείας ἡμῖν ἀποκαλύψεως ἡ διδασκαλία γεγένηται.

On Steck's discovery of the λόγος in 4 Ezra v. 41 f. see Intr. p. lxxv, and on the use made by Resch of this verse to prove ('auf das Deutlichste') St Paul's dependence on the Logia (*Der Paulinismus u. die Logia Jesu* (1904) p. 338 f.) see Kirsopp Lake in *Am. J. of Th.* 1906 p. 107 f., who finds in it rather the suggestion of a smaller and less formal collection of sayings.

ὅτι ἡμεῖς κτλ.] 'that we who are alive, who survive unto the Parousia of the Lord.' These words must not be pressed as conveying a positive and unqualified declaration on the Apostles' part that the Lord would come during their lifetime, if only because as we learn elsewhere in these Epp. they were well aware that the time of that coming was quite uncertain (v. 1, II. ii. 1 ff.). At the same time there can be no doubt that the passage naturally suggests that they expected so to survive (cf. 1 Cor. xv. 51 f.), and we must not allow the fact that they were mistaken in this belief to deprive their words of their proper meaning, as when ἡμεῖς is referred generally to believers who shall be alive at Christ's appearing, or

κοιμηθέντας· ¹⁶ὅτι αὐτὸς ὁ κύριος ἐν κελεύσματι, ἐν

the participles are taken hypothetically 'if we are alive,' 'if we survive.' How far indeed an interpreter may go in the supposed interests of Apostolic infallibility is shown by the attitude amongst others of Calvin who thinks that the Apostles used the first person simply in order to keep the Thessalonians on the alert ('Thessalonicenses in exspectationem erigere, adeoque pios omnes tenere suspensos')! As a matter of fact the near approach of the Parousia here implied would seem, notwithstanding many statements to the contrary, to have been held by St Paul throughout his life: see Kennedy *Last Things* pp. 160 ff., where the evidence of the Epp. down to the closing statement Phil. iv. 5 ὁ κύριος ἐγγύς is carefully examined.

On περιλείπεσθαι see below on v. 17, and on παρουσία see Add. Note F.

οὐ μὴ φθάσωμεν κτλ.] 'shall in no wise precede them that are fallen asleep.' So far from the living having any advantage at the Parousia over those already dead, it would rather be the other way, an assurance which was the more required in view of the prevalent Jewish belief that a special blessing attached to those who survived the coming of the Kingdom: see Dan. xii. 12, Pss. Sol. xvii. 50, *Asc. Isai.* iv. 15 (with Charles's note), and especially 4 Ezra xiii. 24 'scito ergo quoniam magis beatificati sunt qui derelicti super eos qui mortui sunt'; while as showing how the same difficulty continued to linger in the early Christian Church cf. Clem. *Recogn.* i. 52 (ed. Gersdorf) 'Si Christi regno fruentur hi, quos iustos invenerit eius adventus, ergo qui ante adventum eius defuncti sunt, regno penitus carebunt?'

Φθάνειν (ii. 16 note) reappears here in its generally class. sense of 'anticipate,' 'precede,' old Engl. 'prevent' (Wright *Bible Word-Book s.v.*), cf.

Sap. vi. 13, xvi. 28, where, as here, it is followed by an acc.

The double negative οὐ μή is found elsewhere in the Pauline Epp., apart from LXX. citations, only in v. 3, 1 Cor. viii. 13, Gal. v. 16, always apparently with the emphatic sense which it has in class. Gk., and which can also be illustrated from the Κοινή: see e.g. the well-known boy's letter to his father P.Oxy. 119, 14 f. (ii.—iii./A.D.) ἂμ μὴ πέμψῃς οὐ μὴ φάγω, οὐ μὴ πείνω. ταῦτα 'if you don't send, I won't eat, I won't drink; there now!' On the general use of οὐ μή in the Gk. Bible see Moulton *Prolegg.* pp. 39, 187 ff.

16. ὅτι] not parallel to the preceding ὅτι, and like it dependent on λέγομεν, but introducing a justification of the statement just made (οὐ μὴ φθάσ.) by a fuller description of the Lord's Parousia.

αὐτὸς ὁ κύριος κτλ.] Αὐτός ('*Ipse*, grandis sermo' Beng.) draws attention to the fact that it is the Lord in 'His own august personal presence' (Ellic.) Who will descend, and thereby assure the certainty of His people's resurrection (cf. 1 Cor. xv. 23).

For the thought cf. Ac. i. 11, and for καταβαίνειν in a similar eschatological sense cf. Rev. iii. 12, xxi. 2, 10, also Mic. i. 3 ἰδοὺ Κύριος ἐκπορεύεται ἐκ τοῦ τόπου αὐτοῦ, καὶ καταβήσεται ἐπὶ τὰ ὕψη τῆς γῆς.

On ἀπ' οὐρανοῦ see i. 10 note.

ἐν κελεύσματι κτλ.] 'with a shout of command, with an archangel's voice and with God's trumpet'—accompaniments of the descending Lord, evidently chosen with special reference to the awaking of those who were asleep. The three clauses may represent distinct summonses, but the absence of any defining gen. with κελεύσματι makes it probable that it is to be taken as the general idea, which is then more fully described by the two appositional clauses that follow. In

φωνῆ ἀρχαγγέλου καὶ ἐν σάλπιγγι θεοῦ, καταβήσεται ἀπ' οὐρανοῦ, καὶ οἱ νεκροὶ ἐν Χριστῷ ἀναστήσονται

any case it must be kept in view that we are dealing here not with literal details, but with figures derived from the O.T. and contemporary Jewish writings, and that the whole is coloured by the imagery of our Lord's eschatological discourses, especially Matt. xxiv. 30 f.

For the use of ἐν to denote the attendant circumstances of the Lord's descent cf. Lk. xiv. 31, Eph. v. 26, vi. 2, Col. ii. 7; Blass p. 118. Κέλευσμα (ἅπ. λεγόμενον in the N.T., in LXX. only Prov. xxiv. 62 (xxx. 27)) is frequently used in class. Gk. with reference to the 'word of command' in battle (Hdt. iv. 141) or the 'call' of the κελευστής to the rowers (Eur. Iph. in T. 1405): cf. also for a close parallel to the passage before us Philo de praem. et poen. § 19 (ii. p. 928 M.) ἀνθρώπους ἐν ἐσχατιαῖς ἀπῳκισμένους ῥᾳδίως ἂν ἑνὶ κελεύσματι συναγώγοι θεὸς ἀπὸ περάτων. It is not stated by whom the κέλευσμα in the present instance is uttered, perhaps by an archangel, more probably by the Lord Himself as the principal subject of the whole sentence. Reitzenstein (*Poimandres*, p. 5 n.[3]) recalls a passage from the *Descensus Mariae* in which Michael (see below) is described as τὸ κέλευσμα τοῦ ἁγίου πνεύματος.

ἐν φωνῆ ἀρχαγγ.] a more specific explanation of the preceding κέλευσμα. The word ἀρχάγγελος is found elsewhere in the N.T. only in Jude 9, where it is directly associated with Michael, who is generally supposed to be referred to here; cf. Lueken *Michael* (Göttingen, 1898), Volz *Jüd. Eschat.* p. 195 for the part played by Michael in Jewish eschatology, and see also Cheyne *Exp.* VII. i. p. 289 ff. The absence of the artt., however, before φωνῆ and ἀρχαγγέλου makes it very doubtful whether any special archangel is thought of, and for the same reason the gen. both here and in σάλπ. θεοῦ is best treated as possessive—'a voice such as an archangel uses,' 'a trumpet dedicated to God's service' (WM. p. 310).

ἐν σάλπιγγι θεοῦ] In I Cor. xv. 52 this accompaniment is twice referred to as a distinguishing sign of Christ's approach ἐν τῇ ἐσχάτῃ σάλπιγγι· σαλπίσει γὰρ κτλ., the figure apparently being drawn from the parallel description in Joel ii. 1 σαλπίσατε σάλπιγγι ἐν Σειών,...διότι πάρεστιν ἡμέρα Κυρίου, ὅτι ἐγγύς. For similar exx. of trumpet-sounds accompanying the revelations of God cf. Ex. xix. 16, Isa. xxvii. 13, Zech. ix. 14, Pss. Sol. xi. 1, 4 Ezra vi. 23 ('et tuba canet cum sono, quam cum omnes audierint subito expauescent'), and for the speculations of later Judaism on this subject see Weber *Jüd. Theologie* p. 369 f.

καὶ οἱ νεκροί κτλ.] 'and the dead in Christ shall rise first.' The whole phrase οἱ νεκροὶ ἐν Χρ. forms one idea in antithesis to ἡμ. οἱ ζῶντες of the following clause, the significant formula ἐν Χριστῷ (cf. note on i. 1) pointing to the principle of life which was really at work in those who outwardly seemed to be dead.

The resurrection of *all* men does not here come into view, if indeed it is ever taught by St Paul (cf. Titius *Seligkeit* ii. p. 51 f.). All that the Apostles desire to emphasize, in answer to the Thessalonians' fears, is that the resurrection of 'the dead in Christ' will be the first act in the great drama at the Parousia, to be followed by the rapture of the 'living' saints: cf. especially Didache xvi. 6 f. where a 'first' resurrection of the saints alive is similarly assumed, ἀνάστασις νεκρῶν· οὐ πάντων δέ, ἀλλ' ὡς ἐρρέθη· Ἥξει ὁ Κύριος καὶ πάντες οἱ ἅγιοι μετ' αὐτοῦ.

πρῶτον, ¹⁷ἔπειτα ἡμεῖς οἱ ζῶντες οἱ περιλειπόμενοι ἅμα σὺν αὐτοῖς ἁρπαγησόμεθα ἐν νεφέλαις εἰς ἀπάντησιν

The v.l. πρῶτοι (D*G) may perhaps be due to the desire to assimilate the passage to the wholly different πρώτη ἀνάστασις of Rev. xx. 5.

17. ἔπειτα ἡμεῖς κτλ.] 'then we who are alive, who survive'—the qualifying clauses being repeated from v. 15 for the sake of emphasis. Περιλείπομαι is found only in these two vv. in the N.T., but occurs several times in the apocr. books of the LXX. (e.g. 2 Macc. i. 31, 4 Macc. xiii. 18), and in the later Gk. verss. (e.g. Sm. Ps. xx. (xxi.) 13). The word is class. (Hom. *Il.* xix. 230 ὅσσοι δ' ἂν πολέμοιο περὶ στυγεροῖο λίπωνται), and survives in the Κοινή e.g. P.Par. 63, 168 f. (ii./B.C.) ἀγεώργητος περιλειφθήσεται. The thought of the present passage finds a striking parallel in 4 Ezra vii. 28 'reuelabitur enim filius meus Iesus cum his qui cum eo, et iocundabit qui relicti sunt annis quadringentis': cf. also xiii. 24 cited above (v. 15 note).

For ἔπειτα (ἐπ' εἶτα, Hartung *Partik.* i. p. 302) denoting the speedy following of the event specified upon what has gone before, cf. 1 Cor. xv. 6 (with Ellicott's note).

ἅμα] to be closely connected with σὺν αὐτοῖς 'together with them,' 'all together,' in a local rather than in a temporal (Vg. *simul*) sense: cf. v. 10, and for the studied force of the expression see Deissmann *BS.* p. 64 n.².

ἁρπαγησόμεθα] 'shall be caught up' 'snatched up' (Vg. *rapiemur*), the verb in accordance with its usage both in class. Gk. and the LXX. suggesting forcible or sudden seizure, which, as the context proves, is here due to Divine agency (cf. Ac. viii. 39, 2 Cor. xii. 2, 4, Rev. xii. 5), the effect being still further heightened by the mysterious and awe-inspiring accompaniment ἐν νεφέλαις as the vehicle by which the quick and dead are wafted to meet their Lord (Grot. 'tanquam in curru triumphali'). According to Thackeray *Relation of St Paul to Contemporary Jewish Thought* (1900) p. 109 f. no adequate illustration of this use of the 'clouds' has yet been produced from contemporary Jewish or Christian literature, but for partial parallels cf. Mt. xxiv. 30, xxvi. 64 (ἐπὶ τ. νεφελῶν), Rev. i. 7 (μετὰ τ. νεφελῶν), passages which point back ultimately to Dan. vii. 13 ἰδοὺ ἐπὶ (μετὰ Th.) τῶν νεφελῶν τοῦ οὐρανοῦ ὡς υἱὸς ἀνθρώπου ἤρχετο, where the connexion with the present passage is all the closer owing to its primary reference to the glorified people of Israel. Cf. also the description of the taking up of Enoch: 'It came to pass when I had spoken to my sons these men (the angels A) summoned me and took me on their wings and placed me on the clouds' (*Secrets of Enoch* iii. 1).

εἰς ἀπάντησιν κτλ.] lit. 'for a meeting of the Lord into (the) air' (Vg. *obviam Christo in aëra*, Beza *in occursum Domini in aëra*). The thought is that the 'raptured' saints will be carried up into 'air,' as the interspace between heaven and earth, where they will meet the descending Lord, and then either escort Him down to the earth in accordance with O.T. prophecy, or more probably in keeping with the general context accompany Him back to heaven. In any case, in view of the general Jewish tendency to people the 'air' with evil spirits (cf. Eph. ii. 2, and see *Asc. Isai.* vii. 9, *Test. xii. patr.* Benj. iii. 4 τοῦ ἀερίου πνεύματος τοῦ βελίαρ), it can hardly be regarded here as the abode of final bliss: cf. Aug. *de civ. Dei* xx. 20. 2 'non sic accipiendum est, tanquam in aëre nos dixerit semper cum Domino esse mansuros; quia nec ipse utique ibi manebit, quia veniens transiturus est. Venienti quippe ibitur obviam,

τοῦ κυρίου εἰς ἀέρα· καὶ οὕτως πάντοτε σὺν κυρίῳ ἐσόμεθα. ¹⁸ Ὥστε παρακαλεῖτε ἀλλήλους ἐν τοῖς λόγοις τούτοις.

non manenti.' It will be noted that nothing is said here of the physical transformation with which according to St Paul's teaching elsewhere (1 Cor. xv. 35—53, 2 Cor. v. 1—4, Phil. iii. 20 f.) this 'rapture' will be accompanied. The phrase εἰς ἀπάντησιν (frequent in LXX. for Heb. לִקְרַאת) is found c. gen. in Mt. xxvii. 32 (WH. mg.), c. dat. in Ac. xxviii. 15, and is used absolutely in Mt. xxv. 6 : cf. also Mt. xxv. 1 εἰς ὑπάντησιν τοῦ νυμφίου where the closely-related ὑπάντησιν lays stress on 'waiting for' rather than on actual 'meeting.' An interesting instance of the phrase is furnished by Polyb. v. 26. 8 εἰς τὴν ἀπάντησιν 'at his reception,' with reference to the preparations made for the welcome of Apelles in Corinth, with which may be compared P.Tebt. 43, 7 (ii./B.C.) παρεγενήθημεν εἰς ἀπάντησιν of the formal reception of a newly-arriving magistrate. B.G.U. 362. vii. 17 (iii./A.D.) πρὸς [ἀ]πάντη[σιν τοῦ] ἡγεμόνος and the Pelagia-Legenden p. 19 (ed. Usener) εἰς ἀπάντησιν τοῦ ὁσίου ἀνδρός illustrate the genitive-construction of the passage before us. See further Moulton Prolegg. p. 14 n.³.

καὶ οὕτως κτλ.] It was towards this goal, a life of uninterrupted (πάντοτε) communion with his risen and glorified Lord that St Paul's longings in thinking of the future always turned : cf. v. 10, II. ii. 1, 2 Cor. v. 8, Col. iii. 4, Phil. i. 23 σὺν Χριστῷ εἶναι.

Christ is the end, for Christ was the beginning,
Christ the beginning, for the end is Christ.

The contrast with the generally materialistic expectations of the time hardly needs mention (see Intr. p. lxx), but, as showing the height to which even Pharisaic belief occasionally rose, cf. Pss. Sol. iii. 16 οἱ δὲ φοβούμενοι [τὸν, Gebhardt] κύριον ἀναστήσονται εἰς ζωὴν αἰώνιον, καὶ ἡ ζωὴ αὐτῶν ἐν φωτὶ κυρίου καὶ οὐκ ἐκλείψει ἔτι, and 4 Ezra viii. 39, 'sed iocundabor super iustorum figmentum, peregrinationis quoque et saluationis et mercedis receptionis.'

18. ὥστε παρακαλεῖτε κτλ.] Aug. : 'Pereat contristatio, ubi tanta est consolatio' (Serm. clxxiii. 3). For παρακαλεῖν here evidently in its secondary sense of 'comfort' see ii. 11 note ; while, as showing the difference between Christian and heathen sources of comfort, reference may be made to the papyrus-letter of 'consolation' (P.Oxy. 115 (ii./A.D.)) where, after expressing his grief at the news of a friend's death, the writer concludes— ἀλλ' ὅμως οὐδὲν δύναταί τις πρὸς τὰ τοιαῦτα. παρηγορεῖτε οὖν ἑαυτούς, 'but still there is nothing one can do in the face of such trouble. So I leave you to comfort yourselves.' For the whole letter see Add. Note A, and cf. Deissmann New Light on the N.T. (1907) p. 76.

ἐν τοῖς λόγοις τούτοις] 'with these words' viz. vv. 15—17. This is apparently one of the instances where a full *instrumental* sense can be given to ἐν in accordance with a usage not unknown in classical (Kühner³ § 431, 3 a), and largely developed in later Gk., cf. Lk. xxii. 49, 1 Cor. iv. 21, and for exx. from the Κοινή see P.Tebt. 48, 18 f. (ii./B.C.) Λύκος σὺν ἄλλοις ἐν ὅπλοις and the other instances cited by the editors on p. 86. On the consequent disappearance of another of the so-called 'Hebraisms' from the N.T. see Deissmann BS. p. 118 ff., Moulton Prolegg. pp. 12, 61 f., and cf. Kuhring p. 31 f.

V. ¹Περὶ δὲ τῶν χρόνων καὶ τῶν καιρῶν, ἀδελφοί, οὐ χρείαν ἔχετε ὑμῖν γράφεσθαι, ²αὐτοὶ γὰρ ἀκριβῶς

V. 1—11. TEACHING CONCERNING THE SUDDENNESS OF THE ADVENT AND THE NEED OF WATCHFULNESS.

The second difficulty or danger of the Thessalonians was closely connected with the first. So long as they had thought that only those who were actually alive at the time of Christ's Parousia would share in His full blessedness, they had been doubly impatient of any postponement in His coming, lest they themselves might not survive to see that Day. And though the principal ground of their disquiet had now been removed (iv. 13—17), the prevailing restlessness and excitement were such (see Intr. p. xlvi f.), that the Apostles were led to remind their converts of what they had already laid down so clearly in their oral teaching, that 'the day of the Lord' would come as a surprise (vv. 1—5), and consequently that continued watchfulness and self-restraint were necessary on the part of all who would be found ready for it (vv. 6—11).

1—5. 'We have been speaking of Christ's Return. As to the time when that will take place, Brothers, we do not need to say anything further. For you yourselves have already been fully informed that the coming of the Day of the Lord is as unexpected as the coming of a thief in the night. It is just when men are feeling most secure that ruin confronts them suddenly as the birth-pang a travailing woman, and escape is no longer possible. But as for you, Brothers, the case is very different. You are living in the daylight now: and therefore the coming of *the* Day will not catch you unawares.'

1. Περὶ δὲ τ. χρόνων κτλ.] Vg. *de temporibus autem et momentis*, Beza *porro de temporibus et opportunitatibus*. The two words (cf. Ac. i. 7, Dan. ii. 21, vii. 12, Eccles. iii. 1, Sap. viii. 8; P.Lond. I. 42, 23 f. (ii./B.C.) τοσούτου χρόνου ἐπιγεγονότος καὶ τοιούτων καιρῶν) are often distinguished as if they referred to longer and shorter periods of time respectively (Beng.: χρόνων *partes*, καιροί), but χρόνος rather expresses simply duration, time viewed in its extension, and καιρός a definite space of time, time with reference both to its extent and character: cf. Tit. i. 2 f. where this distinction comes out very clearly, ἣν (sc. ζωὴν αἰώνιον) ἐπηγγείλατο ὁ ἀψευδὴς θεὸς πρὸ χρόνων αἰωνίων ἐφανέρωσεν δὲ καιροῖς ἰδίοις. In the present instance therefore χρόνων may be taken as a general description of the 'ages' that may elapse before the Parousia, while καιρῶν draws attention to the critical 'periods' (*articuli*) by which these 'ages' will be marked.

In the N.T. καιρός is very common with an eschatological reference, probably, as Hort suggests (1 *Pet.* p. 51), owing to the manner of its use in Daniel (ix. 27 &c.): cf. Mk. xiii. 33, Lk. xxi. 8, 24, Ac. iii. 19, Eph. i. 10, 1 Tim. vi. 15, Tit. i. 3, Heb. ix. 10, Rev. i. 3, xi. 18, xxii. 10. It should be noted however that it is by no means limited by St Paul to its special use, but is also used of time generally, e.g. Rom. iii. 26, viii. 18, 1 Cor. vii. 29, Eph. v. 16 (with Robinson's note). See further Trench *Syn.* § lvii., and for an interesting discussion of the Gk. idea of καιρός see Butcher *Harvard Lectures on Greek Subjects* (1904) p. 117 ff. The distinction alluded to above survives in mod. Gk. where χρόνος='year,' and καιρός='weather.'

On ἀδελφοί see i. 4 note, and on οὐ χρ. ἔχ. see iv. 9 note.

2. αὐτοὶ γὰρ ἀκριβῶς κτλ.] 'For

οἴδατε ὅτι ἡμέρα Κυρίου ὡς κλέπτης ἐν νυκτὶ οὕτως

yourselves (A.V. 1611 'your selues') know accurately'—a further appeal to the Thessalonians' own experience (cf. ii. 1 note), the addition of ἀκριβῶς being due not only to the stress laid by the Apostles on this point in their oral teaching, but perhaps also to the fact that then as now (see below) that teaching had been based on the actual words of the Lord. For a somewhat similar use of ἀκριβῶς cf. Ac. xviii. 25 where it is said of Apollos ἐδίδασκεν ἀκριβῶς τὰ περὶ τοῦ Ἰησοῦ, though it is going too far to find there with Blass a proof that Apollos made use of a written gospel ('accurate...videlicet non sine scripto euangelio': cf. Knowling E.G.T. ad loc., and see J. H. A. Hart J.T.S. vii. p. 17 ff.). In Eph. v. 15, the only other Pauline passage where the word occurs, it can mean little more than 'carefully' if we follow the best-attested reading βλέπετε οὖν ἀκριβῶς (א*B): if however with א°A ἀκριβῶς belongs to περιπατεῖτε, the thought of strict conformity to a standard is again introduced. The same idea underlies the old Engl. use of 'diligently' by which the word is rendered in the A.V. of Mt. ii. 8 (cf. ἠκρίβωσεν 'inquired diligently' v. 7), as is shown by the translators' own description of their version as 'with the former Translations diligently compared and revised.'

Ἀκριβῶς is found with οἶδα as here in P.Cairo 3, 8 f. (iii./B.C.) ὅπως ἀκριβῶς εἰδῆις, P.Petr. II. 15 (1), 11 (iii./B.C.) εἰδῆσαι ἀκριβῶς; cf. P.Hib. 40, 6 f. (iii./B.C.) ἐπίστασο μέντοι ἀκριβῶς.

ὅτι ἡμέρα Κυρίου κτλ.] an evident reminiscence of the Lord's own teaching Mt. xxiv. 43, Lk. xii. 39: cf. Rev. iii. 3, xvi. 15, and for a similar use of the same figure 2 Pet. iii. 10. The absence of the art. before ἡμέρα is due not only to the fact that the expression had come to be regarded as a kind of proper name, but to the emphasis laid on the character of the day, a day *of the Lord*. It 'belongs to Him, is His time for working, for manifesting Himself, for displaying His character, for performing His work—His strange work upon the earth' (A. B. Davidson, *Theol. of the O.T.* (1904) p. 375).

The phrase is first found in the O.T. in Amos v. 18 ff., where the prophet criticizes the popular expectation that the 'day' was to be a day not of judgment but of national deliverance (perhaps in connexion with phrases like the 'day of Midian' Isa. ix. 4 recalling the victory of Israel over her foes, see W. R. Smith *Prophets of Israel*[2] p. 397 f.). It is very frequent in the later prophecies (e.g. Isa. ii. 12 ff., Zeph. i. 7 ff., Mal. iii. 2, iv. 1), and always with a definite eschatological reference to the term fixed for the execution of judgment: see further A. B. Davidson *op. cit.* p. 374 ff., and Art. 'Eschatology' in Hastings' *D.B.* i. p. 735 ff., also the elaborate discussion in Gressmann *Der Ursprung der israelitisch-jüdischen Eschatologie* (1905) p. 141 ff.

The actual comparison ὡς κλέπτης is not found in the O.T. (but cf. Job xxiv. 14, Jer. xxix. 10 (xlix. 9), Obad. 5), while the addition of ἐν νυκτί, which is peculiar to the present passage, may have led to the belief so widely prevalent in the early Church that Christ would come at night (Lact. *Instt.* vii. 19 'intempesta nocte et tenebrosa,' Hieron. *ad* Mt. xxv. 6 'media nocte'). Ἔρχεται, pres. for fut., lends vividness and certainty to the whole idea (cf. Blass, p. 189).

For Jewish apocalyptic speculations as to the nearness of the End, combined with uncertainty as to its exact date, see Volz *Jüd. Eschat.* p. 162 ff.

ἔρχεται. ³ὅταν ᵀ λέγωσιν Εἰρήνη καὶ ἀσφάλεια, τότε αἰφνίδιος αὐτοῖς ἐπίσταται ὄλεθρος ὥσπερ ἡ ὠδὶν τῇ ἐν

V 3 ὅταν solum ℵ*AG 17 al pauc d g Go Syr (Pesh) Boh Arm Aeth Iren[lat] Tert Cypr Orig[lat] Ambst Hier Theod-Mops[lat] al: ὅταν δὲ ℵᶜBD al Syr (Harcl) Eus Chr Thdt

3. ὅταν λέγωσιν κτλ.] There is good authority for inserting δέ (WH. mg.) after ὅταν, but on the whole ms. evidence is against it, and the verse must be regarded as standing in close (asyndetic) relation to the preceding clause. The subject is left indefinite, but can only be unbelieving men (Beng.: 'ceteri, qui sunt tenebrarum'), while the pres. (instead of the aor.) subj. after ὅταν points to coincidence of time in the events spoken of: it is 'at the very moment when they are saying' &c., cf. Rev. xviii. 9, and see Abbott Joh. Gr. p. 385.

Εἰρήνη κτλ.] a reminiscence of Ezek. xiii. 10 (λέγοντες Εἰρήνη, καὶ οὐκ ἦν εἰρήνη), ἀσφάλεια (Vg. securitas, Clarom. munitio, Ambrstr. firmitas) being added here to draw increased attention to the feeling of security. The latter word is rare in the N.T. occurring elsewhere only twice in Lk. (Go.¹ Ac.¹): in the papyri it is found as a law-term = 'bond,' 'security,' e.g. P.Tebt. 27, 73 f. (ii./B.C.) ἄνευ τοῦ δοῦναι τὴν ἀσφάλειαν.

τότε αἰφνίδιος κτλ.] Cf. Lk. xxi. 34 προσέχετε δὲ ἑαυτοῖς μή ποτε...ἐπιστῇ ἐφ' ὑμᾶς ἐφνίδιος ἡ ἡμέρα ἐκείνη ὡς παγίς.

Αἰ(ε)φνίδιος is found only in these two passages in the N.T., but it occurs several times in the O.T. apocrypha, Sap. xvii. 15 (14) αἰφνίδιος γὰρ αὐτοῖς καὶ ἀπροσδόκητος φόβος ἐπῆλθεν, 2 Macc. xiv. 17, 3 Macc. iii. 24; cf. also O.G.I.S. 339, 18 (ii./B.C.) ἐκ τῆς αἰφνιδίου περιστάσεως. For the form see WH.² Notes p. 157 f., and for the use of the adjective, where we would expect an adverb, to give point and clearness to the sentence see WM. p. 582 f. The adverb is found

in P.Fay. 123, 21 f. (c. A.D. 100) ἀλλὰ αἰφνιδί[[·]]ως εἴρηχεν ἡμῖν σήμερον. In ἐπίσταται (Vg. superveniet, Beza imminet) the idea of suddenness does not belong to the verb itself, though frequently, as here, it is suggested by the context, cf. Lk. xx. 1, Ac. vi. 12, xvii. 5, where ἐφίστημι is used similarly of hostile intent. It occurs elsewhere in the Pauline writings only in 2 Tim. iv. 2, 6. The unaspirated form ἐπίσταται may be due to confusion with the other verb ἐπίσταμαι (WH.² Notes p. 151, WSchm. p. 39).

Ὄλεθρος (class., LXX.) is confined in the N.T. to the Pauline Epp., and, while not necessarily implying annihilation (cf. 1 Cor. v. 5), carries with it the thought of utter and hopeless ruin, the loss of all that gives worth to existence (II. i. 9, 1 Tim. vi. 9): cf. Sap. i. 12 and especially 4 Macc. x. 15 where τὸν αἰώνιον τοῦ τυράννου ὄλεθρον is contrasted with τὸν ἀοίδιμον τῶν εὐσεβῶν βίον. The word is thus closely related to ἀπωλεία (Mt. vii. 13, Rom. ix. 22, Phil. iii. 19): see further J. A. Beet The Last Things (ed. 1905) p. 122 ff.

ὥσπερ ἡ ὠδὶν κτλ.] Another reminiscence of our Lord's teaching, Mt. xxiv. 8, Mk. xiii. 8, cf. Jo. xvi. 21. The same figure is frequent in the O.T. e.g. Isa. xiii. 8, Jer. iv. 31, Hos. xiii. 13, 2 Esdr. xvi. 38 f.—passages which doubtless suggested the Rabbinic expectation of the חֶבְלֵי־הַמָּשִׁיחַ, see Schürer Geschichte³ ii. p. 523 f. (E.Tr. Div. II. ii. p. 154 f.), Weber Jüd. Theol. p. 350 f. The expression is never however used by St Paul in this sense (for the idea cf. 1 Cor. vii. 26), and in the present passage the

M. THESS.   5

γαστρὶ ἐχούσῃ, καὶ οὐ μὴ ἐκφύγωσιν. ⁴ὑμεῖς δέ, ἀδελφοί, οὐκ ἐστὲ ἐν σκότει, ἵνα ἡ ἡμέρα ὑμᾶς ὡς ⌜κλέπτας⌝
καταλάβῃ, ⁵πάντες γὰρ ὑμεῖς υἱοὶ φωτός ἐστε καὶ υἱοὶ

4 κλέπτας AB Boh: κλέπτης ℵDG cet fere omn verss Ephr Chr Theod-Mops[lat]

figure must not be pressed to denote more than the *suddenness* of the coming—

For suddenly
It comes; the dreadfulness must be
In that; all warrants the belief—
'At night it cometh like a thief.'
(R. Browning 'Easter-Day.')

The late ὠδίν (for ὠδίς) is found in the LXX. Isa. xxxvii. 3; cf. in the Κοινή nom. εὐθύριν, P.Grenf. II. 35, 5 (i./B.C.). In οὐ μὴ ἐκφύγ. we have probably another reminiscence of Lk. xxi. (see above), ἵνα κατισχύσητε ἐκφυγεῖν ταῦτα πάντα (v. 36). For the absolute use of the verb in the present passage cf. Ac. xvi. 27, Heb. ii. 3, xii. 25, Sir. xvi. 13 (14), and for οὐ μή see the note on iv. 15.

4. ὑμεῖς δέ κτλ.] Ὑμεῖς emphatic, and conjoined with the following ἀδελφοί suggesting a direct contrast to the unbelieving men of v. 3: cf. Eph. iv. 20. Whatever the past state of the Thessalonians may have been, in the eyes of the Apostles they are no longer (οὐκ ἐστέ) in darkness, the reference being not merely to mental ignorance (Thdt. τὴν ἄγνοιαν), but, as the sequel shows, including also the thought of moral estrangement from God (Chrys. τὸν σκοτεινὸν καὶ ἀκάθαρτον βίον). For the general thought cf. 2 Cor. vi. 14, Eph. v. 8, Col. i. 12. Τό (for ὁ) σκότος, rare in good Attic writers, is the regular form in the N.T.: cf. LXX. Isa. xlii. 16.

ἵνα ἡ ἡμέρα κτλ.] It is possible to give ἵνα here its full telic force (cf. ii. 16) as indicating the Divine purpose for those who are still ἐν σκότει, but it is simpler to find another instance of its well-established late ecbatic use, 'so that the day...': see the note on

iv. 1. Ἡ ἡμέρα can only be 'the day' already referred to (v. 2), the day *par excellence*, the day of judgment, while for καταλάβῃ (Vg. *comprehendat*, Beza *deprehendat*) of 'overtake' in a hostile sense cf. Mk. ix. 18, Jo. xii. 35, and the saying ascribed to the Lord ἐν οἷς ἂν ὑμᾶς καταλάβω, ἐν τούτοις καὶ κρινῶ (Just. M. Dial. 47).

ὡς κλέπτας] By an inversion of metaphor by no means uncommon in the Pauline writings (cf. ii. 7[b] note), the figure of the 'thief' is now transferred from the *cause* of the surprise (v. 2) to its *object*, the idea being that as the 'day' unpleasantly surprises the thief who has failed in carrying through his operations, so 'the day' will 'overtake' those who are not prepared for it. The reading however, though well-attested, is by no means certain, and the dependence of the whole passage on Mt. xxiv. 43 (Lk. xii. 39) may be taken as supporting the easier κλέπτης (WH. mg). Weiss (*Textkritik* p. 17) regards ὑμᾶς ὡς κλέπτας as a 'purely mechanical conformation.'

5. πάντες γὰρ ὑμεῖς κτλ.] a restatement of what has just been said from the positive side, but extended to embrace *all*, and deepened by the relation now predicated of the Thessalonians. They are not only 'in' light, but are 'sons of light,' sharing in the being and nature of light, and also 'sons of day,' ἡμέρας being used apparently not so much generally of the enlightened sphere in which light rules, as with special reference to the 'day' of Christ's appearing already spoken of, in which the Thessalonians in virtue of their Christian standing will have part. On the connexion of light with

ἡμέρας. Οὐκ ἐσμὲν νυκτὸς οὐδὲ σκότους· ⁶ἄρα οὖν μὴ καθεύδωμεν ὡς οἱ λοιποί, ἀλλὰ γρηγορῶμεν καὶ νήφωμεν.

the day of the Lord in O.T. prophecy see such passages as Hos. vi. 5 τὸ κρίμα μου ὡς φῶς ἐξελεύσεται, Mic. vii. 8 f. ἐὰν καθίσω ἐν τῷ σκότει, Κύριος φωτιεῖ μοι...καὶ ἐξάξεις με εἰς τὸ φῶς, and cf. Enoch xxxviii. 4 (with Charles's note), cviii. 11 f. For the 'New Testament' idiom underlying υἱ. φωτ. and υἱ. ἡμ. cf. Lk. xvi. 8, Eph. v. 8 and see Deissmann BS. p. 161 ff., and for the *chiasmus*—σκότους corresponding to φωτός, and νυκτός to ἡμέρας—see Kühner³ § 607, 3. Lft. cites by way of illustration Eur. *Iph. in Taur.* 1025—6 ΙΦ. ὡς δὴ σκότος λαβόντες ἐκσωθεῖμεν ἄν; OP. κλεπτῶν γὰρ ἡ νύξ, τῆς δ' ἀληθείας τὸ φῶς, but the passage is wanting in the best MSS., and is probably a Christian interpolation.

5ᵇ—11. 'Surely then, as those who have nothing to do with the darkness, we (for this applies to you and to us alike) ought not to sleep, but to exercise continual watchfulness and self-control. Night is the general time for sleep and drunkenness. But those who belong to the day must control themselves, and put on the full panoply of heaven. That will not only protect them against sudden attack, but give them the assurance of final and complete salvation. Salvation (we say), for this is God's purpose for us, and He has opened up for us the way to secure it through our Lord Jesus Christ. His death on our behalf is the constant pledge that, living or dying, we shall live together with Him. Wherefore comfort and edify one another, as indeed we know that you are already doing.'

5ᵇ. Οὐκ ἐσμὲν νυκτός κτλ.] For the substitution of the 1st for the 2nd pers. see Intr. p. xliv n.², and for the gen. with ἐσμέν pointing to the *sphere* to which the subjects belong see WM. p. 244.

6. ἄρα οὖν] introduces emphatically the necessary conclusion from the preceding statement, 'the illative ἄρα being supported and enhanced by the collective and retrospective οὖν' (Ellic.). The combination is peculiar to St Paul in the N.T., and always stands at the beginning of sentences, cf. II. ii. 15, Rom. v. 18, vii. 3, 25 &c., Gal. vi. 10, Eph. ii. 19, and see WM. p. 556 f.

μὴ καθεύδωμεν κτλ.] For καθεύδω in its ethical sense of moral and spiritual insensibility cf. Mk. xiii. 36, Eph. v. 14, and contrast the usage in v. 7 and again in v. 10. For ὡς οἱ λοιποί see the note on iv. 13.

ἀλλὰ γρηγορῶμεν κτλ.] Cf. 1 Pet. v. 8 where the same combination of words is found though in a different connexion. In the present passage the words are probably echoes of our Lord's own eschatological teaching; thus for γρηγορῶμεν cf. Mt. xxiv. 42, xxv. 13, Mk. xiii. 35, and for νήφωμεν cf. Lk. xxi. 34, where however the word itself does not occur.

Γρηγορέω (a late formation from ἐγρήγορα, Lob. *Phryn.* p. 118 f., WSchm. p. 104 n.²) is found twenty-three times in the N.T., and occasionally in the later books of the LXX., e.g. Jer. xxxviii. 28, 1 Macc. xii. 27 ἐπέταξεν Ἰωναθὰν τοῖς παρ' αὐτοῦ γρηγορεῖν...δι' ὅλης τῆς νυκτός; cf. also Ign. *Polyc.* i. γρηγόρει ἀκοίμητον πνεῦμα κεκτημένος. From it was formed the new verbal noun γρηγόρησις Dan. TH. v. 11, 14: cf. also the proper name Γρηγόριος.

In addition to this v. and v. 8 νήφω is found in the N.T. only in 2 Tim. iv. 5 (νῆφε ἐν πᾶσιν) and three times in 1 Pet. (i. 13, iv. 7, v. 8). As distinguished from γρηγορέω, a mental attitude, it points rather to a condition of moral alertness, the senses being so exercised and disciplined

68 THE FIRST EPISTLE TO THE THESSALONIANS [V 7, 8

⁷οἱ γὰρ καθεύδοντες νυκτὸς καθεύδουσιν, καὶ οἱ μεθυσκόμενοι νυκτὸς μεθύουσιν· ⁸ἡμεῖς δὲ ἡμέρας ὄντες νήφωμεν, ἐνδυσάμενοι θώρακα πίστεως καὶ ἀγάπης καὶ περικεφαλαίαν

that all fear of sleeping again is removed (Chrys.: γρηγορήσεως ἐπίτασις ἡ νῆψίς ἐστιν): cf. Aristeas 209 where the τρόπος βασιλείας is said to consist in τὸ συντηρεῖν...ἑαυτὸν ἀδωροδόκητον καὶ νήφειν τὸ πλεῖον μέρος τοῦ βίου. 7. οἱ γὰρ καθεύδοντες κτλ.] There is no need to look here for any figurative reference of the words (e.g. Clem. Al. Paed. II. ix. 80, I τουτέστιν ἐν τῷ τῆς ἀγνοίας σκότῳ, Aug. ad Ps. cxxxi. 8): they are simply a statement of the recognized fact that night is the general time when men sleep and are drunken; cf. 2 Pet. ii. 13 ἡδονὴν ἡγούμενοι τὴν ἐν ἡμέρᾳ τρυφήν for the deeper blame associated with revelling in the day-time, and see Mt. xxiv. 48 ff. for the possible source of the passage before us.

The verbs μεθύσκω lit. 'make drunk' and μεθύω 'am drunk' are here virtually synonymous ('ohne merklichen Unterschied,' WSchm. p. 129), and nothing is gained by trying to distinguish them in translation (Vg. ebrii sunt...ebrii sunt, Clarom., Beza inebriantur... ebrii sunt). Νυκτός, gen. of time, cf. χειμῶνος Mk. xiii. 18, and see WM. p. 258.

8. ἡμεῖς δέ κτλ.] 'But let us, since we are of the day, be sober'—the part. having a slightly causal force almost = ὅτι ἡμέρας ἐσμέν. On the other hand the aor. part. ἐνδυσάμενοι is to be closely connected with the principal verb as indicating the manner in which the νήφειν is accomplished, 'having put on' once for all, whether as an antecedent or a necessary accompaniment: cf. 1 Pet. i. 13 ἀναζωσάμενοι...νήφοντες τελείως, ἐλπίσατε ἐπὶ τ. φερομένην ὑμῖν χάριν ἐν ἀποκαλύψει Ἰησοῦ Χριστοῦ.

θώρακα πίστεως κτλ.] The first occurrence of the favourite Pauline figure of armour: cf. Rom. xiii. 12 f. (where there is the same connexion of thought), 2 Cor. vi. 7, x. 4, and for a more detailed account Eph. vi. 13 ff., where however the particulars of the figure are applied somewhat differently, showing that the imagery must not be pressed too closely. For the origin of the simile in each case see the description of Jehovah in Isa. lix. 17 καὶ ἐνεδύσατο δικαιοσύνην ὡς θώρακα, καὶ περιέθετο περικεφαλαίαν σωτηρίου ἐπὶ τῆς κεφαλῆς (cf. Isa. xi. 4 f., Sap. v. 17 ff.), though in his use of it St Paul may also have been influenced by the Jewish conception of the last great fight against the armies of Antichrist (Dan. xi., Orac. Sib. iii. 663 f., 4 Ezra xiii. 10, Enoch xc. 16) as suggested by SH. p. 378.

It should be noted however that in the present instance the weapons spoken of are only those of *defence* in view of the trials which beset believers. Thus we have in the first place θώρ. πίστεως κτλ. 'a breastplate of (or, consisting in) faith and love' (gen. of apposition, Blass p. 98)—a significant complement to the θώρ. τ. δικαιοσύνης of Eph. vi. 14 : 'by faith we are able to realise the Divine will and the Divine power and by love to embody faith in our dealings with men : this is righteousness' (Westcott ad loc.). This is accompanied by περικεφ. ἐλπίδα σωτηρίας 'an helmet the hope of salvation,' where from its eschatological reference σωτηρίας can only be gen. obj. 'hope directed towards salvation,' the mention of 'hope' which does not occur in the Isaian and Ephesian passages being in accord with the dominant teaching of the whole Epistle.

The Hellenistic περικεφαλαία is found eleven times in the LXX., else-

V 9, 10] THE FIRST EPISTLE TO THE THESSALONIANS 69

ἐλπίδα cωτηρίαc· 9ὅτι οὐκ ἔθετο ⌜ἡμᾶς ὁ θεὸς⌝ εἰς ὀργὴν ἀλλὰ εἰς περιποίησιν σωτηρίας διὰ τοῦ κυρίου ἡμῶν Ἰησοῦ [Χριστοῦ], 10τοῦ ἀποθανόντος ⌜περὶ⌝ ἡμῶν ἵνα

9 ἡμᾶς ὁ θεὸς] ὁ θεὸς ἡμᾶς B 37 116   Χριστοῦ om B Aeth   10 περὶ א*B 17 : ὑπὲρ אᶜADG cet Chr Thdt al

where in the N.T. only in Eph. vi. 17. For the growth in the Bibl. conception σωτηρία, which in the Κοινή is frequently = 'health' e.g. B.G.U. 380, 19 ff. (a mother's letter, iii./A.D.) μὴ οὖν ἀμελήσῃς, τέχνον, γράψε μοι περὶ τῆς σωτηρίας [σ]ου, see SH. p. 23 f. The title σωτήρ is discussed by Wendland Z.N.T.W. v. (1904) p. 335 ff., and σώζειν and its derivatives by Wagner Z.N.T.W. vi. (1905) p. 205 ff., where it is shown that in the N.T. the *positive* conception of deliverance to new and eternal life is predominant.

9. ὅτι οὐκ ἔθετο κτλ.] Ὅτι, 'because,' introducing the ground not so much of the hope as of the completed salvation just referred to, which is now described under its two essential aspects of (1) deliverance from wrath, (2) the imparting of eternal life. It is with (1) only that the present v. is concerned and that from (a) a negative (οὐκ ἔθετο κτλ.) and (b) a positive standpoint (ἀλλὰ εἰς περιποίησιν κτλ.).

ἔθετο] While the 'somewhat vague' ἔθετο must not be pressed too far, it clearly carries back the deliverance of the Thessalonians to the direct purpose and action of God, cf. i. 4, ii. 12, II. ii. 13 f., and see Intr. p. lxv. For a similar use of τίθημι cf. Jo. xv. 16, Ac. xiii. 47, 1 Tim. ii. 7, 2 Tim. i. 11, and 1 Pet. ii. 8 (with Hort's note). For ὀργή cf. i. 10 note.

εἰς περιποίησιν σωτηρίας] a difficult phrase from the doubt whether περιποίησιν is to be understood actively of the 'winning' of salvation on the part of man, or passively of the 'adoption' of (consisting in) salvation bestowed by God. In support of the latter view appeal is made to 1 Pet. ii. 9 and Eph. i. 14, but the sense of the former passage (which is taken from Mal. iii. 17) is determined by the use of the word λαός, 'people for a possession,' and in Eph. i. 14 the passive sense, though undoubtedly more natural, is not necessary (cf. Abbott 'a complete redemption which *will give possession*'). And as in the only other passages where the word occurs in the N.T. (II. ii. 14, Heb. x. 39), the active sense is alone suitable, it is better to employ it here also, all the more so because, as Findlay has pointed out, it is the natural sequel of the 'wakeful, soldierlike activity' to which the Thessalonians have already been summoned (vv. 6—8).

The thought of this activity on the part of true believers is not however allowed to obscure the real source of all salvation, namely διὰ τ. κυρ. ἡμ. Ἰησ. [Χριστοῦ], where emphasis is laid not only on the Divine side (κυρίου) of the historic Jesus, but, if Χριστοῦ (omit B aeth) is read, on the fulfilment in Him of God's redemptive purposes. On how this is effected, and the full blessing of salvation as eternal life secured, the next v. proceeds to show.

10. τοῦ ἀποθανόντος κτλ.] a relative clause emphasizing that it is specially to the Lord 'who died' that we must look as the medium of our salvation, the intimate character of the relation between His 'death' and our 'life' being brought out still more clearly if we can adopt the v.l. ὑπέρ (WH. mg.) for the more colourless περί, which is found elsewhere in the Pauline Epp. in a similar connexion only in Rom. viii. 3 (ἁμαρτίας), cf. Gal. i. 4

εἴτε γρηγορῶμεν εἴτε καθεύδωμεν ἅμα σὺν αὐτῷ ζήσωμεν. ¹¹Διὸ παρακαλεῖτε ἀλλήλους καὶ οἰκοδομεῖτε εἷς τὸν ἕνα, καθὼς καὶ ποιεῖτε.

W H. mg. The point cannot however be pressed in view of the 'enfeebling' of the distinction between the two prepositions in late and colloquial Gk.: cf. Moulton *Prolegg.* p. 105. It will be noticed that there is no direct mention here of the accompanying Resurrection of Christ as in i. 10, iv. 14, and generally throughout the Pauline Epp. (Rom. iv. 25, v. 10 &c.), but it is implied in the following ἅμα σὺν αὐτῷ ζήσωμεν. For the doctrinal significance of this whole verse see Intr. p. lxviii f.

ἵνα εἴτε γρηγορῶμεν κτλ.] 'in order that whether we wake or sleep'—the verbs being used no longer in the ethical sense of *v.* 6, but by a slight change of figure as metaphorical designations of life and death. Thdt.: ἐγρηγορότας γὰρ ἐκάλεσε τοὺς ἔτι κατ' ἐκεῖνον τὸν καιρὸν περιόντας· καθεύδοντας δὲ τοὺς τετελευτηκότας. To this particular use of γρηγορέω no Bibl. parallel can be adduced, but καθεύδω, as denoting death, is found in the LXX., Ps. lxxxvii. (lxxxviii.) 6, Dan. xii. 2. Wohlenberg suggests that some proverbial saying may underlie the phrase (cf. 1 Cor. x. 31), and cites by way of illustration Plato *Sym.* 203 A where it is said of Eros διὰ τούτου πᾶσά ἐστιν ἡ ὁμιλία καὶ ἡ διάλεκτος θεοῖς πρὸς ἀνθρώπους, καὶ ἐγρηγορόσι καὶ καθεύδουσι. In its use here the Apostles were doubtless influenced by the perplexity of the Thessalonians which their previous teaching had been directed to meet (iv. 13 ff.).

Εἴτε...εἴτε with the subj., though rare among Attic prose-writers (cf. Plato *Legg.* xii. 958 D εἴτε τις ἄρρην εἴτε τις θῆλυς ᾖ), is common in Hellenistic and late Gk. In the present instance the subj. may be the result of attraction to the principal verb ζήσωμεν, but is perhaps sufficiently explained by the nature of the thought, the 'waking' or 'sleeping' being presented in each case as a possible alternative (Burton § 253).

ἅμα σὺν αὐτῷ ζήσωμεν] 'we should live together with Him'—the use of the aor. ζήσωμεν pointing to this 'life' as a definite fact secured to us by the equally definite death (τ. ἀποθανόντος) of our Lord. It may be noted however that Blass (p. 212) prefers the reading ζήσομεν (A) on the ground that the aor. ζήσωμεν (ℵ *al*) would mean 'come to life again' as in Rom. xiv. 9.

The question whether this 'life' is to be confined to the new life which belongs to believers here, or to the perfected life that awaits them hereafter, can hardly be said to arise. It is sufficient for the Apostle that through union with (ἅμα σύν, iv. 17 note) their Lord believers have an actual part in His experience, and that consequently for them too 'death' has been transformed into 'life'; cf. Rom. xiv. 8 f.

For 'to live' as the most universal and pregnant description of 'salvation' in the apocalyptic teaching of St Paul's day see Volz *Jüd. Eschatologie* p. 306.

11. Διὸ παρακαλεῖτε κτλ.] Cf. iv. 18, διό here taking the place of ὥστε, as serving better to sum up the different grounds of encouragement contained in the whole section iv. 13—v. 10.

καὶ οἰκοδομεῖτε κτλ.] 'and build up each the other' (Vg. *aedificate alterutrum*, Beza *aedificate singuli singulos*)—the first occurrence of a favourite Pauline metaphor, perhaps originally suggested by our Lord's own words (Mt. xvi. 18, cf. vii. 24 ff.), and here used in its widest spiritual

V 12] THE FIRST EPISTLE TO THE THESSALONIANS 71

¹²'Ἐρωτῶμεν δὲ ὑμᾶς, ἀδελφοί, εἰδέναι τοὺς κοπιῶντας ἐν ὑμῖν καὶ προϊσταμένους ὑμῶν ἐν κυρίῳ καὶ νουθετοῦν-

sense (cf. 1 Cor. xiv. 4). Blass (p. 144) traces the unusual combination εἰς τὸν ἕνα (=ἀλλήλους) to Semitic usage, but it finds at least a partial parallel in Theocr. xx. (xxii.) 65 εἰς ἑνὶ χεῖρας ἄειρον. The nearest N.T. parallel is 1 Cor. iv. 6 ἵνα μὴ εἰς ὑπὲρ τοῦ ἑνὸς φυσιοῦσθε κατὰ τοῦ ἑτέρου, 'St Paul's point *there* being the dividing effect of inflatedness or puffing up, as *here* the uniting effect of mutual building up' (Hort *Ecclesia* p. 125 n.¹): cf. also Eph. v. 33 οἱ καθ' ἕνα, and in mod. Gk. the phrase ὁ ἕνας τὸν ἄλλον. καθὼς καὶ ποιεῖτε] Grot. : 'Alternis adhibet hortamenta et laudes : quasi diceret, σπεύδοντα καὶ αὐτὸν ὀτρύνω—festinantem hortor et ipsum.'

V. 12—22. VARIOUS PRECEPTS WITH REGARD TO CHURCH LIFE AND HOLY LIVING.

12—15. From the general exhortation contained in the preceding section (iv. 1—v. 11) the Apostles now turn to define more particularly the duties of their converts (1) to their leaders (*vv.* 12, 13) and (2) to the disorderly and faint-hearted in their number (*vv.* 14, 15)—the counsels in both instances being addressed to the community at large, as shown by the repeated ἀδελφοί (*vv.* 12, 14) without qualification.

12, 13. 'And now to pass before closing to one or two points in this life of mutual service, we call upon you, Brothers, to pay proper respect to those who exercise rule over you in the Lord. Hold them in the highest esteem and love on account of their Divine calling, and thus preserve a spirit of peace in the whole community.'

12. εἰδέναι] evidently used here in the sense of 'know in their true character,' 'appreciate' (Calv. : '*Agnoscere* hic significat Habere rationem aut respectum')—a usage of the word for which no adequate parallel has yet been produced from class. or Bibl. Gk. : cf. however 1 Cor. xvi. 18 ἐπιγινώσκετε οὖν τοὺς τοιούτους, and see Ign. *Smyrn.* ix. καλῶς ἔχει Θεὸν καὶ ἐπίσκοπον εἰδέναι. Bornemann well remarks on the 'Feinheit' displayed in the choice of the word in the present passage : it is knowledge founded on 'Einsicht' that the writers have in view.

τοὺς κοπιῶντας κτλ.] 'them that toil among you, and are over you in the Lord, and admonish you.' In view of the common art. the three participles must be referred to the same persons, in all probability the 'presbyters,' their work being regarded from three different points of view, cf. 1 Tim. v. 17 and see Intr. p. xlvii f.

κοπιῶντας] Κοπιάω in class. Gk. = 'grow weary,' a sense which it also retains in the LXX. (e.g. 2 Regn. xvii. 2, Isa. xl. 30), is generally used in the N.T. (contrast Mt. xi. 28, Jo. iv. 6, Rev. ii. 3) with the derived meaning of 'toil,' 'work with effort,' with reference to both bodily and mental labour (cf. κόπος, i. 3 note). It is a favourite word with St Paul (Epp.¹⁴), who frequently employs it with reference to the laborious character of his own ministerial life (1 Cor. xv. 10, Gal. iv. 11, Phil. ii. 16, Col. i. 29, 1 Tim. iv. 10). Lft. (*ad* Ign. *Polyc.* vi.) derives the metaphor from the toilsome training for an athletic contest. By the use of the word here, as Calvin characteristically remarks, the Apostle excludes from the class of pastors 'omnes otiosos ventres.'

προϊσταμένους] not a technical term of office as shown by its position between κοπιῶντας and νουθετοῦντας, but, in accordance with the general usage of the verb in the N.T. (Rom. xii. 8, 1 Tim. iii. 4, 5, 12, cf. Tit. iii. 8,

τὰς ὑμᾶς, ¹³καὶ ἡγεῖσθαι αὐτοὺς ⌜ὑπερεκπερισσοῦ⌝ ἐν ἀγάπῃ διὰ τὸ ἔργον αὐτῶν. εἰρηνεύετε ἐν ἑαυτοῖς.

13 ὑπερεκπερισσοῦ אAD^(b vel c) cet Chr Thdt : ὑπερεκπερισσῶς BD*G Orig

14), pointing rather to the informal guidance in spiritual matters which the Thessalonian elders exercised 'in the Lord' towards individual members of the Church: cf. Hort *Ecclesia* p. 126, and for the later ecclesiastical use of the verb see Just. M. *Apol.* i. 67, Hermas *Vis.* II. iv. 3. For an 'official' sense attaching to προΐστασθαι in the papyri see P.Tebt. 5, 58 (ii./B.C.) where it is applied to 'the superintendents of the sacred revenues' (τοῖς προεστηκόσι τῶν ἱερῶν προσόδω[ν]), cf. 53, 8 (ii./B.C.); and for a similar use in the inscriptions see Dittenberger *Sylloge²* 318, 8 f. (ii./B.C.), where, in an inscription found close to Thessalonica, a certain Μάαρκυς is described as προϊστάμενος τῶν τε κατὰ κοινὸν πᾶσιν Μακεδόσιν συνφερόντων: cf. also *O.G.I.S.* 728, 4 (iii./B.C.—from the Thebaid) προέστη τῶν κα[θ' αὐτὸν] ἀξίως τῆς πόλεως. The word = 'to practise in business' is discussed by Field *Notes* p. 223 f.: in P.Petr. III. 73, 4 f. (undated) it is used of 'the landlord' of a lodging-house (τοῦ π[ρο]εστηκότος τῆς...συνοικίας).

νουθετοῦντας] Νουθετεῖν (lit. 'put in mind') has apparently always a sense of *blame* attached to it, hence = 'admonish,' 'warn,' cf. v. 14, II. iii. 15. In Col. i. 28 it joined with διδάσκειν, as presenting complementary aspects of the preacher's duty '*warning* to repent, *instructing* in the faith' (Lft.). Outside the Pauline Epp. the word is found in the N.T. only in Ac. xx. 31; cf. 1 Regn. iii. 13, Sap. xi. 10 (11), xii. 2, Pss. Sol. xiii. 8, also Plato *Gorg.* 479 A μήτε νουθετεῖσθαι μήτε κολάζεσθαι μήτε δίκην διδόναι.

13. καὶ ἡγεῖσθαι κτλ.] The exact construction of these words is not unattended with difficulty. Many commentators render 'hold them in love exceeding highly,' connecting ἐν ἀγάπῃ closely with ἡγεῖσθαι on the ground of such partial parallels as ἔχειν τινα ἐν τινι (Rom. i. 28, Thuc. ii. 18, iii. 9). But it is simpler to take the words in the order in which they stand, and to translate with the R.V. 'esteem them exceeding highly in love,' ἐν ἀγάπῃ being then a loose adjunct to the whole phrase ἡγ. αὐτ. ὑπερεκ.: cf. Job xxxv. 2 τί τοῦτο ἡγήσω ἐν κρίσει; The only difficulty is the somewhat strong sense 'esteem' (Thdt.: πλείονος ἀξιοῦν τιμῆς) that is thus given to the generally colourless ἡγεῖσθαι, and for which Lft. can find no nearer parallel than Thuc. ii. 42 τὸ ἀμύνεσθαι καὶ παθεῖν μᾶλλον ἡγησάμενοι ἢ τὸ ἐνδόντες σώζεσθαι 'preferring rather to suffer in self-defence &c.' It is supported however by the analogous use of εἰδέναι (v. 12), and by the general warmth of tone of the whole passage: cf. II. iii. 15 note.

For ὑπερεκπερισσοῦ (ὑπερεκπερισσῶς, WH. mg.) see note on iii. 10.

διὰ τ. ἔργον αὐτῶν] 'for their work's sake,' i.e. both because of their activity in it, and its own intrinsic importance. Calv.: 'Huius operis inaestimabilis est excellentia ac dignitas: ergo quos tantae rei ministros facit Deus, nobis eximios esse oportet.'

εἰρηνεύετε κτλ.] 'be at peace among yourselves'—a precept not to be dissociated from the preceding, but implying that by their affectionate loyalty to their leaders the Thessalonians were to maintain the peace of the whole community (Beza *pacem colite inter vos mutuo*). For εἰρηνεύειν in this sense cf. Mk. ix. 50, Rom. xii. 18, 2 Cor. xiii. 11, Sir. xxviii. 9, 13 (15).

¹⁴ Παρακαλοῦμεν δὲ ὑμᾶς, ἀδελφοί, νουθετεῖτε τοὺς ἀτάκτους, παραμυθεῖσθε τοὺς ὀλιγοψύχους, ἀντέχεσθε τῶν ἀσθενῶν, μακροθυμεῖτε πρὸς πάντας. ¹⁵ ὁρᾶτε μή

If the more difficult but well-attested ἐν αὐτοῖς (אD*GP) is preferred, the meaning will then be 'find your peace through them' i.e. 'through their leadership.' In no case can we render 'be at peace with (i.e. in your intercourse with) them' (Vg. *cum eis*), which would require μετ' αὐτῶν (cf. Rom. xii. 18).

14, 15. A fresh series of instructions still addressed like the preceding to the whole company of believers, and calling upon the (stronger) 'brethren' to extend their aid towards those who are 'weak.'

'Further we call upon you, Brothers, to warn those who are neglecting their proper duties. Let the despondent be encouraged, and those who are still weak in faith be upheld. Cherish a spirit of forbearance towards all men, and take special care that, so far from yielding to the old spirit of revenge, you make it your constant effort to seek the good of all.'

14. νουθετεῖτε τ. ἀτάκτους] Beza *monete inordinatos* rather than Vg. *corripite inquietos*. Ἄτακτος (ἅπ. λεγ. N.T.) primarily a military term applied to the soldier who does not remain in the ranks, and thence used more generally of whatever is out of order. In the present passage the special reference would seem to be to the idleness and neglect of duty which characterized certain members of the Thessalonian Church in view of the shortly-expected Parousia (Intr. p. xlvi f.). Contrast the unbroken front over which St Paul rejoices in Col. ii. 5 χαίρων καὶ βλέπων ὑμῶν τὴν τάξιν καὶ τὸ στερέωμα τῆς εἰς Χριστὸν πίστεως ὑμῶν.

For the meaning of ἄτακτος see further Add. Note G.

παραμυθεῖσθε κτλ.] 'encourage the faint-hearted' (Vg. *consolamini pusillanimes*, Wycl. *counforte ʒe men of litil herte*), whether from over-anxiety regarding their departed friends, or from fear of persecution, or from any other cause leading to despondency. Ὀλιγόψυχος, ἅπ. λεγ. N.T., occurs several times in the LXX. (e.g. Isa. lvii. 15 ὀλιγοψύχοις διδοὺς μακροθυμίαν), as do the corresponding subst. (ὀλιγοψυχία) and verb (ὀλιγοψυχεῖν). For the verb cf. also P.Petr. II. 40 (a), 12 f. (iii./B.C.) μὴ οὖν ὀλιγοψυχήσητε ἀλλ' ἀνδρίζεσθε.

ἀντέχεσθε κτλ.] 'lay hold of the weak' with the added idea of supporting them (Beza *sublevate infirmos*). For ἀντέχεσθαι (N.T. only midd.) in its more primary sense 'hold firmly to' cf. Mt. vi. 24, Lk. xvi. 13, Tit. i. 9, Isa. lvi. 4 ἀντέχωνται τῆς διαθήκης μου; and from the Κοινή such passages as P.Par. 14, 22 f. (ii./B.C.) οὐθενὸς δικαίου ἀντεχόμενοι, P.Amh. 133, 11 ff. (ii./A.D.) καὶ μετὰ πολλῶν κόπων ἀνηκάσαμεν αὐτῶν ἀντασχέσθαι τῆς τούτων ἐνεργίας ἐπὶ τῷ προτέρῳ ἐκφορίου, 'and with great difficulty I made them set to work at the former rent.'

The weak here can only be the spiritually weak (Thdt. τοὺς μὴ ἑδραίαν κεκτημένους πίστιν): cf. Rom. xiv. 1, 1 Cor. viii. 9, 11, ix. 22.

μακροθυμεῖτε κτλ.] 'be long-suffering toward all,' i.e. do not give way to a 'short' or 'quick' temper (ὀξοθυμία) towards those who fail, but be patient and considerate towards them: cf. 1 Cor. xiii. 4, Gal. v. 22, and especially Eph. iv. 2 where μακροθυμία is explained as ἀνεχόμενοι ἀλλήλων ἐν ἀγάπῃ. In this sense μακροθυμία is assigned as an attribute to God Himself, Rom. ii. 4, ix. 22, 1 Pet. iii. 20. Th. Mops. (who confines the reference

τις κακὸν ἀντὶ κακοῦ τινὶ ἀποδῷ, ἀλλὰ πάντοτε τὸ ἀγαθὸν διώκετε ᵀ εἰς ἀλλήλους καὶ εἰς πάντας. ¹⁶ Πάν-

15 διώκετε solum ℵ*ADG 17 37 67** al pauc d g m Vg (?) Go Boh (?) Syr (Pesh) Arm Aeth Ambst Theod-Mops^lat: διώκετε καὶ ℵ^cB al pler Vg (?) Syr (Harcl) Ephr Bas Chr Thdt

to the Church-leaders): '*patientes estote ad omnes*, eo quod hoc necessarium ualde est magistris, ita ut non facile desperent propter peccata, patienter uero suam impleant doctrinam, expectantes semper ut discipuli meliores sui efficiantur.'

15. ὁρᾶτε μή τις κτλ.] 'see that none pay back evil in return for evil to any one': cf. Rom. xii. 17, 1 Pet. iii. 9. The saying, which reflects the teaching of our Lord in such a passage as Mt. v. 43 ff., is often claimed as a distinctive precept of Christianity, and, notwithstanding such isolated maxims from the O.T. as Ex. xxiii. 4, Prov. xxv. 21 f., and the lofty spirit occasionally found in heathen philosophers as in a Socrates (see Plato *Rep.* i. 335), it is certainly true that Christianity first made 'no retaliation' a practical precept for all, by providing the 'moral dynamic' through which alone it could be carried out.

On the durative ὁράω (cognate with our '*beware*') see Moulton *Prolegg.* p. 110 f., and for ὁρᾶτε μή with the subj. cf. Mt. xviii. 10 (Burton §209), also P.Oxy. 532, 15 (ii./A.D.) ὅρα οὖν μὴ ἄλλως πράξῃς. If ἀποδοῖ (ℵ*D^bG) is read, it also must be taken as a subj., formed after the model of verbs in -όω (WM. p. 360 n.²). Both forms can be illustrated from the Κοινή, e.g. P.Par. 7, 11 (i./B.C.) ἐὰν δὲ μὴ ἀποδῷ, B.G.U. 741, 27 (ii./A.D.) ἐὰν δὲ μὴ [ἀ]ποδοῖ: see further Crönert p. 216. The simple δοῖ is found in an illiterate fragment of the iii./B.C., P.Petr. II. 9 (5), 5 ὅπως δοῖ.

ἀλλὰ πάντοτε κτλ.] 'but always pursue after that which is good'—ἀγαθόν being used in the sense of 'beneficial,' 'helpful' (*utile*) as opposed to the preceding κακόν, rather than of what

is morally good (*honestum*): cf. iii. 6 note. For the favourite Pauline διώκειν in the sense of 'pursue,' 'seek eagerly after' (Thpht.: ἐπιτεταμένως σπουδάζειν τι) cf. Rom. ix. 30, Phil. iii. 12, where in both passages it is associated with the correlative καταλαμβάνειν: see also Ex. xv. 9 εἶπεν ὁ ἐχθρός Διώξας καταλήμψομαι. Outside the Pauline Epp. the metaphorical use of the verb in the N.T. is confined to Heb. xii. 14, 1 Pet. iii. 11 (from LXX.); cf. Plato *Gorg.* 507 B οὔτε διώκειν οὔτε φεύγειν ἃ μὴ προσήκει.

16—22. From social duties the Apostles now pass to inculcate certain more directly religious duties.

'At all times cherish a spirit of joyfulness; in unceasing prayer make known your every want; under all circumstances give thanks to God: for only in these ways can God's purposes for you in Christ Jesus be fulfilled. With regard to the gifts of the Spirit, see to it that you do not quench them, or make light of prophesyings. At the same time do not accept these without discrimination. Rather bring everything to the test, and thus keep firm hold of the genuine, while you abstain from evil in whatever form it appears.'

16. πάντοτε χαίρετε] an injunction striking the same glad note that is so often repeated in the Ep. to the other Macedonian Church (Phil. ii. 18, iii. 1, iv. 4), its significance in the present instance being much increased in view of the sufferings already spoken of (i. 6, ii. 14, iii. 2 ff.). For the paradox cf. Rom. v. 3, 2 Cor. vi. 10, and for the true source of this joy see our Lord's own words Jo. xv. 11, xvi. 24, xvii. 13. Leighton's words (cited by Dods) may be recalled: 'All

[V 17—20] THE FIRST EPISTLE TO THE THESSALONIANS 75

τότε χαίρετε, ¹⁷ἀδιαλείπτως προσεύχεσθε, ¹⁸ἐν παντὶ
εὐχαριστεῖτε· τοῦτο γὰρ θέλημα θεοῦ ἐν Χριστῷ Ἰησοῦ
εἰς ὑμᾶς. ¹⁹τὸ πνεῦμα μὴ σβέννυτε, ²⁰προφητείας μὴ

spiritual sorrows, of what nature soever, are turned into spiritual joy: that is the proper end of them; they have a natural tendency that way.' An interesting ex. of the spirit of joy ruling in the early Church is afforded by the names found in the inscriptions—Victor, Nice, Gaudentius, Gaudiosus, Hilaris, Hilaritas (Ramsay *C. and B.* i. p. 493). See also Stanley *Christian Institutions* (1881) p. 250 f.

17. ἀδιαλείπτως προσεύχεσθε] a second precept, not to be interpreted merely as showing how the former precept may be fulfilled, but an independent injunction in thorough accordance with St Paul's constant teaching, cf. Rom. xii. 12, Eph. vi. 18, Col. iv. 2. For the absolute manner (ἀδιαλείπτως, i. 3 note) in which the precept is expressed see the note on iv. 13, and for a striking commentary on it note the constantly interjected prayers in this and the later Ep. (Intr. p. lxv).

For prayer as a part of Church-life cf. Didache xv. 4 τὰς δὲ εὐχὰς ὑμῶν... ποιήσατε ὡς ἔχετε ἐν τῷ εὐαγγελίῳ τοῦ Κυρίου ἡμῶν, and for the conditions under which the whole life of the saint becomes μίαν συναπτομένην μεγάλην...εὐχήν, see Orig. *de Orat.* xii. 2 (ed. Koetschau) 'ἀδιαλείπτως' δὲ προσεύχεται...ὁ συνάπτων τοῖς δέουσιν ἔργοις τὴν εὐχὴν καὶ τῇ εὐχῇ τὰς πρεπούσας πράξεις.

18. ἐν παντὶ εὐχαριστεῖτε] Vg. *in omnibus gratias agite*—ἐν παντί not being 'on every occasion' (Chrys.: ἀεί), but 'in all circumstances,' even in persecutions and trials. Thdt.: μὴ μόνον ἐν τοῖς θυμήρεσιν, ἀλλὰ κἂν τοῖς ἐναντίοις. οἶδε γὰρ τὸ συμφέρον ὁ μεγαλόδωρος. For a similar stress laid by St Paul on universal thanksgiving cf. Eph. v. 20, Phil. iv. 6, Col. iii. 17.

For εὐχαριστεῖν see i. 2 note, and add the late use of the verb by which it is practically = εὔχεσθαι, as in the interesting Christian amulet (vi./A.D. ?) reproduced by Wilcken (*Archiv* i. p. 431 ff.) where after an invocation to God and Christ and the holy Serenus the writer proceeds εὐχαριστῶ...καὶ κλίνω τὴν κεφαλήν [μο]υ... ὅπως διώξῃς ἀπ' ἐμοῦ...τὸν δαίμονα προβασκανίας. May we not have an earlier trace of this usage in P.Tebt. 56, 9 (late ii./A.D.) where the rendering 'pray' seems to suit the context better than the editors' 'give thanks'?

τοῦτο γάρ κτλ.] Τοῦτο, collective with reference to the foregoing precepts, while the θέλημα θεοῦ (iv. 3 note) regarding them is specially defined as resting ἐν Χρ. Ἰησ. not only as their supreme manifestation, but also as the means through whom alone they can be made effective.

For the absence of the art. before εἰς ὑμᾶς 'with regard to you' as well as for the *hyperbaton* cf. Lk. vii. 30 τὴν βουλὴν τοῦ θεοῦ ἠθέτησαν εἰς ἑαυτούς (Field *Notes* p. 60).

19. τὸ πνεῦμα μὴ σβέννυτε] in itself a perfectly general precept but, in view of the προφητείας of the next clause (see note), employed here with special reference to the charismatic gifts which had shown themselves at Thessalonica as afterwards at Corinth (1 Cor. xii., xiv.). Against these apparently a reaction had arisen owing to a certain amount of ἀταξία in their exercise (see Intr.p.xxxiv and cf. 1 Cor. xiv. 29 ff.), and consequently the Apostles found it necessary to warn their readers lest in their dread of over-enthusiasm the χαρίσματα should be extinguished altogether: cf. 2 Tim. i. 6 ἀναμιμνήσκω σε ἀναζωπυρεῖν τὸ χάρισμα τοῦ θεοῦ.

ἐξουθενεῖτε· ²¹πάντα [δὲ] δοκιμάζετε, τὸ καλὸν κατέχετε, ²²ἀπὸ παντὸς εἴδους πονηροῦ ἀπέχεσθε. ²³Αὐτὸς δὲ ὁ θεὸς τῆς

21 πάντα solum ℵ*A al Boh Syr (Pesh) Orig Ephr Bas ⅓ Chr ½ Thdt Tert Orig^lat: πάντα δὲ ℵ^cBDG al d g Vg Go Syr (Harcl) Aeth Clem Bas ⅔ Chr ½ Ambst Theod-Mops^lat

The use of σβέννυτε (for form, WSchm. p. 124) is in accord with the frequent application of the metaphor of fire to the Spirit in Scripture (Ac. ii. 3, xviii. 25, Rom. xii. 11; cf. Plut. *de defect. orac.* § 17, p. 419 B ἀποσβῆναι τὸ πνεῦμα): while μή with the pres. imp. instead of the aor. subj. points to the necessity of desisting from a course of action already going on, as distinguished from avoidance of similar action in the future (Moulton *Prolegg.* pp. 122 f., 247).

20. προφητείας μὴ ἐξουθενεῖτε] an injunction closely related to the foregoing (cf. 1 Cor. xiv. 1 ζηλοῦτε δὲ τὰ πνευματικά, μᾶλλον δὲ ἵνα προφητεύητε), and pointing to the impassioned utterances regarding the deep things of God which so frequently showed themselves in the Early Church under the direct influence of the Spirit: cf. Ac. ii. 17, xix. 6, 1 Cor. xii. 10, Rev. i. 10, and see further McGiffert *Apost. Age* p. 526 ff.

The strong verb ἐξουθενέω 'set at naught,' 'make of no account' (Suid.: ἀντ' οὐδενὸς λογίζομαι) is found in the N.T. only in Lk.[3] and Paul[8], and under the form ἐξουδενεῖν in Mk.[1]. In the LXX. it occurs in four forms ἐξουδενεῖν, -νοῦν, ἐξουθενεῖν, -οῦν: see Lobeck *Phryn.* p. 182.

21. πάντα [δὲ] δοκιμάζετε] The connecting particle δέ, which is amply vouched for, ought probably to be retained here, its omission being easily explained through the influence of the following δο-. In any case whether δέ is retained or not, the whole clause stands in a certain limiting relation to the foregoing precepts: important as 'gifts' and 'prophesyings' are, they cannot be accepted unhesitatingly, but must be put to the test (cf. 1 Jo. iv. 1). Nothing is said as to *how* this διάκρισις πνευμάτων (1 Cor. xii. 10, xiv. 29) is to be effected, but it can only be by a 'spiritual' standard (cf. 1 Cor. ii. 13), and not by the 'rational' inquiry which is sometimes found here, and to which the 'prove' of A.V., R.V. lends a certain colour.

For δοκιμάζω see the note on ii. 4, and for the thought cf. Rom. xii. 2, Phil. i. 10.

τὸ καλὸν κατέχετε] It is not easy to find an adequate English equivalent for τὸ καλόν, but when used in its moral sense the word denotes generally what is good in itself (cf. Arist. *Rhet.* i. 9. 3 καλὸν μὲν οὖν ἐστίν, ὃ ἂν δι' αὑτὸ αἱρετὸν ὂν ἐπαινετὸν ᾖ) as distinguished from τὸ ἀγαθόν what is good in virtue of its results. Thus it is used of *genuine* as opposed to *counterfeit* coin (cf. Xen. *Mem.* iii. 1 διαγιγνώσκειν τό τε καλὸν [ἀργύριον] καὶ τὸ κίβδηλον), and is very appropriate here to denote the goodness which passes muster in view of the testing process just spoken of: cf. the noble comment of the historian Socrates on this verse—τὸ γὰρ καλόν, ἔνθα ἂν ᾖ, ἴδιον τῆς ἀληθείας ἐστίν (*H.E.* iii. 16).

For κατέχω = 'hold fast' cf. Lk. viii. 15, 1 Cor. xi. 2, xv. 2, Heb. iii. 6, 14, x. 23, and see Add. Note H.

22. ἀπὸ παντὸς εἴδους κτλ.] 'from every form of evil abstain.' This rendering may be criticized on two grounds—(1) it takes εἶδος in its quasi-philosophical sense of 'kind,' 'species,' which though frequent in class. writers and more especially in Plato, is not found elsewhere in the N.T., and (2) it treats πονηροῦ, though anarthrous, as a subst. But as re-

εἰρήνης ἁγιάσαι ὑμᾶς ὁλοτελεῖς, καὶ ὁλόκληρον ὑμῶν τὸ

gards (1), apart from such passages as Jos. *Antt.* VII. 80 (iv. 2), x. 37 (iii. 1) εἶδος μέλους, πονηρίας, we have now confirmation of this more popular use of εἶδος from the papyri as when in P.Tebt. 58, 20 f. (ii./B.C.) a taxgatherer undertakes to collect a wheat-tax ἀπὸ παντὸς εἴδους 'from every class'; cf. P.Oxy. 237. viii. 42 f. (ii./A.D.) κατὰ κώμην καὶ κατ' εἶδος 'under villages and classes,' and see P.Fay. 34, 6 f. (ii./A.D.) where ἄλλα εἴδη may be used not of 'other taxes' but of 'other kinds' of produce on which a certain tax (μονοδεσμία) was levied (see editors' note *ad loc.*). While with reference to (2), the anarthrous use of the neut. sing. to denote abstract ideas is too frequent to cause any real difficulty, e.g. Gen. ii. 9 τὸ ξύλον τοῦ εἰδέναι γνωστὸν καλοῦ κ. πονηροῦ, Heb. v. 14 πρὸς διάκρισιν καλοῦ τε καὶ κακοῦ, and cf. Didache iii. 1, apparently a reminiscence of the present passage, φεῦγε ἀπὸ παντὸς πονηροῦ κ. ἀπὸ παντὸς ὁμοίου αὐτοῦ.

The alternative rendering 'abstain from every appearance of evil' (R.V. marg.) has the advantage of taking εἶδος in the same sense as elsewhere in the N.T. (Lk. iii. 22, ix. 29, Jo. v. 37, 2 Cor. v. 7), but, if it is preferred, care must be taken not to impart into the word the idea of 'semblance' as opposed to 'reality': it is rather 'appearance' in the sense of 'outward show,' 'visible form.'

On ἀπέχεσθαι ἀπό see iv. 3 note, and on the more active idea of evil in πονηρός 'malignant' as compared with κακός 'base' see Trench *Syn.* § lxxxiv.

Commentators generally draw attention to the change from τὸ καλόν to παντὸς εἴδους πονηροῦ, for while the good is one, evil has many forms; cf. Arist. *Eth. Nic.* ii. 5. 14 ἔτι τὸ μὲν ἁμαρτάνειν πολλαχῶς ἐστίν,...τὸ δὲ κατορθοῦν μοναχῶς.

It is also of interest to notice that *vv.* 21, 22 are frequently connected by early Christian writers with the agraphon ascribed to our Lord γίνεσθε δόκιμοι τραπεζῖται (for reff. see Suicer *Thesaurus* s.v. τραπεζίτης), and it is at least possible that the writers of our Ep. had this saying of Jesus in mind here: see further Resch *Agrapha* pp. 116 ff., 233 ff., *Paulinismus* p. 408 f., Ropes *Sprüche* p. 142 f.

V. 23, 24. PRAYER.

From these several injunctions the Apostles turn in characteristic fashion to the Divine power in which alone they can be fulfilled. Beng.: 'non meo studio, inquit Paulus, sed divino praesidio muniti eritis.'

23, 24. 'As however without God all your strivings must be in vain we pray that the God of peace Himself will sanctify you through and through, that the whole man may become God's, each part preserved entire and without blame, and found so at the Parousia of the Lord Jesus. Nor need you have any fear regarding this. The very fact that it is God Who is calling is to you the pledge that He will not suffer His calling to become null and void.'

23. ὁ θεὸς τῆς εἰρήνης] a frequent title at the close of the Pauline Epp. (Rom. xv. 33, xvi. 20, 2 Cor. xiii. 11, Phil. iv. 9, (Heb. xiii. 20); cf. II. iii. 16 ὁ κύρ. τ. εἰρ.), and intended to bring out 'the peace' which is not only the one God's characteristic attribute, but which it is His peculiar privilege to bestow, and which in the present passage gains in significance in view of the ἀταξία just spoken of.

For 'Peace' as a Talmudic Name of God see Taylor *Sayings*[2] p. 25 f.; while as further illustrating the personal application of the term it may be noted that in P.Oxy. 41, 27 (iii./iv. A.D.) the prytanis at Oxyrhynchus is popularly acclaimed as εἰρήνη πόλεως.

ἁγιάσαι ὑμᾶς κτλ.] 'sanctify you

πνεῦμα καὶ ἡ ψυχὴ καὶ τὸ σῶμα ἀμέμπτως ἐν τῇ παρου-

wholly'—ἁγιάσαι not being limited to the initial act of consecration, but (as in Rom. xv. 16, Eph. v. 26) pointing to the actual inward sanctification of the Thessalonians' in their whole persons' (Vg. Ambrstr. *per omnia*, Luth. Weizsäcker *durch und durch*). For this ethical sense of ἁγιάζειν cf. Lev. xi. 44 ἁγιασθήσεσθε καὶ ἅγιοι ἔσεσθε, ὅτι ἅγιός εἰμι ἐγώ, and for a full discussion of the word and its synonyms see Westcott *Heb.* p. 346 f. For ὁλοτελής (ἀπ. λεγ. N.T.) cf. Plut. *Mor.* ii. 909 B, Dittenberger *Sylloge*[2] 376, 45 ἀνεισφορίαν, ἣν οὐδεὶς τῶν πρότερον Σεβαστῶν ὁλοτελῆ ἔδωκεν. The adv. ὁλοτελῶς, by which Suidas defines the common ὁλοσχηρῶς, is found in Aq. Deut. xiii. 16 (17).

ὁλόκληρον] a secondary predicate to be taken closely along with τηρηθείη, and as belonging to all three substantives (WM. p. 661): As regards meaning, ὁλόκληρος can hardly be distinguished from ὁλοτελής though, in accordance with its derivation, it draws more special attention to the several parts to which the wholeness spoken of extends, no part being wanting or lacking in completeness. Thus in the LXX. the word is used of λίθοι as yet untouched by any tool (Deut. xxvii. 6, 1 Macc. iv. 47), and it is the regular expression in Philo (*de anim.* § 12, ii. p. 836 M.) and Josephus *Antt.* III. 278 (xii. 2) to denote the *integritas* required both in priests and victims. From this the transition is easy to the metaphorical sense of mental and moral completeness which the word has in the apocr. books of the O.T. (Sap. xv. 3 ὁλόκληρος δικαιοσύνη, 4 Macc. xv. 17 τὴν εὐσέβειαν ὁλόκληρον), and in Jas. i. 4 where it is joined with τέλειος (for distinction between them see Trench *Syn.* § xxii.) and explained as ἐν μηδενὶ λειπόμενος. An interesting parallel to the use

of ὁλόκληρος in the present passage is afforded by the magical papyrus P.Lond. I. 121, 589 f. (iii./A.D.) διαφύλασσέ μου τὸ σῶμα τὴν ψυχὴν ὁλόκληρον, while its original meaning is seen in P.Oxy. 57, 13 f. (iii./A.D.) ὑπὲρ τοῦ ὁλόκληρον (sc. ποιῆσαι) τὴν ἐπίσκεψιν τῶν χωμάτων. The allied subst. ὁλοκληρία (cf. Ac. iii. 16) occurs in the sense of physical wholeness, health, e.g. *B.G.U.* 948, 2 ff. (iv./v. A.D.) εὔχομε...τὰ πε[ρὶ τ]ῆς ὑγίας σου καὶ ὁλοκληρίας σου χάριν, and for the verb see P.Grenf. I. 53, 4 f. (iv./A.D.) ὅπως ὁλοκληροῦντα σὲ ἀπολάβομεν.

ὑμῶν τὸ πνεῦμα κτλ.] The precedent gen. ὑμῶν is unemphatic (cf. Abbott *Joh. Gr.* p. 416), and belongs to each of the following substantives, 'your spirit and your soul and your body,' but this triple subject must not be pressed as if it contained a psychological definition of human nature. St Paul 'is not writing a treatise on the soul, but pouring forth, from the fulness of his heart, a prayer for his converts' (Jowett), and consequently all appeals to the verse in support of a Pauline system of Trichotomy as against the Dichotomy found elsewhere in his Epp. are beside the mark. At the same time it will not do to regard the three subjects as of 'mere rhetorical significance' (de Wette): they are evidently chosen in accordance with the general O.T. view of the constitution of man to emphasize a sanctification which shall extend to man's whole being, whether on its immortal, its personal, or its bodily side: cf. Heb. iv. 12 with Westcott's Add. Note p. 114 ff.

The trichotomist arguments based on the passage will be found fully stated by Ellicott *The Destiny of the Creature*, Serm. v. with the accompanying Notes. For the more important inquiry how far St Paul may have been influenced here by

V 24, 25] THE FIRST EPISTLE TO THE THESSALONIANS 79

σία τοῦ κυρίου ἡμῶν Ἰησοῦ Χριστοῦ τηρηθείη. ²⁴πιστὸς ὁ καλῶν ὑμᾶς, ὃς καὶ ποιήσει.
²⁵Ἀδελφοί, προσεύχεσθε [καὶ] περὶ ἡμῶν.

25 καὶ BD* 4** 6 17 31 37 al pauc Go Syr (Harcl) Arm Orig Chr Theod-Mops^lat : om ℵAD^cG cet f g Vg Boh Syr (Pesh) Aeth Thdt Ambst al

Pharisaic theology see Wohlenberg ad loc., and cf. Jos. Antt. I. 34 (i. 2). For the occurrence of the same trichotomy in Egyptian rites in the order 'soul, body, spirit' see the interesting note by Rev. F. E. Brightman in J.T.S. ii. p. 273 f. ἀμέμπτως] an adverbial adjunct (ii. 10 note) qualifying the whole expression ὁλόκληρον...τηρηθείη : cf. Clem. R. Cor. xliv. 6 ἐκ τῆς ἀμέμπτως αὐτοῖς τετιμημένης (τετηρημένης, Lft.) λειτουργίας. It is not without interest to notice that ἀμέμπτως, which in the N.T. is confined to this Ep., occurs in certain sepulchral inscriptions discovered at Thessalonica, e.g. an inscription of 50 A.D. Εἰσιάδι τῇ συνβίωι ζησάσῃ ἀμέμπτως ἔτη κη...[μνε]ίας χάριν (no. 30 Duchesne et Bayet Mission au Mont Athos p. 29).

ἐν τῇ παρουσίᾳ κτλ.] a temporal clause marking also the condition under which the blameless ὁλοκληρία will be made manifest (cf. ii. 19 note). Wohlenberg prefers to connect the words more closely with τηρηθείη, the thought then being that in the judgment following upon Christ's appearing, while others find themselves the subjects of God's wrath, those who have undergone this triple sanctification will be preserved in bliss. The difference in meaning is not very great, but under no circumstances can the A.V. 'unto (as if εἰς) the coming' be accepted, however true the thought underlying it (cf. Phil. i. 6). For παρουσία see Add. Note F.

24. πιστὸς ὁ καλῶν κτλ.] Chrys. : Ὅρα τὴν ταπεινοφροσύνην. Ἐπειδὴ γὰρ ηὔξατο, μὴ νομίσητέ, φησίν, ὅτι ἀπὸ τῶν ἐμῶν εὐχῶν τοῦτο γίνεται, ἀλλ' ἐκ τῆς προθέσεως, ἧς ὑμᾶς ἐκάλεσεν. Beng. : 'magnam hic versiculus exultationem habet.' For ὁ καλ. ὑμ. which, as always in St Paul, can only refer to God cf. ii. 12 note, and for πιστός in a similar connexion cf. II. iii. 3, 1 Cor. i. 9, x. 13, 2 Cor. i. 18, 2 Tim. ii. 13, Heb. x. 23, xi. 11, Deut. vii. 9, Isa. xlix. 7, Pss. Sol. xiv. 1. The absolute use of ποιήσει is very striking, and sets in bold relief the *doing* with which God accompanies His *calling* : cf. Num. xxiii. 19 αὐτὸς εἶπας οὐχὶ ποιήσει; Ps. xxxvi. (xxxvii.) 5 ἔλπισον ἐπ' αὐτόν, καὶ αὐτὸς ποιήσει. For a similar *certitudo fidei* on the part of St Paul cf. Rom. xvi. 25, Phil. i. 6, and for a like spirit in later Jewish theology see *Apoc. Bar.* xiii. 3, 'Thou shalt therefore be assuredly preserved to the consummation of the times.'

V. 25—28. CONCLUDING INJUNCTIONS AND BENEDICTION.

25—28. 'Meanwhile, Brothers, in your prayers do not forget us. Convey our greetings with the customary holy kiss to all the Brothers. As regards this letter I charge that it be read aloud to all the Brothers. The grace of our Lord Jesus Christ be with you.'

25. Ἀδελφοί, προσεύχεσθε κτλ.] Cf. II. iii. 1, and for a similar request see Rom. xv. 30, Eph. vi. 19, Col. iv. 3, Heb. xiii. 18. If καί is read, it introduces the feeling of reciprocity—'as we have prayed for you, do you also pray for us.'

80 THE FIRST EPISTLE TO THE THESSALONIANS [V 26, 27

²⁶'Ασπάσασθε τοὺς ἀδελφοὺς πάντας ἐν φιλήματι ἁγίῳ. ²⁷'Ενορκίζω ὑμᾶς τὸν κύριον ἀναγνωσθῆναι τὴν ἐπιστολὴν πᾶσιν τοῖς ᵀ ἀδελφοῖς.

27 τοῖς] add ἁγίοις ℵᶜAKLP al pler Vg Go Boh Syr (Pesh Harcl) Arm Chr Thdt Theod-Mops^lat

26. 'Ασπάσασθε κτλ.] an exhortation addressed like the preceding to the whole Church, and not only to those to whom the Ep. was directly sent, presumably the elders. Had any such restriction been intended, it could hardly fail to have been clearly notified, while any difficulty in the general application of the injunction owing to the use of τ. ἀδ. πάντας is met by the want of stress here attaching to πάντας (WSchm. p. 189), the whole phrase being practically equivalent to the more customary ἀλλήλους.

'Ασπάζομαι is of constant occurrence in the papyri for conveying the greetings at the end of a letter, e.g. P.Fay. 119, 25 ff. (c. i./A.D.) ἀσπάζου 'Επαγαθὸν καὶ τοὺς φιλοῦντες ἡμᾶς πρὸς ἀληθίαν.

ἐν φιλήματι ἁγίῳ] 'with a kiss that is holy,' as a token of friendship and brotherly love, cf. Rom. xvi. 16, 1 Cor. xvi. 20, 2 Cor. xiii. 12, in each case the attribute ἅγιον being added to bring out the true character of the φίλημα : see also 1 Pet. v. 14 ἐν φιλήματι ἀγάπης. The practice may have arisen from the customary mode of saluting a Rabbi, Wünsche *Neue Beiträge* p. 339; cf. also F. C. Conybeare in *Exp.* IV. ix. p. 460 ff.

For the first mention of the 'kiss of peace' as a regular part of the Christian service see Just. M. *Apol.* i. 65 ἀλλήλους φιλήματι ἀσπαζόμεθα παυσάμενοι τῶν εὐχῶν, and for full particulars of its liturgical use see art. 'Kiss' in Smith's *D.C.A.*, and Hauck *RE.*³ vi. p. 274. In some parts of Greece the Easter-greeting (Χριστὸς ἀνέστη) is still accompanied by the brotherly kiss.

27. 'Ενορκίζω ὑμᾶς κτλ.] 'Ενορκίζω, not found elsewhere in the Bibl. writings except as a variant in 2 Esdr. xxiii. (xiii.) 25, is apparently a strengthened form of ὁρκίζω (for form, Rutherford *NP.* p. 466 f.), and like it (Mk. v. 17, Ac. xix. 3) is here construed with two accusatives : cf. *I.M.A.* III. 1238 (Christian) ἐνορκίζω ὑμᾶς τὸν ὧδε ἐφεστῶτα ἄνγελον, μή τίς ποτε τολμή(σῃ) κτλ., and see also Ramsay *C. and B.* i. p. 734. For a similar usage of ἐξορκίζω see P.Leid. V. 4. 31 (iii./A.D.) ἐξορκίζω σε τὴν δύναμιν σου, and for ὁρκίζω τινά see Deissmann *BS.* p. 274 ff.

The presence of the adjuration in the present passage has been explained as due either to the Apostle's deep sense of the importance of his Ep. to all without exception, or to a presentiment that a wrong use might be made of his name and authority as in II. ii. 2, iii. 17, or to the fact that the reading of such letters had not yet been officially established. But after all no special reason need be sought. Writing as he did to explain his continued personal absence, and to enforce truths which he felt to be of vital importance to his converts, St Paul naturally took precautions to ensure that his letter should be read and circulated as widely as possible : see Intr. p. xxxiv, and for the change to the 1st pers. sing. to give the appeal a more personal character cf. ii. 18, iii. 5.

ἀναγνωσθῆναι] 'Αναγνωσθῆναι (for construction, Blass p. 241) a timeless aor., and hence lending no support to Alford's view that a special assembly was to be held for this purpose. At the same time it is clear from the context that it is a

^{28}Ἡ χάρις τοῦ κυρίου ἡμῶν Ἰησοῦ Χριστοῦ μεθ' ὑμῶν.

public reading or a reading *aloud* that is alone thought of here. For this sense of ἀναγιγνώσκειν (almost universal in class. Gk., Butcher *Harvard Lect.* p. 230, n.¹) cf. Lk. iv. 16, Ac. xiii. 27, xv. 21, 2 Cor. iii. 15, Col. iv. 16, Rev. i. 3 (with Swete's note), and for the result of this reading aloud in giving the N.T. writings an authoritative character see Sanday *Inspiration* p. 360 f.

Tertullian is sometimes quoted as mentioning Thessalonica and Philippi as churches where the letters of the Apostles were read in the original ('apud quas ipsae authenticae literae eorum recitantur' *de praescr.* 36), but the reference to Thessalonica ('habes Thessalonicenses') is plainly an insertion, clumsy in form, and wanting in the best MSS.

In the papyri ἀναγιγνώσκειν is found = both 'read' and 'read aloud.' Thus for the latter sense cf. P.Grenf. I. 37, 15 (ii./B.C.) ἐπιλέγματος ἀναγνωσθέντος of the reading aloud of a petition, and P.Cairo 29. 3. 1 (ii./A.D.) ἧς ἀναγνωσθείσης of the reading aloud of a will. On the other hand the word must mean simply 'read' in *B.G.U.* 1079 (cited iv. 1 note), and in P.Fay. 20, 23 (iii.—iv./A.D.) where it refers to copies of an edict set up in

public places σύνοπτα τοῖς ἀναγιγνώσκουσιν 'in full view of those who wish to read.'

τὴν ἐπιστολήν] obviously the present letter now drawing to a close, cf. II. iii. 14, Rom. xvi. 22, Col. iv. 16 (WSchm. p. 149).

πᾶσιν τοῖς ἀδελφοῖς] Πᾶσιν emphatic (contrast πάντας v. 26), but not necessarily including others than the combined members of the Thessalonian Church. Ἁγίοις, if read before ἀδελφοῖς (WH. mg.), would produce a combination occurring nowhere else in the Pauline Epp. (cf. however Eph. iii. 5 τ. ἁγίοις ἀποστόλοις), and is better omitted.

28. Ἡ χάρις κτλ.] a concluding benediction in which the favourite Pauline conception of 'grace' takes the place of the ordinary epistolary ἔρρωσο (ἔρρωσθε) or ἐρρῶσθαί σε (ὑμᾶς) εὔχομαι: cf. II. iii. 18, Rom. xvi. 20, 1 Cor. xvi. 23.

A shorter form ἡ χάρις μεθ' ὑμῶν is found in Col. iv. 18, 1 Tim. vi. 21, 2 Tim. iv. 22, Tit. iii. 15 (add πάντων), while this is expanded in various ways in Gal. vi. 18, Eph. vi. 24, Phil. iv. 23. The full trinitarian benediction occurs in 2 Cor. xiii. 13.

The liturgical ἀμήν is found in AD^{bc}KLP &c.: cf. iii. 13 note.

Δεῖ γὰρ ταῦτα γενέσθαι πρῶτον, ἀλλ' οὐκ εὐθέως τὸ τέλος.

Τὰ ἀναγκαῖα πάντα δῆλα.
CHRYSOSTOM.

πιστὸς Δέ ἐςτιν ὁ κύριος, ὃς ςτηρίξει ὑμᾶς καὶ φυλάξει ἀπὸ τοῦ πονηροῦ.

ΠΡΟΣ ΘΕΣΣΑΛΟΝΙΚΕΙΣ Β

ANALYSIS.

I. ADDRESS AND GREETING. i. 1, 2.

II. HISTORICAL AND DOCTRINAL. i. 3—ii. 17.
   1. THANKSGIVING AND PRAYER FOR THE THESSALONIANS' STATE. i. 3—12.
   2. TEACHING CONCERNING THE EVENTS PRECEDING THE LORD'S PAROUSIA. ii. 1—12.
   3. RENEWED THANKSGIVING AND EXHORTATION. ii. 13—15.
   4. PRAYER. ii. 16, 17.

III. CONSOLATORY AND HORTATORY. iii. 1—16.
   1. REQUEST FOR THE THESSALONIANS' PRAYERS. iii. 1, 2.
   2. CONFIDENCE IN THE THESSALONIANS' PROGRESS. iii. 3—5.
   3. CHARGE WITH REGARD TO THE DISORDERLY. iii. 6—12.
   4. EXHORTATION TO THE LOYAL MEMBERS OF THE CHURCH. iii. 13—15.
   5. PRAYER. iii. 16.

IV. SALUTATION AND BENEDICTION. iii. 17, 18.

ΠΡΟΣ ΘΕΣΣΑΛΟΝΙΚΕΙΣ Β

ΠΑΥΛΟΣ καὶ Cιλουανὸς καὶ Τιμόθεος τῇ ἐκκλησίᾳ Θεσσαλονικέων ἐν θεῷ πατρὶ ἡμῶν καὶ κυρίῳ Ἰησοῦ Χριστῷ· ²χάρις ὑμῖν καὶ εἰρήνη ἀπὸ θεοῦ πατρὸς καὶ κυρίου Ἰησοῦ Χριστοῦ.

I. 1, 2. ADDRESS AND GREETING.

1. Παῦλος κτλ.] The address corresponds word for word with the address in I. i. 1 (where see notes) except in the addition of ἡμῶν after πατρί emphasizing that it is the Divine fatherhood in relation to man and not to Christ that is specially in view.

2. ἀπὸ θεοῦ πατρός κτλ.] These words, though unauthentic in I. i. 1, form part of the true text here, and, as in all subsequent Pauline Epp., carry back the customary greeting χάρις κ. εἰρήνη to its ultimate source. Both subjects θεοῦ πατρός and κυρ. Ἰησ. Χρ. are under the government of the same preposition ἀπό, and any distinction between them therefore as the 'ultimate' and the 'mediating' channel of grace and peace (as Findlay), however true in reality, is out of place here. In 2 Jo. 3 the same relation is brought out by the repeated παρά...παρά, which can hardly be distinguished from ἀπό in this connexion, though in accordance with its general sense it may help to draw attention to the *passage* from the giver to the receiver (cf. Lft. on Gal. i. 12).

The addition of ἡμῶν after πατρός is well attested (אAG...Vg Go Boh Syrr), but in accordance with BDP 17 is omitted by WH. Its insertion was doubtless due to its frequent presence in corresponding Pauline formulas.

I. 3.—II. 17. HISTORICAL AND DOCTRINAL.

I. 3—12. THANKSGIVING AND PRAYER FOR THE THESSALONIANS' STATE.

Following upon the Address comes the customary Thanksgiving which, while again closely recalling the Thanksgiving of the First Epistle, presents certain independent features. Thus special stress is now laid on the *progress* of the Thessalonians' faith and love with the consequent *boasting* of the writers on their behalf (*vv.* 3, 4), while the mention of the afflictions from which at the time the Thessalonian Church was suffering is a natural starting-point for an emphatic appeal to the righteous judgment of God, by which the persecuted will be recompensed and the persecutors condemned (*vv.* 5—10). The whole is crowned by a characteristic reference to the Apostles' continual intercession for their converts (*vv.* 11, 12).

3, 4. 'We count it a duty, as well as a privilege, Brothers, to give thanks to God at all times for you, as indeed your own conduct fully merits, in view

86 THE SECOND EPISTLE TO THE THESSALONIANS [I 3, 4

³ Εὐχαριστεῖν ὀφείλομεν τῷ θεῷ πάντοτε περὶ ὑμῶν, ἀδελφοί, καθὼς ἄξιόν ἐστιν, ὅτι ὑπεραυξάνει ἡ πίστις ὑμῶν καὶ πλεονάζει ἡ ἀγάπη ἑνὸς ἑκάστου πάντων ὑμῶν εἰς ἀλλήλους, ὥστε αὐτοὺς ἡμᾶς ἐν ὑμῖν ἐνκαυχᾶσθαι ἐν

of the marvellous growth of your faith and the abounding love which you are all displaying towards one another. So marked indeed are these, that we on our own part are able to make a boast of you in the churches of God, as we think of the endurance and the faith which you have continued to show even among the persecutions and afflictions which are falling upon you at this time.'

3. Εὐχαριστεῖν ὀφείλομεν] Cf. I. i. 2, the addition of ὀφείλομεν in the present passage bringing out the Apostles' sense of thanksgiving as actually a *debt* owing to God in view of their converts' rapid growth in spiritual things (see below). As contrasted with δεῖ 'an obligation in the nature of things,' ὀφείλω expresses 'a special, personal obligation' (Westcott on 1 Jo. ii. 6). It is found combined with εὐχαριστεῖν as here in ii. 13; cf. Clem. R. *Cor.* xxxviii. 4, Barn. *Ep.* v. 3 (ὑπερευχαριστεῖν) vii. 1.

καθὼς ἄξιόν ἐστι] not a mere tautological repetition of ὀφείλομεν for the sake of emphasis (as Jowett), but bringing out the duty of the εὐχαριστία from the *human* standpoint—'it is also merited by your conduct' (Lft.): cf. Phil. i. 7, and for a similar use of ἄξιος see 1 Cor. xvi. 4.

ὅτι] referring back to the principal statement εὐχ. ὀφείλομεν, and in view of the emphatic ὀφείλομεν (see above) best given its full causal significance 'because,' cf. ii. 13 and contrast I. i. 13.

ὑπεραυξάνει] 'groweth exceedingly' (Vg. *supercrescit*, Beza *vehementer augescat*, Wycl. *ouer wexith*), as compared with the ὑστερήματα τ. πίστεως, I. iii. 10.

The verb is another of the verbs compounded with ὑπερ- for which St Paul shows such a marked predilection, cf. ὑπερβαίνω (I. iv. 6), ὑπερεντυγχάνω (Rom. viii. 26), ὑπερνικάω (Rom. viii. 37), ὑπερεκτείνω (2 Cor. x. 14), ὑπερπλεονάζω (1 Tim. i. 14), all, like ὑπεραυξάνω, being ἄπ. λεγόμενα in the N.T.: see also the note on I. iii. 10. Like the simple αὐξάνω in the N.T. (except 1 Cor. iii. 6 f., 2 Cor. ix. 10), the verb is here used intransitively.

καὶ πλεονάζει κτλ.] a fulfilment of the prayer of I. iii. 12. As distinguished from ὑπεραυξάνει, πλεονάζει, which is found in the N.T. outside the Pauline Epp. only in 2 Pet. i. 8, points to *diffusive* rather than *organic* growth, and hence is fittingly used of ἀγάπη, while this love is further characterized as not only individually manifested (ἑνὸς ἑκάστου, cf. I. ii. 11), but as extended to the entire Christian community at Thessalonica (πάντων ὑμῶν εἰς ἀλλήλους). Chrys.: καὶ ὅρα ἀγάπην· οὐ τὸν μὲν ἠγάπων, τὸν δὲ οὔ, ἀλλ' ἴση ἦν παρὰ πάντων.

4. ὥστε αὐτοὺς ἡμᾶς κτλ.] 'so that we on our part...,' the emphatically placed αὐτούς not being simply reflexive, but serving to draw attention to the fact that the Apostles, as well as the Thessalonians, have ground for boasting, inasmuch as it was through their agency, humanly speaking, that the foundations of the Thessalonians' faith were laid.

For ὥστε with inf. cf. I. i. 7 note.

ἐνκαυχᾶσθαι] Ἐνκαυχᾶσθαι (for form, WH.² *Notes* p. 156 f.) instead of the favourite Pauline καυχᾶσθαι (Epp.³⁵) does not occur elsewhere in the N.T., but is found with the same construction as here in Pss. li. (lii.) 3, xcvi. (xcvii.) 7 (ἐγκ-), cv. (cvi.) 47. For

I. 5]   THE SECOND EPISTLE TO THE THESSALONIANS   87

ταῖς ἐκκλησίαις τοῦ θεοῦ ὑπὲρ τῆς ὑπομονῆς ὑμῶν καὶ
πίστεως ἐν πᾶσιν τοῖς διωγμοῖς ὑμῶν καὶ ταῖς θλίψεσιν
αἷς ⌜ἀνέχεσθε⌝, ⁵ἔνδειγμα τῆς δικαίας κρίσεως τοῦ θεοῦ,

I 4 ἀνέχεσθε] ἐνέχεσθε B

the thought cf. I. ii. 19 στέφανος καυχήσεως, and for ἐν indicating the ground of the boasting see WM. p. 292.
ἐν τ. ἐκκλησίαις τ. θεοῦ] i.e. in Corinth and its neighbourhood, cf. 2 Cor. i. 1. For a similar instance of boasting cf. 2 Cor. viii. 1 ff., and for the use made of the present passage by Polycarp see Intr. p. lxxvi f.
ὑπὲρ τῆς ὑπομονῆς κτλ.] 'Υπομονή (I. i. 3 note) is usually found associated with ἐλπίς, and its close union here with πίστις under a common art. has led to the latter's being taken in the sense of 'faithfulness' (Beng.: 'fidelem constantiam confessionis'). But this passive significance of πίστις is, to say the least, very rare in the N.T. (cf. Rom. iii. 3, Gal. v. 22), and the occurrence of the word in its ordinary active sense of 'faith' in the immediately preceding verse makes it more natural to give it the same meaning here. Nor need the added clause ἐν πᾶσιν τ. διωγμοῖς κτλ. cause any difficulty in this respect. It was the very point of the Apostles' boast that the Thessalonians had maintained a true religious 'faith' even in the midst of the 'persecutions' and 'afflictions' which had been both numerous (πᾶσιν) and continuous (ἀνέχεσθε pres.).
For the combination διωγμ. κ. θλίψ. cf. Mt. xiii. 21, Mk. iv. 17, the former being the more special term, with reference to the external persecutions inflicted by enemies of the Gospel (cf. Ac. viii. 1, xiii. 50, 2 Macc. xii. 23), the latter (cf. I. i. 6, note), more comprehensively, afflictions of any kind.
αἷς ἀνέχεσθε] 'which ye are enduring.' Αἷς is generally regarded as an attraction for ὧν ἀνέχεσθε, as elsewhere

in the N. T. ἀνέχομαι is found with the gen. (e.g. 2 Cor. xi. 1, 19, Eph. iv. 2). But such an attraction as this would be unique (WM. p. 204 n.²), and it is simpler to regard αἷς as directly governed by ἀνέχεσθε for which we have class. authority, e.g. Eur. Androm. 980 ξυμφοραῖς δ' ἠνειχόμην. Findlay suggests that the grammatical anomaly may have led to the otherwise interesting variant αἷς ἐνέχεσθε (WH. mg.) 'in which you are involved,' αἷς being then regularly governed by ἐν-: cf. Gal. v. 1 μὴ πάλιν ζυγῷ δουλείας ἐνέχεσθε, P.Fior. 57, 30 (iii./A.D.) ἐνέχεσθε ταῖς λειτουργίαις.

5. 'We have spoken of your heroic faith under persecution, and we gladly dwell upon it, because in itself it affords a proof of what awaits you in the day of God's final judgment, and will then result in your being found worthy of the heavenly Kingdom, for which you are now suffering.'

5. ἔνδειγμα κτλ.] 'a plain token of the righteous judgment of God' (Beza quae res indicium est iusti iudicii Dei). Ἔνδειγμα (ἅπ. λεγ. N.T.) in accordance with its passive form denotes strictly a *result* that has been reached, 'a thing proved,' but as frequently in similar cases where the abstract gives place to the concrete can hardly be distinguished from ἔνδειξις the actual proof by an appeal to facts, cf. Rom. iii. 25 f., 2 Cor. viii. 24, and especially the closely parallel passage Phil. i. 28 μὴ πτυρόμενοι ἐν μηδενί...ἥτις ἐστὶν αὐτοῖς ἔνδειξις ἀπωλείας.

As regards construction, the analogy of this last passage has led to the treating of ἔνδειγμα as a nominative, some such ellipsis as ὅ ἐστιν being

εἰς τὸ καταξιωθῆναι ὑμᾶς τῆς βασιλείας τοῦ θεοῦ, ὑπὲρ

supplied (Blass p. 293). But it is more in keeping with class. usage to regard such noun-phrases as accusatives, in apposition to the whole idea of the foregoing sentence (cf. Rom. viii. 3, xii. 1, 1 Tim. ii. 6, and see further Kühner³ § 406, 6, Riddell *The Apology of Plato* (1877) p. 122). In the present instance, therefore, the meaning is that the heroic faith of the Thessalonians under persecution is in itself a 'proof,' a 'sign' (Est. 'argumentum et indicium') of what God's final judgment in their case will be.

For δικαίας κρίσεως, a phrase not found elsewhere in the Pauline Epp. cf. Rom. ii. 5 δικαιοκρισίας which, however, denotes 'not so much the character of the judgment as the character of the Judge' (SH. p. 56), and for the whole thought see Rom. viii. 18 ff., 2 Cor. iv. 16 ff.

As a literary parallel Garrod aptly cites the lines from Browning's 'Abt Vogler'—

And what is our failure here but a triumph's evidence
For the fulness of the days?

And as still better illustrating the confident appeal to the supreme judgment by which all present sufferings will be set in their true light, Dante's great lines (*Purg.* x. 109—111) may be recalled—

Non attender la forma del martire:
Pensa la succession; pensa che, a peggio,
Oltre la gran sentenza non può ire.

εἰς τὸ καταξιωθῆναι κτλ.] Cf. the common Rabbinic expression 'To be worthy of the future aeon' (Dalman *Worte* p. 97, E. Tr. p. 119).

Καταξιόω, like the simple ἀξιόω (v. 11), denotes not 'make' but 'count worthy,' and is found elsewhere in the N.T. only in Lk. xx. 35 οἱ δὲ καταξιωθέντες τοῦ αἰῶνος ἐκείνου τυχεῖν, Ac. v. 41 ὅτι κατηξιώθησαν ὑπὲρ τοῦ ὀνόματος ἀτιμασθῆναι. In the LXX. it is confined to Maccabees⁴; cf. Aristeas 175 τοὺς δὲ ἥκοντας τιμῆς καταξιῶν μείζονος. It is frequent in Polybius (e.g. i. 23. 3, iv. 86. 8); see also *C.I.A.* III. 690, 9 f. ἀνατροφῆς τῆς αὑτῆς καταξιωθείς.

For εἰς τό with inf., and for the meaning of τ. βασιλ. τ. θεοῦ see the notes on I. ii. 12.

ὑπὲρ ἧς καὶ πάσχετε] cf. Rom. viii. 17, 2 Cor. i. 7, Phil. iii. 10, and Dante *Purg.* xix. 76 f.—

O eletti di Dio, li cui soffriri
E giustizia e speranza fan men duri.

6—10. From the thought of the future recompence awaiting the persecuted Thessalonian Church the Apostles proceed to describe more fully the issue of the Lord's Parousia in an apocalyptic passage closely based on the O.T. as regards both language and imagery (see Intr. p. lix). The form is largely rhythmical, so much so that Bornemann (pp. 329, 336) conjectures that *vv.* 7ᵇ—10ᵃ may be an adaptation of some primitive Christian psalm or hymn.

'We are the more confident of this because it is in accord with God's righteous law to mete out trouble to troublers, and to the troubled rest—a rest which we hope to share along with you at the revelation from heaven of the Lord Jesus attended by the angels, as the instruments of His power, and surrounded by a "fire of flame." Then will He inflict full justice upon all who in wilful ignorance oppose themselves to God, and in consequence disobey the Gospel of Christ. All such shall suffer a fitting penalty. Nothing less than eternal ruin will fall upon them—banishment from the presence of the Lord and from the glory of His might. Yes, from that glory the wicked, your persecutors, will be shut out, for the object of the Lord's coming is to be glorified in His saints and revered

I 6—8] THE SECOND EPISTLE TO THE THESSALONIANS 89

ῆς καὶ πάσχετε, ⁶εἴπερ δίκαιον παρὰ θεῷ ἀνταποδοῦναι
τοῖς θλίβουσιν ὑμᾶς θλίψιν ⁷καὶ ὑμῖν τοῖς θλιβομένοις
ἄνεσιν μεθ' ἡμῶν ἐν τῇ ἀποκαλύψει τοῦ κυρίου Ἰησοῦ
ἀπ' οὐρανοῦ μετ' ἀγγέλων δυνάμεως αὐτοῦ ⁸ἐν πυρὶ φλογός,

in all believers (amongst whom we may reckon you, for you received our testimony) in that great Day.'

6. εἴπερ δίκαιον κτλ.] Εἴπερ ('si quidem') an intensive form, confined in the N.T. to the Pauline writings, which, without implying doubt as to the truth of the condition assumed, lays some stress on it as a condition (cf. Rom. iii. 30, viii. 9, 17; SH. p. 96). That condition is here the exercise of the strict righteousness of God conceived as a *jus talionis*.

For δίκαιον cf. δικαίας κρίσεως (v. 5), and for παρὰ θεῷ ('judice Deo') see WM. p. 493.

ἀνταποδοῦναι κτλ.] Th. Mops. *retribuere his qui tribulant uos retributionem*. For ἀνταποδίδωμι see I. iii. 9 note, and for θλίψις I. i. 6 note. The language as well as the thought (cf. Rom. ii. 6 ff.) is clearly suggested by O.T. prophecy, cf. especially Isa. lxvi. 4, 14 ff., and for a terse description of the close connexion between sin and its 'other half' punishment see Sap. xi. 16 (17) δι' ὧν τις ἁμαρτάνει, διὰ τούτων κολάζεται.

7. ἄνεσιν] Ἄνεσις, lit. 'loosening,' 'relaxing' of the cords of endurance now tightly drawn (cf. Plato *Rep.* i. 349 E ἐν τῇ ἐπιτάσει καὶ ἀνέσει τῶν χορδῶν), is, with the exception of Ac. xxiv. 23 ('indulgence' R.V.), used in the N.T. only by St Paul, and always with the contrast to θλίψις either stated or implied; cf. 2 Cor. ii. 13 (see v. 4), vii. 5, viii. 13. In the apocryphal books of the O.T. it is found also in the more general senses of 'liberty' (1 Esdr. iv. 62) and of 'licence' (Sir. xv. 20 (21), xxvi. 10 (13)): cf. also Aristeas 284 ἐν ταῖς ἀνέσεσι καὶ ῥαθυμίαις, P.Tebt. 24, 73

(ii./B.C.) ἐν ἀν[έ]σει γεγονότας 'becoming remiss.'

In the present passage the 'rest' spoken of (Est.: 'remissionem, relaxationem, scilicet a pressuris hujus mundi') is practically synonymous with the καιροὶ ἀναψύξεως of Ac. iii. 19, where the context again determines the eschatological reference of the phrase: cf. also *Asc. Isai.* iv. 15 'And He will give rest to the godly whom He shall find in the body in this world.'

μεθ' ἡμῶν] i.e. with Paul and his companions, rather than with Christians in general: cf. 2 Cor. i. 7, Phil. i. 30. Oecum.: ἐπάγει τὸ μεθ' ἡμῶν, ἵνα κοινωνοὺς αὐτοὺς λάβῃ καὶ τῶν ἀγώνων καὶ τῶν στεφάνων τῶν ἀποστολικῶν.

ἐν τῇ ἀποκαλύψει κτλ.] Cf. 1 Cor. i. 7, and for the original suggestion of the phrase see Lk. xvii. 30 ᾗ ἡμέρᾳ ὁ υἱὸς τοῦ ἀνθρώπου ἀποκαλύπτεται. Ἐν is not purely temporal but 'in and through' (cf. I. ii. 19 note), the ἀνταπόδοσις being not only associated with the ἀποκάλυψις but actually forming a part of it: cf. 1 Pet. i. 7 (with Hort's note), and on the distinction between ἀποκάλυψις and παρουσία see Add. Note F.

For similar language from Jewish Apocalyptic cf. 4 Ezra vii. 28 (quoted I. iv. 17 note); xiii. 32 'et erit cum fient haec...tunc reuelabitur filius meus quem uidisti uiram ascendentem.'

μετ' ἀγγέλων κτλ.] 'accompanied by angels of His power'—δυνάμεως not being a mere epithet of ἀγγέλων, but, as the accompanying αὐτοῦ shows, pointing directly to the power of the Lord Himself, of which the angels (cf. I. iii. 13 note) were the exponents and ministers. Calv.: '*angelos potentiae*

90 THE SECOND EPISTLE TO THE THESSALONIANS [I 9

Διδόντος ἐκδίκησιν τοῖς μὴ εἰδόσι θεὸν καὶ τοῖς μὴ ὑπακούουσιν τῷ εὐαγγελίῳ τοῦ κυρίου ἡμῶν Ἰησοῦ, ⁹οἵτινες δίκην

vocat, in quibus suam potestatem exseret.'

8. ἐν πυρὶ φλογός] a common figure in O.T. theophanies, and frequently associated as here with the thought of judgment, e.g. Isa. lxvi. 15 ἰδοὺ γὰρ Κύριος ὡς πῦρ ἥξει,...ἀποδοῦναι ἐν θυμῷ ἐκδίκησιν αὐτοῦ καὶ ἀποσκορακισμὸν αὐτοῦ ἐν φλογὶ πυρός. See also Apoc. Bar. xlviii. 39, 'Therefore a fire will consume their thoughts, and in flame will the meditations of their reins be tried; for the Judge will come and will not tarry,' where as elsewhere in the same book (xliv. 15, lix. 2 (with Charles's note), lxxxv. 13) material fire seems to be intended. In St Paul's hands on the contrary the figure has become entirely spiritualized, and there is certainly no thought here of 'fire' as the actual instrument for the destruction of the ungodly, as Kabisch appears to suggest (Eschatologie des Paulus (1893) p. 246).

The v.l. ἐν φλογὶ πυρός (BDG 47 71) appears to be a conformation to Isa. lxvi. 15 (cited above); on the other hand in ἐν πυρὶ φλογός (אAKLP) we may have a reminiscence of LXX. Ex. iii. 2, where however AF read ἐν φλ. πυρ.: cf. Ac. vii. 30 where there is a similar variation of reading.

διδόντος ἐκδίκησιν] not to be connected with πυρός but directly with τ. κυρ. Ἰησοῦ, and serving to bring out further the judicial aspect under which this ἀποκάλυψις is here presented.

Ἐκδίκησις from ἔκδικος (I. iv. 6 note) is full, complete punishment, cf. I Pet. ii. 14 εἰς ἐκδίκησιν κακοποιῶν: elsewhere it has the meaning of 'avenging,' 'vindication' (e.g. Lk. xviii. 7 ff.). The exact phrase δοῦναι ἐκδίκησιν is found only here in the N.T., but it occurs several times in the LXX., e.g. Ezek. xxv. 14: cf. Isa. lxvi. 15 ἀποδοῦναι ἐκδίκησιν, and more particularly for

the thought Deut. xxxii. 35 ἐν ἡμέρᾳ ἐκδικήσεως ἀνταποδώσω. On the power of judgment here ascribed to the Lord Jesus see Intr. p. lxvii.

The v.l. διδούς (D*FG and some Latin authorities) for διδόντος, if it were better attested, would be an instance of the indifference to concord which we find so frequently in the Apocalypse, and in the less educated papyri (Moulton Prolegg. pp. 9, 60).

τοῖς μὴ εἰδόσι κτλ.] 'to them that know not God and to them that obey not the gospel of our Lord Jesus.' The two clauses (note repeated art.) are often referred to the Gentile (I. iv. 5 note) and Jewish (Rom. x. 16 ff.) opponents of the Gospel respectively. But it is doubtful whether any such distinction was in the writers' minds at the time, nor can it be strictly applied, for Gentiles as well as Jews can be taxed with disobedience (Rom. xi. 30), while the wilful ignorance of God which alone can be thought of here (cf. Rom. ii. 14) is elsewhere directly ascribed to Jews (cf. Jer. ix. 6 οὐκ ἤθελον εἰδέναι με). On the whole therefore it is better, and more in keeping with the Hebraistic strain of the whole passage (Findlay), to take both clauses as referring to the same general class, viz. all who as the result of wilful ignorance or disobedience oppose themselves to God: cf. Jer. x. 25 ἔκχεον τὸν θυμόν σου ἐπὶ ἔθνη τὰ μὴ εἰδότα σε καὶ ἐπὶ γενεὰς αἳ τὸ ὄνομά σου οὐκ ἐπεκαλέσαντο, where again the two closely parallel clauses form one extended category.

The substitution of τ. εὐαγγ. τ. κυρ. ἡμ. Ἰησ. for τ. εὐαγγ. τ. θεοῦ (I. ii. 2 &c.) is in accordance with the prominence given to the Lord Jesus throughout the section.

9. οἵτινες] 'men who' ('quippe qui'),

I 10] THE SECOND EPISTLE TO THE THESSALONIANS 91

τίσουσιν ὄλεθρον αἰώνιον ἀπὸ προσώπογ τοῦ κγρίογ καὶ ἀπὸ τῆς Δόξης τῆς ἰσχύος αὐτοῦ, ¹⁰ὅταν ἔλθη ἐνδοξασθῆναι ἐν τοῖς ἁγίοις

the qualitative character of ὅστις, though generally lost in late Gk., being apparently maintained in the Pauline Epp., cf. Rom. i. 25, 1 Cor. iii. 17, Gal. iv. 24, 26, Phil. iv. 3, and see Blass p. 173, Moulton *Prolegg.* p. 91 f.

In the papyri of the Ptolemaic period ὅστις has almost wholly disappeared, its place being taken by the simple ὅς, and in the plural often by ὅσοι (Mayser p. 310).

δίκην τίσουσιν] 'shall pay a penalty.' Δίκη, originally 'custom,' 'usage,' and hence 'right' considered as established usage, came to be extended to a 'process of law' or 'judicial hearing' (e.g. P.Hib. 30, 24 (iii./B.C.) ἡ δίκη σοι ἀναγραφήσετ[α]ι 'the case will be drawn up against you,' P.Reinach 15, 21 (ii./B.C.) ἄνευ δίκης καὶ κρίσεως καὶ πάσης εὑρεσιλογίας 'sans procès, contestation, ni chicane d'aucune sorte'), and then to the result of the lawsuit, 'execution of a sentence,' 'punishment': see Jude 7, Sap. xviii. 11, 2 Macc. viii. 11, and cf. P.Fay. 21, 24 f. (ii./A.D.) τὴν προσήκουσαν δίκη[ν ὑ]πόσχωσι 'may pay the fitting penalty.'

The exact phrase δίκην τίνειν does not occur elsewhere in the N.T. though it is very common in class. writers, cf. Soph. *Electra* 330 ἀλλ' ἴσθι τοι τίσουσά γ' ἀξίαν δίκην, and the other exx. cited by Wetstein. For the verb cf. Prov. xxvii. 12 ζημίαν τίσουσιν, B.G.U. 242, 7 f. (ii./A.D.) [πλ]ηγαῖς πλίσταις με [ἐτ]είσατο.

ὄλεθρον αἰώνιον] a phrase not found elsewhere in the N.T., but cf. 4 Macc. x. 15 τὸν αἰώνιον τοῦ τυράννου ὄλεθρον. As ὄλεθρον (I. v. 3 note) does not necessarily imply *annihilation*, so in itself αἰώνιον need not mean more than 'age-long,' 'age-lasting,' the period over which it extends depending on the nature of the object with which the aeon has to do. Thus in both papyri and inscriptions it is of frequent occurrence with reference to the span of a Caesar's life, cf. B.G.U. 362. iv. 11 f. ὑπὲρ σωτηριῶν καὶ αἰω[νίου] διαμο[νῆ]ς τοῦ κυρίου ἡμῶν (Severus), and for a similar weakened sense of the word see Magn. 188, 12 f. (ii./A.D.) where reference is made to the monies spent by a certain Charidemos during his 'life-long' tenure of the office of gymnasiarch (εἰς γυμνασιαρχίαν αἰώνιον). On the other hand, in view of St Paul's consistent teaching regarding ὁ αἰὼν ὁ μέλλων which is once and for ever to supplant ὁ αἰὼν οὗτος, the thought of 'finality' is necessarily present in the passage before us: the destruction is an 'eternal' one. See further Kennedy *Last Things* p. 316 ff., and the passages cited by Volz *Jüd. Eschat.* p. 286 f. to show that the *eternity* of woe was the ordinary teaching of Jewish writers.

Lachmann's reading ὀλέθριον is only supported by A 17 47 73; cf. Tert. *adv. Marc.* v. 16 'quos ait poenam luituros exitialem, aeternam.'

ἀπὸ προσώπου κτλ.] The words are borrowed, as Tertullian had already remarked (*adv. Marc.* v. 16 'verbis usus Esaiae'), from Isa. ii. 10, 19, 21, and hence ἀπό is best understood neither temporarily nor causally but locally in the sense of *separation from* the face of the Lord. For this pregnant use of the preposition cf. ii. 2, Rom. ix. 3, 2 Cor. xi. 3, Gal. v. 4, and for the thought such passages as Mt. vii. 23, xxv. 41, Lk. xiii. 27 contrasted with Mt. v. 8, 1 Jo. iii. 2, Rev. xxii. 4.

Δόξης, as in I. ii. 12, is the visible glory which is the symbol of the Divine presence, while ἰσχύος (gen. orig.) is the strength by which the Lord is characterized, and from which His glory radiates; cf. Ps. cxlvi. (cxlvii.) 5 μέγας ὁ κύριος ἡμῶν, καὶ μεγάλη ἡ

αὐτοῦ καὶ θαυμασθῆναι ἐν πᾶσιν τοῖς πιστεύσασιν, ὅτι ⌜ἐπι-
στεύθη⌝ τὸ μαρτύριον ἡμῶν ἐφ᾽ ὑμᾶς, ἐν τῇ ἡμέρᾳ ἐκείνῃ.

10 ἐπιστεύθη] ἐπιστώθη 31

ἰσχὺς αὐτοῦ. For the distinction between ἰσχύς *strength* absolutely and κράτος *might*, strength in relation to an end to be gained, see Westcott *Eph.* p. 25 f.

10. ὅταν ἔλθῃ κτλ.] 'whenever He has (or, shall have) come...,' the aor. subj. with ὅταν describing a completed action 'future by virtue of its mood, punctiliar by its tense' (Moulton *Prolegg.* p. 186).

Ἐνδοξασθῆναι is found elsewhere in the N.T. only in *v.* 12, but is common in the LXX., cf. Ex. xiv. 4 ἐνδοξασθήσομαι ἐν Φαραώ, and especially Ps. lxxxviii. (lxxxix.) 8 ὁ θεὸς ἐνδοξαζόμενος ἐν βουλῇ ἁγίων, a verse which may have suggested its use in the present passage.

ἐν τ. ἁγίοις] In accordance with the context these words can refer here only to redeemed men (cf. I. iii. 13 note), the preposition marking them out not as the agents of the Lord's glorification (Chrys. : ἐν, διά, ἐστί), but as the sphere or element in which this glorification takes place; cf. Jo. xvii. 10 δεδόξασμαι ἐν αὐτοῖς.

καὶ θαυμασθῆναι κτλ.] parallel to the preceding clause and with the same wide sweep, cf. Ps. lxvii. (lxviii.) 36 θαυμαστὸς ὁ θεὸς ἐν τοῖς ὁσίοις αὐτοῦ. Bengel's proposal to limit τ. ἁγίοις to converted Jews and πᾶσιν τ. πιστεύσασιν to converted Gentiles is quite untenable.

For ὁ πιστεύσας as an almost technical title for 'one who has accepted the Gospel,' 'a believer,' cf. Ac. iv. 32, xi. 17.

ὅτι ἐπιστεύθη κτλ.] a parenthetical clause catching up the preceding τ. πιστεύσασιν, and expressing the writers' conviction that in the Thessalonians' case the testimony addressed to them had secured the desired result.

While however the general sense is clear, the construction of this clause is admittedly difficult. The words ἐφ᾽ ὑμᾶς are usually connected directly with τὸ μαρτύριον ἡμ., as the order of the sentence naturally suggests, but no other instance of μαρτύριον with ἐπί in this sense is forthcoming (in Lk. ix. 5 ἐπί = 'against') and Findlay's idea of a 'testimony *accosting* (assailing, challenging) you' for which he compares 1 Tim. i. 18, Eph. ii. 7, Rev. xiv. 6 is, to say the least, somewhat far-fetched. We must be content therefore either to regard this as a unique construction, intended to emphasize the direction the testimony took, or (with Lft.) connect ἐφ᾽ ὑμᾶς with ἐπιστεύθη in the sense 'belief in our testimony directed itself to reach you.' WH.² (*Notes* p. 128) favour this latter connexion, but despairing of then finding a proper meaning for ἐπιστεύθη propose the conjectural emendation ἐπιστώθη (read in cod. min. 31) 'was confirmed': 'the Christian testimony of suffering for the faith had been confirmed and sealed upon the Thessalonians.'

ἐν τῇ ἡμέρᾳ ἐκείνῃ] a predicate of time connected with θαυμασθῆναι and rendered emphatic by position. For ἡ ἡμ. ἐκείνη as denoting the day of Christ's final coming cf. Mk. xiii. 32, xiv. 25, Lk. xxi. 34, 2 Tim. i. 12, 18, iv. 8, and for the general meaning of the phrase see note on I. v. 2.

11, 12. A characteristic reference to the writers' constant prayers on their brethren's behalf.

'And now that all this may be brought to pass, our earnest prayer is that our God will count *you* worthy of the heavenly rest for which you are looking. To this end may He mightily animate you with all delight in goodness, and with a whole-hearted activity inspired by the faith you profess. Thus

I 11] THE SECOND EPISTLE TO THE THESSALONIANS 93

¹¹ εἰς ὃ καὶ προσευχόμεθα πάντοτε περὶ ὑμῶν, ἵνα ὑμᾶς ἀξιώσῃ τῆς κλήσεως ὁ θεὸς ἡμῶν καὶ πληρώσῃ πᾶσαν εὐδοκίαν ἀγαθωσύνης καὶ ἔργον πίστεως ἐν δυνάμει,

the full glory of the Lord Jesus will be displayed in you, as you in your turn derive your glory from Him in accordance with the gracious purposes of our God and the Lord Jesus Christ.'

11. εἰς ὅ] 'to which end' with reference to the whole contents of vv. 5—10.

ἵνα ὑμ. ἀξιώσῃ]'Ἀξιόω 'count worthy' (cf. καταξιόω v. 5) occurs seven times in the N.T., and is usually associated as here with the thought of reward (e.g. 1 Tim. v. 17, Heb. iii. 3), cf. however Heb. x. 29 ἀξιωθήσεται τιμωρίας. The verb is frequent in the papyri in the sense of 'beg,' 'entreat,' e.g. P.Tebt. 28, 15 (ii./B.C.) ἀξιοῦμεν ἐμβλέψαντα εἰς τὰ ὑποδεδειγμένα 'we beg you to look into the matters indicated and...'

For ἵνα following προσεύχομαι cf. Mk. xiii. 18, xiv. 35, 38, Phil. i. 9, and for its semi-final force here see the note on I. iv. 1.

κλήσεως] Usually in the N.T. κλῆσις is applied to the initial act of salvation as a Divine invitation (Rom. xi. 29, 1 Cor. i. 26) carrying with it great responsibilities (Eph. iv. 1, 2 Pet. i. 10), and that meaning is by no means impossible here in the sense that on the day of Christ's return the Thessalonians' whole life may be found to have been in harmony with the call once addressed to them. There seems no reason however why the word should not be definitely extended to include the final issue of the calling, much in the sense of τῆς ἄνω κλήσεως in Phil. iii. 14 or κλήσεως ἐπουρανίου in Heb. iii. 1: cf. the similar use of καλέω in I. ii. 12, and see further Intr. p. lxxix.

ὁ θεὸς ἡμῶν] For the expression cf. I. ii. 2 note, and for the change from the 2nd pers. pron. (ὑμᾶς) to the 1st cf. I. v. 5ᵇ note.

καὶ πληρώσῃ κτλ.] 'and may fulfil every delight in goodness and work of faith in power.' The almost technical use of εὐδοκία in the Bibl. writings to denote the good-will of God to man (e.g. Ps. cv. (cvi.) 4, Lk. ii. 14, Eph. i. 5, 9, Phil. ii. 13; cf. Pss. Sol. viii. 39, Enoch i. 8 καὶ τὴν εὐδοκίαν [εὐοδίαν, Charles] δώσει αὐτοῖς) has led to the translation of the A.V. 'all the good pleasure of *his* goodness' (Beza *totum* suae *bonitatis libitum*). But if this had been intended we should have expected the art. before εὐδοκίαν, while the further considerations that ἀγαθωσύνης is never used elsewhere of God (cf. Rom. xv. 14, Gal. v. 22, Eph. v. 9) and that the accompanying parallel clause κ. ἔργον πίστεως must refer to the Thessalonians are both in favour of extending εὐδοκίαν to them also. The word can then only mean the 'good pleasure,' 'delight' in 'goodness' (ἀγαθωσύνης, gen. obj.), which it was the prayer of the Apostles that their converts might evince in full measure.

For εὐδοκία (not found in class. Gk.) in this sense cf. Sir. xxix. 23 (30), xxxv. 14 (xxxii. 18), Pss. Sol. xvi. 12 εὐδοκίᾳ δὲ μετὰ ἱλαρότητος στήρισον τὴν ψυχήν μου, and see the note on εὐδοκέω I. ii. 8. The corresponding subst. εὐδόκησις occurs *O.G.I.S.* 335, 122 (Perg.) κατὰ τὴ[ν τοῦ δήμου ἐπιταγὴν καὶ τὴν βασιλέω]ς εὐδόκησιν.

ἀγαθωσύνης] Ἀγαθωσύνη a late form (WH.² *Notes* p. 159, WSchm. p. 134) found only in the LXX., N.T., and writings derived from them. It is always rendered 'goodness' in A.V., R.V., and 'represents the kindlier, as δικαιοσύνη represents the sterner element in the ideal character: comp. Rom. v. 7' (Robinson *Eph.* p. 200). See further Trench *Syn.* § lxiii., and cf. the valuable note on δίκαιος and

94 THE SECOND EPISTLE TO THE THESSALONIANS [I 12

¹²ὅπως ἐνδοξαcθῆ τὸ ὄνομα τοῦ κυρίου ἡμῶν Ἰησοῦ ἐν ἡμῖν, καὶ ὑμεῖς ἐν αὐτῷ, κατὰ τὴν χάριν τοῦ θεοῦ ἡμῶν καὶ κυρίου Ἰησοῦ Χριστοῦ.

ἀγαθός in Lft. *Notes on Epp. of St Paul* p. 286 f. For ἔργον πίστεως 'activity inspired by faith' cf. I. i. 3 note.

ἐν δυνάμει] an adv. adjunct to πληρώσῃ to bring out the manner of God's working, cf. Rom. i. 4, Col. i. 29, and the Prayer-Book collect for Monday in Easter-week: 'That, as by Thy special grace preventing us Thou dost put into our minds good desires, so by Thy continual help we may bring the same to good effect.'

12. ὅπως] rare with St Paul, and used here probably to vary the preceding ἵνα, cf. 1 Cor. i. 29, 2 Cor. viii. 14 (Blass p. 211).

ἐνδοξασθῇ] cf. *v.* 10 note, and for the reciprocity here implied (ἐν ὑμ. κ. ὑμ. ἐν αὐτῷ) resting on the essential union between the Lord and His people see Jo. xvii. 9 f., 20 ff.

τὸ ὄνομα τ. κυρ. ἡμ. Ἰησοῦ] The use of ὄνομα here goes back to the O.T., where in accordance with its most characteristic usage 'the name of Jehovah' is to be understood as embodying His (revealed) character (see *B.D.B. s.v.* שֵׁם, and cf. Art. 'Name' in Hastings' *D.B.* iii. p. 478 ff.). The glorification of the *name* of the Lord Jesus thus implies the showing forth of the Lord Jesus as He really is, in all the fulness of His person and attributes (cf. Phil. ii. 9 f., Heb. i. 4). With this may be compared the well-established Gk. usage of ὄνομα as a title of dignity or rank, e.g. P.Oxy. 58 (iii./A.D.) where the writer complains of the expense caused to the treasury by the number of persons who have devised 'offices' for themselves (ὀνόματα ἑαυτοῖς ἐξευρόντες), and, after providing for a single trustworthy superintendent, ordains that the remaining 'offices' shall cease (τὰ δὲ λοιπὰ ὀνόματα παύσηται). It should be noted however that very frequently ὄνομα can mean little more than 'person,' e.g. *B.G.U.* 113, 11 (ii./A.D.)ἑκάστῳ ὀνόματι παραγ(ενομένῳ): see further Deissmann *BS.* p. 196 ff., Reitzenstein *Poimandres* p. 17 n.⁶, and cf. the note on iii. 6.

κατὰ τὴν χάριν κτλ.] not merely the norm but the source of the glorification spoken of in accordance with a common derived use of κατά (WM. p. 501). Pelag.: 'Expetit a nobis, quod possumus: ut quod non possumus, largiatur.'

The fact that the art. is not repeated before κυρίου would seem at first sight to imply that both θεοῦ and κυρίου refer to the same person, '(grace) of our God and Lord, Jesus Christ.' But this cannot be pressed in view of the frequent occurrence of κύριος without the art. as practically equivalent to a proper name, and it is more in keeping with general Pauline usage to distinguish between the Father as θεός and Jesus Christ as κύριος, cf. in these Epp. I. i. 1, II. i. 1, 2, ii. 16. We translate therefore as in the R.V., 'according to the grace of our God and the Lord Jesus Christ': see further Middleton *On the Greek Article* (ed. Rose) p. 379 ff.

II. 1—12. TEACHING CONCERNING THE EVENTS PRECEDING THE LORD'S PAROUSIA.

We have seen already what were the circumstances leading up to the writing of this remarkable section— how, on the one hand, St Paul had to do his utmost to allay the restless excitement of which there were increasing signs amongst the Thessalonians, and, on the other, to guard against saying anything to discourage their belief in the near approach of the Lord (Intr. p. xxxviii f.). And it must

II 1] THE SECOND EPISTLE TO THE THESSALONIANS 95

II. ¹'Ερωτῶμεν δὲ ὑμᾶς, ἀδελφοί, ὑπὲρ τῆς παρουσίας τοῦ κυρίου [ἡμῶν] 'Ιησοῦ Χριστοῦ καὶ ἡμῶν ἐπισυνα-

II 1 ἡμῶν om B Syr (Harcl)

be at once admitted that the manner in which he proceeds to do so is at first sight both strange and bewildering. For, instead of conveying his warning in a clear and definite form, the Apostle prefers to embody it in a mysterious apocalyptic picture, which has not only no parallel in his own writings, but is unlike anything else in the N.T., unless it be certain passages in the Revelation of St John (e.g. xiii. 5—8, 12—17, xvi. 9—11). Nor is this all, but the difficulties of the passage are still further increased by the grammatical irregularities and frequent ellipses with which it abounds, and even more by the manifest reserve with which the whole subject is treated.

In the following exposition therefore we shall try and discover as clearly as possible with the aid of the O.T. and the apocalyptic writings of the Apostle's time the meaning of the different words and phrases, leaving the general teaching of the passage to Add. Note I, and the history of the various interpretations that have been offered of it to Add. Note J. The arguments against the authenticity of the Ep. to which it has given rise have already been discussed Intr. p. lxxxv f.

The section opens with an appeal to the Thessalonians not to be led astray by false ideas regarding the coming of the Lord (vv. 1, 2). So far from His Parousia being 'upon them,' it will not take place until after the great Apostasy, culminating in the 'parousia' of the Man of lawlessness (vv. 3, 4). The signs of that 'parousia' are already at work, and it only requires the removal of the presently restraining influence for its full revelation to take place (vv. 5—7)—a revela-

tion which, though it will end in the complete destruction of the 'lawless one,' will bring judgment on all who have set themselves against the Truth (vv. 8—12).

1—4. 'We have been speaking of the great Day of the Lord, but that you may not fall into any mistake as to the Parousia of the Lord by which it will be ushered in, and the assembling of believers by which it will be accompanied, we beg of you, Brothers, not to allow your minds to be unsettled for little or no reason, or to be kept disturbed by any prophetic utterance, or teaching, or letter, any or all of them purporting to come from us, to the effect that the Day of the Lord has actually arrived. Do not, we beg of you, let any man lead you completely astray in this or any other way. For in no case will this Parousia take place until after the great Apostasy, and the consequent revelation of the Man of lawlessness, that son of perdition. So terrible indeed will be his revolt that, as the embodiment of Satanic power, he will be found exalting himself against every one that is spoken of as god, or that is an object of worship. Yes, he will even go the length of seating himself in the Temple of God, and claiming to be God.'

1. Ἐρωτῶμεν δέ κτλ.] For ἐρωτάω see I. iv. 1 note, and for ἀδελφοί see I. i. 4 note.

ὑπὲρ τ. παρουσίας] 'as regarding the Parousia,' the original meaning of ὑπέρ 'on behalf of,' 'in the interest of' being here almost wholly lost sight of, cf. Rom. ix. 27, 2 Cor. i. 8, viii. 23, xii. 8, and such a passage from the Κοινή as P.Tebt. 19, 9f. (ii./B.C.) ὑπὲρ δὲ ὧν σημαίνεις κωμογραμματέων μόλις ἕως τῆς κε χωρισθήσονται, 'regarding the

96 THE SECOND EPISTLE TO THE THESSALONIANS [II 2

γωγῆς ἐπ' αὐτόν, ²εἰς τὸ μὴ ταχέως σαλευθῆναι ὑμᾶς ἀπὸ τοῦ νοὸς μηδὲ θροεῖσθαι μήτε διὰ πνεύματος μήτε

komogramateis whom you mention, they will hardly depart until the 25th.' In no case is there any warrant for the A.V. rendering 'by' as an adjuration (Vg. *per adventum*). For παρουσία see Add. Note F, and for the full title τ. κυρ. Ἰησ. Χρ. see Add. Note D.

ἐπισυναγωγῆς] The word goes back to such a saying of the Lord as Mk. xiii. 27 καὶ ἐπισυνάξει τοὺς ἐκλεκτοὺς αὐτοῦ, and is found elsewhere in the N.T. only in Heb. x. 25 where it is applied to the ordinary religious assembling of believers as an anticipation of the great assembling at the Lord's Parousia: cf. 2 Macc. ii. 7 ἕως ἂν συνάγῃ ὁ θεὸς ἐπισυναγωγὴν τοῦ λαοῦ with reference to the gathering of the tribes into the temporal kingdom of the Messiah. For the verb see Deut. xxx. 4, Ps. cv. (cvi.) 47, Zach. xii. 3, 2 Macc. i. 27, Didache ix. 4, and cf. *O.G.I.S.* 90, 23 (ii./B.C.—the Rosetta stone) τοῖς ἐπισυναχθεῖσιν εἰς αὐτὴν [Λύκων πόλιν] ἀσεβέσιν.

2. εἰς τὸ μὴ τάχ. σαλευθῆναι] 'to the end that you be not readily driven away' from your sober sense, as a ship from its safe anchorage. For this use of σαλεύειν cf. especially Plut. *Mor.* ii. 493 D (cited by Lft.) where ὄρεξιν τοῦ κατὰ φύσιν ἀποσαλεύουσαν is followed almost immediately by ὡς ἐπ' ἀγκύρας τῆς φύσεως σαλεύει. The verb (from σάλος, Lk. xxi. 25), which is very common in the LXX. in its literal sense of the motion produced by winds and storms, is found also figuratively, as here, especially in the Pss. (e.g. ix. 27 (x. 6), xxix. (xxx.) 7): cf. 1 Macc. vi. 8, Pss. Sol. viii. 39, xv. 6, Ac. xvii. 13 (where it is joined with ταράσσειν), Heb. xii. 26 f., also *O.G.I.S.* 515, 47 (iii./A.D.) σαλεύει γὰρ ὡς ἀληθῶς ἡ σωτηρία τῆς πόλε[ως ἐκ κακουργίας.

Ταχέως 'hastily,' 'readily,' the reference being not so much temporal as modal: cf. Gal. i. 6, 1 Tim. v. 22.

ἀπὸ τοῦ νοός] 'from your reason' (Wycl. *from your witte*)—νοός (for form, WSchm. p. 84) being used in its regular Pauline sense of the reasoning faculty, especially on its moral side, the highest part of man's own nature, through which he is most open to Divine influences: cf. 1 Cor. xiv. 14 ff., Phil. iv. 7. The word, which is rare in the LXX. (usually for לֵב or לֵבָב), is found in the N.T. outside the Pauline writings only in Lk. xxiv. 45, Rev. xiii. 18, xvii. 9. Thpht.: παρατραπῆναι ἀπὸ τοῦ νοός, ὃν μέχρι τοῦ νῦν ἔχετε ὀρθῶς ἱστάμενον.

μηδὲ θροεῖσθαι] 'nor yet be disturbed' in accordance with the regular Bibl. use of θροεῖσθαι: cf. Cant. v. 4 καὶ ἡ κοιλία μου ἐθροήθη ἐπ' αὐτόν, and especially Mt. xxiv. 6, Mk. xiii. 7 where, as here, it is used with reference to the Parousia. The present tense should be noted as pointing to a continued state of agitation following upon a definite shock received (σαλευθῆναι).

μήτε διὰ πνεύματος κτλ.] The Apostles now proceed to distinguish three ways in which the θρόησις just spoken of may have been caused, the thrice repeated μήτε dividing the foregoing negation (μηδὲ θροεῖσθαι) into its component parts: 'neither by spirit (i.e. ecstatic utterance, cf. I. v. 19), nor by (reasoned) discourse, nor by letter.'

So far the meaning seems clear, but the introduction of the following words ὡς δι' ἡμῶν has been the cause of much difficulty. As usually understood, they are regarded as a kind of adjectival clause appended to ἐπιστολῆς = 'as though (coming) from us' or 'as though we had written it' (Blass, p. 253, and cf. *B.G.U.* 884, 6 f. (ii./iii.

διὰ λόγου μήτε δι' ἐπιστολῆς ὡς δι' ἡμῶν, ὡς ὅτι ἐνέστηκεν ἡ ἡμέρα τοῦ ⌜κυρίου.⌝ ³μή τις ὑμᾶς ἐξαπατήσῃ κατὰ

2 κυρίου,—sic distinguere conati sunt WH

A.D.) τὰ διὰ τῶν ἐπ[ι]στολῶν αὐτοῦ). But if so, in view of the close parallelism of the preceding clauses, it seems impossible not to extend the qualification to them also. The general meaning would then be that in the event of false teachers arising and appealing in support of their views to some revelation or teaching or letter purporting to come from the Apostles, the Thessalonians were not to be disturbed as if they (the Apostles) were in reality in any way responsible. (Erasm.: 'Paulus non vult eos commoveri, neque per spiritum tanquam a Paulo profectum, neque per sermonem Pauli nomine allatum, neque per epistolam illius iussu aut nomine scriptam.')
A modification of this view, suggested apparently first by Dr Marcus Dods, and since advocated on independent grounds by Askwith (Introd. p. 92 ff.) and Wohlenberg, by which ὡς δι' ἡμῶν, instead of being dependent on the noun-clauses, is rather to be referred back to σαλευθῆναι and θροεῖσθαι as a separate statement, has the advantage of giving διά the same force as in the preceding clauses. But the former connexion is on the whole simpler, nor is there any real difficulty in the use of διά in the qualifying clause instead of παρά or ἀπό. In a friendly letter the use of the prepositions must not be judged with the same strictness as in a classical treatise, more especially when, as here, no important doctrinal issue is at stake. In any case there is no need to fall back on the conjectural reading ὡς δὴ ἡμῶν 'as pretending to be ours,' Field Notes p. 202.
It is only necessary to add that the anarthrous ἐπιστολῆς cannot be referred directly to 1 Thess. (as by Paley Hor. Paul. x. § 3), although the

knowledge that passages in their former Ep., such as iv. 13 ff., had been misunderstood may have been the cause of the writers' referring to 'a letter' at all as amongst the possible sources of error.

ὡς ὅτι ἐνέστηκεν κτλ.] 'as if the day of the Lord is now present' (Vg. quasi instet dies Domini)—ὡς ὅτι being equivalent to the Attic ὡς c. gen. abs. (cf. 2 Cor. v. 19, xi. 21, and see Blass[2], p. 235 f.), and ἐνέστηκεν denoting strictly present time as in Rom. viii. 38, 1 Cor. iii. 22, Heb. ix. 9. Beng.: 'magna hoc verbo propinquitas significatur; nam ἐνεστὼς est praesens.' The verb is very common in the papyri and inscriptions with reference to the current year, e.g. P.Oxy. 245, 6 (i./A.D.) εἰς τὸ ἐνεστὸς ιβ (ἔτος), Magn. 100 b, 26 ἐν τῶι ἐνεστῶτι ἐνιαυτῶι.
It may be added that in late Gk. ὡς ὅτι also appears in a sense hardly differing from the simple ὅτι, e.g. Dion. Hal. Antt. ix. 14 ἐπιγνοὺς ὡς [om. ὡς, Kiessling] ὅτι ἐν ἐσχάτοις εἰσὶν οἱ κατακλεισθέντες ἐν τοῖς λοφοῖς, C.P.R. 19, 3 (iv./A.D.) πρώην βίβλια ἐπιδέδωκα τῇ σῇ ἐπιμελείᾳ ὡς ὅτι ἐβουλήθην τινὰ ὑπάρχοντά μου ἀποδόσθαι (Jannaris, § 1754, Moulton, Prolegg. p. 212).

3. μή τις ὑμ. ἐξαπατήσῃ] A general warning leading up to the statement of the following clause. In their margin WH. suggest placing a comma at κυρίου, and thus connecting the words elliptically with what has gone before—'(we say this) lest any one should....' But the ordinary connexion is simpler, and more in keeping with our Lord's saying which may well have been in the writers' minds: βλέπετε μή τις ὑμᾶς πλανήσῃ· πολλοὶ γὰρ ἐλεύσονται κτλ. (Mt. xxiv. 4 f.).

Ἐξαπατάω, a strengthened form of

98 THE SECOND EPISTLE TO THE THESSALONIANS [II 3

μηδένα τρόπον· ὅτι ἐὰν μὴ ἔλθῃ ἡ ἀποστασία πρῶτον
καὶ ἀποκαλυφθῇ ὁ ἄνθρωπος τῆς ⌜ἀνομίας⌝, ὁ υἱὸς τῆς

3 ἀνομίας ℵB al pauc Sah Boh Orig ⅓ Cyr-Hier al: ἁμαρτίας ADG al pler Lat (Vet Vg) Syr (Pesh Harcl) Go Iren^lat Orig ⅔ Hipp Eus Ephr Chr Orig^lat Ambst Theod-Mops^lat al plur

ἀπατάω (1 Tim. ii. 14), is confined in the N.T. to the Pauline writings, cf. Rom. xvi. 18, 1 Cor. iii. 18. For the rare use of the prohibitory subj. in the 3rd pers. cf. 1 Cor. xvi. 11 (Burton, § 166).
κατὰ μηδένα τρόπον] i.e. not only not in any of the three ways already specified, but 'in no way'—evidently a current phrase, cf. P.Amh. 35, 28 (ii./B.C.), P.Lond. III. 951, 4 f. (iii./A.D.). Thdt.: πάντα κατὰ ταὐτὸν τὰ τῆς ἀπάτης ἐξέβαλεν εἴδη.
ὅτι ἐὰν μὴ ἔλθῃ κτλ.] an elliptical sentence, the apodosis being lost sight of in view of the length of the protasis, but too clearly implied in what precedes to occasion any difficulty: 'because *the Parousia of the Lord will not take place* unless there come the Apostasy first.'
It is not so easy, however, to determine in what this Apostasy consists. In late Gk. ἀποστασία is found as an equivalent of ἀπόστασις (Lob. *Phryn.* p. 528) in the sense of political defection or revolt, e.g. Plut. *Galba* i. κάλλιστον ἔργον διαβαλὼν τῷ μισθῷ, τὴν ἀπὸ Νέρωνος ἀποστασίαν προδοσίαν γενομένην, and the same meaning has been attached to it here, as when it has been referred to the revolt of the Jews from the Romans (Schöttgen *Hor. Heb.* i. p. 840). But the usage of both LXX. and in N.T. is decisive against any such interpretation. Thus in Josh. xxii. 22 the word is directly applied to rebellion *against the Lord* (ἐν ἀποστασίᾳ ἐπλημμελήσαμεν ἔναντι τοῦ κυρίου), and in 1 Macc. ii. 15 to the efforts of the officers of Antiochus Epiphanes to compel the people to sacrifice to idols (οἱ καταναγκάζοντες τὴν ἀποστασίαν...ἵνα θυ-

σιάσωσιν), cf. also 2 Chron. xxix. 19, Jer. ii. 19; while in Ac. xxi. 21, the only other passage in the N.T. where it occurs, we read of ἀποστασίαν...ἀπὸ Μωυσέως, with which may be compared the use of the corresponding verb ἀφίσταμαι in 1 Tim. iv. 1, Heb. iii. 12; cf. M. Anton. iv. 29 ἀπόστημα κόσμου ὁ ἀφιστάμενος καὶ χωρίζων ἑαυτὸν τοῦ τῆς κοινῆς φύσεως λόγου. Whatever then the exact nature of the apostasy in the present connexion, it must at least be a *religious* apostasy, and one moreover, as the use of the def. art. proves, regarding which the Apostles' readers were already fully informed. In this conclusion we are confirmed when we pass to the next words.
καὶ ἀποκαλυφθῇ] 'and (so) there be revealed (the man of lawlessness)'— a second historical condition preceding the Lord's Parousia, or rather, giving καί its full consecutive force (I. iv. 1 note), the sign in which the just-mentioned ἀποστασία finds its consummation.
The emphatic ἀποκαλυφθῇ by which the appearance of this sign is described is very significant, not only as marking the 'superhuman' character of the coming spoken of, but as placing it in mocking counterpart to the ἀποκάλυψις of the Lord Jesus Himself, cf. i. 7 and note the repetition of the same verb in vv. 6, 8 of this chapter. For other exx. of hostile powers assuming the semblance of what they oppose see 2 Cor. xi. 13 ff., Rev. ii. 2, and cf. *Asc. Isai.* iv. 18 where it is said of Beliar that he 'manifested himself and acted openly in this world.'
ὁ ἄνθρωπος τ. ἀνομίας] the man, that

ἀπωλείας, ⁴ὁ ἀντικείμενος καὶ ὑπεραιρόμενος ἐπὶ πάντα λεγόμενον θεὸν ἢ σέβασμα, ὥστε αὐτὸν εἰς τὸν ναὸν τοῦ θεοῦ

is, of whom 'lawlessness' is the true and peculiar mark—ἀνομίας being used here, as elsewhere in the N.T., to describe the condition not of one living without law, but of one who acts contrary to law, and thus as practically equivalent to the v.l. ἁμαρτίας (WH. mg.): cf. 1 Jo. iii. 4 ἡ ἁμαρτία ἐστὶν ἡ ἀνομία, and as illustrating the active sense belonging to the word cf. P.Par. 14, 27 f. (ii./B.C.) ἀφορήτῳ δὲ ἀνομίᾳ ἐξενεχθέντες. The lawless one is thus none other than Belial (cf. 2 Cor. vi. 15) in accordance with the Bibl. usage by which בְּלִיַּעַל is rendered by ἀνόμημα (Deut. xv. 9), ἀνομία (2 Regn. xxii. 5), or ἀποστασία (3 Regn. xx. (xxi.) 13 A), and in keeping with the (erroneous) Rabbinical derivation of the word from בְּלִי 'without' and עֹל 'yoke,' i.e. one who will not accept the yoke of the law (see *Jew. Encycl. s.v.* 'Antichrist'). 'Law, in all its manifestations is that which he [the Antichrist] shall rage against, making hideous application of that great truth, that where the Spirit is, there is liberty' (Trench *Hulsean Lectures* p. 136; cf. *Syn.* § lxvi. p. 227 f.).

ὁ υἱὸς τ. ἀπωλείας] a second distinguishing epithet: so completely has the lawless one fallen under the power of 'perdition' (cf. Jo. xvii. 12) that it may be regarded as his ultimate destination, cf. 1 Regn. xx. 31 υἱὸς θανάτου οὗτος i.e. 'destined to death.' The thought of *final doom* is, however, only indirectly present in the description (cf. note on ὄλεθρος, i. 9). Here rather, as elsewhere in his Epp. (Rom. ix. 22, Phil. i. 28, iii. 19, 1 Tim. vi. 9), St Paul employs ἀπώλεια in direct antithesis, either stated or implied, to σωτηρία, full and complete blessedness, in harmony with the usage of the word (and its allied terms) in the LXX. and the later writings of the Jews: cf. I. v. 3 note, and see further Kennedy *Last Things* p. 119 ff., Volz *Jüd. Eschat.* p. 282 f. The phrase 'sons of perdition' (=בְּנֵי הָאֲבַדּוֹן) is found in *Jubilees* x. 3, with reference to those who perished in the Flood.

4. ὁ ἀντικείμενος κ. ὑπεραιρόμενος κτλ.] a continued description of the lawless one in two participial clauses bound together under the vinculum of a common article. The first clause is generally taken as a participial subst. = 'the adversary' (cf. Lk. xiii. 17, Phil. i. 28, 1 Tim. v. 14), but if so, care must be taken not to refer the description to Satan himself. Rather, as *v.* 9 shows, the being spoken of is the tool or emissary of Satan, working in his name and power (κατ' ἐνέργειαν τ. Σατανᾶ), and, as such, is further distinguished as 'the exalter of himself against every one called god or object of worship.' Beng.: 'effert se corde, lingua, stilo, factis, per se, per suos.'

Ὑπεραίρομαι is found in the N.T. only here and in 2 Cor. xii. 7 (bis); cf. 2 Chron. xxxii. 23, and see the note on i. 3. For πάντα λεγ. θεόν cf. 1 Cor. viii. 5, and for the comprehensive σέβασμα (Vg. *quod colitur*, Beza *numen*) denoting everything held in religious honour, see Ac. xvii. 23, and cf. Sap. xiv. 20, xv. 17, Bel 27 Th., also *Apol. Arist.* xii. οὐ γὰρ ἠρκέσθησαν [οἱ Αἰγύπτιοι] τοῖς τῶν Χαλδαίων καὶ Ἑλλήνων σεβάσμασιν.

ὥστε] See note on I. i. 7.

τ. ναὸν τ. θεοῦ] These words were understood of the actual temple at Jerusalem by Irenaeus (*adv. Haer.* v. 30. 4), but this view was modified by Chrysostom and the Antiochenes who extended them metaphorically to the

7—2

καθίcαι, ἀποδεικνύντα ἑαυτὸν ὅτι ἔcτιν θεόc—. ⁵Οὐ μνημονεύετε ὅτι ἔτι ὢν πρὸς ὑμᾶς ταῦτα ἔλεγον ὑμῖν; ⁶καὶ νῦν τὸ κατέχον οἴδατε, εἰς τὸ ἀποκαλυφθῆναι αὐτὸν

Church or Churches of Christ: Chrys.: οὐ τὸν ἐν Ἱεροσολύμοις μόνον, ἀλλὰ καὶ καθ᾽ ἑκάστην ἐκκλησίαν (v.l. εἰς τὰς πανταχοῦ ἐκκλησίας); Thdt.: 'ναὸν' δὲ 'θεοῦ' τὰς ἐκκλησίας ἐκάλεσεν; Th. Mops.: ' "in Dei templis," hoc est, et in domibus orationum'; cf. Hier. *Ep.* 121 'in templo Dei uel Ierosolymis, ut quidam putant, uel in ecclesia, ut uerius arbitramur.' In favour of the latter interpretation is the undoubtedly figurative use of the expression elsewhere in the Pauline Epp., e.g. 1 Cor. iii. 16 f., vi. 19, 2 Cor. vi. 16, Eph. ii. 21. On the other hand, the nature of the context, the use of such a local term as καθίσαι, and the twice-repeated def. art. (τὸν ναὸν τοῦ θεοῦ) all point to a literal reference in the present instance, a conclusion in which we are confirmed when we keep in view the dependence of the whole passage upon the description of Antiochus Epiphanes in Dan. xi. 36 f. (see below), and upon the language of the Parousia-discourses in Mt. xxiv. 15, Mk. xiii. 14 (cf. Dan. xii. 11).

καθίσαι] 'takes his seat.' The verb is intrans. as generally in the N.T. (contrast 1 Cor. vi. 4, Eph. i. 20, and cf. Ev. Pet. 3). For the construction with εἰς cf. Mk. xiii. 3 (WM. p. 516).

ἀποδεικνύντα ἑαυτόν κτλ.] 'Ἀποδείκνυμι, lit. 'show off,' 'exhibit,' is frequently used in late Gk. = 'nominate' or 'proclaim' to an office, e.g. Jos. *Antt.* VI. 35 (iii. 3) ἱκέτευον ἀποδεῖξαί τινα αὐτῶν βασιλέα, O.G.I.S. 437, 92 (i./B.C.) οἱ ὑφ᾽ ἑκατέρων τῶν δήμων ἀποδειχθέντες ἄνδρες ἐπὶ τῶν συλλύσεων. This gives excellent sense in the present passage, and, while simplifying the construction of the following ὅτι clause (WM. p. 781), draws more pointed attention to the impious nature of the claim advanced in it.

We translate therefore 'proclaiming himself that he is god.' For the suggestion of this trait in the character of the lawless one cf. Ezek. xxviii. 2 ἀνθ᾽ οὗ ὑψώθη σου ἡ καρδία, καὶ εἶπας Θεός εἰμι ἐγώ, and for the whole description see Dan. xi. 36 f. καὶ ὑψωθήσεται ἐπὶ πάντα θεόν, καὶ ἐπὶ τὸν θεὸν τῶν θεῶν ἔξαλλα λαλήσει,...καὶ ἐπὶ τοὺς θεοὺς τῶν πατέρων αὐτοῦ οὐ μὴ προνοηθῇ...ὅτι ἐν παντὶ ὑψωθήσεται κτλ.

5—7. 'You cannot have forgotten that while I was still with you, I was in the habit of telling you these things. And since then you have had experience for yourselves of the working of that power by which the full revelation of the lawless one is kept in check until his appointed time shall have arrived. The full revelation we say—for the spirit of lawlessness is already at work, though in secret, until he who at present is keeping it in check is taken out of the way.'

5. Οὐ μνημονεύετε ὅτι κτλ.] Est.: 'Tacita obiurgatio.' Calv.: 'Observanda etiam Pauli mansuetudo, qui quum acrius excandescere posset, tantum leniter eos castigat.'

For μνημονεύειν cf. I. i. 3 note, and for the construction εἶναι πρός cf. I. iii. 4 note. The use made of ἔτι as against the Pauline authorship of the Ep. is discussed Intr. p. xc.

6. καὶ νῦν τὸ κατέχον οἴδατε] 'and now you know that which restraineth' —νῦν having its full *temporal* sense in keeping with the emphasis laid in the context on the *present* working of the power of lawlessness (cf. v. 7). It must not, however, be taken as if it actually belongs to κατέχον (cf. however Jo. iv. 18 καὶ νῦν ὃν ἔχεις), or be opposed to the preceding ἔτι ὤν which yields no good sense, but rather be placed in contrast with the

following ἀποκάλυψις ἐν τῷ αὐτοῦ καιρῷ: 'for the present (i.e. practically 'so far as regards the present') the Thessalonians know only the restraining power: what is restrained is not yet revealed.' See further Bornemann's elaborate note *ad loc.* It is more difficult to determine what we are to understand by τὸ κατέχον. That the verb is here used in the sense of 'restrain,' 'hold back,' rather than of 'hold fast' (as in I. v.21), is too generally admitted to require further proof (see Add. Note H): while, as we have just seen, whatever is intended must clearly be something which was actually at work at the time when the Ep. was written, and of which moreover its readers had personal knowledge. Nor is this all, but, as the occurrence of the same phrase in the masc. (ὁ κατέχων, *v.* 7) proves, this impersonal principle or power is capable also of manifesting itself under a personal form. When these different considerations are taken into account, it will be recognized how much is to be said for the view that goes back as far as Tertullian ('quis nisi Romanus status?' *de Resurr.* c. 24; cf. *Apol.* c. 32), and which has since won the support of the great majority of ancient and modern scholars, that we have here a veiled description of the restraining power of law and order, especially as these were embodied at the time in the Roman Empire or its rulers. And in this view we are further confirmed when we remember that St Paul had already found a 'restraining power' in the Roman officials both at Paphos (Ac. xiii. 6 ff.) and at Thessalonica itself (Ac. xvii. 6 ff.), and that it was doubtless these and similar experiences that afterwards led him to write to the Romans of '*the powers* that be' as 'ordained of God,' and of 'rulers' as 'not a terror to the good work, but to the evil' (Rom. xiii. 1, 3). There is nothing unlikely, then, to say the least, in his having the same thought in his mind on the present occasion, while the fact that he does not give more definite expression to it is not only in accord with the generally cryptic character of apocalyptic writings, but may also be due to prudential motives, seeing that afterwards he is to speak of this power as being 'taken out of the way' (*v.* 7).

This last particular indeed appears to be decisive against the only other interpretation of τὸ κατέχον which requires to be mentioned, namely that it refers to the working of the Holy Spirit (Severianus ap. Cramer *Cat.* vi. 388, 'τὸ κατέχον,' φησί, τὴν τοῦ Ἁγίου Πνεύματος χάριν), or more generally to a limit of time fixed by Divine decree (Thdt.: ὁ τοῦ θεοῦ τοίνυν αὐτὸν ὅρος νῦν ἐπέχει φανῆναι; Th. Mops.: τοῦ θεοῦ [λέγων] τὸν ὅρον) with special reference (so Thdt.) to Mt. xxiv. 14, as indicating one of the limits by which this condition will be attained. For then ὁ κατέχων (*v.* 7) can only be God Himself, and it seems impossible to conceive of any adequate sense in which the words ἕως ἐκ μέσου γένηται can be applied to Him (cf. Swete's note on Th. Mops. *ad loc.*). That however this restraining power acts in accordance with the Divine purpose is proved by the words that follow.

[For a modification of this view according to which the Man of lawlessness is the imperial line with its rage for deification, and the restraining power the Jewish State, see Warfield *Exp.* III. iv. p. 30 ff.; and cf. Moffatt *Hist. N. T.* p. 143.]

εἰς τὸ ἀποκαλυφθῆναι κτλ.] The 'revelation' (*v.* 3 note) of the lawless one is not immediate (Chrys.: οὐκ εἶπεν ὅτι τάχεως ἔσται), but like the revelation of the Lord Jesus Himself (cf. 1 Tim. vi. 14 f.) will take place in the 'season' (I. v. 1) appointed for him by God, and which can therefore be described emphatically as 'his' (αὐτοῦ ℵ*AKP, ἑαυτοῦ ℵᶜBDGL).

ἐν τῷ αὐτοῦ καιρῷ· ⁷τὸ γὰρ μυστήριον ἤδη ἐνεργεῖται τῆς ἀνομίας· μόνον ὁ κατέχων ἄρτι ἕως ἐκ μέσου γένηται. ⁸καὶ τότε ἀποκαλυφθήσεται ὁ ἄνομος, ὃν ὁ κύριος ['Ιη-

8 Ἰησοῦς אAD*G al pauc Lat (Vet Vg) Sah Boh Syr (Pesh Harcl) Arm Aeth Iren^lat Hipp Orig ⅔ Const Ath Cyr-Hier Bas Chr Thdt ⅔ al Tert Hil Ambst Orig^lat Theod-Mops^lat : om BD^c al pler Orig ½ Macar Ephr Thdt ⅔ Vig

For the insertion of ἐν before καιρῷ cf. Rom. iii. 26, xi. 5, 2 Cor. viii. 14; and for similar language applied to the coming of the Messiah cf. Pss. Sol. xvii. 23 εἰς τὸν καιρὸν ὃν οἶδας σύ, ὁ θεός.

7. τὸ γὰρ μυστήριον κτλ.] a confirmatory explanation of the preceding statement, in which the main stress is evidently laid on τὸ μυστήριον both on account of its isolated and emphatic position in the sentence, and from its contrast with the preceding ἀποκαλυφθῆναι: the revelation, that is, of the lawless one, just spoken of, will be a revelation only, for, as a matter of fact, the principle of which he is the representative is already at work, though as yet only in secret.

For this the regular Bibl. sense of μυστήριον pointing to a secret to be revealed see Robinson *Eph.* p. 234 ff., where the different shades of meaning attached to the word in the Pauline writings are fully discussed, and for ἐνεργεῖται cf. I. ii. 13 note.

μόνον] There is no need to find a case of ellipsis here as in *v.* 3, μόνον belongs to ἕως, and introduces the limitation in the present working of τὸ μυστ. τ. ἀνομ., while the order of the following words is rhetorical, ὁ κατέχων ἄρτι being placed before ἕως for the sake of emphasis (cf. Gal. ii. 10 μόνον τῶν πτωχῶν ἵνα μνημονεύωμεν, and see WM. p. 688, Buttmann p. 389).

For the meaning of ὁ κατέχων see note on *v.* 6, and for ἄρτι, strictly present time, as compared with the more subjective ἤδη 'already,' see the note on I. iii. 6, and cf. Kühner³ §§ 498, 499.

ἐκ μέσου γένηται] Nothing is said as to *how* the removal spoken of is to be effected, nor can the absence of ἄν with the subj. in this clause be pressed, as if it lent additional certainty to the fact, in view of the general weakening of ἄν in later Gk., leading to its frequent omission, especially after such temporal particles as ἕως, ἕως οὗ &c.: see WM. p. 371, and add such passages from the Κοινή as P.Oxy. 259, 30 (i./A.D.) ἕως ἑαυτὸν αὐτ[ὸ]ν ποιήσω, 294, 15 f. (i./A.D.) ἕως ἀκούσω φάσιν παρὰ σοῦ περὶ ἁπάντων.

For ἐκ μέσου cf. 1 Cor. v. 2, Col. ii. 14.

8—10. 'Then indeed the lawless one will be revealed, only however to find himself swept away by the breath of the Lord's mouth, and brought utterly to naught by the manifestation of the Lord's Parousia. In what mocking counterpart will *his* parousia then appear! With what activity on the part of Satan will it be accompanied! How it will make itself known by all manner of false miracles and false signs and false wonders, as well as by every kind of unrighteous device calculated to deceive those who are already on the path of destruction, seeing that they have no affinity with the Truth by which alone they can be saved!'

8. καὶ τότε ἀποκαλυφθήσεται ὁ ἄνομος] Not until ὁ κατέχων has been removed, can the revelation of ὁ ἄνομος take place, but 'then' it will no longer be delayed. For the solemn and emphatic κ. τότε cf. Mt. xxiv. 10, 14, 30, 1 Cor. iv. 5.

Ὁ ἄνομος is clearly to be identified with ὁ ἄνθρ. τ. ἀνομίας (*v.* 3), while

II 8] THE SECOND EPISTLE TO THE THESSALONIANS 103

σοῦς] ⌜ἀνελεῖ⌝ τῷ πνεγματι τοŷ cτόματος αγτοŷ καὶ καταργήσει

ἀνελεῖ] ἀναλοῖ ℵ* Orig (non semper)

ἀποκαλυφθήσεται recalls ἀποκαλυφθῇ (v. 3) and ἀποκαλυφθῆναι (v. 6). 'Thrice, with persistent emphasis, ἀποκαλύπτεσθαι is asserted of ὁ ἄνομος, as of some portentous, unearthly object holding the gazer spell-bound' (Findlay).

For the idea of a world-crisis on the fall of the Roman Empire in Jewish apocalyptic literature see Apoc. Bar. xxxix. 7, 'And it will come to pass when the time of his consummation that he should fall has approached, then the principate of My Messiah will be revealed': cf. 4 Ezra v. 1 ff. Similar evidence from Rabbinical sources is given by Weber Jüd. Theologie p. 366.

ὃν ὁ κύριος κτλ.] a relative sentence describing the fate of ὁ ἄνομος in language borrowed from Isa. xi. 4 πατάξει γῆν τῷ λόγῳ τοῦ στόματος αὐτοῦ, καὶ ἐν πνεύματι διὰ χειλέων ἀνελεῖ ἀσεβῆ. Ἀνελεῖ is a post-class. fut. from ἀναιρέω, the verb, which is very common in Acts, not being found elsewhere in the Pauline Epp., but occurring in Heb. x. 9 in the sense of 'remove,' 'do away with.' Beza renders it in the passage before us by absumet, while the Lat. verss. have interficiet.

The marginal reading ἀναλοῖ has the advantage of offering a ready explanation of the genesis of certain other variants—ἀναλώσει (Dᶜ KL al pler) being then due to grammatical emendation, and the unusual ἀνελοῖ (D*G 17 67**) to a simple interchange of a and ε, or to a mingling of ἀναλοῖ and ἀνελεῖ (see Zimmer). But the evidence for ἀνελεῖ (ABP 23 31 al) is too strong to be easily set aside, even with the further possibility of its being a conformation to LXX. Isa. xi. 4 (cited above).

τ. πνεύμ. τ. στόμ. αὐτ.] a perfectly general statement not to be limited to any actual 'word' of the Lord (Thdt.: φθέγξεται μόνον; Th. Mops.: 'spiritu oris, hoc est, uoce'), still less to the work of the Third Person of the Holy Trinity (as Athan. ad Serap. i. 6 ad fin.), but emphasizing that, terrible as was the power of the lawless one, the mere 'breath' of the Lord's mouth will be sufficient for his destruction. In addition to Isa. xi. 4 (cited above), where according to the old (incorrect) Jewish interpretation the 'wicked' is the future arch-enemy of the Jews, cf. Job iv. 9 ἀπὸ δὲ πνεύματος ὀργῆς αὐτοῦ (sc. Κυρίου) ἀφανισθήσονται, and see also Sap. xi. 20 (21), Pss. Sol. xvii. 27, 41, Enoch lxii. 2, 4 Ezra xiii. 38 ('perdet eos sine labore').

καὶ καταργήσει κτλ.] Καταργέω, rare in class. Gk. and the LXX. (2 Esdr.[4]), occurs twenty-five times in the Pauline writings (elsewhere in N.T. only Lk.[1], Heb.[1]), and in accordance with its derivation (κατά causative and ἀργός = ἀεργός) means literally 'render idle or inactive,' and hence 'abolish,' 'bring to naught': cf. especially with the present passage 2 Tim. i. 10 Χρ. Ἰησοῦ, καταργήσαντος μὲν τὸν θάνατον φωτίσαντος δὲ ζωὴν καὶ ἀφθαρσίαν διὰ τοῦ εὐαγγελίου. As showing the different shades of meaning that may be attached to the word, Vaughan (on Rom. iii. 3) states that the A.V. gives it no less than seventeen different renderings in the twenty-seven places of its occurrence in the N.T. It is found also in the Κοινή in a much weakened sense, e.g. P.Oxy. 38, 17 (i./A.D.) καταργοῦντός με χειρότεχνον ὄντα 'hinders me in my trade.'

For the thought in the present passage cf. Isa. xxvi. 10 ἀρθήτω ὁ ἀσεβής, ἵνα μὴ ἴδῃ τὴν δόξαν Κυρίου, and for the meanings to be assigned to ἐπιφάνεια and παρουσία see Add.

τῇ ἐπιφανείᾳ τῆς παρουσίας αὐτοῦ, ⁹οὗ ἐστὶν ἡ παρουσία κατ' ἐνέργειαν τοῦ Σατανᾶ ἐν πάσῃ δυνάμει καὶ σημείοις καὶ τέρασιν ψεύδους ¹⁰καὶ ἐν πάσῃ ἀπάτῃ ἀδικίας τοῖς ἀπολλυμένοις, ἀνθ' ὧν τὴν ἀγάπην τῆς ἀληθείας οὐκ

Note F. Chrys.: ἀρκεῖ παρεῖναι αὐτόν, καὶ πάντα ταῦτα ἀπόλωλε· στήσει τὴν ἀπάτην καὶ φανεὶς μόνον.

9. οὗ ἐστὶν ἡ παρουσία κτλ.] a second relative clause resuming the ὅν of v. 8, and describing the working of the lawless one, as the former had described his doom. As the Lord Jesus has His Parousia, the lawless one has his (cf. Rev. xvii. 8 τὸ θηρίον... πάρεσται), in which he shows himself the representative and instrument of Satan. Th. Mops.: 'adparebit ille Satana sibi inoperante omnia.' Beng.: 'ut ad Deum se habet Christus, sic e contrario ad Satanam se habet antichristus, medius inter Satanam et perditos homines.'

As distinguished from δύναμις potential power, ἐνέργεια is power in exercise, operative power ('*potentia*, arbor: *efficacia*, fructus,' Calv. on Eph. i. 19), and except here and in v. 11 is always confined in the N.T. to the working of God; cf. especially with the present passage Eph. i. 19 f. κατὰ τὴν ἐνέργειαν...ἣν ἐνήργηκεν ἐν τῷ χριστῷ, and for a similar use in the inscriptions with reference to the pagan gods cf. *O.G.I.S.* 262, 4 (iii./A.D.) προσενεχθέντος μοι περὶ τῆς ἐνεργείας θεοῦ Διὸς Βαιτοκαίκης.

ἐν πάσῃ δυνάμει...ψεύδους] the sphere in which the parousia of the lawless one makes itself known; cf. Mt. xxiv. 24, Mk. xiii. 22, also Rev. xiii. 14, xix. 20. As regards construction both πάσῃ and ψεύδους belong to all three substantives, ψεύδους being best understood as a gen. of quality (cf. Jo. viii. 44), without however excluding the further thought of effect, aim. False in themselves, the works spoken of lead also to falsehood.

For the combination δυν. κ. σημ. κ. τέρ. cf. Ac. ii. 22, Rom. xv. 19, 2 Cor. xii. 12, Heb. ii. 4, and for the distinction between them see Trench *Syn.* § xci., SH. p. 406. Similar portents are ascribed to the Beliar-Antichrist in *Asc. Isai.* iv. 4 ff., *Orac. Sib.* iii. 63 ff.

10. ἀπάτῃ] 'deceit,' 'deceitful power,' in accordance with the regular N.T. use of the word, e.g. ἀπάτη τ. πλούτου (Mk. iv. 19), τ. ἁμαρτίας (Heb. iii. 13); cf. 4 Macc. xviii. 8 λυμεὼν ἀπάτης ὄφις. If in 2 Pet. ii. 13 we can read ἀπάταις (but see Bigg *ad loc.*) we seem to have an ex. of the word in its Hellenistic sense of 'pastime,' 'pleasure'; cf. Polyb. ii. 56, 12 and see Deissmann *Hellenisierung* p. 165 n.[5]. Moeris: 'Ἀπάτη, ἡ πλάνη παρ' Ἀττικοῖς...ἡ τέρψις παρ' Ἕλλησιν.

ἀδικίας] 'unrighteousness,' 'wrongdoing' of every kind, cf. Rom. i. 18, ii. 8 where, as here and in v. 12, it is opposed to ἀλήθεια, and Plato *Gorg.* 477 c where it is coupled with σύμπασα ψυχῆς πονηρία. By its union with ἀπάτη, ἀδικία is evidently thought of here as an active, aggressive power which, however, can influence only τ. ἀπολλυμένοις, the use of the 'perfective' verb marking out those so described as having already *ideally* reached a state of ἀπώλεια; cf. 1 Cor. i. 18, and see Moulton *Prolegg.* p. 114 f.

ἀνθ' ὧν] 'in requital that,' 'for the reason that'—a class. phrase occurring several times in the LXX., but in the N.T. only here and in Luke (Gosp.[3], Ac.[1]): cf. ἀντὶ τούτου Eph. v. 31.

τῆς ἀληθείας] may be understood of truth generally as contrasted with τὸ ψεῦδος (v. 11), but is better limited

II 11, 12] THE SECOND EPISTLE TO THE THESSALONIANS 105

ἐδέξαντο εἰς τὸ σωθῆναι αὐτούς· ""καὶ διὰ τοῦτο πέμπει αὐτοῖς ὁ θεὸς ἐνέργειαν πλάνης εἰς τὸ πιστεῦσαι αὐτοὺς τῷ ψεύδει, ¹²ἵνα κριθῶσιν ⌈πάντες⌉ οἱ μὴ πιστεύσαντες τῇ ἀληθείᾳ ἀλλὰ εὐδοκήσαντες τῇ ἀδικίᾳ.

12 πάντες BD al plur Orig ¼ Hipp Chr Thdt : ἅπαντες ℵAG 12 17 31 Orig ¾ Cyr-Alex

to 'the truth' κατ' ἐξοχήν, the truth of the Gospel, in accordance with its use elsewhere with the art. (2 Cor. iv. 2, xiii. 8, Eph. iv. 24), while the insertion of τ. ἀγάπην shows that those spoken of had not only not 'welcomed' (ἐδέξαντο, I. ii. 13 note) this truth, but had no *liking* for it, no *desire* to possess it.
According to Westcott (on 1 Jo. ii. 5) this is the only instance in the N.T. where the gen. after ἀγάπη 'marks the object of love'; Abbott (*Joh. Gr.* p. 84) adds Lk. xi. 42 παρέρχεσθε τὴν κρίσιν καὶ τὴν ἀγάπην τοῦ θεοῦ '[just] judgment and love toward God.'

11, 12. 'That is why God uses Satan as His instrument in punishing them, visiting them with a fatal delusion in believing this (great) Lie. False belief becomes thus the proof of falseness, and sentence is passed upon all who refused to believe the truth, and made evil their good.'

11. πέμπει] pointing not merely to the permissive will of God (Th. Mops.: 'concessionem Dei quasi opus eius'), but to the definite judicial act by which, according to the constant teaching of Scripture, God gives the wicked over to the evil which they have deliberately chosen, cf. Ps. lxxx. (lxxxi.) 12 f., Rom. i. 24, 26, 28, and for similar teaching in Gk. drama see Aesch. *Pers.* 738 ἀλλ' ὅταν σπεύδῃ τις αὐτός, χὠ θεὸς συνάπτεται, *Fragm.* 294 (ed. Nauck) ἀπάτης δικαίας οὐκ ἀποστατεῖ θεός.

εἰς τὸ πιστεῦσαι τῷ ψεύδει] 'to the end that they should believe the lie'— the thought of *purpose*, and not mere

result (I. ii. 12 note) being undoubtedly uppermost here in accordance with the leading thought of the main sentence.
For τῷ ψεύδει 'the lie' as contrasted with τὴν ἀλήθειαν (v. 10) cf. Rom. i. 25 οἵτινες μετήλλαξαν τὴν ἀλήθειαν τοῦ θεοῦ ἐν τῷ ψεύδει. 'Among the Persians "the Lie" (*Drauga*, akin to the Avestan demon *Druj*) is a comprehensive term for all evil' (Moulton *Exp. T.* xviii. p. 537).

12. ἵνα κριθῶσιν πάντες] 'in order that they might all be judged,' any idea of *condemnation* being derived from the context, and not from κριθῶσι *per se*: see Lft. *Fresh Revision of Engl. N.T.*³ p. 69 ff. for a full discussion of κρίνειν and its compounds. For κρίνω in its wider sense of 'resolve' cf. P.Grenf. I. 30, 5 f. (ii./B.C.) διὰ γραμμάτων ἐκρίναμεν σημῆναι.
The reading πάντες is well-attested, but the stronger and rarer ἅπαντες (WH. mg.) has good grounds to be considered, both as less likely to be substituted by the copyists, and as better suiting the emphatic position here assigned to it. Beng.: 'late ergo et diu et vehementer grassatur error ille.'
For the evidence (by no means decisive in the N.T., Blass p. 161) that in the Κοινή, as in Attic writers, the use of πᾶς or ἅπας was determined on the ground of euphony, πᾶς being found after a vowel, and ἅπας after a consonant, see Mayser p. 161 f.

οἱ μὴ πιστεύσαντες κτλ.] Cf. 1 Cor. xiii. 6. By a usage characteristic of Bibl. writers (but cf. Polyb. ii. 12. 3)

¹³ Ἡμεῖς δὲ ὀφείλομεν εὐχαριστεῖν τῷ θεῷ πάντοτε περὶ ὑμῶν, ἀδελφοὶ ἠγαπημένοι ὑπὸ Κυρίου, ὅτι εἵλατο ὑμᾶς

εὐδοκεῖν (I. ii. 8 note) is generally construed with ἐν, but here according to the best texts (א*BD*G as against א^cAD^cKLP) it is followed by the simple dat. as in 1 Macc. i. 43, 1 Esdr. iv. 39, Rom. i. 32 (συνευδοκεῖν), and late writers generally (e.g. Polyb. ii. 38. 7, iii. 8. 7). The verb is found c. acc. Mt. xii. 18, Heb. x. 6, and with εἰς 2 Pet. i. 17. For the general thought of the verse in Jewish literature cf. *Apoc. Bar.* liv. 21 'For at the consummation of the world there will be vengeance taken upon those who have done wickedness according to their wickedness, and Thou wilt glorify the faithful according to their faithfulness.'

II. 13—15. RENEWED THANKS-GIVING AND EXHORTATION.

From the terrible picture they have been conjuring up the Apostles turn with a sigh of relief to give God thanks on their converts' behalf in view of the salvation which He has worked for them—a salvation beginning in His eternal choice, and to be completed by their sharing in the glory of the Lord Jesus Christ Himself (*vv.* 13, 14). The two verses thus form 'a system of theology in miniature' (Denney), and in characteristic Pauline fashion lead up to the practical exhortation to the Thessalonians to hold fast to what they have been taught (*v.* 15).

13—15. 'But not to dwell on this melancholy picture, what a different prospect opens itself up before us! What an unceasing debt of gratitude we owe to God on your behalf, Brothers beloved not only of us but of the Lord! Is it not the case that from the beginning God purposed your salvation, and not only purposed, but accomplished it through the sanctifying influence of the Holy Spirit, and your belief in the Truth? It was to this salvation indeed that He called you by the Gospel-message of which we were privileged to be bearers, and those who finally obtain it will obtain also the glory which belongs to it—the glory which is Christ's own. Such then being the Divine purpose regarding you, see to it that you on your own part, Brothers, stand firm, keeping fast hold of all sound doctrine and practice as you have learned them from us both by word and by letter.'

13. Ἡμεῖς δέ κτλ.] See the notes on i. 3, the emphatic ἡμεῖς in the present passage lending additional stress to the writers' keen sense of indebtedness to God for the good estate of the Thessalonian Church. For ἀδ. ἠγ. ὑ. Κυρ. see I. i. 4 note.

ὅτι εἵλατο κτλ.] Εἵλατο (for form, WH.[2] *Notes* p. 172) is used of the Divine election in Deut. xxvi. 18 Κύριος εἵλατό σε...λαὸν περιούσιον (cf. προείλε(α)το Deut. vii. 6 f., x. 15), but does not occur elsewhere in the N.T. in this connexion: cf. Phil. i. 22 and see Intr. p. lxxix. In the present instance the reference would seem to be to the *eternal* choice or purpose of God (1 Cor. ii. 7, Eph. i. 4, 2 Tim. i. 9), as otherwise (cf. note on ἐκλογή I. i. 4) the qualifying ἀπ' ἀρχῆς would almost have required some distinguishing addition such as τ. εὐαγγελίου (cf. Phil. iv. 15).

It is possible however that the real reading is not ἀπ' ἀρχῆς but ἀπαρχήν (WH. mg.), a thoroughly Pauline word (Rom. viii. 23, xi. 16, xvi. 5, 1 Cor. xv. 20, 23, xvi. 15), which might fairly be applied to the Thessalonians as the 'first-fruits' (Vg. *primitias*) of Macedonia, seeing that their conversion followed that of the Philippians by only a few weeks, and

II 14, 15] THE SECOND EPISTLE TO THE THESSALONIANS 107

ὁ θεὸς ⌜ἀπ' ἀρχῆς⌝ εἰς σωτηρίαν ἐν ἁγιασμῷ πνεύματος καὶ πίστει ἀληθείας, ¹⁴εἰς ὃ ἐκάλεσεν ὑμᾶς διὰ τοῦ εὐαγγελίου ἡμῶν, εἰς περιποίησιν δόξης τοῦ κυρίου ἡμῶν Ἰησοῦ Χριστοῦ. ¹⁵Ἄρα οὖν, ἀδελφοί, στήκετε, καὶ κρατεῖτε τὰς παραδόσεις ἃς ἐδιδάχθητε εἴτε διὰ λόγου

13 ἀπ' ἀρχῆς אD al pler d g Syr (Pesh) Arm Aeth Chr Thdt Ambst Vig Theod-Mops^lat al : ἀπαρχὴν BG al pauc Vg Syr (Harcl) Boh Did Amb al

was attended by such striking results (cf. I. i. 8, iv. 10).
For σωτηρία as denoting completed blessedness see I. v. 8 note.

ἐν ἁγιασμῷ πνεύματος καὶ πίστει ἀληθείας] In view of the obvious parallelism of the clauses it is natural to understand the two genitives in the same way, and if so they may be taken either objectively, a 'sanctification' having for its object the 'spirit' and a 'faith' that has for its object 'truth,' or as genitives of the *causa efficiens*, 'sanctification by the Spirit and faith by the truth.' In the former case πνεῦμα can only be the human spirit: in the latter it must be the Holy Spirit of God. To this latter rendering the absence of the art. is no real objection, and it is supported by the recurrence of the same phrase in 1 Pet. i. 2 where the Third Person of the Trinity is clearly intended (see Hort *ad loc.*).

For ἁγιασμός cf. note on I. iv. 7, and with πίστις ἀληθείας contrast οἱ μὴ πιστεύσ. τ. ἀληθείᾳ (*v.* 12).

14. ἐκάλεσεν] the historical fulfilment of the Divine purpose expressed in εἵλατο: cf. I. ii. 12, v. 24, notes.

εἰς περιποίησιν δόξης] 'unto the obtaining of the glory' (Vg. *in acquisitionem gloriae*, Weizs. *zum Erwerb der Herrlichkeit*). For περιποίησις cf. I. v. 9 note, and for δόξα I. ii. 12 note.

15. Ἄρα οὖν, ἀδελφοί, στήκετε κτλ.] The practical conclusion from what has just been said. The work of God, so far from excluding all human effort, rather furnishes the reason for it and the pledge of its final success: cf. Phil. ii. 12 f., iii. 12.

For ἄρα οὖν see I. v. 6 note, and for στήκετε I. iii. 8 note.

κ. κρατεῖτε τ. παραδόσεις] Cf. 1 Cor. xi. 2 τ. παραδόσεις κατέχετε, and for the relation of κρατεῖν and κατέχειν see Add. Note H. The construction of κρατεῖν with the acc. (as generally in the N.T.—acc.[38], gen.[8]) may be due simply to the tendency to enlarge the sphere of the acc. in later Gk. (Hatzidakis p. 220 ff.), but serves also in the present instance to lay emphasis on the παραδόσεις as being already in the Thessalonians' possession; cf. Rev. iii. 11 κράτει ὃ ἔχεις. Beng.: '*tenete*, nil addentes, nil detrahentes.'

In themselves these παραδόσεις (cf. iii. 6) included both the oral and written teaching on the part of the Apostles (Thdt.: λόγους, οὓς καὶ παρόντες ὑμῖν ἐκηρύξαμεν, καὶ ἀπόντες ἐγράψαμεν) with the further thought imbedded in the composition of the word itself of the ultimate authority whence that authority was derived: cf. 1 Cor. xi. 23 ἐγὼ γὰρ παρέλαβον ἀπὸ τοῦ κυρίου, ὃ καὶ παρέδωκα ὑμῖν.

In the inscriptions Treasure Lists and Inventories are frequently known as παραδόσεις, the articles enumerated being 'handed over' (παρέδοσαν *C.I.A.* I. 170, 2 (v./B.C.)) by one set of officers to their successors; see Roberts-Gardner p. 256.

For the fact and contents of a Christian 'tradition' in the Apostolic

εἴτε δι' ἐπιστολῆς ἡμῶν. ¹⁶Αὐτὸς δὲ ὁ κύριος ἡμῶν
Ἰησοῦς Χριστὸς καὶ [ὁ] θεὸς ὁ πατὴρ ἡμῶν, ὁ ἀγαπήσας
ἡμᾶς καὶ δοὺς παράκλησιν αἰωνίαν καὶ ἐλπίδα ἀγαθὴν ἐν
χάριτι, ¹⁷παρακαλέσαι ὑμῶν τὰς καρδίας καὶ στηρίξαι ἐν
παντὶ ἔργῳ καὶ λόγῳ ἀγαθῷ.

16 ὁ om BD*K 17 37 Orig Chr^cod

Age see Mayor *Jude* pp. 23, 61 ff., and for the possibility that we have here (cf. Rom. vi. 17, xvi. 17) a reference to an early catechism or creed, based upon the sayings of Christ, which was used by the first missionaries, see Seeberg *Katechismus* pp. 1 ff., 41 f. The title of οἱ κρατοῦντες, applied by eccles. writers to Christians, is probably due to this passage (LS. s.v. κρατέω).

II. 16, 17. PRAYER.

A prayer is again interjected that the exhortation spoken of may be fulfilled in the Thessalonians' case. Chrys.: πάλιν εὐχὴ μετὰ παραίνεσιν· τοῦτο γάρ ἐστιν ὄντως βοηθεῖν.

16, 17. 'May our Lord Jesus Christ Himself and God our Father Who loved us, and in His Divine bounty bestowed upon us abiding comfort and good hope, comfort your hearts and strengthen you to do and to say everything that is right.'

16. Αὐτὸς δὲ ὁ κύριος ἡμ. κτλ.] The invocation is identical with I. iii. 11 except that ὁ κύρ. Ἰησ. Χρ. is now placed first, and that the def. art. is substituted before πατήρ for the more ordinary καί, while the first ὁ before θεός is doubtful. The order (cf. 2 Cor. xiii. 13, Gal. i. 1) may have been determined by the immediately preceding reference to the glory of the Lord Jesus (*v.* 14), or be due to the fact that He is the intermediary through whom the purposes of God for His people are carried out. In either case we have another striking ex. of the equal honour ascribed to the Son with the Father throughout these Epp. (Intr. p. lxvi). Chrys.: ποῦ νῦν εἰσιν οἱ τὸν υἱὸν ἐλλατοῦντες; Thdt.: τῇ τῆς τάξεως ἐναλλαγῇ τὴν ὁμοτιμίαν δεικνύων. ὁ ἀγαπήσας ἡμ. κ. δοὺς κτλ.] The two participles under the vinculum of the common art. belong to ὁ θεός alone, and the use of the aor. shows that the reference is to the definite historical act in which the Gospel originated.

For παράκλησις see I. ii. 3 note, and for αἰωνίαν (for form, WSchm. p. 96) as bringing out the 'final and abiding' character of this 'comfort' compared with the transitory joys of earth see i. 9 note. Ἀγαθήν 'good' both in its character and results; cf. I. iii. 6, v. 15, and for the phrase ἀγαθὴ ἐλπίς in Gk. literature see Dem. *Cor.* 258 (§ 120) δεῖ δὲ τοὺς ἀγαθοὺς ἄνδρας ἐγχειρεῖν μὲν ἅπασιν ἀεὶ τοῖς καλοῖς, τὴν ἀγαθὴν προβαλλομένους ἐλπίδα.

ἐν χάριτι] not the human disposition in which the gifts just spoken of were received, but the Divine favour or bounty by which the 'consolation of Israel' was freely extended to those who were Gentiles by birth, cf. i. 12 note.

17. παρακαλέσαι κτλ.] For παρακαλεῖν see I. ii. 11, iii. 2 notes, and for στηρίζειν see I. iii. 2 note.

Παντί and ἀγαθῷ refer to both the intervening nouns (cf. *v.* 9), and the whole expression is of the most general character 'whatever you may do or say,' any attempt to limit λόγῳ to specific Christian doctrine (Chrys.: δόγματα, Calv.: 'sana doctrina') being quite out of place.

III. ¹ Τὸ λοιπὸν προσεύχεσθε, ἀδελφοί, περὶ ἡμῶν, ἵνα ὁ λόγος τοῦ κυρίου τρέχῃ καὶ δοξάζηται καθὼς καὶ πρὸς ὑμᾶς, ²καὶ ἵνα ῥυσθῶμεν ἀπὸ τῶν ἀτόπων καὶ πονη-

III. 1—16. CONSOLATORY AND HORTATORY.

The writers now pass to teaching of a more directly consolatory and hortatory character, and, as in their former Epistle (I. v. 25), accompany it with the request for their readers' prayers.

III. 1, 2. REQUEST FOR THE THESSALONIANS' PRAYERS.

1, 2. 'Nor do we only pray for you, we ask further that you, Brothers, should pray for us, and especially that the word of the Lord may have the same swift and glorious course everywhere that it has already had amongst you. To this end do you pray that we may be rescued from the perverse and evil men who are at present placing obstacles in our path—for it is not every one who has a true faith in Christ.'

1. Τὸ λοιπὸν προσεύχεσθε κτλ.] The request is another proof of the closeness of the bond which the Apostles recognized as existing between their 'brethren' and themselves (Intr. p. xliv), while as regards its contents (for the sub-final ἵνα see note on I. iv. 1) it is significant that in the first instance it is of the furtherance of their work rather than of any ease or advantage to themselves that they think.

For τὸ λοιπόν cf. I. iv. 1 note, and for προσεύχεσθε περί I. v. 25 note.

ὁ λόγος τ. κυρίου] 'the word of the Lord' Jesus in accordance with the general practice of the Epp. (Add. Note D). The use of the title in the present section is very marked, occurring as it does four times in vv. 1—5.

τρέχῃ] 'may run' emphasizing the living, active nature of the word in the Apostles' eyes, and their ardent desire that it may speed ever onward on its victorious course: cf. I. i. 8. The figure, which falls in with St Paul's well-known fondness for metaphorical language from the stadium (Rom. ix. 16, 1 Cor. ix. 24 ff., Gal. ii. 2, v. 7, Phil. ii. 16, 2 Tim. iv. 7), is derived from the O.T., see especially Ps. cxlvii. 4 (cxlvi. 15) ἕως τάχους δραμεῖται ὁ λόγος αὐτοῦ, and the splendid imagery of Ps. xviii. (xix.) directly cited in Rom. x. 18. Findlay aptly recalls Vergil's lines on *Fama* beginning 'Mobilitate viget, viresque adquirit eundo' (*Aen.* iv. 175 ff.).

καὶ δοξάζηται] the inner recognition following on (καί consec.) the outward progress of the word: cf. Ac. xiii. 48 ἀκούοντα δὲ τὰ ἔθνη ἔχαιρον καὶ ἐδόξαζον τὸν λόγον τοῦ θεοῦ, and for the thought see Tit. ii. 10. On the deepened significance of δοξάζω in Bibl. Gk. see SH. p. 44, and for the slightly stronger ἐνδοξάζω cf. i. 10, 12. As illustrating the N.T. usage, the following invocation from the long magical papyrus P.Lond. I. 121, 502 ff. (iii./A.D.) is noteworthy: κυρία Ἶσις...δόξασόν με (μοι Pap.), ὡς ἐδόξασα τὸ ὄνομα τοῦ υἱοῦ(ς) σου Ὥρου (cf. Reitzenstein *Poimandres* p. 22 n.⁶).

καθὼς κ. πρὸς ὑμᾶς] For this use of πρός with acc. cf. I. iii. 4 note, and for the fact see I. i. 5 ff., ii. 1, 13.

2. καὶ ἵνα ῥυσθῶμεν κτλ.] a second and more personal need for which the prayers of the Thessalonians are asked, and which, though independent of the first, is closely connected with it: cf. Rom. xv. 30 f., and note the striking verbal parallel in Isa. xxv. 4 ἀπὸ ἀνθρώπων πονηρῶν ῥύσῃ αὐτούς. Thdt.: διπλῆ μὲν ἡ αἴτησις εἶναι δοκεῖ, μία δὲ ὅμως ἐστί. τῶν γὰρ πονηρῶν ἀνθρώπων ἡττωμένων, ἀκωλύτως καὶ ὁ τοῦ κηρύγματος συντρέχει λόγος.

110 THE SECOND EPISTLE TO THE THESSALONIANS [III 3

ῥῶν ἀνθρώπων, οὐ γὰρ πάντων ἡ πίστις. ³Πιστὸς δέ

For the meaning of ῥυσθῶμεν (late pass. aor., WSchm. p. 131)=*eripiamur* (Beza) rather than *liberemur* (Vg.), see the note on I. i. 10, and contrast the construction with ἀπό, not ἐκ, in the present passage, laying stress perhaps on the deliverance itself rather than on the power from which it is granted, cf. Rom. xv. 31, 2 Tim. iv. 18, and from the LXX. Ex. ii. 19 ἐρρύσατο ἡμᾶς ἀπὸ τῶν ποιμένων. For a late instance of ῥύεσθαι ἀπό see P.Lond. II. 413, 3 f. (iv./A.D.) ἐ[ὔχομ]αι σ[.]ῶ τῷ θεῷ περὶ [τῆ]ς σ[ωτ]ηρίας ἵνα ῥύσει σαὶ ἀπό....

τ. ἀτόπων κ. πονηρῶν ἀνθρώπων] Ἄτοπος, originally='out of place,' 'unbecoming,' is used in class. Gk. especially in Plato in the sense of 'marvellous,' 'odd' (e.g. *Legg.* i. 646 B τ. θαυμαστοῦ τε καὶ ἀτόπου), from which the transition is easy to the ethical meaning of 'improper,' 'unrighteous' in later Gk., e.g. Philo *Legg. Alleg.* iii. § 17 (i. p. 97 M.) παρ᾽ ὃ καὶ ἄτοπος λέγεται εἶναι ὁ φαῦλος· ἄτοπον δέ ἐστι κακὸν δύσθετον, and such a passage from the Κοινή as P.Petr. III. 43 (3), 17 f. (iii./B.C.), where precautions are taken against certain discontented labourers ἵνα μὴ ἄτοπ[ό]ν τι πράξωσιν: cf. also *B.G.U.* 757, 21 (i./A.D.) where ἕτερα ἄτοπα are ascribed to certain marauders who had pulled to pieces a farmer's sheaves of wheat, and the very interesting public notice contained in P.Fior. 99 (i./ii. A.D.) to the effect that the parents of a prodigal youth will no longer be responsible for his debts or for ἄτοπόν τι πράξη[ι].

It is in this sense accordingly, implying something morally amiss, that, with the exception of Ac. xxviii. 6, the word is found in the LXX. and the N.T. (Job iv. 8, xi. 11 &c., Prov. xxiv. 55 (xxx. 20), 2 Macc. xiv. 23, Lk. xxiii. 41, Ac. xxv. 5), and in the passage before us it is best given some such rendering as 'perverse' or 'froward' rather than the 'unreasonable' of A.V., R.V. Similarly πονηρός (as frequently in the LXX., e.g. Gen. xxxvii. 20, Ps. lxxvii. (lxxviii.) 49, Esth. vii. 6; cf. Hatch *Essays* p. 77 f.) is used not so much of passive badness as of active harmfulness, while the prefixed art. shows that the writers have here certain definite persons in view, doubtless the fanatical Jews who at the time were opposing their preaching in Corinth (Ac. xviii. 12 ff.), as they had already done in Thessalonica and Beroea (Ac. xvii. 5, 13): cf. I. ii. 14 ff.

οὐ γὰρ πάντων ἡ πίστις] 'for not to all does the Faith belong' (Luth. *denn der Glaube ist nicht jedermanns Ding*). For a similar *meiosis* cf. Rom. x. 16 ἀλλ᾽ οὐ πάντες ὑπήκουσαν τῷ εὐαγγελίῳ. As illustrating the form of the sentence, Wetstein quotes the proverbial saying, οὐ παντὸς ἀνδρὸς ἐς Κόρινθον ἐσθ᾽ ὁ πλοῦς (Strabo viii. 6. 20).

III. 3—5. CONFIDENCE IN THE THESSALONIANS' PROGRESS.

From the want of *faith* on the part of men, the Apostles turn to the thought of the *faithfulness* of the Lord Jesus (cf. 2 Tim. ii. 13) with the view moreover of reassuring not themselves, but their converts.

3—5. 'We have spoken of the want of faith in certain quarters. However this may be, know assuredly that the Lord is faithful. He will set you in a firm place. He will protect you from the attacks of the Evil One. And seeing that He will do this, we have confidence that you on your part will not come short, but will continue as at present to do the things which we are enjoining. May the Lord direct you into the love of God and into the patience of Christ.'

3. Πιστός] recalling the πίστις of the previous verse. For a similar word-play cf. Rom. iii. 3.

III 4, 5] THE SECOND EPISTLE TO THE THESSALONIANS 111

ἐστιν ὁ κύριος, ὃς στηρίξει ὑμᾶς καὶ φυλάξει ἀπὸ τοῦ πονηροῦ. ⁴πεποίθαμεν δὲ ἐν κυρίῳ ἐφ᾽ ὑμᾶς, ὅτι ἃ παραγγέλλομεν [καὶ] ποιεῖτε καὶ ποιήσετε. ⁵Ὁ δὲ κύριος

III 4 καὶ om ℵAD* d (g) Boh

ὃς στηρίξει ὑμ. κτλ.] Not only will the Lord 'set them in a firm place' (στηρίξει, for form, WM. p. 110), but He will also 'protect' (φυλάξει, Vg. *custodiet*) them there from external assaults: cf. for the thought Jo. xvii. 12. For στηρίζειν (I. iii. 2 note) cf. 1 Pet. v. 10 ὁ δὲ θεὸς πάσης χάριτος... αὐτὸς καταρτίσει, στηρίξει, σθενώσει, and for the constr. φυλάσσειν ἀπό cf. Ps. cxl. (cxli.) 9 φύλαξόν με ἀπὸ παγίδος ἧς συνεστήσαντό μοι, and see Buttmann p. 192.

ἀπὸ τ. πονηροῦ] The precise sense to be attached to these words is best determined by the meaning assigned them in the petition of the Lord's Prayer ῥῦσαι ἡμᾶς ἀπὸ τοῦ πονηροῦ (Mt. vi. 13), of which we have apparently a reminiscence here (cf. Col. i. 13, and see Feine *Jesus Christ und Paulus* p. 252 f.). As the general consensus of modern scholarship is to understand πονηροῦ there as masc. rather than as neut. in accordance with the predominant usage of the N.T. (Mt. v. 37, xiii. 19, 38, Eph. vi. 16, 1 Jo. ii. 13 f., iii. 12ª, v. 18 f. as against Lk. vi. 45, Rom. xii. 9), and the unanimous opinion of the Gk. commentators, we follow the same rendering here, and translate 'from the evil one': a rendering, it may be noted further, which forms a fitting antithesis to ὁ κύριος of the preceding clause, and is moreover in thorough harmony with the prominence assigned shortly before to the persons of Satan and his representative (ii. 1—12), and more especially to the *evil men* (πονηρῶν ἀνθρώπων) of the preceding clause. See further Lft.'s note *ad loc.* and the same writer's *Revision of the Engl. N.T.*³ p. 269 ff., and especially the exhaustive discussion by Chase *The Lord's Prayer* p. 112 ff.

4. πεποίθαμεν δέ κτλ.] The assurance that it is the Lord Who is protecting the Thessalonians gives the Apostles a corresponding confidence that the Thessalonians themselves will faithfully fulfil their part. Chrys.: δεῖ μὲν γὰρ τὸ πᾶν ἐπ᾽ αὐτὸν ῥίπτειν, ἀλλ᾽ ἐνεργοῦντας καὶ αὐτούς, τοῖς πόνοις ἐμβεβηκότας καὶ τοῖς ἀγῶσι.

For ἐν κυρίῳ (see I. iv. 1), as the ground with correspondingly new resources in which all St Paul's hopes and desires are centred, cf. Gal. v. 10, Eph. iv. 17, Phil. ii. 19, 24, and for ἐφ᾽ ὑμᾶς, instead of the class. dat., as marking the *direction* of the confidence displayed cf. Mt. xxvii. 43, 2 Cor. ii. 3, Ps. cxxiv. (cxxv.) 1.

ὅτι ἃ παραγγέλλομεν κτλ.] For a similar use of ὅτι introducing the objective statement of the Apostle's confidence cf. Phil. ii. 24. Under ἃ παραγγέλλομεν must be understood not such injunctions as had already been given (e.g. I. iv. 1—12), but rather, as the resumption of the same verb in *v.* 6 proves, those that immediately follow, and which, on account of their hardness, are further prefaced by a short ejaculatory prayer.

For παραγγέλλω see I. iv. 11 note, and as bringing out the idea of transmission contained in the word cf. P.Grenf. I. 40, 6 f. (ii./B.C.) ἔκρινον γράψαι σοι ὅπως εἰδὼς παραγγείλης καὶ τ[οῖς] ἄλλοις ἱερεῦσι.

5. Ὁ δὲ κύριος κατευθύναι κτλ.] Ὁ κύριος can only be the Lord Jesus as in *vv.* 1, 3, 4, any reference to the Holy Spirit (as Basil *de Spiritu sancto* c. 21 and most of the Gk. commentators) being outruled if only on the

κατευθύναι ὑμῶν τὰς καρδίας εἰς τὴν ἀγάπην τοῦ θεοῦ καὶ εἰς τὴν ὑπομονὴν τοῦ χριστοῦ.

⁶ Παραγγέλλομεν δὲ ὑμῖν, ἀδελφοί, ἐν ὀνόματι τοῦ

ground that ὁ κύριος is never so employed in the N.T. (not even in 2 Cor. iii. 18).

For κατευθύνω see I. iii. 11 note: its metaphorical use is further illustrated by Aristeas 18 κατευθύνει τὰς πράξεις καὶ τὰς ἐπιβολὰς ὁ κυριεύων ἁπάντων θεός.

εἰς τ. ἀγάπην τ. θεοῦ κ. εἰς τ. ὑπομονὴν τ. χριστοῦ] The close parallelism of the two clauses makes it natural (as in ii. 13) to understand the genitives in the same way, and as the subjective interpretation of the second clause is rendered almost necessary by the regular meaning of ὑπομονήν in the N.T., 'constancy,' 'endurance' (I. i. 3 note) not 'patient waiting' (ἀναμονήν, cf. I. i. 10), we are similarly led to think of τ. ἀγαπὴν τ. θεοῦ as the love which is God's special characteristic, and which He has displayed towards us; cf. Rom. v. 5, viii. 39, 2 Cor. xiii. 13, Eph. ii. 4, and see Abbott *Joh. Gr.* p. 84.

The use of the art. before χριστοῦ is significant as emphasizing the connexion of the 'patience' spoken of not merely with the earthly trials of the Saviour, but with these trials as the inevitable lot of the suffering servant of Jehovah. Cf. for the general thought Heb. xii. 1 f., Rev. iii. 10, and see Ign. *Rom.* x. 3 ἔρρωσθε εἰς τέλος ἐν ὑπομονῇ Ἰησοῦ Χριστοῦ, where however Lft. (*ad loc.*) inclines to the meaning 'patient waiting for Christ.'

III. 6—12. CHARGE WITH REGARD TO THE DISORDERLY.

It is 'in the Lord,' as has just been shown, that the Apostles' trust for their converts is centred. At the same time they are anxious that these should not forget the responsibilities resting on themselves. And accordingly in a section, in which the severity of the language shows the serious nature of the evils complained of, they once more (cf. I. v. 14 f.) rebuke the idle and disorderly behaviour, which at the time certain members of the Thessalonian community were displaying.

6—12. 'In order, however, that this happy result may be attained, we again on our part urge you—and yet not we, but the Lord—not in any way to associate with a brother who is not living a well-ordered life in accordance with our teaching. For you yourselves cannot but be conscious that you ought to follow our example. When we were with you, we did not depend on others for our support. Rather in toil and moil, night and day, we worked that we might not lay an unnecessary burden upon any of you. You must not indeed suppose that we have not the right to maintenance, but we waived our right in order to set an example for you to follow. And not only so, but we gave you a positive precept to this effect. For you cannot have forgotten that while we were with you, we were in the constant habit of urging upon you that "If any will not work, neither let him eat." And we are the more led to go back upon this, because information is reaching us regarding certain of your number who are living ill-ordered lives, and, instead of attending to their own business, are busy with what does not concern them. It is such as these that we urge and entreat in the Lord Jesus to attend quietly to their own work and earn their own living.'

6. Παραγγέλλομεν δὲ ὑμῖν, ἀδελφοί] In introducing their παραγγελία the Apostles adopt a tone at once of affection and of authority—of affec-

κυρίου ᵀ Ἰησοῦ Χριστοῦ στέλλεσθαι ὑμᾶς ἀπὸ παντὸς ἀδελφοῦ ἀτάκτως περιπατοῦντος καὶ μὴ κατὰ τὴν παράδοσιν ἣν ⌜παρελάβετε⌝ παρ' ἡμῶν. ⁷αὐτοὶ γὰρ οἴδατε πῶς δεῖ μιμεῖσθαι ἡμᾶς, ὅτι οὐκ ἠτακτήσαμεν ἐν ὑμῖν

6 κυρίου solum BD* d Cypr: add ἡμῶν אG cet g Vg cet verss Ambst Theod-Mops^lat   παρελάβετε BG al pauc g ½ Go Syr (Harcl) Arm Orig ½ Bas (?) Thdt: παρελάβοσαν א*A 17 Bas (non semper)

tion, because it is to their 'brethren' that they appeal, and of authority, because it is as the representatives of one Jesus, Who had been made known both as Lord and Christ, that they enforce their charge.

ἐν ὀνόματι τ. κυρ. Ἰησ. Χρ.] practically synonymous here with διὰ τ. κυρ. Ἰησ. (I. iv. 2 note), though the introduction of the common O.T. periphrasis (cf. Ex. v. 23, Deut. xviii. 22, Jer. xi. 21) lays greater stress on the personality and consequent authority of the person spoken of: cf. i. 12 note, and for a full discussion of this and similar expressions see the exhaustive monograph by W. Heitmüller *Im Namen Jesu* (Göttingen, 1903).

A similar usage occurs in the Κοινή where ὄνομα with the gen. often stands for the dat. of the name of the person addressed, e.g. Ostr. 670 Πανίσκος... ὀνό(ματι) [ὀνό(ματος), Wilcken] Πασήμιος κτλ. (other exx. in Herwerden).

στέλλεσθαι ὑμᾶς κτλ.] Στέλλειν originally = 'set,' 'place,' and hence 'bring together,' 'make compact' as e.g. of shortening the sails of a ship (Hom. *Il.* i. 433, *Od.* iii. 11), by a natural transition came to denote generally 'restrain,' 'check,' and is found in the midd. in the sense of 'draw or shrink back from' anything, whether from fear (Hesych.: στέλλεται· φοβεῖται) or any other motive as in Mal. ii. 5 ἀπὸ προσώπου ὀνόματός μου στέλλεσθαι αὐτόν, 3 Macc. i. 19 αἱ δὲ καὶ προσαρτίως ἐσταλμέναι ('die sich ganz zurückgezogen halten' Kautzsch, and cf. Grimm's note *ad loc.*): cf. Hipp. *Vet. med.* 10 (ed. Foesius)

οὔτ' ἂν ἀπόσχοιντο ὧν ἐπιθυμεοῦσιν, οὔτε στείλαντο, and see the old gloss quoted in Steph. *Thesaur. s.v.* where στέλλεσθαι is explained by ἀφίστασθαι, ἀναχωρεῖν. This gives the clue to its meaning here (Vg. *ut subtrahatis vos*) and in 2 Cor. viii. 20 στελλόμενοι (Vg. *devitantes*) τοῦτο μή τις ἡμᾶς μωμήσηται, the only other place where it is found in the N.T. Thdt.: τὸ στέλλεσθαι ἀντὶ τοῦ χωρίζεσθαι τέθεικε. The compound ὑποστέλλω (-ομαι) is used in the same sense in Ac. xx. 20, 27, Gal. ii. 12, Heb. x. 38; cf. Deut. i. 17, Job xiii. 8, Sap. vi. 7 (8).

παντὸς ἀδελφοῦ] Notwithstanding his faults, the title of 'brother' is not denied to the disorderly person, even while duty to the 'brotherhood' requires that he be avoided; cf. 1 Cor. v. 11.

ἀτάκτως] See Add. Note G.

κατὰ τ. παράδοσιν κτλ.] For παράδοσιν see ii. 15 note, and for παρελάβετε see I. ii. 13 note.

The marginal reading παρελάβοσαν is well-attested, and, if adopted, must have its subj. supplied from the collective ἀπὸ παντὸς ἀδελφοῦ. The termination in -οσαν receives however scanty warrant from the papyri (Moulton *Prolegg.* p. 52), and in the present instance may have originated 'in an ocular confusion with -οσιν (παράδοσιν) in the corresponding place of the line above' (WH² *Notes* p. 172).

7. αὐτοὶ γὰρ οἴδατε] Cf. I. i. 5, ii. 1, 5, 11 &c.; Intr. p. xliv.

μιμεῖσθαι ἡμᾶς] The verb μιμέομαι, repeated in *v.* 9, is found elsewhere in

⁸οὐδὲ δωρεὰν ἄρτον ἐφάγομεν παρά τινος, ἀλλ' ἐν κόπῳ καὶ μόχθῳ νυκτὸς καὶ ἡμέρας ἐργαζόμενοι πρὸς τὸ μὴ ἐπιβαρῆσαί τινα ὑμῶν· ⁹οὐχ ὅτι οὐκ ἔχομεν ἐξουσίαν, ἀλλ' ἵνα ἑαυτοὺς τύπον δῶμεν ὑμῖν εἰς τὸ μιμεῖσθαι ἡμᾶς. ¹⁰καὶ γὰρ ὅτε ἦμεν πρὸς ὑμᾶς, τοῦτο παρηγγέλλομεν

the N.T. only in Heb. xiii. 7, 3 Jo. 11; it occurs several times in the apocr. books of the O.T., cf. also Aristeas 188 μιμούμενος τὸ τοῦ θεοῦ διὰ παντὸς ἐπιεικές. For the thought of the present passage see I. i. 6 note. οὐκ ἠτακτήσαμεν] another instance of *meiosis* (cf. *v.* 2, I. ii. 15), embodying the ground of the Thessalonians' knowledge just spoken of. For ἀτακτέω see Add. Note G.

8. δωρεάν] 'gratis' as frequently in the LXX. (Gen. xxix. 15, Ex. xxi. 2 &c.): cf. Rom. iii. 24, 2 Cor. xi. 7, also P.Tebt. 5, 249 ff. (ii./B.C.) ἐπιρίπτειν...ἔργα δωρεὰν μηδὲ μισθῶν ὑφειμένων 'to impose labour gratis or at reduced wages.' In Jo. xv. 25 (LXX.), Gal. ii. 21 the word has the further sense of 'uselessly,' 'without sufficient cause.'

ἄρτον ἐφάγομεν] a general expression for taking food of any kind (cf. Mk. iii. 20, Lk. xiv. 1), corresponding to the Heb. אָכַל לֶחֶם (Gen. iii. 19, 4 Regn. iv. 8).

ἀλλ' ἐν κόπῳ κτλ.] See the notes on I. ii. 9, and as further illustrating the meaning of the phrase νυκτ. κ. ἡμ. cf. Magn. 163, 7 f. ἀδιαλείπτως θέντα τὸ ἔλαιον ἡμέρας τε καὶ νυκτός.

9. οὐχ ὅτι οὐκ ἔχομεν ἐξουσίαν] a limitation introduced to avoid any possible misconception as to the Apostolic claim to gratuitous support: cf. I. ii. 6 and especially 1 Cor. ix. 4, 7—14 where St Paul traces this same 'right' (ἐξουσίαν, *v.* 4) to the enactment of the Lord Himself (*v.* 14, Lk. x. 7 f.); see also 1 Tim. v. 18, Didache xiii. 1 πᾶς δὲ προφήτης ἀληθινὸς...ἄξιός ἐστι τῆς τροφῆς αὐτοῦ. For this later sense of ἐξουσία (primarily 'liberty of action') to de-

note a definite 'claim' or 'right,' with the further idea of 'authority' over others, cf. its frequent technical use in the papyri in connexion with wills and contracts, e.g. P.Oxy. 491, 3 (ii./A.D.), ἐφ' ὃν μὲν περίειμι χρόνον ἔχειν μ[ε] τὴν τῶν ἰδίων ἐξου[σί]αν 'so long as I survive I am to have power over my own property,' 719, 25 (ii./A.D.) ἐξουσίας σοι οὔσης ἑτέροις παρ[αχωρεῖν] 'the right resting with you to cede to others.'

For the use of οὐχ ὅτι = οὐ λέγομεν ὅτι (...ἀλλά) in the N.T. for the purpose of avoiding misconception cf. 2 Cor. i. 24, iii. 5, Phil. iv. 17; WM. p. 746.

ἀλλ' ἵνα ἑαυτοὺς τύπον κτλ.] a second, and in the present instance, the main reason of the Apostles' self-denying toil: not only did they desire to remove any hindrance from the free diffusion of the Gospel (cf. I. ii. 9), but also by their own daily lives and conduct to impress more forcibly upon their converts' hearts the real significance of their message.

For ἑαυτούς with reference to the 1st pers. plur. cf. I. ii. 8 note. It is of interest to notice that this usage does not seem to have extended to the sing. except in the case of very illiterate documents, e.g. B.G.U. 86, 5 (ii./A.D.) συνχωρῶ μετὰ τὴν ἑαυτοῦ τελευτὴν τοῖς γεγονόσι α[ὑτ]ῷ ἐκ τῆς συνούσης αὐτοῦ γυναικός (cf. Moulton *C.R.* xv. 441, xviii. 154). With τύπος (I. i. 7 note) cf. the use of ὑποτύπωσις in 1 Tim. i. 16, 2 Tim. i. 13, the metaphor there, according to Lft. (on Clem. R. *Cor.* v. *ad fin.*), being due to the art of sculpture, 'the first rough model.'

10. καὶ γὰρ ὅτε ἦμεν κτλ.] Cf. I.

III 11, 12] THE SECOND EPISTLE TO THE THESSALONIANS 115

ὑμῖν, ὅτι εἴ τις οὐ θέλει ἐργάζεσθαι μηδὲ ἐσθιέτω.
¹¹ἀκούομεν γάρ τινας περιπατοῦντας ἐν ὑμῖν ἀτάκτως,
μηδὲν ἐργαζομένους ἀλλὰ περιεργαζομένους· ¹²τοῖς δὲ
τοιούτοις παραγγέλλομεν καὶ παρακαλοῦμεν ἐν κυρίῳ

iii. 4, the only difference being that, in view of *v.* 6, τοῦτο παρηγγέλλομεν is substituted for προελέγομεν. For similar references by St Paul to his previous public teaching cf. 1 Cor. xi. 23, xv. 1.
ὅτι εἴ τις οὐ θέλει κτλ.] 'that if any one is not willing (Beng.: 'nolle vitium est') to work, neither let him eat.' Pelag.: 'Haec sit inquietudinis non solum poena, sed etiam emendatio.'
For ὅτι which is here equivalent to little more than our inverted commas see WM. p. 683 n.¹, and for illustrations of the maxim, which was apparently a proverbial Jewish saying based on Gen. iii. 19, see the passages cited by Wetstein, especially Bereschith R. ii. 2 'ego vero si non laboro, non edo,' xiv. 12 'ut, si non laborat, non manducet': cf. also Didache xii. 3 εἰ δὲ θέλει πρὸς ὑμᾶς καθῆσαι, τεχνίτης ὤν, ἐργαζέσθω καὶ φαγέτω. According to Resch (*Agrapha,* p. 240 ff., *Paulinismus,* p. 409 f.) the saying in its present form may have been derived from a logion of the Lord Himself.
For εἰ...οὐ see WM. p. 599, Jannaris, § 1807ᵇ, and for the strong negative μηδέ (*ne quidem*) with the imperative cf. Eph. v. 3.

11. ἀκούομεν γάρ κτλ.] Fresh news from Thessalonica had reached the writers since the despatch of their first Epistle, perhaps through the bearer of that Epistle on his return, of such a character as to lead them to single out the offenders, who were evidently known to them, for direct rebuke.
For the pres. ἀκούομεν instead of the perf. cf. 1 Cor. xi. 18 (Burton, § 16, Gildersleeve *Syntax* § 204), and for its construction with the acc.

and part. to describe an actually existing state see Buttmann p. 302 f.
μηδὲν ἐργαζομένους ἀλλὰ περιεργαζομένους] 'doing no business but being busy bodies'—a translation suggested by Ellic. which has the merit of preserving the play of words in the original: cf. Beza 'nihil agentes, sed inaniter satagentes,' Est. 'nihil operantes, sed circumoperantes,' and amongst more modern renderings Ew., Schm. 'keine Arbeit treibend, sondern sich herumtreibend,' Zöckl. 'nicht schaffend, sondern vielgeschäftig,' Jowett 'busy only with what is not their own business.' The same play on the original Gk. words is found in Dem. *Phil.* iv. 150 σοὶ μὲν ἐξ ὧν ἐργάζει καὶ περιεργάζει τοὺς ἐσχάτους ὄντας κινδύνους. For other exx. of paronomasia from the Pauline Epp. see *v.* 13, Rom. i. 20, xii. 3, 1 Cor. vii. 31, 2 Cor. iv. 8, Phil. iii. 2 f. (WM. p. 794 f., Blass, p. 298 f.).
Περιεργάζομαι, ἅπ. λεγ. N.T. (cf. περίεργος Ac. xix. 19, 1 Tim. v. 13), is found in the same sense as here in Sir. iii. 23 (24) ἐν τοῖς περισσοῖς τῶν ἔργων σου μὴ περιεργάζου: cf. Plato *Apol.* 19 B, where it is said of Socrates in an accusatory sense, περιεργάζεται ζητῶν τά τε ὑπὸ γῆς καὶ τὰ ἐπουράνια, and for a significant ex. from the inscriptions see *C.I.A.* III. 74, 14 f. ὃς ἂν δὲ πολυπραγμονήσῃ τὰ τοῦ θεοῦ ἢ περιεργάσηται, ἁμαρτίαν ὀφιλέτω κτλ. Quintilian defines περιεργία as 'supervacua operositas' (viii. 3. 55): cf. M. Anton. x. 2 τούτοις δὴ κανόσι χρώμενος, μηδὲν περιεργάζου.

12. τ. δὲ τοιούτοις παραγγέλλομεν κτλ.] The παραγγελία is now addressed directly to the ἄτακτοι themselves in so far as they possess the above-

8—2

116 THE SECOND EPISTLE TO THE THESSALONIANS [III 13, 14

Ἰησοῦ Χριστῷ ἵνα μετὰ ἡσυχίας ἐργαζόμενοι τὸν ἑαυτῶν ἄρτον ἐσθίωσιν. [13]Ὑμεῖς δέ, ἀδελφοί, μὴ ἐνκακήσητε καλοποιοῦντες. [14]εἰ δέ τις οὐχ ὑπακούει τῷ λόγῳ ἡμῶν

mentioned characteristics—τοῖς τοιούτοις, cf. Mt. xix. 14, Rom. xvi. 18, 1 Cor. v. 11.

For παρακαλοῦμεν cf. I. ii. 12 note, and for ἐν κυρ. Ἰησ. Χρ. cf. I. iv. 1 note.

ἵνα μετὰ ἡσυχίας κτλ.] It is not enough that they should not be disorderly, they must also work, and that too 'with quietness' for their own maintenance.

Ἡσυχία (elsewhere in N.T. only Ac. xxii. 2, 1 Tim. ii. 11 f.; cf. ἡσυχάζειν I. iv. 11, and for a class. parallel [Dem.] *Exord. Or.* 1445 ἔχειν ἡσυχίαν καὶ τὰ ὑμέτερα αὐτῶν πράττειν) differs from ἠρεμία in denoting tranquillity arising from *within* rather than from *without* (Ellic. on 1 Tim. ii. 2).

For the force of μετά see the note on I. i. 6, and cf. P.Lond. I. 44, 17 f. (ii./B.C.) μεθ' ἡσυχίας ἀναλύειν.

III. 13—15. EXHORTATION TO THE LOYAL MEMBERS OF THE CHURCH.

After the digression caused by the rebuke of the disorderly, the writers, fearing that their example may have a bad effect, address a special word of exhortation to the main body of their readers.

13—15. 'On the other hand as regards the rest of you, Brothers, we exhort you not to fail in doing the right thing, but to persevere in your honourable course. And in order that you may do this, there is nothing for it but to mark the man who is disregarding what we have said in this Epistle, and not in any way to associate with him, in order that thereby he may be shamed. And yet in saying this, we need hardly caution you that you are not to treat him as if he were in any sense an enemy, but rather to counsel him as a brother.'

13. Ὑμεῖς δέ] 'But you'—whatever may have been the conduct of others. Thdt.: μὴ νικήσῃ τὴν ὑμετέραν φιλοτιμίαν ἡ ἐκείνων μοχθηρία.

μὴ ἐνκακήσητε] Ἐνκακέω (for form, WH.[2] *Notes* p. 157 f.) from κακός 'cowardly' is found elsewhere in N.T. only in Lk. xviii. 1, 2 Cor. iv. 1, 16, Gal. vi. 9, Eph. iii. 13: cf. Polyb. iv. 19. 10 τὸ μὲν πέμπειν τὰς βοηθείας ...ἐνεκάκησαν 'they omitted through cowardice to send assistance.'

For the use of the aor. subj. in 2nd pers. after μή, which is comparatively rare in Paul, see Moulton *Prolegg.* p. 122 ff.

καλοποιοῦντες] 'doing the fair, the noble thing' rather than 'conferring benefits' (ἀγαθοποιοῦντες): cf. the double exhortation in 1 Tim. vi. 18 ἀγαθοεργεῖν, πλουτεῖν ἐν ἔργοις καλοῖς.

The verb καλοποιέω is not found elsewhere in the N.T. (for similar compounds, Lob. *Phryn.* p. 199 f.), but for the thought see Gal. vi. 9 τὸ δὲ καλὸν ποιοῦντες μὴ ἐνκακῶμεν, where, as here, καλός carries with it the thought not only of what is right in itself (I. v. 21 note), but of what is *perceived* to be right (1 Tim. v. 25 τὰ καλὰ πρόδηλα), and consequently exercises an attractive power. See further for this sense of καλός the interesting discussion by Lock, *St Paul* p. 117 ff.

14. τῷ λόγῳ ἡμῶν διὰ τῆς ἐπιστολῆς] 'our word (sent) through the (present) epistle' (Th. Mops. *interpr.*: 'uerba quae per epistolam loquimur'). The interpretation favoured by some of the older commentators by which διὰ τ. ἐπιστ. is rather to be connected with what follows in the sense 'by means of a letter (from you) do you notify' (cf. Tind. *sende vs worde of him by a letter*) is exposed to the well-founded

III 15] THE SECOND EPISTLE TO THE THESSALONIANS 117

διὰ τῆς ἐπιστολῆς, τοῦτον σημειοῦσθε, μὴ συναναμίγνυσθαι αὐτῷ, ἵνα ἐντραπῇ· ¹⁵καὶ μὴ ὡς ἐχθρὸν ἡγεῖσθε,

objections that it is inconsistent with the natural order of the words, and with the use of the demonstrative τῆς (I. v. 27 note), which points to an existing letter rather than to one to be written afterwards.

τοῦτον σημειοῦσθε] 'of this man take note' (Vg. *hunc notate*). Σημειόομαι (ἄπ. λεγ. N.T.) means to 'mark or notify for oneself,' and from being used in a neutral or even favourable (Ps. iv. 7) sense came also to have the idea of disapprobation connected with it, e.g. Polyb. v. 78. 2 (of a sinister omen) σημειωσάμενοι τὸ γεγονός. The ordinary usage of the word is illustrated by Aristeas 148 παραδέδωκεν ὁ νομοθέτης σημειοῦσθαι τοῖς συνετοῖς εἶναι δικαίους, *O.G.I.S.* 629, 168 (Palmyra, ii./A.D.) ὁ κράτιστος ἐσημ(ε)ιώσατο ἐν τῇ πρὸς Βάρβαρον ἐπιστολῇ.

It may be added that with the grammarians σημείωσαι is used in the sense of 'nota bene,' and that in the ostraca and papyri σεσημείωμαι is the regular term for the signature to a receipt or formal notice, as when in P.Oxy. 237. vii. 29 (ii./A.D.) the prefect gives legal validity to the ὑπομνηματισμός by the words ἀνέγνων· σεσημ(είωμαι).

μὴ συναναμίγνυσθαι αὐτῷ] lit. 'not to mix yourselves together up with him' (Vg. *ne commisceamini cum illo*, Beza *ne commercium habete cum eo*) —the expressive double compound being found elsewhere in the N.T. only in 1 Cor. v. 9 μὴ συναναμίγνυσθαι πόρνοις: cf. Hos. vii. 8 Α Ἐφράιμ ἐν τοῖς λαοῖς αὐτοῦ συνανεμίγνυτο. For the corresponding adj. in the Κοινή see P.Oxy. 718, 16 f. (ii./A.D.) ἀρούρας τῆς βασιλικῆς συναναμίγους εἶναι τῇ ὑπαρ[χούσῃ μοι γῇ].

ἵνα ἐντραπῇ] 'in order that he may be put to shame' (Vg. *ut confundatur*, Beza *ut erubescat*), following the late metaphorical sense of ἐντρέπω, cf. Ps. xxxiv. (xxxv.) 4, 1 Cor. iv. 14, Tit. ii. 8, and from the Κοινή such passages as P.Par. 47, 3 f. (ii./B.C.) [ε]ἰ μὴ μικρόν τι ἐντρέπομαι, 49, 29 f. (ii./B.C.) γίνεται γὰρ ἐντραπῆναι. The corresponding subst. ἐντροπή (= αἰσχύνη) is found in 1 Cor. vi. 5, xv. 34. For its sense of αἰδώς as in class. Gk. (e.g. Soph. *Oed. Col.* 299) cf. the late magical papyrus P.Lond. I. 46, 16 f. (iv./A.D.) δὸς ἐντροπὴν τῷ φανέντι πρὸ πυρός.

In the midd. the verb = 'reverence,' and contrary to class. usage is construed in the Bibl. writings with the acc., e.g. Sap. ii. 10, Mk. xii. 6, Heb. xii. 9.

15. καὶ μὴ ὡς ἐχθρόν κτλ.] a clause added to prevent any possible misunderstanding of the foregoing. Throughout the conduct enjoined has in view the final amendment of the offender (Th. Mops.: 'ut modis omnibus increpatione, obsecratione, doctrina reducatis eum ad id quod honestum est'): cf. Didache xv. 3 ἐλέγχετε δὲ ἀλλήλους μὴ ἐν ὀργῇ ἀλλ' ἐν εἰρήνῃ, and Clem. R. *Cor.* xiv. 3 χρηστευσώμεθα αὐτοῖς [τοῖς ἀρχηγοῖς τῆς στάσεως] κατὰ τὴν εὐσπλαγχνίαν καὶ γλυκύτητα τοῦ ποιήσαντος ἡμᾶς.

For the softening effect of ὡς 'as if he were an enemy' cf. Blass p. 246 n.¹, and for ἡγέομαι and νουθετέω see the notes on I. v. 13, I. v. 12, respectively. As further illustrating the 'stronger' sense of ἡγέομαι in the former passage see M. Anton. iv. 1 where the best texts read ὁρμᾷ μὲν πρὸς τὰ ἡγούμενα ('moves towards things preferred') in the sense of προηγούμενα in the parallel passage v. 20 (see Crossley's note *ad loc.*).

III. 16. Prayer.

16. 'May the Lord, from whom all peace comes, Himself give you His

118 THE SECOND EPISTLE TO THE THESSALONIANS [III 16—18

ἀλλὰ νουθετεῖτε ὡς ἀδελφόν. ¹⁶Αὐτὸς δὲ ὁ κύριος τῆς εἰρήνης δῴη ὑμῖν τὴν εἰρήνην διὰ παντὸς ἐν παντὶ τρόπῳ. ὁ κύριος μετὰ πάντων ὑμῶν. ¹⁷Ὁ ἀσπασμὸς τῇ ἐμῇ χειρὶ Παύλου, ὅ ἐστιν σημεῖον ἐν πάσῃ ἐπιστολῇ· οὕτως γράφω. ¹⁸ἡ χάρις τοῦ κυρίου ἡμῶν Ἰησοῦ Χριστοῦ μετὰ πάντων ὑμῶν.

peace at all times and in all ways. The Lord be with you all.'

16. Αὐτὸς δέ κτλ.] For αὐτὸς δέ see I. iii. 11 note, and for ὁ κύρ. τ. εἰρ., here evidently the Lord Jesus (cf. v. 5), see I. v. 23 note. The Hellenistic opt. δῴη (for δοίη) is found again in the N.T. in Rom. xv. 5, 2 Tim. i. 16, 18 (WSchm. p. 120). For διὰ παντός 'continually,' as distinguished from πάντοτε 'at all times' see Westcott's note on Heb. ix. 6, and cf. P.Lond. I. 42, 6 (cited in note on I. i. 3).

The v. l. ἐν παντὶ τόπῳ (A*D*G 17 Vg Go) doubtless arose through the desire to conform a somewhat awkward phrase (cf. παντὶ τρόπῳ Phil. i. 18, κατὰ πάντα τρόπον Rom. iii. 2) to the more common expression (cf. I. i. 8, 1 Cor. i. 2, 2 Cor. ii. 14, 1 Tim. ii. 8).

μετὰ πάντων ὑμῶν]—even with the disorderly brother, cf. v. 18 and for πάντων used with a similar emphasis see the Benedictions in 1 Cor. xvi. 24, 2 Cor. xiii. 13.

III. 17, 18. SALUTATION AND BENEDICTION.

17, 18. 'I add this salutation with my own hand, signing it with my name Paul, as I am in the habit of doing. May the grace of our Lord Jesus Christ be with you all.'

17. Ὁ ἀσπασμὸς τῇ ἐμῇ χειρὶ Παύλου] Cf. 1 Cor. xvi. 21, Col. iv. 18, and for a similar use of ἀσπασμός in the Κοινή see P.Oxy. 471, 67 f. (ii./A.D.) ἀναμενόντων...τὸν ἀσπασμόν 'waiting to salute him,' and cf. the note on ἀσπάζομαι I. v. 26.

Παύλου is gen. in apposition with ἐμῇ in accordance with a common Gk. idiom (Kühner³ § 406, 3).

ὅ ἐστιν σημεῖον κτλ.] namely the fact of St Paul's writing the salutation with his own hand, and not merely the insertion of the immediately preceding words, which as a matter of fact are found elsewhere only in two of his Epp. (1 Cor., Col.). Because however St Paul does not always pointedly direct attention to the autographic nature of the salutations is in itself no proof that he did not write them: cf. Intr. p. xcii and see Add. Note A. In the present instance he may have considered a formal attestation of the clearest kind the more necessary in view of the false appeals that had been made to his authority in Thessalonica (see note on ii. 2).

οὕτως γράφω] with reference to the characters in which vv. 17, 18 were written, which the Thessalonians would henceforth recognize as his: cf. Gal. vi. 11. Any reference to an ingeniously-framed monogram (Grot.: 'certum quendam nexum literarium') used by the Apostle for his signature is quite unnecessary.

18. ἡ χάρις τοῦ κυρίου κτλ.] The substance of the Pauline ἀσπασμός, embodying the Apostle's favourite idea of 'grace,' and by the significant addition of πάντων extending it to 'all' alike, even those whom he had just found it necessary to censure (cf. v. 16 note).

As in the First Ep. (cf. I. v. 28 note) a liturgical ἀμήν has found its way into certain MSS. (ℵᶜADGKLP).

ADDITIONAL NOTES

Καθὼς καὶ ὁ ἀγαπητὸς ἡμῶν ἀδελφὸς Παῦλος κατὰ τὴν δοθεῖσαν αὐτῷ σοφίαν ἔγραψεν ὑμῖν, ὡς καὶ ἐν πάσαις ἐπιστολαῖς λαλῶν ἐν αὐταῖς περὶ τούτων, ἐν αἷς ἐστὶν δυσνόητά τινα.

2 Pet. iii. 15, 16.

NOTE A.

St Paul as a Letter-Writer.

Φιλοφρόνησις γάρ τις βούλεται εἶναι ἡ ἐπιστολὴ σύντομος, καὶ περὶ ἁπλοῦ πράγματος ἔκθεσις καὶ ἐν ὀνόμασιν ἁπλοῖς.
Demetrius *de Elocutione* 231 (ed. Roberts, p. 176).

'Als einen Ersatz seiner persönlichen Wirkung schreibt er seine Briefe. Dieser Briefstil ist Paulus, niemand als Paulus; es ist nicht Privatbrief und doch nicht Literatur, ein unnachahmliches, wenn auch immer wieder nachgeahmtes Mittelding.'
U. von Wilamowitz-Moellendorff *Die Griechische Literatur des Altertums* p. 157 (in *Die Kultur der Gegenwart* I. 8, Berlin, 1905).

We have already seen that the Thessalonian Epistles are true 'letters,' and not doctrinal treatises, and that, in adopting this method of communicating with his scattered Churches, St Paul found a means of communication admirably suited alike to his own temperament, and to the circumstances under which he wrote. The use of a 'letter' indeed for religious purposes was not altogether without precedent. It was by a letter that Jeremiah communicated God's will regarding them to the Jewish captives in Babylon (Jer. xxix.)[1], and by a letter again, to come down to Christian times, that the Council at Jerusalem announced their decision to the Gentile Churches (Ac. xv.)[2]. But, notwithstanding these partial parallels, St Paul was apparently the first to recognize the full possibilities that lay in a letter as a means of conveying religious instruction[3]. And as there is good reason to believe that in the Thessalonian Epistles we have the earliest of his extant writings (see p. xxxvi f.), this is a fitting opportunity for trying to form as clear an idea as possible of the outward form and method of the Pauline correspondence.

Towards this, recent discoveries in Egypt have lent most valuable aid. For though it is somewhat remarkable that no copy of a Pauline Epistle, or any part of one, on papyrus, belonging to the first three centuries, has yet come to light[4], the ordinary papyrus letters of the Apostle's time enable

The Pauline Epistles are true letters. Light thrown on them by recent discoveries of papyri.

---

[1] Cf. in the Apocrypha the so-called Epp. of Jeremiah and Baruch, and 2 Macc. i. 1, 10. Renan (*Saint Paul* (1869) p. 229 n.[2]) refers also to the *iggéret* or *risâlet*, which the Jewish synagogues were in the habit of addressing to one another on points of doctrine or practice.

[2] 'Letters of recommendation' (ἐπι-στολαὶ συστατικαί) were common, Ac. ix. 2 (xxii. 5), xviii. 27; cf. Rom. xvi. 1, 2, 2 Cor. iii. 1, and for a pagan example see the first of the papyrus-letters reproduced on p. 127.

[3] An exception is sometimes made in favour of the Epistle of James; but see Sanday *Inspiration* p. 344 f.

[4] There are various fragments be-

122 THE EPISTLES TO THE THESSALONIANS

us to picture to ourselves with great distinctness what must have been the exact *format* of the Pauline autographs.

Papyrus as a writing material. Thus there can be no doubt that, like other letter-writers of his time, St Paul wrote his letters on papyrus. The costlier pergament, which was used for copies of the O.T. books[1], was not only beyond the Apostle's slender means, but would have been out of keeping with the fugitive and occasional character he himself ascribed to his writings[2]. And he would naturally fall back upon a material which was easily procurable, and whose use for the purposes of writing had already a long history behind it[3].

The manufacture of papyrus. In itself papyrus is derived from the papyrus-plant (*Cyperus papyrus* L.)[4], and was prepared for the purposes of writing according to a well-established process, of which the elder Pliny (*N.H.* xiii. 11—13) has left a classical account.

According to this, the pith (βύβλος) of the stem of the papyrus-plant was cut into long strips (*philyrae*), which were laid down vertically to form a lower or outward layer. Over this a corresponding number of strips were then placed horizontally; and the two layers were pressed together to form one sheet (*scheda*), the process being assisted by a preparation of glue, moistened, when possible, with the turbid water of the Nile, which was supposed to add strength to it[5]. After being dried in the sun, and

longing to the fourth and fifth centuries, amongst which Dr Kenyon (Hastings' *D.B.* v. p. 354) includes one containing 2 Thess. i. 1—ii. 2 (Berlin Museum P. 5013); but, in a private communication to the present writer, he states that, in reality, this is not on papyrus, but on vellum. The important papyrus containing about one-third of the Ep. to the Hebrews (P.Oxy. 657) is certainly not later than the fourth century, perhaps the end of the third.

[1] These are probably referred to in τὰς μεμβράνας of 2 Tim. iv. 13, as compared with τὰ βιβλία, the ordinary papyrus-rolls.

[2] The very fact that Josephus mentions that the letter of the Jews to Ptolemy Philadelphus was written on parchment (διφθεραί, *Antt.* xii. 89 (ii. 11)) shows that this was unusual.

[3] The earliest extant papyrus-writing is a statement of accounts, dated in the reign of Assa, the last King of the fifth dynasty in Egypt, about 3580—3536 B.C. (Kenyon *Palaeography of Greek Papyri* p. 14). According to Sir E. M. Thompson (*Greek and Latin Palaeography* p. 33), papyrus continued

to be manufactured in Egypt for writing purposes down to the tenth century of our era. Recently attempts have been made to supply *charta* according to the ancient model from the papyrus-plants growing near Syracuse. In addition to the authorities quoted, see the essay on 'Ancient Papyrus and the mode of making paper from it' by Prof. Ezra Abbot, reprinted in his *Critical Essays* (Boston, 1888) p. 137 ff.

[4] The most probable derivation of the word 'papyrus' is from the Egyptian *pa-p-yôr*, 'the (product) of the river,' i.e. 'the river-plant' (see *Encycl. Bibl.* col. 3556). The plant is mentioned in Job viii. 11; in Ex. ii. 3 the תֵּבַת גֹּמֶא was a 'chest of paper-reed,' or a papyrus-boat, cf. Isa. xviii. 2 ἐπιστολὰς βυβλίνας. For the Gk. word πάπυρος cf. P.Leid. S p. 97 col. 1ª, 8, 11 (ii./B.C.), and (παπύρους) P.Par. 55 *bis* col. 1 and 2 (ii./B.C.), and for the adj. P.Leid. U col. 2ª, 6 f. (ii./B.C.) πλοῖον παπύρινον, ὃ καλεῖται Αἰγυπτιστὶ Ῥώψ. See further Mayser p. 37.

[5] This appears to be the correct interpretation of Pliny's 'turbidus

ST PAUL AS A LETTER-WRITER 123

rubbed down with ivory or a smooth shell to remove any roughness, the sheet was ready for use—a *scripturabilis facies*.

The size of the sheets thus formed would obviously vary according to the quality of the papyrus; but Dr Kenyon has shown that for non-literary documents the size in ordinary use would be from 5 to 5½ inches in width, and from 9 to 11 inches in height[1]. *Size of papyrus-sheets.*

For a brief note, like the Epistle to Philemon, a single sheet would therefore suffice, but, when more space was required, it was easily procurable by fastening the requisite number of sheets together to form a roll[2], the beginning (πρωτόκολλον) and the end (ἐσχατοκόλλιον), as the parts most usually handled, being not infrequently strengthened by attaching extra strips of papyrus at the back. These rolls would seem to have been generally sold in lengths of twenty sheets (*scapi*), the cost of two sheets being at the rate of a drachma and two obols each, or a little over a shilling of our money[3].

As a rule the original writing was confined to one side of the papyrus-sheet, that side being chosen on which the fibres lay horizontally (*recto*), which was therefore smoother for the purpose. But occasionally, when space failed, recourse was had also to the back (*verso*)[4]. The *verso* was also frequently used for some other writing of less importance, or for scribbling purposes, much as we use the back of an old letter[5]. *Recto and Verso.*

The matter was arranged in columns (σέλιδες, *paginae*) of from two to three inches wide, which were as a rule placed close together, so that there *Width of columns.*

---

liquor vim glutinis (dat.) praebet,' as elsewhere he recognizes only the form *glutinum*, and not *gluten*, according to which *glutinis* would be a genitive: cf. Birt *Das antike Buchwesen* (1882) p. 231 f., and for the whole of Pliny's description see Gardthausen *Griechische Palaeographie* (1879) p. 31 f., Thompson *op. cit.* p. 30 f., Kenyon *op. cit.* p. 15.

[1] *Op. cit.* p. 16 ff.

[2] Cicero (*ad Fam.* xii. 30. 1) speaks of so delighting in his correspondence with Cornificius, that he desires to send him 'not letters but rolls.'

[3] Thompson *op. cit.* p. 28; cf. Karabacek *Führer durch die Papyrussammlung* (1904) of the Rainer Museum at Vienna, p. xvi. Karabacek also refers (p. xv) to the different qualities of papyrus-paper, such as the *Charta claudia*, a very white paper, and the *Charta salutatrix*, a favourite form for ordinary correspondence. The finest of all was the *Hieratica*, while the *Emporetica*, made out of the rougher

layers served much the purposes of brown paper amongst ourselves.

[4] Cf. Ezek. ii. 9 f. 'a roll of a book ...written within and without,' and Rev. v. 1 βιβλίον γεγραμμένον ἔσωθεν καὶ ὄπισθεν, the roll was so full that the contents had overflowed to the *verso* of the papyrus (but see Nestle *Text. Crit. of the Gk. N.T.* p. 333). A similar peculiarity distinguishes the long magical papyrus P.Lond. 1. 121 (iii./A.D.). On the distinction between *Recto* and *Verso* see especially Wilcken in *Hermes* xxii. (1887) p. 487 ff.: cf. *Archiv* i. p. 355 f.

[5] The letter P.Gen. 52 is written on the *verso*, the writer explaining— χάρτην (χάρτιον, Wilcken *Archiv* iii. p. 399) καθαρὸν μὴ εὑρὼν πρὸς τὴν ὥραν εἰς τοῦ[τ]ον ἔγραψα. See also the interesting caricature from the back of a papyrus (ix./B.C.) reproduced in Erman and Krebs *Aus den Papyrus der Königlichen Museen* [*zu Berlin*], Berlin, 1899, p. 6.

124   THE EPISTLES TO THE THESSALONIANS

would be little room for the marginal annotations St Paul is sometimes credited with having made, unless we are to think of these as inserted at the top or bottom of the sheet.

Ink and pen. To complete our survey of the writing-materials, it is sufficient to notice that the black ink (μέλαν, or μέλαν γραφικόν) ordinarily used was prepared from a mixture of soot and gum-water[1] and that a rush or reed (κάλαμος, or κάλαμος γραφικός) served as a pen (cf. 3 Jo. 13 διὰ μέλανος καὶ καλάμου)[2].

A papyrus-roll. When finished, the roll was rolled round upon itself, and fastened together with a thread[3], and in ordinary letters the address or title was then written on the back of the roll. In the case of more important literary works, which would be preserved in libraries, a σίλλυβος, or small strip of papyrus containing the title, was frequently attached to the end of the roll for the purpose of identification[4].

Mode of reading. In order to ascertain its contents, the reader held the roll with two hands, unrolling it with his right, and with his left hand rolling up what he had finished reading[5]: a practice which enables us to understand the imagery of Rev. vi. 14 ὁ οὐρανὸς ἀπεχωρίσθη ὡς βιβλίον ἑλισσόμενον (ἑλισσόμενος ℵ), where the expanse of heaven is represented as parting asunder, 'the divided portions curling up and forming a roll on either hand' (Swete *ad loc.*).

St Paul's employment of an amanuensis. From these more general details that help to throw light on the outward method of the Pauline correspondence, it is necessary now to turn to one or two particulars that affected its contents. Amongst these a first place must be given to the fact that as a rule St Paul, following a well-established custom (Norden *Kunstprosa* ii. p. 954 ff.), seems to have

---

[1] Pliny *N.H.* xxxv. 6. The excellent quality of this ink is shown by the way it has preserved its colour after the lapse of so many years. At the same time by not sinking into the texture of the paper like our modern inks, it readily lent itself to being washed completely off: hence Col. ii. 14 ἐξαλείψας τὸ...χειρόγραφον (see Williams' note *ad loc.* in *C.G.T.*).

[2] Directions for buying papyrus, pens, ink &c. will be found in P. Grenf. II. 38 (cf. Witkowski *Epp.* no. 55), a letter of i./B.C. For illustrations of the ordinary writing-materials see Erman and Krebs *op. cit.* p. 8 f., and the above-cited *Führer* through the Rainer collection at Vienna p. 6.

[3] The wooden-roller (ὀμφαλός, *umbilicus*) with projecting knobs or tips (κέρατα, *cornua*) would seem to have been confined to the costlier editions of literary works (Gardthausen *op. cit.*

p. 52 f., Kenyon *op. cit.* p. 23). And the same would be the case with the φαινόλης or φαιλόνης, the 'cover' by which more valuable works were protected. Birt (*op. cit.* p. 65) finds a reference to this 'cover,' and not to the Apostle's 'travelling-cloke,' in the φελόνη of 2 Tim. iv. 13.

[4] Specimens of these σίλλυβοι have been recovered: see P.Oxy. 301, 381.

[5] Cf. Lucian *imag.* c. 8 βιβλίον ἐν ταῖν χεροῖν εἶχεν, ἐς δύο συνειλημμένον· καὶ ἐῴκει τὸ μέν τι ἀναγνώσεσθαι αὐτοῦ, τὸ δὲ ἤδη ἀνεγνωκέναι (cited Gardthausen p. 52). Seneca, who prided himself on his brevity, breaks off a letter with the remark that no letter should 'fill' the left hand of the reader (*Ep.* 45 'quae non debet sinistram manum legentis implere'), implying that, were it longer than a single sheet, the reader would require to use both hands (Birt p. 62).

dictated his letters. This at least is the most obvious interpretation of such a passage as Rom. xvi. 22 ἀσπάζομαι ὑμᾶς ἐγὼ Τέρτιος ὁ γράψας τὴν ἐπιστολὴν ἐν κυρίῳ, where, unless we are to think of Tertius' writing a *copy* of the letter the Apostle had previously penned, we can only regard him as the actual scribe. Further confirmation of this practice is afforded by 2 Thess. iii. 17, a verse which sets the authenticating signature of the Apostle in direct contrast with the rest of the letter as written by someone else: cf. 1 Cor. xvi. 21, Col. iv. 18.

To such a mode of procedure the Egyptian papyri again offer striking confirmation, the signature being often in a different hand from the body of the document itself, as when a letter on land-distribution by three officials, Phanias, Heraclas, and Diogenes, is endorsed at the bottom by the second of these ('Ηρακλ(ᾶς) σεση(μείωμαι)), the letter itself having no doubt been written by a clerk (P.Oxy. 45 (i./A.D.) with the edd. note)[1].

In speaking of St Paul's amanuensis, we must not however think of a professional scribe (ταχυγράφος, *notarius*), but rather of some educated friend or companion who happened to be with the Apostle at the time (cf. Rom. xvi. 21). The writing would then be of the ordinary, non-literary character, though doubtless more than the usual care would be taken in view of the importance of the contents. The words, in accordance with general practice, would be closely joined together. Contractions, especially in the way of leaving out the last syllables of familiar words[2], would be frequent. And, as a rule, accents and breathings would be only sparingly employed. The bearing of these facts upon the various readings that crept later into the Pauline texts is at once obvious. But for our present purpose it is more important to ask, How much was St Paul in the habit of leaving to his amanuensis? Did he dictate his letters word for word, his scribe perhaps taking them down in some form of shorthand[3]? Or was

Significance of this fact

---

[1] Mahaffy (P.Petr. I. p. 48) finds here the clue to the correct interpretation of the πηλίκα γράμματα of Gal. vi. 11—the large, irregular characters of the man who wrote but little, as compared with the smaller, cursive hand of his more practised amanuensis: cf. for a striking illustration of this the facsimile of Pap. 215 in the *Führer* to the Rainer collection (p. 68), where the rude, uncial signatures of two consenting parties are clearly distinguishable from the more cultured hand in which the body of the contract is written. But Ramsay (*Hist. Comm. on Galatians* p. 466) is probably nearer the mark in saying that by the use of 'large' letters the Apostle desired rather to draw special attention to the 'importance' of the following sentences, in accordance with a well-established custom in ancient times.

[2] Kenyon's statement (*Palaeography* p. 33) that the omission of the *middle* portion of words is not found in Gk. papyri now requires modification: cf. P.Amh. 35, 55 (ii./B.C.) βα(σιλι)κῶν, where the editors point out that the scribe first wrote βι, and then added κων to distinguish it from βι = βα- (σιλέως) in the previous line, and see also Kenyon himself (P.Lond. III. p. 91) where κλ κοι = κλήρου κατοικοῦ is allowed as 'one of the very few exceptions' to his own above-stated rule.

[3] For the practice of shorthand amongst the ancients see art. 'Nota' in Smith's *Dict. of Gk. and Rom. Antt.*, and cf. Kenyon *op. cit.* p. 33. To the literature there adduced may be added an art. by F. G. W. Foat *On old Greek Tachygraphy* in *J.H.S.* xxi. (1901)

126 THE EPISTLES TO THE THESSALONIANS

he content to supply a rough draft, leaving the scribe to throw it into more formal and complete shape? It is true that to these questions no definite answer can be given. In all probability the Apostle's practice varied with the special circumstances of the case, or the person of the scribe whom he was employing. More might be left to the discretion of a Silvanus or a Timothy, than of a Tertius. But, in any case, the very fact that such questions can be put at all shows how many of the difficulties regarding the varied style and phraseology of the different Epistles might be solved, if we had only clearer knowledge of the exact conditions under which they were severally written[1].

Possibility of quotations

Nor can we leave out of sight the possibility that, when dictating, St Paul may frequently have held some letter he was answering in his hand, and that consequently quotations from his correspondents' language, which we should now in print at any rate distinguish by the use of inverted commas, may have found their way into his answer, or at any rate suggested the exact form of the language employed[2].

In a suggestive paper in the *Expositor* (v. vi. p. 65 ff.) Dr Walter Lock has applied this possibility to the elucidation of 1 Cor. viii. 1—9, and more recently Dr Rendel Harris (*Exp.* v. viii. p. 169 ff.) has tried in the same way to disentangle from our existing 1 Thessalonians traces of a lost letter previously addressed by the Thessalonians to St Paul. Some of the points raised may perhaps seem to the ordinary reader over-subtle, and capable of simpler explanation. But the idea is a fruitful one, and may yet be found to do good service in the explanation of various Pauline linguistic and grammatical anomalies[3].

and marginal annotations.

Another possibility is that what were originally marginal annotations now form part of the Pauline Epistles. What more natural, it has been argued, than that St Paul should have read over his letter, after his scribe had finished writing it, and jotted down in the margin explanatory comments or additions, which afterwards found their way into the text[4]. That marginal annotations of this kind were added later is well known;

---

p. 238 ff., which contains a general résumé of the present state of the question.

[1] Cf. Sanday *Inspiration* p. 342, and for the possibility that in the 'dictation' and 'revision' of the fourth Gospel, which early tradition asserts (especially *Can. Murat.* p. 10 a.), we may have a key to the differences between it and the Apocalypse see Swete *Apoc.* p. clxxix f.

In an art. in the *Churchman* for June 1906 (summarized in *Exp. T.* xvii. p. 433) Bishop Moule cites a mode of procedure from the modern mission-field which may have some bearing on the point before us. According to

this when a European missionary in China desires to send a message, he first writes it down in his own Chinese, and then submits it to a 'writer,' who drafts it afresh into the correct classical phraseology. After revision it is then sent out by the missionary, 'as his own authentic message.'

[2] Cf. Weizsäcker *Apost. Age* ii. p. 102 ff.

[3] For its application to the Ep. to the Philippians see Kennedy *Phil.* p. 403 in *E.G.T.*

[4] See especially Laurent *Neutest. Studien* (Gotha, 1866) p. 3 ff., and cf. Renan *Saint Paul* (1869) p. 232.

ST PAUL AS A LETTER-WRITER 127

but it is very doubtful whether any of them can be traced back to St Paul
himself. The general form of an ordinary papyrus-letter left, as we have
already seen, little room for them. And such a phrase for example as
ἔμπροσθεν τοῦ κυρίου ἡμῶν Ἰησοῦ ἐν τῇ αὐτοῦ παρουσίᾳ (1 Thess. ii. 19), which
Laurent (p. 28 f.) cites in support of this view, may just as readily have
formed part of the original writing.

We are on surer ground when we turn to the undoubted light which General
the correspondence of the time throws upon the *general form* of the form
Pauline letters. That form, as is well known, consists as a rule of an of the
Address or Greeting, a Thanksgiving, Special Contents, Personal Salu- letters.
tations, and an Autographic Conclusion. And when full allowance has
been made for difference in character and tone, it is remarkable how
closely this structure resembles the structure of an ordinary Greek
letter.

This will perhaps be best shown by giving one or two specimens of Examples
the latter. We begin with a short letter from Oxyrhynchus, of date of papy-
A.D. 16, in which the writer Theon recommends to the notice of his rus-
brother Heraclides the bearer of the letter Hermophilus. A letter of
P.Oxy. 746. recom-
menda-
Θέων Ἡρακλείδηι τῶι ἀδελφῶι tion.
πλεῖστα χαίρειν καὶ ὑγιαίνειν.
Ἑρμόφιλος <ὁ> ἀποδ[ι]δούς σοι τὴν
ἐπιστολήν [ἐ]στ[ι] . [. .] . κ[. .]μ . φ[.]ηρι
[.]ερίου, καὶ ἠρώτησέν με γράψαι σοι.
[π]ροφέρεται ἔχειν πραγμάτιον
[ἐν τῆι] Κερκεμούνι. τοῦτο οὖν ἐάν
σοι φα[ί]νηται σπουδάσεις κατὰ τὸ
δίκαιον. τὰ δ' ἄλλα σεαυτοῦ ἐπιμελοῦ
ἵν' ὑγιαίνῃς.
ἔρρωσο.
(ἔτους) γ Τιβερίου Καίσαρος Σεβαστοῦ Φαῶφι γ.

On the *verso* is written the address:

Ἡρακλείδηι βα(σιλικῶι) γρ(αμματεῖ)
Ὀξυ(ρυγχίτου) Κυνοπ(ολίτου)

the round brackets indicating the resolution of the abbreviations
employed.

The general similarity of the Address and the closing Salutation to A letter of
the ordinary Pauline practice is at once obvious, and the same may be invitation.
said of the following letter of invitation from the Faiyûm, belonging to the
year A.D. 84.
B.G.U. 596:

Δίδυμος Ἀπολλωνίωι
τῶι τιμιωτάτωι
χαίρειν.
Καλῶς ποιήσεις συνελθὼν
[Ἀ]ιλουρίωνι τῶι κομίζον-
τί σοι τὸ ἐπ[ι]στ[ό]λιον, ὅπως

128 THE EPISTLES TO THE THESSALONIANS

εἰς τὴν ἑωρτὴν (sic) περιστε-
ρείδια ἡμεῖν ἀγοράσηι,
καὶ ἐρωτηθεὶς κατελ-
θὼν συνευωχηθῇ[ι]
ἡμεῖν. Τοῦτ[ο] οὖν ποιή-
σας ἔσῃ μοι μεγάλην
χάριταν (sic) κατ[α]τεθειμ[έ]νο(ς).
Ἄσπασαι τοὺς σοὺς πάντας.
Ἔρρωσο.
(ἔτους) τρίτου Αὐτοκράτορος
Καίσαρος Δομιτιανοῦ
Σεβαστοῦ Γερμανικοῦ Παχ(ὼν) ιε̄.

The address is again on the *verso* :

Εἰς Βακχιάδα [ἀπόδος Ἀπολλωνίωι] τῶι τιμιωτ[ά(τωι)].

A letter from a mother to her children.

Our next example still more closely recalls a Pauline letter, as, in addition to more formal resemblances, it contains an earnest prayer to the writer's god Serapis for the welfare of her children. This letter was also discovered in the Faiyûm, and belongs to the end of the second, or the beginning of the third, century of our era.

B.G.U. 332 :

Σεραπιὰς τοῖς τέκνοις Πτολεμαίῳ καὶ Ἀπολιναρίᾳ καὶ
Πτολεμαίῳ πλεῖστα χαίρειν.
Πρὸ μὲν πάντων εὔχομαι ἡμᾶς ὑγιαίνιν, ὅ μοι πάντων
ἐστὶν ἀνανκαιότερον. Τὸ προ[σ]κύνημα ἡμῶν ποιῶ παρὰ τῷ
κυρίῳ Σεράπιδι, εὐχομένη ἡμᾶς ὑγιαίνοντες ἀπολαβεῖν,
ὡς εὔχομαι ἐπιτετευχότας. Ἐχάρην κομισαμένη γράμματα,
ὅτι καλῶς διεσώθητε. Ἀσπάζου Ἀμμω[ν]οῦν σὺν τέκνοις καὶ
συμβίῳ καὶ τοὺς φιλοῦντάς σε. Ἀσπάζεται ἡμᾶς Κυρίλλα
καὶ ἡ θυγάτηρ Ἑρμίας Ἑρμίας (sic), Ἑρ[μ]ανοῦβις ἡ τροφός, Ἀθηναῒς ἡ δέσκα-
λος, Κυρίλλα, Κάσια, [. .]μ . . νις, Σ[. . .]ανος, Ἔμπις, οἱ ἐνθάδε πάντες.
Ἐρωτηθεὶς οὖν πρ[ᾶγμ]α πράσσις γρ[άψ]ε μοι, εἰδὼς ὅτι, ἐὰν γράμματά
σου λάβω, ἱλαρά εἰμι περὶ τῆς σωτηρίας ἡμῶν.
Ἐρρῶσθαι ἡμᾶς εὔχομαι.

On the *verso* this letter has two addresses, one in the original hand to the effect

Ἀπόδος Πτολε Χ μαίῳ τῷ τέκνῳ.
Ἀσπάζου . . . .

and the second in a different hand

Ἀπόδ(ος) Πτολεμαίῳ Χ ἀδε(λ)φῷ Ἀπολινα[ρί]ας.

It would appear therefore that the first recipient Ptolemaios had afterwards forwarded his mother's letter to his brother of the same name, and his sister Apolinaria.

A letter of consolation.

To these three letters I am tempted to add in full the pagan letter of consolation already referred to (see I. iv. 18 note) as, apart from similarity in outward form, its contents stand in such striking contrast to the bright and hopeful character of the Epistles before us.

P.Oxy. 115 (ii./A.D.):

Εἰρήνη Ταοννώφρει καὶ Φίλωνι
εὐψυχεῖν.
καὶ
οὕτως ἐλυπήθην ἔκλαυσα ἐπὶ
τῶι
Εὐμοίρωι ὡς ἐπὶ Διδυμᾶτος
ἔκλαυσα, καὶ πάντα ὅσα ἦν κα-
θήκοντα ἐποίησα καὶ πάντες
οἱ ἐμοί, Ἐπαφρόδειτος καὶ Θερμού-
θιον καὶ Φίλιον καὶ Ἀπολλώνιος
καὶ Πλαντᾶς. ἀλλ' ὅμως οὐδὲν
δύναταί τις πρὸς τὰ τοιαῦτα.
παρηγορεῖτε οὖν ἑαυτούς.
εὖ πράττετε. Ἀθὺρ ᾱ.

On the verso

Ταοννώφρει καὶ Φίλωνι.

Nothing would be easier than to multiply examples[1], but these must suffice to show the amount of truth there is in Deissmann's dictum that the Pauline letters 'differ from the messages of the homely Papyrus leaves from Egypt not as letters, but only as the letters of *Paul*' (*BS.* p. 44): while they also make clear how frequently the actual phrases employed are drawn from the current epistolary language of the Apostle's time[2]. This is naturally most noticeable in the more formal parts of the letter such as the address or the closing salutation[3]; but it is by no means confined to these, as will be seen from the preceding Notes on such passages as I. i. 2, 3, ii. 9, iv. 1, 13, II. ii. 3, iii. 2[4].

Current epistolary phrases.

Similarly with the authenticating signature. Reference has already been made to the fact that this was apparently generally added in St Paul's own hand in accordance with general practice[5]. And it is enough to add

St Paul's signature.

[1] An excellent collection of the letters belonging to the Ptolemaic period will be found in Witkowski's *Epistulae Privatae Graecae* (Leipzig, Teubner, 1906).

[2] For the existence of similar expressions in Latin letters see Tyrrell and Purser *The Correspondence of M. T. Cicero* (3rd ed. Dublin, 1904) i. p. 56 ff.

[3] This point did not escape the notice of the older commentators. Thus Theodore of Mopsuestia writes with reference to I. i. 1 (ed. Swete): τὸ χάρις ὑμῖν οὕτως τίθησιν ὥσπερ ἡμεῖς τὸ χαίρειν ἐν ταῖς προγραφαῖς τῶν ἐπιστολῶν εἰώθαμεν· τὸ ἐν θεῷ πατρὶ τεθεικώς, ὡς καὶ ἡμεῖς τὸ ἐν κυρίῳ γράφομεν. Cf. also Theodoret on II.

i. 2 : τὸ δὲ ἐν θεῷ πατρί ἔοικεν τῷ παρ' ἡμῶν ἐν ταῖς ἐπιστολαῖς γραφομένῳ· καὶ γὰρ ἡμεῖς εἰώθαμεν γράφειν· 'ὁ δεῖνα τῷ δεῖνι ἐν κυρίῳ χαίρειν.' On the original formula see Dr G. A. Gerhard's dissertation 'Die Formel ὁ δεῖνα τῷ δεῖνι χαίρειν' forming the first part of his *Untersuchungen zur Geschichte des griechischen Briefes* (*Philologus* lxiv. (N. F. xviii.), 1905, p. 27 ff.).

[4] Further evidence pointing in the same direction will be found in the Dean of Westminster's Note 'On some current epistolary phrases' in his great commentary on *St Paul's Epistle to the Ephesians*.

[5] Cf. Cic. *ad Attic.* viii. 1, Suet. *Tib.* 21, 32, Dion Cass. lviii. 11.

130   THE EPISTLES TO THE THESSALONIANS

that the οὕτως γράφω (like our 'signed') with which the Apostle draws attention to it in II. iii. 17 finds a ready parallel in the σεσημείωμαι (generally contracted into σεση), with which so many of the Egyptian papyrus-letters and ostraca close.

Mode of despatch of the Pauline letters. The only other point requiring notice is the mode of despatch of the Pauline letters. By this time the Imperial Post, established by Augustus[1], was in full operation, but its use was strictly limited to state and official needs, and ordinary correspondence could only be sent by special messenger, or by favour of some friend or passing traveller[2]. Even had it been otherwise, it is obvious that many of the Apostle's communications could only have been entrusted with safety to a Christian messenger in full sympathy with their object[3]. The messenger's part would thus be an important one. And there can be little doubt that to St Paul's messengers there often fell the task of reinforcing and supplementing the Apostolic message to the Churches addressed[4].

---

[1] Suet. *Aug.* 49. In this, as in so many other customs of his court, Augustus doubtless followed a Persian model (Friedlaender *Sittengeschichte Roms*[2] ii. p. 8, cf. i. p. 395).

[2] Cic. *ad Attic.* i. 9. 1, Pliny *Ep.* vii. 12, Mart. iii. 100. 1.

[3] According to a modern traveller, even to this day, in view of the perils attending correspondence at the hands of the Turkish postal authorities, Christians in Macedonia 'are forced to employ private couriers of their own creed and nationality' (G. F. Abbott *Tale of a Tour in Macedonia* p. 275).

[4] For the union of messenger and letter cf. P.Grenf. I. 30 (ii./B.C.), *B.G.U.* 1009 (ii./B.C.).

NOTE B.

Did St Paul use the Epistolary Plural?

The question of whether St Paul ever uses the epistolary plural is one of some general interest, and has also a direct bearing upon the interpretation of several passages in our Epistles. It is a question which has sometimes been answered very definitely in the negative, as when it has been categorically maintained that St Paul never uses the 1st pers. plur. except with reference to more than one person (Hofmann *Die heil. Schrift neuen Testaments* (1862) i. p. 147 and *passim*), or, more guardedly, that in those Epistles where several names occur in the address all subsequent 1st persons plur. must be referred to them, except where the context demands a still wider reference, as e.g. to Christians in general (Zahn *Einl. in d. N.T.* i. pp. 150 ff., 219 f.). Laurent, on the other hand, as positively declares (*SK.* 1868 p. 159 ff., *Neutest. Stud.* p. 117 f.) that, so far at least as the Thessalonian Epistles are concerned, the 1st pers. plur. is always to be referred to St Paul alone as a kind of *pluralis maiestaticus*, being used by the Apostle when he speaks in his official capacity, while as a private individual he uses the singular. As a matter of fact, however, as Karl Dick has shown in his elaborate monograph *Der schriftstellerische Plural bei Paulus* (Halle, 1900), no such hard and fast rule on either side can be carried consistently through without doing constant violence to the sense. And the general conclusion at which Dick arrives after a complete survey of the evidence is that St Paul uses the 1st pers. plur. with such a wide variety of *nuances* and shades of meaning, that the *pluralis auctoris* may well have a place amongst them, wherever it is found to be most in keeping with the context, and the circumstances of writing at the time.

The question not to be decided categorically,

Nor in this would the Apostle cause any undue difficulty to his readers. For if the use of the 1st pers. plur. for the 1st pers. sing. seems only to have existed to a very limited extent in classical Gk. (cf. Kühner³ II. i. § 371. 3, Gildersleeve *Syntax* § 54), in later writers it is very common (e.g. Polyb. i. 41. 7 πειρασόμεθα, Jos. *Vita* 10 (2) ἐβουλήθην...εἴπομεν...ᾤμην). And, what is still more pertinent to our present inquiry, this plural can now be illustrated from the ordinary correspondence of St Paul's time.

but in the light of the evidence of classical and later Greek,

We must be careful indeed not to overstrain the evidence in this direction, as some of the instances which are usually cited are by no means certain, owing to the possibility that the writer may be including those around him, members of his family or friends, in the plural reference. Thus in the first of Dick's two examples *B.G.U.* 27 (not 41, as Dick), 5 ff. εἰς γῆν ἐλήλυθα...καὶ ἐξε[κ]ένωσα μὲν (or ἐξεκενώσαμεν)...καὶ παρεδέξατο ἡμᾶς ὁ τόπος, the corn-merchant, who is its author, seems undoubtedly to be

and especially of the ordinary correspondence of the Apostle's time.

132   THE EPISTLES TO THE THESSALONIANS

thinking of his comrades as well as of himself, when he uses the plural[1], and similarly in the illiterate *B.G.U.* 596, 1 ff. (i./A.D.) καλῶς ποιήσεις... κατελθὼν συνευωχηθῆ[ι] ἡμεῖν. Τοῦτ[ο] οὖν ποιήσας ἔσῃ μοι μεγάλην χάριταν (*sic*) κατ[α]τεθειμ[έ]νο(ς), there is again no reason why the reference in ἡμεῖν and μοι should be identical[2].

Other examples can however now be cited in which it seems impossible to establish any distinction between the two numbers. For example, in the opening salutation of P.Par. 43 (ii./B.C.) we find εἰ ἔρρωσθαι, ἔρρωμαι δὲ καὐτοί, the plur. reading καὐτοί being here regarded as 'certain' by Witkowski (*Epp.* p. 55) as against καὐτός (Letronne); and with this may be compared such documents as P.Tebt. 58 (ii./B.C.) εὑρήκαμεν...εὗρον... βεβουλεύμεθα, P.Hib. 44 (iii./B.C.) ἐγράψαμεν...ὁρῶντες...ὤιμην, and, from a much later date, P.Heid. 6 (iv./A.D.) πιστεύομεν...γράφω καὶ φλυαρήσω... δυνηθῶμεν. Evidence to the same effect is afforded by the Inscriptions, as in *O.G.I.S.* 484, possibly a rescript of Hadrian, in which the sing. and plur. are interchanged in a truly astonishing manner, e.g. 1 ... λοῦμεν, 2 [μετεπεμ]ψάμην, βουληθείς, 13 ἔδοξεν ἡμεῖν, 27 ἐδοκιμάσαμεν, 31 ἐπίστευον, 41 δίκαιον ἡγησάμην, 54 νομίζω (see Dittenberger's note *ad loc.*).

The consequent possibility of such a usage in the Pauline Epistles. Special circumstances to be taken into account in the case of 1, 2 Thessalonians.

It is unnecessary to go on multiplying instances. These are sufficient to prove the possibility, to say the least, of the use of ἡμεῖς for ἐγώ in a writer of St Paul's time. And if, accordingly, we find passages in his Epistles where the 1st pers. plur. seems to be best understood of the Apostle alone, we need not hesitate so to apply it.

On the other hand in view of the fact that in several of his Epistles (1 Cor., Gal., Phil., Philemon) St Paul, after starting with an address from several persons, employs the 1st sing. throughout in the body of the letters, the continued use of the 1st pers. plur. throughout the Thessalonian Epistles is surely significant, and may be taken as indicating a closer and more continuous joint-authorship than was always the case at other times. And as we are further supported in this conclusion by all that we know regarding the special circumstances under which the two Epistles were written (see Intr. p. xxxiv f.), we shall do well to give its full weight to this normal use of the plural in them, and to think of it as including St Paul's two companions along with himself wherever on other grounds it is possible.

[1] Cf. Moulton *Prolegg.*[2] p. 246 as against p. 86 of the 1st edition.
[2] See the whole letter on p. 127 f.

NOTE C.

The Thessalonian Friends of St Paul.

In view of the strength of the ties which bound St Paul to the Thessalonian Church, it is not surprising to find that several of its members were afterwards reckoned amongst his close personal friends.

Amongst these a first place is naturally given to Jason who was his host at Thessalonica, and who must subsequently have joined St Paul on his missionary journeyings, if, as is generally thought, he is to be identified with the Jason who unites with the Apostle in sending greetings from Corinth to the Roman Christians (Rom. xvi. 21). In this case too we get the further information regarding him that he was a Jew by birth (cf. οἱ συγγενεῖς μου l.c.), and his name consequently is to be explained as the Grecized form of the Heb. Jesus or Joshua[1]. 1. Jason.

More prominently mentioned in connexion with St Paul's later history is a certain Aristarchus of Thessalonica (Ac. xx. 4). He was with the Apostle on his last journey to Jerusalem, and afterwards accompanied him and St Luke on the voyage to Rome (Ac. xxvii. 2). Bishop Lightfoot thinks that on this occasion he did not accompany St Paul all the way, but that, when the Apostle's plans were changed at Myra, Aristarchus continued in the Adramyttian vessel to his own home in Thessalonica (*Philipp.*[2] p. 34 f.). But if so, he certainly rejoined St Paul later in Rome, and apparently shared his captivity, to judge from the language of Col. iv. 10 'Ἀρίσταρχος ὁ συναιχμάλωτός μου. It is possible however that his captivity was voluntary, as in Philemon 24 he is spoken of simply as St Paul's fellow-worker (συνεργός), while the title συναιχμάλωτος is transferred to Epaphras (v. 23)— a circumstance that lends a certain colour to the suggestion that St Paul's companions took turns in sharing his captivity with him[2]. 2. Aristarchus.

It is sometimes thought that Aristarchus is included in the οἱ ὄντες ἐκ περιτομῆς of Col. iv. 11, and that consequently he was a Jew by birth; but that clause is better understood as referring only to Mark and Jesus Justus. The fact that Aristarchus was one of the deputation bearing the offerings of the Gentile Churches for the poor saints at Jerusalem (Ac. xx. 4) points rather to his own Gentile origin (cf. Klöpper, Peake *ad loc.*).

As illustrating the connexion of the name with Thessalonica, it may be

---

[1] Cf. Jos. *Antt.* xii. 239 (v. 1) ὁ μὲν οὖν Ἰησοῦς Ἰάσονα αὐτὸν μετωνόμασεν, and see Deissmann *BS.* p. 315 n.[2].

[2] It is of course possible that the title συναιχμάλωτος is applied to Aristarchus in a *spiritual* sense (cf. Rom. vii. 23, 2 Cor. x. 5, Eph. iv. 8) like σύνδουλος (Col. i. 7, iv. 7), and συστρατιώτης (Phil. ii. 25, Philem. 2): see Lft. *Philipp.*[2] p. 11 n.[6].

134   THE EPISTLES TO THE THESSALONIANS

mentioned that in an inscription containing a list of politarchs recently discovered at Thessalonica the list begins with 'Αριστάρχου τοῦ 'Αριστάρχου: see Dimitsas 'Η Μακεδονία (Athens, 1896) p. 428, inscr. 368 (cited by Burton *Am. Journ. of Theol.* ii. p. 608).

3. Secundus.   Closely associated with Aristarchus in Ac. xx. 4 is another Thessalonian, Secundus, of whom we know nothing further, though again it is not without interest to notice that the same name occurs among the Thessalonian politarchs in the list on the triumphal Arch (*C.I.G.* 11. 1967; cf. Intr. p. xxiii), and is also found on a memorial inscription of the year 15 A.D., discovered in a private house in the Jewish quarter of Thessalonica, which runs 'Απολλωνίῳ...Εὔτυχος Μαξίμου καὶ Σεκοῦνδα οἱ θρεπτοὶ τὸν βωμὸν μνείας χάριν κτλ. (Duchesne no. 59, p. 43), and with which may be compared Γάϊος 'Ιούλιος Σεκοῦνδος Πρίμῳ τῷ ἰδίῳ τέκνωι μνήμης χάριν (*ibid.* no. 78, p. 50).

4. Gaius.   This last inscription recalls yet another Macedonian friend of St Paul, the Gaius of Ac. xix. 29 Γαῖον καὶ 'Αρίσταρχον Μακεδόνας. Beyond however this juxtaposition with Aristarchus, there is no evidence definitely connecting Gaius with Thessalonica, though again we may notice the occurrence of the name in the list of politarchs (*C.I.G.* 11. 1967). The name was evidently a common one even in the Gk. world, and is borne by two other friends of St Paul, Gaius of Derbe (Ac. xx. 4), and Gaius of Corinth (Rom. xvi. 23, 1 Cor. i. 14), as well as by 'Gaius the beloved' to whom St John addresses his Third Epistle (3 Jo. 1).

5. Demas.   There remains still a fifth possible Thessalonian as holding a place for a time in the circle of St Paul's more immediate friends. In Philem. 24 a certain Demas is described along with the Thessalonian Aristarchus as a συνεργός of the Apostle (cf. Col. iv. 14). And when later this same man in the hour of his defection is described as going to Thessalonica (2 Tim. iv. 10) it is at least a fair surmise that he did so, because this was his native town[1]. His name at least is not Heb. but Gk. (see Meyer on Col. iv. 14, and cf. *C.I.G.* III. 3817 Δημᾶς καὶ Γάϊος), and under its full form Demetrius[2] appears twice in the already frequently cited list of politarchs (*C.I.G.* 11. 1967), as well as in that other list referred to under Aristarchus—Πολιταρχούντων 'Αριστάρχου τοῦ 'Αριστάρχου,...Δημητ[ρίου] τοῦ 'Αντιγόνου, which, according to Dimitsas, is to be dated between 168 B.C. and the Christian era (see Burton *ut s.* p. 608).

A later instance of the name is afforded by the martyr Demetrius who perished at Thessalonica in the persecution under Maximian (Intr. p. xxiv).

---

[1] Chrys. *Hom.* X. *in II ad Tim.* εἵλετο μᾶλλον οἴκοι τρυφᾶν 'he chose to live in luxury at home.'

[2] For the simple Δημᾶς cf. P.Petr. III. 49, 7, *B.G.U.* 10, 12 (ii./A.D.).

NOTE D.

The Divine Names in the Epistles.

Καὶ ὁ θεὸς αὐτὸν ὑπερύψωσεν, καὶ ἐχαρίσατο αὐτῷ τὸ ὄνομα τὸ ὑπὲρ πᾶν ὄνομα, ἵνα ἐν τῷ ὀνόματι Ἰησοῦ πᾶν ΓΌΝΥ ΚΆΜΨΗ ἐπουρανίων καὶ ἐπιγείων καὶ καταχθονίων, καὶ πᾶϲα ΓλῶϲϲΑ ἐξομολογήϲΗΤΑΙ ὅτι ΚΥΡΙΟΣ ΙΗΣΟΥΣ ΧΡΙΣΤΟΣ εἰς δόξαν θεοῦ πατρός. Phil. ii. 9—11.

The early date of the Epp. to the Thessalonians, combined with the generally undogmatic character of their contents, makes their evidence as to the view taken of the Person of Christ in the Apostolic Church specially significant. It is of importance therefore, as helping us to understand that view, to examine more closely than was possible in the Commentary the Names by which the Lord is here spoken of.

We begin naturally with the human Name *Jesus* which, standing by itself, is found only in two passages: *Jesus.*

I. i. 10 ὃν ἤγειρεν ἐκ [τῶν] νεκρῶν, Ἰησοῦν τὸν ῥυόμενον ἡμᾶς ἐκ τ. ὀργῆς τ. ἐρχομένης.

I. iv. 14 εἰ γὰρ πιστεύομεν ὅτι Ἰησοῦς ἀπέθανεν κ. ἀνέστη, οὕτως καὶ ὁ θεὸς τ. κοιμηθέντας διὰ τοῦ Ἰησοῦ ἄξει σὺν αὐτῷ.

This rare occurrence of the Name by which the Saviour was familiarly known during His earthly life may seem at first sight somewhat surprising, but is in entire accord with the general trend of Pauline teaching, the centre of which is to be found not in the earthly but in the heavenly and exalted Christ[1]. Only when, as in the foregoing passages, the reference to the historic facts of the Saviour's life is so direct as to make any other Name less suitable does St Paul use it alone without any other title.

Thus, to refer briefly to his later usage, in the four principal Epp. the name Ἰησοῦς is found alone ten times, five times with (2 Cor. iv. 10 (*bis*), 11, xi. 4 (ἄλλον Ἰησοῦν), Gal. vi. 17), and five times without (Rom. iii. 26, 1 Cor. xii. 3, 2 Cor. iv. 5, 11, 14) the article. In the Epp. of the Captivity it is found only twice, Eph. iv. 21 (with art.), Phil. ii. 10 (without art.). In the Ep. to the Colossians and the Pastoral Epp. it is not found at all.

Its use is characteristic of the Ep. to the Hebrews, and of the Apocalypse of St John where, except in the opening Greeting (i. 5) and in the Benediction (xxii. 21), Ἰησοῦς always stands alone.

---

[1] Thus Deissmann, while insisting on the identity between the historical and the exalted Christ, says: 'Christ is for him [Paul] first of all a present living Being: the "exalted" Christ is the central point of his Christian thoughts' (*In Christo Jesu* p. 80). See also a suggestive passage in Dean Robinson's *Ephesians* p. 23 ff.

136   THE EPISTLES TO THE THESSALONIANS

2. *Christ, the Christ.*   The Name *Christ* by itself is also comparatively rare, occurring four times altogether:

I. ii. 6 δυνάμενοι ἐν βάρει εἶναι ὡς Χριστοῦ ἀπόστολοι.
I. iii. 2 Τιμόθεον...διάκονον τοῦ θεοῦ ἐν τῷ εὐαγγελίῳ τοῦ χριστοῦ.
I. iv. 16 οἱ νεκροὶ ἐν Χριστῷ ἀναστήσονται πρῶτον.
II. iii. 5 ὁ δὲ κύριος κατευθύναι ὑμῶν τὰς καρδίας...εἰς τὴν ὑπομονὴν τοῦ χριστοῦ.

On two of these occasions the Name is accompanied by the def. art., and, as generally, when this is the case, is used in its official sense of 'the Christ,' 'the Messiah' (I. iii. 2, II. iii. 5: see notes *ad loca*)[1]. On the other hand in I. ii. 6 the anarthrous Χριστοῦ must have its full force as a Proper Name: it is as emissaries of 'Christ,' belonging to Him, and despatched on His service, that the Apostles might, had they so willed it, have claimed their full right of maintenance. Similarly in I. iv. 16 the phrase οἱ νεκροὶ ἐν Χριστῷ forms in reality a single idea 'the-dead-in-Christ.'

3. *Christ Jesus.*   The combination *Christ Jesus*, which denotes the Saviour alike in His official and personal character, and whose use in the N.T. is confined to St Paul[2], occurs twice, both times in the characteristic formula ἐν Χριστῷ Ἰησοῦ:

I. ii. 14 τῶν ἐκκλησιῶν τοῦ θεοῦ τῶν οὐσῶν ἐν τῇ Ἰουδαίᾳ ἐν Χριστῷ Ἰησοῦ.
I. v. 18 τοῦτο γὰρ θέλημα θεοῦ ἐν Χριστῷ Ἰησοῦ εἰς ὑμᾶς.

The early Christian formula Ἰησοῦς Χριστός, where the Names follow the historical order, and in which stress is laid on the religious significance Jesus has for believers, is not found in these Epp. at all.

4. *Lord, the Lord.*   We now come to *Lord*, or *the Lord*, the frequency of whose occurrence entitles it to be regarded as the distinctive Name of these Epp.[3]. It is found in all twenty-two times, eight times with, and four times without the article. And though the two usages cannot be so clearly distinguished

---

[1] On the history of the title 'the Christ' see Westcott *Epp. of St John* p. 189 ff., where it is shown that, unless in the disputed passage Dan. ix. 25 f., the name is not applied to the expected Divine King and Saviour of Israel in the O.T., but is so used in some of the later books of the Jews.

[2] Cf. Ac. xvii. 3, where, in accordance with AD, WH. read Χριστὸς Ἰησοῦς in the margin: also xviii. 5, 28 τὸν χριστὸν Ἰησοῦν.

[3] The history of the title 'the Lord' as a designation of Jesus is attended with much difficulty, and cannot be followed out here, but for the Jewish and Synoptic usage reference may be made to Dalman *Worte* p. 266 ff.

(E. Tr. p. 324 ff.), while the new import attaching to ὁ κύριος as a Divine title, in contrast with its pagan use, is well brought out by Deissmann in his *New Light on the N.T.* p. 79 ff. Whether St Paul himself intended it so or not, Deissmann thinks that his first readers can hardly have failed to find in the designation, as applied to Jesus, 'a tacit protest against other "Lords," or even against the "Lord," as the Roman emperor was beginning to be called' (p. 81). Cf. the insidious plea addressed to Polycarp on his way to trial: 'Τί γὰρ κακόν ἐστιν εἰπεῖν, Κύριε Καῖσαρ, καὶ θῦσαι καὶ διασώζεσθαι;' (Eus. *H.E.* iv. 15. 13).

as in the case of Χριστός and ὁ χριστός, the fact that almost two-thirds of the occurrences are anarthrous is sufficient to show how completely by this time the word had come to be recognized as a Proper Name[1]. The passages are as follows:

I. i. 6 μιμηταὶ ἡμῶν ἐγενήθητε καὶ τοῦ κυρίου.
    8 ἐξήχηται ὁ λόγος τοῦ κυρίου.
  iii. 8 ἐὰν ὑμεῖς στήκετε ἐν κυρίῳ.
   12 ὑμᾶς δὲ ὁ κύριος πλεονάσαι.
  iv. 6 διότι ἔκδικοϲ Κγ́ριοϲ περὶ πάντων τούτων.
   15 λέγομεν ἐν λόγῳ κυρίου.
    „ οἱ περιλειπόμενοι εἰς τὴν παρουσίαν τοῦ κυρίου.
   16 αὐτὸς ὁ κύριος ἐν κελεύσματι...καταβήσεται.
   17 εἰς ἀπάντησιν τοῦ κυρίου εἰς ἀέρα.
    „ οὕτως πάντοτε σὺν κυρίῳ ἐσόμεθα.
  v. 2 ἡμέρα Κυρίου ὡς κλέπτης...ἔρχεται.
   12 τοὺς...προϊσταμένους ὑμῶν ἐν κυρίῳ.
   27 ἐνορκίζω ὑμᾶς τὸν κύριον.
II. i. 9 ὄλεθρον αἰώνιον ἀπὸ προϲώπογ τογ κγρίογ.
  ii. 2 ὡς ὅτι ἐνέστηκεν ἡ ἡμέρα τοῦ κυρίου.
   13 ἀδελφοὶ Ἡγαπημένοι ὑπὸ Κγρίογ.
 iii. 1 προσεύχεσθε...ἵνα ὁ λόγος τοῦ κυρίου τρέχῃ.
   3 πιστὸς δέ ἐστιν ὁ κύριος.
   4 πεποίθαμεν δὲ ἐν κυρίῳ ἐφ' ὑμᾶς.
   5 ὁ δὲ κύριος κατευθύναι ὑμῶν τὰς καρδίας.
  16 αὐτὸς δὲ ὁ κύριος τῆς εἰρήνης.
   „ ὁ κύριος μετὰ πάντων ὑμῶν.

In some of these passages the Name may seem at first sight to refer to God rather than to Christ, as e.g. in the passages derived from the LXX. (I. iv. 6, II. i. 9, ii. 13), but as in the vastly preponderating number of instances it can only apply to the Son, it is better so to refer it throughout, in accordance with St Paul's general usage elsewhere[2].

When we do so, the varied connotations in which we find it used throw a flood of light upon the depth of meaning which thus early in the history of the Church had come to be read into the simple title. It stands no longer, as apparently it generally did for the disciples during the earthly lifetime of Jesus, for Rabbi or Rabboni, a title which from St John's interpretation they must have understood in a sense differing

---

[1] In addition to the passages cited above, the anarthrous κύριος with reference to Christ is used by St Paul in such passages as Rom. xiv. 6, xvi. 2, 1 Cor. vii. 22, x. 21, xvi. 10, 2 Cor. iii. 16 ff., Eph. ii. 21, &c. It is found as a title of address (κύριε) to a superhuman person in Rev. vii. 14, with which Swete (ad loc.) compares such passages from O.T. Apocalyptic as Dan. x. 16 f., Zech. iv. 5, 13. In the Κοινή, apart from its legal sense of 'guardian' (cf. Archiv iv. p. 78 ff.), κύριος is very common as a general title of respect in addressing officials, or near relatives, e.g. P.Leip. 110, 1 f. (iii.–iv./A.D.) Σαραπίω]ν τῇ κ[υ]ρίᾳ μου μητρί...24 f. τὴν κυρίαν μου ἀδελφὴν πολλὰ προσαγόρευε Ταῆσιν.

[2] Perhaps uniform usage, if we except quotations from the O.T., e.g. 2 Cor. vi. 17 f.: see Stanton Jewish and Christian Messiah p. 158 n.[7].

little from 'Master' (xx. 16, cf. Mt. xxiii. 8, xxvi. 25, 49, Mk. x. 51). But, in accordance with a tendency of which we find clear traces very shortly after the Resurrection (Ac. ii. 36 κύριον αὐτὸν καὶ χριστὸν ἐποίησεν ὁ θεός, τοῦτον τὸν Ἰησοῦν ὃν ὑμεῖς ἐσταυρώσατε), it is now employed as a brief and comprehensive description of Jesus as the Divine Lord, risen, glorified, and exalted[1].

This is seen most clearly in the use of the title in connexion with the actual Parousia of the Lord and the events associated with it (I. iv. 15 ff., v. 2, II. ii. 2). But it comes out also in the other references to which the foregoing passages bear witness.

Thus it is 'the word' of the 'Lord' which the Apostles find to be sounding forth in every place (I. i. 8, cf. II. iii. 1), and to which they look as embodying a direct communication to themselves (I. iv. 15 note). It is 'in the Lord,' in whom their ideal 'Christian' life is actually lived out[2], that the Thessalonians are encouraged to stand firm (I. iii. 8, cf. II. iii. 3 f.), and to the same 'Lord' that the Apostles pray to perfect in their converts the graces (I. iii. 12, II. iii. 5, 16), of which He Himself is the perfect example.

Nothing indeed can be more significant of the hold which this aspect of Christ has taken of St Paul than that when calling upon the Thessalonians to be 'imitators' of himself and of his fellow-writers, he does not add, as we might have expected, 'and of Jesus,' or even 'and of the Christ,' but 'and of the Lord' (I. i. 6), thereby pointing not merely to the supreme pattern to be copied, but to the living power in which alone this 'imitation' could be accomplished, and man's highest end successfully reached[3].

How completely however the Apostle recognized that the earthly 'Jesus' and the heavenly 'Lord' were one and the same is proved by the next combination that meets us.

5. *Lord Jesus.*

That combination is the *Lord Jesus*, and the first occasion on which it is used throws into striking relief at once the Divine glory and the human character of Him to whom it refers:

I. ii. 15 τῶν καὶ τὸν κύριον ἀποκτεινάντων Ἰησοῦν.

He whom the Jews had slain was not only 'the Lord'—'Him whom

---

[1] According to Kennedy *E.G.T.* ad Phil. ii. 6: 'This position of Κύριος is the reward and crowning-point of the whole process of His voluntary Humiliation.' And later (*ad* ii. 11) the same writer well remarks: 'The term "Lord" has become one of the most lifeless words in the Christian vocabulary. To enter into its meaning and give it practical effect would be to recreate, in great measure, the atmosphere of the Apostolic Age.'

[2] 'The *Christ* of the privileged position is the *Lord* of the holy life: if in Christ we are in heaven, in the Lord we must live on earth' (Robinson *Eph.* p. 72).

[3] 'Paul craved in a perfect Example one who was not only in the graces of human character all that man should be, but who had attained to that destiny for which man was made. This he found in the Christ in whom Man had overcome death, and been crowned with everlasting life' (Somerville *St Paul's Conception of Christ* p. 291).

THE DIVINE NAMES IN THE EPISTLES 139

they were bound to serve' (Jowett)—He was moreover 'Jesus,' their Saviour. And so, from another point of view, when in their Second Ep. the Apostles refer to the revelation in and through which God's righteous ἀνταπόδοσις will be accomplished, it is pointedly described as:

II. i. 7 ἐν τῇ ἀποκαλύψει τοῦ κυρίου Ἰησοῦ ἀπ' οὐρανοῦ.

The other passages in which the same combination occurs, and which are equally deserving of study, are:

I. ii. 19 τίς γὰρ ἡμῶν ἐλπὶς...ἔμπροσθεν τοῦ κυρίου ἡμῶν Ἰησοῦ ἐν τῇ αὐτοῦ παρουσίᾳ;
iii. 11 ὁ κύριος ἡμῶν Ἰησοῦς κατευθύναι τὴν ὁδὸν ἡμῶν.
13 ἐν τῇ παρουσίᾳ τοῦ κυρίου ἡμῶν Ἰησοῦ.
iv. 1 παρακαλοῦμεν ἐν κυρίῳ Ἰησοῦ.
2 τίνας παραγγελίας ἐδώκαμεν ὑμῖν διὰ τοῦ κυρίου Ἰησοῦ.
II. i. 8 τῷ εὐαγγελίῳ τοῦ κυρίου ἡμῶν Ἰησοῦ.
12 ὅπως ἐνδοξασθῇ τὸ ὄνομα τοῦ κυρίου ἡμῶν Ἰησοῦ ἐν ὑμῖν.
ii. 8 ὁ ἄνομος, ὃν ὁ κύριος [Ἰησοῦς] ἀνελεῖ.

Apart from any special considerations which may have led to the use of this compound Name in the above passages, we cannot forget that in itself it formed the shortest and simplest statement of the Christian creed (Ac. xvi. 31, Rom. x. 9)—a statement moreover 'so completely in defiance of the accepted dogma about the Christ, so revolutionary in its effects on the character of the believer, that it was viewed as springing from Divine inspiration. "No man," said Paul in writing to the Corinthians, "can say that Jesus is Lord, but by the Holy Spirit" (1 Cor. xii. 3)[1].'

On the other hand, this makes the comparative rarity of the title in the Pauline Epistles, other than those to the Thessalonians, all the more remarkable. In the Ep. to the Galatians it is not found at all. In the relatively much longer Epp. to the Corinthians it occurs only seven times (1 Cor. v. 4 (bis), 5, xi. 23, xii. 3, 2 Cor. iv. 14, xi. 31), while only a single instance of its use can be produced from each of the Epp. to the Ephesians (i. 15), Philippians (ii. 19), and Colossians (iii. 17), the explanation probably being a growing preference on St Paul's part for the still more comprehensive and expressive combination, the *Lord Jesus Christ*[2].

Already, indeed, in our Epp. we find this full Name completely established, occurring as it does five times in the First and no less than nine times in the short Second Epistle.

6. Lord Jesus Christ.

---

[1] Somerville op. cit. p. 12 f. For the idea of the suffering Messiah as not pre-Christian see Stanton op. cit. p. 122 ff.

[2] The combination κύριος χριστός or χριστὸς κύριος is not found in the Pauline Epp.: to the Apostle it would have been a pleonasm. The latter form is however found in Lk. ii. 11, and in 1 Pet. iii. 15 we read κύριον δὲ τὸν Χριστὸν ἁγιάσατε ἐν ταῖς καρδίαις ὑμῶν, the words being a quotation from Isa. viii. 13 with τὸν Χριστόν substituted for the original αὐτόν. Cf. also χριστὸς Κύριος used of an earthly king in Lam. iv. 20, and the description of the Messianic King in Pss. Sol. xvii. 36 καὶ βασιλεὺς αὐτῶν χριστὸς κύριος, and in xviii. 8 χριστοῦ κυρίου—all passages, however, where we may have a mistranslation of the Heb. מְשִׁיחַ יְהוָה, 'the Lord's anointed.'

140   THE EPISTLES TO THE THESSALONIANS

I. i. 1, II. i. 1 τῇ ἐκκλησίᾳ Θεσσαλονικέων ἐν...κυρίῳ Ἰησοῦ Χριστοῦ.
  3 μνημονεύοντες...τῆς ὑπομονῆς τῆς ἐλπίδος τοῦ κυρίου ἡμῶν Ἰησοῦ Χριστοῦ.
  v. 9 εἰς περιποίησιν σωτηρίας διὰ τοῦ κυρίου ἡμῶν Ἰησοῦ [Χριστοῦ]: cf. II. ii. 14.
  23 ἐν τῇ παρουσίᾳ τοῦ κυρίου ἡμῶν Ἰησοῦ Χριστοῦ: cf. II. ii. 1.
  28, II. iii. 18 ἡ χάρις τοῦ κυρίου ἡμῶν Ἰησοῦ Χριστοῦ μεθ' (μετὰ πάντων) ὑμῶν.
II. i. 2 χάρις ὑμῖν καὶ εἰρήνη ἀπὸ...κυρίου Ἰησοῦ Χριστοῦ.
  12 κατὰ τὴν χάριν...κυρίου Ἰησοῦ Χριστοῦ.
  ii. 16 αὐτὸς δὲ ὁ κύριος ἡμῶν Ἰησοῦς Χριστός.
  iii. 6 παραγγέλλομεν...ἐν ὀνόματι τοῦ κυρίου Ἰησοῦ Χριστοῦ.
  12 παρακαλοῦμεν ἐν κυρίῳ Ἰησοῦ Χριστῷ.

None of these passages call for special remark beyond the evidence which they afford of the appropriateness of the full Name with all its associations for Addresses, Benedictions, and solemn Charges of any kind— a usage which the testimony of the later Epp. abundantly confirms[1].

---

[1] There is a useful paper on 'The Chief Pauline Names for Christ' with Tables by F. Herbert Stead in *Exp.* III. vii. p. 386 ff. Cf. also von Soden's famous Essay on *Das Interesse des apostolischen Zeitalters an der evangelischen Geschichte* (in *Theologische Abhandlungen* Carl von Weizsäcker gewidmet) p. 118 f.

NOTE E.

On the history of εὐαγγέλιον, εὐαγγελίζομαι.

'Euāgeliō (that we cal the gospel) is a greke worde, & signyfyth good, mery, glad and ioyfull tydinge, that maketh a mannes hert glad, and maketh hym synge, daunce, and leepe for ioye.'
Tindale (after Luther) *Prologue to N.T.*, 1525.

Εὐαγγέλιον and εὐαγγελίζομαι are two of the great words of the Christian vocabulary, and in view of the facts that the former occurs eight times in our Epistles, forming indeed the key-word of one of their most important sections (I. ii. 1—12), and that the latter is found here (I. iii. 6), and nowhere else in the Pauline Epistles, in its earlier or more general sense, a brief Note may be devoted to recalling one or two facts in their history.

The subst. εὐαγγέλιον, which is very rare in the singular in classical Gk.[1], means originally the *reward* for good tidings (Hom. *Od.* xiv. 152, 166), and is used with greater frequency in the plural in the sense of *thank-offerings* made on behalf of such tidings, e.g. Aristoph. *Eq.* 654 εὐαγγέλια θύειν, Xen. *Hell.* iv. 3. 14 ἐβουθύτει ὡς εὐαγγέλια; cf. *O.G.I.S.* 4, 42 f. εὐαγγέλια κ. σωτήρια ἔ[θ]υσε.

Usage in classical Gk.

Afterwards in later Gk. it came to be extended to the *good tidings* themselves, as in Lucian *Asin.* 26, and on several occasions in Plutarch.

and later Gk.

In the LXX. it is found only once, where it reverts to its original Homeric meaning (2 Regn. iv. 10 ᾧ ἔδει με δοῦναι εὐαγγέλια)[2], while the verb, apart from the passages in which it is specially associated with good news (of victory 1 Regn. xxxi. 9, of the birth of a son Jer. xx. 15), is also found on several occasions with reference to tidings of any kind (2 Regn. xviii. 19, 20 (*bis*), 26), following in this the Heb. בִּשֵּׂר, which in 1 Sam. iv. 17 is actually used of mournful tidings (cf. Dalman *Worte* p. 84 (Engl. Tr. p. 103))[3].

The LXX.

---

[1] It would appear to have dropped altogether out of general use in the Κοινή. At least I have been able to find no instance of it in the papyrus collections to which I have access. In his art. on the title Εὐαγγελιστής in *Z.N.T.W.* i. p. 336 ff. A. Dieterich cites an inscription from Asia Minor in which, with reference to the birthday of the σωτήρ Augustus, it is said— ἦρξεν δὲ τῷ κόσμῳ τῶν δι' αὐτὸν εὐαν- γελ[ίων] (*O. G. I. S.* 458, 40).

[2] In 2 Regn. xviii. 22, 25 we should probably read εὐαγγελία (not εὐαγγέλια), in view of v. 20 ἀνὴρ εὐαγγελίας.

[3] It is a curious fact, in view of its later history, that εὐαγγελίζω should be the word used by Agrippina to convey to Nero the 'good news' (!) that his attempt upon her life had failed—καὶ ὅτι σώζοιτο εὐηγγέλικε δῆθεν αὐτῷ (Dion Cass. lxi. 13).

142 THE EPISTLES TO THE THESSALONIANS

In addition to these passages, however, εὐαγγελίζομαι is used in the Psalms to herald the righteousness and salvation of God, as in Ps. xxxix. (xl.) 10 εὐηγγελισάμην δικαιοσύνην, a phrase which Keble renders—

Thy righteousness aloud,
Good tidings of great joy I tell.

Cf. also Ps. xcv. (xcvi.) 2 εὐαγγελίζεσθε...τὸ σωτήριον αὐτοῦ. And more especially in Deutero-Isaiah we find it in contexts which pave the way for its full Christian meaning. Thus in Isa. xl. 9 the prophet summons a messenger to ascend a high mountain, and proclaim to Sion and Jerusalem the glad tidings of God's appearing (ἐπ' ὄρος ὑψηλὸν ἀνάβηθι, ὁ εὐαγγελιζόμενος Σείων...ὁ εὐαγγελιζόμενος Ἱερουσαλήμ)[1], and similarly in lii. 7 (cf. Nah. i. 15 (ii. 1)) we are called upon to admire the swift-footed messengers, as they carry their joyful message over the mountains of Judah and Jerusalem (ὡς πόδες εὐαγγελιζομένου ἀκοὴν εἰρήνης, ὡς εὐαγγελιζόμενος ἀγαθά). And still more pointedly this same 'evangelic' office is claimed by the servant of the Lord himself—Πνεῦμα Κυρίου ἐπ' ἐμέ, οὗ εἵνεκεν ἔχρισέν με εὐαγγελίσασθαι πτωχοῖς (lxi. 1).

The Gospels. This last passage indeed from our Lord's own use of it in Lk. iv. 18 f. may be said to have set the stamp upon εὐαγγελίζομαι as the most fitting term to describe the true character of the message of the new Messianic King. And it is in special relation to that message accordingly that we find it repeatedly used by St Luke (viii. 1, ix. 6 &c.).

It can only be an accident, therefore, that he finds no occasion to use the corresponding subst. in his Gospel (but cf. Ac. xv. 7 speech of Peter, xx. 24 speech of Paul), as do both St Mark and St Matthew.

St Mark's usage in this respect is very instructive, as apart from i. 1 where we seem to have a trace of εὐαγγέλιον in its later meaning of a 'record' of the Lord's life and words (see below), the word is used in v. 14 to draw attention to the nature of the proclamation of Jesus (κηρύσσων τὸ εὐαγγέλιον τοῦ θεοῦ), as contrasted with the proclamation of His forerunner (v. 4 κηρύσσων βάπτισμα μετανοίας), and again in v. 15 to indicate the 'nucleus' of Christian teaching embodied in this proclamation (πιστεύετε ἐν τῷ εὐαγγελίῳ: see Swete's notes ad loca). And in the same way St Matthew employs it with reference to the glad news of the 'kingdom' in which the Messianic hopes and blessings are centred and fulfilled (iv. 23, ix. 35, xxiv. 14, cf. xxvi. 13).

Other N.T. writings. It is all the more surprising, therefore, that in the case of the other writers of the N.T., with the exception of St Paul, the use of the two words is by no means so common as we might have expected. Neither St James in his Epistle, nor St John in his Gospel and Epistles, uses either term, though the latter in the Apocalypse employs the subst. once (xiv. 6), and the verb in the active twice (x. 7, xiv. 6)[2]. St Peter

---

[1] In the original Heb. it is Sion and Jerusalem who act as 'evangelists': cf. **Aq. Sm. Th.** εὐαγγελιζομένη Σιών. For an echo of the LXX. rendering see Pss. Sol. xi. 2 κηρύξατε ἐν Ἱερουσαλὴμ φωνὴν εὐαγγελιζομένου, ὅτι ἠλέησεν ὁ θεὸς Ἰσραὴλ ἐν τῇ ἐπισκοπῇ αὐτῶν.

[2] For the rare active εὐαγγελίζω,

ON ΕΥΑΓΓΕΛΙΟΝ, ΕΥΑΓΓΕΛΙΖΟΜΑΙ 143

in his First Epistle has the subst. once (iv. 17), and the verb three times (i. 12, 25, iv. 6): and in the Epistle to the Hebrews the verb occurs twice (iv. 2, 6).

In the case of St Paul, however, both words occur with a frequency, St Paul. which shows how strongly he had been attracted by them, as the most fitting terms to describe the message with which he had been entrusted: and it is to his influence accordingly that we must look for the prominence which they and their equivalents have since gained in the language of Christendom[1].

Thus the subst. εὐαγγέλιον is found no less than sixty times in his Epistles, occurring in all except the Epistle to Titus: while the verb, apart from its exceptional usage in 1 Thess. iii. 6, is found twenty times (once in a quotation from the LXX.) in its distinctive Christian sense.

Naturally in so widely extended a list of examples, the two words are used with a considerable variety of application, as when the subst. is used absolutely as a convenient summary of the whole contents of the Christian message (Rom. x. 16 &c.), or defined more particularly in its relation to God (1 Thess. ii. 2 &c.), or to Christ (1 Thess. iii. 2 &c.), or to the Apostle himself as entrusted with its proclamation (1 Thess. i. 5, 2 Thess. ii. 14 &c.). In another important set of passages St Paul draws attention to characteristic aspects of this message by such phrases as ἡ ἀλήθεια τ. εὐαγγελίου (Gal. ii. 14), or ἡ πίστις τ. εὐαγγελίου (Phil. i. 27).

Of the later usage of εὐαγγέλιον to denote the 'book' in which Ecclesi-Christ's teaching is recorded, as distinguished from that teaching in astical itself, there is no instance in the N.T., unless perhaps in Mk. i. 1 ἀρχὴ usage. τ. εὐαγγελίου Ἰησοῦ Χριστοῦ (cf. Hos. i. 2 ἀρχὴ λόγου Κυρίου ἐν Ὡσῆε)[2], and we must look for the earliest witnesses in this direction to such passages as Didache viii. 2 ὡς ἐκέλευσεν ὁ Κύριος ἐν τῷ εὐαγγελίῳ αὐτοῦ, xv. 4 ὡς ἔχετε ἐν τῷ εὐαγγελίῳ τοῦ Κυρίου ἡμῶν, where a written Gospel (apparently St Matthew's from the nature of the accompanying citations) seems to

which is found only in later Gk., see the passage already cited from Dion Cassius, and cf. P.Amh. 2, 16 (a Christian hymn, iv./A.D.) παισὶν δ' [ε]ὐαγγέλιζε λέγων, Πτωχοὶ βασιλείαν.... Note also the interesting use of the adj. with reference to the Lord's Prayer in the Christian amulet B.G.U. 954, 13 ff. (vi./A.D.) ὅπως ὑγιανῶ...εἰπεῖν τὴν εὐαγγελικὴν (αγγελικην Pap.) εὐχὴν ⁿᵘ [οὕτως? Πάτερ ἡμῶν...]: cf. Wilcken Archiv i. p. 431 ff.

[1] The ordinary Engl. rendering 'gospel' is the modern form of the Anglo-Saxon 'godspell' = 'God (i.e. Christ) story,' as may be seen in King Alfred's translation of 2 Cor. iv. 4 'onlihtnes Crīstes godspelles' (in his version of Bede's Eccl. Hist. 122), and in Aelfric's Homily on Mt. xi. 4 ff. 'and ðearfan bodiað godspel.' For other examples of this use of the word see A. S. Cook Biblical Quotations in Old English Writers (1898) Index s.v. 'godspell.' According to Skeat (Concise Etym. Dict., 1901) the A.S. 'godspell' was originally 'good spell,' a tr. of εὐαγγέλιον.

[2] In Rev. xiv. 16 (ἄλλον ἄγγελον... ἔχοντα εὐαγγέλιον αἰώνιον εὐαγγελίσαι), which is also cited in this connexion, 'St John has in view not the Gospel as a whole, but rather a gospel which is a particular aspect of it, the gospel of the Parousia and the consummation which the Parousia will bring' (Swete ad loc.).

144   THE EPISTLES TO THE THESSALONIANS

be clearly intended, or Ign. *Philad.* v. προσφυγὼν τῷ εὐαγγελίῳ ὡς σαρκὶ Ἰησοῦ καὶ τοῖς ἀποστόλοις ὡς πρεσβυτερίῳ ἐκκλησίας, where Ignatius distinguishes between two classes of writings included in our N.T.—τὸ εὐαγγέλιον the Gospel or Gospels, and οἱ ἀπόστολοι the Apostolic Epistles[1]. The plural εὐαγγέλια with direct reference to our four canonical Gospels is first found in the well-known passage in Just. M. *Apol.* i. 66 οἱ γὰρ ἀπόστολοι ἐν τοῖς γενομένοις ὑπ' αὐτῶν ἀπομνημονεύμασιν, ἃ καλεῖται εὐαγγέλια. In the same way the title εὐαγγελιστής, which in the N.T. describes the man who brought the first news of the Gospel-message to any new region (Ac. xxi. 8, Eph. iv. 11, 2 Tim. iv. 5; cf. Eus. *H. E.* v. 10. 2 of Pantaenus), was afterwards applied to the 'writer' of a 'Gospel,' as by Hippolytus and Origen[2].

[1] For a different interpretation of the passage, according to which τὸ εὐαγγέλιον retains its original sense of 'the teaching,' not 'the book,' see Bishop Lightfoot's note *ad loc.*

[2] Cf. *Encycl. Bibl. s.v.* 'Evangelist,' and on the heathen use of the title see especially Dieterich's art. in *Z.N.T.W.*

i. p. 336 ff. Curtius (*Ges. Abhandlungen* i. p. 532 f.) recalls, as illustrating the Hellenistic practice of laying special stress on the first proclamation of a happy discovery, that the shepherd Pixodaros, who accidentally found the stone-bridge at Ephesus, received the heroic name Euangelos (Vitruv. x. 7).

NOTE F.

Παρουσία. Ἐπιφάνεια. Ἀποκάλυψις.

The three words παρουσία, ἐπιφάνεια, ἀποκάλυψις are used in our Epistles with reference to the return of the glorified Lord. All have interesting histories. And it may be well briefly to recall these, in order to determine as exactly as possible the different shades of meaning between them.

i. Παρογcίa.

In classical Gk. the word παρουσία denotes generally *presence*, e.g. Classical Aesch. *Pers.* 171 ὄμμα γὰρ δόμων νομίζω δεσπότου παρουσίαν, Thuc. vi. 86 Gk. πόλει δὲ μείζονι τῆς ἡμετέρας παρουσίας (=ἡμῶν τῶν παρόντων), but it is also found in the closely-related sense of *arrival*, e.g. Eur. *Alc.* 209 ἀλλ᾽ εἶμι καὶ τὴν σὴν ἀγγελῶ παρουσίαν, Thuc. i. 128 Βυζάντιον γὰρ ἑλὼν τῇ προτέρᾳ παρουσίᾳ. The same usage may also be illustrated from later Gk. Thus in Polyb. Later Gk. iii. 41. 1 certain events are summarized as having taken place from the beginning of the war ἕως εἰς τὴν Ἀννίβου παρουσίαν 'until the arrival of Hannibal,' and further on in the same chap. (8) Publius, when informed of the arrival of the enemy (παρεῖναι τοὺς ὑπεναντίους) is said not to have believed it διὰ τὸ τάχος τῆς παρουσίας. In xviii. 31. 4, on the other hand, the reference is rather to a coming that has not yet taken place, C. Cornelius counselling Philip to send ambassadors to Rome ἵνα μὴ δοκῇ τοῖς καιροῖς ἐφεδρεύων ἀποκαραδοκεῖν τὴν Ἀντιόχου παρουσίαν[1].

With this general usage of the word may be compared such a passage The from the Κοινή as P.Oxy. 486, 15 (ii./A.D.), where a certain Dionysia, who Papyri. is engaged in a lawsuit, petitions for leave to return home as the care of her property demands her 'presence' (χρῄζει μου τῆς παρουσία[ς]): cf. P.Par. 45, 5 (ii./B.C.) κὰ αὐτὸς παρέσομαι ταχύ, 46, 18 (ii./B.C.) παραχρῆμα παρέσομαι πρὸς σέ.

But along with this it is important to notice that παρουσία occurs frequently in the papyri as a kind of *terminus technicus* with reference to the 'visit' of the king, or some other official. Thus in P.Petr. II. 39 (e), 18 (iii./B.C.), as emended (see note on I. ii. 19), it is used of a royal visit by a Ptolemy to a district which was mulcted to provide a

---

[1] Cf. the verb in Diod. Sic. xvii. 8 περὶ ταῦτα δ᾽ ὄντος αὐτοῦ, παρῆσάν τινες ἀπαγγέλλοντες πολλοὺς τῶν Ἑλλήνων νεωτερίζειν, 'there came some that told him'—a passage that is of significance for Lk. xiii. 1 (Field *Notes* p. 65).

M. THESS. 10

146   THE EPISTLES TO THE THESSALONIANS

στέφανος, and similarly in P.Tebt. 48, 13 f. (ii./B.C.) we hear of an extra levy of wheat imposed πρὸς τὴν τοῦ βασιλέως παρουσίαν: see also P.Tebt. 116 (ii./B.C.), an account including items incurred ἐν το(ῖς) βα(σιλέως) παρουσίας (57), and P.Grenf. II. 14 (b), 2 (iii./B.C.) announcing preparations ἐπὶ τὴν παρουσίαν τὴν Χρυσίππου, and cf. Dittenberger *Sylloge*² 226, 84 ff. (iii./B.C.) τῶν δὲ ἀρχόντων συναγαγόντων ἐκλησίαν καὶ τήν τε παρουσίαν ἐμφανισάντων τοῦ βασιλέως¹.

Other instances might easily be given, but these are sufficient to suggest an interesting comparison with the N.T. usage of the word to denote the Parousia of their King or Lord for which His people are to make ready. And we fall back upon them the more gladly because for this particular sense of the word the Jewish sacred writings give us little help.

Greek O.T.

In the LXX. παρουσία is found only once as a variant for πορεία (BS) in the A text of 2 Esdr. xii. 6 (= Neh. ii. 6) ἕως πότε ἔσται ἡ παρουσία σου, and the same untechnical sense marks its few occurrences in the Apocrypha, as when in Judith x. 18 the report is spread of the 'arrival' or 'presence' of Judith (ἡ παρουσία αὐτῆς) in the camp of Holofernes, or as when Judas, on hearing of the inroad of Nicanor, communicates to his followers τὴν παρουσίαν τοῦ στρατοπέδου (2 Macc. viii. 12; cf. 2 Macc. xv. 21, 3 Macc. iii. 17).

Jewish apocalyptic writings.

Nor is the case substantially different in the later apocalyptic writings. It is true that in *Apoc. Bar.* xxx. 1 'And it will come to pass after these things, when the time of the advent of the Messiah is fulfilled, and He will return in glory,' Dr Charles draws attention to the fact that the word translated 'advent' (ܡܐܬܝܬܐ) was an ordinary rendering of παρουσία, which may therefore have been found in the Gk. version of the book. And with this there may be compared two passages in the *Test. xii. patr.* in the first of which the word is used with reference to God (Jud. xxii. 3 ἕως παρουσίας τοῦ θεοῦ τῆς δικαιοσύνης), and in the second with reference to John Hyrcanus regarded as the prophet of the Highest, i.e. the Messiah (Lev. viii. 15 ἡ δὲ παρουσία αὐτοῦ ἀγαπητή ἐστιν ὡς προφήτης). But these instances—aud I have not been able to discover any others²— are hardly sufficient in themselves to suggest an established use of the term with reference to the Messiah in Jewish writers³.

---

¹ As showing the burden that these and similar 'visits' often imposed, the petition of the priests of Isis at Philae may be recalled in which they complain that the officials resorting to the temple ἀναγκάζουσι ἡμᾶς παρουσίας αὐτοῖς ποιεῖσθαι οὐχ ἑκόντας (*C.I.G.* iii. 4896 (ii./B.C.)): see further Wilcken *Ostraka* i. p. 274 ff., and for an additional ex. of the word cf. Wilcken *Ostr.* 1372 (i./A.D.) πυροῦ...οὗ ἔλαβες ἀπὸ θησαυροῦ εἰς τὴν παρουσίαν Φλάκος ἡγήμων (for Φλάκκου ἡγεμόνος).

² In the interesting passage in *Test. Abraham* § xiii. A where Abel is appointed judge μέχρι τῆς μεγάλης καὶ ἐνδόξου αὐτοῦ [*sc.* θεοῦ] παρουσίας, we read also of a δευτέρα παρουσία when all souls κριθήσονται ὑπὸ τῶν δώδεκα φυλῶν τοῦ Ἰσραήλ, but a Christian interpolator has evidently been at work here (see James *The Testament of Abraham* p. 50, in *Texts and Studies* ii. 2).

³ Cf. Teichmann *Paul. Vorstellungen von Auferstehung u. Gericht*

ΠΑΡΟΥΣΙΑ. ΕΠΙΦΑΝΕΙΑ. ΑΠΟΚΑΛΥΨΙC 147

In these circumstances it would seem as if for the definite N.T. The usage of the term to describe the coming of the glorified Christ, we Gospels. must look directly to the impression produced upon His disciples' minds by the words of the Lord Himself. For though neither in St Mark nor in St Luke is He represented as having used the term, it is found four times in the great eschatological discourse in Matt. xxiv. (vv. 3, 27, 37, 39). And without discounting the possibility of the hand of a later redactor, there is after all no reason why the first Evangelist should not on this occasion supply the word, which most faithfully represents the original language of Jesus.

If so, we have at once a full and satisfactory explanation of the fact The N.T. that the term παρουσία is definitely employed as a *term. techn.* by all the Epistles. Apostolic writers. St James uses it twice in this sense (v. 7, 8), St Peter— or whoever wrote the Second Epistle of that name—thrice (2 Pet. i. 16, iii. 4, 12), St John once (1 Jo. ii. 28), while by St Paul, apart from several occurrences with the more general meaning of 'presence' as opposed to 'absence' (1 Cor. xvi. 17, 2 Cor. vii. 6 f., Phil. i. 26, ii. 12; cf. 2 Cor. x. 10), the word is used seven times of the 'Parousia' of the Lord Jesus (1 Thess. ii. 19, iii. 13, iv. 15, v. 23, 2 Thess. ii. 1, 8, 1 Cor. xv. 23), and once of its mocking counterpart (2 Thess. ii. 9). And though in all these passages the primary reference is eschatological, to a definite coming that had not yet been fully manifested, it is impossible not to notice how appropriate the word was to emphasize the nearness and the certainty of that 'coming.' So near was it that it was not so much a 'coming' as already a 'presence' of the Lord with His people, a *permanent* presence moreover, which not even absence from sight for a little while could really interrupt, and which, when fully re-established, would last for ever[1].

To complete our survey of the history of the word it may be added Ecclesi-that this technical use of the term has become firmly established in astical the ecclesiastical writers, though by them it is extended also to the writers. First Coming of the Lord, a use which is never found in the N.T. Thus Ignatius *Philad.* ix. writes ἐξαίρετον δέ τι ἔχει τὸ εὐαγγέλιον, τὴν παρουσίαν τοῦ σωτῆρος ἡμῶν Ἰησοῦ Χριστοῦ, τὸ πάθος, αὐτὴν τὴν ἀνάστασιν, where the position of παρουσίαν shows that the Incarnation must be intended, while in Justin Martyr the teaching regarding the double Parousia is fully developed: see *Dial.* 14 (Otto II. 32 D), 49 (II. 158 B), and especially 31 (II. 98 E) δύο παρουσίας αὐτοῦ γενήσεσθαι ἐξηγησάμην, μίαν μὲν

---

p. 11 n.[1]. According to Volz *Jüd. Eschat.* p. 189, the *term. techn.* for the coming of God on the Great Day seems rather to have been ἐπισκοπή.

[1] Cf. Ewald *Die drei ersten Evangelien* p. 333 (though it should be noted that the actual expression *Shekinah* never occurs in the O.T.): 'The παρουσία Χριστοῦ perfectly corresponds with the שְׁכִינָה of God in the O.T.—the permanent dwelling

of the King, where His people ever behold Him, and are ever shielded by Him. During the present imperfect state He is not so actually and fully present as His people hope and long for;...even when the expression more immediately denotes *the advent*, it still always includes the idea of *a permanent dwelling from that coming onwards*' (quoted by Cremer p. 238).

10—2

148   THE EPISTLES TO THE THESSALONIANS

ἐν ᾗ ἐξεκεντήθη ὑφ᾽ ὑμῶν, δευτέραν δὲ ὅτε ἐπιγνώσεσθε εἰς ὃν ἐξεκεντήσατε. Cf. also Tertull. *Apol.* 21, Clem. *Recogn.* i. 49, 69.

ii. 'Επιφάνεια.

Later Gk. The subst. ἐπιφάνεια is not found at all in classical, but is frequent in later Gk. to denote any sudden appearance or manifestation (e.g. of the dawn Polyb. iii. 94. 3, of the enemy i. 54. 2), and is used more particularly with reference to the intervention of the higher powers on behalf of their worshippers. Thus in Diodorus Siculus we read of the honours due to Isis διὰ τὴν ἐν ταῖς θεραπείαις ἐπιφάνειαν (i. 25), and in Dion. Hal. *Antt.* ii. 68. 1 it is declared to be a worthy act τὴν ἐπιφάνειαν ἱστορῆσαι τῆς θεᾶς, ἣν ἐπεδείξατο ταῖς ἀδίκως ἐγκληθείσαις παρθένοις.

The Inscriptions. A similar use is found in the inscriptions where the word is employed not only of divine assistance (e.g. *O.G.I.S.* 331, 52 τὰς ἐξ αὐτοῦ [τοῦ Διὸς τοῦ Σαβαζίου] γενομένας ἐπιφανείας), but is extended in characteristic fashion to the accession of a Roman Emperor as in *Inscriptions of Cos* 391 [ἐ]νιαυτοῦ πρώτου τᾶς [Γαΐ]ου Καίσαρος...ἐπιφανείας. In Magn. 157 c, 6 the predicate of ἐμφανέστατος [θεός] is bestowed on Claudius[1].

Greek O.T. In the canonical books of the LXX. the word is found only three times, in passages (2 Regn. vii. 23, Esth. v. 1, Amos v. 2) none of which throws much light on its special meaning. But in 2 and 3 Maccabees it occurs several times with reference to God's supernatural interpositions τὰς ἐξ οὐρανοῦ γενομένας ἐπιφανείας (2 Macc. ii. 21) on behalf of His people. Thus in 2 Macc. iii. 24, on the appearance of Heliodorus to confiscate the money in the Treasury, 'the Sovereign of spirits and of all authority caused a great manifestation (ἐπιφανίαν μεγάλην),' so that all who had presumed to come in with him were stricken with fear; and in xiv. 15 the Jews are represented as making solemn supplication to Him Who, alway 'making manifest His presence, upholdeth them that are His own portion' (μετ᾽ ἐπιφανείας ἀντιλαμβανόμενον τῆς ἑαυτοῦ μερίδος): cf. also 2 Macc. xii. 22, 3 Macc. ii. 9, v. 8, 51. In 2 Macc. v. 4 the word is used of an apparition announcing misfortune[2].

With this use of the subst. there should also be compared the fre-

---

[1] See further Thieme *Die Inschriften von Magnesia* p. 34 ff. Moulton (*Proleg.* p. 102 n.[3]) has pointed out that ἐπιφανής as the regular appellation of Ptolemy V. can no longer be translated 'illustrious,' but is = 'manifest,' much in the sense of the Sanskrit *Avatar*; cf. *O.G.I.S.* 90, 6 (Rosetta stone) θεοῦ 'Επιφανοῦς Εὐχαρίστου with Dittenberger's note, where a number of parallel passages are cited. See also Schürer[3] i. p. 192 f.

[2] In his valuable note on the use of ἐπιφάνεια with reference to God in the *Journal of Biblical Literature and Exegesis* i. p. 16 ff. (reprinted in *Critical Essays* (Boston, 1888) p. 454 ff.), Prof. Ezra Abbot draws attention to the instructive example from the Additions to Esther Text B vii. 6 (Fritzsche *Lib. Apocr. Vet. Test.* p. 71) where the sun and light of Mordecai's dream are said to represent ἐπιφάνια τοῦ θεοῦ in the deliverance of Jews. Similar instances of the word are also quoted from Josephus, as when in connexion with the dividing of the waters of the Red Sea Moses is described as ὁρῶν τὴν ἐπιφάνειαν τοῦ θεοῦ (*Antt.* II. 339 (xvi. 2)).

ΠΑΡΟΥΣΙΑ. ΕΠΙΦΑΝΕΙΑ. ΑΠΟΚΑΛΥΨΙΣ 149

quent use of the verb in the Psalms to denote God's making His face to shine upon His people, e.g. Ps. xxx. (xxxi.) 17, cxvii. (cxviii.) 27; while the corresponding adj. ἐπιφανής is applied by the LXX. translators to the great day of the Lord in Joel ii. 31 (iii. 4), Hab. i. 7, Mal. i. 14 (cf. Judg. xiii. 6 A) evidently in the sense of 'manifest' of all, through a misunderstanding on their part of the original Hebrew נוֹרָא, 'terrible.'

In the N.T. ἐπιφάνεια is used only by St Paul, and, with the exception of 2 Thess. ii. 8, only in the Pastoral Epp. (1 Tim. vi. 14, 2 Tim. i. 10, iv. 1, 8, Tit. ii. 13). In all these passages it is rendered 'appearing,' both in A.V. and R.V., and except in 2 Tim. i. 10 (cf. Tit. ii. 11, iii. 4 ἐπεφάνη), where it is used of Christ's First Coming (διὰ τ. ἐπιφανείας τ. σωτῆρος ἡμῶν Χριστοῦ Ἰησοῦ), has a definite eschatological reference. The same is the case in 2 Thess. ii. 8 καταργήσει τ. ἐπιφανείᾳ τ. παρουσίας αὐτοῦ, where the A.V., probably on account of the following παρουσίας, wrongly renders it 'brightness' (Vg. *illustratione*)[1], for which the Revisers have substituted 'manifestation.' This last is probably as accurate a rendering as we can get for the word in English, involving as it does the idea of something striking—a conspicuous intervention from above[2]. The

In ecclesiastical writers ἐπιφάνεια has the same double reference as Ecclesiπαρουσία, and when referring to the First Coming of Christ is sometimes astical distinguished by a characterizing epithet such as ἔνσαρκος (Eus. *Demonstr.* writers. *Evang.* viii. p. 226)[3]. Hence too it came to be applied not only to the day sacred to Christ's Nativity (e.g. Epiphan. *de Haer.* ii. *ad fin.* οὔτε ἐν τῇ ἡμέρᾳ τῶν ἐπιφανίων, ὅτε ἐγεννήθη ἐν σαρκὶ ὁ κύριος), but also to the day of His Baptism as in the oration of Gregory of Nazianzus inscribed εἰς τὰ Ἐπιφάνια. For its reference to the Second Coming it is sufficient to refer to the letter of Dionysius, preserved in Eus. *H. E.* vii. 24, where in close connexion with τῆς ἐνδόξου καὶ ἀληθῶς ἐνθέου τοῦ Κυρίου ἡμῶν ἐπιφανείας we are assured of τῆς ἡμετέρας ἐκ νεκρῶν ἀναστάσεως καὶ τῆς πρὸς αὐτὸν ἐπισυναγωγῆς καὶ ὁμοιώσεως. From Greg. Naz. *Orat.* iii. p. 77 A it would appear that the word was also applied by ecclesiastical writers to saints or martyrs.

iii. Ἀποκάλυψις.

Ἀποκάλυψις, though not wholly[4], is distinctively a Biblical word, and is Greek used euphemistically for עֶרְוָה in 1 Regn. xx. 30 (εἰς αἰσχύνην ἀποκαλύψεως O.T. μητρός σου), and metaphorically in the apocryphal book of Sirach, where it is applied to the revelation of a man's deeds in the hour of death (xi. 27 ἐν συντελείᾳ ἀνθρώπου ἀποκάλυψις ἔργων αὐτοῦ), and to the revealing of secrets (xxii. 22 μυστηρίου ἀποκαλύψεως, xlii. 1 ἀποκαλύψεων λόγων κρυφίων). The corresponding verb ἀποκαλύπτειν is however much more common,

---

[1] Alford aptly recalls Milton's fine line,—'far off His coming shone.'
[2] Chrys. *Hom. ix. in II. ad Tim.*: Ἐπιφάνεια δὲ λέγεται διὰ τὸ ἐπάνω φαίνεσθαι, καὶ ἄνωθεν ἀνατέλλειν.
[3] Suid.: Ἐπιφάνεια...ἡ τοῦ σωτῆρος ἡμῶν Ἰησοῦ Χριστοῦ ἔνσαρκος οἰκονομία.

[4] It occurs a few times in Plutarch (e.g. *Mor.* 70 F). To the class. and late Gk. instances of the verb given by the dictionaries may now be added the new class. fragment in P.Oxy. 413, 166 f. ἀ[ποκ]άλυψον ἵνα ἴδω αὐτήν.

150   THE EPISTLES TO THE THESSALONIANS

and is already definitely applied to the revelations of God to men, e.g. 1 Regn. ii. 27 τάδε λέγει Κύριος Ἀποκαλυφθεὶς ἀπεκαλύφθην, iii. 21 ἀπεκαλύφθη Κύριος πρὸς Σαμουήλ, and especially such passages from the Theodotion version of Daniel as ii. 19 ἐν ὁράματι τῆς νυκτὸς τὸ μυστήριον ἀπεκαλύφθη, 22 ἀποκαλύπτει βαθέα καὶ ἀπόκρυφα, 28 θεὸς ἐν οὐρανῷ ἀποκαλύπτων μυστήρια.

N.T.   These passages, combined with our Lord's own words Lk. xvii. 30 κατὰ τὰ αὐτὰ ἔσται ᾗ ἡμέρᾳ ὁ υἱὸς τοῦ ἀνθρώπου ἀποκαλύπτεται, give the key to the use of the subst. in the N.T., where it is applied exclusively to communications that proceed from God or Christ, or to the Divine unveiling of truths that have been previously hidden. It is thus the exact correlative of μυστήριον as that word is used in the N.T.[1], as when in the Gospels it is employed with reference to our Lord Himself as the light given to dispel heathen darkness (Lk. ii. 32 φῶς εἰς ἀποκάλυψιν ἐθνῶν), or sums up the visions granted to St John on Patmos under the significant title Ἀποκάλυψις Ἰησοῦ Χριστοῦ (Rev. i. 1). Similarly in 1 Pet. we read of the 'praise and glory and honour' which are to be made known ἐν ἀποκαλύψει Ἰησοῦ Χριστοῦ (i. 7; cf. v. 13, iv. 13), where, as in 1 Thess. ii. 19 (see note), the preposition is not to be understood simply as referring to a contemporaneous event, but rather as implying the means 'in and through' which the finding unto praise spoken of is to be brought about (cf. Hort 1 Pet. p. 44).

Pauline   The word is, however, pre-eminently a Pauline one, occurring in all the
Epp.   groups of the Epp. except the Pastorals, and always in its higher or spiritual sense. Thus it is δι' ἀποκαλύψεως Ἰησοῦ Χριστοῦ (Gal. i. 12) that the Apostle himself received the Gospel, and it is through a similar revelation that he elsewhere claims to have been entrusted with the Divine secret of the extension of that Gospel to the Gentiles (Eph. iii. 3 κατὰ ἀποκάλυψιν ἐγνωρίσθη μοι τὸ μυστήριον, cf. Gal. ii. 2). The whole of Christianity indeed according to the Pauline view may be summed up as 'a revelation of a mystery' (Rom. xvi. 25 ἀποκάλυψιν μυστηρίου), and consequently ἀποκάλυψις is in its turn the means by which men enter into the knowledge of its highest truths (Eph. i. 17 πνεῦμα σοφίας καὶ ἀποκαλύψεως ἐν ἐπιγνώσει αὐτοῦ, cf. 1 Cor. xiv. 6, 26, 2 Cor. xii. 1, 7). As however this knowledge is at present necessarily limited, it is to the final 'revelation of our Lord Jesus Christ' (1 Cor. i. 7 τ. ἀποκάλυψιν τ. κυρίου ἡμ. Ἰησοῦ Χριστοῦ) that we are taught to look for the complete fulfilment of the work begun now. Then, in accordance with the 'revelation of the righteous judgment of God' (Rom. ii. 5 ἀποκαλύψεως δικαιοκρισίας τ. θεοῦ), justice will be meted out to all (2 Thess. i. 7), and the whole creation will rejoice in 'the revelation of the sons of God' (Rom. viii. 19 τ. ἀποκάλυψιν τ. υἱῶν τ. θεοῦ)[2].

In all these passages it will be noticed that, notwithstanding a considerable latitude of application, the fundamental idea of the word is always the same—an unveiling of what already exists, though hitherto

---

[1] Reference may again be made to Dean Armitage Robinson's valuable note, *Eph.* p. 234 ff.

[2] Cf. Westcott's note, *Introduction*

to the Study of the Gospels[6] (1881) p. 9 n.[1], on which the above summary is based, also the same writer's *Eph.* p. 178 f.

ΠΑΡΟΥCIA. ΕΠΙΦΑΝΕΙΑ. ΑΠΟΚΑΛΥΨΙC   151

it has been hidden, or at best only imperfectly known: an unveiling which, though it may pass through a long and varying process, finally reaches its climax in the full revelation of the now unseen, though ever-present Lord.

The religious history of the word outside the Canon need not detain us. In view of what has been said, it will be obvious how readily it lent itself as a title to the large class of writings, both Jewish and Christian, which, dealing with what lay outside the immediate range of human experience and knowledge, aimed at exhorting and consoling those to whom they were addressed in the dark days on which they had fallen. 'Tracts for the Times,' as they have been called, they were also 'Tracts for Bad Times[1],' and with widely-differing degrees of insight sought by the aid of symbolism and eschatological speculation to disclose to men the hidden but ever-present rule and purposes of God[2]. *Jewish and Christian Apocalypses.*

iv. *Summary.*

If we have been correct in the foregoing distinctions between the three words, it will be seen that, while all may be used to describe the Return of the now exalted and glorified Lord, they do so from three distinct points of view. *General distinctions between*

The first, παρουσία, lays stress on the 'presence' of the Lord with His people, which, while existing now, will only at that Return be completely realized. *παρουσία,*

The second, ἐπιφάνεια, draws attention to His 'presence' as the result of a sublime 'manifestation' of the power and love of God, coming to His people's help. *ἐπιφάνεια,*

The third, ἀποκάλυψις, reminds us that the 'manifestation' is also a 'revelation' of the Divine plan and purpose which has run through all the ages, to find its consummation at length in the 'one far-off divine event,' to which the whole Creation is slowly moving. *and ἀποκάλυψις.*

[1] Cf. C. A. Scott, *Revelation* (in *The Century Bible*) p. 27.
[2] For a brief account of these 'apocalypses' see Swete *Apoc.* p. xviii ff.
Full particulars, with references to the relative literature, will be found in Schürer[3] iii. p. 181 ff.

NOTE G.

On ἀτακτέω and its cognates.

The three words ἀτακτέω, ἄτακτος, and ἀτάκτως are only found in the Thessalonian Epistles amongst the writings of the N.T. In these circumstances it may be well to bring together a few passages illustrating their usage both from classical and from later Gk., more particularly as the exact meaning to be attached to them has an important bearing upon the view we form of a certain section of the Thessalonian Church at the time of St Paul's writing.

1. Ἄτακτος. Classical writers.

In doing so we begin with the adj. ἄτακτος, which means primarily 'out of order,' 'out of place,' and hence, like the Latin *inordinatus*, is readily employed as a military term to denote a soldier who does not keep the ranks, or an army advancing in disarray. It is found in this sense in Xen. *Oec.* viii. 4, where an ἄτακτος is contrasted with a τεταγμένη στρατιά, and a suggestive example of the same usage is afforded by Dem. *Phil.* i. 50, where the great orator indignantly condemns the want of preparation with regard to the war—ἄτακτα ἀδιόρθωτα ἀόριστα ἅπαντα—compared with the care bestowed—οὐδὲν ἀνεξέταστον οὐδ' ἀόριστον—upon games and festivities.

From this the transition is easy to disorderly or irregular living of any kind as in Plato's reference to ἄτακτοι ἡδοναί (*Legg.* ii. 660 B, cf. vii. 806 C), or in Plutarch's rebuke of those who, neglecting a 'sane and well-ordered life' (ὑγιαίνοντος κ. τεταγμένου βίου), hurl themselves headlong into 'disorderly and brutal pleasures' (τὰς ἀτάκτους κ. ἀνδραποδώδεις ἡδονάς, *de lib. educ.* § 7 p. 5 A; cf. ἀκόλαστα κ. ἄτακτα, *de def. orac.* § 20 p. 420 E).

Greek O.T.

The word is not found in the canonical books of the LXX., but in *Sap.* xiv. 26 the corresponding subst. occurs in the phrase γάμων ἀταξία, with which are associated μοιχεία κ. ἀσέλγεια. On the other hand the more primary sense of the adj. is well illustrated in 3 Macc. i. 19, where it is used to describe the 'disorderly rush' (δρόμον ἄτακτον) of the newly-married brides into the street at the siege of Jerusalem[1].

---

[1] An interesting use of ἄτακτος, though it throws no light on the meaning of the word in our Epp., is afforded by the Tribal Lists in the Inscriptions, where it is applied to a city that has been granted, but has not yet exercised the privilege of self-assessment (e.g. *C.I.A.* I. 243, 36 ἄτακτος πόλις: see Roberts-Gardner p. 290). Εὔτακτος is found as a proper name in an inscription discovered at Thessalonica—Λ(ούκιος) Σέξτιος Εὔτακτος (no. 114, Heuzey et Daumet p. 280).

ON ΑΤΑΚΤΕΩ AND ITS COGNATES 153

The usage of ἀτάκτως naturally follows similar lines, as when in Thuc. iii. 108 we read that many of the Peloponnesians, after the defeat of Olpae, perished when hurrying ἀτάκτως κ. οὐδενὶ κόσμῳ to reach their camp, whereas the Mantineans through the excellence of their order (μάλιστα ξυντεταγμένοι) were able to effect a retreat[1]: while for the more metaphorical sense we can point to such a phrase as πλημμελῶς κ. ἀτάκτως in Plato *Tim.* 30 A, or to Isocr. *Evagr.* 197 E οὐδὲ πρὸς ἐν ἀτάκτως οὐδ' ἀνωμάλως διακείμενος, ἀλλ' ὁμοίως τὰς ἐν τοῖς ἔργοις ὁμολογίας ὥσπερ τὰς ἐν τοῖς λόγοις διαφυλάττων.

2. 'Ατάκτως. Classical writers.

A late example to much the same effect is afforded by the discovery in the Fayûm of the fragment of a philosophic work concerning the gods, belonging to the second century, in which the words occur δεῖ τῶν [ἀν]θρώπων ἄρχειν [τῶν] πράξεων ἐκεί[νου]ς δὲ εὐθὺς ἐφέπεσθαι, οὐκ ἀτάκτως μέντοι ἀλλ' εἰμα[ρ]μέ[νως]. τοῦ γὰρ ἀστόχως...(P.Fay. 337, 16 ff.).

Late Gk.

We come now to ἀτακτέω. Like its adj., it is frequently applied to soldiers marching out of order, or quitting the ranks (e.g. Xen. *Cyr.* vii. 2. 6), and hence is extended to every one who does not perform his proper duty, as in Xen. *Oec.* v. 15 where the ἀτακτοῦντες are contrasted with τοῖς ποιοῦσιν ἃ δεῖ ποιεῖν. Cf. P.Par. 26, 15 (ii./B.C.) ὑπέδειξαν ὡς ἂν εὐτακτηθησομένων ἡμῖν τῶν καθηκόντων.

3. 'Ατακτέω. Classical writers.

In later Greek this ethical sense is very common, as when, by Philostratus I., the verb was applied to children who dreaded punishment 'if they had done any thing amiss' (εἴ τι ἀτακτήσειαν *Vit. Soph.* p. 230, ed. Kayser), or generally speaking to any irregularities on the part of men (οἱ γὰρ ὑπὲρ τοιούτων ἀτακτοῦντες *Vit. Ap.* p. 17, ψυχαὶ ἀτακτοῦσαι p. 338).

Later Gk.

In these circumstances we are prepared to take both the verb and its cognates metaphorically in the Thessalonian Epp., as indeed the context clearly demands. And the only question that remains is whether they are to be understood positively of actual wrong-doing, or in a more negative sense of a certain remissness in the conduct of life.

Thessalonian Epp.

Of the Gk. commentators Chrysostom apparently inclines to the former view, as when in his Homily on I. v. 14 he describes the ἄτακτοι as πάντες οἱ παρὰ τὸ τῷ θεῷ δοκοῦν πράττοντες...πάντες οἱ ἁμαρτάνοντες. On the other hand Theodoret confines the ἀταξία complained of to idleness—ἀτάκτους τοὺς ἀργίᾳ συζῶντας ἐκάλεσεν (*ad* I. v. 18): τῇ ἀργίᾳ συζῶσιν (*ad* II. iii. 11).

And of this latter view, at least in a slightly modified form, we have lately received unexpected confirmation in two striking examples of the use of ἀτακτέω in the Κοινή, much about the time of St Paul's writing. The first occurs in P.Oxy. 275 (A.D. 66) in a contract of apprenticeship, according to which a father binds himself not to take away his son during a certain specified period, with the further condition that if there are any days on which the boy 'fails to attend,' or 'plays the truant' (ὅσας δ' ἐὰν ἐν τούτῳ ἀτακτήσῃ ἡμέρας, 24 f.), he is to produce him for an equivalent number of days after the period is over.

The Papyri.

[1] Symmachus uses the word in 4 Regn. ix. 20 to describe the driving of Jehu—ἀτάκτως ἄγει (Heb. בְּשִׁגָּעוֹן, madly).

154 THE EPISTLES TO THE THESSALONIANS

The second also comes from Oxyrhynchus in a similar contract, dated about one hundred and twenty years later, P.Oxy. 725, according to which a weaver's apprentice is allowed twenty holidays in the year, 'but if he exceeds this number of days from idleness or ill-health or any other reason' (ἐὰν δὲ πλείονας τούτων ἀργήσῃ [ἢ ἀσ]θενήσῃ ἢ ἀτακτήσῃ ἢ δι' ἄλλην τιν[ὰ αἰ]τίαν 39 ff.), he has to make his absences good without wages.

If then these instances can be taken as typical of the ordinary colloquial sense of the verb, we can understand how readily St Paul would employ it to describe those members of the Thessalonian Church who, without any intention of actual wrong-doing, were neglecting their daily duties, and falling into idle and careless habits, because of their expectation of the immediate Parousia of the Lord.

NOTE H.

On the meanings of κατέχω.

The verb κατέχω is found in our Epistles in two distinct senses:
(1) 'Hold fast':
    I. v. 21 τὸ καλὸν κατέχετε.
(2) 'Hold back':
    II. ii. 6 νῦν τὸ κατέχον οἴδατε.
    7 μόνον ὁ κατέχων ἄρτι ἕως ἐκ μέσου γένηται.

Both meanings are well-established, but in view of the importance of the passages in which they occur, it will not be out of place to bring together a few passages from the Κοινή, which may help to illustrate them.

The first meaning 'hold fast' is best reached through κατέχω as a perfective of ἔχω = 'possess,' as in 1 Cor. vii. 30, 2 Cor. vi. 10 ὡς μηδὲν ἔχοντες κ. πάντα κατέχοντες[1], with which may be compared P.Amh. 30, 26 f. (ii./B.C.) where, in an official report regarding the ownership of a house, proofs were adduced to establish that a certain Marres κατεσχηκέναι τὴν οἰκίαν ('had become owner of the house'), and the corresponding use of the subst. κατοχή = bonorum possessio in B.G.U. 140, 24 ff. (c. i./A.D.), ὅμως κατ[ο]χὴ[ν] ὑ[πα]ρχόντων ἐξ ἐκείνου τοῦ μέ[ρ]ους τοῦ διατάγματος. i. κατέχω = 'hold fast.'

From this the transition is easy to the sense 'take possession of,' 'lay hold of,' and accordingly in the interesting rescript regarding the Third Syrian War, ascribed with all probability to Ptolemy III. himself, the King narrates how certain ships, acting in his interest, sailed along the coast of Cilicia to Soli, and took on board τὰ ἐκ[εῖ?]σε κατασκεθέντ[α χρή]ματα 'the money that had been seized there' (P.Petr. II. 45, ii. 3 f., cf. P.Petr. III. p. 335 f.).

In this passage, it will be noticed, the verb is practically = κρατεῖν. And, as a matter of fact, we find it used interchangeably with κρατεῖν in the long Petition of Dionysia (P.Oxy. 237 (ii./A.D.)) regarding the 'right of ownership' (κατοχή) of a property (οὐσία) which she claimed: see especially col. viii. 22 f. and 34 f., τὰς Αἰγυπτιακὰς γυναῖκας...κατέχειν τὰ ὑπάρχοντα τῶν ἀνδρῶν and κατά τινα ἐπιχώριον νόμον κρατεῖται τὰ ὑπάρχοντα.

Other examples of the more legal or technical uses of the terms, which cannot be discussed here, are—for the verb, P.Tebt. 5, 47 (a Royal ordinance, ii./B.C.) [κρατεῖ]ν ὧν κατεσχήκασι κλή(ρων), and for the subst., P.Oxy. 713, 36 (i./A.D.), where an applicant declares for registration his 'right' (κατοχήν)

---

[1] Cf. Magn. 105, 51 (ii./A.D.), where the right of possession in certain territory is expressed by the formula 'ἵνα ἔχωσιν κατέχωσίν τε καρπί[ζ]ωνταί τε.'

to certain arourae that had belonged to his mother. Cf. also the important legal rescript, P.Strass. 22 (iii./A.D.). More important for our present purpose are the instances of the verb in a slightly metaphorical sense, as when a letter-writer of the second century accuses his correspondent of 'being oppressed by an evil conscience' (ὑπὸ κακοῦ συνειδότος κατεχόμενος, P.Oxy. 532, 22 ff.), or as when a would-be purchaser of confiscated property declares that in a certain contingency she will not be 'bound' by her promise (P.Amh. 97, 17 f. (ii./A.D.) οὐ κατασχε[θ]ήσομαι τῇ [ὑ]ποσχέσει)[1].

And if we accept the view, which has recently found strong support, that the κάτοχοι of the Serapeum are to be regarded as those 'possessed' by the spirit of the god[2], we have further evidence pointing in the same direction.

If, on the other hand, we incline to the older view, according to which they are to be thought of as a species of monks, living for the time being 'in retreat' (ἐν κατοχῇ) within the temple-precincts[3], we are prepared for the further modifications in the meaning of κατέχω, according to which it gains the sense of 'detain,' 'arrest,' while κατοχή signifies 'the place of custody,' 'the gaol.'

Thus in P.Lond. II. 342, 7 f. (ii./A.D.) a charge is laid against one Sempronius of attempting to lay hands on the relatives of the petitioner as ἐπιπλόους or boat-overseers (προφάσι τοῦ κατέχειν ἐπιπλόους τοὺς συνγενεῖς μου), while in a fragmentary letter in the same collection (422), belonging to the fourth century, directions are given to arrest a certain individual and 'put him in irons' (σιδηρῶσαι αὐτόν) for selling stolen camels, and it is added κατέχεται ἡ γυνή ('his wife is already arrested'). Similarly in B.G.U. 372, 16 (ii./A.D.) we read of a man who is 'arrested' (κατεχόμενον) as a tramp: while κατοχή = 'custody' appears in such passages as P.Amh. 80, 9 (iii./A.D.) [ἐ]γλύσωσίν με [τῆς κα]τοχῆς, B.G.U. 323, 11 f. (Byz.) [εἰ]ς κατοχὴν ποιήσω πάντα τὰ ὄντ[α ἐν τῷ] μου χωρίῳ ξένα πρόσωπα.

ii. κατέχω = 'hold back.'

These last examples bring us to the second main use of κατέχω which we set out to illustrate, in which the thought of 'holding fast,' 'arresting,' passes into the thought of 'holding back,' 'detaining,' as may be seen from a single papyrus in which the verb occurs with both meanings.

A *beneficiarius* of one village addresses a letter to the comarchs of

---

[1] Cf. Jo. v. 4 ᾧ δήποτε κατείχετο νοσήματι (A).

[2] See especially E. Preuschen *Mönchtum und Serapiskult* 2te Aufl. Giessen, 1903. Wilcken (*Archiv* iv. 207) cites in support of this view an inscription from Priene to the effect— ἀπὸ τῶν τραπεζῶν ὧν ἂν δῆμ[ος κοσμῆι, δεδόσθω] [τ]οῖς κατεχομένοις ὑπὸ τοῦ θεοῦ (Priene 195, 28 f. (ii./B.C.)). Cf. also Dittenberger, *O. G. I. S.* ii. *Addenda* p. 549 f.

[3] 'Inclusio voluntaria in Serapieio a vita coenobitarum nonnullorum haud multum diversa' (Herwerden *Lex. s.v.* κατοχή). With this view Kenyon (*British Museum Papyri* I. p. 29 ff.) in the main agrees, nor does it seem possible to attach any other meaning to such a phrase as ὑπὲρ τοῦ ἀπολελῦσθαί σε ἐκ τῆς κατοχῆς (P.Lond. I. 42, 26 f. (ii./B.C.)), than that the person spoken of had been 'released from his seclusion.' See also the references to the use of κατοχή in Mayser p. 22 f.

ON THE MEANINGS OF ΚΑΤΕΧΩ

another, bidding them deliver up to the officer whom he sends a certain Pachoumis ὃν κατεσχήκατε, 'whom you have arrested,' and then, after enjoining them if they have anything to say in his favour to come along with him and say so, the writer adds—ὅρα μὴ κατάσχητε τὸν ὑπηρέτη<ν>, 'see that you do not detain the officer' (P.Oxy. 65 (iii.—iv./A.D.)). Earlier examples of the same usage are afforded by P.Fay. 109, 11 (i./A.D.) μὴ κατάσχῃς Κλέωνα, P.Tebt. 315, 19 f. (ii./A.D.) ἐὰν δέ σέ τι κατέχῃ, and the illiterate B.G.U. 775, 12 (ii./A.D.) μὴ κατάσχῃ[ς] οὖν τὸ κλειδίν μου. It is hardly necessary to carry the evidence further, but, for the sake of its intrinsic interest, reference may be made to the heathen (*Archiv* ii. p. 173) Charm which Crum prints in his *Coptic Ostraca* no. 522 beginning—Κρόνος ὁ κατέχων τὸν θυμὸν ὅλων τῶν ἀνθρώπων κάτεχε τὸν θυμὸν Ὥρι....

NOTE I.

The Biblical Doctrine of Antichrist[1].

Παιδία, ἐσχάτη ὥρα ἐστίν, καὶ καθὼς ἠκούσατε ὅτι ἀντίχριστος ἔρχεται, καὶ νῦν ἀντίχριστοι πολλοὶ γεγόνασιν· ὅθεν γινώσκομεν ὅτι ἐσχάτη ὥρα ἐστίν. 1 Jo. ii. 18.

The whole subject of Antichrist is surrounded with difficulties, and raises many questions which are altogether outside the scope of this Commentary. The utmost that can be attempted here is to supply a few Notes, tracing the historical growth of the idea in the sacred Scriptures and in the apocalyptic writings of the Jews, with the view of further illustrating and confirming the interpretation given to the Man of lawlessness in the foregoing pages[2].

The name Antichrist.
1. The actual name Antichrist is first found in the Johannine Epistles (1 Jo. ii. 18, 22, iv. 3, 2 Jo. 7), but the main idea underlies St Paul's description of the Man of lawlessness in 2 Thess. ii. 1—12, while, from the manner in which both writers refer to this mysterious figure, it is evident that they had in view an oral tradition current at the time (1 Jo. iv. 3 ἀκηκόατε, 2 Thess. ii. 6 οἴδατε). Any attempt therefore to understand the doctrine of Antichrist as it meets us in the N.T. must naturally begin with this tradition, so far as it is now possible to trace it.

Possible connexion with a Babylonian myth.
2. Here, according to the latest view, we are carried very far back. Gunkel in his epoch-making book *Schöpfung und Chaos* (1895) would have us find the roots of the Jewish doctrine of Antichrist in the primitive Babylonian dragon myth of a monster (Tiâmat) who opposed the Creator (Marduk) in the beginning and was overcome by Him, but who, it was believed, would in the last days again rear his head in rebellion only to

---

[1] The following Note in a condensed form appears in *The Standard Dictionary of the Bible* under the title 'Antichrist and the Man of Sin.'

[2] On the whole subject, in addition to the special literature cited in the course of the Note, reference may be made to the articles on 'Antichrist' by Bousset in the *Encycl. Bibl.*, by James (under the title 'Man of Sin') in Hastings' *D.B.*, by Moffatt (under the title 'False Christs') in Hastings' *D.C.G.*, by Ginsburg in the *Jewish Encyclopaedia*, and by Sieffert in Hauck *RE.*[3], and to the Excursuses in their Commentaries on the Thessalonian Epistles by Bornemann and Findlay. Thackeray has a useful Note in his Essay on *The Relation of St Paul to Contemporary Jewish Thought* (1900) p. 136 ff., and the elaborate study *Zur Lehre vom Antichrist* by Schneckenburger-Boehmer in the *Jahrbücher für Deutsche Theologie* iv. (1859) p. 405 ff. may still be consulted with advantage.

be finally crushed. And more recently this view has been adopted and developed on independent lines by Bousset in his elaborate monograph on *Der Antichrist* (1895, translated into English, with a new Prologue by A. H. Keane, under the title *The Antichrist Legend*, 1896).

It is impossible here to examine in detail the evidence adduced by those writers, but their investigations have made it practically certain that this myth had reached Palestine, and is alluded to in the O.T. (see artt. 'Rahab' and 'Sea-Monster' in Hastings' *D.B.*). At the same time its influence must not be exaggerated. Whatever part it may have had in familiarizing the Jews with the idea of an arch-enemy of God, it exercised little influence on the development of the idea amongst them, and many of the traits ascribed to Antichrist, which are to be found in the eschatological commentaries of Irenaeus, Hippolytus, and other early writers, and which, because unsupported by anything he can find elsewhere, Bousset is inclined to refer back to some such esoteric doctrine, are more naturally explained as the result of the imaginations of these commentators themselves, working on the data supplied to them by the Scriptures.

3. In any case we are on surer ground when we turn to those data, *Antichrist in the O.T.* and, in proceeding to examine them, we may start from the general Jewish belief in a fierce attack that would be directed against Israel in the end of the days by some hostile person or power, but which would be finally frustrated by the action of Jehovah or His Messiah. The conception which the Jewish writers formed of the exact nature of this attack was naturally largely influenced by their particular circumstances at the time, but, as it first meets us, it is generally thought of as proceeding from the heathen nations of the world.

Thus in Ps. ii., which Friedländer regards as the real source ('Quelle') *Psalms.* of the later Antichrist legend[1], we have a graphic picture of the rebellion of the world-kingdoms 'against the Lord and against His Anointed,' coupled with the assurance that all such rebellion, because directed against Jehovah Himself, is hopeless, and, if persevered in, can only result in the complete overthrow of the nations: while in the exilic Psalm xciii. (xciv.) the Psalmist comforts the oppressed Israelites with the reminder that the Lord cannot have any alliance with 'the throne of lawlessness' (*v*. 20 μὴ συνπροσέσται σοι θρόνος ἀνομίας), but will cause their lawlessness to recoil upon all evil-doers (*v*. 23 ἀποδώσει αὐτοῖς τὴν ἀνομίαν αὐτῶν)[2].

The thought of the same contest ending in the same way meets us *Post-exilic* also in the post-exilic prophets, as for example in the description of the *Prophets.* onslaught by Gog from the land of Magog, as the type of the world's

---

[1] *Der Antichrist in den vorchristlichen jüdischen Quellen* (1901) p. 128 —an Essay in which much valuable evidence is gathered together both from the O.T., and the later data of the Midrash and Talmud, in proof of the Jewish doctrine of Antichrist, whatever may be thought of its main thesis that during the last century B.C. Beliar was the embodiment of the antinomian spirit which pervaded the Jewish sect of מִינִים.

[2] Cf. also the striking linguistic parallels between Ps. lxxxviii. (lxxxix.) and 2 Thess. i. and ii. adduced by Bornemann p. 356 f.

160 THE EPISTLES TO THE THESSALONIANS

power, against God's people who 'dwell securely' (Ezek. xxxviii., xxxix.)[1], or of the final assault against Jerusalem to which all nations of the earth go up, and which again ends in the intervention and universal headship of God (Zech. xii.—xiv.).

Daniel. It is however in the visions and prophecies of the Book of Daniel (B.C. 168—165) that we find the real starting-point of many of the later descriptions of Antichrist, and especially in the picture that is there presented of Antiochus IV., called Epiphanes[2]. No other foreign ruler was ever regarded by the Jews with such hatred on account both of his personal impieties (1 Macc. i. 24 אV ἐλάλησεν ὑπερηφανίαν μεγάλην), and of his bitter persecution of their religion, and, accordingly, he is here portrayed as the very impersonation of all evil. Some of the traits indeed ascribed to him are of such a character (see vii. 8 b, 20 b, 21, 25, xi. 36—45) that it has often been thought that the writer had not so much Antiochus as the future Antichrist directly in view. And, though this is not exegetically possible, it is easy to understand how his description influenced the Apostolic writers in their account of the arch-enemy of God and man (cf. e.g. 2 Thess. ii. 4 with Dan. xi. 36 f., and Rev. xiii. 1—8 with Dan. vii. 8, 20, 21, 25, viii. 24, xi. 28, 30; and see Driver *Daniel* p. xcvi ff.).

With the fall of Antiochus and the rise of the Maccabean kingdom, the promise of deliverance, with which Daniel had comforted God's people during their dark days, received its proximate fulfilment. But when the nation again fell under a foreign yoke, the old fears were once more revived, and received a fresh colouring from the new powers by which the Jewish nation now found itself opposed.

Antichrist in later Jewish writings. 4. In determining the Jewish views regarding Antichrist during this period, much difficulty is caused by the uncertainty regarding the exact date of some of the relative writings, and the possibility of their having received Christian interpolations in the form in which they have come down to us. The following references, however, deserve notice.

Psalms of Solomon. In the Pharisaic *Psalms of Solomon* (48—40 B.C.) Pompey as the representative of the foreign power that had overthrown Zion is described as the personification of sin (ii. 1 ὁ ἁμαρτωλός), and even as the dragon (*v.* 29 ὁ δράκων), perhaps an unconscious survival of the dragon-myth[3]: and in Ps. xvii. 13 if we may adopt Ewald's conjectural reading, which has been generally approved by the editors, of ὁ ἄνομος (ὁ ἄνεμος in all the

---

[1] For the later connexion of Gog and Magog with the story of Antichrist cf. Rev. xx. 7 f. The actual identification of Gog with Antichrist, however, does not occur till the seventh century, and even then only in Jewish sources (Bousset art. 'Antichrist' in *Encycl. Bibl.* § 12).

[2] The epithet Epiphanes is generally rendered 'the illustrious,' but its real meaning, as seen when the title is stated in full θεὸς ἐπιφανής, is the 'god made manifest' (cf. Add. Note F, p. 148). For a graphic description of the circumstances of his reign see E. Bevan, *Jerusalem under the High Priests* (1904), and for the general interpretation of the visions of Dan. vii.—xii. see Porter *The Messages of the Apocalyptical Writers* (1905) p. 125 ff.

[3] See Charles *The Ascension of Isaiah* p. liv.

MSS.), we have another epithet applied to Pompey which, if used technically, is proper to the Beliar-myth (see below). It may, however, in the present instance mean no more than 'heathen' as in 1 Cor. ix. 21.

Similarly in the *Apocalypse of Baruch* which, though belonging to *Apocalypse of* the last decade of the 1st cent. A.D., is in the main a true Jewish writing, *Baruch.* we have a description of the destruction of the 'lost leader' of the enemies of Israel by the Messiah on Mount Zion (xl. 1, 2), where again Pompey may be thought of. And in 4 Ezra v. 1—6, belonging to about the same *4 Ezra.* time, after an enumeration of the signs of the last times, and the coming of the fourth (Roman) Empire, after the third (Greek) Empire has passed away in disorder ('post tertiam turbatam' ed. Bensly)[1], we read of one who 'shall rule whom they that dwell upon the earth look not for' ('et regnabit quem non sperant qui inhabitant super terram'), a mysterious being, who is generally identified with the future Antichrist[2].

In none of these passages, it will be noticed, have we more than a God-opposing being of human origin, but it has recently been pointed out with great cogency by Dr Charles (*Ascension of Isaiah* p. lv ff.)[3] that, in the interval between the Old and the New Testaments, a further development was given to the Jewish belief in Antichrist through the influence of the Beliar-myth.

In the O.T. 'belial' is never strictly speaking a proper name, but denotes 'worthlessness,' 'wickedness[4].' From its frequent occurrence, however, along with another noun in such phrases as 'daughter' (1 Sam. i. 16), 'man' (1 Sam. xxv. 25), and especially 'sons' (Deut. xiii. 13, Judg. xix. 22 &c.) of 'belial,' it is obvious how readily the idea lent itself to personification, while it is not without significance in our present inquiry that in those latter passages it is rendered in the LXX. by παράνομος (e.g. Deut. xiii. 13 ἐξήλθοσαν ἄνδρες παράνομοι).

In the later pseudepigraphical literature of the Jews this humanizing or rather demonizing process is carried still further, until the title regularly appears as a synonym for Satan or one of his lieutenants.

Thus in the *Book of Jubilees* (ii./B.C.) we read 'Let Thy mercy, O Lord, *Jubilees.* be lifted up upon Thy people...and let not the spirit of Beliar rule over *Testa-* them' (i. 20, cf. xv. 33, ed. Charles). And similar references to Beliar as *ments of* a Satanic spirit are frequent in the *Testaments of the xii Patriarchs* *the xii* (ii./B.C., in part at least): see e.g. Reub. iv. 7, vi. 3, Levi iii. 3, xviii. 12. *Patri-archs.*

---

[1] Gunkel (in Kautzsch *Pseudepigrapha* p. 359) prefers to supply 'diem' after 'post tertiam' (=μετὰ τὴν τρίτην ἡμέραν, Blass), and understands the three 'days,' as the secret apocalyptic number, which denotes the world-rule until its destruction: cf. the three-and-a-half 'days' of Rev. xi. 9, and see *Schöpfung u. Chaos* pp. 268 n.[1], 269 n.[1].

[2] Cf. L. Vaganay *Le Problème Eschatologique dans le iv*[e] *Livre d'Esdras* (Paris, 1906) p. 86 f.

[3] See also Friedländer *op. cit.* p. 118 ff.

[4] The origin of the word בְּלִיַּעַל is disputed, but the old derivation from בְּלִי 'without' and יַעַל 'profit' is still strongly supported. For an interesting discussion, in which Dr Cheyne finds in the word a modification of the Babylonian *Bililu* in the sense of the 'land without return,' i.e. the underworld, see *Exp. T.* viii. and ix. *s.v.* 'Belial' in the Indices.

162 THE EPISTLES TO THE THESSALONIANS

Sibylline Oracles. The most interesting passage, however, for our purpose is contained in the third book of the *Sibylline Oracles*, in a section which in the main goes back to the same early date, where Beliar is depicted as a truly Satanic being accompanied by all the signs that are elsewhere ascribed to Antichrist[1]. The passage is as follows:

ἐκ δὲ Σεβαστηνῶν[2] ἥξει Βελίαρ μετόπισθεν
καὶ στήσει ὀρέων ὕψος, στήσει δὲ θάλασσαν
ἠέλιον πυρόεντα μέγαν λαμπράν τε σελήνην,
καὶ νέκυας στήσει καὶ σήματα πολλὰ ποιήσει
ἀνθρώποις·

* * * * *

καὶ δύναμις φλογόεσσα δι' οἴδματος ἐς γαῖαν ἥξει,
καὶ Βελίαρ φλέξει καὶ ὑπερφιάλους ἀνθρώπους
πάντας, ὅσοι τούτῳ πίστιν ἐνεποιήσαντο.

Orac. Sib. iii. 63 ff. (ed. Rzach).

With this passage should also be compared *Orac. Sib.* ii. 167 f. where it is stated that 'Beliar will come and do many signs to men'

καὶ Βελίαρ θ' ἥξει καὶ σήματα πολλὰ ποιήσει
ἀνθρώποις,

though here the originally Jewish origin of the passage is by no means so certain.

Rabbinical writings. In the same way it is impossible to lay too much stress in the present connexion on the speculations of Rabbinical theology regarding the person of Antichrist in view of the late date of our authorities[3]. But we may accept, as in the main reflecting the views of the Jews about the beginning of the Christian era, the general conception of a powerful ruler to be born of the tribe of Dan[4] and uniting in himself all enmity against God and hatred against God's people, but whom the Messiah will finally slay by the breath of His lips[5].

Antichrist in our Lord's teaching. 5. We can see how readily this idea would lend itself to the political and materialistic longings of the Jews, and it is only therefore what we should expect when we find our Lord, true to His spiritual ideals, saying nothing by which these expectations might be encouraged in the

---

[1] Cf. 4 Ezra v. 4 'et relucescet subito sol noctu, et luna interdie,' *Asc. Isai.* iv. 5 'et eius verbo orietur sol noctu, et luna quoque ut sexta hora appareat, efficiat.' For later Christian references to the wonders of Antichrist see Bousset *The Antichrist Legend* p. 175 ff.

[2] This reference to the Σεβαστηνοί, by whom we naturally understand 'the race of Augustus,' has caused difficulty in accepting this as a purely Jewish picture, but, unless it is to be regarded as a later interpolation (Schürer[3] iii. p. 441, Engl. Tr. II. iii. p. 284), it is probably to be understood of the inhabitants of Sebaste-Samaria.

[3] None of these are earlier than the second century A.D.

[4] Support was lent to this view by such passages as Gen. xlix. 17, Deut. xxxiii. 22, Jer. viii. 16; cf. the omission of Dan in Rev. vii. 5 ff., and see further Friedländer *op. cit.* c. ix *Die Abstammung des Antichrist aus Dan.*

[5] See Weber *Jüd. Theologie* p. 365.

BIBLICAL DOCTRINE OF ANTICHRIST

minds of His hearers, but contenting Himself with warning them against false teachers, the 'false Christs' and the 'false prophets' who would be ready 'to lead astray, if possible, even the elect' (Mt. xxiv. 24, Mk. xiii. 22). Even too, when in the same discourse He seems to refer to a single Antichrist, the reference is veiled under the mysterious figure derived from Daniel of the 'abomination of desolation standing ($\dot{\epsilon}\sigma\tau\eta\kappa\acute{o}\tau a$) where he ought not' (Mk. xiii. 14; cf. Mt. xxiv. 15). A similar reticence marks His words as recorded by St John, if here again, as is most probable, He has Antichrist in view: 'I am come in my Father's name, and ye receive me not: if another shall come in his own name, him ye will receive' (v. 43).

6. Slight, however, though these references in our Lord's recorded teaching are, they would naturally direct the attention of the Apostolic writers to the traditional material lying to their hands in their treatment of this mysterious subject, and, as a matter of fact, we have clear evidence of the use of such material in the writings of at least two of them. *Antichrist in the Apostolic writers.*

Thus, apart from his direct reference to the Jewish belief in Beliar in 2 Cor. vi. 15 ('And what concord hath Christ with Beliar?'), St Paul has given us in 2 Thess. ii. 1—12 a very full description of the working of Antichrist, under the name of the Man of lawlessness, in which, as we have already seen (comm. *ad loc.*), he draws freely on the language and imagery of the O.T. and of the speculations of later Judaism. It is unnecessary to recapitulate the evidence, but for the sake of completeness it may be well to summarize briefly the leading features in the Pauline picture. *St Paul.*

(1) 'The mystery of lawlessness' is already at work, though for the moment it is held in check by a restraining person or power, probably to be identified with the power of law or government, especially as these were embodied at the time in the Roman State. (2) No sooner has this restraining power been removed (cf. 4 Ezra v. 4, *Apoc. Bar.* xxxix. 7) than a general 'apostasy' results, which finds its consummation in the 'revelation' of 'the Man of lawlessness.' (3) As 'the opposer' he 'exalteth himself against all that is called God' (cf. Dan. xi. 36 f.) and actually 'sitteth in the temple of God, setting himself forth as God'—the description being again modelled on the Danielic account (cf. Dan. viii. 13, ix. 27, xi. 31, xii. 11), and the 'lying wonders' by which his working is distinguished being illustrated by such passages as *Orac. Sib.* iii. 64 f., *Asc. Isai.* iv. 5 (see above). (4) Powerful as this incarnation of wickedness seems to be, the Lord Jesus at His Parousia will 'slay him with the breath of His mouth,' the words being a quotation from Isa. xi. 4, a passage which the Targum of Jonathan afterwards applied to the destruction of Armilus the Jewish Antichrist[1], and whose use here St Paul

---

[1] For Armilus (ארמילוס) i.e. Romulus, as the name of the chief adversary of the people of Israel, in later Rabbinism see Schürer³ ii. p. 533 (Engl. Tr. II. ii. p. 165); cf. Bousset *The Antichrist Legend* p. 105, Castelli *Il Messia secondo gli Ebrei* (1874) p. 239 ff.

164 · THE EPISTLES TO THE THESSALONIANS

may well have drawn from the Jewish tradition of his time (cf. the use of the same passage in Pss. Sol. xvii. 27, 39, 4 Ezra xiii. 10). The whole description, it will thus be seen, is of a very composite character[1], though at the same time it is so definite and detailed[2], that it is hardly to be wondered at that there has been a constant endeavour to find its suggestion in some historical personage of the writer's own time[3]. But though the sacrilegious conduct of Caligula (Jos. *Antt.* xviii. 261 (viii. 2), Tac. *Hist.* v. 9, Suet. *Calig.* xxii. 33) may have influenced the writer's language in *v.* 4, the real roots of the conception lie elsewhere, and it is rather, as we have seen, in the O.T. and in current Jewish traditions that its explanation is to be sought[4].

St John. The Apocalypse.

7. The same may be said, in part at least, of the various evil powers which meet us in the Johannine Apocalypse. The first wild Beast of the Seer (Rev. xiii.—xx.) vividly recalls the horned wild Beast of Dan. vii., viii., and the parallels that can be drawn between the language of St John and of St Paul (cf. Rev. xii. 9, xiii. 1 f. with 2 Thess. ii. 9 f.; xiii. 5 ff., xiv. 11 with ii. 4, 10—12; xiii. 3 with ii. 9 ff.) point to similar sources as lying at the roots of both. On the other hand the Johannine descriptions have now a direct connexion with contemporary secular history which was largely wanting in the earlier picture. This is seen noticeably in the changed attitude towards the power of Rome. So far from this being regarded any longer as a restraining influence, it is rather the source from which evil is to spring[5]. And we can understand therefore how the city of Rome and its imperial house supply St John with many of the characteristics under which he describes the working of Antichrist, until at length he sees all the powers of evil culminate in the Beast of c. xvii., who, according to the interpretation of Bousset (adopted by James in Hastings' *D.B.*), is partly representative of an individual who 'was, and is not, and shall be present' (*v.* 8 ἦν καὶ οὐκ ἔστιν καὶ πάρεσται), that is a *Nero redivivus*; partly of a polity, namely that of Rome.

---

[1] 'The ἄνομος-expectation of 2 Thessalonians is not the arbitrary invention of an individual, but only the expression of a belief which had a long historical development, and was at the time universally diffused' (Gunkel *Schöpfung u. Chaos* p. 221).

[2] 'There is scarcely a more matter-of-fact prediction in the Bible' (Findlay *Thessalonians* p. 219). The whole Appendix on 'The Man of Lawlessness' is a clear and well-balanced statement on this difficult subject, to which the present writer gladly acknowledges his indebtedness both in this and the following Note.

[3] E.g. Caligula (Spitta *Urchristentum* i. p. 294 ff.), Nero (Schmiedel *Handcommentar* II. i. p. 30 f.); see further Add. Note J.

[4] 'We have here a Jewish-Christian dogma, which is to be understood by means of the history of religious reflexion, and very indirectly by means of the history of the Caesars' (Gunkel *Schöpfung u. Chaos* p. 223).

[5] For the effect of the imperial persecutions, initiated by Nero in A.D. 64, in leading St John to regard their authors as the direct vassals of Satan, see Swete *Apoc.* p. lxxviii ff. The whole of this interesting section 'Antichrist in the Province of Asia' should be studied in connexion with the subject of this Note.

BIBLICAL DOCTRINE OF ANTICHRIST 165

8. There remain only the references in the Johannine Epistles to *The* which, it will be remembered, we owe the name of Antichrist. In these, *Epistles.* conformably to the writer's main object, the spiritual side of the conception is again predominant. Thus, after indicating some of the main elements in Christian Truth, St John passes in I. ii. 18 to the conflict into which at 'a last hour' Truth will be brought with Falsehood, and in token of this points to the decisive sign by which this crisis will be known, namely, the coming of 'Antichrist,' the absence of the article in the original showing that the word has already come to be used as a technical proper name. Nor does 'Antichrist' stand alone. Rather he is to be regarded as 'the personification of the principle shown in different antichrists' (Westcott *ad loc.*), who, by their denial that 'Jesus is the Christ,' deny in like manner the revelation of God as Father (ii. 22), and, consequently, the true union between God and man (iv. 3).

It is, therefore, into a very different atmosphere that we are intro- Present duced after the strange symbolism of the Apocalypse, and the scenic signi- representation of the Pauline description. And one likes to think that ficance the last word of Revelation on this mysterious topic is one which leaves of Anti- it open to every one to apply to the spiritual workings of evil in his own christ. heart, and in the world around him, a truth which has played so large a part in the history of God's people in the past, and which may still pass through many varying and progressive applications, before it reaches its final fulfilment in the 'dispensation of the fulness of the times' (Eph. i. 10).

NOTE J.

On the interpretation of 2 Thess. ii. 1—12.

Ἐχρῆν δὲ τὸν μὲν ἕτερον τῶν ἄκρων καὶ βέλτιστον υἱὸν ἀναγορεύεσθαι τοῦ θεοῦ διὰ τὴν ὑπεροχήν, τὸν δὲ τούτῳ κατὰ διάμετρον ἐναντίον υἱὸν τοῦ πονηροῦ δαίμονος καὶ Σατανᾶ καὶ διαβόλου.

Orig. c. Cels. vi. 45 (ed. Koetschau II. 116).

Varied interpretations of the passage.

There are few passages in the N.T. for which more varied interpretations have been proposed than for 2 Thess. ii. 1—12. It is impossible to attempt to give a full account of these here[1]. But it may be well at least to indicate the main lines along which the exegesis of the passage has run. In doing so we shall follow as far as possible the historical order, for, though the different schools of interpreters cannot be rigidly distinguished according to periods of time, there have been on the whole certain clearly marked cycles in the method of interpretation applied to this difficult and mysterious passage.

i. The Ante-Nicene Church.

i. The Ante-Nicene Church. General view.

In the Early Church the ecclesiastical writers, amidst considerable differences in detail, agreed in regarding the whole passage as a *prophecy* which, at the time when they wrote, was still unfulfilled. Rightly interpreting the Parousia as the personal Return of the Lord for the Last Judgment, they saw in the Man of lawlessness an equally definite personality, who was to be manifested at the close of the world's history, but who for the time being was held in check by a restraining influence, generally identified, from the time of Tertullian[2] onwards, with the power of the Roman Empire.

---

[1] Special excursuses are devoted to the passage in most of the commentaries: see especially those of Lünemann, Bornemann and Wohlenberg among the German expositors, and of Eadie, Gloag, and Findlay among the English. The article on 'Antichrist' by Rev. F. Meyrick in Smith's *D.B.* contains many interesting details. Cf. also Döllinger *The First Age of Christianity* (tr. by Oxenham, 4th ed. 1906) Appendix 1., and W. Bousset *The Antichrist Legend* (Eng. Tr. by Keane, London, 1896), where the patristic evidence is given very fully. E. Wadstein has collected much curious material in his essay on *Die eschatologische Ideengruppe: Antichrist-Weltsabbat-Weltende und Weltgericht* (Leipzig, 1896) p. 81 ff., and for the conceptions of Antichrist from the xvth to the xxth century see H. Preuss *Die Vorstellungen vom Antichrist im späteren Mittelalter, bei Luther, und in der Konfessionellen Polemik* (Leipzig, 1906).

[2] *De Resurr.* c. 24 'quis nisi Romanus status?' Elsewhere Tertullian

Of this line of interpretation we find traces already in the Didache xvi. and in Justin Martyr *Dial.* 110, and it is clearly enunciated by Irenaeus who presents a vivid picture of a personal Antichrist 'diabolicam apostasiam in se recapitulans,' and 'seducens eos qui adorant eum, quasi ipse sit Christus' (*adv. Haer.* v. 25. 1). Elsewhere (v. 30. 2) he ascribes to Antichrist a Jewish origin, tracing his descent, in accordance with O.T. prophecy (Jer. viii. 16), to the tribe of Dan—a view that was shared by Hippolytus (*de Antichristo* c. 14)[1]. Origen is equally definite in looking for a single being, υἱὸν τοῦ πονηροῦ δαίμονος καὶ Σατανᾶ καὶ διαβόλου, who is to be opposed κατὰ διάμετρον to the Christ (*c. Celsum* vi. 45 f. ed. Koetschau II. 115 ff.), and similarly Cyril of Jerusalem speaks of Antichrist as Satan's 'organ,' who will take his place in the Temple of Jerusalem, when not one stone of the old building has been left standing upon another, and adds the pious wish that he himself may be spared from seeing the horrors of that day (*Catech.* xv. 7).

<small>Early Greek writers.</small>

The Latin commentators follow on much the same lines[2]. By 'Ambrosiaster' the Antichrist is not named, but, arising out of the circumcision he is to kill the saints and restore liberty to Rome. The working of this mystery of iniquity had already begun with Nero, who had killed the Apostles, and from him it had passed on to Diocletian and Julian. 'Ambrosiaster' appears to identify ὁ ἄνομος with the devil.

<small>The Latin commentators.</small>

Pelagius says pointedly 'Nisi Antichristus uenerit, non ueniet Christus,' and then goes on to describe how the 'homo peccati' ('diaboli scilicet') will attempt to revive the Temple and its worship with the view of persuading the Jews to accept him 'pro Christo[3].' For this the false doctrines already at work were preparing the way: the only restraining influence was the 'regnum, quod nunc tenet.'

Differences in this general view were naturally caused, according as τὸ μυστήριον τῆς ἀνομίας was found in the political or in the religious sphere[4]:

<small>Differences in detail.</small>

says that Christians should pray for the Emperor, because ' clausulam saeculi acerbitates horrendas comminantem Romani imperii commeatu scimus retardari ' (*Apol.* c. 32).
[1] Cf. c. 6, ἐν περιτομῇ ὁ Σωτὴρ ἦλθεν εἰς τὸν κόσμον, καὶ αὐτὸς [i.e. the Antichrist] ὁμοίως ἐλεύσεται. Elsewhere (c. 15) Hippolytus describes the Antichrist as τύραννος καὶ βασιλεύς, κριτὴς δεινός, υἱὸς τοῦ διαβόλου.
[2] For 'Ambrosiaster' and Pelagius see the List of Commentaries.
[3] The passage may be given in full according to the correct reading of the Karlsruhe MS., kindly supplied by Prof. Souter; in this short extract it differs in nine places from the text of the Pseudo-Jerome in Migne: 'Supra omnipotentiam et aeternitatem se iactabit et sacramenta culturae diuinae corrigere uel augere se dicet, et templum Hierusolymae restaurare temptabit omnesque legis caerimonias reparare tantum ut ueritatis Christi euangelium soluat, quae res Iudaeos eum pro Christo suscipere persuadebit, in suo, non in dei, nomine uenientem.'
[4] In Chrysostom we find again the attempt to associate Nero with Antichrist: Νερῶνα ἐνταῦθά φησιν ὡσανεὶ τύπον ὄντα τοῦ ἀντιχριστοῦ...καὶ καλῶς εἶπε, τὸ μυστήριον· τουτέστιν, οὐ φανερῶς, ὡς ἐκεῖνος, οὐδὲ ἀπηρυθριασμένως (*Hom.* iv. *in II. ad Thess.*). Theodoret, on the other hand, thinks that the Apostle has in view the heresies that were beginning to spring up (τὰς ἀναφυείσας αἱρέσεις) within the Church itself. According to Ephrem Syrus (*Comm. in*

while it is further significant to notice, in view of later developments, that, according to the testimony of Augustine[1], there were already some who, despairing apparently of finding a consistent literal interpretation for the different details, had come to apply it in a general way to all forms of evil as they arose in the Church.

ii. The Middle Ages.

ii. The Middle Ages.

During the earlier portion of the Middle Ages this prophetic interpretation of the passage as an inspired description of what was actually to happen in the great Day of the Lord continued to prevail, not however without such modifications as were required by the changing relations between Church and State, and the divisions that were arising within the Church itself. Already too there were increasing signs of the tendency, afterwards to become so marked, to find at least partial fulfilments of the prophecy in contemporary historical events.

The Eastern Church.

Thus in the Eastern Church, struggling for bare existence against the forces of Islamism, Muhammad was readily identified with Antichrist, while in the Western Church the arrogant pretensions of some of the Church's own rulers had already begun to lead to whispers of the possibility of a Papal Antichrist. It is a curious fact indeed that the first traces of such a view seem actually to have come from an occupant of the Papal See itself, when, towards the close of the sixth century, Gregory I., in denouncing the claims of the contemporary Byzantine patriarch, went the length of saying that whoever arrogates to himself the title of 'universal priest' is a precursor of Antichrist and described the title as 'erroris nomen, stultum ac superbum vocabulum, perversum, nefandum, scelestum vocabulum, nomen blasphemiae[2].' Four centuries later Arnulph, Bishop of Orleans, declared much to the same effect at the Council of Rheims (A.D. 991) that if the Roman Pontiff was destitute of charity, and puffed up with knowledge, he was Antichrist. It was only therefore giving statements such as these a general application when in the twelfth century Joachim of Floris in his *Enchiridion in Apocalypsim* began to trace a correspondence between the warnings of the Apocalypse and the evils of his time—a mode of interpretation which another Franciscan, John Oliva, followed up by asserting that in the opinion of some Antichrist would be a 'pseudo-papa[3].'

The Western Church. First hints of the possibility of a Papal Antichrist.

Development of

When such hints were thrown out within the Church itself, one can readily understand that they were eagerly laid hold of by all who, on grounds

---

Ep. Pauli, Venice 1893, p. 193) Antichrist is to be a circumcised Jew of the tribe of Judah ('ex ipso populo et ex tribu Judae, neque in praeputio, sed in circumcisione') who, imitating the coming of the Lord, is to take his place in the Church itself, but who for the time being is 'restrained' by the Jewish Temple-worship and afterwards by the preaching of the Apostles (see further Wohlenberg, p. 194 f.).

[1] *De Civ. Dei* xx. 19 'alii...non putant dictum, nisi de malis et fictis, qui sunt in Ecclesia.' Augustine himself despaired apparently of finding a correct interpretation for the passage: 'Ego prorsus quid dixerit, me fateor ignorare' (*ut s.*).

[2] *Ep.* xxxiii. lib. vii. p. 891, *Opera* III. Migne.

[3] See Swete *Apoc.* p. ccviii f.

INTERPRETATION OF 2 THESS. ii. 1—12

of liberty or morality, found themselves obliged to oppose the Roman
hierarchy, and that the identification of the Papacy with Antichrist
gradually became a commonplace amongst the sects. At first apparently
it was only an individual that was thought of, but from this the transition
was easy to a succession of individuals or a polity, as when Wycliffe asserted
of the Pope generally that he did not seem to be 'the vicar of Christ,
but the vicar of Antichrist[1],' and in the last year of his life (1384) wrote a
treatise *De Christo et suo adversario Antichristo*, in which he identified
the Pope with Antichrist for twelve reasons, many of these being applicable
to the Pope *as such*.

this view amongst opponents of the Hierarchy.

iii. *The Reformed Church.*

The reference of Antichrist to the Papal Hierarchy continued to be the
prevailing view of the Reformers. And such stress was laid on it by
Luther in the great controversial writings of 1520 and succeeding years[2] that
it found a place in the Articles of Smalkald which, under his influence, were
adopted in 1537 by a number of evangelical theologians as their rule of
faith[3]. In England both Houses of Convocation decreed in 1606 that
'if any man shall affirm that the intolerable pride of the Bishop of Rome,
for the time still being, ... doth not argue him plainly to be the Man of Sin,
mentioned by the Apostle, he doth greatly err[4].' And a few years later the
Translators of our A.V. complimented King James for having by means of
his tractate *Apologia pro Juramento Fidelitatis* 'given such a blow to that
man of sin, as will not be healed.' A section of the Westminster *Confession
of Faith* is devoted to defending the same view. And, with a few honourable
exceptions, the equation 'the Pope, or the Papacy, is Antichrist' may be
said to have been the prevailing view of Protestant exegetes for a period of
about two hundred years[5].

iii. The Reformed Church. Prevailing view, Papacy = Antichrist.

---

[1] *Dial.* 31. 73 'videtur papam non esse Christi vicarium, sed vicarium antichristi.' Elsewhere he goes the length of saying that no man is better fitted to be the vicar of Satan than the Roman pontiff himself (' ut sit vicarius principalis Satanae et praecipuus antichristus' *de Blasphemia* c. 3), and characterizes his legates as 'a latere antichristi.'

[2] On 11th Oct. 1520 Luther writes, 'Jetzt bin ich um vieles freier, nachdem ich endlich gewiss geworden bin, dass der Papst der Antichrist ist' (*Briefwechsel*, ed. Enders ii. 491), and to this conviction he clung to the end of his life; see Preuss *op. cit.* p. 145 ff.

[3] In the later authoritative Latin translation of these Articles the reference runs as follows: 'Haec doctrina praeclare ostendit, papam esse ipsum verum Antichristum, qui supra et contra Christum sese extulit et evexit, quandoquidem Christianos non vult esse salvos sine sua potestate, quae tamen nihil est, et a deo nec ordinata nec mandata est. Hoc proprie loquendo est se efferre supra et contra deum, sicut Paulus 2 Thess. ii. loquitur.'

[4] Cardwell *Synodalia* i. p. 379.

[5] The position of Calvin (Comm. ad *loc.*) is interesting. While agreeing in the general reference of Antichrist to the Papacy ('Quid, obsecro, est se efferre supra omne quod numen reputatur, si hoc Papa non facit?'), he finds the restraining influence in the limited diffusion of the Gospel. Not till the Gospel was preached to the

170   THE EPISTLES TO THE THESSALONIANS

Rise of new methods of interpretation.

But not to dwell further on a system of interpretation which has nothing to commend it except the ease with which it lends itself to partisan purposes[1], it is of more importance to trace the rise of certain new methods of apocalyptic interpretation, which have powerfully affected the view taken of this passage in modern times.

iv. Modern Views.

iv. Modern Views.
(1) The *ideal view*.

(1) Amongst these a prominent place must be given to the tendency to regard the whole conception in a purely ideal manner. Unable to agree with a method of interpretation in which personal references and animosities played so large a part, the followers of this system understood the passage in a general or spiritual sense. The concrete individual traits of the Pauline picture were wholly ignored, or else treated simply as symbolic representations of certain great principles always at work in the Church and the world.

Of this tendency C. L. Nitzsch is a striking example[2]. In the Appendix to his Essays *De Revelatione* (1808), starting from the assumption that the παρουσία is a 'factum ideale,' not to be looked for at any definite time or place, but whenever and wherever faith needs to be strengthened, he goes on to say that, as regards the Man of lawlessness, no such man ever has existed or apparently will exist ('nusquam quisquam fuit nec in posterum futurus esse videtur'). St Paul, that is to say, in his whole representation was influenced by subjective considerations, and without any regard to the historic truthfulness of his picture desired only the edification of his readers.

Later modifications.

Others who followed in this direction, without perhaps going the same length, or losing sight so entirely of objective realities, were such expositors as Pelt in Germany, who lays down as a preliminary condition to his whole discussion that St Paul was looking for no visible Return of Christ[3], and Jowett in England, who for a guide to the Apostle's meaning in this particular passage lays stress on his 'habitual thought' as revealed in such passages as Col. ii. 8, 16, or the spiritual combat of Rom. vii.

whole world, would the Man of Sin be manifested ('Haec igitur dilatio erat, donec completus esset Evangelii cursus: quia gratuita ad salutem invitatio ordine prior erat').

[1] It is hardly to be wondered at that many Romanist scholars (*e.g.* Estius †1613) should adopt the methods of their opponents, and retaliate by asserting that the Pauline apostacy was rather to be found in defection from Rome, and that consequently Luther and his followers were the real Antichrist. At the same time it is right to notice that to the Jesuit scholars Ribeira (†1601) and Alcasar (†1613) belongs the credit of inaugurating more scientific methods in the interpretation of the Apocalypse: see Swete *Apoc*. p. ccix f.

[2] On Nitzsch's position see especially Bornemann p. 428 ff.

[3] P. 185 '...tenentes, illum Christi adventum a Paulo non visibilem habitum.' De Wette is even more explicit in declaring that 'whoever finds more than a subjective outlook of the Apostle into the future of the Christian Church from his own historical position falls into error,' and that to expect any actual embodiment of Satan is 'contrary alike to the reflective understanding and the pious feeling.'

The practical advantages of this view are at once apparent. The prophecy is made universally applicable, and lessons can be drawn from it for all succeeding generations of readers, whatever the special circumstances in which they find themselves. But this result is only reached by depriving the very literal and precise statements of the passage of all definite meaning, and consequently we are not surprised to find that a large and influential body of English expositors, while applying the truths of the prophecy continuously throughout the whole course of the world's history lay stress at the same time on their final and complete embodiment at the English end of the days. Amongst supporters of this view it is sufficient to expositors. mention such names as Alford, Ellicott, Eadie, Alexander, Dods, and most recently Findlay, according to whom, 'The ideal Antichrist conceived by Scripture, when actualized, will mould himself upon the lines of the Antichrists whose career the Church has already witnessed' (p. 231). But however true this may be as an *application* of the Apostle's words, it contributes little or nothing to their *interpretation*[1], or to the exact meaning they must have conveyed to their first writer or readers. So far from their conceiving an 'ideal' Antichrist, 'there is scarcely,' in Findlay's own words already quoted elsewhere (p. 164), 'a more matter-of-fact prediction in the Bible.' And it is not until the expositor has succeeded in forming some idea of the genesis and reference of its varied details, that he can hope to apply with any degree of success the underlying law or principle to present-day needs. It is only therefore in keeping with the growth of the historical spirit that alongside of this more subjective school of criticism, there should have been a determined attempt to find the real key to the passage in the historical circumstances of the time when it was written.

For the rise of this method of interpretation, which is generally known (2) The as the *praeterist* or *historical* to distinguish it from the *futurist* or historical *predictive* method, we can go back as far as Grotius who in his *Annotationes* Begin- (Paris, 1644), starting from the untenable position that the Epistles were nings of written in the second year of Caligula, found the fulfilment of the passage in this view. that Emperor's desire to set up a statue of himself in Jerusalem (Jos. *Antt.* xviii. 261 (viii. 2), cp. Suet. *Calig.* xxii. 33), the restraining power being the proconsul Vitellius, 'vir apud Judaeos gratiosus et magnis exercitibus imperans,' and the ἄνομος, who was wrongly dissociated from the Man of lawlessness himself, Simon Magus. Wetstein on the other hand identified the Man of lawlessness with Titus, on the ground that his army brought their standards into the Temple, offered sacrifices to them, and proclaimed the Emperor as αὐτοκράτωρ (Jos. *B.J.* vi. 6. 1), while Döllinger preferred to think of the youthful Nero, restrained by the efforts of the dull Claudius.

Apart too from these distinctive references to the Imperial House Varieties another important band of scholars sought the apostasy referred to rather in its ap- in the revolt of the Jews from the Roman yoke—the restraining power plication. being found either in their leaders who were against the revolt (Le Clerc), or in the prayers of the Christians who warded off for a time the destruction

---

[1] For some good remarks on the difficulty caused by confusing these two very different things see Denney *Thess.* p. 317 f.

of Jerusalem (Schöttgen), or, if an individual had to be sought, in the influence of such a man as James the Just (Wieseler). It soon became obvious indeed that this system lent itself to almost endless modifications and combinations in accordance with the predilections of its supporters. And we can understand therefore the relief with which in the beginning of last century an application of it was hailed, which for a time seemed to command widespread assent.

The Nero Redivivus theory.

Its author was Kern[1] who, starting with the postulate that the whole passage was written under the influence of the Apocalypse, found the Man of lawlessness in the widespread belief in *Nero Redivivus*, the restraining power in Vespasian and his son Titus, and the apostasy in the wickedness of the Jews in their war against the Romans. This line of interpretation was adopted by Baur[2], Weizsäcker[3], Holtzmann[4], and Schmiedel[5], to mention only a few representative names. But apart from the consideration that, if accepted, it would be fatal to the authenticity of the Epistle, in which we have already found good reason for believing (Intr. p. lxxvi ff.), it is wrecked on the fact that the παρουσία referred to by St Paul cannot be understood of the period of the destruction of Jerusalem, as the theory requires, but only of the second and personal coming of the Lord Jesus Himself. On this the evidence of the Epistles is quite decisive. And in view of it it is unnecessary to spend time in showing that, even were it otherwise, the precise traits of the Pauline picture are not fulfilled in Caligula, Nero[6], or any other Emperor of the period, though we must not lose sight of the fact that some of the actions of the first-named may have influenced the Apostle's language[7].

(3) *The traditional view.*

The real roots of his delineation are however, as we have already had occasion to notice, to be sought elsewhere. And it is one of the great services of what may be known as the *traditional* view to have drawn

---

[1] *Tübinger Zeitschrift für Theologie* ii. 1839, p. 145 ff.

[2] *Theol. Jahrbücher* xiv. 1855, p. 141 ff., translated as Appendix III. to the Engl. ed. of *Paul, His Life and Works* (Lond. 1873—5).

[3] *Das apost. Zeitalter* p. 521, Engl. Tr. ii. p. 193 f. 'It is impossible that anything else can have been meant than the Neronic Antichrist, who at present is delayed by the living Emperor, and who in his own time will be supported by the deceit of false prophecy (cf. Rev. xiii).'

[4] *Einl.*[3] p. 217 'Zur Conception eines Bildes wie Apoc. 13...hat Nero gesessen.'

[5] *Hand. Comm.* zu 2 Thess. ii. 1—12 'Nur die zeitgeschichtliche Deutung hat wissenschaftliches Recht.'

[6] So strong an opponent of the Epistle's authenticity as Wrede says pointedly, 'Die Deutung der Stelle auf Nero ist jedenfalls gründlich erschüttert' (*Echtheit* p. 1). Similarly Pfleiderer (*Urchristentum*[2] p. 97 f., Engl. Tr. i. p. 138 f.) while postulating the close affinity of the Pauline representations with Rev. xiii., xvii., xix., xx., admits that 'the distinctive features which in the Johannine apocalypse point to the legend of the return of Nero are completely wanting in 2 Thess.'

[7] For the relation of the Pauline picture to Caligula see Klöpper *Der zweite Brief an die Thess.* p. 53, and cf. Spitta *Urchristentum* i. p. 148 'Es handelt sich hier eben um die Anwendung der Caligula-Apokalypse auf eine neue Zeit.'

INTERPRETATION OF 2 THESS. ii. 1—12

attention afresh to how largely the whole delineation grew out of the Jewish experiences of the Apostle. For not only did the uncompromising hostility of his Jewish fellow-countrymen suggest to St Paul the source whence the crowning development of evil was to manifest itself (see pp. xxviii, xxxi f.), but he was led to fall back on O.T. prophecy and current Jewish Apocalyptic for the actual details which he worked up into his dread picture.

This line of interpretation is by no means new. From the earliest times the dependence of many traits in the Pauline Antichrist upon the godless king in Daniel have been clearly recognized. But it is only in more recent years that increasing knowledge of the sources has made it possible to trace systematically the Jewish tradition lying at the base of the N.T. passage. According to Bousset (*Encyc. Bibl.* col. 179) the credit of breaking fresh ground in this direction belongs to Schneckenburger[1]. And now Bousset himself has endeavoured to carry the tradition still further back, and to find in the Antichrist legend 'a later anthropomorphic transformation' of the old Babylonian Dragon myth, which he regards as 'one of the earliest evolved by primitive man[2].' The data on which this theory is built up are too uncertain to make it more than a very plausible conjecture (cf. p. 159), nor, after all, even if it were more fully established, would it have any direct bearing on our inquiry, for certainly all thought of any such mythical origin of the current imagery was wholly absent from St Paul's mind[3]. In the meantime, then, we must be content with re-emphasizing that it is to the Jewish apocryphal and pseudepigraphic writings, and especially to the prophetical books of the Greek O.T., and the eschatological teaching of Jesus, that we must principally look for light on the outward features of the Pauline representation.

Possible relation to primitive myth.

General conclusion.

---

[1] See the survey of his writings by Böhmer in the *Jahrbücher für Deutsche Theologie* iv. (1859) p. 405 ff.

[2] *The Antichrist Legend* p. 13 ff.

[3] Cf. Preuschen *Z.N.T.W.* ii. p. 169 n.1.

INDEXES

I. SUBJECTS.

Achaia, xlv, 11
Acts of Apostles, parallels with, xlii
Agrapha of our Lord, 39, 66, 77, 115
Amanuensis, St Paul's employment of an, xc f., 124 ff.
Analysis of the Epistles: 1 Thess., 2; 2 Thess., 84
Angels, lxx, 45, 89
Antichrist, Biblical doctrine of, 158 ff.; views regarding, at different periods in the history of the Church, 166 ff.
Aorist: of inception, 17; expressing immediate past, 32
Apostle, title of, 21
Armilus, 163
Article: emphatic, 13, 49, 105, 112; demonstrative, 81, 117; absence of the, 4, 14, 48, 51, 64, 75, 94
Authenticity of the Epistles: 1 Thess., lxxii ff.; 2 Thess., lxxvi ff.

Benediction, 81
Brother, xliv, 8; brotherly-love, 52 f.

Cabiri, xlvi
Call, the Divine, 26, 51, 79, 93
Chiasmus, 67
Christ, the title of, 136; the doctrine of, lxvi ff.
Church, St Paul's use of the term, 4
Church-life in Thessalonica, xlvi ff., 71 ff.
Commentaries on the Epistles, cii ff.
Compound-verbs, St Paul's love for, liii, 40
Conversion, 13
Crown, 35

Date of the Epistles, xxxv ff.
Day of the Lord, 64
Death: of Christ, 57, 69 f.; of believers, 55 ff.
Destruction, eternal, 91
Dichotomy and trichotomy, 78 f.
Divinity of our Lord emphasized, lxvi f.

Election, 8, 106
Emphasis in the N. T., lvii
Epistolary formulae, 129

M. THESS.

Eschatology, lxix ff.
Ethical teaching, lxxi

Faith, 6; and works, 6, 94; and love, 40, 68
Friends, St Paul's Thessalonian, 133 f.

Gentiles, 31, 49
Glory, 27
God, doctrine of, lxiv ff.
Gospel, the Apostolic, lxv, 8 f., 17 ff.; see also p. 141 ff.
Grace, 4, 81
Greeting, Apostolic form of, 4 f.

Heart, 19
Heathen-world: its immorality, 48 ff.; its hopelessness, 56
Heavens, the, 14 f.
Hellenism, St Paul and, lv, lvii
Hope, 7

Impurity, 48 ff.
Infinitive: consecutive with ὥστε, 11; explanatory, 17; articular, 38, 47; with πρὸς τό, 24; with εἰς τό, 26, 31, 42, 53
Inscriptions, Greek, use made of, viii f.; see Index III. 1 (a)
Integrity: of 1 Thess., lxxvi; of 2 Thess., lxxxviii f.

Jesus, the name of, 135; the words of, lix ff.; Jesus and Paul, lxii
Jews, opposition of, to St Paul, xxviii f., xxxi f.; condemnation of, 29 ff.
Joy, 10, 74 f.
Judaea, 29
Judaistic literature, use made of, ix; see Index III. 2
Judge, Christ as, lxvii
Judgment, the Last, 88 ff.

Kingdom, xxviii f., 27
Kiss, 80

Letter-writer, St Paul as a, xxxiv, xli ff., 121 ff.

12

Life with Christ, lxviii f., lxx f., 62, 70
Lord, the name of, lxvii, 136 ff.; the word of the, 12, 58, 109
Love, 7

Macedonia, xlv, 11
Man of lawlessness, 98 ff.
Manual labour, xlvii, 54, 114 f.
Manuscripts, Greek, of the Epistles, xciii ff.
Meiosis, 30, 110, 114
Metaphors derived from the way, 13, 26, 43; the athletic ground, 17, 71, 109; the home, 21 f., 25, 33; building, 37, 70; warfare, 68; inversion of metaphors, 22, 66
Michael, 60
Morals, lessons in Christian, 45 ff.
Muhammad and Antichrist, 168

'Name,' significance of, 94, 113
Nero redivivus, lxxxvii, 172

Old Testament, Greek, relation of language to, liv, lviii f.
Order of the Epistles, xxxix

Papacy and Antichrist, 168 f.
Papyrus, manufacture of, 122 f.; examples of papyrus-letters, 127 ff.
Papyri, Greek, use made of, viii f.; see Index III. 1 (*b*)
Parousia of Christ, lxix f., 59 ff.; of Antichrist, 98 ff.
Participle: present part. with art., 11, 15, 26, 39, 79; with οὐ, 19; for the ind., 25
Patristic authorities for the text, xcix ff.
Paul as a man, xliii f.; as a missionary, xliv ff.; 'I Paul,' 34, 39
Peace, 4, 77
Persecution at Thessalonica, xxxii, 10, 87
Philippians, Epistle to the, coincidences with, liii
Place of writing of the Epistles, xxxv, xxxix
Plays on words, 19, 54, 110, 115
Plural, epistolary, 131 f.
Prayer: instances of, in the Epistles, lxv; addressed to Christ, lxvi; the duty of, 75
Prepositions, uses of, in late Greek, 12, 20, 38, 62, 95, 109
Prophesyings, 76

Quotations in Pauline Epistles, 126

Rabbinical literature cited, 35, 49, 54, 77, 88, 115
Readings, some variant, discussed, 5, 10, 21, 30, 37, 38, 45, 51, 66, 85, 90, 92, 103, 105, 106, 113
Resurrection of Jesus, 15, 57; of believers, 60
Retaliation forbidden, 74
Rhythm, supposed, in Pauline Epp., lvi
Roman Empire as the restraining power, lxx, lxxxviii, 101

Salvation, 69
Satan, 34 f., 39, 111
Sayings of Jesus, reminiscences of, lix ff.
Signature, authenticating, xcii, 129 f., and see Index IV. *s.v.* γράφω
Silvanus, 3
Sleep, figurative use of, 55 ff.
Son, Christ as, lxvi
Soteriology, lxviii f.
Spirit: doctrine of the Holy Spirit, lxviii; spiritual gifts, 75 f., 96; spirit of man, 78
Structure, general, of the Epistles, xlviii ff.
Studies, special, on the Epistles, cviii f.
Style of the Epistles, lvi f.

Text, Greek, adopted, vii f.; authorities for, xciii ff.
Thanksgiving: the Apostolic, 5, 27, 41, 86, 106; the duty of, 75
Thessalonica, the city of, xxi ff.; St Paul's connexion with, xxvi ff.; general character of Church of, xlvi ff.
Timothy, 3 f., 37; as supposed author of 2 Thess., lxxxix ff.
Title of the Epistles, 3
Tradition, 107 f.
Truth and falsehood, 104 f.
Type, 11

Verse-divisions, unusual, in the WH. text, 6, 20, 25
Versions, ancient, of the Epistles, xcvi ff.
Versions, renderings from various: early English, 9, 10, 12, 14, 20, 33 f., 50, 55, 73, 86; A.V. of 1611, 13, 64; German, 32, 50, 78, 107, 110, 115; Latin, 6, 7, 12, 17, 22, 28, 40, 41, 42, 55, 68, 73, 78, 86, 107, 115
Vocabulary of the Epistles, lii ff.; of 2 Thess., lxxix f.

Will of God, 48
Women, position of, in Macedonia, xxvii
Wrath, Divine, 15

Zoroastrianism, lxxi

II. AUTHORS.

The main object of this Index is to supplement the lists of authorities in the Table of Abbreviations and in the Introduction VII and VIII. As a rule, therefore, no references are given to the grammatical, lexical, and textual works that are there described, or to the commentators on the Epistles, though occasionally, in the case of works most frequently cited, a general reference has been added for the sake of completeness. It should be noted further that the majority of references are to actual quotations, and not to mere citations of the authors specified.

Abbot, Ezra, 122, 148
Abbott, Edwin A., 13 and *passim*
Abbott, G. F., xxi, xxv, 130
Abbott, T. K., 51, 69
Aeschylus, 14, 38, 56, 105, 145
Antipater of Thessalonica, xxi
Antoninus, Marcus, 98, 115, 117
Aristides, 25, 28, 99
Aristophanes, 141
Aristotle, xlvii, 19, 47, 76, 77
Arnulph, 168
Athanasius, 103
Augustine, 21, 48, 55, 61, 62, 168

Bacon, 43
Bacon, B. W., xxxviii, xlii, lxxxviii
Bahnsen, lxxviii
Barnabas, 52, 86
Bartlet, xxxvii, xliii
Basil, 111
Baur, F. C., xxxix, lxxiii ff., lxxviii, lxxxvi, 172
Bechtel, 27
Beet, J. A., 65
Bevan, E., 160
Bigg, xlvii, 104
Birt, 123 f.
Blass, viii, xxix, lvi, 6 and *passim*
Boehmer, see Schneckenburger
Böklen, lxxi
Bousset, lxii, lxxi, lxxxvii, 35, 158, 159, 162, 163, 166, 173
Briggs, lxvii
Brightman, 79
Brooke, A. E., xciii
Browning, R., 66, 88
Bruce, A. B., lxiv, lxx
Brückner, xxxvi
Burton, xxiii, 134
Butcher, 63, 81

Cameniata, xxiv, xxvi
Carr, A., lv
Castelli, 163
Catullus, 56
Charles, R. H., ix, lxxviii, lxxxvii; and see Index III. 2
Chase, 14, 15, 111, 193
Cheyne, 60, 161
Chrysostom, xlvi, 57, 82, 134, 149
Cicero, xxii, 16, 48, 56, 123
Clemen, xxxi, xxxvi, xxxvii, lxxvi, lxxviii
Clement of Alexandria, 68
Clement of Rome, 9, 79, 117; Pseudo-Clement, 15
Clementine Homilies, 39
Clementine Recognitions, 59
Colani, lxvii
Conybeare, F. C., 56, 80, and see Index IV. *passim*
Cook, A. S., 143
Cousinéry, xxi
Cromwell, O., 20
Cumont, F., lxxi, 14, 193
Curtius, E., lv, 144
Cyril of Jerusalem, 167

Dalman, 27, 88, 136, 141
Dante, 88
Davidson, A. B., 64
Davidson, S., lxxviii
Deissmann, viii, liii, lvi, lxix, 3, 4, 62 and *passim*
Delitzsch, F., xlvii
Demetrius, 121
Demosthenes, 16, 30, 108, 115, 116, 152
Dick, K., 131
Dieterich, A., 141
Dimitsas, 134

12—2

INDEXES

Diodorus Siculus, 20, 31, 40, 145, 148
Dion Cassius, 19, 54, 141
Dion Chrysostom, 19
Dion Halicarnassus, 97, 148
Dobschütz, von, xlv, lv
Döllinger, 166
Driver, 160
Drummond, R. J., lxii
Duchesne and Bayet, xxi, xxiii, and see Index III. 1 (a).

Edersheim, xlvii
Ellicott, 33, 78, 116
Ephrem Syrus, 167
Epictetus, 17, 37, 40, 46
Epiphanius, 149
Epistle Vienne and Lyons, lxxvii
Erman and Krebs, 123 f.
Euripides, 15, 50, 67, 87, 145
Eusebius, 149
Everling, lxx, 39
Ewald, xxxix, 147, 160

Fabricius, 3
Feine, lxii, 111
Firmicus, xlvi
Foat, 125
Friedländer, L., 130
Friedländer, M., 159, 161, 162
Fritzsche, 22, 23, 40, 43

Gardner, see Roberts
Gardthausen, 123 f.
Geldart, 32
Gerhard, G. A., 129
Gfrörer, lxxxvii
Gibbon, xxiv
Gifford, 40
Ginsburg, 158
Goguel, lxii
Gorgias, 56
Gregory, C. R., xcix
Gregory of Nazianzen, 149
Gregory of Nyssa, lii
Gressmann, 64
Grill, 14
Gunkel, lxxxvii, 158, 161, 164

Harnack, xxxvi, xlv, lxxviii, 8, 11, 21, 193
Harris, Rendel, xxx, 13, 126
Hart, ix, 64
Hartung, 61
Hatch, 23 and *passim*
Hausrath, lxxxix
Hawkins, 32
Heinrici, lvii
Heitmüller, W., 113
Hermas, lxxiii, 72
Herodotus, xxi, 21
Heuzey and Daumet, xxi, and see Index III. 1 (a)

Hicks, E. L., lv, 31, 54, 192
Hilgenfeld, lxxviii, lxxxvii
Hippocrates, 113
Hippolytus, 167
Hollmann, lxxxv
Holtzmann, lxvii, lxix, lxxxi, lxxxiii, 172
Homer, 38, 50, 61, 113, 141
Horace, 20, 33, 48
Hort, xxvii, xlviii, 4, 9, 21, 26, 42, 63, 71, 72, 89, 193, 194

Ignatius, lxxiii, lxxvii, 6, 67, 71, 112, 144, 147
Irenaeus, lxxiii, lxxvii, 99, 167
Isidore of Pelusium, xlvi
Isocrates, 153

James, M. R., 158, and see Index III. 2
Jannaris, 46
Jebb, R. C., 23
Jerome, xlvii, 12, 55, 64, 100
Joachim, 168
Josephus (ed. Niese), 20, 29, 77, 78, 100, 122, 131, 133, 148, 164
Jülicher, xxxi, lxii, lxxi, lxxv, lxxviii, lxxx
Juncker, lxvi
Justin Martyr, xxix, lxxvii, 66, 72, 144, 147

Kabisch, 90
Kaftan, lxii
Karabacek, 123
Kautzsch, ix
Keble, 142
Kennedy, H. A. A., lxix, lxx, 27, 31, 59, 91, 99, 126, 138
Kenyon, F. G., 8, 122 ff., 156, and see Index III. 1 (b)
Kern, lxxviii, 172
Klöpper, xxxix, 133
Knowling, xxvii, xxxvi, lxii, lxxv,. lxxvi, 48, 64
Krauss, 21
Krebs, see Erman

Lactantius, 15, 64
Lake, Kirsopp, 58
Laqueur, R., 42
Laurent, xxxix, 126, 131
Leake, xxi
Leighton, 75
Lietzmann, 6, 28
Lightfoot, J. B., lvii, lxvi, lxxix, 6, 20, 21, 71, 94, 105, 111, 114, 133 and *passim*
Livy, 35
Lobeck, xlvi
Lock, W., xli, xlv, 32, 116, 126
Locke, John, xlii

II. AUTHORS

Lucian, xxiii, 52, 124, 141
Lueken, 60
Luther, 169

Mahaffy, xxvi, 125, and see Index III. 1 (b)
Manen, van, lxxvi
Mathews, Shailer, lxix
Mayor, J. B., 35, 108
McClellan, 193
McGiffert, xxxvi, xxxvii, lxxviii, 76
McLean, Norman, xciii
Menegoz, xxxvi, lxiv
Meyrick, 166
Middleton, 94
Moffatt, xxxvi, lxxvi, xc, 101
Mommsen, xlvi
Monteil, lxiii
Moule, 126
Moulton, J. H., viii, ix, lxxi, 11, 22, 105 and *passim*
Moulton, W. F., 57
Mozley, F. W., 15
Musonius, 20
Myers, 62

Nägeli, lv and *passim*
Nestle, 38, 52, 123
N. T. in Ap. Fathers, lxxiii, lxxvii
Nietzsche, xliv
Nitzsch, C. L., 170

Oliva, 168
Origen, xxxiv, 21, 166, 167

Paley, xxx, 97
Peake, 133
Pelagia-Legenden (ed. Usener), 62
Pfleiderer, lxxxvii, 172
Philo (cited by sections and by Mangey's pages), 12, 36, 49, 60, 78
Philodemus, 19
Philostratus, 153
Pindar, 33
Plato (ed. Stallbaum), 18, 24, 34, 50, 54, 70, 72, 74, 104, 110, 115, 152, 153
Pliny, xxii, 33, 122 ff.
Plutarch, 26, 76, 78, 96, 98, 152
Pollux, 12
Polybius (ed. Schweighäuser), 17, 18, 20, 46, 51, 62, 105, 116, 117, 131, 145
Polycarp, lxxvii, cx
Porter, F. C., 160
Preuschen, E., 156, 173
Preuss, H., 166
Purser, see Tyrrell

Quintilian, 115

Radford, 11

Ramsay, W. M., xxvii, xxix, xxxvi, xli, xlv, lv, lxiv, lxx, 7, 29, 125 and *passim*
Reinach, T., 31
Reitzenstein, 60, 94, 109, and see Index IV. *passim*
Renan, xli, xlvi, 121, 126
Rendall, xxxvii
Resch, A., lx, 39, 58, 77, 115
Reuss, lxxx
Riddell, 88
Ritschl, 15
Roberts and Gardner, 11 and *passim*
Robinson, J. Armitage, 4, 29, 93, 102, 129, 135, 138
Ropes, 58, 77
Round, Douglass, xxxvii

Sabatier, xlii, lxiv
Sanday, xxxiv, lvi, lxvi, lxix, 14, 81, 121, 126
Sanday and Headlam, 4 and *passim*
Sandys, xxiv
Schäder, E., lxix
Schettler, lxviii
Schmidt, J. E. C., lxxviii
Schneckenburger-Boehmer, 158, 173
Schöttgen, 54, 98, 172
Schrader, lxxiii
Schürer, 65, 148, 151, 162, 163
Scott, C. A., 151
Seeberg, lxvii, 51, 108
Seneca, 124
Severianus, 38, 101
Sieffert, 158
Skeat, 143
Smith, W. R., 64
Socrates, 76
Soden, von, xxxiv, lxxv, xcv, 140
Söderblom, 141
Somerville, 138, 139
Sophocles, 49, 91, 117
Souter, A., ix, xciv, xcix, cii, civ
Spitta, lxxxix ff., 39, 164, 172
Stanley, A. P., 75
Stanton, V. H., 137, 139
Stead, F. H., 140
Steck, lxxv, 58
Strabo, xxi, xxiii, 110
Suetonius, 130, 164
Swete, 38, 81, 101, 126, 137, 142, 143, 151, 164

Tacitus, xxix, 31, 164
Tafel, xxi, xxii
Tatian, 52
Taylor, xlvii, 35, 77
Teichmann, lxx, 146
Tertullian, 30, 81, 91, 101, 166
Thackeray, St John, 61, 158
Theocritus (ed. Ziegler), 56, 71
Theodoret, xxiv

Theophilus, 52
Theophrastus, 19
Thompson, E. M., 122 ff.
Thucydides, 30, 145, 153
Thumb, A., ix, 193
Tindale, 141
Tischendorf, xciii
Titius, lxx, 49, 60
Trench, R. C., 7, 99 and *passim*
Turner, C. H., xxxvi, cii
Tyrrell and Purser, 129

Vaganay, 161
Vaughan, 103
Vergil, 56, 109
Vischer, lxxxvi
Volz, lxvii, lxix, 56, 60, 64, 70, 91, 99, 147

Wadstein, 166
Wagner, 69
Warfield, 101
Weber, F., 9, 60, 65, 103, 162
Weber, V., xxxvii
Weinel, xlv, xlviii
Weiss, B., xxxii, lxxiv, 37, 66
Weiss, J., lvi

Weizsäcker, lxxxi, 3, 126, 172
Wellhausen, lxix
Wendland, 69
Wernle, xlv, lxxxiii, lxxxvi
Westcott, 6, 31, 52, 68, 78, 86, 105, 118, 136, 150
Wette, de, lxxviii
Wieseler, 12, 172
Wilamowitz-Moellendorff, 121
Wilcken, lxiv, 35, 46, 48, 75, 123, 143
Wilke, 23
Williams, A. L., 124
Wilson, A. J., lvii
Witkowski, 129, 132, and see Index IV. *passim*
Wrede, lxii, lxxxi ff.
Wright, 59
Wünsche, 80
Wycliffe, 169

Xenophon, 10, 26, 47, 49, 76, 141, 152, 153

Zahn, xlv, lxvi, lxxvii, lxxviii, lxxxv, 3 and *passim*
Zimmer, F., xciii, 5

III. REFERENCES.

I. INSCRIPTIONS AND PAPYRI.

(a) INSCRIPTIONS.

C.I.A.
Corpus Inscriptionum Atticarum (Berlin, 1873—).

	PAGE		PAGE		PAGE
I. 170	. 107	II. 444	. 54	III. 74	. 115
243	. 152	III. 23	. 18	690	. 88
II. 403	. 11				

C.I.G.
Corpus Inscriptionum Graecarum, ed. A. Boeckh (Berlin, 1828—).

I. 84	. 25	III. 3817	. 134	IV. 9313	. 56
II. 1967	. 134	4896	. 146	9439	. 56
3037	. 37				

Cos
Inscriptions of Cos, by W. R. Paton and E. L. Hicks (Oxford, 1891).
no. 391 . . 148

Crum
Coptic Ostraca, by W. E. Crum (London, 1902).
no. 522 . . 157

Duchesne et Bayet
Mémoire sur une Mission au Mont Athos, by L'Abbé Duchesne and M. Bayet (Paris, 1876).
p. 29 . . . 79 | p. 43 . . . 134 | p. 50 . . . 134

Heuzey
Mission Archéologique de Macédoine, by L. Heuzey and H. Daumet (Paris, 1876).
p. 280 . . 152 | p. 282 . . 29

I.G.S.I.
Inscriptiones Graecae Siciliae et Italiae, ed. G. Kaibel (Berlin, 1890).

no. 549	. 56	no. 929	. 56	no. 1879	. 56
830	. 24	956	. 8		

I.M.A.
Inscriptiones Graecae Insularum Maris Aegaei, edd. H. von Gaertringen and W. R. Paton (Berlin, 1895—).
III. 1238 . . 80

J.H.S.
Journal of Hellenic Studies.

	PAGE		PAGE		PAGE
xviii. 333	. . xxvii				

Kaibel
Epigrammata Graeca, ed. G. Kaibel (Berlin, 1878).

no. 247 . . 22

Magn.
Die Inschriften von Magnesia am Maeander, ed. O. Kern (Berlin, 1900).

no. 33	. . 26	no. 105	. 9, 155	no. 163	. . 114
85	. . 26	109	. . 37	179	. . 57
90	. . 6	113	. 18, 24	188	. . 91
100	. . 97	157	. lxvi, 148		

Michel
Recueil d'Inscriptions Grecques, ed. Ch. Michel (Paris, 1900).

no. 459 . . 50

O.G.I.S.
Orientis Graeci Inscriptiones Selectae, ed. W. Dittenberger, 2 vols. (Leipzig, 1903—05).

no. 4	. . 141	no. 335	. . 93	no. 485	. . 25
90	. 8, 96, 148	339	. . 65	515	. . 96
194	. . 22	437	. . 100	629	. xxix, 117
227	. . 41	444	. . 51	646	. . 19
262	. . 104	484	. xxix, 132	728	. . 72
331	. . 148				

Pergamene
Die Inschriften von Pergamon [in Altertümer von Pergamon viii.], ed. M. Fränkel (Berlin, 1900—).

no. 248 . . 26

Priene
Die Inschriften von Priene, ed. H. von Gaertringen (Berlin, 1906).

no. 195 . . 156

Revue des Études Grecques.
xv. 142 . . xxix

Sylloge[2]
Sylloge Inscriptionum Graecarum, 2nd Edit., ed. W. Dittenberger, 2 vols. and Index (Leipzig, 1888—1901).

no. 153	. . 21	no. 318	. 36, 72	no. 376	. . 78
255	. . 41				

Wilcken Ostr.
Griechische Ostraka, ed. U. Wilcken, 2 vols. (Leipzig, 1899).

ii. no. 670 . . 113 | ii. no. 1153 . . 54 | ii. no. 1372 . . 146

(b) PAPYRI.

P.Alex.
Bulletin de la Société archéologique d'Alexandrie ii., ed. G. Botti (Alexandria, 1899).

no. 4 . . 34

III. REFERENCES   185

P.Amh.
The Amherst Papyri, edd. B. P. Grenfell and A. S. Hunt (London, 1900—01).

Part I. nos. 1—9.
no. 2 . . 143

Part II. nos. 10—201.

no.			no.			no.		
30	.	. 155	66	.	. 9	97	.	. 156
33	.	. 42	78	.	29, 50	133	.	. 5, 73
35	.	98, 125	80	.	. 156	141	.	. 26
46	.	. 25	93	.	. 41			

B.G.U.
Griechische Urkunden, from the Berlin Museum.

Vol. I. nos. 1—361 (1895).

no.			no.			no.		
10	.	. 134	140	.	. 155	246	.	lxiv, 42
27	lxiv,	55, 131	147	.	. 54	297	.	. 22
86	.	. 114	174	.	lxvi	323	.	. 156
113	.	. 94	242	.	. 91	332	.	. 128

Vol. II. nos. 362—696.

no.			no.			no.		
362	.	62, 91	385	.	. 12	612	.	. 48
372	.	. 156	594	.	. 40	632	.	. 5
380	.	. 69	596	.	127, 132			

Vol. III. nos. 697—1012.

no.			no.			no.		
741	.	. 74	844	.	. 6	954	.	. 143
757	.	. 110	884	.	. 96	1009	.	. 130
775	.	. 157	948	.	. 78	1011	.	. 23

Vol. IV. (in progress).

no. 1039 . . 46 | no. 1079 . 46, 81

P.Cairo
Greek Papyri from the Cairo Museum, ed. E. J. Goodspeed (Chicago, 1902).

no. 3 . 57, 64 | no. 5 . . 35 | no. 29 . . 81

C.P.R.
Corpus Papyrorum Raineri archiducis, I. Griechische Texte, ed. C. Wessely (Vienna, 1895).

no. 19 . . 97 | no. 27 . . 44 | no. 32 . . 33

P.Fay.
Fayûm Towns and their Papyri, edd. B. P. Grenfell, A. S. Hunt, and D. G. Hogarth (Egyptian Exploration Fund, London, 1900).

no.			no.			no.		
20	.	. 81	109	.	. 157	123	.	. 65
21	.	. 91	119	.	. 80	337	.	. 153
34	.	. 77						

P.Fior.
Papiri Fiorentini, ed. G. Vitelli (Milan, 1905—06).

Part I. 1—35.
no. 9 . . 32

Part II. 36—105.
no. 57 . . 87 | no. 99 . . 110

P.Gen.
Les Papyrus de Genève, I. Papyrus Grecs, ed. J. Nicole (Genève, 1896—1900).

no. 52 . . 123 | no. 54 . . 13

P.Grenf. I.

An Alexandrian Erotic Fragment, and other Greek Papyri, chiefly Ptolemaic, ed. B. P. Grenfell (Oxford, 1896).

no.	PAGE	no.	PAGE	no.	PAGE
15	. 9	37	. 81	41	. 35
18	. 22	40	. 111	53	. 78
30	. 105, 130				

P.Grenf. II.

New Classical Fragments, and other Greek and Latin Papyri, edd. B. P. Grenfell and A. S. Hunt (Oxford, 1897).

no. 14 . . 146 | no. 35 . . 66 | no. 38 . . 124

P.Heid.

Heidelberger Papyrus-Sammlung, I. *Die Septuaginta - Papyri und andere altchristliche Texte,* ed. A. Deissmann (Heidelberg, 1905).

no. 6 . 6, 47, 132

P.Hib.

The Hibeh Papyri I., edd. B. P. Grenfell and A. S. Hunt (Egypt Exploration Fund, London, 1906).

no.	30	. . 91	no. 44	. . 132	no. 49	. . 25
	40	. . 64				

P.Leid.

Papyri graeci Musei antiquarii publici Lugduni-Batavi, ed. C. Leemans, 2 vols. (1843, 1885).

no. S . . 122 | no. U . . 122 | no. V . . 80

P.Leip.

Griechische Urkunden der Papyrussammlung zu Leipzig, I., ed. L. Mitteis (Leipzig, 1906).

no. 110 . . 137 | no. 119 . . 32

P.Lond.

Greek Papyri in the British Museum, 3 vols. (London, 1893, 1898, 1907).

Vol. I. nos. 1—138, ed. F. G. Kenyon.

no.	3	. . 22	no. 44	. . 116	no. 121	. 78, 109, 123
	42 . 6, 63, 118, 156		46	. . 117		

Vol. II. nos. 139—484, ed. F. G. Kenyon.

no. 342 . . 156 | no. 413 . . 110

Vol. III. nos. 485—1331, edd. F. G. Kenyon and H. J. Bell.

no. 951 . . 98 | no. 1178 . . 41

P.Oxy.

The Oxyrhynchus Papyri, edd. B. P. Grenfell and A. S. Hunt (Egyptian Exploration Fund, London, 1898, 1899, 1903, 1904).

Part I. nos. 1—207.

no.	38	. . 103	no. 57	. . 78	no. 115	. 62, 129
	41	. . 77	58	. . 94	119	. . 59
	45	. . 125	65	. . 157	126	. . 24

Part II. nos. 208—400.

no.	237 20,32,77,117,155	no. 261	. . 50	no. 294	. 46, 102
	245 . . 97	275	. . 153	301	. . 124
	259 . 49, 102	292	. 10, 46, 53	381	. . 124

III. REFERENCES

Part III. nos. 401—653.

no.			no.			no.		
413	.	149	486	.	145	496	.	23
471	.	26, 118	491	.	114	532	.	74, 156

Part IV. nos. 654—839.

no.			no.			no.		
657	.	122	719	.	114	744	.	46
713	.	155	725	.	154	745	.	xxiii
718	.	117	726	.	19	746	.	127

P.Par.

Paris Papyri in *Notices et Extraits* XVIII. ii., ed. Brunet de Presle (Paris, 1865).

no.			no.			no.		
7	.	74	42	.	8, 35	49	.	117
10	.	12	43	.	132	55	.	122
14	.	73	45	.	145	63	.	61
26	.	153	47	.	23, 117			

P.Petr.

The Flinders Petrie Papyri (in the Proceedings of the Royal Irish Academy—"Cunningham Memoirs," nos. viii., ix., xi.), 3 vols. (Dublin, 1891, 1893).

Part I. nos. 1—30, ed. J. P. Mahaffy.

no. 11 . . 37 | no. 29 . . 53

Part II. nos. 1—50, ed. J. P. Mahaffy.

no.			no.			no.		
9	.	74	39	.	35, 145	45	.	155
15	.	64	40	.	73			

Part III. nos. 1—146, edd. J. P. Mahaffy and J. G. Smyly.

no.			no.			no.		
42	.	53	49	.	134	73	.	72
43	.	22, 110						

P.Reinach

Papyrus Grecs et Démotiques, ed. Th. Reinach (Paris, 1905).

no. 15 . . 91

P.Strass.

Griechische Papyrus der Kaiserl. Universitäts- und Landesbibliothek zu Strassburg I., ed. Fr. Preisigke (Strassburg, 1906).

no. 22 . . 156

P.Tebt.

The Tebtunis Papyri, 2 vols. (University of California Publications, London, 1902, 1907).

Part I. nos. 1—264, edd. B. P. Grenfell, A. S. Hunt, and J. G. Smyly.

no.			no.			no.		
5	49, 72, 114, 155		43	.	62	58	.	41, 77, 132
19	.	95	47	.	23	61	.	51
24	.	23, 89	48	.	62, 146	74	.	51
27	.	65	56	.	75	116	.	146
28	.	93						

Part II. nos. 265—689, edd. B. P. Grenfell, A. S. Hunt, with the assistance of E. J. Goodspeed.

no. 314 . . 55 | no. 315 . . 157 | no. 410 . . 53

P.Tor.

Papyri graeci regii Taurinensis Musei Aegyptii, ed. A. Peyron, 2 vols. (Turin, 1826, 1827).

no. 1 . . 8

II. JUDAISTIC WRITINGS.

Apoc. Bar.
The Apocalypse of Baruch, ed. R. H. Charles (London, 1896).

	PAGE		PAGE		PAGE
i. 4	. 31	xxx. 1 . . 146	xlviii. 49	. . 27
xi. 4	. 56	xxxix. 7 . 103, 163	lix. 2	. . 90
xiii. 3	. 79	xl. 1, 2 . . 161	lxxii. 2	. lxvii
xv. 8	. 27	xliv. 15 . . 90	lxxxv. 13	. . 90
xx. 6	. lxix	xlviii. 39 . . 90		

Aristeas
Aristeae ad Philocratem Epistula, ed. P. Wendland (Leipzig, 1900).

no. 79	. . 53	no. 188	. . 114	no. 284	. . 89
148	. . 117	209	. . 68		

Asc. Isai.
The Ascension of Isaiah, ed. R. H. Charles (London, 1900).

iv. 4 ff.	. . 104	iv. 16	. 45, 58	vi.—xi.	. . 14
5	. 162, 163	18	. . 98	vii. 9	. . 61
15	. 59, 89				

Ass. Mos.
The Assumption of Moses, ed. R. H. Charles (London, 1897).

i. 15 . . 56 | x. 14 . . 56

Bel
27 . . 99

Didache
The Teaching of the Twelve Apostles, ed. H. de Romestin, 2nd Edit. (Oxford, 1885); and ed. A. Harnack (Texte und Untersuchungen ii. 1 and 2, Leipzig, 1884).

iii. 1	. . 77	xiii. 1 . . . 114	xvi. 6 f.	. . 60
ix. 4	. . 96	xv. 3 . . . 117	7 .	. . 45
xii. 3	. . 115	4 . . . 75		

Enoch
The Book of Enoch, tr. from the Ethiopic and ed. by R. H. Charles (Oxford, 1893).

i. 8	. . 93	lxii. 2	. xvii, 103	xc. 16	. . 68
xxxviii. 4	. . 67	lxix. 27	. . lxvii	cviii. 11 f.	. . 67
xlv. 3	. lxvii				

1 Esdras
iv. 62 . . . 89

2 Esdras
xii. 6 . . . 146

4 Ezra
The Fourth Book of Ezra, edd. R. L. Bensly and M. R. James (Texts and Studies iii. 2, Cambridge, 1895).

v. 1 ff.	. 103, 161	vii. 28	. 45, 61, 89	xiii. 24	. 59, 61
4 .	. 162, 163	32	. . 56	32	. . 89
41 f.	. xxxiii, 58	42	. . 27	33	. . 68
vi. 6 .	. lxvii	viii. 39	. . 62	38	. . 103
23 .	. . 60	61	. . lxix	52	. . 45
55 f.	. . 31	xiii. 10	. . 164		

III. REFERENCES

Jubilees
The Book of Jubilees, ed. R. H. Charles (London, 1902).

	PAGE		PAGE		PAGE
i. 20	161	xxiii. 1	56	xxxvi. 18	56
xv. 33	161	xxiv. 30	15		

Judith
x. 18 . . . 146

1 Maccabees
vi. 8 . . . 96 | xii. 27 . . . 67

2 Maccabees

	PAGE		PAGE		PAGE
i. 27	96	vii. 37	23	xii. 44	56
31	61	viii. 11	91	xiv. 15	148
ii. 7	96	12	146	17	65
21	148	xii. 22	148	23	110
iii. 24	148	23	87	xv. 21	146
v. 4	148				

3 Maccabees

i. 19	152	iii. 17	146	v. 8, 51	148
ii. 9	148	24	65		

4 Maccabees

x. 15	65, 91	xv. 17	78	xviii. 8	104
xiii. 18	61				

Orac. Sib.
Oracula Sibyllina, ed. A. Rzach (Vienna, 1881).

ii. 167 f.	162	iii. 64 f.	163	iii. 663 f.	68
iii. 63 ff.	104, 162	286 f.	lxvii	iv. 40 ff.	lxvii

Pss. Sol.
The Psalms of Solomon, edd. H. E. Ryle and M. R. James (Cambridge, 1891); and ed. O. von Gebhardt (*Texte und Untersuchungen* xiii. 2, Leipzig, 1895).

ii. 1, 29	160	xiii. 8	72	xvii. 27, 41	103, 164
iii. 16	62	xiv. 1	79	36	139
iv. 8	19	xv. 6	96	38	31
viii. 39	93, 96	xvi. 12	44, 93	39	164
ix. 7	8	xvii. 13	160	50	59
xi. 1, 4	60	23	102	xviii. 8	139
2	142				

Sap.
The Wisdom of Solomon.

i. 12	65	vi. 13	59	xiv. 20	99
ii. 10	117	viii. 8	63	26	152
23	51	xi. 10	72	xv. 3	78
iii. 8	45	16	89	17	99
v. 17	68	20	103	xvi. 28	59
vi. 7	113	xii. 2	72	xvii. 15	65

Sayings[2]
Sayings of the Jewish Fathers, 2nd Ed., by C. Taylor (Cambridge, 1897).
p. 25 . . . 77 | p. 68 . . . 35

Secrets of Enoch
The Book of the Secrets of Enoch, tr. from the Slavonic by W. R. Morfill, and ed. by R. H. Charles (Oxford, 1896).

	PAGE		PAGE		PAGE
iii. 1	61	xliv. 2	15		

Sir.
The Wisdom of Jesus the son of Sirach, or *Ecclesiasticus*.

		PAGE			PAGE			PAGE
iii. 23	.	115	xxii. 16	.	44	xxix. 23	.	93
xi. 27	.	149	22	.	149	xxxv. 14	.	93
xv. 20	.	89	xxvi. 10	.	89	23	.	23
xvi. 13	.	66	xxviii. 9, 13	.	72	xlii. 1	.	149

Testament of Abraham
Ed. M. R. James (*Texts and Studies* ii. 2, Cambridge, 1892).

§ xiii. A . . 146

Test. xii. patr.
The Testaments of the Twelve Patriarchs, ed. R. H. Charles (Oxford, 1908).

Benj. iii. 4	.	61	Levi vi. 11	.	32	Levi xviii. 12	.	161
Jos. xx. 4	.	56	,, viii. 15	.	146	Reub. iv. 7	.	161
Jud. xxii. 3	.	146	,, xviii. 11	.	44	,, vi. 3	.	161
Levi iii. 3	.	161						

IV. GREEK WORDS.

This is intended to be primarily an Index to the Greek words discussed in the Introduction and Notes, and not a Concordance to the Epistles: in the case, however, of characteristic words and phrases, references have sometimes been given to passages which are not directly annotated. A few additional references have also been inserted, principally to lexical and grammatical authorities, in the hope that they may prove useful to the student. The abbreviations employed for this purpose are explained in the list of abbreviations, p. xiii ff.

ἀγαθός, I. iii. 6, v. 15, II. ii. 16
ἀγαθωσύνη, II. i. 11
ἀγαπάω, I. iv. 9; ἠγαπημένος ὑπό, I. i. 4, II. ii. 13
ἀγάπη, I. i. 3, iii. 6, II. iii. 5 (ἀγ. τ. θεοῦ)
ἀγαπητός, I. ii. 8
ἄγγελος, II. i. 7; cf. Nägeli p. 38
ἁγιάζω, I. v. 23
ἁγιασμός, I. iv. 7, II. ii. 13
ἅγιος, I. i. 5 f., iv. 8; οἱ ἅγιοι, I. iii. 13, II. i. 10
ἁγιωσύνη, I. iii. 13; cf. Nägeli p. 43
ἀγνοέω, I. iv. 13
ἄγω, I. iv. 14
ἀγών, I. ii. 2
ἀδελφός, I. i. 4; p. xliv, cf. Witkowski *Epp*. p. 38
ἀδιαλείπτως, I. i. 2, ii. 13, v. 17
ἀδικία, II. ii. 10
ἀήρ, I. iv. 17
ἀθετέω, I. iv. 8
Ἀθῆναι, I. iii. 1
αἱρέομαι, II. ii. 13; cf. Nägeli p. 19 f.
αἰφνίδιος, I. v. 3
αἰώνιος, II. i. 9, ii. 16
ἀκαθαρσία, I. ii. 3, iv. 7
ἀκοή, I. ii. 13
ἀκούω, II. iii. 11
ἀκριβῶς, I. v. 2
ἀλήθεια, II. ii. 13; ἡ ἀλήθεια, II. ii. 10, 12
ἀληθινός, I. i. 9
ἀληθῶς, I. ii. 13
ἅμα σύν, I. iv. 17, v. 10
ἁμαρτία, I. ii. 16, II. ii. 3
ἄμεμπτος, I. iii. 13
ἀμέμπτως, I. ii. 10, iii. 13, v. 23
ἀμήν, p. 45
ἀνάγκη, I. iii. 7
ἀναιρέω, II. ii. 8
ἀναμένω, I. i. 10
ἀναπληρόω, I. ii. 16

ἀνέχομαι, II. i. 4
ἄνθρωπος, I. ii. 4; ὁ ἄνθρ. τ. ἀνομίας, II. ii. 3
ἀνίστημι, I. iv. 14, 16
ἀνομία, II. ii. 3, 7
ἄνομος, II. ii. 8
ἀνταποδίδωμι, I. iii. 9, II. i. 6
ἀντέχομαι, I. v. 14
ἀντί, I. v. 15; ἀνθ' ὧν II. ii. 10
ἀντίκειμαι, II. ii. 4
ἄξιος, II. i. 3
ἀξιόω, II. i. 11
ἀξίως τ. θεοῦ, I. ii. 12
ἀπαγγέλλω, I. i. 9
ἀπάντησις, I. iv. 17
ἅπαξ καὶ δίς, I. ii. 18
ἀπαρχή, p. 106; cf. Wilcken *Ostr.* i. p. 345 f.
ἅπας, II. ii. 12
ἀπάτη, II. ii. 10
ἀπέχω, I. iv. 3, v. 22; cf. Nägeli p. 54 f.
ἀπό, I. i. 8, ii. 6, II. i. 9
ἀποδείκνυμι, II. ii. 4
ἀποδίδωμι, I. v. 15
ἀποθνήσκω, I. iv. 14, v. 10
ἀποκαλύπτω, II. ii. 3, 6, 8; p. 149 f.
ἀποκάλυψις, II. i. 7; p. 149 ff.
ἀποκτείνω, I. ii. 15
ἀπόλλυμι, II. ii. 10
ἀπορφανίζομαι, I. ii. 17
ἀποστασία, II. ii. 3
ἀπόστολος, II. ii. 6
ἀπώλεια, II. ii. 3
ἄρα οὖν, I. v. 6, II. ii. 15
ἀρέσκω (θεῷ), I. ii. 4, 15, iv. 1
ἁρπάζω, I. iv. 17
ἄρτι, I. iii. 6, II. ii. 7
ἄρτος, II. iii. 8, 12
ἀρχάγγελος, I. iv. 16; cf. Nägeli p. 48 f.
ἀρχή, II. ii. 13
ἀσθενής, I. v. 14

192   INDEXES

ἀσπάζομαι, I. v. 26
ἀσπασμός, II. iii. 17
ἀσφάλεια, I. v. 3
ἀτακτέω, II. iii. 7; p. 153 f.
ἄτακτος, I. v. 14; p. 152
ἀτάκτως, II. iii. 6, 11; p. 153
ἄτοπος, II. iii. 2
αὐτός, ὁ, I. iii. 11, iv. 16, v. 23, II. ii. 16, iii. 16
Ἀχαία, I. i. 7 f.; p. xlv

βάρος, I. ii. 7
βασιλεία, I. ii. 12, II. i. 5

γάρ, I. ii. 1, 20; καὶ γάρ, I. iii. 4
γαστήρ, I. v. 3
γίνομαι· γέγονα, I. ii. 1; ἐγενόμην, I. i. 7, iii. 4 f., II. ii. 7; ἐγενήθην, I. i. 5 (bis), 6, ii. 5, 7, 8, 10, 14
γινώσκω, I. iii. 5
γράφω, οὕτως, II. iii. 17; for the authenticating signature cf. *Mél. Nic.* p. 130 ff.
γρηγορέω (ethical), I. v. 6, (metaphorical) I. v. 10

δεῖ, p. 86
δέομαι, I. iii. 10
δέχομαι, I. i. 6, ii. 13, II. ii. 10
δῆμος, ὁ, p. xxiii
διά, c. gen. I. iii. 7, iv. 2, 14, II. ii. 2 (ὡς δι' ἡμῶν); c. acc. I. i. 5 (δι' ὑμᾶς)
διάκονος, I. iii. 2
διαμαρτύρομαι, I. iv. 6
δίδωμι, I. iv. 2, 8; δῴη, II. iii. 16
δίκαιος, II. i. 5, 6; cf. Lft. *Notes* p. 286 f.
δικαίως, I. ii. 10
δίκην τίνω, II. i. 9
διό, I. iii. 1, v. 11
διότι, I. ii. 8; cf. Mayser p. 161
διωγμός, II. i. 4
διώκω, I. v. 15
δοκιμάζω, I. ii. 4 (bis), v. 21
δόλος, I. ii. 3
δόξα, I. ii. 6, 12, 20, II. i. 9, ii. 14
δοξάζομαι, II. iii. 1
δουλεύω, I. i. 9
δύναμις, I. i. 5, II. i. 7; ἐν δυνάμει, II. i. 11, ii. 9
δωρεάν, II. iii. 8; cf. Nägeli p. 35 f.

ἐάν, I. ii. 7; with ind. iii. 8; ἐὰν μή, II. ii. 3; for ἄν, p. 22; cf. Conybeare *Selections* p. 91 f.
ἑαυτοῦ, I. ii. 7, 12; ἑαυτῶν (for 1st pers. plur.) I. ii. 8, II. iii. 9; cf. Schmid *Attic.* i. p. 82
ἐγείρω, I. i. 10
ἐγώ (emphatic), I. ii. 18, iii. 5
ἔθνος, I. ii. 16, iv. 5; cf. Nägeli p. 46
εἰ, I. iv. 14; εἰ οὐ, c. ind., II. iii. 10, 14

εἰδέναι, I. iv. 4
εἶδος, I. v. 22
εἴδωλον, I. i. 9
εἰμὶ πρός, I. iii. 4, II. ii. 5
εἴπερ, II. i. 6
εἰρηνεύω, I. v. 13
εἰρήνη, I. i. 1, v. 3; ὁ θεὸς (κύριος) τ. εἰρήνης, I. v. 23, II. iii. 16
εἰς, I. i. 5, iv. 8; εἰς τό c. inf. (result), I. ii. 12, (purpose) II. ii. 11
εἷς ἕκαστος, I. ii. 11, II. i. 3; εἷς τὸν ἕνα, I. v. 11
εἴσοδος, I. i. 9, ii. 1
εἴτε (with the subj.), I. v. 10
ἐκ, I. ii. 6
ἐκδίκησιν δοῦναι, II. i. 8
ἔκδικος, I. iv. 6; cf. Soph. *Lex. s.v.*, Hicks *C.R.* i. p. 44
ἐκδιώκω, I. ii. 15
ἐκκλησία Θεσσαλονικέων, I. i. 1, II. i. 1; ἐκκλησίαι τ. θεοῦ, I. ii. 14, II. i. 4
ἐκλογή, I. i. 4
ἐκφεύγω, I. v. 3
ἐλπίς, I. i. 3, ii. 19, iv. 13, v. 8; ἐλπὶς ἀγαθή, II. ii. 16
ἐμός, II. iii. 17
ἔμπροσθεν τ. θεοῦ (κυρίου), I. i. 3, ii. 19, iii. 9, 13
ἐν· I. iv. 7, 16; for εἰς, i. 8; instrumental, iv. 18; θεῷ πατρί, i. 1; Χρ. Ἰησοῦ, ii. 14; κυρίῳ, iii. 8; λόγῳ κυρίου, iv. 15; ὀνόματι τ. κυρίου, II. iii. 6
ἐναντίος, I. ii. 15
ἔνδειγμα, II. i. 5
ἐνδοξάζομαι, II. i. 10, 12
ἐνδύω, I. v. 8
ἐνέργεια, II. ii. 9, 11
ἐνεργέω, I. ii. 13, II. ii. 7
ἐνίστημι, II. ii. 2; cf. Mayser p. 371
ἐνκακέω, III. ii. 13
ἐνκαυχάομαι, II. i. 4
ἐνκόπτω, I. ii. 18
ἐνορκίζω, I. v. 27
ἐντρέπομαι, II. iii. 14; cf. Anz *Subsidia* p. 13 f., Witkowski *Epp.* p. 47
ἐξαπατάω, II. ii. 3
ἐξέρχομαι, I. i. 8
ἐξηχέω, I. i. 8
ἐξουθενέω, I. v. 20; cf. Soph. *Lex. s.v.*
ἐξουδενέω
ἐξουσία, II. iii. 9; cf. Reitzenstein *Poimandres* p. 48
ἔξω, οἱ, I. iv. 12
ἔπειτα, I. iv. 17
ἐπί, c. gen. I. i. 2; c. dat. iii. 7, 9, iv. 7; c. acc. ii. 16, II. i. 10, iii. 4
ἐπιβαρέω, I. ii. 9, II. iii. 8
ἐπιθυμία, I. ii. 17, iv. 5
ἐπιποθέω, I. iii. 6
ἐπιστολή, I. v. 27, II. ii. 2, 15, iii. 14, 17

IV. GREEK WORDS

ἐπιστρέφω, I. i. 9; cf. Anz Subsidia p. 7.
ἐπισυναγωγή, II. ii. 1
ἐπιφάνεια, II. ii. 8; p. 148 f.
ἐπιφανής, pp. 148, 160
ἐργάζομαι, I. ii. 9, iv. 11, II. iii. 8, 10, 11, 12
ἔργον (πίστεως), I. i. 3, II. i. 11; διὰ τ. ἔργον, I. v. 13
ἐρωτάω 'rogo,' I. iv. 1, v. 12, II. ii. 1; cf. Thumb Hellen. p. 121
ἐσθίω, II. iii. 10
ἔτι, II. ii. 5
εὐαγγελίζομαι, I. iii. 6; p. 141 ff.
εὐαγγέλιον, τό, I. ii. 4; ἡμῶν, I. i. 5, II. ii. 14; τ. θεοῦ, I. ii. 2, 8, 9; τ. χριστοῦ, I. iii. 2; τ. κυρίου ἡμ. Ἰησοῦ, II. i. 8; p. 141 ff.
εὐδοκέω, I. ii. 8; iii. 1; c. dat. II. ii. 12
εὐδοκία, II. i. 11
εὐσχημόνως, I. iv. 12
εὐχαριστέω, I. i. 2; ἐν παντὶ εὐχ., I. v. 18
εὐχαριστία, I. iii. 9
ἐφίστημι, I. v. 3
ἕως (conj.), II. ii. 7

ζάω, I. iii. 8, v. 10; θεὸς ζῶν, I. i. 9
ζητέω, I. ii. 6

ἢ οὐχί, I. ii. 19
ἡγέομαι, I. v. 13, II. iii. 15
ἤδη, II. ii. 7
ἡμέρα, ἡ, I. v. 4; ἡμέρα κυρίου, v. 2; ἡ ἡμέρα ἐκείνη, II. i. 10; υἱοὶ ἡμέρας, I. v. 5
ἤπιος, p. 21; cf. Herwerden Lex. s.v.
ἡσυχάζω, I. iv. 11
ἡσυχία, II. iii. 12

θάλπω, I. ii. 7; cf. Thumb Hellen. p. 215, Mél. Nic. p. 249
θαυμάζω, II. i. 10
θέλημα (θεοῦ), I. iv. 3, v. 18; cf. Hort 1 Pet. p. 142 f.
θέλω, I. ii. 18, II. iii. 10; οὐ θέλω ἀγνοεῖν, I. iv. 13
θεοδίδακτος, I. iv. 9
θεός, ὁ, p. lxiv; θεὸς πατήρ, p. lxv
Θεσσαλονικεύς, I. i. 1, II. i. 1
θλίβω, I. iii. 4, II. i. 6, 7
θλῖψις, I. i. 6, iii. 3, 7, II. i. 4, 6
θροέομαι, II. ii. 2
θώραξ (πίστεως), I. v. 8; for the 'militia Christi' see Harnack's Essay (1905), and cf. Cumont Relig. orient. p. xiii ff.

ἴδιος, I. ii. 14; τὰ ἴδια, iv. 11
ἱερόδουλοι, p. 14; cf. Herwerden Appendix s.v.

Ἰησοῦς, p. 135 ff.; cf. Chase Credibility of Acts p. 205 f.
ἱκανὸν λαβεῖν, p. xxix
ἵνα final, I. ii. 16, v. 10; semi-final, iv. 1, v. 4, II. i. 11, iii. 1; ἵνα μή, I. iv. 13
Ἰουδαῖος, I. ii. 14
ἰσχύς, II. i. 9

καθάπερ, I. ii. 11; καθάπερ καί, iii. 6, 12; iv. 5
καθεύδω (ethical), I. v. 6; (literal) v. 7; (metaphorical) v. 10
καθίζω, II. ii. 4
καθώς, I. i. 5; καθ. οἴδατε, p. xliv καί in comparison, I. ii. 5; contrasting, ii. 18
καιρός· πρὸς καιρὸν ὥρας, I. ii. 17; ἐν τῷ αὐτοῦ καιρῷ, II. ii. 6; χρόνοι κ. καιροί, I. v. 1; cf. Revue d. Études grecques xv. p. 4
κακός, I. v. 15
καλέω, I. ii. 12, iv. 7, v. 24, II. ii. 14
καλοποιέω, II. iii. 13; cf. Soph. and Herwerden Lex. s.v.
καλός, I. v. 21
καρδία, I. ii. 4, 17 (προσώπῳ οὐ καρδίᾳ), iii. 13 (στηρίξαι καρδίας)
καταλαμβάνω, I. v. 4
καταλείπω, I. iii. 1
καταξιόω, II. i. 5; cf. Anz Subsidia p. 38
καταργέω, II. ii. 8
καταρτίζω, I. iii. 10; cf. Mayser p. 20 f.
κατευθύνω, I. iii. 11, II. iii. 5
κατέχω, I. v. 21; II. ii. 6, 7; p. 155 ff.
καύχησις, I. ii. 19
κεῖμαι, I. iii. 3
κέλευσμα, I. iv. 16
κενός, I. ii. 1; εἰς κενόν, iii. 5
κηρύσσω, II. ii. 9
κλέπτης, I. v. 2, 4
κλῆσις, II. i. 11
κοιμάομαι, I. iv. 13 ff.
κολακία, I. ii. 5
κοπιάω, I. v. 12
κόπος, I. i. 3, iii. 5; κόπος κ. μόχθος, ii. 9, II. iii. 8
κρατέω, c. acc., II. ii. 15; p. 155
κρίνω, II. ii. 12
κρίσις, II. i. 5
κτάομαι, I. iv. 4
κύριος, p. 136 ff.; cf. Hort 1 Pet. p. 30 ff., and for the legal use of κύριος in the papyri see Archiv iv. p. 80 ff.
κωλύω, I. ii. 16

λαλέω, I. i. 8; cf. McClellan Gospels p. 383 ff.
λόγος, I. i. 5; ὁ λόγος, i. 6; θεοῦ, ii. 13; κυρίου, i. 8, iv. 15, II. iii. 1; ἡμῶν,

194　INDEXES

II. iii. 14; κολακίας, I. ii. 5; ἀκοῆς,
ii. 13; ἐν τ. λόγοις, iv. 18; διὰ λόγου,
II. ii. 2, 15; ἔργῳ κ. λόγῳ, ii. 17
λοιπός· οἱ λοιποί, I. iv. 13, v. 6; λοιπόν,
iv. 1; τὸ λοιπόν, II. iii. 1

Μακεδονία, I. i. 7 f., iv. 10; p. xlv
μακροθυμέω, I. v. 14
μᾶλλον (intensive), I. iv. 1, 10
μαρτύριον, II. i. 10
μαρτύρομαι, I. ii. 12
μάρτυς, I. ii. 5, 10
μεθύσκομαι, I. v. 7
μεθύω, I. v. 7; cf. Reitzenstein
  Poimandres p. 240 f.
μέλλω, I. iii. 4
μέν (solitarium), I. ii. 18
μέσος, I. ii. 7; ἐκ μέσου, II. ii. 7
μετά, I. i. 6, II. iii. 12
μεταδίδωμι, I. ii. 8
μή with pres. imp., I. v. 19; with aor.
  subj., II. iii. 13; μή πως, I. iii. 5
μιμέομαι, II. iii. 7, 9
μιμητής, I. i. 6, ii. 14
μνείαν ποιεῖσθαι, I. i. 2; μνείαν ἔχειν,
  iii. 6
μνημονεύω, c. gen. I. i. 3; c. acc.
  II. ii. 9
μόνον, II. ii. 7
μόνος, I. iii. 1
μόχθος v. κόπος
μυστήριον, II. ii. 7; cf. Hatch Essays
  p. 57 ff.

ναός, II. ii. 4
νεκρός, I. i. 10, iv. 16
νεφέλη, I. iv. 17
νήπιος, I. ii. 7
νήφω, I. v. 6, 8; cf. Hort 1 Pet. p. 65 f.
νουθετέω, I. v. 12, 14, II. iii. 15
νοῦς, II. ii. 2
νῦν, I. iii. 8, II. ii. 6
νύξ, I. v. 2, 5, 7; νυκτὸς κ. ἡμέρας,
  I. ii. 9, iii. 10, II. iii. 8

ὁ demonstrative, I. v. 27, II. iii. 14
ὁδός, I. iii. 11
οἶδα, I. i. 4; καθὼς οἴδατε, I. i. 5, p. xliv
οἰκοδομέω, I. v. 11
οἶος, I. i. 5
ὄλεθρος, I. v. 3; ὀλ. αἰώνιος, II. i. 9
ὀλιγόψυχος, I. v. 14
ὁλόκληρος, I. v. 23
ὅλος, I. iv. 10
ὁλοτελής, I. v. 23
ὁμείρομαι, I. ii. 8
ὄνομα, II. i. 12, iii. 6; cf. Herwerden
  s.v., and Mél. Nic. p. 253
ὁποῖος, I. i. 9
ὅπως, II. i. 12
ὁρᾶτε μή, I. v. 15
ὀργή, ἡ, I. i. 10, ii. 16

ὁσίως, I. ii. 10
ὅστις, II. i. 9; cf. Dieterich Untersuchungen p. 199 f.
ὅταν with aor. subj., II. i. 10
ὅτε, I. iii. 4, II. iii. 10
ὅτι demonstrative, I. i. 5, ii. 13, iii. 4
  causal, I. iv. 16, v. 9, II. i. 3, ii. 13
οὐ with part., I. ii. 4; οὐ μή, I. iv. 15;
  οὐχ ὅτι, II. iii. 9
οὐδέ, I. ii. 3
οὐρανός, I. i. 10, iv. 16, II. i. 7
οὔτε, I. ii. 5, 6
οὕτως, I. ii. 4, iv. 14, II. iii. 17 (οὕτως
  γράφω)
οὐχί, I. ii. 19
ὀφείλω, II. i, 3, ii. 13

πάθος, I. iv. 5
πάντοτε, I. i. 12, ii. 16, iii. 6, iv. 17,
  v. 15, 16; II. i. 3, 11, ii. 13
πάπυρος, p. 122
παρά c. gen., I. ii. 13, iv. 1, II. iii. 6,
  8; c. dat. II. i. 6
παραγγελία, I. iv. 2
παραγγέλλω, I. iv. 11, II. iii. 4, 6, 10, 12
παράδοσις, II. ii. 15, iii. 6
παρακαλέω, I. ii. 12; c. ἵνα, I. iv. 1;
  c. inf. iv. 10
παράκλησις, I. ii. 3, II. ii. 16
παραλαμβάνω, I. ii. 13, iv. 1; παρελάβοσαν p. 113, cf. Conybeare Selections
  p. 32
παραμυθέομαι, I. ii. 11, v. 14
παρουσία, I. ii. 19, iii. 13, iv. 15, v. 23,
  II. ii. 1, 8, 9; cf. p. 145 ff.
παρρησιάζομαι, I. ii. 2
πᾶς, I. iii. 12, 13, v. 26, II. iii. 16, 18;
  ἐν παντί, I. v. 18; διὰ παντός, II. iii.
  16
πάσχω, I. ii. 14, II. i. 5
πατήρ, I. ii. 11; (of God) I. i. 1, 3,
  iii. 11, 13, II. i. 1, 2, ii. 16, cf.
  p. lxv f.
Παῦλος (emph.), I. ii. 18
πείθω, II. iii. 4
πειράζω, I. iii. 5
πέμπω, II. ii. 11
περὶ δέ, I. iv. 9, v. 1
περιεργάζομαι, II. iii. 11
περικεφαλαία, I. v. 8
περιλείπομαι, I. iv. 15, 17
περιπατέω, I. ii. 12
περιποίησις, I. v. 9, II. ii. 14
περισσεύω, I. iii. 12, iv. 1, 10
περισσοτέρως, I. ii. 17
πιστεύω, I. iv. 14; ὁ πιστεύων, I. i. 7,
  ii. 10, 13; ὁ πιστεύσας, II. i. 10;
  πιστεύομαι c. acc. I. ii. 4
πίστις, ἡ, II. iii. 2; πρὸς τ. θεόν, I. i. 8;
  ἔργον πίστεως, I. i. 3, II. i. 11; πίστις
  κ. ἀγάπη, I. iii. 6, v. 8
πιστός, I. v. 24, II. iii. 3

IV. GREEK WORDS

πλάνη, I. ii. 3, II. ii. 11
πλεονάζω, I. iii. 12, II. i. 3
πλεονεκτέω, I. iv. 6
πλεονεξία, I. ii. 5
πληροφορία, I. i. 5
πληρόω, II. i. 11
πνεῦμα, I. v. 19, 23, II. ii. 2, 13; of Christ, II. ii. 8; πνεῦμα ἅγιον, I. i. 5, 6, iv. 8
ποιέω, I. v. 24
πονηρός, I. v. 22, II. iii. 2, 3
πορνεία, I. iv. 3
πρᾶγμα, I. iv. 6
πράσσω, I. iv. 11
προΐστημι, I. v. 12
προλέγω, I. iii. 4, iv. 6
προπάσχω, I. ii. 2
πρός c. acc. after verb of rest, I. iii. 4, II. ii. 5, iii. 1; πρὸς τό c. inf., I. ii. 9
προσευχή, I. i. 2
προσεύχομαι, I. v. 17; προσεύχομαι ἵνα, II. i. 11, iii. 1
προσώπῳ οὐ καρδίᾳ, I. ii. 17
πρόφασις, I. ii. 5
προφητεία, I. v. 20
προφήτης, I. ii. 15
πρῶτον, I. iv. 16
πῦρ, II. i. 8
πῶς, I. i. 9; τὸ πῶς, iv. 1

ῥύομαι (ἐκ), I. i. 10, (ἀπό) II. iii. 2; cf. Anz *Subsidia* p. 19 f.

σαίνομαι, I. iii. 3; see also σιαίνομαι
σαλεύω, II. ii. 2
σάλπιγξ, I. iv. 16
Σατανᾶς, I. ii. 18, II. ii. 9
σβέννυμι, I. v. 19
σέβασμα, II. ii. 4
σημεῖον, II. ii. 9, iii. 17
σημειόομαι, II. iii. 14
σιαίνομαι, p. 38; cf. also *Z.N.T.W.* viii. p. 242
Σιλουανός, I. i. 1, II. i. 1
σκεῦος, I. iv. 4
σκότος, I. v. 4 f.
σπουδάζω, I. ii. 17
στέγω, I. iii. 1, 5
στέλλομαι, II. iii. 6
στέφανος, I. ii. 19; cf. Herwerden *Lex. s.v.*
στήκω, I. iii. 8, II. ii. 15; cf. Conybeare *Selections* p. 42
στηρίζω, I. iii. 2, 13, II. ii. 17, iii. 3; cf. Anz *Subsidia* p. 20 f.
συμφυλέτης, I. ii. 14
σύν v. ἅμα
συναναμίγνυμαι, II. iii. 14
συνεργός, p. 37
σῴζω, I. ii. 16, II. ii. 10
σῶμα, I. v. 23

σωτηρία, I. v. 8, 9, II. ii. 13

ταχέως, II. ii. 2
τέκνον, I. ii. 7, 11
τέλος εἰς, I. ii. 16
τέρας, II. ii. 9
τηρέω, I. v. 23
τίθημι, I. v. 9
τιμή, I. iv. 4
Τιμόθεος, I. i. 1, iii. 2, 6, II. i. 11
τίνω, II. i. 9
τό with inf., I. iii. 3
τοιγαροῦν, I. iv. 8
τοιοῦτος, II. iii. 12
τόπος, I. i. 8
τότε, II. ii. 8
τρέχω, II. iii. 1
τρόπος, II. ii. 3, iii. 16
τροφός, I. ii. 7
τύπος, I. i. 7, II. iii. 9; cf. Herwerden *Lex. s.v.*

ὑβρίζω, I. ii. 2
υἱός (of Christ), I. i. 10; φωτὸς κ. ἡμέρας, v. 5; τ. ἀπωλείας, II. ii. 3
ὑπακούω, II. i. 8, iii. 14
ὑπέρ, I. iii. 2, II. i. 4, 5, ii. 1; p. 69
ὑπεραίρομαι, II. ii. 4
ὑπεραυξάνω, II. i. 3
ὑπερβαίνω, I. iv. 6
ὑπερεκπερισσοῦ, I. iii. 10, v. 13
ὑπό, I. ii. 14
ὑπομονή, I. i. 3, II. i. 4, iii. 5
ὑστέρημα, I. iii. 10

φθάνω, I. ii. 16, iv. 15
φιλαδελφία, I. iv. 9
φίλημα, I. v. 26
Φίλιπποι, I. ii. 2
φιλοτιμέομαι, I. iv. 11
φλόξ, II. i. 8
φυλάσσω, II. iii. 3
φωνή, I. iv. 16
φῶς, I. v. 5

χαίρω, I. iii. 9, v. 16
χαρά, I. i. 6, ii. 19 f., iii. 9
χάρις, I. i. 1, v. 28, II. i. 2, 12, ii. 16, iii. 18
χείρ, I. iv. 11, II. iii. 17
χρείαν ἔχειν, I. i. 8
Χριστός, p. 136 ff.
χρόνος, I. v. 1; see also καιρός

ψεῦδος, II. ii. 9, 11
ψυχή, I. ii. 8, v. 23

ὠδίν, I. v. 3
ὥρα, I. ii. 17
ὡς ἐάν, I. ii. 7; ὡς ὅτι, II. ii. 2
ὥστε consecutive, I. i. 4

www.ingramcontent.com/pod-product-compliance
Lightning Source LLC
Chambersburg PA
CBHW050432240426
43661CB00055B/2356